Don Casey's
Complete Illustrated
Sailboat
Maintenance
Manual

Don Casey

INTERNATIONAL MARINE/McGRAW-HILL
Camden, Maine • New York • Chicago • San Francisco • Lisbon • London • Madrid •
Mexico City • Milan • New Delhi • San Juan • Seoul • Singapore • Sydney • Toronto

To Olga—
for sharing the fireflies
and paying my
cosmic salary with her smile.

The McGraw·Hill Companies

1 2 3 4 5 6 7 8 9 10 DOC DOC 0 9 8 7 6

© 2006 by International Marine

Library of Congress Cataloging-in-Publication Data
  Casey, Don.
Don Casey's complete illustrated sailboat maintenance manual / Don Casey.
      p.   cm. Includes index.
  ISBN 0-07-146284-8 (hardcover : alk. paper)
  1. Sailboats—Maintenance and repair—Amateurs'
  manuals.   I. Title.
  VM351.C325 2005
  623.822´3´0288—dc22   2005015441

Questions regarding the content of this book should be addressed to
McGraw-Hill/International Marine
P.O. Box 220
Camden, ME 04843
www.internationalmarine.com

Questions regarding the ordering of this book should be addressed to
The McGraw-Hill Companies
Customer Service Department
P.O. Box 547
Blacklick, OH 43004
Retail customers: 1-800-262-4729
Bookstores: 1-800-722-4726

Illustrations by the author, Jim Sollers, Rob Groves, Paul Mirto, Kim Downing, Jamie Downing, Peter Compton. Design by Ann Aspell, modified by Shannon Swanson.

CONTENTS

INTRODUCTION

Buy me.

    Was that too direct? I'm sorry, but my particular calling is to help fellow boaters and I simply cannot give you any better advice than those two words. The money-saving, time-saving, and boat-saving information you will find between these two covers could fill six books. That, in fact, is exactly what this is—six books bound together in one volume. Better still, the six books included are the best available on their particular subjects. Profusely illustrated and with concise, carefully honed text, these books shine the bright light of comprehension into the darkest corners of boat care and improvement. I cannot imagine any boatowner or boat buyer—sail or power—failing to profit from owning this book.

    Sailboat owners will instantly see their own boats, their own problems, their own wants in the illustrations, so allow me a short aside to the powerboaters. These books were written with sailboats in mind, but the rounded hulls in the drawings don't make them less applicable to powerboats any more than repairing sailboats reduces the boatyard fiberglass wizard's ability to patch a powerboat hull. Hull repair is hull repair. Refinishing is refinishing. The wiring for sail and power comes off the same spool, the terminals from the same bin. And if your propulsion is diesel, you won't find a more helpful resource than *Troubleshooting Marine Diesels*, included here. So take a close look. Despite the word "sailboat" in the book titles, you are likely to find here just what you need.

    Perhaps I should also address those without a boat. The first book in this volume is an indispensable guide to evaluating the condition of boats. It shows you what to look for and how to interpret what you see. It is a short course, really, in boat surveying. If you use it, it can save you the potentially disastrous mistake of buying a boatload of trouble. Boatowners will find this book equally useful for recognizing potential problems in their own boats early, before they lead to more serious consequences.

    The second and third books in this collection are guides to refinishing and to hull and deck repair, a propitious pairing since these two nearly always happen simultaneously. One book instructs on the full range of fiberglass repair, from modest to heroic. In it you will find expert guidance for using sealants correctly to prevent leaks, for repairing dull or damaged gelcoat, for dealing with osmotic blisters, for repairing impact damage, and even for core replacement. The other book shows you how to get the best possible result from a can of paint or varnish or resin, how to deal with worn-out nonskid, how to apply vinyl graphics and much more.

    The fourth book, *Sailboat Electrics Simplified*, takes ALL the mystery out of 12-volt electrical systems. Electrical manuals tend to be complicated, even incomprehensible to the layman. That is decidedly not the case here. With plain illustrations and everyday language, this book shows you how to avoid or correct onboard electrical problems. You will not find a more usable guide to boat electrics.

    Troubleshooting Marine Diesels comes next. Adding this book to your library is like retaining an exceptionally knowledgeable diesel mechanic—except that when a problem arises you will be reaching for your wrenches rather than your wallet. Master mechanic Peter Compton has crafted a series of flow charts that lead from symptom directly to likely causes. I *never* leave the dock without this amazing book aboard.

Perhaps you have never thought of buying a canvaswork book. If not, then you get a real bonus in *Don Casey's Complete Illustrated Sailboat Maintenance Manual.* The ability to sew opens the door to an infinite number of excellent boat enhancements and reduces their costs to no more than the fabric and the thread. *Canvaswork and Sail Repair* provides step-by-step instructions, from

making your first hesitant stitches through confidently building a dodger, with interior upholstery falling somewhere in the middle. Clean, fun, and instantly gratifying, canvaswork is my favorite boat-husbandry discipline and it could become yours.

That completes the tour. Six books between two covers focused on one idea—to give you the information you need to improve and maintain your boat to a high standard without spending so much money that it takes the enjoyment out of boating.

"There aren't many experiences
more ripe with promise
than buying a boat."

Inspecting
the Aging
Sailboat

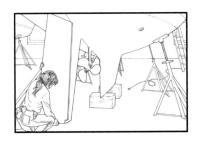

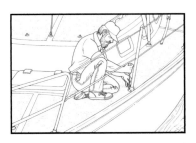

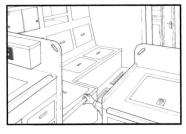

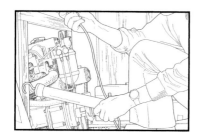

INTRODUCTION

There are a few well-cared-for yachts into their second century of service, but most boats built 100 years ago, or even 50 years ago, are long gone—a pile of gray ash in the bottom of a boatyard stove or a punky skeleton buried in the mud of some creek or canal. Neglect is fatal to wooden boats.

In noticeable contrast, almost every sailboat larger than a skiff and built in the last 35 years, unless lost to violent weather or navigational mishap, is still around. Most see regular service. Even those sitting dirt-covered along the back fence of a boatyard are rarely beyond redemption. The reason for this new immortality is a change in the construction material.

In the late 1940s a handful of boat manufacturers abandoned the practice of constructing hulls from wood in favor of molding hulls from a war-developed synthetic polymer, reinforcing this plastic with glass fibers. Within a dozen years, virtually all production boats were being constructed of glass-reinforced plastic. Because the word "plastic" had become synonymous in 1950s America with "cheap and inferior," boat manufacturers sought to avoid this taint by calling their new construction material "fiberglass."

Plastic boats were cheaper, mostly because simplified construction techniques allowed for mass production. This made boat ownership affordable for millions who were previously excluded. As for being inferior, the ability of plastic boats to tolerate slipshod maintenance soon became legendary. Whether the addition of millions of undistinguished and poorly maintained boats to the shorelines and waterways represented a social good is certainly debatable, but for the individual, cheaper and more durable boats were surely better.

Fiberglass boats aren't completely impervious to neglect, and they can be damaged. Moreover, a boat is more than simply a hull; many of the assembled components offer less durability. Wood used to reinforce and stiffen is subject to rot. Metal parts corrode or fatigue. Fabrics tear and mildew. Machinery wears out. While these conditions are rarely fatal—a fiberglass boat in almost any condition can be restored—the issue is value. Is making needed repairs economically sound? The answer to this question will vary according to who is considering it. A boat that should be avoided by an owner who leaves all repairs to the yard could be a bargain for the skilled do-it-yourselfer.

SURVEYING A BOAT FOR PURCHASE

There aren't many experiences more ripe with promise than buying a boat. When you find the very craft you have been dreaming about sulking impatiently on a cradle or shifting restlessly in a slip, perfect days on the water suddenly play through your mind. You step aboard and run your fingers over her in a lover's caress. Look how perfect she is. This is the one! You stand at the helm, gripping the wheel, feeling the wind through your hair, the sun on your back, the motion of . . .

SNAP OUT OF IT!

Are those cracks in the gelcoat? Should the deck crackle like that? Are those rivets in the rubrail, and why are they loose? Why doesn't the head door close? Why are there brown streaks beneath the portlights? Are those water marks inside the galley cabinets? Should there be rust on the keel bolts? What is that bulge in the hull?

If any of these indicate real trouble (and some of them do), it is about to become your trouble. It is going to be your money paying for the repair or, God forbid, your feet treading water. So be still your beating heart; shopping for a boat is about looking for the warts.

But where do you look? And what do you look for? And when you find something, how do you know what it means? That's what this book is all about.

Wait a minute. Isn't finding a boat's problems the job of the surveyor, a real surveyor? Absolutely. If your dream boat is going to cost a substantial (by your definition) amount, a professional survey is essential. A seller is far more likely to make financial concessions based on the findings of a formal survey than on your whining about the very same things. If you plan to finance or insure the boat, a survey will be required anyway. And an experienced surveyor brings a depth of knowledge that is likely to result in findings you might overlook. So why would you want to bother with any of this if you're going to hire a pro?

Consider this. The cost to have a boat professionally surveyed runs about $10 to $15 per foot, plus travel and expenses. Haulout costs can add $3 or $4 per foot, and if you want an engine evaluated, tack on another $300 or more. You want to invest this much money only once in a boat you don't yet own, meaning that before you commission a survey, you want to be 99 percent certain that it isn't going to reveal any defects serious enough to send you looking for a different boat.

If you don't plan to hire a surveyor—a common course of action where the cost of the boat is relatively low—then you need to be 100 percent sure of the boat's condition. In either case, if you are shopping for a boat, you need to be able to look at the various candidates with a critical eye and understand the implications of what you see.

DETERMINING THE NEEDS OF YOUR OWN BOAT

That a potential buyer needs to carefully determine a boat's overall condition is obvious, but why would an owner want to survey his or her own boat? The most important reason is safety. A single cracked wire terminal can drop the rig in a heartbeat. Unbacked cleats under load can tear free of the deck and whip through the air with potentially deadly consequences. Serious delamination reduces actual hull strength to a fraction of what is required. Chafed wire insulation can leave you treading water while your boat burns to the waterline.

The second reason is economy. Backing up cleats is sure to be cheaper than salvaging a boat released from her mooring in a blow. Caulking stanchion bases is cheaper than the major surgery of deck-core replacement. A single terminal fitting is a fraction of the cost of a whole new rig. By replacing a corroded through-hull, you could avoid rebuilding a submerged engine.

The third reason is pride. Part of the reward of owning a boat is keeping her in nice condition. An essential part of this is recognizing problems and understanding their ramifications. Most boatowners keep a weather eye open for anything irregular, but boat problems are often hidden from casual view until they become obvious in some spectacular or disheartening way. Periodic stem-to-stern surveys can reveal attention-needing conditions well before they get out of hand.

Catching potential problems early, before they have a chance to work their mischief, requires a thorough and focused examination and a discerning eye. There is nothing particularly difficult about assessing the condition of a boat; it is an essential skill for every boatowner, though too often neglected. In the pages that follow, you will learn where to look and what to look for. Take the time to develop this skill and you will save money, the occasional skipped heartbeat, and perhaps even disaster.

HULL

The hull is the most important component of any boat. It keeps the water out and the boat afloat, and it provides the foundation for all other components. A condemned mast, engine, or deck can be replaced, but a condemned hull dooms the boat. Always start your survey with the hull.

A fair number of wood hulls are still around, but the number gets smaller every year. While well-cared-for wood hulls are remarkably long lived, such care is sadly rare. An aging wood hull is infinitely more likely to have serious problems than one constructed of fiberglass. Effectively surveying a wood hull requires specialized techniques not covered here, but some guidance in probing wood for rot can be found in "Interior."

Metal is primarily a custom boat material in the United States, but a number of European production boats have been constructed of steel or aluminum. The main risk with metal hulls is corrosion. Determining their condition essentially requires examining every square inch for telltale signs—pitting and scaling, bubbled paint, or a powdery coating. A surveyor will bang suspicious spots vigorously with a hammer.

Fiberglass is the construction material of virtually all production sailboats built in the United States. If you own a sailboat or are looking to buy one less than 35 years old, there is an overwhelming likelihood that the boat's hull will be fiberglass. Unlike wood or metal, the troubles found in fiberglass hulls are rarely natural decomposition. More often they stem from poor construction techniques or impact damage.

Determining with a high degree of certainty the condition of a fiberglass hull requires little more than good observation skills and a basic understanding of the conditions you're looking for. Laboratory tests to determine the internal condition of the laminate are rarely employed, even by professional surveyors, because they rarely reveal conditions inconsistent with the surveyor's field observations.

Look, listen, and wonder. Sharp eyes, sensitive ears, and a deductive mind are the most important tools in the fiberglass-boat surveyor's kit.

FAIR AND TRUE?

Fair means smooth and regular—without humps or flat spots. True means accurately shaped—true to her designed lines. Both are good indicators of quality and may also reveal repairs.

HULL SIDES

Standing at the stern, position your eye near the hull, then slowly move sideways so you see more and more of the hull. Concentrate on the "horizon" of the hull, watching for it to jump or dip instead of move away smoothly. Glossy hulls are more revealing; wet the hull if it is dull, but don't confuse waves in the layer of water with irregularities in the hull. A flexible batten can help you position a flaw precisely.

Hard spots. Hard spots reveal themselves as bumps or ridges in the hull. Inside the boat you will generally find a bulkhead or other structural member at the hard spot. The hard spot is caused by the hull flexing over the rigid member. Most boats reveal hard spots to the observant eye, but if the bump is pronounced, the hinging may have broken the glass fibers. Suspect some weakening of the hull.

Flat spots. Because thin fiberglass depends upon curvature to make it stiff, designed flat areas of the hull will be thicker and/or stiffened to compensate. Flat spots in the curved parts of a hull indicate trouble. They occasionally occur because the manufacturer removed the hull from the mold too soon, but more often they indicate weakness, damage, or a poorly executed repair. Rigging tension can dimple a flimsy hull around the chainplate attachment points. A weak hull may permanently deflect if stored in a cradle or supported by screw stands for a long time. Any impact that flattens the hull has broken or delaminated the fiberglass. Amateur repairs often "bridge" a hole rather than matching the original contour of the hull. All of these require corrective measures.

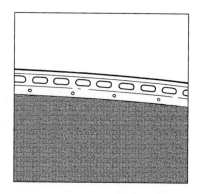

Print-through. Often the weave of the underlying fabric is visible in the surface of the hull, especially if the gelcoat still has its gloss. Dark colors show print-through more. A light print-through is probably not serious, but anything more than that suggests poor layup technique. Hull construction begins with a layer of gelcoat sprayed into the polished mold, then one or two layers of chopped-strand mat (CSM) begins the laminate schedule. Mat is important because it is the most watertight fabric and it provides the best foundation for a strong gelcoat bond. That it also yields the smoothest surface is an ancillary benefit, so if you see significant print-through, the manufacturer failed to put sufficient mat between the woven fabric and the gelcoat. Premature gelcoat failure is a likely consequence.

LINES

Walk (or row) away from the hull, then circle it slowly, looking at the shape of the hull.

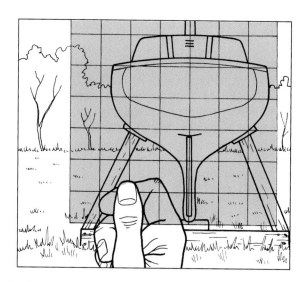

Symmetry. From directly forward and astern, the hull should appear symmetrical and the keel perpendicular to the deck. Sighting the hull through the gridwork of a plastic plotter simplifies this determination. Any detectable difference from one side to the other suggests major trouble.

Distortion. From either side, look for any change in the flow of the sheer. Overtight stays can permanently distort the hull, revealed by a break in the sheerline, usually at the mast station. Improper support during storage can also cause permanent hull distortion.

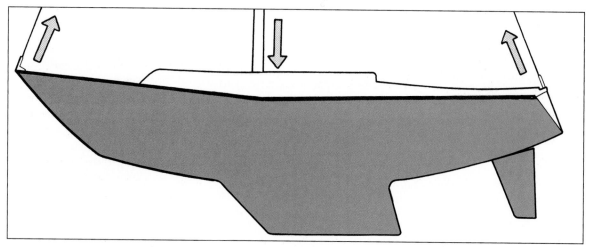

SCANTLINGS

Older fiberglass hulls are generally of consistent thickness, but hulls built in the last 15 years are likely to be thinner above the waterline than below. This lowers costs and may improve performance, but it makes a weaker hull. Current models may be more than 1 inch thick near the keel and less than ¼ that at the rail. Whether or not the loss in strength matters depends on how the boat will be used.

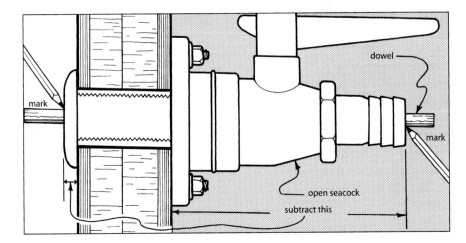

Without special equipment, you need a hole in the hull to determine its thickness. Any through-bolted hardware on the hull provides an opportunity to observe the hull thickness because you can extract a bolt. You can measure the thickness at through-hull fittings by dismantling just the hose connection. Hulls sometimes have extra thickness at through-hull locations, but you should be able to determine this by examining the inside of the hull around the through-hull. Except in extreme cases, determining the hull thickness has limited absolute value, but comparative hull thicknesses can be useful in evaluating boats from different manufacturers.

HULL IDENTIFICATION NUMBER

SINCE 1972 BOAT MANUFACTURERS have been required to mold a 12-character hull identification number (HIN) into the transom. The prescribed code is easy to decipher. It generally looks something like this: PEA74155L485.

The first three characters are the manufacturer, the next five the model designation and the production number in the series. In this case the boat is a Pearson, coded model 74, and it is number 155 in the series. It could be the 155th boat built, but manufacturers sometimes begin a series with 100 or some other number.

Of course it's likely you already know what kind of boat you're looking at, so it is the last four numbers that are most useful. The first two are the month and year this particular model was certified by the Coast Guard. Month designations are A (January) through L (December). Year designations are 0 through 9; you have to guess the decade. The last two numbers are the model year of the boat. Keep in mind that model year often runs from August through July rather than January through December. So the HIN ending with L485 tells you that this particular model was certified in December of 1984 or, judging from the hull number (155), more likely 1974 and that it was built in 1984 or 1985. The molded-in model year can confirm or refute representations made by the seller, and the year of certification gives you a clue to the success of this particular design. TIP: New boats tend to reveal design flaws that result in some redesign, so most models are better after a year or two in production.

Sometimes manufacturers don't follow the prescribed code exactly. If you can't figure it out, call the manufacturer.

SIGNS OF STRESS OR TRAUMA

Fiberglass generally reveals stress problems with cracks in the gelcoat. The cracks can be very fine and hard to see; get close to the hull and lay your finger against the spot you are examining to ensure that your eyes focus properly. A dye penetrant such as Spot Check (available from auto-parts suppliers) can highlight hairline cracks.

Don't confuse stress cracks with surface crazing; crazing is a random pattern of cracks—something like the tapped shell of a boiled egg just before you peel it—that occurs over large areas of the boat. Stress cracks are localized and generally have an identifiable pattern to the discerning eye.

IMPACT DAMAGE

A collision serious enough to damage the hull usually leaves a scar, but sometimes the only visible record of the event is a pattern of concentric cracks in the gelcoat. Impact with a sharp object, like the corner of a dock, leaves a bull's-eye pattern. Impact with a flat object, like a piling or a seawall, tends to put the stressed area in parentheses. Tap the hull with a plastic mallet or a screwdriver handle in the area of the impact and listen for any dull-sounding areas, which indicate delamination. Examine the hull inside for signs that the impact fractured the glass.

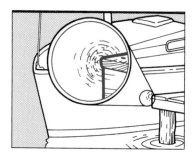

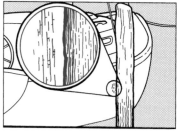

PANTING

Panting occurs when poorly supported sections of the hull flex as the boat drives through the waves. This problem is also called oilcanning, taking its name from the domed bottom you push in and let spring back on a small oilcan. Panting usually occurs in relatively flat areas of the hull near the bow, but it may also occur in flat bilge areas and unreinforced quarters. The classic sign is a series of near-parallel cracks, sometimes crescent shaped, in the gelcoat. If you can move any portion of the hull by pushing on it, the hull lacks adequate stiffness. Left unchecked, panting can result in fatigue damage to the laminate and eventually a hinge crack all the way through the hull.

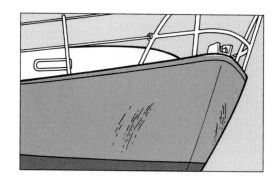

TRANSVERSE DAMAGE

An impact on one side of a boat often results in damage to the opposite side as the force is transferred by some rigid member or just by the box effect—push on one corner of a box and all corners are distorted. Because hulls are designed to resist outside assault, the damage to the nonimpacted side—where the stress is applied from inside the hull—is often greater than to the impacted side. When you find any evidence of impact damage, always check the opposite side of the boat for collateral damage.

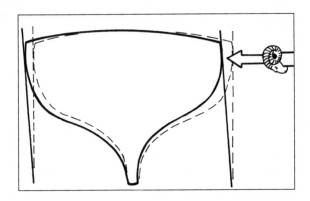

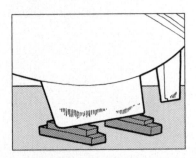

WEEPING

Any spot on the hull that remains damp more than a few hours after the boat is hauled indicates water has penetrated the surface of the hull. Scrape away paint and you are likely to find a crack that requires repair. Weeping from an encapsulated keel can indicate a serious problem if the ballast is iron; water incursion causes the iron to rust and swell, distorting and even bursting the fiberglass. Examine the bottom of the keel and the rudder most carefully for signs of weeping.

REPAIRS

Done well, a repair is almost impossible to detect, but this is not a concern because a proper repair will be just as strong as the original laminate. Inferior repairs are generally easier to detect. We have already mentioned flat spots. Also look for variations in the color and texture of the hull surface. It is hard to match gelcoat exactly, and careful observation will usually reveal any patching. Gelcoat paste used in a repair can also develop a porous look compared to the billiard-ball smoothness of the original gelcoat. If the hull has been painted, look for a crescent-shaped ridge that will mark a less-than-perfectly-sanded patch.

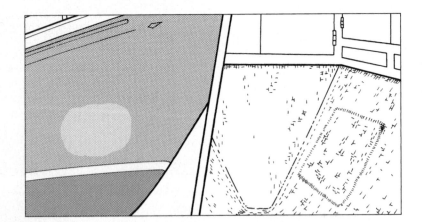

Repairs are more visible inside the hull. Any signs of lifting around the edge of a patch suggests grinding—essential for a strong repair—was inadequate. The repair shouldn't be trusted. Where you find evidence of a repair, sound the hull in a regular pattern over the entire repair area to detect voids or delamination.

DELAMINATION

Delamination in fiberglass is the functional equivalent of rot in a wooden boat. Well-constructed solid-fiberglass hulls (meaning not cored) almost never delaminate unless they have suffered impact damage or unless water has penetrated the gelcoat (see the next section). This is because proper hull-construction technique—adding each layer before the previous one has cured—results in the resin linking chemically into a solid mass. Occasionally a manufacturer defeats this by leaving an uncompleted hull in the mold over a weekend; but most know—and do—better.

Introduce core into the formula and the likelihood of delamination increases dramatically. A core divides the hull into three distinct layers—the outer skin, the core, and the inner skin—with the bond between them strictly mechanical. Polyester resin adheres chemically to itself with amazing tenacity, but it has never been very good at adhering to other materials. At the slightest provocation it will release its grip on the core material, regardless of what it is.

PERCUSSION TESTING

Tapping a fiberglass hull is akin to spiking a wooden one. Use a plastic mallet or the handle of a screwdriver to give the hull a light rap. If the laminate is healthy, you will get a sharp report. If it is delaminated, the sound will be a dull thud. Your hull is sure to play more than two notes, but map all suspect returns; then check inside the hull to see if a bulkhead, tank, or bag of sail is responsible. If not, it is the laminate.

It is essential to do a thorough evaluation of a cored hull because core delamination is unfortunately common and robs the hull of much of its designed strength. Tap every 2 or 3 inches over the entire surface of the hull. Be especially suspicious of the area around through-hull fittings and near signs of skin damage or repair. Percussion testing can also reveal filler patches.

GELCOAT PROBLEMS

Most gelcoat problems are cosmetic, but a few suggest underlying structural defects.

CHALKING

Well-applied gelcoat will last a decade with little or no maintenance, perhaps twice that long if protected with a regular application of wax. Eventually the exposed surface erodes and the gelcoat loses its gloss. To determine whether the gloss can be restored, buff an inconspicuous area with rubbing compound (formulated for fiberglass). If the gloss returns before the gelcoat becomes transparent, you may get a few more years from the surface; otherwise, painting is the preferred way to restore the gloss.

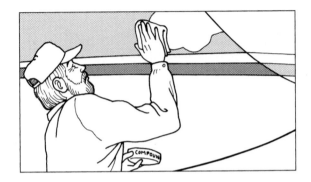

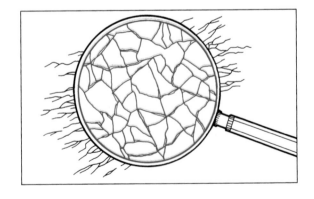

no color change; can probably be buffed out

color change; gelcoat repair required

SCRATCHES

If scratches don't penetrate the gelcoat, they can usually be buffed out with rubbing compound. Deep scratches are easily repaired with gelcoat putty.

CRAZING

Close examination of the gelcoat, especially on boats built in the '60s and '70s, may reveal a random eggshell-like pattern of fine cracks which is usually caused by temperature expansion (and contraction) of the hull. It is prevalent in older boats because the gelcoat was thicker and thus less flexible. Correcting this condition requires filling the cracks with epoxy and painting the repaired surface.

parallel cracks under the transom are probably from excessive backstay tension

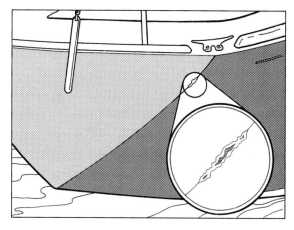

STRESS CRACKING

Unlike crazing, stress cracks are usually localized and exhibit a discernible pattern. As previously mentioned, stress cracks can indicate impact damage or panting. They are a valuable clue for a number of other conditions detailed in this chapter. If you find cracks in the gelcoat, figure out why they are there before moving on.

VOIDS

The reluctance of glass fabric to take a sharp bend causes it to pull away from the gelcoat on inside corners during the layup process, creating voids. On a hull, this condition is generally confined to the stem, the corners where the hull sides intersect the transom, and the turn of the hull flange. Percussion testing reveals voids and may break them open. Voids are a cosmetic flaw and easily repaired with gelcoat putty.

BLISTERS

Blisters reveal themselves as bumps in the surface of fiberglass and are easily detected by simply examining the hull. A blister can be as small as a ladybug or as big as your hand.

GELCOAT BLISTERS

Blisters occur because free water-soluble chemicals inside the laminate exert an osmotic pull on water outside, and some water molecules find a way through the slightly permeable gelcoat. As more water is attracted into the enclosed space, internal pressure builds. The water molecules aren't squirted back out the way they came in because they combine with the attracting chemicals into a solution with a larger molecular structure. Instead, the pressure pushes the covering gelcoat into a dome—a blister.

Break a sample blister to assess the condition. Wear goggles because pressures can exceed 150 psi and the liquid that comes spraying out is acid. Scrub out the blister with water and a brush and examine the underlying laminate. If the laminate is perfect—the usual finding—the blister is primarily a cosmetic flaw, although taking steps to prevent water from reaching the laminate may be prudent.

LAMINATE BLISTERS

If the laminate is damaged, repairs will be more extensive, but this is still not a dangerous condition as long as the number of blisters is small. Use a knife point to find the depth of the damage. Laminate blisters most often occur between the initial layer(s) of mat and the first layer of woven roving— probably because the manufacturer was religious about getting the initial mat laid into the mold while the gelcoat was still chemically active, but was less exacting about the timing for completing the layup. Or it may be due to a failure to roll the roving sufficiently against the resin-stiffened mat to eliminate all voids. Whatever the reason, laminate blisters below the first layers of mat are no more dangerous than gelcoat blisters.

If additional layers of the laminate are involved in the blister, the area will have to be treated like any other delamination. How serious the problem is depends on the number and size of the laminate blisters.

POX

For pox, examine the bottom as soon as it comes out of the water. In the early stages blisters can shrink and even disappear altogether. If the bottom is covered with hundreds of blisters, the boat has pox. Boat pox is a much more serious condition than a handful of blisters scattered over the bottom of a 15-year-old hull. It is a systemic condition and will only worsen unless remedial action is taken.

To cure boat pox you must grind away all the gelcoat below the waterline. Just opening and filling the blisters won't do because a hull with pox is saturated throughout and won't dry out unless the gelcoat is removed. Once the hull is dry, which can take several months, the usual process is to apply a new barrier coat of epoxy or vinylester. The cost to have this done professionally is between $300 and $400 per foot of boat length. Most of this is labor, so the cost if you do it yourself is much more modest, but it is a nasty job at best.

MOISTURE CONTENT

Floating fiberglass hulls absorb moisture, sometimes a significant amount. Water makes the boat heavier, and it puts the gelcoat and laminate at risk for blisters. The only way to determine the absolute moisture content is to cut a plug from the hull, weigh it, oven-dry it, then weigh it again. The difference in the two weights is the moisture content. But unless you have reason to believe that the laminate is saturated, this type of testing is unnecessary.

MOISTURE METERS

Professional surveyors use moisture meters, and boatyards sometimes have a moisture meter available. These typically measure electromagnetic capacitance and convert that into percentage of moisture content. Moisture-meter readings are notoriously misleading. For example, readings as high as 25 percent are not uncommon, but the actual moisture content of saturated fiberglass laminate is unlikely to exceed 4 percent. Despite claims to the contrary, moisture meters tell you very little about the interior of the laminate. Generally you must remove the bottom paint to even get a reading from the fiberglass.

These limitations don't mean moisture-meter readings are useless. A series of moisture-meter readings can identify areas of the hull that are wet relative to other areas. And meter readings taken over time should flatten out, giving you an indication that the hull has reached its driest state. On a boat that has been out of the water for several weeks, a reading around 5 percent suggests the hull is dry.

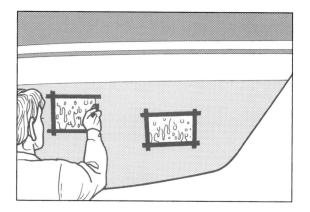

PLASTIC

You can accomplish much the same thing with 6-inch squares of plastic freezer bag. To see if a hull is wet, tape several squares to different locations on the hull, using electrical tape and sealing all four edges. After 24 hours, check the plastic. If moisture has condensed on the interior surface, the hull is wet. This works best when the day is sunny and relatively warm.

To monitor the drying process, do this test periodically over a period of weeks or months. When the plastic remains dry even in bright sunlight, the hull is dry.

KEEL

The occurrence of keel problems seems to be directly related to the keel's aspect ratio. The greater the chord—the keel's fore and aft dimension—the less vulnerable the keel.

ALIGNMENT

Keels on wooden sailboats are often found to have taken a twist or cant, but fiberglass boats only rarely exhibit this condition. Occasionally manufacturers remove the hull from the mold too soon and the keel or keel pad moves before the laminate reaches full cure. A straightedge held at arm's length will let you check the keel against the mast or the horizontal plane of the deck.

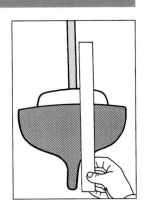

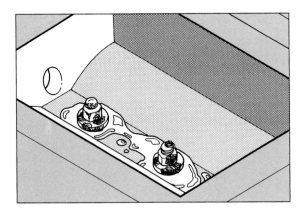

ATTACHMENT

Quality bronze or stainless steel keel bolts can last half a century or longer, but they are susceptible to life-shortening corrosion when wet or exposed. If the keel-to-hull joint isn't completely sealed, stainless steel keel bolts are likely to develop crevice corrosion. Bilge water is more likely to be the catalyst, so manufacturers often encapsulate the tops in resin to seal them. This undoubtedly extends the lives of the bolts, but it precludes easy examination. Fortunately catastrophic keel-bolt failure on an otherwise sound fiberglass boat is highly unlikely; but to be certain you can have the keel X-rayed. If the bolts are exposed, visually check them for corrosion and signs of leakage. They should have a generous shoulder washer under the nut. For every 1,500 pounds of external ballast, the keel should have at least 1 square inch of bolt sectional area; this is called Nevin's Rule.

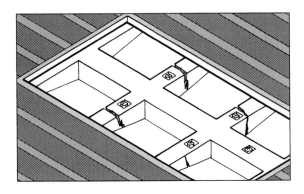

Hull attachment. When the keel is bolted directly to the hull, the bolts should pass through floor "timbers" or a reinforcing grid. Check the timbers and grid for any signs of stress cracking.

Stub-keel attachment. Bolting the ballast keel to a molded stub keel is generally a stronger design. Check the keel-to-stub joint for any signs of movement. Separation at the joint puts stainless steel keel bolts at risk for crevice corrosion, and their integrity will be in question unless they are inspected.

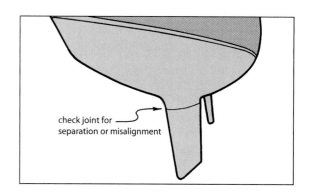

check joint for separation or misalignment

Encapsulated ballast. When the keel is a hollow part of the hull filled with ballast, problems are rare. Check both sides of the keel for swelling; if the ballast is iron—common in boats built outside the United States—water intrusion can cause it to rust and expand. The bottom of the keel is most damage prone, so be sure to examine it carefully. This requires having the yard lift the boat or at least reposition the keel blocks.

Also check the bilge to make sure the top of the ballast cavity is sealed. If this part of the bilge can hold standing water, set a glass in it and pour water into the bilge and the glass to the same level. Check in a couple of days; if the level of the bilge water is lower than the level of the water in the glass, the bilge is leaking into the keel cavity.

If you suspect water intrusion, drill a couple of exploratory holes through or near the bottom of the keel. Use only a hand drill or a battery-operated drill for this. If there is water in the cavity, the holes will serve as drains, and they also allow you to determine the ballast material. Find and repair the leaks into the cavity, then repair the drilled holes with epoxy laminate (see *Sailboat Hull and Deck Repair*).

GROUNDING

Going aground in mud or sand is usually harmless, but striking rock or coral while under way subjects the hull to a pile-driver-like blow. When the impact is to the lowest part of the keel, the lever effect multiplies the already considerable forces and concentrates them. Any signs of damage to the front or the bottom of the keel should have you carefully examining the area where the keel joins the hull. A bump in front of the keel or a dimple behind it suggests serious damage. Remove the bottom paint to check for cracks. Also examine these areas from inside the hull.

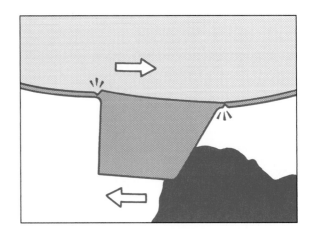

CENTERBOARDS

Except in lightly built racers, fiberglass construction has eliminated most of the problems that traditionally plagued wooden centerboarders—except fouling—but there are a few conditions to be on the lookout for.

Board. Check metal centerboards with a straightedge to make sure they have not been bent by grounding. A bent centerboard can usually be pressed or hammered back into true. Fiberglass centerboards are constructed much like rudders and should be inspected as detailed in the rudder section on page 26.

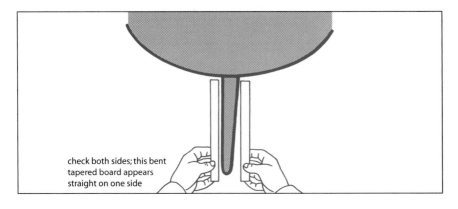

check both sides; this bent tapered board appears straight on one side

Trunk. The monocoque construction made possible by fiberglass usually yields a strong and leak-free center-board trunk. The case is typically an integral, molded feature of the hull and should be examined in the same manner as the rest of the hull. In a keel/centerboard configuration where the centerboard is entirely housed within the ballast keel, the likelihood of leakage or structural problems is low. To inspect the interior of the case, the boat must be hoisted enough for the board to be fully lowered.

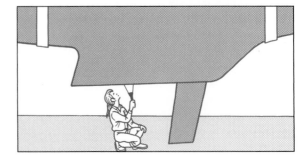

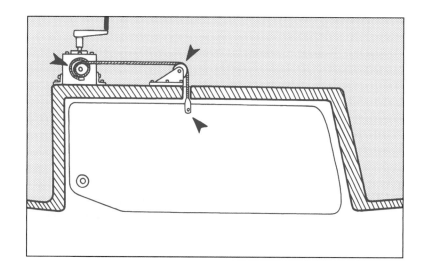

Pendant. Inspect the wire pendant for rust and broken strands. Look for wear on the fitting that lets the pendant into the boat. If the pendant runs in a groove over the top of the centerboard, look for marks outside the groove that might suggest that the pendant is slipping out of the groove, which risks jamming the board.

Pivot pin. Check the pivot pin (or the hole) for wear by trying to move the lowered board up and down or fore and aft. The pivot pin on most centerboard boats is essentially a shoulder bolt passing through both sides of the trunk. Check the grommets on either end for resilience and for signs of leakage.

The pin on a keel/centerboard is usually inaccessible, captured by resin plugs on either side. It can be the source of leakage into the ballast cavity, indicated by weeping around the pin (inside the trunk) after the boat has otherwise dried out. If the pin isn't loose or weeping, it generally requires no further attention, although stainless steel pins are subject to crevice corrosion. Determining the condition of the pin requires extraction.

RUDDER

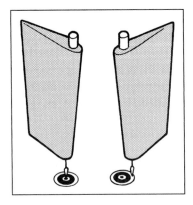

A sailboat rudder should have nearly neutral buoyancy so it neither floats nor sinks when the boat heels. Wood satisfies this requirement, and some early fiberglass sailboats had wood rudders, but most sailboat rudders are foam-filled or hollow fiberglass constructions.

SPADE RUDDERS

Spade rudders are built around the lower end of a length of tube or bar stock, with the tiller or steering quadrant attached to the upper end. The stock both turns the rudder and attaches it to the boat.

1 Check the vertical alignment of the rudder (above). Observe the bottom of the rudder blade as someone else moves the tiller or wheel from hard over to hard over. If the stock is bent it will be obvious.

2 Tie or lock the tiller or wheel, then try to turn the blade. If it moves, the internal structure of the rudder is broken or the filler has deteriorated, and the rudder will have to be rebuilt.

3 Examine the rudder port—where the stock enters the hull—and the hull around it. If the rudder comes under the strain of grounding or catching a line, will the stock bend or will it pry a hole in the bottom of the boat? A strong rudder installation requires reinforcement of the rudder tube well above the hull.

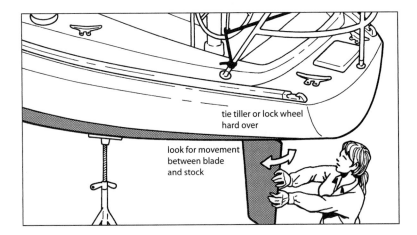

tie tiller or lock wheel hard over

look for movement between blade and stock

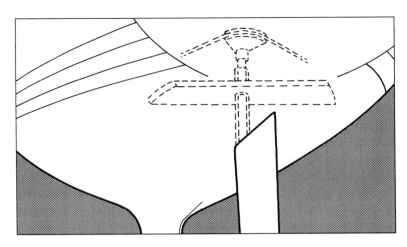

KEEL-HUNG

Hinging the rudder to the aft end of the keel provides fewer opportunities for rudder damage but is only possible with a keel that runs well aft.

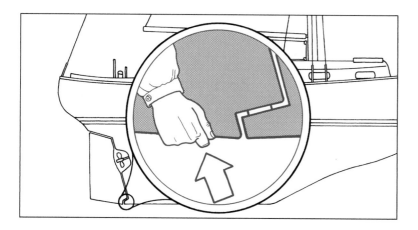

1 Shake the rudder blade at the bottom. Some play in the heel fitting is acceptable, but the socket shouldn't be elongated or the pin obviously worn.

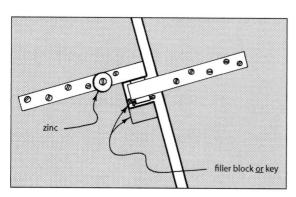

zinc

filler block or key

2 If the rudder hinges on pintles and gudgeons, check them for wear. Also check to make sure they are well mounted to both the hull and the rudder. They should have keys or filler blocks to prevent them from coming unshipped, and generally they should be protected with zinc anodes.

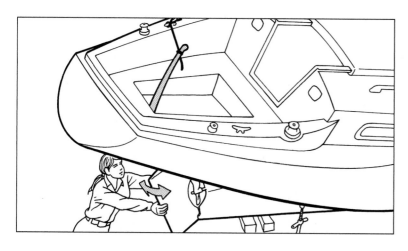

3 Check the rudder/stock attachment by locking the steering and trying to turn the blade.

SKEG-MOUNTED

To gain some of the advantages of a keel mounting without the disadvantages of a long keel, rudders are often attached to a leading skeg. Check a skeg-mounted rudder exactly as one hinged to the keel. In addition, examine the skeg carefully, paying particular attention to its alignment and its attachment to the hull.

OUTBOARD RUDDERS

The advantage of an outboard rudder is that the stock doesn't penetrate the hull. In fact, there is no stock; the tiller (or quadrant) is attached directly to the blade. The rudder is, however, vulnerable to collision from the rear. Examine the aft edge of the rudder, and check the pintles and gudgeons.

CONSTRUCTION

Occasionally rudders are constructed by wrapping fiberglass cloth around the core, but more often they are molded in two shell-like halves, then bonded together around the stock and the core.

Water intrusion. Rudder skins are typically thin, making the rudder relatively fragile. Examine the rudder (and the centerboard) carefully for cracks or weeping. Pay particular attention to the bottom of the rudder and to the area where the rudderstock passes through the skin. Inspection of the latter usually requiring the aid of a mirror. Water inside the rudder alters its buoyancy, is potentially damaging to the rudder's interior framework, and is a freeze risk in winter.

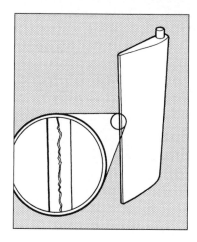

Center split. The joint between the two halves of molded rudder blades fails regularly. Examine every inch of the joint for signs of separation.

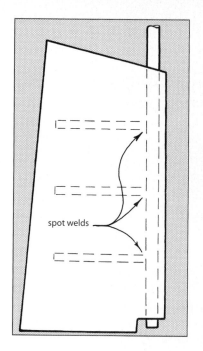

spot welds

Broken framework. With the tiller or wheel locked, if you can move the rudder, the interior framework is probably broken. Too often the internal framework is little more than two or three metal straps or rods spot-welded to the stock. When these welds break, the rudder rotates on the stock. Any movement of the rudder on the stock means the rudder must be cut apart and rebuilt.

CUTLESS BEARING AND PROPELLER

The Cutless bearing provides a bearing surface for the shaft where it exits the hull. Cutless bearings are generally a splined rubber tube inside a bronze housing.

1 Try to move the shaft side-to-side and up-and-down. Some play is normal, but if the shaft rattles, the Cutless bearing is worn and needs replacing.

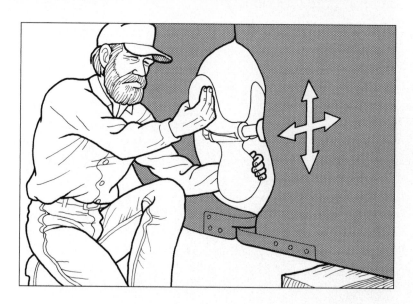

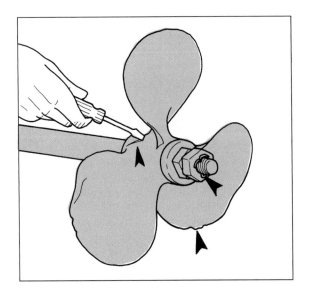

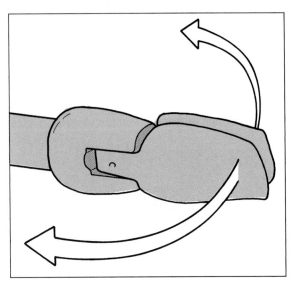

2 Examine the prop for nicks, corrosion, and bent blades. Scratch the hub to check the prop for galvanic corrosion: yellow is good, pink is bad. Look at the condition of the threads at the end of the shaft, and make sure the retaining nuts are tight and secured with a cotter pin.

3 If the prop is supposed to feather or fold, make sure it operates smoothly.

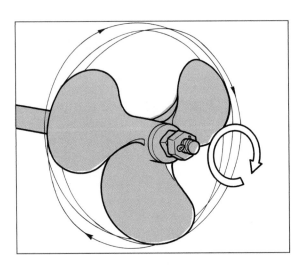

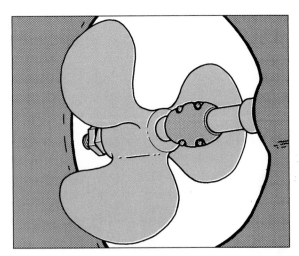

4 Rotate the prop to check the shaft for any bend.

5 The shaft should have a zinc collar in good condition (even if electrically isolated with a rubber coupling). The zinc should not be against the Cutless bearing or it will restrict the lubricating flow of water to the bearing.

THROUGH-HULL FITTINGS

Through-hull fittings are not very complicated—nothing more than a threaded pipe with an integral flange on one side, a clamping nut on the other.

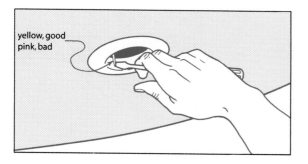

yellow, good
pink, bad

BRONZE

A patina on bronze skin fittings usually indicates nothing more than surface tarnish. Scratch the bronze with the corner of a screwdriver; if the exposed metal has a pinkish hue, the zinc has leeched out of the bronze and the remaining alloy is probably brittle. The fitting should be replaced.

PLASTIC

Early plastic through-hulls were brittle and dangerous, but the best modern ones are made of glass-reinforced resin (Marelon)—much like the hull they are usually installed in. Their biggest advantage is that they are not subject to corrosion. Some sailors object to plastic through-hulls below the waterline, but there is no evidence that Marelon through-hulls fail more often than bronze ones. It is unlikely that many of the old brittle through-hulls are still around, but unfortunately cheap plastic skin fittings intended for topside use are still available. Give all plastic fittings a good rap with a plastic mallet to check them. Make sure that only plastic nuts and plastic seacocks are used on plastic through-hulls; never mix bronze and plastic.

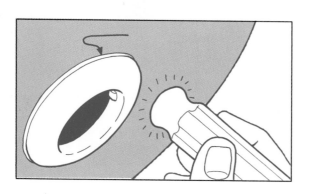

BEDDING

Check all around the through-hull flange for a continuous bead of bedding. If there is any indication that the seal has broken, the edges of the laminate around the hole may be exposed to water. The through-hull should be removed, cleaned, and rebedded in polyurethane sealant. Tap the hull around all skin fittings for evidence of delamination.

DECK

Unless you are terribly ham-fisted at the helm, it is the deck that sustains the worst treatment. You walk on it, carefully perhaps when the boat was new, but later with no more concern than you give a concrete sidewalk. It lies horizontal beneath the sun, like a staked-out Foreign Legionnaire. It is coated with salt, assaulted by acid rain. The freeze-thaw-freeze cycle of winter moisture in crevices and cracks, like clicks of a jack, pry the deck apart.

To endure, a deck needs to be strong, but weight carried high in a boat reduces stability, so first it needs to be light. Heavy abuse and light construction—not a combination that suggests longevity. In addition, decks are usually landscapes of corners, angles, and textures, each introducing new problems into the equation.

Glass-reinforced plastic is inherently flexible, but most of us want the deck to be stiff, to feel solid underfoot. Stiffening the deck without adding excessive weight requires cored construction—with all the potential problems that implies. You can shy away from a cored hull, but limiting yourself to boats without cored deck makes for extremely slim pickings.

Despite this, more deck problems (excluding the hull-to-deck joint) are the result of poor care and maintenance than of poor design and construction. Leaving the deck uncovered through the winter is murder on the laminate. Failure to properly bed deck hardware is a death warrant for the core.

Deck repairs are likely to be more costly and/or time consuming than comparable hull repairs. The angles and textures complicate laminate repair. Core is more likely to be involved. The deck is laden with a wide array of hardware which may have to be removed. And access to the underside of the deck is almost certain to be restricted.

Identifying deck problems early and taking the appropriate corrective action can prevent more serious damage. You should carefully survey the deck of your own boat at least once a year.

HULL-TO-DECK JOINT

Perhaps the very best clue to the overall construction of a boat is the hull-to-deck joint. Conscientious manufacturers make sure these joints are strong and will remain watertight long after the warranty expires.

Hull-to-deck joints generally fall into one of three categories, each with advantages and drawbacks. Identifying the type your boat has will make examination easier.

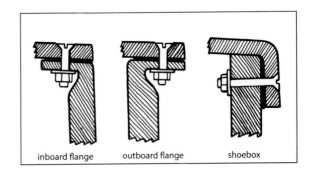

inboard flange   outboard flange   shoebox

CHECKING THE JOINT

1 From inside look for any signs of past leakage—discoloration, dust rivulets, etc. Much of the joint may be inaccessible, but sample segments may be observed from the forepeak and the cockpit lockers.

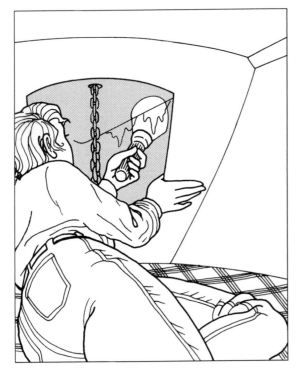

2 From outside, be suspicious if you see a fillet of caulk along either edge of the rail.

3 To fully inspect the joint, remove the covering rail or molding.

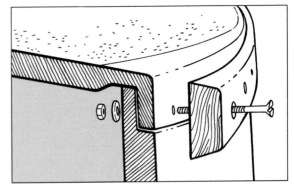

FASTENING

1 Pop rivets are soft by design and a poor way to join the deck to the hull. The pulsating stresses on the joint eventually stretch the rivet and allow the joint to loosen.

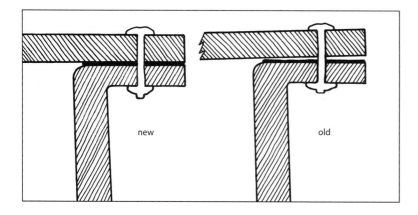

new   old

2 Self-tapping screws are better than pop rivets, but the strength of the joint is limited to the grip the threads have on the laminate. This is likely to be inadequate in rough seas or any kind of collision.

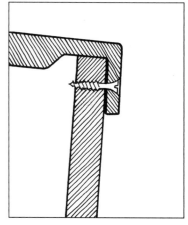

3 The best joints are fastened together with stainless steel bolts on about 6-inch centers. Wider spacing can allow the joint to separate between fasteners. Manufacturers sometimes let the toerail or rubrail bolts serve double duty—perfectly acceptable.

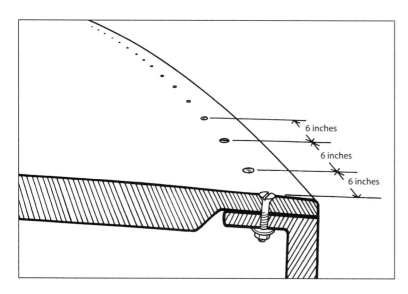

6 inches

6 inches

6 inches

TRACKING A LEAK

LEAKS DON'T ALWAYS leave a trail behind, but you can set a trap for the sneaky ones. Using a washable marker, simply draw a horizontal line high on the interior of the hull everywhere you have access. After the next hard rainstorm or wet beat to weather, inspect the line. Leaks will be flagged with a blurry break in the line and probably a streak of color down the hull. You can wash off the marker after your test, or leave it as an active monitoring system.

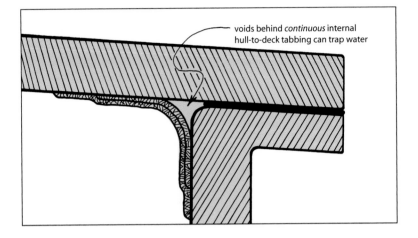

voids behind *continuous* internal hull-to-deck tabbing can trap water

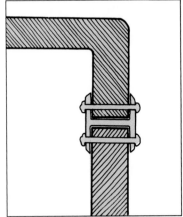

4 A few manufacturers have strengthened the joint by tabbing the hull and deck together with fiberglass. This generally makes a strong, watertight joint, but be sure it has not been done in such a way that it causes the joint to trap water, especially if the boat will be subjected to freezing temperatures.

5 Occasionally you may come across an older boat with the hull and deck joined by an H-shaped extrusion. This has proven to be a very poor method and should be avoided.

SEALANT

With the rail or molding removed, check to make sure the joint is fully caulked and the sealant still supple. Petroleum-based sealants eventually harden; the proper sealant for the hull-to-deck joint is polyurethane. A night inspection with a helper shining a bright light on the joint inside the boat can reveal otherwise undetectable separations.

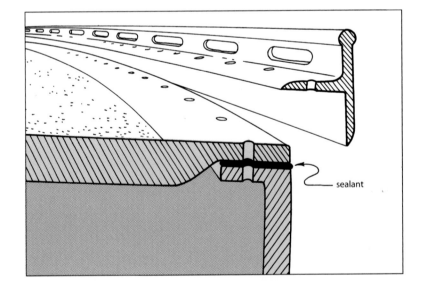

sealant

SURFACE DAMAGE

The gelcoat surface of the deck almost always has a shorter life than that of the hull. Some well-meaning manufacturers tried to compensate for this by making the deck gelcoat thicker, but this generally made matters worse.

CRAZING

Crazing is caused by temperature expansion and is more common on early fiberglass boats. Crazing is typically widespread, often covering most or all of the smooth deck surfaces. True crazing, i.e., not caused by flexing of the underlying laminate, is a cosmetic condition easily repaired with high-build epoxy primer.

STRESS CRACKING

Stress cracks are evidence that the deck has flexed beyond the capacity of the gelcoat. Stress cracks are usually localized, although lightly built boats sometimes exhibit stress cracks over every inch of the deck.

Alligatoring. A random pattern of stress cracks over a wide area is sometimes called alligatoring. Caused by excessive flexing of the underlying laminate, it looks similar to crazing, but with a much larger pattern. Alligatoring often indicates core delamination, which destroys the deck's stiffness and allows the top skin to flex.

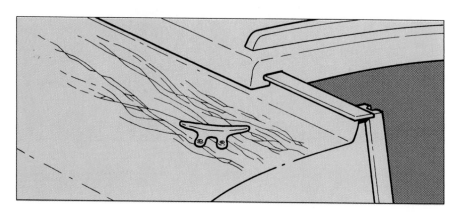

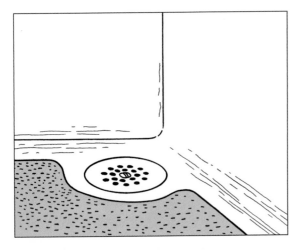

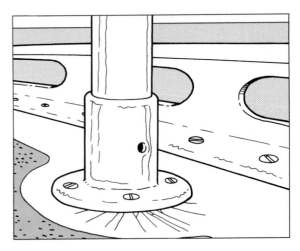

Parallel cracks. Hinge cracks are a common condition, caused by repeated flexing of the deck at a weak location. Look for parallel hinge cracks where the cockpit sides meet the sole and where the side decks intersect the trunk. Repairs require strengthening and/or stiffening the area.

Star cracks. Star cracks result from "pinpoint" stresses. The most common deck star cracks radiate from the bolt holes under stanchion bases—a direct result of the deck being levered up (or down) by force applied to the top of the stanchion. A backing plate that spreads the stresses is the usual preventative measure.

BREAKOUT

Because of the numerous corners in a deck mold, gelcoat voids are all too common. It is not unusual to find a boat with a flawless hull and a deck as pockmarked as a rural road sign. Voids in the flat expanse of the deck suggest inferior layup technique; but if they are confined to sharp outside corners of deck features, they show only that the designer was more concerned with style than with the realities of production fiberglass layup. Deck traffic quickly breaks out sizable voids; so an older boat without open voids means either good design and layup or voids that have been repaired. Check for voids by percussion testing the deck.

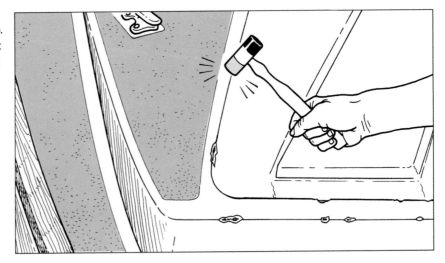

NONSKID

Most fiberglass boats have texture molded into the deck to provide secure footing. The design challenge—met with varying success—has always been to make the texture rough enough without being uncomfortable. Over time, traffic wears away sharp edges and painting fills depressions, reducing nonskid qualities. Check the deck wet and with marginal shoes; inadequate traction is as dangerous as a weak hull.

CORE PROBLEMS

Almost every decked fiberglass sailboat has core in the deck, usually end-grain balsa. Balsa is light and resists saturation when installed properly. Plywood is often substituted in hardware-mount areas for its higher compression strength. Relatively flat areas of the deck may be cored entirely with plywood. Plywood is stiffer and stronger, but much less resistant to saturation. Several types of plastic foam are also used as core material.

DELAMINATION

Crackling underfoot suggests delamination. Percussion test the deck to find and map delaminated areas. A delaminated deck often exhibits humps and alligatoring.

Domestic builders have been conscientious about using only marine-grade plywood for plywood cores, but a number of imported boats were built with lesser grades. The glue in these plywoods dissolves when they get wet and the plywood delaminates, losing all structural integrity. Such decks become springy and must be totally reconstructed.

WET CORE

Wet core can feel and sound squishy underfoot; water pumping out around deck-mounted hardware is a sure sign. Water usually enters deck core material through improperly sealed hardware mounting holes. If percussion testing reveals delamination near a piece of hardware—saturated core may sound less hollow than dry delamination, but not sharp like healthy core—remove the hardware and probe the core with a tissue-wrapped screwdriver; moisture on the tissue suggests a wet core.

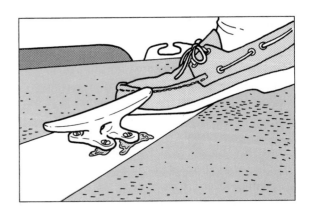

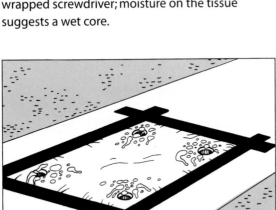

Seal the mounting holes—top and bottom—with plastic, then check the plastic at the end of a sunny day; condensation inside the plastic suggests moisture in the core.

You can confirm suspected wet core by drilling into it through the top skin. If the core is saturated, the material the drill brings out will be wet.

Foam cores are generally unaffected by moisture, but wet foam is still a serious condition. The hydraulic pumping action from just walking on a saturated deck tends to hammer the skins apart, and if the boat is subject to freezing conditions, the expansion rips them apart. Regardless of core material, the space between the inner and outer deck skins must be dry.

ROT

Balsa resists rot, but if it remains saturated for a long period, the effect is the same: the core becomes mushy and weak and separates from the sandwiching skins. Probing the core with a wire through a hole in the skin will give you a clue as to the integrity of the core material.

Plywood rots and virtually disintegrates if it is allowed to remain wet. A soft deck suggests rotten core. This is easily confirmed with a wire probe.

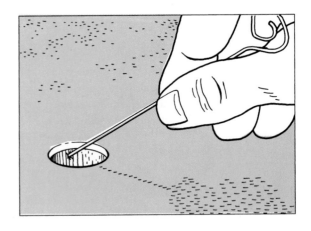

Hatches must be strong and watertight. Even hatches with a high coaming need a gasket to be truly watertight. Modern hatches depend entirely on gaskets.

DECK HATCHES

1   Check the integrity of the hatch; wooden hatches tend to come apart if they aren't well maintained, and fiberglass hatches are sometimes so thin, especially on the sides, that they crack or split.

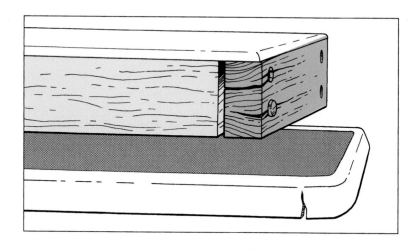

2   Gaskets are almost invariably kept in service long past their useful life. Check the gasket to make sure it is still supple. Also inspect the hinges, support, and latch for distortion or corrosion.

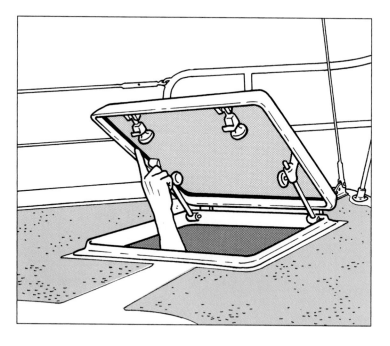

COMPANIONWAY HATCH

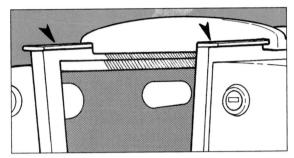

1 Carefully inspect the rabbets or notches that retain a sliding companionway hatch; hatches sometimes stress-crack in the bottom of the rabbet, and a healthy jerk will separate the hatch from the boat.

2 For easy hatch operation, the rails should be perfectly straight. Overtight stays can cause distortion; loosen the backstay tension and check the rails again. If the beds for the rails aren't flat, fairing them with epoxy putty, then reinstalling the rails will generally cure a "sticky" hatch.

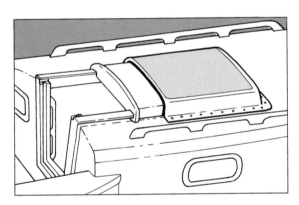

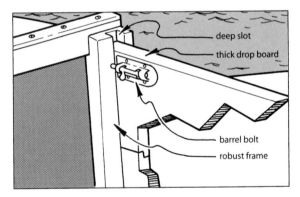

deep slot

thick drop board

barrel bolt

robust frame

3 Don't expect a sliding hatch to be truly watertight; a sea hood over its forward end helps. Sea hoods need to be well fastened to the deck and strong enough to stand on.

4 It may be possible to construct a companionway door as strong as dropboards, but it rarely happens. Outside of protected waters, dropboards are essential. Make sure they are thick enough to take a breaking wave. The slot for the hatch boards should also be up to the task—deep, with plenty of material on both sides. Barrel bolts to hold the boards in place are a good feature.

COCKPIT LOCKERS

1 The most essential concern is keeping the lid in place. Hinges are often inadequate; the fiberglass should fail before the hinge does. Make certain each hatch has a securable latch strong enough to hold if the contents of the locker fall against the inside of the lid in a knockdown.

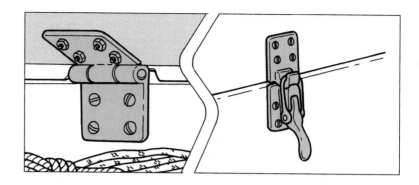

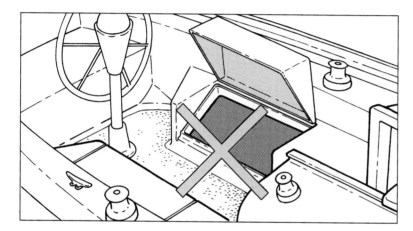

2 Cockpit hatches rarely have a gasket, depending on deep coamings to channel the water away. Such coamings should never be low enough for cockpit flooding to flood the hatch.

COCKPIT FLOODING

COCKPIT DESIGN IS NOT TECHNICALLY a survey issue, but that is little consolation if you strengthen hatch boards and locker latches but still end up treading water. A companionway at cockpit-sole level is dangerous, and keeping the lower board in place is a poor substitute for a bridge deck. Cockpit drains are almost always too small; they should be capable of lowering the water below the level of the hatch coamings in a matter of seconds, capable of emptying the cockpit entirely in a minute or two.

PORTLIGHTS

Portlights must be leak free and strong enough to resist a boarding wave. If they are fixed, they should be clear, and if they are opening, they should seal with a light turn on the dogs.

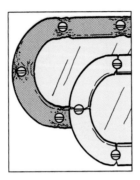

1 Check frames for damage or distortion. Plastic frames have a poor record of durability. Aluminum frames tend to corrode, sometimes beyond use. Bronze and stainless give few problems.

2 Check the gasket on opening ports. If it is not soft and supple, replace it. Overtightening the dogs in an effort to get a "dead" gasket to seal is the biggest cause of damage to opening ports; a couple of easy turns on the dogs should be sufficient.

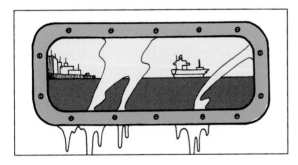

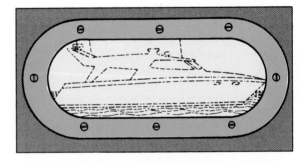

3 Water stains beneath a deadlight suggest that the port needs to be removed and rebedded. Beneath an opening port, water stains may only reflect that the port was left open when it should have been closed.

4 Over time plastic portlights get scratched and sometimes craze. Replacing them is not difficult if the frames are sound, and clear portlights make a big difference in both the appearance of the boat and the view from the cabin.

DECK HARDWARE

Part of a deck survey is an examination of the hardware attached to the deck. Spars, rigging, and steering systems are covered elsewhere in this book.

MOUNTING

Oil-discharge plaques and speed-log bevels can be mounted with screws, but virtually every other item of deck hardware should be through-bolted to the deck. All items that might come under stress—such as cleats, winches, pulpits, and stanchion bases—need a generous backing plate on the underside of the deck. Metal, preferably stainless steel, is the material of choice; wood backers tend to compress, and fiberglass laminate, unless obtrusively thick, is too flexible.

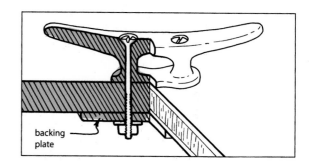

backing plate

BEDDING

1 Below deck, check for signs of leakage—water stains, dust rivulets, mildew, corrosion on the mounting bolts or backing plate. On deck, examine all sides of the base of each item; a properly bedded item sits on a thin "gasket" of sealant. Anywhere there is a void or the base sits hard against the deck is a potential leak. Sealant beaded or filleted around the edge of the base is a sure sign of leakage. Sealant below deck is also a sign of a leakage problem; backing plates should never be bedded.

2 Depending on sealant to keep water out of core material is an invitation to disaster. If the hardware is installed on a cored area, remove a mounting bolt and probe the hole with wire. Top-quality boats have solid laminate in designed hardware-mount areas. If the core is exposed in the hole, the mounting holes should be drilled oversize, filled with epoxy, then redrilled for the bolts (see *Sailboat Hull and Deck Repair*). Bedding is still required.

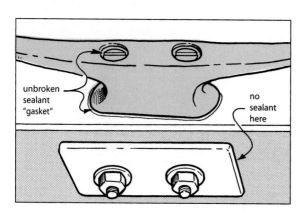

unbroken sealant "gasket"

no sealant here

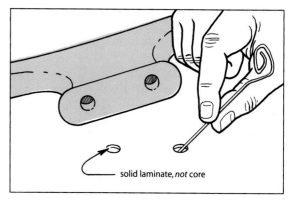

solid laminate, *not* core

WINCHES

Turn each winch drum backward (usually counterclockwise) slowly and listen to the pawls. You should hear two distinct clicks, and both pawls should seat at each click with a solid snap. Make a complete revolution, then do it again reversing your effort at each click to make sure the pawls seat in each tooth of the gear. Insert the winch handle and turn it backward to check the spindle pawls the same way. Now spin the drum; it should spin easily, halted only by the drag of the pawls. If the winch is stiff or the pawls fail to click properly, the winch needs at best to be dismantled, cleaned, and lubricated; but the condition could be more serious. Winches almost always contain dissimilar metals, and if they are not properly cared for, corrosion can do serious damage. To fully determine the condition of a winch, you must dismantle it.

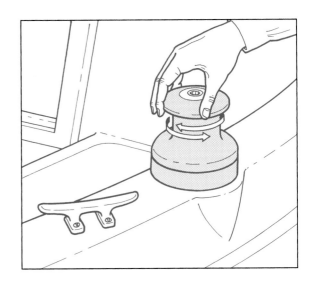

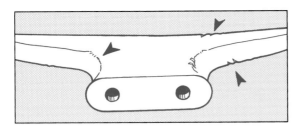

CLEATS

Run your fingers over all cleats, especially under the horns. Cleats should have no sharp edges and no rough areas, and they should be of an appropriate size for the line they are intended to belay.

HINGES

Hinges essential to keeping water out of the interior of the boat should be cast or machined from solid bronze or stainless steel and should have oversize pins. Anchor lockers seem especially prone to inadequate hinges (and ridiculous latches if they have one at all). Watch out for cast zinc (Zamak) hardware, which looks strong enough but isn't.

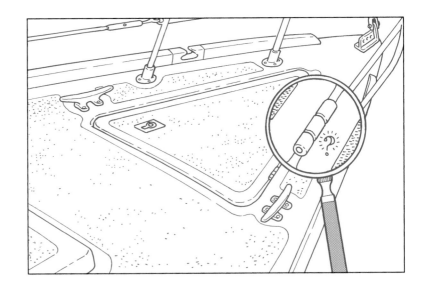

PULPITS

Both the pulpit and the pushpit should feel strong and rigid. A flimsy pulpit is dangerous. Tubing diameter should be at least 1 inch, and welds should be continuous and well finished.

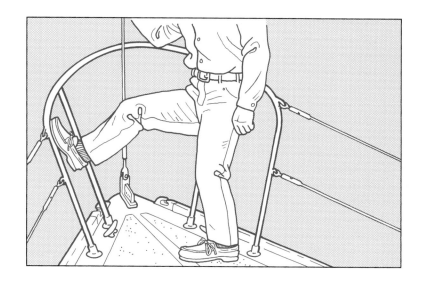

STANCHIONS AND LIFELINES

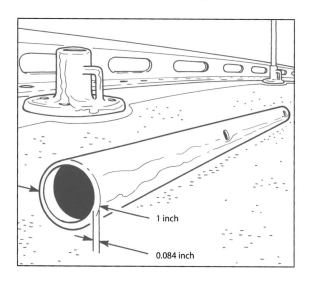

1 inch

0.084 inch

1 Stanchions made of ⁷⁄₈-inch, 16-gauge tubing will bend with as little as 130 pounds of pressure, woefully inadequate to stop a flying body (yours). Check stanchions to make sure they are at least 1 inch in diameter and at least 14 gauge—that is, a wall thickness of 0.084 inch.

2 Proper spacing for stanchions is 6 to 8 feet. In addition to being through-bolted to metal backing plates, the stanchion bases should exhibit no signs of distortion. Peeling plating suggests that the base is zinc, a poor substitute for bronze or stainless steel.

3 Lifelines tend to fail where the line passes through stanchions and at the end fittings. Examine ends carefully, especially under locknuts. If the fittings are swaged, examine them for cracks with a magnifying glass. Rust appearing through the plastic covering of the cable suggests crevice corrosion, and the safest course is to condemn the wire and replace it.

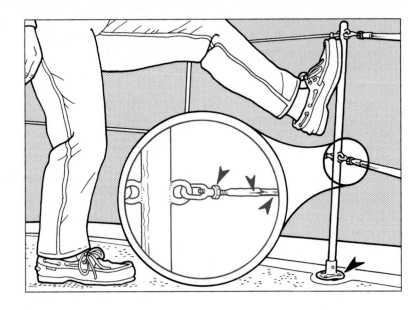

TRACKS AND TRAVELERS

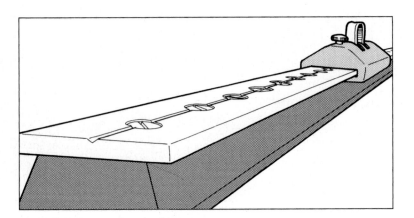

Sight along tracks to observe their contour. Tracks and travelers should be adequately stiff and fastened well enough to remain flat. Track cars should slide easily. Cars on a traveler should move easily even under substantial load.

CANVAS

Most sailboats have at least a canvas cover for the furled mainsail. Many boats exhibit a wide array of exterior canvas items.

COVERS

Compare the underside of the canvas to the exposed side; little discernible difference suggests the canvas has a number of years left. Feel the canvas and flex it; acrylic canvas is stiff like brown paper when new, soft like flannel when it is nearing replacement time. Examine all seams for broken or worn stitching.

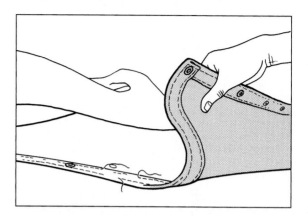

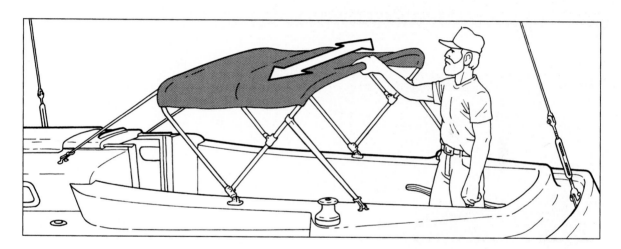

DODGERS AND BIMINIS

Check the condition of the canvas and stitching as above. Dimple the top with your finger and pour water into it; leakage means the top is near the end of its life. Check for torn or corroded fasteners. Fogged plastic windows will require replacement. Move the frame side to side; some movement is almost unavoidable, but it should be slight for a dodger and not excessive for a Bimini. Because they invariably serve also as a handrail, flexible frames can be dangerous. If the boat will be used outside protected waters, frames should be $7/8$- or 1-inch heavy-wall (14-gauge) steel tubing, and the hinges and mounting hardware should be steel or bronze, not zinc or plastic.

RIG

The rig is a sailboat's engine. As with any engine, the failure of a single component can leave you dead in the water, but a rigging failure is also likely to drop the mast like an axed pine. Murphy's Law gives you a clue as to which way it will fall relative to your location on the boat; and once the mast ricochets over the side, your vexed boat will try to commit hari-kari by jerking the jagged mast into the side of the hull with each rolling wave. Even if you sail only on Lake Tranquillity and your fine German auxiliary diesel has only two engine hours on it, it is the height of folly to ignore the rig.

The mast and guy wires holding the TV antenna over the roof of your bungalow is essentially a fixed structure, but a sailboat rig is essentially a machine. The mast jerks at the wires and fittings with each tack, each jibe, each passing wave. Hanks slide over wire, lines run over sheaves, and booms lift and drop like a wind-speed indicator. Even when you are motoring along on a calm day, the wires and fittings are dancing to the piston's beat. The tensions result in stretching and distortion, the constant motion in wear and fatigue.

On top of all of this is the issue of exposure, often compounded by the abundant presence of corrosive salts. It is a marvel that sailboat rigs hold up as well as they do. One thing is for certain: destructive forces are at work every day on your rig, and if you aren't on the lookout for them, something will eventually succumb, perhaps with disastrous, even deadly, consequences. Inspecting the rig is not merely advisable; it is an essential responsibility of sailboat ownership.

Much of what you need to inspect is four stories or more overhead, so surveying the rig is much easier when the mast is out of the boat. But the rig should be gone over completely at least every year; so unless you pull the mast that often, plan on an annual trip to the "truck" in a bosun's chair. Pay attention to the safety issues—two halyards, a safety line around the mast, and no snapshackles—and there is no reason that you can't look forward to these ascensions. Take a camera up with you and shoot a few pictures of the masthead; later they will come in handy to show you what shackle or block you need up there without making two trips. Use the rest of the chip or film for some great overhead shots of your boat.

MAST AND BOOM

In recent years a handful of production boats have been outfitted with laminated carbon fiber spars, not unlike giant and very stiff fishing rods. The unstayed carbon fiber mast may well be the rig of the future, offering strength, light weight, and simplicity, but for now masts and booms are almost invariably extruded aluminum. Surveying a fiberglass sailboat will likely require an evaluation of aluminum spars.

STRAIGHT

It is desirable to examine spars when they are out of the boat and well supported on several level horses, but this isn't always possible. If the mast is up, release the tension on all the stays and shrouds to allow the mast to take its natural shape. With your eye at the heel of the mast, sight toward the masthead to check for any fore-and-aft or athwartship bend. On horses, roll the mast 180 degrees to separate sag from bend. If you can take the curvature out of a standing mast with hand tension on a shroud, the bend is of no consequence. If the mast exhibits a kink or an S-curve, consult a sparmaker.

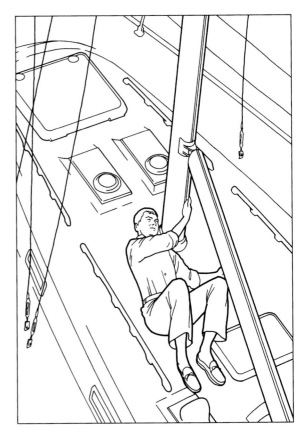

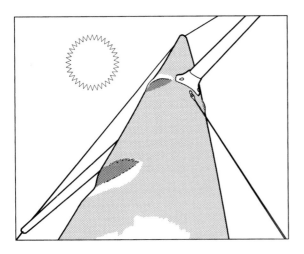

DENTS AND RIDGES

Spars get much of their strength from the curvature of the tube walls. A sizable dent in a spar is a serious defect and may weaken a spar enough to make it untrustworthy. Booms may show the effects of banging against the rigging during an all-standing jibe. Sight the length of the spar all the way around. Look also for ridges that can occur when an unsupported section of the mast "pumps" unabated for years. If you find dents or ridges, consult a sparmaker. Spars sometimes exhibit slight regular undulations that can occur during manufacture and are of no consequence.

CRACKS

The usual alloy in aluminum booms and masts is 6061—strong but brittle. The walls of an aluminum spar will crack if overstressed. Examine the mast and boom carefully around every piece of attached hardware, looking for cracks radiating from the fastener holes. Pay special attention to the spreader base area on a mast, and to center-sheeting or hydraulic-vang attachment points on a boom. Also check for splitting at the ends of the spar caused by corrosion swelling of the end caps.

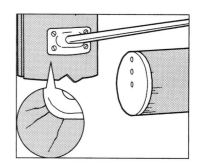

WELDS

Tapered masts are welded at the top, and the full length of the weld(s) should be examined for cracks with a magnifying glass or a loupe. Examine all other welds on the mast, especially the ends of the welds—where cracks usually start. Welding is common in spar manufacture, but be suspicious of welded repairs since welding destroys the temper of the surrounding aluminum.

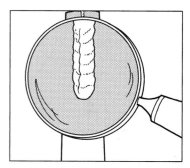

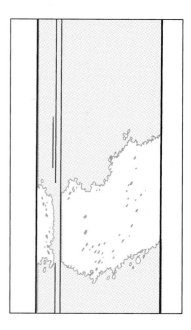

SURFACE CONDITION

Most aluminum spars are anodized; a few are coated with polyurethane. Either treatment will protect an aluminum spar for decades as long as the coating remains intact. Unfortunately breaches are common, some accidental from chafe, others made purposely when hardware is mounted to the mast. Look for scars in the spots where halyard shackles or eyesplices lie against the mast with the sails both up and down. Tying off external halyards and giving the mast an annual coat of wax goes a long way toward extending the life (and maintaining the appearance) of a mast.

Oxidation. For all metal parts on a sailboat, corrosion is the enemy, but on aluminum it is also a friend. The white powdery coating of oxide that forms on the surface of aluminum tends to protect the underlying metal from further corrosion. A surface coating of oxide has little significance regarding the integrity of a spar, but it does tell you that the anodizing is no longer protecting the aluminum. It is time to have the spar reanodized or painted.

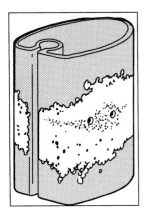

Corrosion. Pitting is another matter. If the corrosion has progressed to the point that the surface of the metal is heavily pitted, the strength of the spar has been compromised. You can estimate the extent of the damage by gauging the depth of the pitting and comparing it to the wall thickness of the spar. For example, if the pitting seems to be about $\frac{1}{10}$ of the wall thickness, 10 pits are approximately equivalent to a pit-size hole in the mast. Estimate the number of pits, divide by 10, then multiply that number by the area of a single pit-size hole (πr^2) and compare the result with the area of a pair of $\frac{1}{4}$-inch holes (0.10 square inches); a couple of in-line hardware-mounting holes in a mast have little effect on the spar's strength. If your result is much greater, the spar is weakened. Always err in your depth estimates on the side of safety.

HIDDEN CORROSION

1 Damaging mast corrosion is most likely to occur at the heel of the mast, especially if it sits in a wet bilge area or if the step lacks an adequate drain. Unfortunately, the corrosion is likely to be on the inside of the mast, one reason the mast must be out of the boat to conduct a thorough survey. If corrosion is breaking through at the heel of a standing mast, damage is almost certain to be extensive and require a new mast or a spliced replacement section at the heel, unless you are willing to shorten the spar.

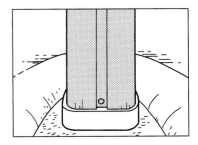

2 Corrosion is likely at the partners, especially where the boot clamps to the spar. Remove the boot to check. Corrosion may also be hidden by the deck collar and the wedges, but this is less likely if the area under the boot is corrosion free.

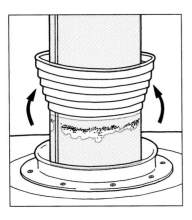

3 Attaching stainless steel fittings or using stainless steel fasteners on an aluminum spar leads to galvanic corrosion. To inspect the mast under fittings attached with threaded fasteners, lubricate the screws with penetrating oil, then remove them with an impact driver to avoid rounding the slot. Rivets have to be drilled out. If the threads in mounting holes are in good shape, clean them with a wire brush (or "chase" them with a tap) and reinstall the fitting. Insulate the fitting from the mast by bedding it in silicone. Coat fastener threads with a locking compound (Loctite) or a corrosion inhibitor (Tef-Gel).

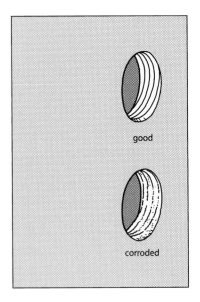

good

corroded

STEP

The mast step holds the bottom of the mast in position and must take the compression load exerted by the mast when the rigging is tensioned. Mast steps should be troublefree, but there are problems to be on the lookout for.

DECK STEP

1 If the deck is dished around the mast step, the support below deck—typically a bulkhead or a beam—is inadequate or perhaps rotten.

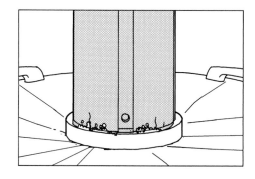

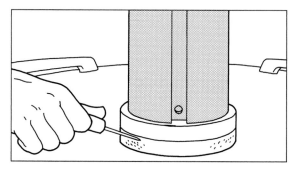

2 The mast step often sits on a wooden or laminated base to spread the load. Spike a wooden base to check for rot.

3 Make sure the step has a good drain that isn't plugged. Water standing inside the mast quickly results in damaging corrosion.

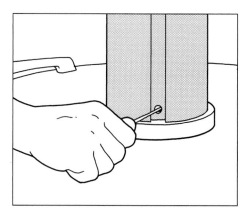

KEEL STEP

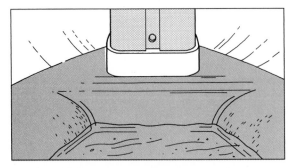

1 The mast should never be stepped directly on the keel. It should sit on a reinforced floor to transfer the load to the hull and to keep the heel of the mast above any bilge water.

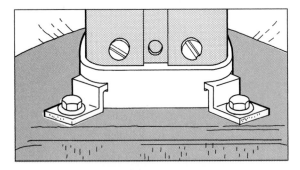

2 Should the rigging fail, the heel of the mast could cause serious damage and even injury if it comes free of the step. Make sure the mast is bolted to the step and the step is bolted or clamped to the floor.

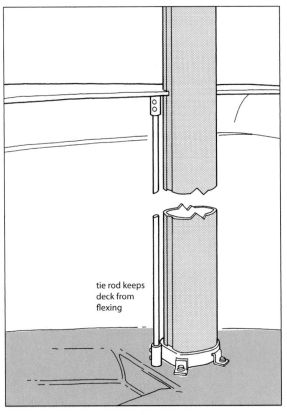

tie rod keeps deck from flexing

3 Make sure the step has a good drain that isn't plugged. A well-secured bulkhead or a tie rod near the partners is required to keep the deck from moving up the mast.

PARTNERS

A keel-stepped mast should have a weather boot clamped tightly around the mast and the deck flange; check below for telltale signs of leakage. Check also that the mast is properly aligned and securely wedged at the partners. A canvas coat over the boot adds years to the boot's useful life.

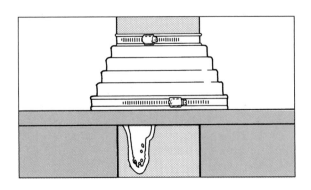

CAP

The cap fitting at the top of the mast usually provides attachment points for stays, cranes for halyard blocks, and a base for masthead gear like lights and wind indicators. Corrosion is less likely at the cap fitting than at the heel fitting, but if the mast is out of the boat, it is a good idea to remove the cap fitting in order to check the inside of the mast. In any case, go over the cap fitting carefully, looking for cracks at welds and bends and for wear where the rigging is attached.

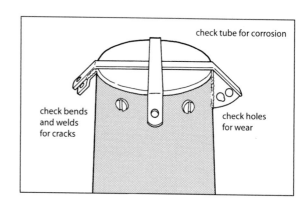

check tube for corrosion

check bends and welds for cracks

check holes for wear

SHEAVES, BLOCKS, AND HALYARDS

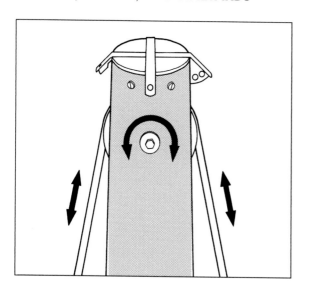

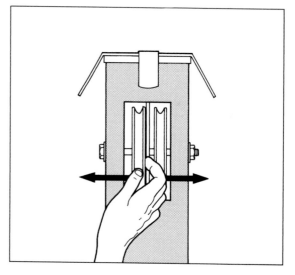

1 Also at the masthead are the sheaves for the main and jib halyards. Bearings aren't necessary for the low-speed rotation of sheaves, but make sure the sheaves rotate with the movement of the halyards. If the sheaves jam under load, it results in wear of both the halyard and the sheave, and makes sail hoisting and dousing more difficult. Greasing the axle bolt may be all that is required to correct this situation.

2 Check for side-to-side play of the sheaves. If the halyard can jump the sheave and jam, someday it will, and at the worst possible time. Shimming the side plates should solve this problem.

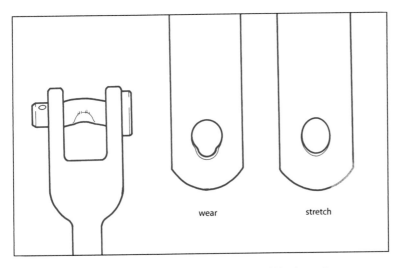

wear   stretch

3 Check all clevis pins that attach rigging or halyard blocks to the cap fitting. Pins should be straight and unworn. Check also the holes in the cap fitting for elongation. Some elongation as a result of wear is tolerable, but if an aluminum fitting shows any sign of having been stretched, failure is imminent.

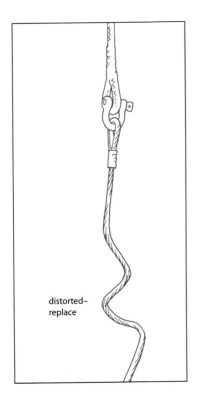

distorted–replace

4 Now is a good time to check halyards. Wire halyards that exhibit any broken strands or are kinked or curled must be replaced. Rope halyards should not show wear or have the sisal-like stiffness that signals the weakening effect of sun damage. Check also splices and shackle attachments.

TANGS

Cap shroud tangs are sometimes a feature of the cap fitting, but more often they are attached below the cap with a bolt that passes through both tangs and the mast. Lower shroud tangs may be similarly attached or part of the spreader socket. Look for mast corrosion under the tang, and distorted holes or mounting bolts. The safest course is to pull tang bolts to check for corrosion. Tangs often develop cracks where they are bent, so examine all bends—on both sides of the tang—with great care, at least with the aid of a magnifying glass and preferably with a dye penetrant, crack-detection process (Spot Check).

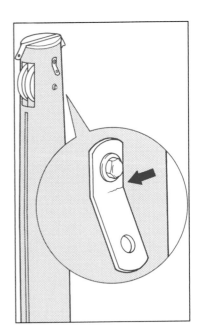

MASTHEAD GEAR

While you are at the top of the mast, check to see that all masthead lights work. Check antenna and wind instrument mountings as well as the condition of the equipment. Be certain the radio is not on. Examine all exposed wiring and make sure it is protected with grommets in all entry holes. On the way down, check the steaming and/or the deck (spreader) lights.

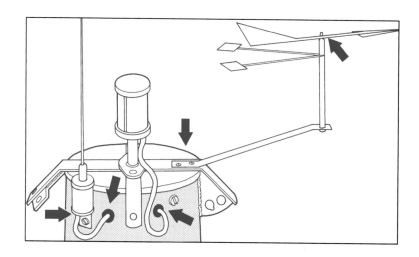

ASCENDING SAFELY

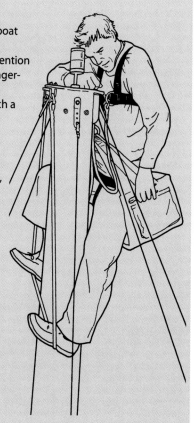

GOING TO THE TOP of the mast need not be scary or uncomfortable. Every boat should be equipped with a sturdy bosun's chair with around-the-back and between-the-legs straps. First check the halyard carefully, paying special attention to splices and shackle attachments. Using snapshackles is an inherently dangerous way to attach yourself to the halyard, but if your halyards are fitted with snapshackles, wire the shackle where it cannot be opened. In addition, attach a line to the halyard above the shackle with a rolling hitch and tie it to the lift ring on the chair. Now rig a safety line with a loose rolling hitch around the mast and attach it to the chair, or for greater safety, to a sailing (chest) harness. You will slide the safety line up the mast as you go, and should the halyard drop you, the safety line hitch will tighten and jam against the mast, preventing a fall. Attach a second safety line to allow you to secure yourself above the spreaders before releasing the line below the spreaders. Tying this extra line off to a shackle at the masthead will give you complete confidence in your security while you conduct your inspection.

Reel winches are dangerous for hoisting someone up the mast because the line is never cleated, only held by a friction brake. If you have the help available, going up on dual halyards is the safest method, but you will be momentarily unprotected when you have to unshackle one of the halyards to pass it around a spreader; so use a safety line around the mast even if you are attached to two halyards.

Take up an additional piece of line to serve as a rope step that will allow you to stand and get your eyes above the masthead.

SPREADERS

Spreaders are especially prone to a number of problems. Spend adequate time examining the spreaders to assure yourself of their soundness.

CONDITION

Spreaders may be wood, even on an aluminum mast. Wooden spreaders should be finished bright on their underside, so that problems with the wood will be immediately visible, but their top surface should be painted, to better resist exposure. Examine wooden spreaders carefully for checking or splitting. Use a spike or an ice pick to check for rot. Aluminum spreaders are generally superior and less likely to develop problems, but they may corrode where they contact the wire.

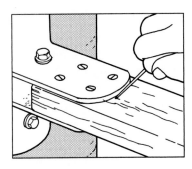

SOCKETS

1 Spreader sockets should never be screwed or riveted to an aluminum mast, although far too often that is exactly how they are attached. Pressure on the spreader, such as that applied by a backwinded genoa during a tack, tries to lever the socket off the mast, flexing the mast wall. Move the tip of the spreader and observe the socket; if it moves easily, either the fasteners are loose or the spar wall is cracked. Remove the spreader socket to determine the exact condition.

2 Unless the spreader sockets are separated by compression tubes or a special compression fitting, tensioning the upper shrouds tends to squeeze the mast. Properly installed sockets are bolted through compression tubes or a fitting that allows the socket to sit snug against the mast but prevents the mast wall from being distorted by the shroud tension. Check the pins in articulating sockets for bend or wear.

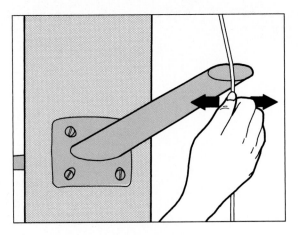

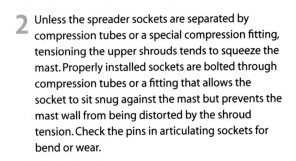

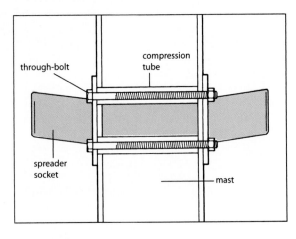

through-bolt

compression tube

spreader socket

mast

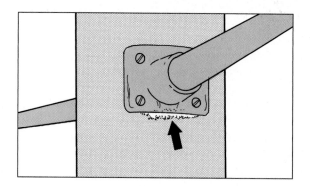

3 If the sockets are stainless steel rather than cast aluminum, examine the bottom edges of the socket where it lies against the mast. If you find oxidation in the crack between the two parts, the mast is corroding under the socket and you should remove the socket to determine the seriousness of the condition.

SPREADER TIPS

1 Wooden spreaders require metal inserts to prevent the wire from splitting the tip. Check to make sure the inserts are there and that the wire has not worn through them.

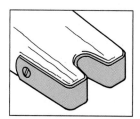

2 Spreader tips must be secured to the shroud with either clamps or seizing. The tips should be enclosed to protect sails from damage. Rubber boots trimmed to be open on the underside are preferable to rigging tape because they are less likely to encourage corrosion.

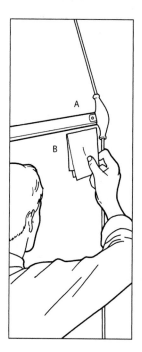

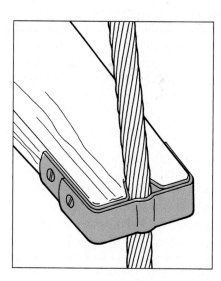

3 The angle the spreader makes with the wire must be the same above and below the spreader; otherwise the out-of-column compression may cause the spreader to collapse with catastrophic consequences. Take a protractor up the mast with you, or simply fold a sheet of paper to the top angle, then turn it over and check under the spreader.

GOOSENECKS, SHEETS, AND VANGS

The attachment of the mast to the boom, if it is robust, is generally troublefree except for fastener corrosion. Check for secure attachment. Also examine the fitting for cracks. Roller-furling goosenecks are more complicated and should be tested to see if they operate properly.

Examine bails for wear and for loose or inadequate attachment. Look for signs of corrosion around stainless steel bails. Hydraulic vangs are capable of applying damaging stresses; check around their mount plates carefully.

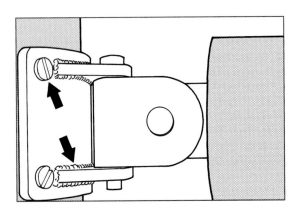

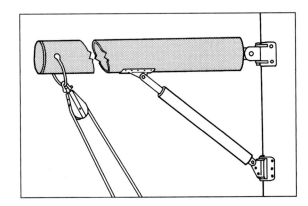

STAYS AND SHROUDS

Like the battery in your car or the spark plugs in an outboard, stays and shrouds need to be replaced periodically. How long the wire will last depends on how and where the boat is used, but except in extreme conditions, stainless steel rigging should give at least 5 years of service and may well last 15 years or longer.

WIRE

1 Typically a matter of design rather than condition, the size of stays and shrouds should nevertheless be checked. As a rule of thumb, the combined strength of the shrouds on one side should be at least 1.5 times the boat's displacement. Stays can be the same size as the shrouds but are often one size larger for added safety and to resist the wear from hanks.

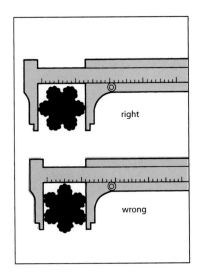

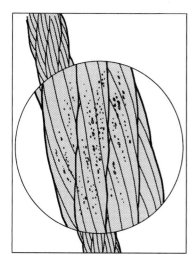

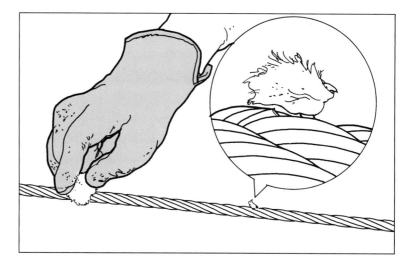

2 Some uniform discoloration is common with stainless steel rigging, but rigging that is heavily rusted, discolored in some areas but not others, or pitted even mildly should not be trusted.

3 The classic sign that rigging wire should be condemned is broken strands. Wiping the wire with a cotton ball will flag broken strands, appropriately known as meathooks. A single broken strand, because it is a reliable indicator of the condition of the other strands, is sufficient to condemn a length of wire.

ROD

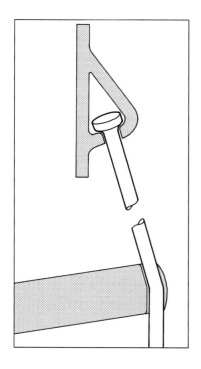

1 Rod rigging is stronger for its size and stays tuned better, but it gives no warning before it fails. If the failure is not at the formed ends, it is almost always at the point where the rod bends over a spreader. Check both of these areas carefully for cracks.

2 Discontinuous rod rigging eliminates bend in the rod. Failure is rare, but check the formed ends for cracks or signs of uneven loading.

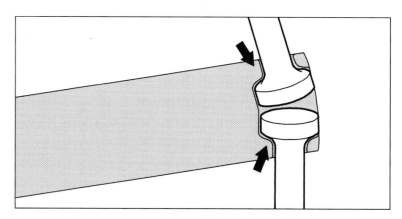

SWAGED END FITTINGS

Stays and shrouds can be attached by splicing or clamping their ends into eyes, but special end fittings are far more common.

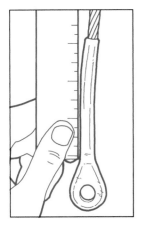 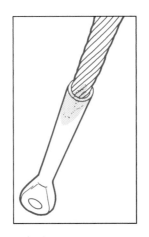 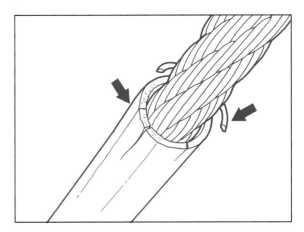

1 Lay a straightedge alongside the tubular part of swaged fittings. If it is curved—banana shaped—the swage is defective and should be condemned.

2 Water running down the wire into the interior of the swage leads to corrosion damage. A bloom of rust around the top of lower swaged fittings (upper fittings generally don't have this problem) suggests that the swage has already lost some strength and may soon be untrustworthy.

3 Swages are rolled onto the wire and depend upon compression for strength. Even a microscopic crack, like unbuttoning a sleeve, will release a swage's grip. Failure of a swage at the deck end of a stay or shroud is by far the most common rigging failure. Examine every swage and condemn any that have cracks. A dye crack detector gives more reliable results.

MECHANICAL END FITTINGS

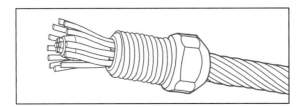 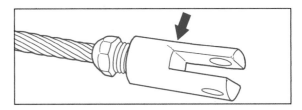

1 Properly installed mechanical fittings—Sta-Lok and Norseman—are troublefree and can be reused over and over, with replacement of only the internal cone required. If you need assurance that the fitting has been properly installed, open it: the wires should be evenly spaced and close neatly over the cone.

2 If any fork fittings are installed (eye fittings are almost always preferable), check the base of the jaws carefully. Uneven loading tends to place all the stress on one side of the fitting, leading to failure.

TURNBUCKLES

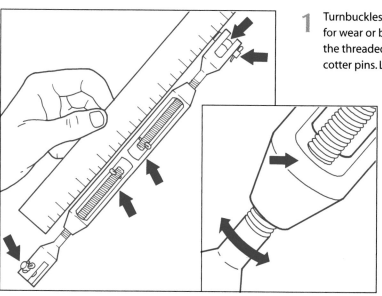

1 Turnbuckles should be straight. Check the clevis pins for wear or bending. Make sure both the pins and the threaded studs are secured with split rings or cotter pins. Locking nuts on the studs are unreliable.

2 Stainless steel turnbuckles tend to gall, effectively welding the threaded studs to the body. Check turnbuckles for ease of operation; well-maintained turnbuckles spin easily from fully extended to fully contracted when not under load, but there shouldn't be excessive play in any of the components.

TOGGLES

There must be a toggle at every deck fitting and at both ends of any stay that carries sail. There is no disadvantage to having toggles at the upper end of all stays and shrouds.

1 Toggles should be sized properly for the attached turnbuckle. Check for wear, cracks, and bent clevis pins. Pinholes in the surface of a cast bronze toggle are sure signs of "blow holes" in the casting, and the toggle should not be trusted.

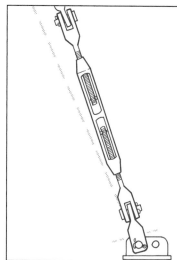

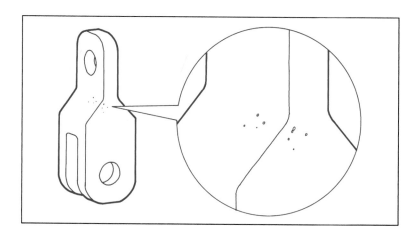

2 Look for inadequate fork depth, especially at the stem fitting. If the toggle "bottoms out" on the fitting, the pull on the turnbuckle is unfair and will lead to damage or failure.

TENSION

Excessive rigging tension tends to distort the shape of the boat, sometimes doing permanent damage. Loose stays and shrouds are easier on the boat but can be hard on the rigging in any kind of seaway. Stays and shrouds should be snug but not violin-string tight.

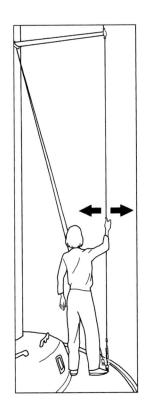

BACKSTAY ADJUSTERS

Check manual backstay adjusters as you would any other turnbuckle. Check hydraulic adjusters by pumping them to a predetermined tension and then monitoring the gauge for bleed off. Check all fittings for leakage and examine hoses for cracks that signal replacement is required. Make sure the pressure can be released, preferably in a controlled manner that maintains adequate tension on the stay.

CHAINPLATES

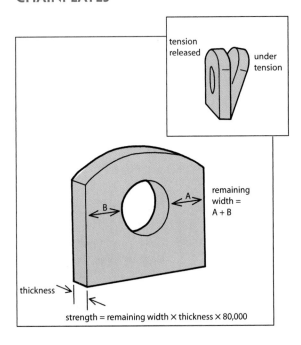

tension released

under tension

remaining width = A + B

thickness

strength = remaining width × thickness × 80,000

1 Alignment is critical. Relieve the tension on each chainplate and see if it moves out of alignment. Misalignment subjects the chainplate to flexing, and it puts uneven stresses on the pins and jaws of the attached toggle and turnbuckle.

2 Chainplates should be *at least* as strong as the shrouds they are attached to. Because the load can sometimes be concentrated on one side of the pinhole, it's best if chainplates are twice as strong as the shrouds. To calculate the strength of a chainplate, multiply its thickness by the remaining width (the total width minus the hole diameter), and then multiply that by the per-square-inch tensile strength of the chainplate material—about 80,000 pounds for common stainless steel. Compare your calculation to the strength of the wire (see table opposite). Watch out for chainplates that have been drilled out for heavier rigging: this can actually weaken them.

3 Examine chainplates for cracks, especially in bends and around the pinhole. Misalignment causes the strap to flex every time a tack or movement of the mast releases tension on the attached shroud or stay. Motoring can also set up resonant vibrations in the rigging that flex the chainplate hundreds of thousands of times, causing the metal to fatigue. Mast tangs are subject to the same problem.

4 Water collects around chainplates just below deck level, trapped by the caulking that prevents intrusion into the cabin below. Standing in a collar of water is highly damaging to stainless steel, often leading to crevice corrosion and ultimately to chainplate failure. The only way to inspect a chainplate thoroughly is to remove it and have it X-rayed, or at least do a dye test on it. Any cracks, pits, or other flaws should condemn a chainplate.

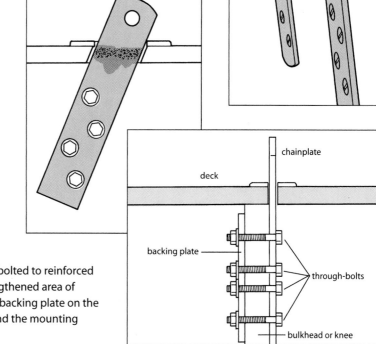

5 Chainplates should be through-bolted to reinforced bulkheads or knees or to a strengthened area of the hull, and they should have a backing plate on the opposite side. Check the bolts and the mounting holes for wear or distortion.

BREAKING STRENGTH OF 1 X 19 STAINLESS STEEL (302/304) WIRE ROPE

Diameter (inches)	Strength (pounds)	Diameter (inches)	Strength (pounds)
1/16	500	1/4	8,200
3/32	1,200	9/32	10,300
1/8	2,100	5/16	12,500
5/32	3,300	3/8	17,500
3/16	4,700	7/16	22,500
7/32	6,300	1/2	30,000

—Courtesy of *Rigger's Apprentice.*

ROLLER FURLING

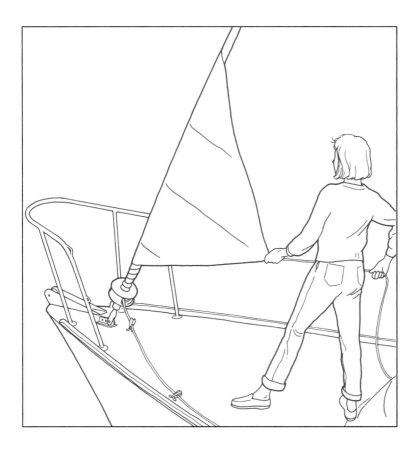

1 Roller-furling design varies with manufacturer, but the requirement to roll the sail under tension is common to all types. Crank extra pressure on the backstay with the backstay adjuster or by tightening the turnbuckle, then open and furl the headsail. It should be quite easy if the sail is luffing; otherwise the furler requires servicing.

2 Drop the sail to check the luff groove. Sight up the bare extrusion for twists or other defects. Examine the swivel, the halyard, the drum, and the furling line. Rehoist and tension the sail.

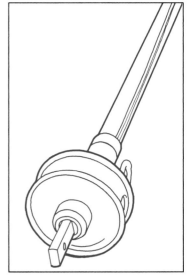

SAILS

A professional surveyor generally gives sails only the most cursory inspection, often simply listing the inventory and assigning each sail a one- or two-word description of condition—"nearly new," "serviceable," etc. For the purchase of a racer, the only sure way to assess sails—a big portion of the boat's value—is to take a knowledgeable sailmaker aboard and fly each sail in the inventory. For less exacting requirements, you can get a good idea of the quality and condition of the sails aboard by examining them.

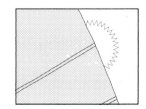

1 Crisp sailcloth suggests that a sail is new or has seen very little use. Old or sunburned sails are soft. Stand on the shady side of a hoisted sail and if it shows pinholes in the panels (not needle holes), it is in its twilight years.

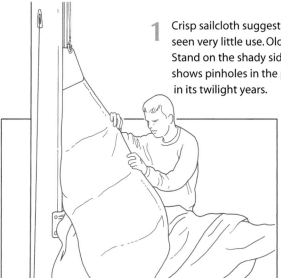

2 Examine the sail for obvious defects—rips, patches, abrasions, broken stitching, torn cringles. This is easiest if you can spread the sail on a lawn or floor, but you can also inspect a sail by hoisting it incrementally. Examine one side as the sail goes up, the other as you lower it.

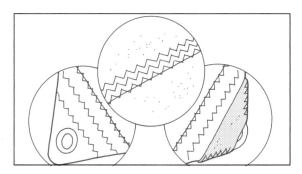

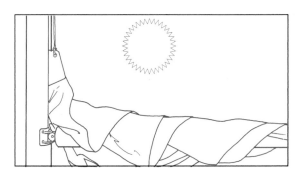

3 It isn't possible to determine how a sail sets without flying it, but triple stitching at panel seams, heavy corner patches, and hand-finished leather chafe protection suggest quality construction.

4 If possible, determine where and how the sail has been stowed. Any part of a sail that has been constantly exposed to the sun for a season or two is damaged, even if the rest of the sail is perfect.

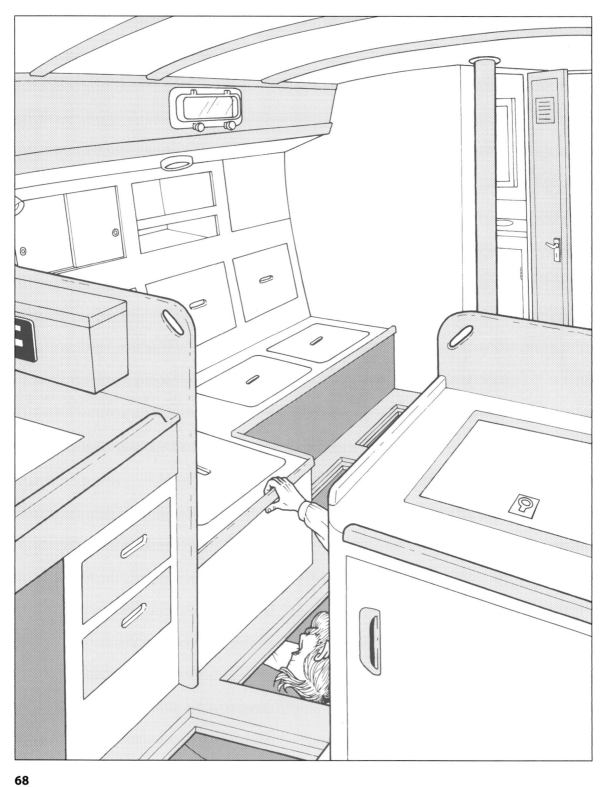

INTERIOR

Surveying the outside of a boat requires an occasional trip below. You have already been below to check the attachment of the keel, the hull-to-deck joint, and the security of the chainplates. But now we are going to concentrate on the boat's interior components.

The interior of a boat is a trap. Manufacturers discovered long ago that attractive interiors sell boats. If you don't believe it, go to a boat show and compare the amount of time shoppers spend below to the time they spend on deck. Nice woodwork and plush upholstery are essential to getting signatures on the dotted line.

There is nothing wrong with having a great-looking interior—but never use interior decor to judge a boat. Far too many manufacturers building to a budget have scrimped elsewhere to put money into their boats' interiors. This strategy is often successful financially, but intellectually—and perhaps morally—it is bankrupt. Coordinated colors and rubbed varnish don't account for much when the wind pipes up and the seas start to crest.

Don't misunderstand; a cozy, woody interior is a definite plus over a boat with the interior charm of a refrigerator, but you should not be overly influenced by a boat's below-deck look. Treat a fab interior as a bonus or as a tie-breaker, but not as a major selection criterion.

What's behind the wood and fabric is what you're most interested in. Is the deck hardware through-bolted with generous backing plates? Are all through-hull fittings accessible? Are electrical wires secure or are they free to chafe dangerously against raw glass as the boat pitches and rolls? A couple of sheets of veneered plywood can hide a plethora of flaws and omissions. Make sure both the intent and the function of the interior design is nothing more sinister than to give the boat added appeal.

Cabinets and furniture can also seriously complicate some emergencies. Imagine sailing into submerged debris; if the hull was holed below the waterline, could you get to the damaged area to stem the flow from inside?

Look at the cabin of a boat critically. Fight the tendency to form an opinion based on a pleasing decor. Interior varnish and velvet have almost exactly the same significance as a nice shade of red engine paint; they don't give a reliable indication of anything.

BULKHEAD ATTACHMENT

Rarely are bulkheads installed solely to divide up the living space. They are an integral component of the boat's design, providing critical and essential strengthening, but they must be well attached to do the job.

1 Bulkheads attach to the hull with laminated strips of fiberglass tape— called tabbing. Check to make sure they are tabbed continuously to both the hull and the deck. Tabbing on only one side of the bulkhead or a single layer of tape are typical deficiencies to look for.

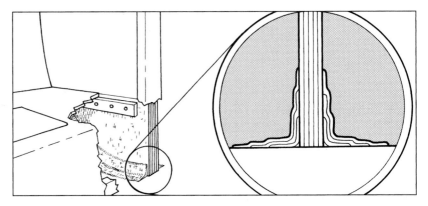

2 Tabbing rarely comes loose from the hull but often releases from the bulkhead. Use a thin, flexible knife or a feeler gauge to check. If the blade slips between the tabbing and the bulkhead, the bulkhead is adrift. If all the tabbing has released, it will need to be ground away and replaced. Use epoxy resin rather than polyester. For less extensive tabbing failure, you can inject the space with polyurethane adhesive (5200) and reattach the tab with staggered screws. Make sure rigging tension hasn't lifted the bulkhead.

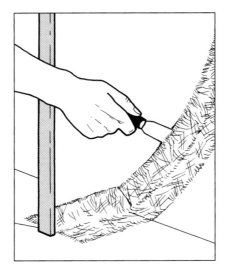

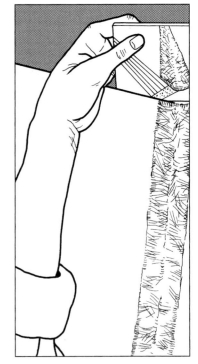

3 Look at whether the bulkhead sits hard against the hull. To avoid introducing hardspots, bulkheads should sit on foam spacers contoured to also provide a fillet for the tabbing. This is widely acknowledged as the "right" way to install bulkheads, but only the most conscientious builders take the trouble.

STRINGERS AND FLOORS

Wide expanses of fiberglass are often stiffened by the fore-and-aft edges of built-in furniture, but where furniture is absent, stringers are glassed to the hull. They are sometimes disguised by the construction of a shelf above them. Floors strengthen the hull in the bilge area, supporting the cabin sole and often carrying the stresses from the keel.

1 Make sure stringers are firmly attached to the hull along their entire length.

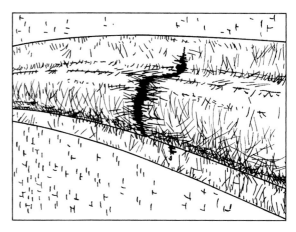

2 Check the surface of the stringer. Any cracks or tears render the stringer ineffectual. The damage must be repaired and the stringer reinforced.

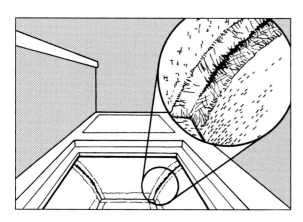

3 Examine floors for cracks. A hard grounding sometimes breaks floors or tears them from the hull. A tear suggests the repair should include additional strengthening.

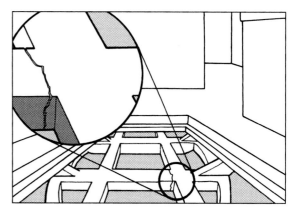

4 Some boats use a molded interior waffle grid to strengthen the hull and distribute keel and rigging loads. Check every inch of the grid for cracks, and make sure it is securely bonded to the hull.

INTERIOR PANS

Fiberglass hull liners have replaced plywood furniture in many production boats. Liners vary from strong and well-engineered structural components to flimsy inserts with purely cosmetic value. In this latter case, the absence of interior reinforcement is likely to allow the hull to flex and distort.

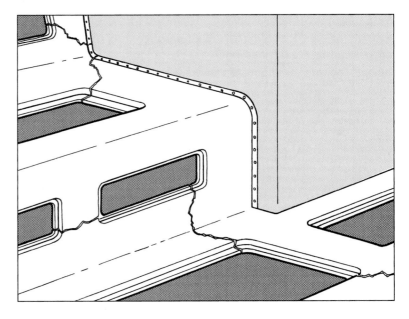

1 Cracks in the pan suggest inadequate pan strength and hull distortion. In the long term, this can be dangerous.

2 Poorly designed liners can block access to the hull, a potentially serious flaw in an emergency. Check the liner for hull access.

DISTORTION

Occasionally an interior bulkhead or beam will prove to be inadequate. Stresses on the hull and deck—typically imposed by rigging tension—bow or buckle the reinforcing member.

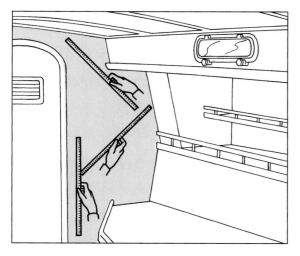

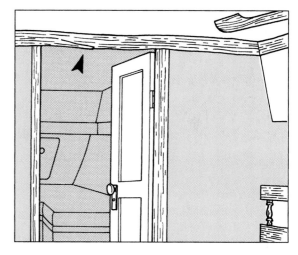

1 Lay a straightedge in a variety of orientations against one side of every interior bulkhead. Any significant bowing is a serious defect.

2 Examine support beams for sagging or cracks. Beams with a bit of upward arc are stronger than straight beams.

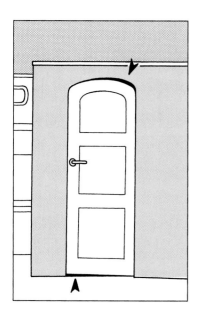

3 Look at how cabin and cabinet doors fit. If they no longer fit their frames or openings, the interior has changed shape. A head door that drags or jams, for example, typically indicates movement of one of the bulkheads on either side of the opening, probably the one under the mast.

SIGNS OF LEAKAGE

Interior fittings and equipment can be damaged by water—not to mention the discomfort a soggy bunk can cause. The cabin should be virtually watertight.

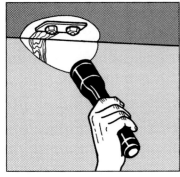

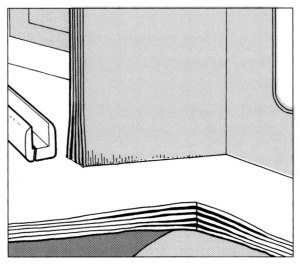

1 With a strong light, examine bulkheads and the interior of the hull for runnels—water tracks outlined with dust, rust, or salt. The source of such leaks is usually obvious, and the offending gasket or mounting bolt will need to be renewed or rebedded.

2 Plywood members and furniture will show signs of delamination if they remain wet. Look especially close at plywood soles and the lower portion of bulkheads.

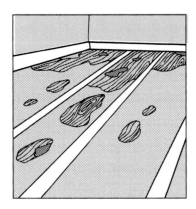

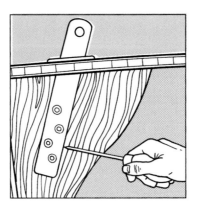

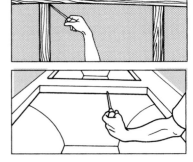

3 Black stains under varnish or bubbles under paint (or varnish) finishes are sure signs of water damage.

4 Use a sharpened spike or an ice pick to check interior wood for rot. Spike knees and bulkheads around chainplate attachments; beams and compression posts; sole panels and wooden floors.

TANKAGE

Replacing a leaking tank can be inordinately expensive because the boat is often built around the tank. Inspect all tanks for condition and security. In a prepurchase survey, you may also want to know the capacity; a close estimate can be made by measuring the tank. To get the capacity in gallons, divide the volume of the tank in cubic inches by 231.

1 Examine all tanks for construction material. Diesel fuel dissolves zinc, so diesel tanks should not be copper or galvanized. Integral fuel tanks are also a bad idea because fiberglass is not completely impermeable. Fiberglass tanks almost always give water an off taste. Aluminum tanks—all too common in production boats—quickly corrode. Monel is an excellent (but expensive) tank material; stainless steel is less desirable because it is subject to corrosion. Polyethylene provides the best value and fewest problems of any material for all tank applications.

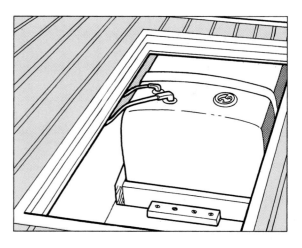

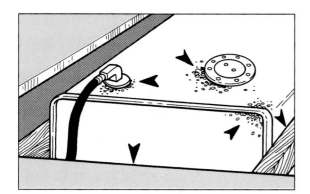

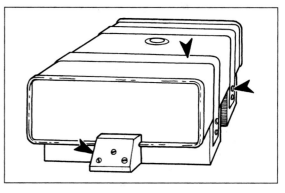

2 Look for corrosion in steel and aluminum tanks; check the bottom inside the tank and check outside where the tank bears against supports or other parts of the boat. Visually inspect for leakage; if possible, fill the tank and check it again after several days undisturbed.

3 All tanks must be securely mounted, unable to move even if the boat is inverted. Give chocks and straps a thorough inspection. Look for any signs of past movement. Bearing surfaces should be impermeable to discourage moisture retention.

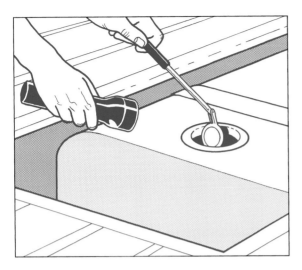

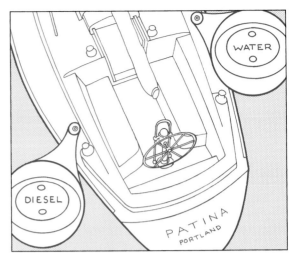

4 Tanks larger than about 5 gallons should have internal baffles to prevent the liquid from surging inside the tank. Outside weld marks are not a sure sign of baffling; view the interior of the tank through the inspection port with a light and a mirror.

5 Water and fuel fills should not be near each other, and each should be clearly labeled. Fuel vent fittings should be located as high as possible to prevent water intrusion. Both fill and vent lines (and fuel lines, as well) should be labeled "USCG A1" or "B1."

HEAD

Discharge laws vary from place to place, but a holding tank and a securable Y-valve to allow direct discharge offshore will meet most state and local codes.

1 Holding tanks must be vented to the outside to allow the escape of explosive methane.

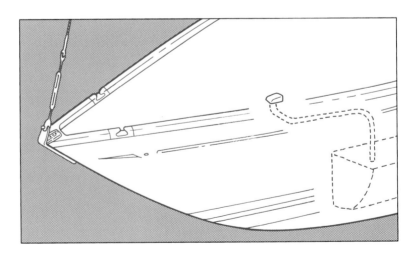

2 The discharge line from the head must be looped well above the waterline to prevent back-siphoning. If an antisiphon valve is installed in the loop, check its operation by blowing through a piece of hose fitted over the nipple. (To minimize odor from an antisiphon valve, vent it overboard.)

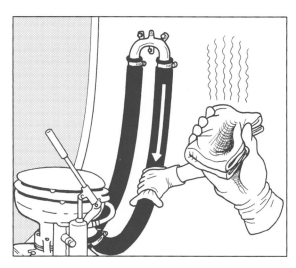

3 Wipe the outside surface of the discharge line with a damp cloth, then smell the cloth. If it has picked up an odor, the hose is the wrong type for this application.

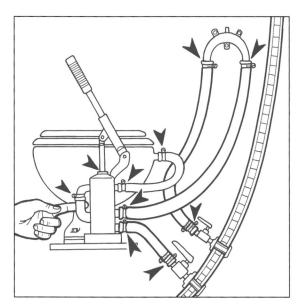

4 Check the head and all hose connections for fresh signs of leakage.

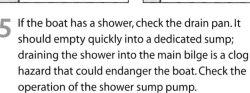

5 If the boat has a shower, check the drain pan. It should empty quickly into a dedicated sump; draining the shower into the main bilge is a clog hazard that could endanger the boat. Check the operation of the shower sump pump.

GALLEY

The functionality of a galley is more often a matter of design than condition, but there are some universal requirements.

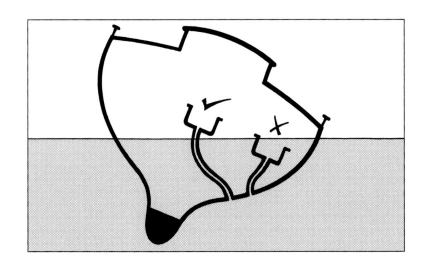

1 Where is the sink drain? Sinks should be located near the centerline of the boat. Those located near the hull can flood the cabin when the boat heels to that side.

2 If the stove will be used underway, it must be gimbaled fore-and-aft, and it must have sufficient ballast to overcome the weight of a full pot sitting on the burner.

3 Where propane is the galley fuel, a solenoid shutoff at the tank with a warning light in the galley is essential. The supply line must be continuous from the tank, except for the inclusion of a flexible segment to a gimbaled stove.

4 Propane tanks must be mounted on deck well clear of any deck openings, or in a vaportight locker with an overboard drain that will not submerge when the boat heels. The bottle(s) should be fitted with a pressure gauge.

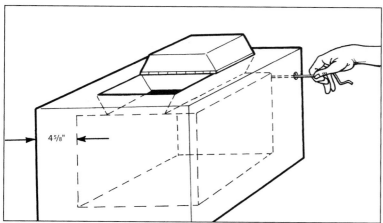

4 5/8"

5 Factory ice-chest insulation—if there is any at all—is too often a couple of inches of fiberglass batting. To be efficient, a refrigerator or icebox requires a minimum of 4 inches of urethane foam on all sides. Measure the distance between inner and outer walls and subtract about ⅝ inch (for the two skins). Probe to determine the insulation material.

6 Air-cooled refrigeration should be located where the air flowing across the condenser will be coolest, which means not in the engine room.

SEACOCKS

The safest number of through-hull fittings is zero. The usual number is at least seven. Always keep in mind that the only thing keeping your boat afloat is the clamps and hoses connected to these fittings.

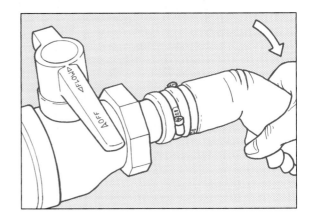

1 Squeeze or flex all hoses connected to the seacocks. Any that show cracks or hardening require replacement.

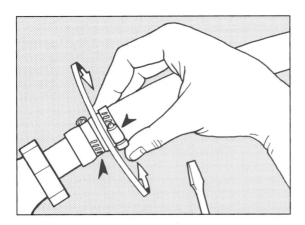

2 Check every below-the-waterline hose connection for dual clamps. Even all-stainless clamps corrode, usually at their lowest point or beneath the screw housing. Loosen each clamp and rotate it 360 degrees to inspect it, then retighten it.

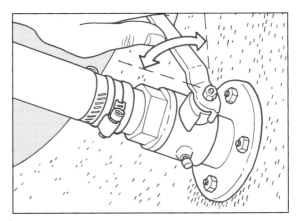

3 Every through-hull fitting that is (or could be) below the waterline should be equipped with a seacock. Gate valves are inherently unsafe and must not be substituted. Operate each seacock to make sure it is in good working order. Unused seacocks have an annoying tendency to freeze, rendering them worthless, and replacement generally requires a haulout.

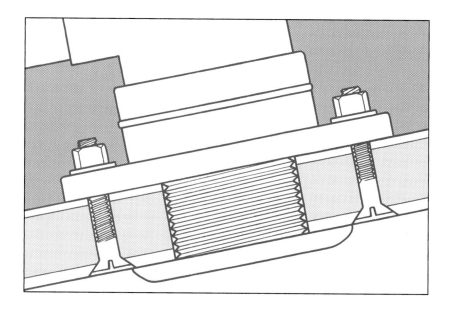

4 Make sure all seacocks are bolted to the hull, not just threaded onto the through-hull fitting. If the seacock is bronze, the bolts should also be bronze; a pile of corrosion on them will tell you the bolts are steel. Also make sure that the through-hull and the seacock are the same material; never mix bronze and plastic.

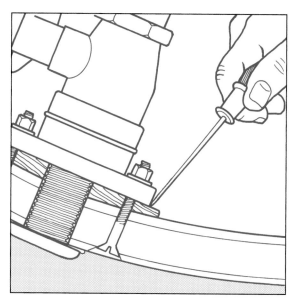

5 Seacocks are often installed on backer blocks to accommodate the contour of the hull. If the backer block is wood, spike it to make sure it has not gone spongy.

no bolts in flange

gap under flange

6 Check the seacock for any signs of leakage. Traditional tapered-plug seacocks are particularly prone to leaking, and if the nut has to be so tight to stop the leak that the handle can't be turned, the seacock needs servicing and perhaps replacement.

BILGE PUMPS

No sailboat bigger than a dinghy should be without at least one bilge pump, and most boats require two or more.

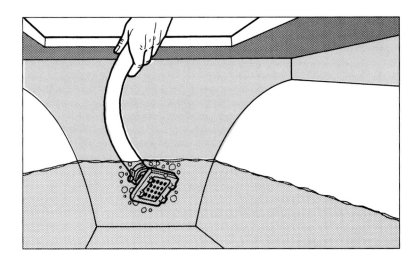

1 An operable manual bilge is essential equipment even if the boat is equipped with an array of electric pumps. Check the pickup to make sure it is clog protected. Pump the handle to make sure the pump will prime and move water out of the boat efficiently.

2 Automatic bilge pumps should also have an ON position in case the float switch fails. Run electric pumps to check their operation.

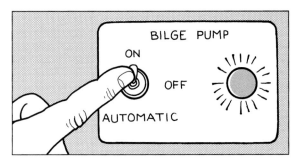

3 Find where all pumps discharge. Outlets must always remain above water or they will siphon water into the boat, causing the pump to run until it kills the battery; then the boat will fill.

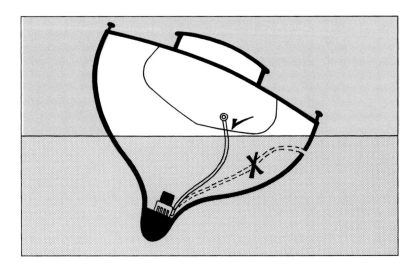

COMFORT AND SAFETY

While you are in the cabin, consider the design features that have comfort and safety implications. Some can be improved—at your expense. Others you are likely to simply live with.

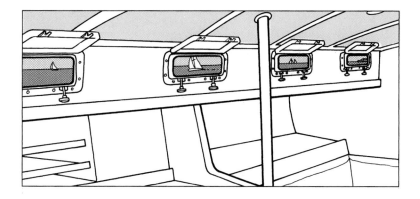

1 Fixed ports and a single forward hatch make for an uncomfortable boat when the mercury rises. It is unlikely that a boat will have too much ventilation. Check the number of hatches, opening ports, and effective ventilators.

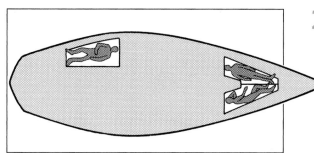

2 V-berths are great in port—if they are long enough and don't come to a point—but they are worthless at sea. At least one bunk well aft to serve as a sea berth is essential if anyone plans to sleep underway. Check bunks for length (long) and width (not too wide) and location (aft).

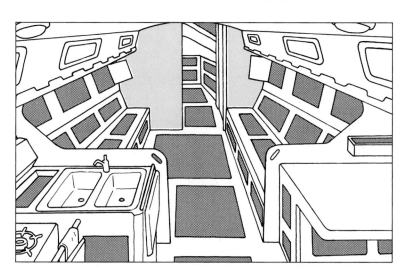

3 Depending on the intended use of the boat, stowage capacity can be an important factor. A heavier-displacement cruising boat should be able to swallow up a mountain of gear and supplies. Light-displacement boats have less carrying capacity and smaller locker spaces.

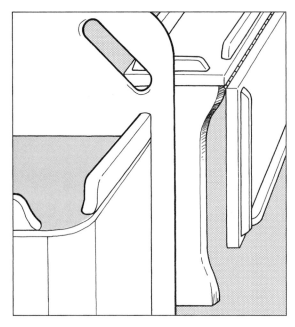

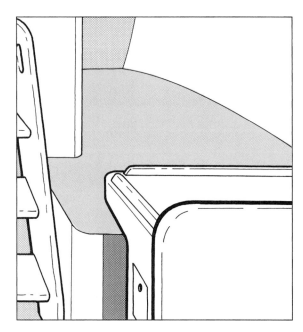

4 Look at shelves, counters, and tables to see if items will stay put when the boat heels. High fiddle rails can prevent a great deal of irritation and innumerable accidents.

5 Sharp corners are dangerous in the cabin of a pitching boat. So are wide spaces. Fall against the furniture and other surfaces in the cabin to see if an unexpected fall is likely to cause injury.

6 Unexpected falls are far less likely if the cabin has ample strong, intelligently spaced handholds. Make sure you can pass from one end of the cabin to the other without releasing your grip.

DECOR

Now you can admire the varnished trim and the beautiful fabric on the settee cushions. So they're pretty, but what condition are they in?

1 Check all the upholstery for soiling, wear, tear, and open seams. Pay special attention to zippers: metal zippers are almost certain to be corroded beyond use, and so are plastic zippers if the slide is metal.

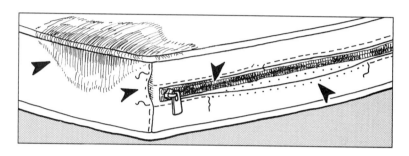

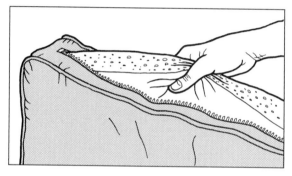

2 Check the foam. Firm foam is essential for comfort. Old foam tends to crumble and go soft. Quality replacement foam can be expensive.

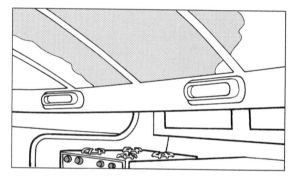

3 If the headliner is fabric, observe its color and condition. Some vinyls tend to yellow with age, and all can be affected by galley smoke.

4 Look at the condition of mica on bulkheads, tables, and countertops. Burns and some stains are permanent.

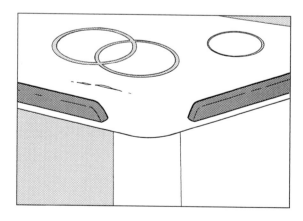

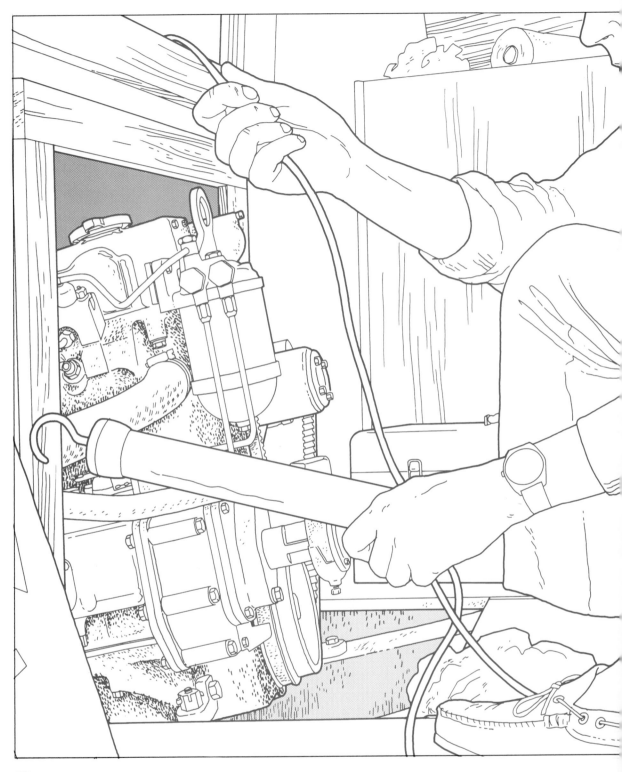

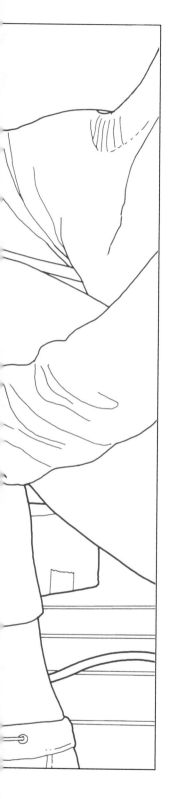

ENGINE
AND STEERING

t is time to remove engine hatches and cockpit-locker panels and examine the other half of the interior, the half occupied by the engine, cables, filters, and steering gear.

A truly comprehensive evaluation of the condition of an inboard engine requires a specialized examination by a qualified marine mechanic. In-depth engine evaluations are generally beyond the capability of even a professional surveyor. But there are key indicators that can give you a reasonably good idea of the condition of a boat's engine.

A lot of obvious engine problems go undetected for a long time because engine spaces are almost always dark. The most important engine-surveying tool is a bright light. A fluorescent drop light is ideal.

In this chapter, our focus is primarily on diesel engines. Gasoline engines have not been installed in production sailboats in the United States for more than 20 years. There are still thousands of older sailboats with gasoline engines, of course; but since a gasoline engine doesn't add value to the boat, there is little need to know more than whether the engine runs and meets stringent safety requirements. When a gasoline engine reaches the end of its useful life, most owners elect to repower with diesel.

Outboard engines are omitted here altogether. It is a simple matter to take an outboard engine in the sizes generally found on a sailboat to a qualified outboard mechanic for testing.

An oil-coated engine and black bilges have always suggested indifferent maintenance, but today they have additional implications. Pumping out oily bilge water can result in a substantial fine. It is now even more important for an engine to be well maintained and for bilges to be kept clean.

ENGINE ACCESS

If you are surveying your own boat, you already know about the access compromises the manufacturer made in order to minimize the interior space lost to the engine installation. There are boats in which the stuffing box is only accessible once the engine is removed. The time to discover such absurdities is before you buy. Here is a sample of access questions, but in general you should be able to get to every side of the engine.

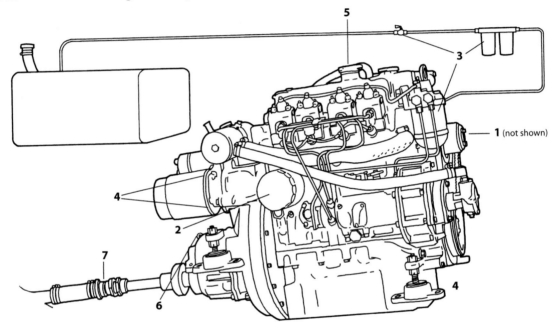

1 Where is the raw-water pump? Flexible impellers have to be replaced periodically—and it should be a simple job.

2 Can you get to the oil filter? Can you get a strap wrench around the canister and have room to turn it?

3 Are the fuel filters likewise accessible, and can you easily reach the fuel-supply shutoff valve?

4 Can you get a wrench on both starter mounting bolts? What about servicing the alternator?

5 Is there room above the oil filler to turn up a can of oil?

6 Can you reach the transmission dipstick?

7 Can you get two wrenches on the stuffing box? If so, will you be able to apply enough force to release and retighten the locknut?

VISUAL CLUES

Shine a bright light on the engine and look it over slowly and carefully with a critical eye. Streaks, cracks, stains, and shiny spots all need explanation.

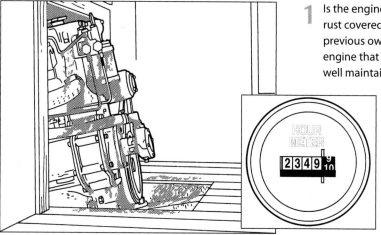

1 Is the engine clean and nicely painted or dirty and rust covered? This may tell you more about the previous owner than about the engine, but an engine that looks new is more likely to have been well maintained.

How many hours does the engine have? A functioning hour meter is essential for properly scheduling maintenance. A well-maintained auxiliary diesel should easily run 5,000 hours between overhauls. Well-kept maintenance logs are a major plus.

2 Look for leaks of any kind. Touch your finger to the underside of all hose and fuel connections. Rub across the bottom of the fuel pump and all fuel filters. Check bleed screws on the injector pump. Examine the catch pan under the engine and the bilge for dripping oil.

3 Squeeze all coolant hoses; if they're hard and brittle, soft and spongy, or cracked, they need replacing. Look for kinks that might restrict flow. Examine both hoses and fuel lines anywhere they might be rubbing; the lively movement of a running diesel can quickly wear through a chafing line.

Check the zinc pencil on the heat exchanger. If it is badly corroded or missing, check the exchanger more carefully for evidence of corrosion.

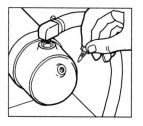

4 Open the pressure cap on the expansion tank; if it feels oily, dip some of the coolant out into a clear glass and let it settle. Oil in the coolant suggest a blown head gasket (bad) or a cracked water jacket (worse).

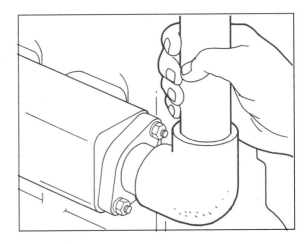

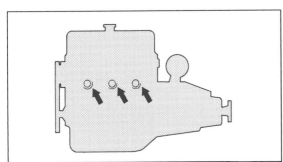

5 Check the exhaust system from the engine to the transom. Be especially suspicious of copper or stainless steel standpipes and water-jacketed exhausts. Give the section that connects to the manifold a good jerk; hot diesel gases eat at the pipe, eventually loosening or destroying it.

6 Locate every freeze plug and examine each for signs of rust or leakage.

GASOLINE ENGINES

GASOLINE IS VERY DANGEROUS in a boat because it is highly volatile and the heavier-than-air fumes can collect in the bilge. If you are inspecting a boat with a gasoline inboard, there are additional things to look for.

1. Does the tank show any signs of corrosion? A leaking tank can be deadly.
2. The potential consequences of a gasoline tank coming adrift are horrific, so make especially sure the tank is securely chocked and strapped.
3. Are all connections to the top of the tank? Bottom fittings are both dangerous and illegal.
4. The fill pipe should be flexible, not rigid, and the vent line must be outboard and equipped with a flame arrestor screen.

5. Are both the tank and the deck fill electrically grounded to the engine to bleed off static electricity?
6. Is the deck fill located where an overflow cannot enter the boat?
7. A functioning fuel shutoff at the tank is mandatory.
8. Look for flexible—not rigid—fuel lines rated for gasoline. Spring clamps should never be used on gasoline lines. Make sure the separator bowl isn't glass.
9. The carburetor must be down-draft and equipped with an approved flame arrestor.
10. Make sure the boat has a functional bilge blower, vented overboard, with the pickup in the lowest dry part of the bilge. An intake vent lower than the carburetor intake is also required.

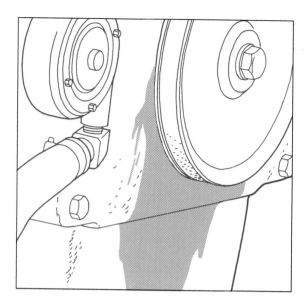

7 Check both the front and the back of the engine for signs that either oil seal is leaking.

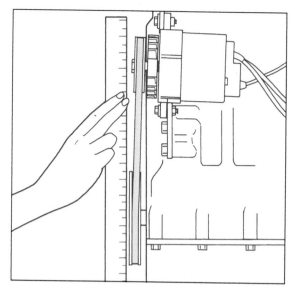

8 Check the engine and the surrounding bulkheads for telltale black fluff that indicates excessive belt wear. If you find belt fluff, check the alignment of the various pulleys with a straightedge. Misalignment can be a serious problem or one easily solved with spacers. A corrosion-roughened pulley can also be the problem.

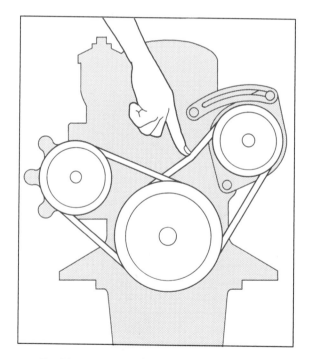

9 Check belt tensions. With moderate finger pressure, you should be able to depress the longest span about ³⁄₈ inch.

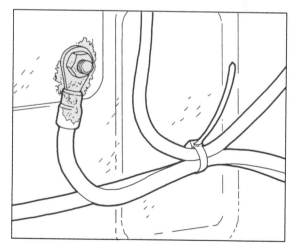

10 Examine all wiring connections for corrosion and all wire runs for support.

MOUNTING AND ALIGNMENT

Occasionally someone reports that the engine fell off the bearers into the bilge. It can't be a pleasant event, but there were almost certainly adequate warning signs.

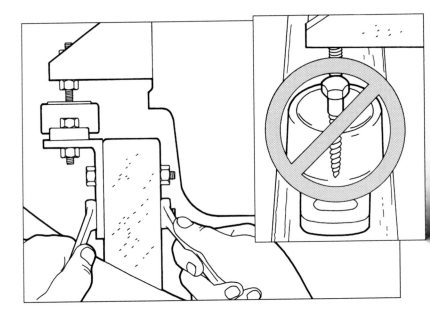

1 Check the engine mounts. Put a wrench on every nut and bolt that attaches the mounts to both the engine and the bed to make sure they are tight. Engine mounts are too often secured to the bearers with lag screws; where heavy weather is possible, mounts must be through-bolted to the bearers.

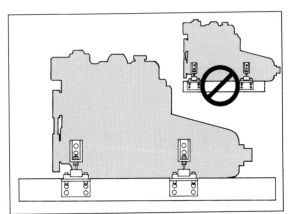

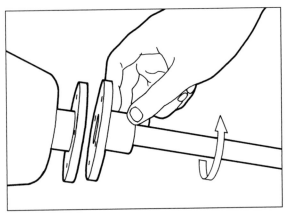

2 The engine bearers under a diesel need to be robust to take the punishment; they should be substantially longer than the engine. Be particularly suspicious of the bearers in a boat that has been repowered from gasoline to diesel. Check the bearers closely to make sure they are securely attached to the hull. Check wooden bearers for splits, cracks, and rot.

3 Rotate the propeller shaft to check for alignment. A short shaft with a rigid coupling will not show misalignment unless you remove the coupling bolts and separate the coupling slightly. Misalignment can usually be corrected by turning the adjustment nuts on the engine mounts, but this should only be checked and adjusted with the hull afloat. Flexible couplings are not a substitute for good engine alignment.

STUFFING BOX

Fiberglass sailboats generally pass the prop shaft to the outside of the hull in the least complicated way—through a tube glassed into the hull and connected to the stuffing box with a length of rubber hose. Flax packing in the stuffing box is compressed against the shaft to seal it.

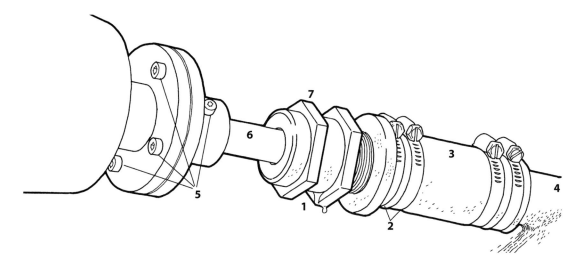

1 Check the stuffing box for leakage. A slight drip is often recommended to cool the stuffing, but more that six drops per minute is excessive. If tightening doesn't seal the fitting, repacking is needed.

2 The clamps that are on the hose connecting the stuffing box to the stern tube typically corrode on the bottom. Release and rotate them to check, then retighten. The hose should be double-clamped at both ends.

3 Check the hose for hardening or splitting. The shaft must be removed—or at the very least extracted from the coupling—to install a replacement.

4 Check the stern tube carefully for fractures or separation from the hull.

5 Check all coupling bolts and set screws to make sure they are in place and tight.

6 Make sure there is adequate space between the coupling and the stuffing box to slide the nut back for repacking.

7 Come back to the stuffing box and touch it immediately after running the prop for a while. If it is hot, the packing is too compressed and needs to be replaced. Excessive tightening will score the shaft.

EXHAUST SMOKE

After you have made all your visual inspections, it is time to start the engine. If you're doing a pre-purchase survey, be sure this is the first time the engine has been started today: easy starting of a cold diesel is the best indicator of its overall state.

Position yourself to see the exhaust as the engine starts. A good-running diesel will not smoke at all under load, but it may smoke at start-up and at idle.

1 White exhaust smoke generally indicates moisture in the cylinders, but it can also suggest low cylinder compression. If the smoke clears up quickly, the cause is probably nothing more than condensation inside the engine. If smoking continues, the engine may have a blown head gasket (or maybe a cracked head). Unfortunately, a normal wet exhaust can also generate white smoke.

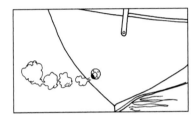

2 If the exhaust smoke is blue, the engine is burning oil. If the blue smoke continues, suspect the piston rings; the engine needs major work. If the smoke clears up, the valve guides are likely worn and letting oil drain into the cylinder when the engine is stopped. Unless the engine is also hard to start, this condition can probably be ignored until you have other reason to rebuild the head.

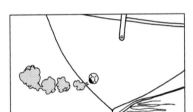

3 Black smoke is caused by excessive fuel or too little air. If you start the engine using the "cold start" button, black smoke is likely to result, but it should quickly clear. A puff of black smoke is also common when you accelerate, as the engine momentarily overloads. Continuing black smoke usually indicates problems with the injectors or the high-pressure pump; but less serious causes can be motoring into a strong headwind (overloading), a clogged air filter, a restricted exhaust system, or an oversize propeller.

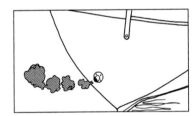

RUNNING THE ENGINE

One of the best tests of an inboard engine is to run it under load to see exactly how it performs.

1 With a fully charged battery, a diesel engine should start easily. Long cranking suggests low compression.

2 Uneven running at idle speeds is not uncommon, but it should smooth out when the prop is engaged and the engine is put under load. Uneven running under load means one or more cylinders are misfiring. The problem could be something as relatively innocuous as a plugged fuel filter (the misfiring should get worse as you increase the engine speed), or it could be a major—and costly—mechanical problem. It is time for a mechanic.

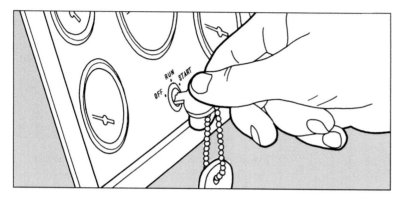

3 Look at the gauges. After a few minutes under load, oil pressure should be close to what is specified in the owner's manual and the engine should reach optimum operating temperature—about 180 degrees for a freshwater-cooled diesel, 150 for one cooled with raw water. The ammeter should show a substantial charge initially (commonly around 30 amps), a slight tilt to the plus side later.

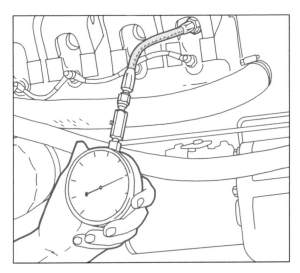

4 Take another look at the engine and the exhaust system, while the engine is running, to see if they are spewing any liquids or gases. Do the pulleys run true? Diesel engines are notoriously noisy, but do you hear any discordant clanks, any noise that seems extraordinarily loud? Having listened to other diesel engines will prove helpful here.

5 A compression test is an excellent diagnostic tool. Have a mechanic perform this test, or if you have the equipment, do it yourself. Readings that are consistent between cylinders and close to the engine-maker's specifications (see the owner's manual) suggest that pistons, rings, and valves are all healthy.

IS THE ENGINE BIG ENOUGH?

THE RULE OF THUMB FOR AN INBOARD auxiliary installation is 3 horsepower per ton of displacement. Of course this also depends on the boat and what you want the engine to do. A narrow, easily driven hull can get away with less power; more will be needed if the boat is beamy and has to shoulder its way through the water. And if you expect to power your way into strong headwinds, you may need 4 or even 5 horsepower per ton.

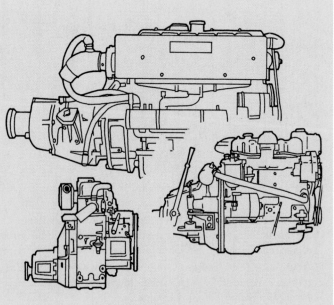

OIL

After you shut the engine down, pull the dipsticks on both the engine and the transmission. You are interested in more than whether the oil is at the right level.

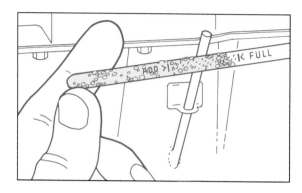

1 Bubbles on the engine-oil dipstick indicate water in the sump. The usual source is a failed head gasket, but there are other possibilities. Don't expect the engine oil in a diesel to stay as clear as it does in a gasoline engine.

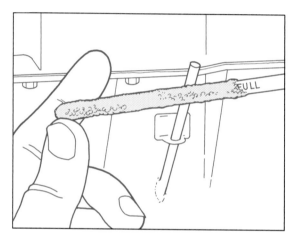

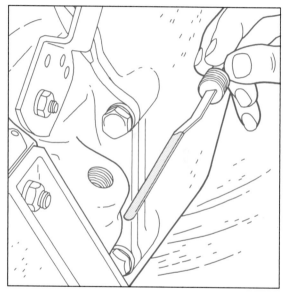

2 If the engine oil looks like a chocolate milkshake, a lot of water has gotten into the oil. This is more typical with raw-water cooling, and is more damaging to the engine. It usually indicates a crack in the water jacket, often caused by overheating due to a scale buildup. A seal failure on a gear-driven water pump can also let water into the oil.

3 Milky gear-case fluid also indicates saltwater intrusion. In this case, the usual source is a hole in the transmission-oil cooler.

The simplest steering gear is a tiller bolted to the rudderhead, but as boats get larger, heavier steering forces require impractically long tillers. Wheel steering can generate the needed power without sweeping the cockpit.

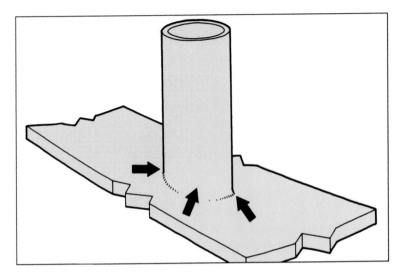

RUDDERPOST

1 Check the rudderstock tube for any signs of separation from the hull.

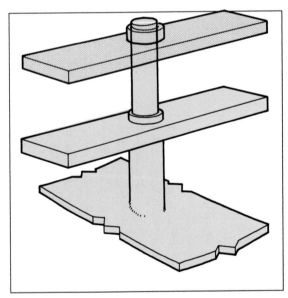

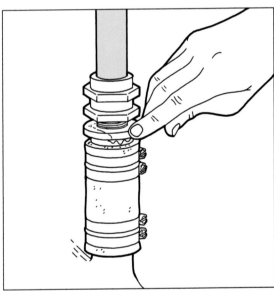

2 Either the top of the tube or the top of the rudderstock should be rigidly supported. Otherwise the top of the tube is almost certain to move when the rudder is under load.

3 If the tube ends below the waterline, it will be fitted with a stuffing box. No water should enter the hull around the rudderstock.

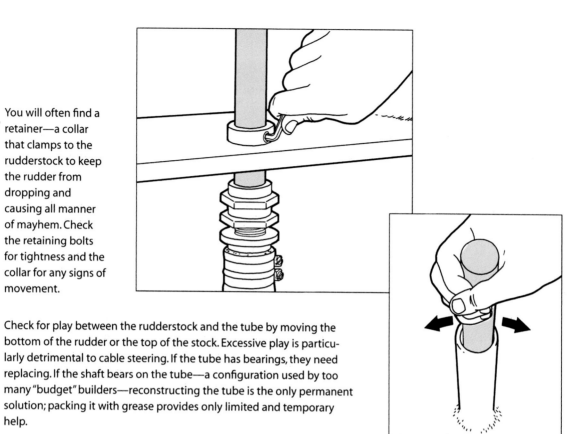

4 You will often find a retainer—a collar that clamps to the rudderstock to keep the rudder from dropping and causing all manner of mayhem. Check the retaining bolts for tightness and the collar for any signs of movement.

5 Check for play between the rudderstock and the tube by moving the bottom of the rudder or the top of the stock. Excessive play is particularly detrimental to cable steering. If the tube has bearings, they need replacing. If the shaft bears on the tube—a configuration used by too many "budget" builders—reconstructing the tube is the only permanent solution; packing it with grease provides only limited and temporary help.

TILLERS

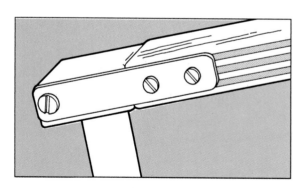

1 Play in a tiller takes the pleasure out of steering. Check the tiller to make sure the clamp bolt holes are not elongated and the bolts are snug. The tiller should fit tightly to the rudderhead.

2 Tillers are often laminated from woods that are strong and/or attractive, but not rot resistant. Check the tiller, particularly underneath, for black spots beneath the varnish, and probe its rudderstock end for rot.

CABLE STEERING

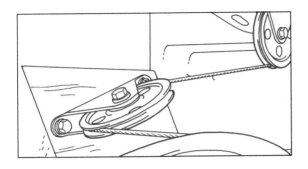

1 Check the cables for wear and to make sure they aren't loose. Any broken strands mean it is time to replace the cables. With the wheel hard over in both directions, the cables should be just tight enough to give off a musical note when you thump them—but not a high note. Both the sheave bearings and the cables should be well oiled.

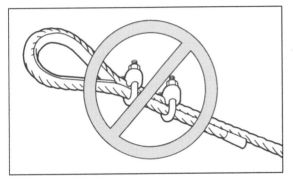

2 Cable ends should have mechanical fittings (Norseman) or thimbles retained by two compression sleeves (Nicopress); knots or rigging clamps are not acceptable.

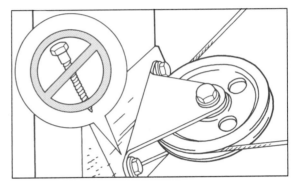

3 Check all sheave attachments. The pressure exerted on the sheaves is substantial, and they must be through-bolted—not screwed—to adequate structural members.

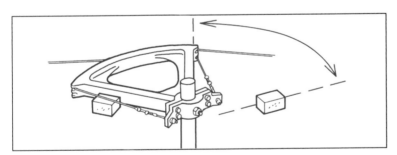

4 Check the attachment of the quadrant to the rudderstock. No movement between the rudder and the quadrant should be possible. Solid stops should limit the quadrant movement to no more than 70 degrees.

5 After you have made sure the cables are tight, rotate the wheel slowly from stop to stop and back. It should turn smoothly; if it is jerky, the chain and sprocket need servicing, and you will need to remove the compass to get to them.

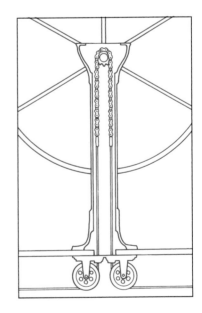

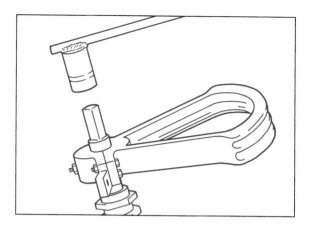

6 Check the emergency tiller—every wheel-steered boat should have one—to make sure it fits the rudderhead and has sufficient clearance to operate properly.

GEARED STEERING

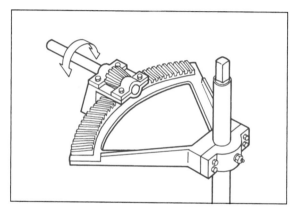

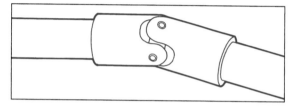

2 Check universal joints for play. Failure to keep these joints packed in grease leads to destructive wear and corrosion.

1 With the rudder centered and held rigid, move the wheel to check for play in the worm gear or between the pinion and geared quadrant. Because wear is usually in only one area of the gear, attempts to remove the play by adjusting the mesh often fail; replacement parts are generally required.

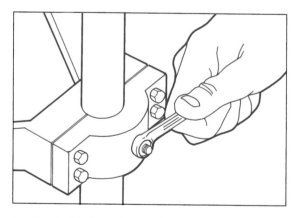

3 Check all bolts and screws for tightness. There should be no play between the quadrant or the worm steerer and the rudderstock.

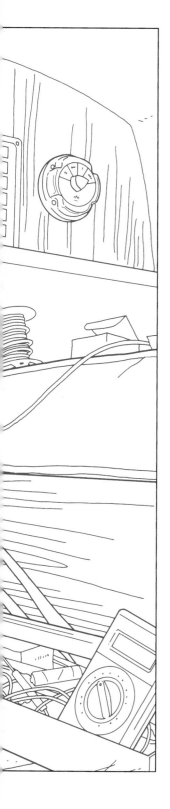

ELECTRICAL SYSTEM

There was a time—not so long back—when newspapers reported with alarming regularity the demise of boater after boater launched into the next world by the sudden ignition of gasoline that had maliciously accumulated in the bilge. Even then the catalyst was often electrical: a spark from the battery-selector switch as the skipper routinely switched on the power.

Fortunately gasoline explosions are less common today due to more stringent engine-installation requirements, one of which is a vaporproof selector switch. But boats still catch fire and burn to the waterline, a particularly disheartening event when the shore is far away. Boat fires today are almost invariably caused by some malfunction of the electrical system, and equally invariably these disasters could have been avoided. Failure to pay close attention to a boat's electrical system is a potentially fatal error.

Even if the consequences of an electrical failure aren't as dire, it is certain to render some piece of equipment inoperable. You may find yourself ankle-deep in bilge water, in traffic lanes without running lights, or unable to start the engine. For most of us, a functioning electrical system is essential, yet there could hardly be a more unfriendly environment for electrical equipment than a boat, particularly a boat operated in salt water.

The DC electrical system of a typical sailboat is not very complicated. There may be a dozen or more circuits, but each one is essentially the same as all the others—two wires running from the battery terminals (through the main selector switch) to two terminals on the piece of electrical equipment, with a fuse or breaker in the hot (+) side of the circuit. More than one item may be connected to a given circuit, but each one is still connected across the two primary wires—like rungs between the rails of a ladder.

If the boat has a generator and AC-powered equipment aboard, extra caution is needed. AC can kill you, especially in the damp environs of a boat. Limit your survey of AC equipment to flipping switches. If the equipment doesn't work, get a qualified electrician to sort it out.

BATTERY

Start a survey of a boat's 12-volt electrical system by examining the batteries. A separate starter battery prevents inattentive power consumption from leaving the boat without the use of the engine.

1 Battery size and capacity have a direct relationship. Is the house battery large enough to operate the equipment aboard? For a more accurate assessment, add up the anticipated daily amp-hour consumption of the various electrical items (see sidebar); this should not exceed 1/2 of the house battery's amp-hour rating. If it does, the battery is too small.

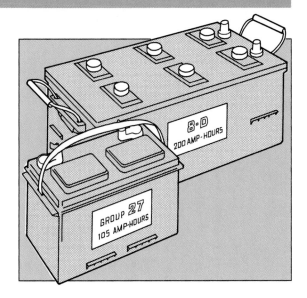

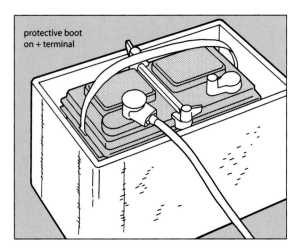

protective boot on + terminal

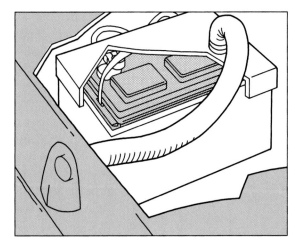

2 Make sure the batteries are in an acidproof box and securely clamped or strapped. Sailors have been severely injured in knockdowns when a battery came adrift and fell on them.

3 Make sure the battery locker is well ventilated. Batteries generate hydrogen gas when they are being charged, and any accumulation is an explosion risk.

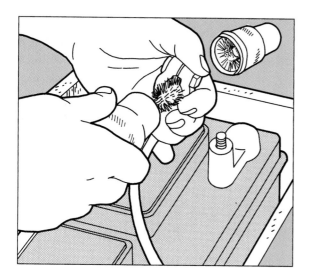

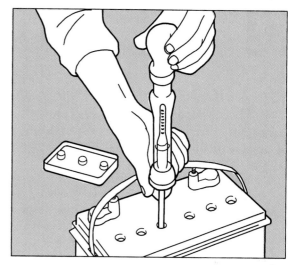

4 Corroded terminals can stop the flow of current out of and into the battery. Terminals and cable clamps should be clean and tight. Positive terminals should be protected by a lid on the battery box or with rubber boots.

5 To determine the condition of a wet-cell battery, check each cell with a hydrometer. A fully charged cell will have a specific gravity (SG) reading of around 1.265. If you can't charge all cells to this SG, the battery has probably lost capacity. If the highest cell reading differs by more than 0.050 from the lowest, the battery is bad.

DAILY LOAD

A QUICK INVENTORY of the electrical equipment aboard can give you a rough idea of the necessary battery capacity. For example, a 25-watt light consumes about 2 amps (watts ÷ volts [12] = amps), or 2 amp-hours every hour. If you expect to run 4 of these lights for 4 hours each day, the amp-hour requirement is 32. For good battery life, batteries should not be discharged below 50 percent of their capacity; so 100 watts of light for 4 hours requires at least 64 amp-hours of battery capacity (limiting discharge to 30 percent will almost double battery life). Manufacturers list actual current requirements for their equipment, but here is a list of typical ratings to help you assess how well battery capacity (and charging capacity) matches the equipment aboard.

Incandescent lights	2.1 amps
Fluorescent lights	0.7
Fans	1.2
Masthead anchor light	0.8
Depthsounder	0.2
VHF-standby	0.5
VHF-transmit	5.5
Loran	0.5
Radar	3.5
Refrigeration	5.5
Windlass	90.0
Starter motor	300.0

—courtesy of *This Old Boat*

BREAKER PANEL

Any boat with more than one electrical circuit should be equipped with a fuse panel or breaker panel. Every circuit must be protected with a fuse or breaker. Dual batteries require a selector switch.

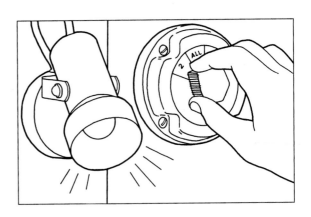

1 Turn on a light and rotate the main selector switch slowly through every position. The light should come on and stay on continuously until you return to the off position. If the light flickers or goes out between positions, the switch is faulty and will ruin the alternator. The switch should be vaporproof.

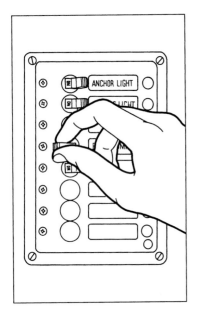

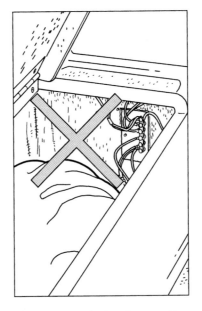

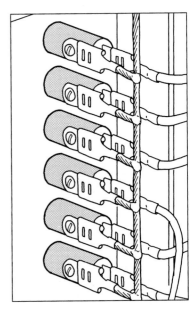

2 Fuses are foolproof and inexpensive; breakers can make neither claim. Throw and reset each breaker on the panel to check that it operates properly.

3 Make sure the breaker panel is not located where it can get wet. Consider the back of the panel as well; the wiring should not be exposed in a sail locker or the engine compartment.

4 Open the breaker or fuse panel and examine the wire connections. They should be brightly soldered and neat. This often tells you a great deal about all the wiring in the boat.

WIRE AND CONNECTORS

It isn't practical nor necessary to examine every run of wire, but making sure end connections are tight and uncorroded goes a long way toward avoiding unexpected failures. Any loose connections—not bolted to a terminal—should be sealed, preferably with heat-shrink tubing.

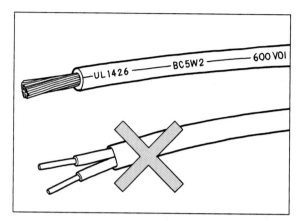

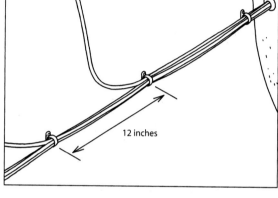

1 Solid wire has no place on a boat. It tends to work-harden and fracture. All wiring should be stranded copper suitable for wet locations. The best is tinned Type III (Class K). This type will be labeled Marine Grade, Boat Cable, BC, BC5W2, or UL1426 on the insulation. Other acceptable wire types include MTW, AWM, THWN, and XHHW.

2 Wire runs should be supported about every 12 inches with nonmetallic clips or ties. Look for grommets where wire passes through bulkheads and dividers.

3 Color-coded insulation makes troubleshooting much easier. The American Boat and Yacht Council (ABYC) recommends specific colors for specific circuits, but as a practical matter, any color scheme simplifies tracing a circuit.

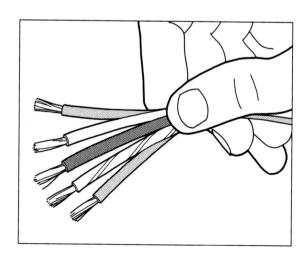

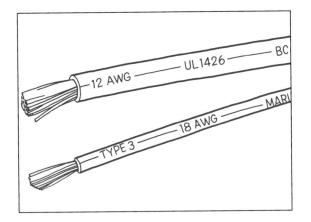

4 Look at the wire sizes; higher loads and/or longer runs necessitate heavier gauges. Factory-installed wiring is almost always too small. In a 12-volt system, a 5-amp load 15 feet from the panel calls for #18 AWG wire if a 10-percent voltage drop is tolerable; but to deliver essentially full voltage (no more than a 3-percent drop) requires #12 AWG.

WIRE SIZE

LIGHTS ARE TYPICALLY UNAFFECTED BY A 10-percent voltage drop, but most motors suffer and may not operate at all. Some electronics are also intolerant of low voltage. It is not necessary to immediately rewire circuits that appear to be functioning, but it is a good practice to size all new wire runs to limit the voltage drop to 3 percent. ABYC recommends nothing smaller that #16 AWG outside of a sheath (i.e., a duplex enclosure) no matter how short the run.

The wire length in the table is the distance from the panel to the device and back.

CONDUCTOR SIZES FOR 3 PERCENT VOLTAGE DROP

Amps at 12V	Wire run in feet									
	10	15	20	25	30	40	50	60	70	80
5	18	16	14	12	12	10	10	10	8	8
10	14	12	10	10	10	8	6	6	6	6
15	12	10	10	8	8	6	6	6	4	4
20	10	10	8	6	6	6	4	4	2	2
25	10	8	6	6	6	4	4	2	2	2
30	10	8	6	6	4	4	2	2	1	1
40	8	6	6	4	4	2	2	1	0	0
50	6	6	4	4	2	2	1	0	2/0	2/0

—courtesy of *This Old Boat*

ALTERNATOR

Alternators are generally black and white—they are either working or they aren't. A look at the ammeter when the engine is running may be the only check required, but checking the voltage at the battery is a good idea.

1 With the alternator running, voltage measured across the charging battery should be at least 13.5 volts. If less, the alternator isn't charging.

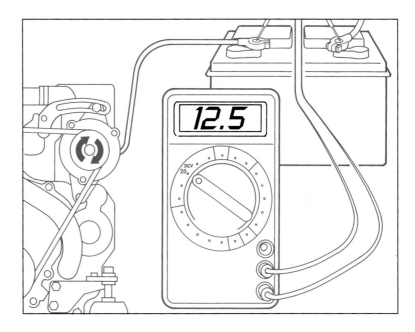

2 If the voltage across the battery terminals is above 14.4 volts, there is a problem with the voltage regulator, and it is damaging the batteries. A rotten-egg odor is a sure sign of overcharging.

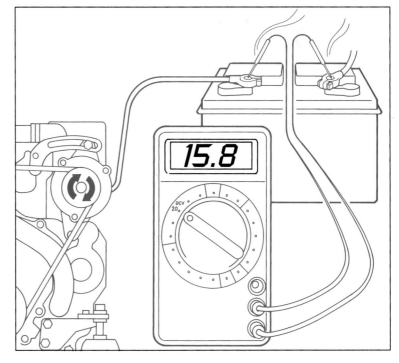

PUMPS AND MOTORS

Electrical equipment, especially bilge pumps, should be checked to make sure they are working properly.

1 Run all electrical equipment and listen for noisy bearings or erratic operation. After a few minutes of run time, touch the motor housing to check for overheating.

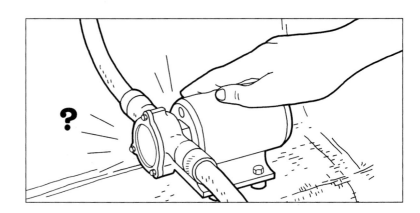

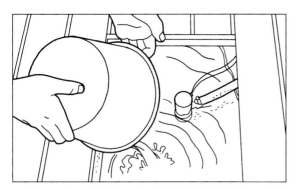

2 Pour water into the bilge to activate the float switch on the automatic bilge pump. Never run pumps dry. Now is also a good time to make sure the discharge line is as short and straight as possible and that it's unobstructed; check valves are not desirable.

3 Check all connections for corrosion. In wet areas like the bilge, look for the bright green corrosion that signals current leakage. Wires should never lie in water.

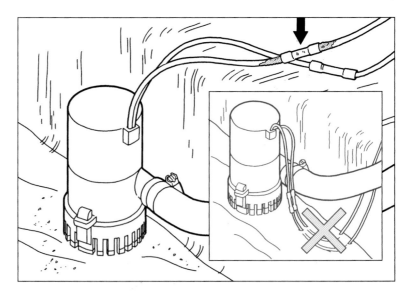

LIGHTS

Again, the obvious test is to turn on each light to see if it works. Failure may be the fault of the bulb, the switch, the connections, the socket, or the fuse (or breaker)—generally in that order of likelihood.

1 Unscrew incandescent bulbs and check the socket for rust. Sockets not intended for boats have steel parts that quickly disintegrate in the marine environment.

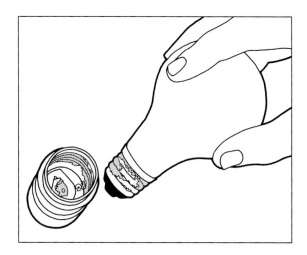

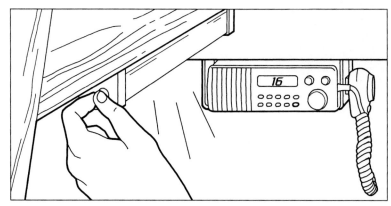

2 With the radio and other onboard electronics operating, switch on fluorescent fixtures to check for interference. Better-quality lights have "noise" suppression circuitry but may still cause interference in certain conditions. Moving the fixture or screening the tube may be necessary.

3 Running lights and other deck-mounted electrics need close scrutiny for corrosion of connections, sockets, and mountings.

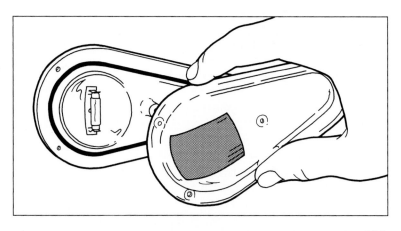

ELECTRONICS

The lay survey of electronics is generally limited to turning on the various pieces of equipment to see if they operate properly.

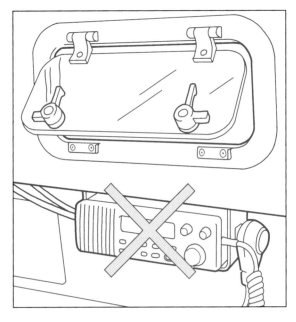

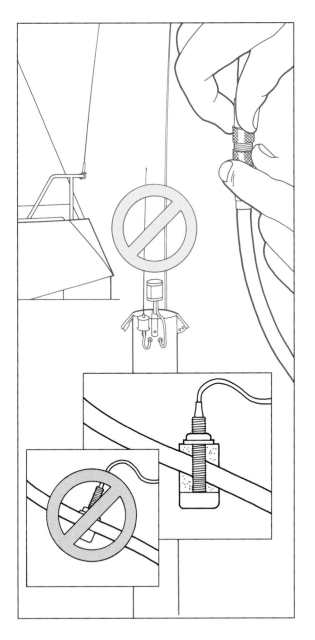

1 Each piece of electronic gear should be located for convenient operation but out of harm's way. Even "waterproof" electronics will have fewer problems if kept dry. Direct sunlight can cause condensation to fog the inside of displays.

2 Power, transducer, and antenna connections should all be tight and corrosion free. Check also the location and condition of transducers and antennas. Transducers should be properly oriented and out of turbulence. VHF antennas should be mounted as high as possible. GPS antennas should be located where they have an unobstructed view of the sky, but they should NOT be mounted high.

3 Antenna leads and power leads should not be bundled together, and neither should run near potential sources of interference—motors, fluorescent lights, and charging circuits.

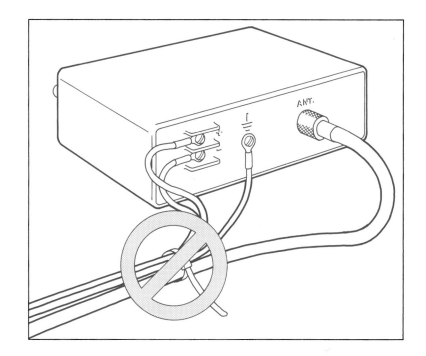

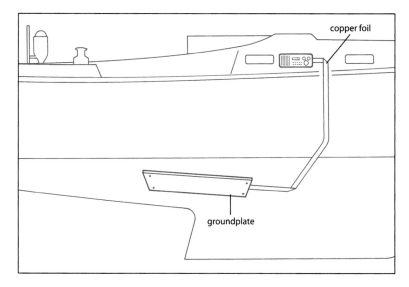

copper foil

groundplate

4 Ham and single-sideband radios (and Loran) will not perform well without an adequate grounding system. Be sure ham and SSB radios are connected to a generous groundplate.

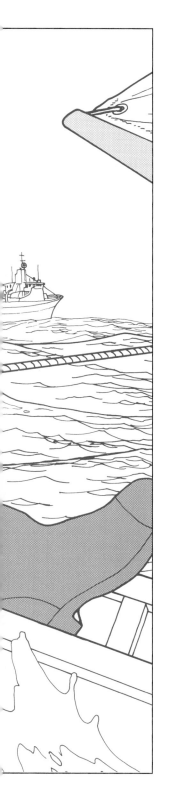

OTHER CONSIDERATIONS

The decision to purchase a particular boat, or even the decision to invest in the boat you already own, doesn't depend entirely on the boat's condition. Suitability is a factor. If you expect to win silver, you need a boat that is fast. If you want to live aboard, a certain level of comfort is essential. If you're going to cross an ocean, reliability takes on added significance.

Some aspects of a boat assessment can take place away from the actual boat. You might read a review of this model in a consumer magazine. You might note which boats consistently lead the fleet in printed race results. You could seek out current or previous owners of sisterships. Contacting the secretary of an owner's association can be a gold mine of valuable information. Even an old press release, magazine ad, or sales brochure can sometimes be insightful: if, for example, it touts a stiffer hull in 1983, what does that say about the 1981 model you are considering?

Sometimes the name of a particular designer is expected to "say it all," but no architect gets the delicate balance of boat design exactly right every time. And to expedite production, builders often make scores of design changes without consulting or even informing the architect.

The reputation of the manufacturer can be your best clue to anticipating the quality of a boat, but boat companies change hands. Commitment to quality can easily change with ownership—or just due to economic reality.

The price of a boat is rarely much affected by the inventory of equipment aboard, but quality equipment in good condition does add to the value of the boat. If you are comparing two or more similar boats, a list of the included equipment should be part of your assessment. For your own boat, a comprehensive equipment survey will save you trouble and money in the event of an insurance claim.

DESIGN

Despite phenomenal advances in the textile industry, it remains true that you can't make a silk purse out of a sow's ear. And no matter how well built or meticulously maintained, a tub is still a tub.

1 Honestly assess how you will use a boat. A fat double-ender is poorly suited for summer weekends on Long Island Sound. Don't consider an 8-foot draft if you're planning an Intracoastal trip to the Bahamas. Adding weather cloths to a lightly built club racer doesn't make it a bluewater cruiser. And a retired ocean-racing greyhound is a poor cruiser choice for a retired husband and wife.

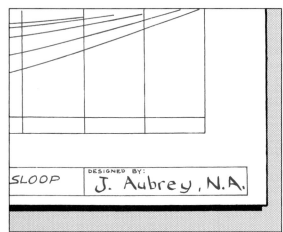

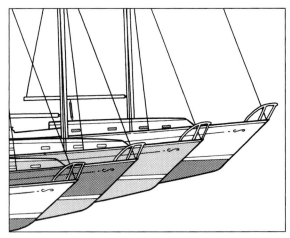

2 Who is the designer? Does his reputation mesh with your needs; i.e., is the designer known for drawing flyers, bay sailers, or passagemakers? Is this one of his better designs? A telephone call to a still-working designer can answer questions you may not even know to ask.

3 How many of these boats were built? A long production run suggests an especially successful design, a valuable recommendation if the boat suits your needs.

REPUTATION

Boats tend to earn a reputation. They are "sweet" or "bulletproof" or "junk." Builders likewise become known for the kinds of boats they turn out.

1 Talk to other sailors about the boats you are considering. Don't depend on a single "expert"; individual opinions are shaded by personal preferences. Talk to various sailors, ask "Why?" often, and look for consensus.

2 Sailboat manufacturers come and go. That a boat manufacturer is no longer in business reflects only on their business skills, not the quality of their boats. Some built terrible boats that disappeared with the company. Just as many built excellent boats, finding themselves unable to compete against cheaper offerings. The fate of the manufacturer is of little practical consequence to the owner of an older sailboat.

PERFORMANCE

Speed may not seem important, but sitting still while other boats glide by will soon tarnish a sailboat's other merits. Even a barge will sail when the wind pipes up, so to find out how well a boat sails, take her out in light air. For a bluewater boat, heavy-air performance is equally important, suggesting a second sea trial.

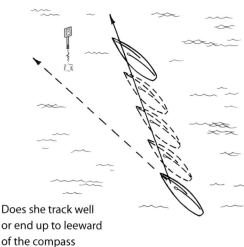

1 Does the boat balance well, or does she want to round up if you ease your pull on the tiller?

2 Does she track well or end up to leeward of the compass course?

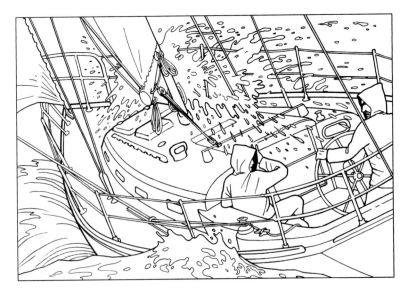

3 Is she easy to sail, or does cranking in the genoa sheet test your strength?

4 How close to the wind will she keep moving well? This is half the angle between tacks.

5 An ocean vessel should carry sail and remain dry in moderate conditions.

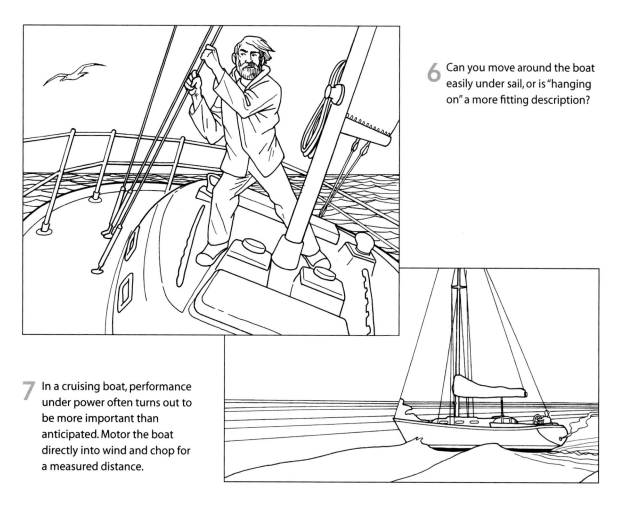

6 Can you move around the boat easily under sail, or is "hanging on" a more fitting description?

7 In a cruising boat, performance under power often turns out to be more important than anticipated. Motor the boat directly into wind and chop for a measured distance.

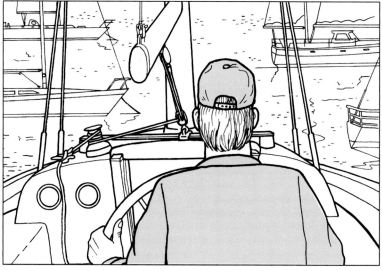

8 How does she handle under power in close quarters?

For the inexperienced sailor, sea trials have limited value as a boat evaluation tool. If you are a neophyte, give more weight to the boat's reputation. In other words, buy a boat that you know is capable and its performance will improve with your skills.

ACCOMMODATIONS

If you plan to "live" on the boat—overnight or longer—then the accommodation plan also needs to perform. We have already assessed the construction and safety of various cabin features ("Interior"); here we are talking about how well the design fits your needs.

1   Will every crewmember have a comfortable bunk and adjacent storage for clothes and other belongings?

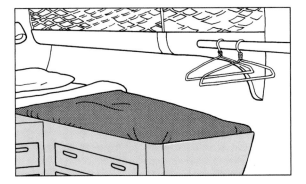

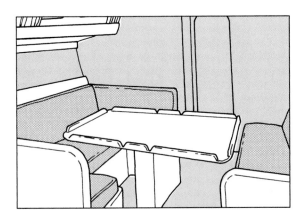

2   Will the table seat everyone comfortably at mealtimes?

3   Does the galley make turning out a multicourse meal a joy or a chore?

4   Is the cabin a cozy, dry, and well-ventilated haven for the entire crew in inclement weather? Can everyone move around, or is the only passage often blocked by the table or the cook?

EQUIPMENT

Because you may be tempted to depend on it, poor equipment is worse than no equipment. Check the gear aboard for quality, condition, and suitability.

1 Good ground tackle is essential for a cruising sailboat. Anchors should be ample in size and suitable in type for the expected bottom conditions. Check chains for corrosion, lines for abrasion, shackles for bent pins and absent safety wire.

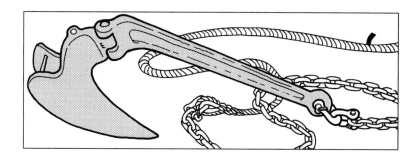

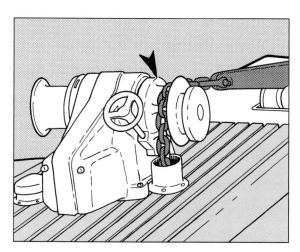

2 When the ground tackle is heavy, a functioning windlass is essential. Make sure the wildcat or gypsy fits the chain aboard.

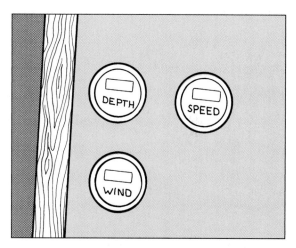

3 Most boats of any size are equipped with some electronic gear. A VHF radio and a depthsounder are almost always useful. The value of other electronics depends entirely on whether you will use them.

4 Coast Guard safety gear is essential. Make sure the boat is equipped with fire extinguishers, life jackets, and the necessary flares and horns.

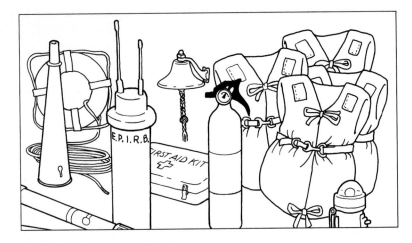

5 Lockers should contain adequate fenders and docklines and a sturdy boathook.

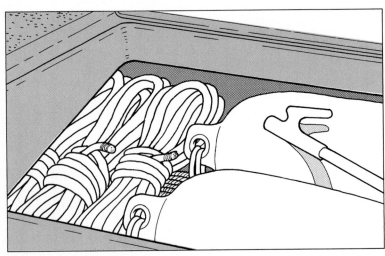

gear aboard

Avon Redcrest—good condition
6 hp Johnson—tired
6-man Switlik raft in cannister
2 harnesses
canvas bosun's chair—
good condition

6 List other gear like liferafts, dinghies, awnings, cushions, flags, windscoops, swim ladder, and bosun's chair. Anything aboard in good condition that you would otherwise buy gives the boat added value for you.

VALUE

The value of a boat to you is whatever you're willing to pay for it; but for the purchase to be a sound investment, you don't want to pay too much. The trick is to figure out how much the seller thinks the boat is worth—a number that tends to decrease the longer the boat is on the market.

1 BUC Research semiannually publishes their *Used Boat Guide*, which lists market values for most production boats built in the last 30 years. However, unless recent sales of a specific boat have been reported, the guide's price may be out-of-date. BUC also gets its information from brokers and dealers, who have been known to misreport sale prices to keep the BUC value up.

2 NADA has long published used car prices, but only recently ventured into the used boat arena with their *Used Boat Price Guide*. Far fewer boat sales preclude the level of accuracy of the car guide, particularly for sailboats, but this guide can provide another clue to a boat's value.

3 Look in newspapers and magazines for advertisements for similar boats. Look at back issues as well as current ones; values of older boats change slowly. Keep in mind that the listed price is what the seller is asking. Selling price is likely to be 10 to 20 percent less, sometimes lower.

4 As with real estate, yacht brokers subscribe to a listing service. A cooperative broker can provide you with the asking price of every boat of a particular type offered for sale by any participating broker—which is most brokers in North America and the Caribbean, and beyond.

5 *Practical Sailor* has occasionally published a comparative chart of used boat prices. Again, these are asking prices, but the value of the chart is that it suggests relative values, allowing you to get more information from ads. For example, if the chart shows boat B is worth about 25 percent less than boat A, and there are three boat As in the newspaper for 20 grand, a $15,000 asking price is about right for a boat B.

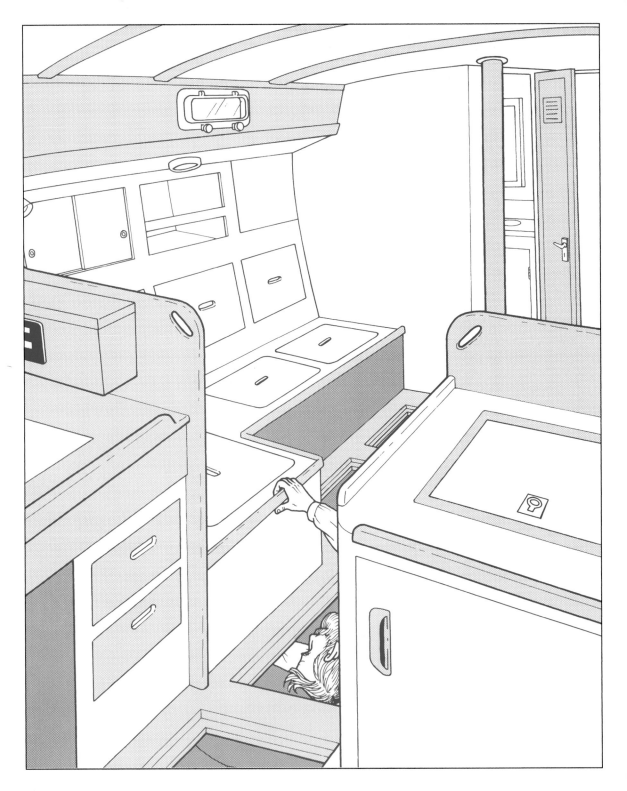

BOAT-BUYER'S 30-MINUTE SURVEY

The process of buying a used boat can be overwhelming. You look at one boat, then another, then another. To bring some order to this effort, most shoppers settle on one boat early on that becomes the standard. Subsequent boats are compared and eliminated if they don't displace the standard. This scheme works pretty well, but the problem is the basis for selecting the standard.

Sailboat buyers tend to make their selection based mostly on how a boat looks and how sumptuous the interior is. If the boat selected this way surveys well, everything is fine. But suppose the surveyor reports that the cored hull is delaminated so extensively that repair costs will exceed the value of the boat. At the very least you're out the cost of the survey, and if you ranked the other boats only against the standard, you may have to start all over.

Of course if you did your own assessment of the selected boat prior to commissioning a professional, you would have found the delamination and saved the cost of a survey. That puts money back in your pocket, but still leaves you back at square one as far as buying a boat. You either have to make a second pick from memory—hardly a good plan—or you have to take a second look at all the candidates.

What if you had discovered the hull delamination the first time you looked at the chosen boat? You wouldn't now be facing the prospect of setting up appointments to take a second look at a bunch of boats you're not going to buy. Look at boats squint-eyed rather than wide-eyed and you will minimize the number of surprises when you come back to your top choice or two for a closer examination.

It is impractical to fully assess every boat you look at, but about 30 minutes of focused scrutiny will catch all the obvious problems and give you a good idea of the overall quality and condition of the boat. The trick is to know exactly what you're looking for and not allow yourself to be distracted by joinerwork and varnish. Remember that you're not trying to learn the condition of everything; if the boat passes muster, you'll be back.

Boats are almost always consistent, so if your quick survey turns up quality or maintenance problems, these are likely to be representative. However, bear in mind that if a boat has passed through several hands, repairs and modifications may reflect the differing levels of skill and/or care of the various owners.

To do a quick survey, you'll need a good flashlight and either a thin-blade screwdriver or a plastic-handled awl. Take a pen and pad to record your findings.

HULL

A boat has to have eye appeal or you won't be happy with it, but don't fall in love. A pretty shape should just qualify a boat for consideration. Conversely, if you hate the lines, save everyone's time and don't even go aboard.

1 **Topsides.** Keeping the side of your face just clear of the topsides, walk quickly around the hull. You are looking for irregularities in the surface—bumps, flat spots, hardspots, or damage. Also watch the flow of the hull-to-deck joint for signs of separation.

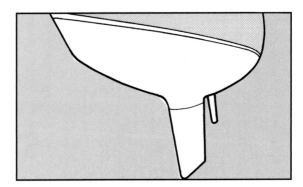

2 **Bottom.** Make a second, slower pass around the boat, this time examining the bottom. Look particularly for signs of blisters—bumps—or blister repairs—flat spots—but note any flaw that catches your eye.

3 **Keel.** If there is a keel joint, check it for tightness. Examine the leading edge and bottom of the keel for signs of hard grounding.

4 **Hull delamination.** With the handle of your screwdriver, tap the hull around all through-hull fittings, including transducers and rudder fittings, and in the area of any flaws you noted in your two circuits of the hull. These are the likely places for delamination to start.

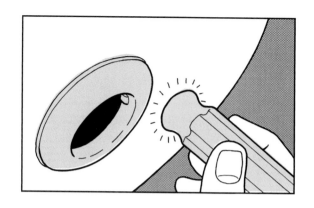

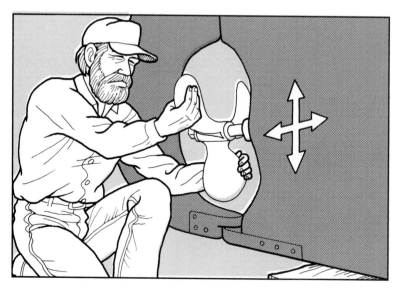

5 **Rudder.** Push on the trailing edge of the rudder to see if it operates smoothly; look for movement between the shell and the stock. Shake the leading edge to check the pintles and rudder tube for play.

6 **Prop.** Shake the prop to check the Cutless bearing. Note the condition of the prop.

DECK

If you discover problems in your examination of the hull that eliminate this boat from consideration, you can stop there. Otherwise, it is time to go aboard. Out of courtesy and to broaden your exposure to boats, you may want to go aboard anyway.

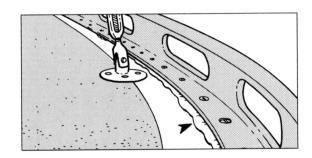

1 **Deck delamination.** Start at the bow and sound the deck and cabintop about every foot or two with the handle of your screwdriver. Most old fiberglass sailboats have some delamination in the deck; you are looking for a big problem.

2 **Bedding.** As you sound your way around the deck, look for beads of silicone or other caulk along toerails and around window frames. This is a sure sign of leakage in these areas.

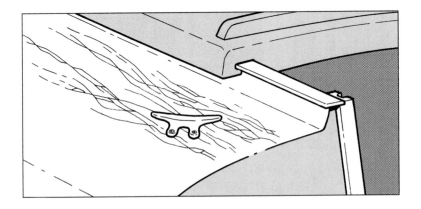

3 **Gelcoat cracks.** Also keep an eye out for stress cracks in the gelcoat as you sound. Large areas of stress cracking are likely to respond to your tapping with the dull thud of delamination.

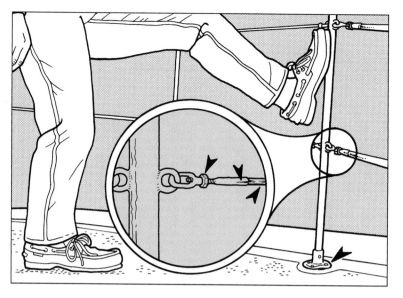

4 **Stanchions and lifelines.** Check stanchions to see if they are erect and sturdy. Check the end fittings on lifelines for corrosion and cracking. Also note any rust stains breaking through the plastic coating.

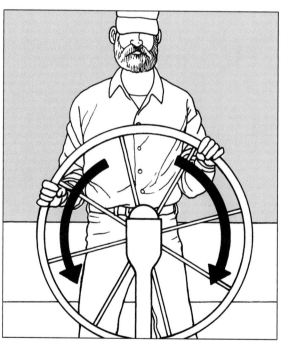

5 **Helm.** Move the tiller or turn the wheel to check for binding or play.

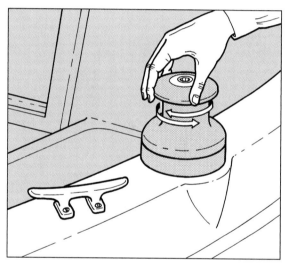

6 **Winches.** Rotate each winch once around, listening for the regular musical click of pawls that will suggest that the winch is clean and appropriately lubricated.

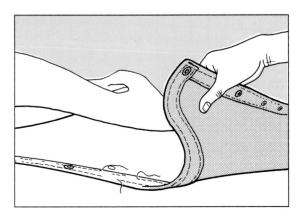

7 **Canvas.** Give all the canvas on deck a quick once-over, observing vibrancy and feeling the cloth for age clues. Check the stitching and look for chafe and tears.

8 **Working sails.** Uncover any sail stowed on a boom. It isn't necessary to spread the sail; you can guess its condition by examining the leech near a batten pocket. Pull out the first 3 or 4 feet of a roller-furled sail for the same reason. Also note if the sail rolls out and back in easily.

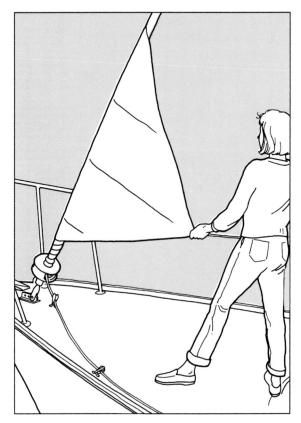

RIG

Before you go below, take a quick look at the rig. You are mainly looking for damage or corrosion, but it takes no additional time to note the mast section and wire diameter in order to get a feel for how strongly the boat is rigged.

1 **Mast.** Sight up the mast to see if it is straight. Look for dimples or ridges. Note the condition of the protective finish.

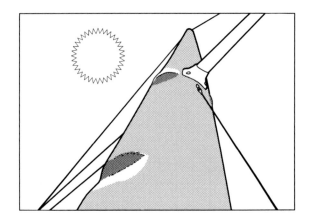

2 **Step.** Inspect the base of a deck-stepped mast for signs of corrosion. Note also the condition of the step and the contour of the deck; dishing around the step suggests inadequate mast support.

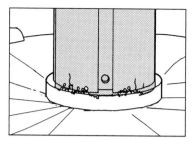

3 **Spreaders.** From the stern, see if the tip elevation of port and starboard spreaders match. Do the spreaders bisect the angle the shroud makes as it passes over the tip? Move the upper shrouds vigorously fore and aft, watching the spreader bases to see if they are solidly attached to the mast.

4 **Rigging.** If lower end fittings are swaged, make a quick inspection of each one to see if it is cracked or bent. Also check the wire near the swage for broken strands. When the end fittings are mechanical, check the wire only.

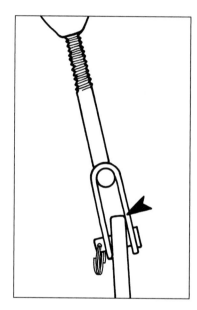

5 **Chainplates.** As you check end fittings, note also the size and condition of the chainplates. Are they properly aligned with the attached shroud or stay?

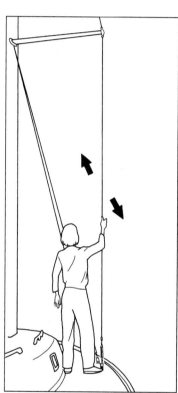

It is time to go below. Take a minute or two to take in the layout and note any special features, but then get right back to your examination. Start at the forepeak and work aft, peering into every compartment and lighting its dark recesses with your flashlight to check (for) the following:

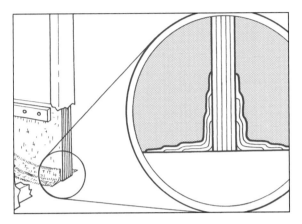

1 **Leaks.** Look for salt crystals, dust rivulets, and water stains. Tracks high on the hull are usually from deck-joint problems; other leaks are less serious if they haven't already caused damage.

2 **Tabbing.** Find access to some bulkhead tabbing and check it. Bulkheads should be tabbed on both sides with several layers. Plastic laminate should have been removed in the tabbing area. The tabbing should extend onto the bulkhead at least 3 inches—more as boats get larger. Check with your screwdriver to see that it is attached.

3 **Chainplates.** Chainplates should be accessible and through-bolted to strong structural members. Inaccessible chainplates prevent assurance that they are in good condition.

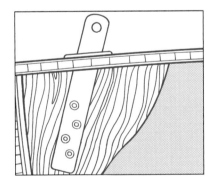

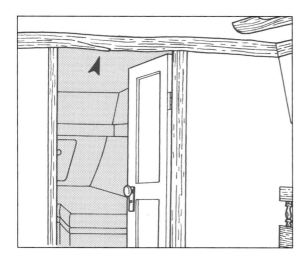

4 **Mast support.** Check the bulkhead or beam that supports a deck-stepped mast; it should be solid and undistorted. If the mast is keel-stepped, check the supporting floors for cracks or rot. Also examine the step and mast base for corrosion.

5 **Door alignment.** Look at cabin and cabinet doors. Some misalignment is common, but if the door jams or has been trimmed, the hull is flexing and wrenching the bulkheads.

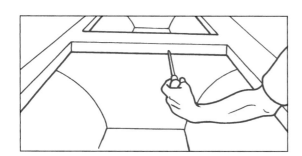

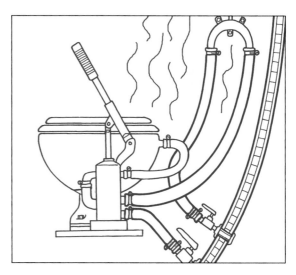

6 **Rot.** Tap around the edges of the cabin sole and at the bottom of bulkheads. If you get a dull report, try the pointed end of your awl or screwdriver on the wood. Check wooden engine bearers.

7 **Head.** Is the head installation legal? Is the toilet dry and clean or leaky and disgusting?

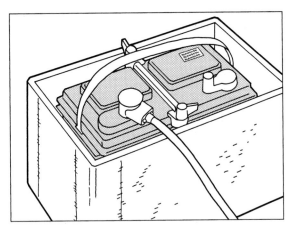

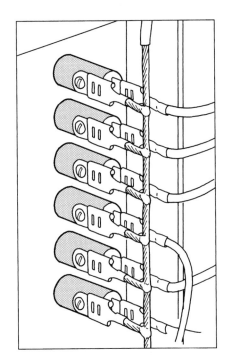

8 **Batteries.** If the batteries are in the boat, are they clean and are the terminals corrosion free? How old are they?—they generally have a date on them. Common deep-cycle batteries rarely last much longer than 5 years; heavy-duty marine batteries can last 10 years or more.

9 **Electrics.** If the face of the switch panel is hinged, open it and look inside. Otherwise check the electrical wiring in two or three locations for size, type, and support, and for the condition of the connections. Switch on each electrical item as you work your way through the cabin.

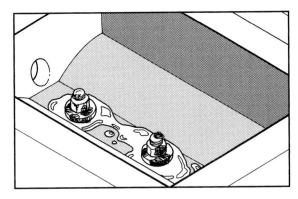

10 **Through-hull fittings.** Do you observe any through-hulls with gate valves or no valve at all? Do seacocks appear clean and operational or green and frozen? The flange of a properly installed seacock will be through-bolted on a flat surface.

11 **Keel bolts.** Pull up the floorboards and look at the keel bolts for corrosion or signs of leakage. Note if the material under the washers or backing plates is solid or cracked.

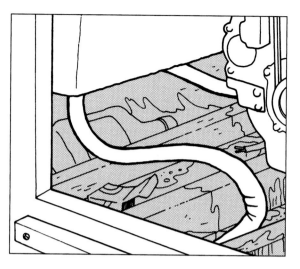

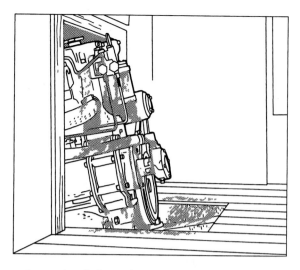

12 **Bilge.** Is the bilge clean and dry or full of oil and debris? Is the boat equipped with a manual bilge pump in addition to the electric one, and do both have short, straight discharge runs?

13 **Engine.** Is the engine a rusting lump or painted and clean? Is the compartment black with oil or belt dust? Rub across the underside of engine surfaces and fuel pumps to check for fresh leaks.

14 **Other sails.** Pull a corner of each sail out of its bag and see if the cloth has lost its body or if the edges show chafe or fraying.

IMPRESSION

Before you leave the boat, make a note of any significant findings. Now is also a good time to categorize this boat.

1 **Classic or condo.** First-time boat buyers tend to look at sailboats in terms of how much space they have. Think a minute about the boats that attracted you to sailing. Is this boat destined to be a classic, or is it a floating condo?

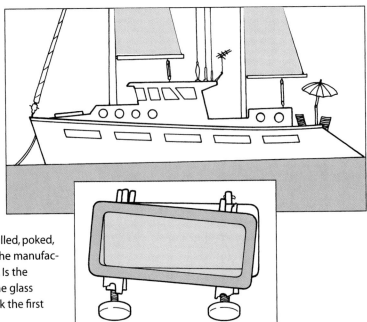

2 **Quality or budget.** Now that you've pulled, poked, and prodded, determine for yourself if the manufacturer cut corners to hold the cost down. Is the hardware plastic, the interior finish of the glass rough? Are the portlights going to break the first time someone dogs them down tight?

3 **Light or heavy.** For protected waters you want a boat light enough to sail well but not so light that you worry about the hull cracking like an egg. For offshore sailing you want a boat heavy enough to take the punishment of a storm, but not so heavy that you need a storm to make her sail. How would you characterize the construction of this boat?

4 **Use or neglect.** It is important to determine whether a boat is showing her age because she has been used or because she's been neglected. Use suggests that, at the very least, essential maintenance has been done; surprises are less likely. Neglect gives various destructive forces an opportunity to gain a foothold; long-term neglect is almost always costly.

HIRING A PROFESSIONAL

If you are 99 percent sure that the boat you are buying is sound, why do you need to spend the money on a professional survey?

Well, first there is that 1 percent. But even if you like the odds, chances are a survey is going to be required. If you plan to insure an aging sailboat, expect the insurance company to require a current survey. If you need financing for your purchase, the bank is also likely to demand proof of the value of your floating collateral. And even if they don't demand a survey, they will require insurance. You can see where that leads. So if you have to pay for a survey anyway, it makes incontrovertible sense to have it done before the problems it turns up are yours.

Perhaps a more compelling argument for having a professional survey is that it is likely to save instead of cost you money. When the value of a boat is in the thousands of dollars, most sellers expect any purchase agreement to be contingent upon a satisfactory survey. The seller will have to correct significant flaws or at the very least renegotiate the selling price, and the dollars involved often far exceed the survey cost.

Can't the seller refuse and let the deal collapse? Sure, but even if you go away as a buyer, the seller knows the problems with the boat won't. Unless the survey is awful—and it shouldn't be if you've already checked out the boat carefully—there is usually a genuine desire on the part of both parties to hold the deal together. Sometimes the owner knows the boat has undisclosed problems, but probably more often the survey findings are news. It can take a couple of days for the owner to assimilate this new knowledge and come to grips with the fact that his or her boat is worth less than originally thought. Patience and a willingness to cut the seller a little slack can lead to a transaction that satisfies both parties.

A third reason for a survey is that the professional surveyor has no vested interest. When you have really fallen for a particular boat, the rose-colored glasses can be thick enough to blind you to her faults. Seeing them listed in black and white can be just the slap you need.

FINDING A COMPETENT SURVEYOR

Marine surveying is an unregulated service. A flyer on the marina bulletin board or a listing in the Yellow Pages is all that is needed to get into the business. But because someone calls themselves a surveyor doesn't mean they really are one. A significant percentage of so-called professional surveys aren't worth the paper they are printed on, much less the hundreds of dollars the "surveyor" charged. In a medical system that didn't require training, internship, or licensing for doctors, would you select a pediatrician at random from telephone listings, or would you check with other parents? Finding a good surveyor requires a bit of effort, but it will be time well invested.

Sometimes finding a surveyor is easy; you ask around at the marina and one name keeps coming up.

But more often, asking other boatowners just elicits a shrug. A boatowner that hasn't changed boats in a few years has little reason to be current on surveyors.

Ask the manager of the boatyard you use. Boatyard operators see surveyors at work all the time. They hear sellers complain about nit-picking, buyers complain about dependability or overcharging. They are asked to do work that isn't needed and later see problems that a survey should have picked up. But boatyard managers sometimes see surveying as an appropriate sideline business, given their expertise. Because of the potential conflict of interest—more findings mean more work for the yard—the two U.S. surveying associations (see below) strictly prohibit surveyors from being engaged in the boatyard business (or as brokers or marine vendors). However, only about 20 percent of surveyors belong to a professional association, so such by-laws have no significance for the other 80 percent.

Brokers always have a list of surveyors they can recommend. Keep in mind, though, that it is in the broker's best interest for the survey to be clean, so a local surveyor known for her thoroughness may be purposely omitted from your broker's list. Never accept a single recommendation from a broker, and carefully check out all surveyors recommended by the broker before making a selection.

There are two professional associations for surveyors in the U.S.—the National Association of Marine Surveyors and the Society of Accredited Marine Surveyors. Both can provide listings of member surveyors in your area. Membership is no assurance that a surveyor is competent, but these associations do have minimum experience requirements. They also sponsor periodic seminars and recommend uniform survey practices. A surveyor who is a member of NAMS or SAMS usually notes this in ads and on business cards. Contact NAMS at 1-800-822-NAMS, www.nams-cms.org; reach SAMS at 1-800-344-9077, www.marinesurvey.org.

Another source of surveyor recommendations is your insurance agent. No matter how you come to choose a surveyor, you should make sure that the survey will be acceptable to both your lender and your insurer before you have it done. Insurers especially can have defined survey requirements, and if the survey you provide fails to meet their requirements, they may refuse to accept it. Select your surveyor from a list provided by your agent and you avoid this situation.

Being on the agent's list may be the best recommendation anyway. Unlike the broker, the boatyard operator, or even other sailors, the insurance company shares your keen interest in finding out everything that is wrong with this boat, especially anything that might cost money or result in personal injury. Start your search with a call to your insurance agent, then confirm your choice by checking accreditations and recommendations.

COST

Costs vary geographically, and like the price of almost every other service, they tend to rise over time. Currently you should anticipate being charged between $10 and $12 per foot for a sailboat under 40 feet, and up to about $15 per foot for boats larger than that. (As boats get longer they also get wider and more complicated.)

Many surveyors also charge travel time, including billing you for mileage. If you want the surveyor to participate in a sea trial, there is likely to be an hourly charge for that. If the boat is in the water, add haulout costs of $3 to $4 per foot. Few surveyors are qualified to determine the condition of the engine, so expect to spend another $300 to $400 if you want the engine thoroughly inspected.

Adding everything up, $20 to $25 per foot for both boat and machinery will give you a fair estimate of actual out-of-pocket cost. An $800 survey adds 10 percent to the cost of an $8,000 35-footer but only 1 percent if the boat's price is $80,000. And you are likely to pay for the survey in the first case since the price is already at the bottom of the range at $8,000; but almost any flaw discovered in the second case will lower the selling price by more than $800. That means there is no real cost to the buyer in the latter case; the survey actually saves the buyer money.

The actual monetary cost or benefit of a survey varies; the constant is that a survey inserts a known cost into the equation and takes out surprise costs. If you aren't required by an insurer or lender to survey the boat, then you have to evaluate the cost against the potential benefit. If the survey cost doesn't exceed 2 percent of the contract price, having the boat surveyed will almost always save you money.

WHAT TO EXPECT

Survey reports can be long or short. They can be informative or simply descriptive. They can be narrative or multiple choice. They can describe all of a boat's faults or only those due to wear and tear.

Surveyors tend to follow a pattern in all their surveys, so ask a perspective surveyor for a sample survey to make sure you will be getting the information you want. Be cautious of long surveys that list every item aboard and comment on the condition of everything. Better surveyors confine their comments to things that need pointing out.

Since you have already looked the boat over carefully, it is a good idea to tell the surveyor about any specific concerns. If you are worried about blisters or bulkhead attachments or the strength of the rudder tube, ask the surveyor to comment on those items.

Ask your surveyor if he or she has ever surveyed a sistership to the boat you are considering. A surveyor with extensive prior experience with this model may know what trouble to be especially on the lookout for.

You should also tell the surveyor how you plan to use the boat. Knowing, for example, that you expect to take this particular boat offshore, your surveyor might comment on rigging-wire size and mast section where he might otherwise have ignored these deficiencies (for your intended use) simply because they are standard for this particular boat.

Most surveyors would probably prefer to be left alone to concentrate on the job at hand, but attending the survey will be instructive for you and allow you to get detailed explanations of significant findings. If you want to be there while the boat is surveyed, tell your prospective surveyor up front. If it is clear you aren't welcome, you may be happier with a different surveyor.

Expect your surveyor to spend several hours aboard, to wriggle into every space and compartment, and to give you a written report within a couple of days of the survey. The report should reflect his or her findings in adequate detail and offer recommendations to correct any deficiencies. If you request it, a valuation will also be a part of the report.

If repairs will be made prior to closing the sale, plan on bringing the surveyor back to inspect the work.

"Wooden boats regularly
die early deaths of natural causes;
fiberglass boats
must be assassinated."

Sailboat
Hull & Deck
Repair

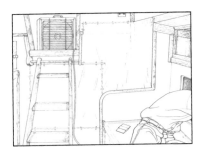

INTRODUCTION:

BEAUTY IS MORE THAN SKIN DEEP

Fiberglass.

Legendary yacht designer L. Francis Herreshoff has—somewhat inelegantly, it seems to me—called this versatile material "frozen snot." Maybe so, but how many of Herreshoff's beautiful wooden boats have ended up as lobster condominiums or fuel for a boat shed stove, while snot-built boats of the same age, no matter how undeserving of immortality, continue to ply the world's oceans, bays, and estuaries? Wooden boats regularly die early deaths of natural causes; fiberglass boats must be assassinated.

Don't get me wrong; I love wooden boats, and in particular I love Herreshoff's wooden boats. There is something magical about taking straight lumber and manipulating it into the flowing contours of a boat. The craftsmanship of the builder is obvious: planks steamed to linguini and worried into compound curves, knees cut from a natural crook to harness the tree's full strength, precise dovetail joints wedding shelf and beam. Such craft is far less evident in a hull formed by painting a boat-shaped mold with a thick layer of fiber and sticky glop. That the dried glop pops out of the mold with the same graceful curves yields no redemption.

But it isn't redemption that is called for; it's perspective. If we open the leaded glass doors in the galley of one of Mr. Herreshoff's classic wooden yachts, we are likely to encounter fine china. Why not wooden plates, woven bowls? Because china dishes—molded bone-reinforced clay—are infinitely more serviceable.

Likewise molded glass-reinforced plastic boats.

Fiberglass is malleable, durable, and easy to maintain. These characteristics, widely known, have made fiberglass the overwhelming material of choice for boat construction for more than three decades. If you want a boat to display, wood has much to recommend it, but for a boat to *use*, fiberglass is hard to beat.

A lesser-known virtue of fiberglass is that it is easy to repair. A fiberglass hull's seamless nature leads many boatowners to conclude that repair must be difficult. Any assertion to the contrary too often elicits raised eyebrows. In the pages that follow, we hope to quell the skeptics with astoundingly clear explanations, but the only way you can fully purge yourself of any nagging doubts is to buy a can of gelcoat paste or a bit of glass cloth and resin and give it a whirl. You'll wonder what you were worried about.

While this book is confined to hull and deck repairs to fiberglass boats, it is not limited to fiberglass repairs. Fiberglass boats are not *all* fiberglass. Decks, for example, may be cored with plywood, balsa, or foam, railed with aluminum, covered with teak, outfitted with bronze, interrupted with acrylic, penetrated with stainless steel, and booted with rubber. Virtually all of these components require regular maintenance and occasional repair, and they must be assembled properly and carefully if the boat is to be dry.

Watertight joints are our first order of business. Boatowners today don't need even a passing acquaintance with oakum caulking and firming irons; molded hulls are completely seamless, and rare is the fiberglass *hull* that leaks, no matter how old. Deck leaks are, unfortunately, another matter. The dirty little secret of fiberglass boats is that most are only slightly more watertight than a colander. Spray? Rain? Wash-down water? A significant amount of all three finds its way below.

Deck leaks don't just wet the contents of lockers, drip on bunks, and trickle across soles; they destroy wood core, corrode chainplates, and delaminate bulkheads. Identifying and eliminating leaks is essential. This book details the most effective technique for sealing joints and bedding hardware, and it provides specific sealant recommendations for various uses. It instructs you in portlight replacement, hull-to-deck joints, and centerboard trunk repairs. It also shows you how to test your work and how to locate pesky leaks.

Often all that is wrong with a fiberglass hull is a chalky surface or a few scratches. Restoring the gloss can be the easiest of repairs to fiberglass; it is where we begin our exposition of this material.

The ravages of time affect decks more than hulls. An older fiberglass deck is likely to be webbed with hairline cracks, even pocked with open voids, and may have stress cracks radiating from corners or from beneath hardware. Fortunately there are easy ways to repair these blemishes. Step-by-step instructions for restoring the deck to perfection are provided.

Deck repairs are complicated by the necessity of providing effective nonskid surfaces. Owners of boats with molded-in nonskid will find the included instructions for renewing those surfaces useful. Those with planked decks will be more interested in the section detailing the care and repair of teak overlay.

Eventually, of course, a hull-and-deck-repair book for fiberglass boats must come around to repairs requiring fiberglass lay-up, but not without first providing clear and concise descriptions of the various materials to be used. When should you use polyester resin and when epoxy? What is vinylester? Cloth, mat, or roving? You will find answers to these questions and more in Chapter 4.

Armed with an understanding of the materials involved and guided by clear illustrations, you are ready to take on more complicated repairs. Chapter 5 shows you how to repair deck delamination and how to replace spongy core. Chapter 6 focuses on hull repairs—dealing with gouges, repairing blisters, and reconstructing after impact damage. A quick look in Chapter 7 at repairing common rudder and keel problems, and you will have taken the cannon.

When all boats were built of wood, a truly professional repair required the skills of someone with years of experience. Not so with fiberglass. Pay attention and give it a try, and you will discover that there is virtually no repair to a fiberglass hull or deck that a motivated owner can't do as well (if not as quickly) as a pro.

Frozen snot, indeed!

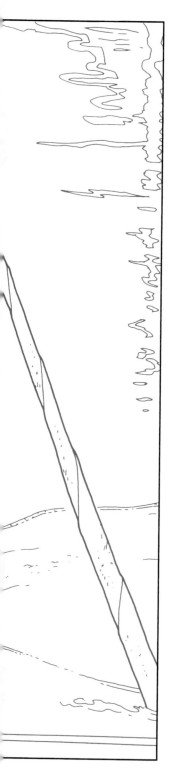

LEAKS

Leaks are insidious. A tiny leak, left unattended for months or years, can easily result in damage that will cost thousands of dollars to have repaired, or take innumerable hours if you make the repairs yourself.

There are the obvious things: ruined interior varnish below leaking ports, mildewed upholstery from trickles from the hull-to-deck joint, a punky cabin sole from "mysterious" rainwater intrusion.

As serious as these are, they're small potatoes. The biggest risk from leaks is to the deck core, and you may not see any evidence of a leak until major damage is already done.

The decks of most fiberglass boats are made up of a plywood or balsa core sandwiched between two skins of fiberglass. (Closed-cell foam, more resistant to saturation but no less susceptible to delamination, is found in relatively few production boats.) If water penetrates the fiberglass skin and gets into the core, the result is likely to be failure of the bond between the core and the skin(s). This core delamination weakens the deck. Delamination is accelerated if the boat is subjected to temperatures that cause the trapped water to freeze and expand.

The water entering a cored deck cannot get back out; the flow is one way, like filling a jug. Balsa cores become saturated and mushy. Plywood soon rots. In both cases, the only solution is cutting away the fiberglass skin and replacing the core. After you do this job once, knowing full well that it could have been prevented with four-bits' worth of caulk and an hour's worth of effort, you will become religious about maintaining a watertight seal around any hole in the deck.

CHOOSING A SEALANT

You walk into a marine store and there they are, dozens of different cartridges and tubes standing on shelves, stacked in bins, and hanging in blister cards. Geez, how many different kinds of marine sealants can there be?

Three. That's it. Three. Understand these three and you have the selection process whipped.

POLYSULFIDE

Polysulfide is the Swiss Army knife in marine sealants; you can use it for almost everything. Often called Thiokol (a trademark for the polymer that is the main ingredient of all polysulfide sealants regardless of manufacturer), polysulfide is a synthetic rubber with excellent adhesive characteristics. As a bedding compound it allows for movements associated with stress and temperature change, yet maintains the integrity of the seal by gripping tenaciously to both surfaces. Polysulfide is also an excellent caulking compound since it can be sanded after it cures and it takes paint well.

Use polysulfide for everything except plastic. Polysulfide bonds as well to plastic surfaces as to any other, but the solvents in the sealant attack some plastics, causing them to harden and split. Specifically, don't use polysulfide to bed plastic portlights, either acrylic (Plexiglas) or polycarbonate (Lexan). Don't use it to bed plastic deck fittings (including portlight frames); plastic marine fittings are generally either ABS or PVC, and polysulfide will attack both. Any plastic fitting made of epoxy, nylon, or Delrin—such as quality plastic through-hull fittings—may be safely bedded with polysulfide.

The black caulking between the planks of a teak deck is polysulfide. For this application, a two-part polysulfide gives the best results. Because polysulfide adheres well to teak (a special primer improves adhesion), and because it is unaffected by harsh teak cleaners, it is also the best choice for bedding teak rails and trim.

Polysulfides are the slowest curing of the three types of sealant, often taking a week or more to reach full cure.

POLYURETHANE

Polyurethane is the bulldog of marine sealants— once it gets a grip, it doesn't turn loose. Polyurethane is such a tenacious adhesive that its bond should be thought of as permanent; if there is any likelihood that you will want to separate the two parts later, don't use polyurethane to seal them.

Use polyurethane anywhere you want a permanent joint. This is the best sealant for the hull-to-deck joint. It is also a good choice for through-hull fittings and for toerails and rubrails, but not if they are raw teak because some teak cleaners soften it. Like polysulfide, polyurethane should not be used on most plastics—acrylic, polycarbonate, PVC, or ABS.

The cure time for polyurethane is generally shorter than polysulfide, but still may be up to a week.

SILICONE

Silicone can seem like the snake oil of the marine sealant trio. A bead of this modern miracle is too often expected to cure any and every leak. And it

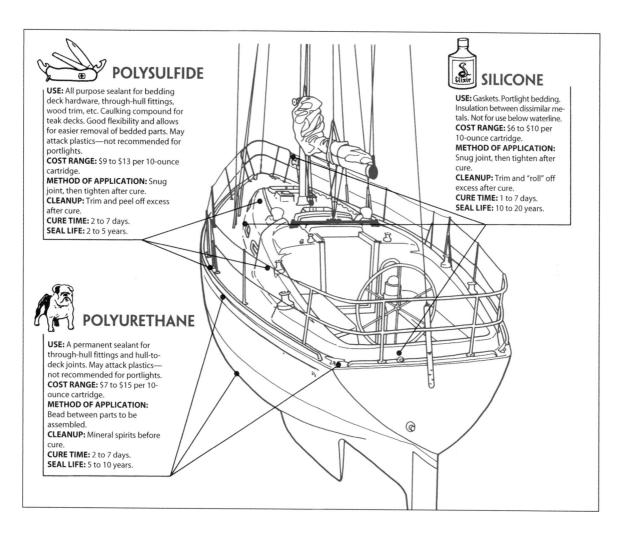

POLYSULFIDE

USE: All purpose sealant for bedding deck hardware, through-hull fittings, wood trim, etc. Caulking compound for teak decks. Good flexibility and allows for easier removal of bedded parts. May attack plastics—not recommended for portlights.
COST RANGE: $9 to $13 per 10-ounce cartridge.
METHOD OF APPLICATION: Snug joint, then tighten after cure.
CLEANUP: Trim and peel off excess after cure.
CURE TIME: 2 to 7 days.
SEAL LIFE: 2 to 5 years.

SILICONE

USE: Gaskets. Portlight bedding. Insulation between dissimilar metals. Not for use below waterline.
COST RANGE: $6 to $10 per 10-ounce cartridge.
METHOD OF APPLICATION: Snug joint, then tighten after cure.
CLEANUP: Trim and "roll" off excess after cure.
CURE TIME: 1 to 7 days.
SEAL LIFE: 10 to 20 years.

POLYURETHANE

USE: A permanent sealant for through-hull fittings and hull-to-deck joints. May attack plastics—not recommended for portlights.
COST RANGE: $7 to $15 per 10-ounce cartridge.
METHOD OF APPLICATION: Bead between parts to be assembled.
CLEANUP: Mineral spirits before cure.
CURE TIME: 2 to 7 days.
SEAL LIFE: 5 to 10 years.

does—for about as long as it used to take the magic elixir salesman to slip out of town. Then the bead releases its grip, and what started out as a tube full of promise ends up as a dangling rubber worm. All is not lost—with a hook and the right wrist action, you can at least catch dinner.

Silicone sealant is a gasket material—period. If you think of silicone's adhesive abilities as temporary at best, you will find it is the best product for a number of sealing requirements. It is the only one of the marine sealant trio than can be safely used to bed plastic. It is an excellent insulator between dissimilar metals—use it when mounting stainless hardware to an aluminum spar. It is the perfect gasket material between components that must be periodically dismantled—beneath hatch slides, for example.

Silicone retains its resilience for decades and is unaffected by most chemicals, but it should not be used below the waterline. Because it depends upon mechanical compression to maintain its seal, silicone is not the best choice for sealing hardware on a cored deck. Exposed silicone is a magnet for dirt but repels paint like an opposite pole, so never fillet with silicone, and don't use this sealant on any surface you plan to paint.

Silicone sealants typically set in a few minutes and usually reach full cure in less than 24 hours.

A USEFUL HYBRID

THERE IS A BIG ADVANTAGE TO USING A SEALANT with good adhesive properties. An adhesive sealant maintains its seal even when stresses pull or pry the bedded components apart, the sealant stretching and compressing like the bellows joining the two sides of an accordion.

This accordion effect would be especially useful for plastic portlight installations where the portlights are not bolted in place but rather clamped between an inner and outer frame. As the cabin sides expand and contract with temperature changes or flex with rigging stresses, the space between the frames varies.

Applied properly (see "Rebedding Deadlights"), silicone sealant can accommodate these variations, but it is not easy to set the portlight in a uniform thick-ness of silicone. Although silicone has amazing elasticity, its lack of adhesion means it must always be under pressure to maintain a watertight seal. If the gasket formed by the cured silicone is thin anywhere around the portlight, the seal is sure to fail, probably sooner rather than later.

Either polysulfide or polyurethane would provide a more dependable seal, but polysulfide is certain to attack the plastic, and polyurethane prohibits any future disassembly. Fortunately a chemist somewhere, one who undoubtedly owns a boat and tried to bed plastic portlights, cooked up a new goo that is part silicone and part polyurethane. Marketed by BoatLife as Life Seal, this is a more durable sealant than silicone for portlights and other plastic fittings.

REBEDDING DECK HARDWARE

Fiberglass boats are notorious leakers. Wood is, to a degree, self-sealing; a leak swells the wood, pinching off further leakage. Not so with fiberglass. Once the seal between the fiberglass and the hardware is broken, it will leak unabated until you reseal it. The seal can be broken by stress, by deterioration, or by temperature changes. Wrenching the top of a lifeline stanchion can break the seal at the base. Sunlight and chemicals erode sealants. In cold weather the deck may literally contract away from the hardware.

Every seal on the deck (and hull) of a fiberglass boat should be carefully examined at least annually, and at any sign of failure, the joint should be opened, cleaned, and resealed. This modest investment is guaranteed to return greater relative dividends than even your most profitable stock fund.

1 Gather all the necessary materials. If you are using a cartridge—economical if you have quite a bit of rebedding to do—you need a caulking gun. Have masking tape and adhesive cleaner on hand to control squeeze-out.

2 Remove the fitting. This is usually the hardest part of the job, either because access to the fasteners is difficult to gain or because the bolts are frozen—or both. Access sometimes requires removing headliners or cabinetry, but don't try to avoid this by simply running a bead of sealant around the fitting. If you do that, eventually you will still be removing the fitting, only this time in preparation for major deck repair.

For access to the fasteners securing wooden components, the bungs hiding the bolt heads will have to be removed. This can be accomplished by drilling a small hole in the center of the bung and threading a screw into it; when the point of the screw finds the screw head below the bung, continuing to turn the screwdriver will lift the bung. Extracting bungs this way can sometimes damage the bung hole. A safer method is to drill the bung with a bit slightly smaller than the diameter of the bung, then carefully remove the remaining ring of material with a small chisel.

If the fitting was installed with polyurethane, removing the fasteners may have little effect. Trying to pry the fitting loose is likely to result in damage to the deck and the fitting. Debonding products are now available that can coax cured polyurethane sealant to release its grip.

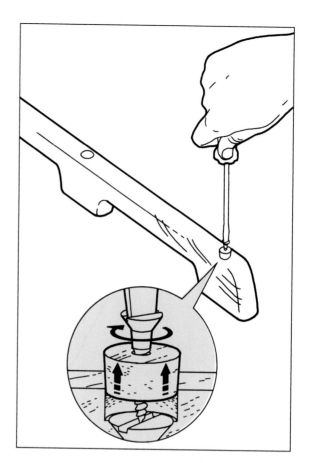

HEADLINERS

HEADLINERS ARE AS VARIED AS BOATS. If the headliner is fiberglass, you likely cannot remove it (without removing the deck). Occasionally manufacturers bolt hardware to the deck before installing it over the headliner. You will have to cut or drill the headliner beneath the fasteners to gain access. Reinstall the hardware with longer bolts through spacers and a backing plate that covers the cutout.

When the headliner is made up of panels, it is usually captured by trim pieces screwed in place. Panels may also attach with Velcro.

Sewn headliners are typically stapled to wooden strips across the overhead. You can't see the staples because they are through the excess material on the back side at the seams. You gain access by removing the trim piece at the forward or aft end of the liner and pulling the liner loose at that end. Work the staples out with a flat screwdriver at the seams until you uncover the desired area. Be sure you use Monel staples when you replace the liner. For more on headliners, see *Canvaswork and Sail Repair.*

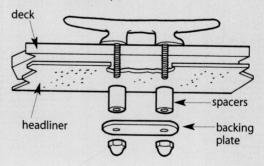

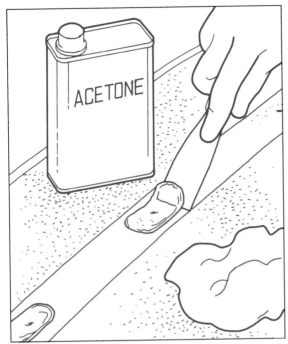

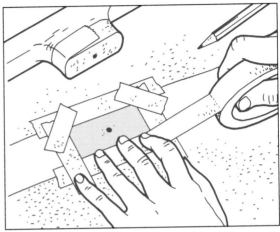

3   Clean off the old bedding. Every trace of the old sealant must be removed. Use a blade, sandpaper, or a wire brush as required, and clean both the deck and the fitting with acetone.

4   Mask adjacent areas. Cleaning up the squeeze-out with solvent takes twice as long as masking and is ten times more messy. Dry-fit the part and trace around it with a pencil. This is the time to strengthen the mounting location if required (see "Deck Repairs"). Mask the deck 1/8 inch outside the pencil line and mask the edge of the fitting.

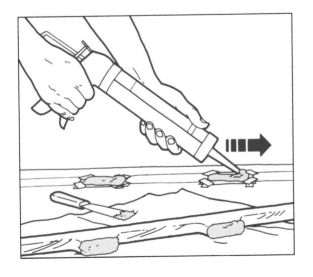

5   Coat both surfaces with sealant. Cut the tip of the tube or cartridge at a 45° angle—close to the tip for a thin bead, farther back for a thicker bead. (Cartridges have an inner seal you will have to puncture with an ice pick.) Apply the sealant with a forward motion, pushing the bead in front of the nozzle. Coat both surfaces to make sure there will not be any gaps in the bond; use a putty knife to spread the sealant evenly, like buttering bread. Before inserting the mounting bolts—not screws—run a ring of sealant around each just below the head. NEVER apply sealant around the fasteners on the underside of the deck; if the seal with the outer skin breaks, you want the water to pass into the cabin where it will be noticed.

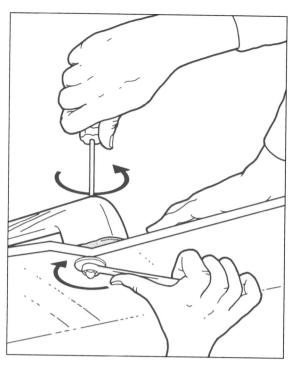

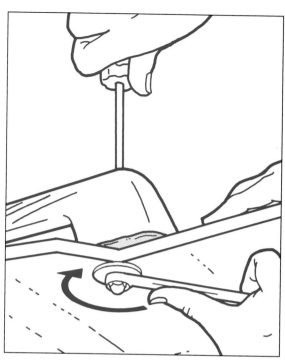

6 Assemble the parts and "snug" the fasteners enough to squeeze sealant out all the way around.

7 Wait until the sealant partially cures—30 minutes for silicone, 24 hours for polysulfide or polyurethane—then fully tighten the bolts by turning the nuts only to prevent breaking the seal around the shank of the bolt. If the fitting is attached with screws, withdraw them one at a time, run a bead of sealant around the shank beneath the head, reinstall each in turn, then drive them all home evenly.

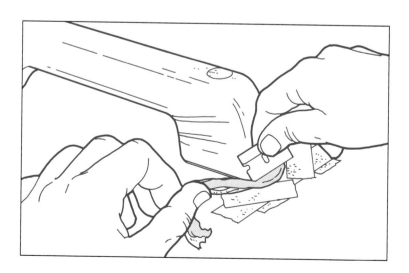

8 Trim away the excess squeeze-out by running a razor blade around the fitting, then peeling away the masking tape. Never leave a fillet around the edge; silicone attracts dirt, polyurethane yellows, and polysulfide weakens in the sun, so you want the least amount of sealant visible—only the thin edge beneath the fitting. Install new bungs, matching color and grain and setting them with varnish.

PREPARING A CORED DECK FOR NEW HARDWARE

As good as marine sealants are, you should never depend on them to keep water out of the core of a deck or hull. Anytime you drill or cut a hole in the deck, seal the exposed core with epoxy before mounting any hardware. If you are rebedding old hardware for the first time, be certain that the core has been properly sealed, or follow this procedure before reinstalling the fitting.

1 Drill all fastener holes oversize. A large hole—for a through-hull fitting, for example—doesn't need to be cut oversize.

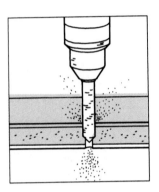

2 Remove all the core within ½ inch of the hole. You can do this easily with a bent nail chucked into a power drill. Vacuum the pulverized core from the cavity; whatever you can't remove will act as a filler.

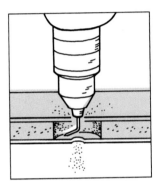

3 Fill the cavity with epoxy. The most secure way is a two-step process. First seal the bottom hole with duct tape, then pour catalyzed epoxy into the top hole. When the cavity is full, puncture the tape and let the epoxy run out back into your glue container. Filling the cavity with unthickened epoxy allows the epoxy to better penetrate the edge of the core. Retape the bottom hole. If there are several mounting holes, fill each and drain in turn until all have been treated and all bottom holes resealed.

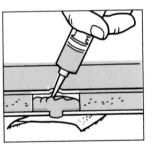

The second step is to thicken the epoxy (the same mix you have already poured through the holes) with colloidal silica to a mayonnaise consistency. Now fill each cavity level with the deck and allow the epoxy to cure fully.

4 Redrill the mounting holes through the cured epoxy. Sand and clean the area that will be under the fitting. Now you are ready to bed the new hardware as detailed in the previous section.

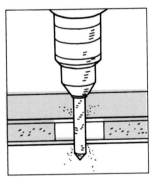

SEALING CHAINPLATES

When water finds its way below, very often the culprit is a leaking chainplate. Chainplates' propensity to leak is understandable; they are bedded under moderate fixed stress, but once under sail the windward chainplates are alternately yanked and eased while the leeward chainplates are virtually released. This tries the grip of any sealant. They are also stressed in unfair directions by poor sheet leads, shroud encounters with the dock, and by the use of shrouds for body support or as handholds for coming aboard. When the seal fails, rain and spray gathered by the attached shroud or stay runs down the wire and across the turnbuckle directly to the chainplate.

As annoying and potentially damaging as a leak into the cabin is, the larger risk is often from chainplates that appear to be watertight. The danger is usually not to the deck; most manufacturers know enough not to have chainplate openings located in a cored section of the deck (but you should check yours). It is the rig that is at risk. If the seal at the deck breaks, water penetrates, but additional sealant lower on the chainplate stops the leak before it enters the cabin. This results in the chainplate sitting in a ring of water. Despite the corrosion resistance of stainless steel, this situation will, over time, almost certainly result in chainplate failure. Because the erosion is hidden by the deck and/or sealant, the only way to detect this problem—short of catastrophic failure—is to pull the chainplate and examine it. If you have never fully examined your chainplates, or if it has been a few years, you are strongly urged to pull them before you rebed them.

1 Remove the trim plate if there is one. This can usually be taped up out of the way, but rebedding is much easier if you disconnect the shroud or stay by slackening the turnbuckle and pulling the pin. Disconnect only one shroud at a time. Before releasing a stay always set up a halyard to support the mast.

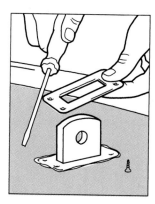

2 Pull the mounting bolts below deck and extract the chainplate. It is only necessary to remove the chainplate if you want to check it for signs of corrosion. If it doesn't come out easily, pass a long, round screwdriver shaft through the pinhole and support the end on a wooden block while lifting on the handle.

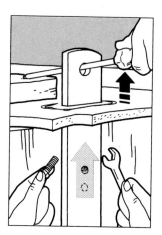

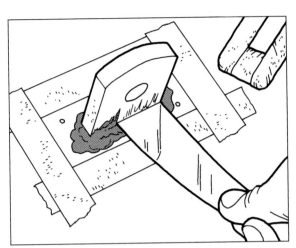

3 Dig all of the old caulk from the hole. A piece of hacksaw blade can be useful for this, but be careful not to enlarge the hole through the deck; the tighter the chainplate fits, the less it will move, and the longer your bedding job will last. Clean the deck, trim plate, and chainplate of old bedding. Examine the chainplate in the caulk area carefully; any pitting, cracks, or brown discoloration indicate replacement. Wipe down the deck, trim plate, chainplate, and the inside of the hole with acetone.

4 Reinstall the chainplate if you removed it. Dry-fit the trim plate and trace around it with a pencil. Mask the deck outside of the pencil line, the chainplate above the trim plate, and the top surface of the trim plate. Push a generous bead of polysulfide sealant into the space between the chainplate and the deck all the way around the chainplate. Use the flat of a flexible putty knife to force sealant into the crack. Butter the deck and the bottom of the trim plate with sealant.

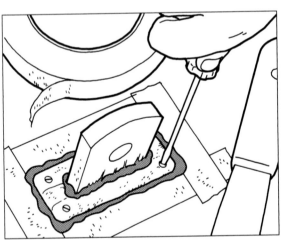

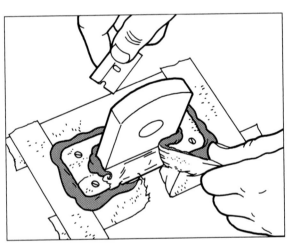

5 Fit the trim plate in position and install its fasteners. Because the trim plate screws are generally quite small, there is little to be gained by two-stage tightening, so tighten these screws fully. Sealant should squeeze out of the slot and all around the plate.

6 When the sealant is sufficiently cured, trace around the trim plate and the chainplate with a razor blade and remove the masking.

SEALING PORTHOLES—A TEMPORARY SOLUTION

When a porthole develops a leak, what you should do is rebed it properly. But maybe you're 500 miles offshore, and removing a porthole doesn't seem like a very good idea. Or maybe your end-of-season haulout is only three weeks away. Or maybe you just don't have the time or the inclination to get involved in such a job at the moment. You could just let the sucker leak, but a more sensible solution is a temporary repair.

1 Wipe the frame, cabin side, and portlight thoroughly with *alcohol* to remove any oil or grease. *Never use acetone or other strong solvents on plastic portlights or hatches.*

2 Mask both the portlight and the cabin side about ⅛ inch from the frame.

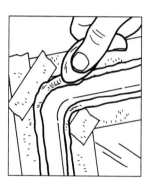

3 Push a thin bead of silicone sealant into the corners the frame forms with the portlight and with the cabin side. Drag a fingertip or a plastic spoon through the bead to form a concave fillet all the way around both edges of the frame.

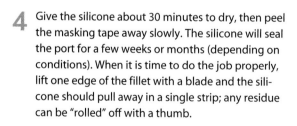

4 Give the silicone about 30 minutes to dry, then peel the masking tape away slowly. The silicone will seal the port for a few weeks or months (depending on conditions). When it is time to do the job properly, lift one edge of the fillet with a blade and the silicone should pull away in a single strip; any residue can be "rolled" off with a thumb.

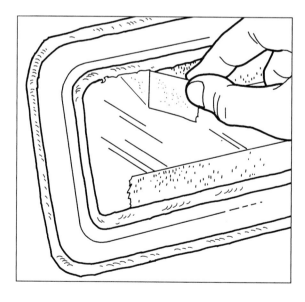

Opening portholes are rebedded like any other piece of hardware—by removing them, cleaning away all old caulk, buttering the cabin side and the outside flange with fresh sealant, snugging the fasteners, then tightening fully after the sealant has cured. Use polysulfide if the frames are metal, silicone (or a silicone hybrid) if they are plastic.

Getting a watertight seal around a fixed port is a bit more exacting.

1 Dismantle the deadlight. The deadlight pane is typically captured between inner and outer trim rings bolted together, either by through-bolts or by machine screws that thread into sockets on the outer ring.

NOTE: You may find a rubber gasket between the inner frame and the plastic pane. This is not a seal; it's a spacer. Boat manufacturers often installed acrylic windows thinner than the space between the trim rings, making up the difference with a rubber gasket. If you aren't replacing the pane, you will need this gasket. If it has hardened or deteriorated, cut a new one. Don't use soft gasket material; this will allow the pane to be pushed away from the outer frame, probably resulting in seal failure. Eliminating the gasket altogether by installing thicker portlights is the best plan (see next section).

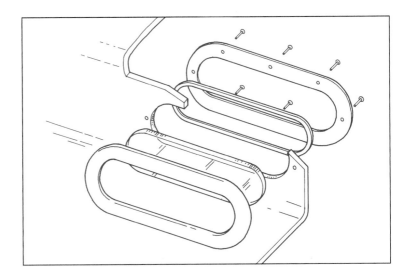

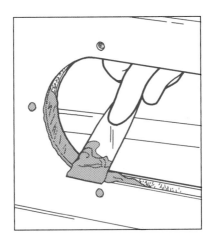

2 Remove all traces of old sealant and wipe all the surfaces with rubbing (isopropyl) alcohol. Check the edges of the cutout in the cabin side. If there is exposed core, dig it out beyond the screw holes and fill the cavity with epoxy thickened with colloidal silica. After the epoxy cures, redrill the fastener holes.

3 Reassemble the cleaned parts and mask both the portlight and the cabin side at the edge of the outer frame. Disassemble.

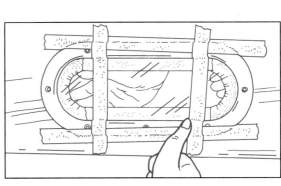

4 Tape the inside ring in place, then position the pane—with the gasket, if fitted—in position inside the cutout. A couple of strips of tape across the pane and frame inside the cabin will hold the pane in place.

5 Back up on deck, fill the space between the plastic and the cabin side with silicone-based adhesive sealant (Life Seal or equivalent). Continue applying sealant to the pane and cabin side until the unmasked edges of both are coated. Distribute the bedding with a putty knife.

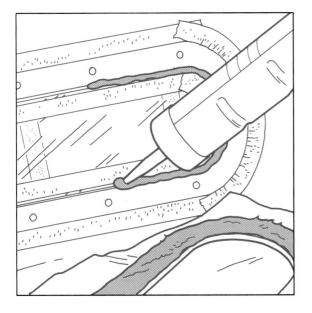

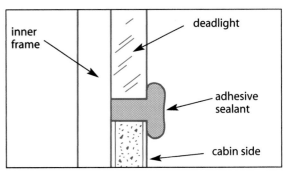

inner frame

deadlight

adhesive sealant

cabin side

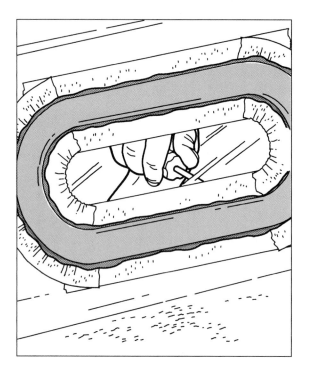

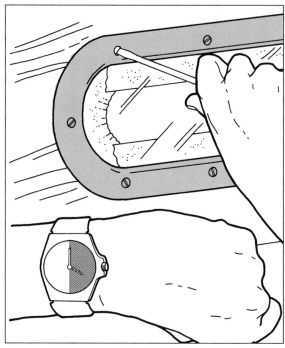

6 Butter the underside of the outside ring and install it. Snug the mounting bolts or machine screws until sealant squeezes from under every edge of the ring. If the rings are through-bolted, don't forget to put a bead of sealant under the head of each fastener.

7 Let the silicone cure for 30 minutes, then tighten the screws.

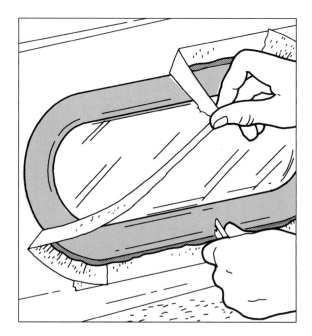

8 Run a new razor blade around both edges of the outside frame, then peel away the masking tape.

REPLACING PORTLIGHTS

Old acrylic portlights get scratched, cloudy, and crazed, but because this happens gradually we often fail to notice until they are almost opaque. Replacing portlights is easy and inexpensive. You are sure to be amazed at the difference it will make in both the look of the boat and the clarity of the view.

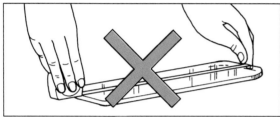

1 Measure the opening. Don't blindly copy the old pane. Mount the inner and outer frames without a pane and measure the space between them. This is the correct thickness for your new plastic—perhaps a few thousandths thinner to allow for expansion. Using a rubber gasket to fill the space is a poor compromise.

Also look at how the old portlight fits the opening. Often the corner radius of the opening and that of the pane are completely different, resulting in excessive gap at the corners. The new plastic should fit the opening (or the frame if it has a capturing flange) with an even gap of about ⅛ inch all the way around. If the old pane isn't a good fit, cut a stiff paper pattern.

2 Take the measurements and patterns to the plastics supplier and have the pieces cut, or buy a sheet of plastic the proper thickness and cut them yourself. Both acrylic and polycarbonate can be cut and drilled with standard woodworking tools, but the edges must be well supported to prevent chipping. Special plastics blades will give the best results. Scrape away any slag with the back (smooth edge) of a hacksaw blade, then file or sand out any chips to eliminate any points that might lead to cracking. Leave the protective film on the plastic while fabricating and mounting.

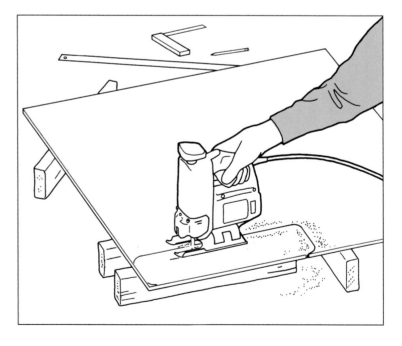

3 Dry-fit the new portlight and trace around the inside of both frames with the corner of a razor blade to cut the protective film. Dismantle the assembly and peel the film from the edges of the plastic.

4 Bed the new pane as detailed in the previous section. When the sealant is cured, trace the frame with a blade and peel away the protective film.

ACRYLIC OR POLYCARBONATE?

WHEN CHOOSING THE MATERIAL FOR REPLACEMENT PORTLIGHTS, you have two choices. Acrylic—sold under such brand names as Plexiglas, Lucite, and Acrylite—is the plastic you are most likely to be replacing. Manufacturers use it because it is adequate and relatively cheap. Those may be good enough reasons for you to chose acrylic as well. Acrylic can be brittle and has historically exhibited a tendency to craze. Crazing is less of a problem with today's formulations, but stressed acrylic still cracks. However, for spans typical of boat portlights, acrylic of appropriate thickness is unlikely to break even in extreme conditions.

Polycarbonate—most familiar as Lexan—is not just a better acrylic. It is an entirely different thermoplastic and has an impact resistance roughly 20 times greater than acrylic. Polycarbonate's remarkable strength makes it the undisputed best choice for the wide spans of hatches and oversize windows, but it is probably overkill for most portlight installations. Polycarbonate is softer than acrylic and thus easier to scratch, and it tends to darken with age.

With the cost of polycarbonate about 2½ times that of acrylic, there is little reason to spend the extra money for polycarbonate portlights unless you are heading out to the high latitudes. Acrylic provides adequate strength for all but the most extreme conditions, is more scratch-resistant, and will remain bright longer. Of course if you would feel more secure with bulletproof portlights, that's what you should install.

Acrylics and polycarbonates are both available with coatings to make them more scuff-resistant, but in the marine environment these coatings invariably peel off like a bad sunburn. Opt for the less expensive basic untreated plastic; lost luster can be easily restored with a quality plastic polish.

Both plastics are easy to fabricate with common woodworking tools. Polycarbonate shows less tendency to chip, but more tendency to heat up in the cut and bind the blade. Lubricate the blade with beeswax or bar soap, and use a moderate blade speed.

DEAD FRAMES

THREADED SOCKETS, ESPECIALLY IN ALUMINUM frames, are prone to corrode and may strip when you back out the mounting screws. If that happens, you can still reuse the frames by drilling through the

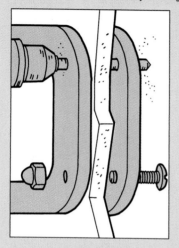

outside frame (down the center of the stripped sockets), countersinking the new holes, and through-bolting the frames with barrel screws or with oval-head screws and cap nuts.

Sometimes aluminum frames are so corroded underneath that they simply disintegrate when dismantled; if that happens, you can buy new frames from the original manufacturer, special order frames through Bomar, Vetus den Ouden), or Hood Yacht Systems, or have them fabricated by a local machine shop.

Deadlights are sometimes installed without a frame, captured in a rubber gasket like an old automobile windshield. The gasket may have a metal or plastic insert to "lock" it in position. Rubber-mounted deadlights are more often found on small boats and are probably safe enough for a boat used inshore. You work a new pane into the gasket with the aid of a soap solution and a rounded prying tool—like putting a tire on a rim—but by

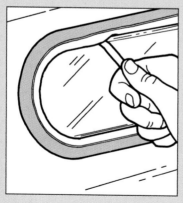

the time it is time to replace the pane, the rubber gasket is usually too brittle to stretch over the plastic without tearing. You may be able to find replacement gaskets, but if the boat will be operated outside of protected waters, where the punch of a boarding wave could push the portlight out of the gasket, consider reinstalling the pane with a rigid mounting system.

If you don't object to the change in look, one of the most secure methods of installing a deadlight is to simply cut the plastic pane an inch or so larger than the opening all around and

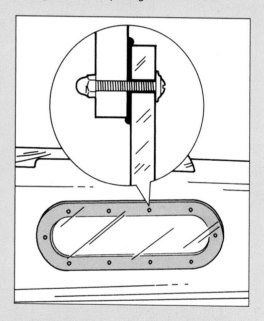

through-bolt the pane directly to the cabin side—well-bedded, of course. Drill the mounting holes a drill size or two oversize to allow the plastic to expand and contract. Space the holes at roughly 12 times the thickness of the pane. Don't countersink the holes; the wedge effect of countersunk fasteners will eventually crack the plastic. Instead, use panhead bolts (preferably with oversize heads) or use finishing washers under oval-head bolts. Hide the raw edges of the hole in the cabin side with trim.

MAST BOOTS

Leaks around a keel-stepped mast indicate boot failure. The time to install a new mast boot (or coat) is when the mast is being stepped. Universal molded replacement boots are available, but a cheaper, more versatile, and more durable alternative is a section of inner tube; your nearest tire dealer probably has a bin full of discards that would provide a suitable section.

Slip the boot up the mast inside out and upside down. Once the mast is stepped and the rubber chocks are in place, slide the boot down and clamp the lower end to the mast with a boot clamp (a BIG hose clamp). Now turn the top of the boot down over the clamp—like rolling down a sweatsock—and stretch it over the deck flange. A clamp around the flange completes the seal. If the mast has an extruded sailtrack, before installing the boot, fill the track in the clamp area with polysulfide sealant or epoxy putty and let the compound dry.

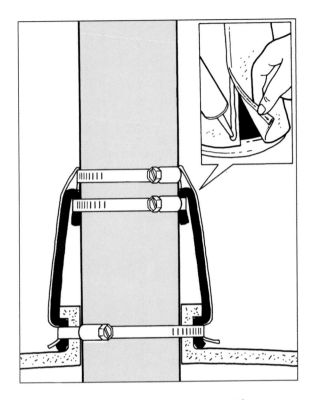

Extend the life of the boot by protecting it with a canvas coat. Cut the canvas so the edges overlap and "button" them with a bead of polyurethane after the coat is installed. The canvas should be captured under its own clamp on the mast, but it can share the flange clamp with the boot.

HULL-TO-DECK JOINT

In older fiberglass boats, deck joints are often an annoying source of leaks. Rare is the old fiberglass boat that doesn't exhibit a bead of silicone somewhere along the edge of the caprail or toerail, placed there in some past ill-fated attempt to stop the intrusion.

Better fastening techniques and better joint compounds have improved hull-to-deck joints, and these improvements can be applied to older boats.

EVALUATING THE JOINT

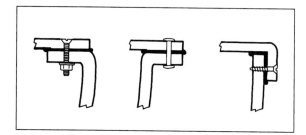

1 Most hull-to-deck joints fall into one of three categories: inboard flange, outboard flange, or shoebox. The best joints are fiberglassed together into a single strong and leak-free unit, but few boats are built this way. Most are joined mechanically with rivets, screws, or bolts, and depend on sealant to keep water out.

2 Gaining clear access to the deck joint almost always involves removing the rail, which requires bedding anyway. The outboard flange is generally the easiest joint to reseal. Cabin joinery can make access to the other types impossible without virtually dismantling the interior. In such cases, a compromise repair may be the best alternative.

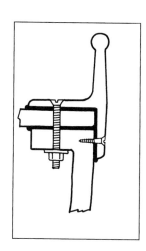

REBEDDING

How big the job of repairing a leaking hull-to-deck joint is depends almost entirely on how much dismantling is required to get to the joint fasteners. The good news is that if you do it right, you are unlikely to need to do it again for at least 20 years. Don't cut corners.

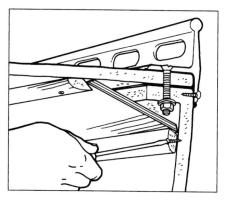

1 Remove the rail. Metal rails may be through-bolted (best), screwed in place (a distant second), or sometimes riveted (bad). Wood rails will be bolted or screwed; drill out the bungs to get at the heads of the fasteners. The nuts are often accessible behind easily removed panels in the cabin.

2 Remove mechanical fasteners holding the joint together. Don't be surprised if these are widely spaced; manufacturers often installed only a sufficient quantity to hold the flange together until the rail was installed, depending on the rail fasteners to do double duty. Grind the heads off any rivets and punch them out.

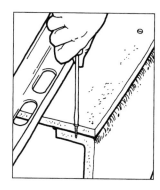

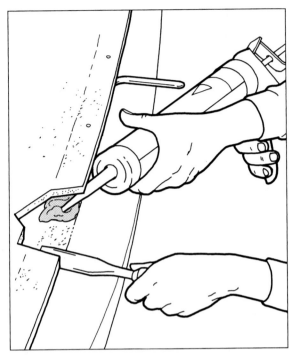

3 Reef out old bedding compound. Early fiberglass boats were bedded with an oil-based mastic that eventually dries out and shrinks. For a secure seal, all the old caulking must be removed. Clean the joint thoroughly with acetone, using a sharpened putty knife to separate the flanges as much as possible without damaging the laminate.

FIBERGLASSING

THE BEST SOLUTION FOR A LEAKING hull-to-deck joint is to join the two parts permanently with fiberglass lay-up. This can be done either inside or outside, depending on access and the design of the joint. Instructions for laying up fiberglass are provided in "Laminate Repair."

4 With the flange pried open, fill the gap with polyurethane sealant (3M 5200 or equivalent). For a permanent seal, it is imperative to have a continuous line of sealant that passes both outboard and inboard of the fastener holes.

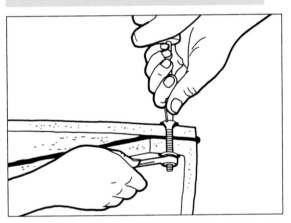

6 Reinstall the rail, bedding it as detailed earlier. Be sure to use backing plates or at least oversize shoulder washers under nuts holding slotted rail or T-track.

5 Refasten the flange. Through-bolt if possible. If not, use self-tapping screws, not rivets. Generously bed the bolts or screws in sealant.

CENTERBOARD TRUNKS

Wooden centerboard trunks are notorious leakers, but fiberglass trunks seldom leak except around the pivot pin. This is easily avoided by making the pin part of an internal frame that slips inside the case, but more often the pivot pin in a true centerboard boat—one without an external keel—passes through the trunk from inside the boat, sealed on either side by rubber grommets. When the grommets harden, a leak occurs. Tightening the nut is not the solution and may distort the case enough to jam the centerboard. Stop the leak by replacing the grommets.

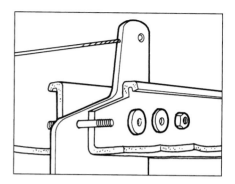

Pulling the pivot pin with the boat afloat will admit a significant flow. This is a job better done with the boat out of the water. Be sure the centerboard is well supported when you pull the pivot pin or the board will drop out of the trunk.

In a keel/centerboard boat, the pivot pin usually passes through the stub keel. A leak here cannot be repaired effectively with grommets or sealant. Details for repairing the pivot pin of a keel/centerboard boat are provided in "Keel and Rudder Damage."

THROUGH-HULL FITTINGS

Through-hull fittings last a very long time, but occasionally require replacement. Modifications to the boat may necessitate an additional through-hull, but the prudent skipper will minimize the number of holes through the hull of his boat by tying into existing through-hulls whenever practical.

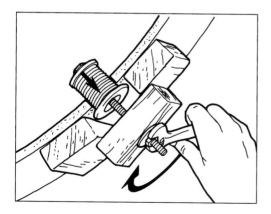

1 Removal of the old through-hull is easy with the aid of a long bolt and a washer large enough to sit on the through-hull. With the retaining nut or seacock removed, pass the bolt through the through-hull and through a wooden block outside the hull. Block the ends of the wood clear of the hull and tighten the nut on the bolt.

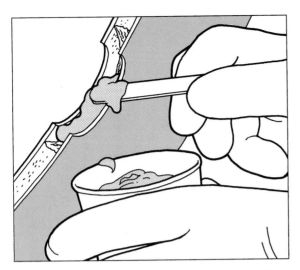

2 The hull must be solid around a through-hull. If the hull is cored, hollow an area around the hole at least as large as the flange of the seacock and fill the hollow with epoxy thickened to mayonnaise consistency with colloidal silica.

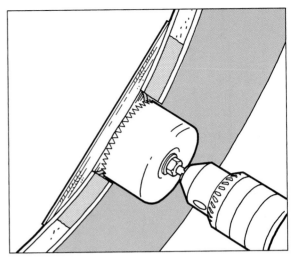

3 Fitting a flat seacock flange to the concave inner surface of a hull requires a contoured backer block. A backer block also spreads the load on the hull. The easiest backer block is a ring cut from plywood and shaped to the hull with a sander, but if you use plywood, saturate it with epoxy before you install it (cured), or the slightest seacock leak will quickly destroy it. Laminating incrementally larger circles of fiberglass to the hull to build up a flat island is a better approach (see "Laminate Repair" for laminating instructions). Capturing the flange bolts under the laminated pad to eliminate bolt holes through the hull makes a very nice installation. Drill the center hole in the pad (from outside) after the laminates cure.

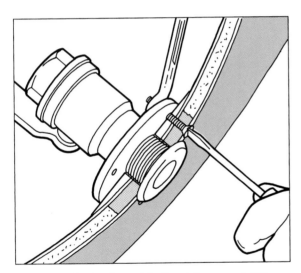

4 Assemble the through-hull and the seacock. If the through-hull bottoms out into the seacock, you need additional pad thickness. If you have not glassed in studs, drill and countersink mounting holes through the hull. Bolt the seacock in place; never install a seacock by simply threading it onto the through-hull. Bed the mounting bolts well.

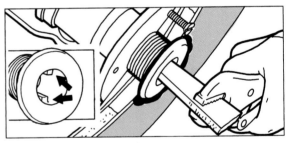

5 Remove the through-hull, turning it with a file, steel plate, or hardwood wedge against the internal ears. Butter the hole, the edge, and the through-hull threads and flange with polyurethane sealant. Reinstall the through-hull and tighten; caulk should squeeze out all around the outside flange. Clean away the excess and use some of it to fair the heads of the flange bolts.

PRESSURIZING TO FIND LEAKS

Some leaks into the cabin are obvious, but most aren't. Water may leak through the deck, then travel along the top of a headliner 10 feet or more before finding an exit and dripping out. The traditional way of finding leaks is to flood the deck, moving the hose incrementally "up" the deck until the drip appears. This method often fails. Here is a method that requires a bit more effort, but it will locate every leak.

1   Shut all seacocks and close all hatches.

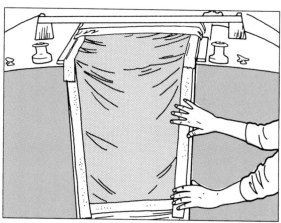

2   Use duct tape to seal all openings you don't expect to be airtight, i.e., ventilators, cockpit hatches, hawsepipes, etc. Seal the companionway with plastic sheeting (a garbage bag will be adequate) edge-taped over the hatch and the dropboards.

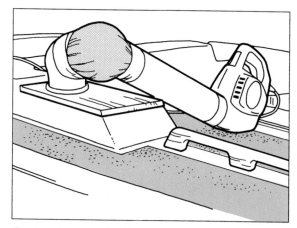

3   Insert the nozzle of a small electric leaf blower into an open ventilator or deck plate and seal it with tape. A shop-vac with the hose on the "blow" side will also serve.

   With the blower running (give it five minutes to pressurize all the internal spaces), sponge soapy water over all ports, hatches, and hardware. Anywhere you see bubbles, you have a deck leak.

   After you rebed the identified fitting, you can pressure-test again to confirm that the leak is

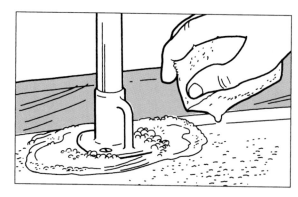

resolved, but don't leave the tape in place for more than a few hours—never overnight—or you will have great difficulty removing it.

RESTORING THE GLOSS

Production fiberglass boats are built by laying multiple laminates into a boat-shaped mold. The interior of the mold is polished mirror-bright and coated with a releasing agent (wax); then the first layer, called gelcoat, is sprayed onto the mold surface. The initial layer of fiberglass is applied to the "back" side of the gelcoat, and additional layers are added until the builder achieves the desired thickness.

This is opposite of the way most other products are manufactured, where the last step in production is to spray on the finish—presumably the reason it's called the finish. Gelcoat is the start.

Gelcoat also differs from paint in other important ways. The bond between paint and the underlying surface is mechanical—that Passion Fruit Crimson enamel on your old Roadmaster is hanging on (or not) by gripping microscopic scratches put there by sanding or chemically etching the metal. Between gelcoat and the underlying laminates, the bond is chemical; the resin saturating the first layer of glass material combines with the exposed surface of the gelcoat to form a single mass—not unlike pouring warm gelatin over cold. This is called chemical cross-linking, and it occurs because gelcoat resin and the polyester resin used to saturate the layers of fiberglass material are the same basic product. Gelcoat is essentially pigmented polyester resin.

Gelcoat resin has poor flow characteristics. Good paints are self-leveling—like water—drying to a smooth, glossy finish, but gelcoat resin behaves more like plaster, taking on the texture of the application tool. It can be thinned and sprayed to get a reasonably smooth finish, but the "wet-look" gloss characteristic of new fiberglass boats is due entirely to the highly polished interior surface of the mold.

Gelcoat is much thicker than a paint finish. For example, the dry film thickness (DFT) of a typical polyurethane finish (Awlgrip) is 1.5 to 2 mils (0.0015 to 0.002 inch) thick. The thickness of the gelcoat layer of a boat just popped from the mold is 20 mils, give or take 3 or 4 mils. In other words, the paint on a painted surface is typically thinner than a single page of this book, while a layer of gelcoat will normally be about 10 pages thick.

A well-applied gelcoat (like everything else, there are quality differences between manufacturers) will generally last 10 years with minimal or no care. Protected with an annual coat of wax and compounded in later years, gelcoat can maintain its gloss for 20 years or more. The longevity of gelcoat is due primarily to its thickness. When the surface dulls and chalks, the "dead" layer can be abraded off and the fresh surface underneath polished to restore the gloss.

Thickness can also be the enemy. If the builder applies the gelcoat too thickly—often done with the best intentions on early fiberglass boats—it eventually cracks like dried mud. A faulty resin formulation can also cause cracking and crazing.

Except for color matching, gelcoat repairs are easy and straightforward.

BUFFING

The most common surface malady of fiberglass boats is a dull finish. This is brought on almost entirely by exposure and can be delayed significantly by regularly waxing the gelcoat. When unprotected gelcoat becomes dull and porous, perhaps even chalky, waxing will no longer restore the gloss. The damaged surface must be removed by buffing the gelcoat with rubbing compound.

START WITH A CLEAN SURFACE

1 Wash. Scrub the surface thoroughly with a solution of 1 cup of detergent per gallon of water; choose a liquid detergent, such as Wisk. To make the solution even more effective, fortify it with trisodium phosphate (TSP), available at any hardware store. If the surface shows any signs of mildew, add a cup of chlorine bleach to the mix. Rinse the surface thoroughly and let it dry.

2 Degrease. Soap solutions may fail to remove oil or grease from the porous gelcoat. To degrease the surface, sweep it with an MEK-soaked rag. (Acetone can also be used, but the slower-evaporating MEK holds contaminants in suspension longer.) Protect your hands with rubber gloves and turn the rag often, changing it when a clean area is no longer available.

3 Dewax. Rubbing compound works like very fine sandpaper, and wax on the surface can cause uneven cutting. In addition, if the surface has silicone on it (nine boats out of ten do), the compound drags the silicone into the bottom of microscopic scratches, which will cause you grief if you ever paint the hull. Wipe the hull with rags soaked in toluene or a proprietary dewax solvent. Wipe in a single direction, usually diagonally downward toward the waterline.

CHOOSE THE RIGHT COMPOUND

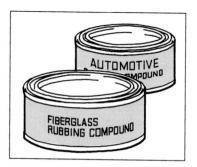

Gelcoat is much softer than paint and requires a gentler rubbing compound. Select a compound formulated for fiberglass. If the gelcoat is in especially bad shape, the heavier abrasion of an automotive compound can provide faster surface removal, but it must be used with caution to avoid cutting through.

PLUG IN

Rubbing compound can be buffed out by hand if the area is small, but hand-buffing an entire boat is not recommended. An orbital polisher is far cheaper than an artificial elbow. Don't try chucking a buffing disk into your electric drill; it will eat right through the gelcoat, or you'll burn up the drill running it slow.

THE RIGHT PRESSURE

How much of the surface the compound removes relates directly to how much pressure you apply. Since you always want to remove as little gelcoat as necessary, never use any more pressure than is required. You will have to experiment with how much that is.

Whether you are compounding a small repair by hand or an entire hull with the aid of a machine, the process is the same. Working a small area at a time, apply the compound to the surface by hand, then buff it with a circular motion. Use heavier pressure initially, then progressively reduce the pressure until the surface becomes glassy.

If the gelcoat shows swirl marks, buff them out with a very fine finishing compound.

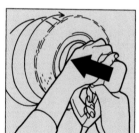

SANDING

Sometimes the dead layer of old gelcoat is so deep that removing it with rubbing compound becomes interminable. In that case, the process can be accelerated by sanding the surface first. This only works if the gelcoat is thick; if you sand through the gelcoat, it is too thin to restore and you will have to paint the surface to restore its gloss.

HIGH SPEED AND HIGH RISK

1 The safest way to sand gelcoat is by hand, but you can slash the time required to remove the dead surface layer by using a power sander. You will need a ¼-sheet finishing sander—called a palm sander. Load it with 120-grit aluminum-oxide paper (it's brown). It is a good idea to start in an inconspicuous spot to make sure your gelcoat is thick enough to take this treatment. Keep in mind that the sander is working at about 200 orbits per second, so keep it moving and don't sand any area more than a few seconds. Apply only as much pressure as needed to maintain contact. This first pass removes most of the material; if the gelcoat doesn't get transparent, good results from the remaining steps are likely.

2 Don't let the sander run over any high spots, ridges, or corners, or it will cut through the gelcoat regardless of how thick it is. Change paper when the amount of sanding dust diminishes.

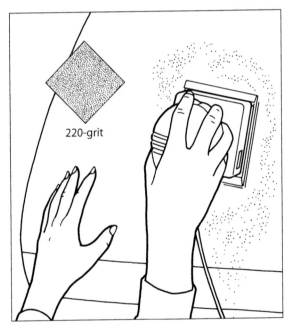

220-grit

3 When you have run the sander over the entire area, change to 220-grit paper and do it again.

WET SAND

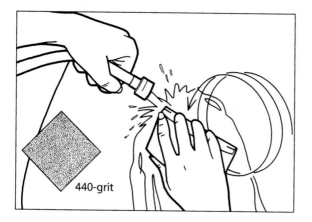

440-grit

1 Remove the scratch marks power sanding left behind by wet sanding the surface with 400-grit wet-or-dry (silicone carbide) sandpaper. Hand sand with a circular motion, keeping a trickle of water running on the sanding area.

2 To ensure a uniform surface, backing sandpaper with a rubber or wooden block is usually a good idea, but when the grit is very fine—320 or higher—you will get the same results and perhaps better control from finger-backed sanding. Fold the sandpaper as shown to keep the paper from sanding itself and to provide three fresh faces from each piece of paper.

3 Wear cloth garden gloves—the kind with the hard dots—to save the tips of your fingers.

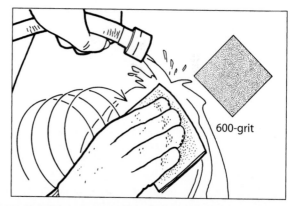

600-grit

4 Make a final pass with 600-grit wet-or-dry paper and the surface should be ready to buff to a like-new gloss.

WHAT?

THE HIGH SPEEDS OF PALM SANDERS—about 14,000 rpm—can result in an ear-damaging shriek. **Earplugs** are available from any drugstore for about a buck; buy a pair and use them. Not only will they save your hearing, but by eliminating the fatigue that accompanies such an assault on the senses, they actually make this job much easier.

SCRATCH REPAIR

Scratches are less visible on gelcoat than on paint since they don't cut through to some different color base. If the surrounding gelcoat is in good condition, always make surface damage repairs with gelcoat rather than paint. Even though the gelcoat application may initially be rough, it can be sanded smooth and polished to blend imperceptibly with the rest of the hull. For dealing with deeper gouges that also damage the underlying laminates, see "Hull Repairs."

OPENING A SCRATCH FOR REPAIR

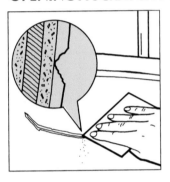

Never try to repair a scratch by simply painting over it with gelcoat. Gelcoat resin is too thin to fill the scratch, and if the resin is thickened to a paste, the paste bridges the scratch rather than filling it. To get a permanent repair, draw the corner of a scraper or screwdriver down the scratch to open it and put a chamfer on both sides.

GELCOAT CHOICES

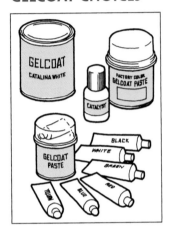

You will find gelcoat available as both a resin and in a thicker putty form called paste. Paste is what you want for scratch repair. Kits containing a small amount of gelcoat paste and hardener along with a selection of pigments can be purchased for less than $20.

WHAT COLOR IS WHITE?

THE HARDEST PART OF A REPAIR TO THE SURFACE of a fiberglass boat is matching the color. Even professionals that do gelcoat repairs daily have difficulty getting a perfect match. This is one of the few places that may call for conditioning yourself to be happy with a self-assessment of "not bad."

You can purchase gelcoat as unpigmented resin, in a kit with a half-dozen different colors of inorganic pigments, or in "factory" colors for the most popular boats. Because pigments fade, if a boat has seen a few years in the sun, even factory colors won't match exactly.

For small repairs to a white boat, a kit with pigments should serve; getting close is much easier with white, and once the repair is buffed out to a gloss, small shading differences will be unnoticeable.

For colored hulls and larger repairs, getting an adequate match is more difficult. It essentially requires tinting an ounce of gelcoat with one drop of pigment at a time and touching the

resulting mix to the hull until you get a match. Keep track of the number of drops of each tint per ounce to reach the right color. Guys, get your wives or girlfriends to help you with this part; men are eight times more likely to have defective color vision—a minus that becomes a plus if your repair is slightly off (you won't notice).

For additional assistance in matching colors, see *Sailboat Refinishing.*

CATALYZING

The hardener for gelcoat is the same as for any polyester resin—methyl ethyl ketone peroxide, or MEKP. Gelcoat resin usually requires 1 to 2 percent of hardener by volume (follow the manufacturer's instructions). As a general rule, four drops of hardener will catalyze 1 ounce of resin at 1 percent. The mix shouldn't kick (start to harden) in less than 30 minutes. Hardening in about two hours is probably ideal. *Always err on the side of too little hardener.* Also be certain to stir in the hardener thoroughly; if you fail to catalyze every bit of the resin, parts of the repair will be undercured.

SPREADING GELCOAT PASTE

1 Original gelcoat is chemically bonded to the underlying laminates, but this molecular bond applies only to lay-up; the bond between a long-cured hull and an application of fresh gelcoat over a ding or scratch is strictly mechanical—just like paint. Wiping the scratch with styrene just prior to coating *can* partially reactivate the old gelcoat and result in some chemical crosslinking, but as a practical matter this step is usually omitted.

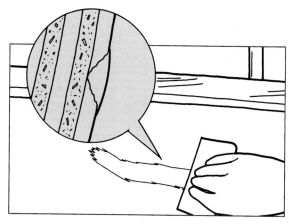

2 Apply gelcoat paste like any other putty; a plastic spreader works best. Let the putty bulge a little behind the spreader; polyester resin shrinks slightly as it cures, and you're going to sand the patch anyway. Just don't let it bulge too much or you'll make extra work for yourself.

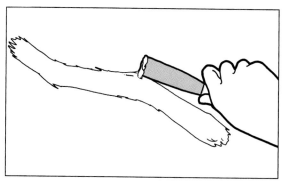

3 Scrape up any excess beyond the patch area.

COVERING THE REPAIR

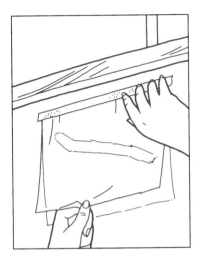 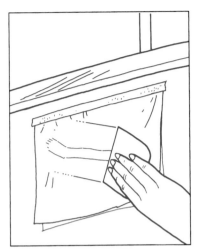 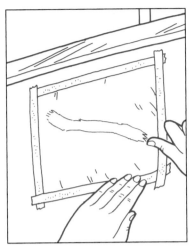

Gelcoat will not fully cure in air. Large repairs require a coating of polyvinyl alcohol (PVA) to seal the surface (see "Laminate Repair"), but to seal a scratch repair, cover it with a sheet of plastic. A section of kitchen "zipper" bag works especially well because it tends to remain smooth and the gelcoat will not adhere to it. Tape one edge of the plastic to the surface just beyond the repair, then smooth the plastic onto the gelcoat and tape down the remaining sides.

SANDING AND POLISHING GELCOAT REPAIRS

After 24 hours, peel away the plastic. The amount of sanding required will depend on how smoothly you applied the gelcoat.

1 For a scratch repair, a 5-inch length of 1 x 2 makes a convenient sanding block. Wrap the block with 120- or 150-grit paper, and use the narrow side to confine your sanding to the new gelcoat. Use short strokes, taking care that the paper is sanding only the patch and not the surrounding surface. Never do this initial sanding without a block backing the paper.

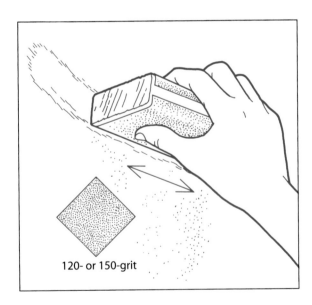

120- or 150-grit

2 When the new gelcoat is flush, put 220-grit wet-or-dry paper on your block and wet sand the repair, feathering it into the old gelcoat until you can detect no ridge with your fingertips.

3 Switch to 400-grit wet-or-dry, abandoning the block, and wet sand the surface until it has a uniform appearance. Follow this with 600-grit wet-or dry.

4 Dry the area and use rubbing compound to give the gelcoat a high gloss. On small repairs, you can buff the gelcoat up to a gloss by hand. Give the repair area a fresh coat of wax. If your color match is reasonably good, the repair will be virtually undetectable.

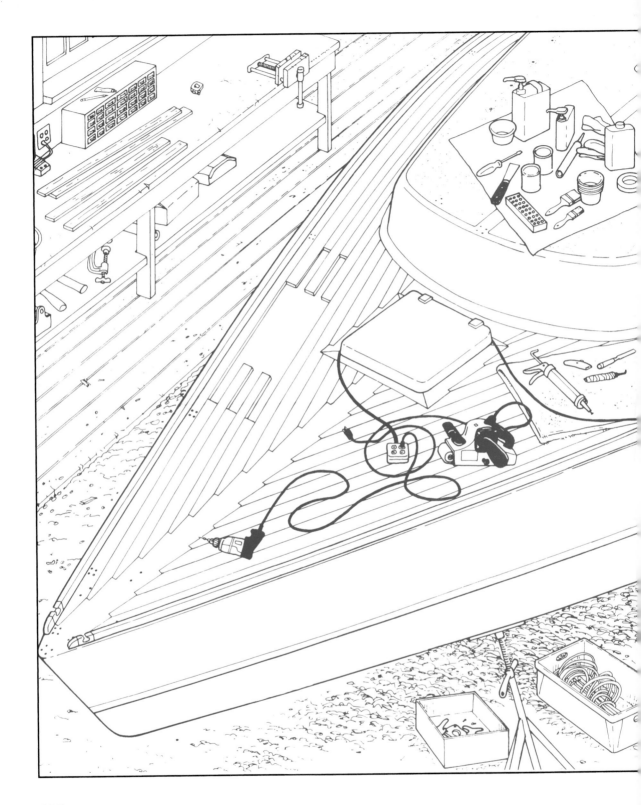

DECK REPAIRS

A fiberglass boat is typically molded in two sections: the hull and the deck. Most of the furniture and machinery is installed inside the open hull before the deck goes on—like filling a box before putting on the lid.

If you stay off the rocks and don't smash into the dock, the hull has a pretty good life—coddled by the water and always half in the shade. The deck, on the other hand, is born to a life of abuse. It sits out in the sun like a piece of Nevada desert. It is assaulted by rain, pollution, and foot. It is eviscerated by openings, pierced by hardware, pried by cleat and stanchion.

You might think that to stand up to such treatment, decks are as strongly built as the hull they cover. You'd be wrong. Weight carried low in a boat has little detrimental impact—a builder can make the hull as thick as he feels like—but weight carried high reduces stability. A deck must first be light; strength is defined by "strong enough." As a result, the need for deck repairs is far more common than the need for repairs to the hull.

Deck repairs can also be more complicated (but not necessarily "harder"). While the surface of a hull is flat or uniformly curved and relatively featureless, a deck is a landscape of corners, angles, curvatures, and textures. Damage often extends under deck-mounted hardware. Backside access may be inhibited by a molded headliner. And to provide stiffness without weight, deck construction generally involves a core.

In this chapter we will confine repairs to surface damage. This is hardly a constraint; most deck problems are limited to the deck's top surface.

RECOGNIZING STRESS CRACKS

Stress cracks are easy to identify by their shape. Typically the cracks run parallel or fan out in starburst pattern. You will see parallel cracks in molded corners, such as around the perimeter of the cockpit sole or where the deck intersects the cabin sides. These suggest weakness in the corner. Parallel cracks also show up on either side of bulkheads or other stiffening components attached to the inside surface of the hull or deck. The concentration of flexing stresses at such "hard spots" causes the gelcoat, and sometimes the underlying laminate, to crack.

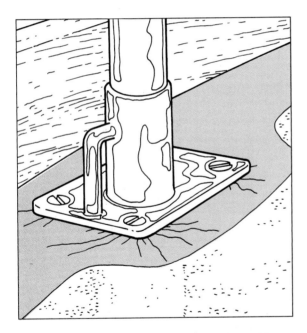

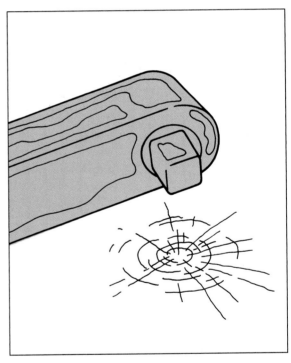

Starburst cracks are also caused by flexing, but in this case the movement centers at a point rather than along an edge. The most common starburst cracking extends from beneath stanchion mounts, brought about by falling against lifelines or by pulling oneself aboard with the top of the stanchion, which literally levers the deck up around the socket mounting holes.

Another cause of starburst cracking is point impact, such as dropping an anchor or a heavy winch handle on deck. (Exterior impact may instead result in concentric cracks—like the pattern of a target.)

ELIMINATING THE CAUSE

Backing plates.
Starburst cracking can usually be stopped by installing generous backing plates on the underside of the deck beneath the offending hardware to spread the load. Wooden plates are the easiest to fabricate, but stainless steel or bronze are better because of their resistance to crushing. Bevel the edges of the backing plate to avoid causing a hard spot. Polished stainless steel plates with threaded holes make for an attractive installation.

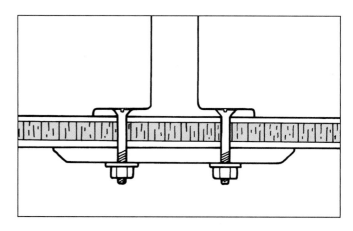

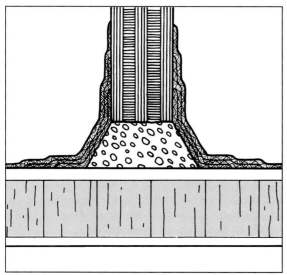

Hard spots.
Hard spots are more common on the hull than the deck, and usually appear where bulkheads attach. Stress cracks around hard spots are likely to return unless you eliminate the hard spot. This typically involves detaching the offending fixture, shaving some material from the edge, then reattaching it mounted on a foam spacer. Realistically, the work required may exceed the benefit, but anytime a bulkhead is detached or a new bulkhead is installed, it should always be mounted with a foam spacer.

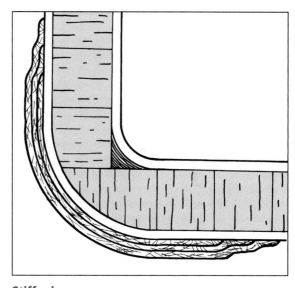

Stiffening.
Stress cracks related to general laminate weakness, such as those that too often appear around cockpit soles, can be prevented by stiffening the area with additional laminates. Laminating instructions are provided in "Laminate Repair." In this case you are trying to add stiffness, not strength, which translates into laminate thickness; use fiberglass mat to quickly build additional thickness.

REPAIRING THE CRACKS

Cracks in the deck typically affect only the gelcoat layer, and perhaps the first layer of mat beneath the gelcoat. Repairs are identical to scratch repair detailed in the previous chapter, except that you may need to remove deck hardware to get full access to the damage. Occasionally flexing has been so severe that stress cracks extend into the woven fabric of the laminate. When this is the case, the strength of the laminate is compromised, and the area must be ground out and relaminated to restore it. Detailed instructions for this type of repair are found in "Hull Repairs."

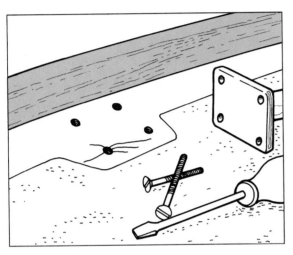

1 Gain access to the entire length of the crack.

2 Open the crack with the corner of a cabinet scraper.

3 Fill it with gelcoat paste.

4 Sand and buff.

VOIDS

Voids are thankfully rare in the flat expanses of hull lay-up, but all too common in fiberglass decks. Voids occur when the first layer of cloth is not compressed against the gelcoat (or when a subsequent laminate is not compressed against the previous one). They are often as much a consequence of design as of workmanship. While crisp angles and corners may look stylish, they are more difficult to mold with glass fabric. The fabric resists being forced into a tight corner and after saturation may take a more natural shape, pulling away from the gelcoated mold. The result is a void—a pocket of air beneath the thin gelcoat, perhaps "bird caged" with a few random strands of glass. The first time pressure is applied, the gelcoat breaks away like an eggshell, revealing the crater beneath.

Deck voids are a cosmetic problem and easily repaired.

1 Break away the cracked gelcoat to fully expose the void.

2 Use a rotary grinding point chucked in your drill to grind the interior surface of the cavity. Chamfer the gelcoat all around the void.

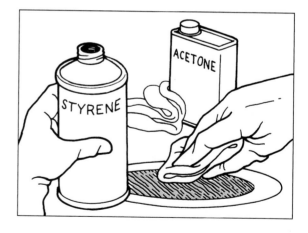

3 Clean the cavity with acetone. For a better bond, wipe the cavity with styrene.

4 Fill the cavity to the bottom of the gelcoat with a putty made from polyester resin and chopped glass. Be sure you use laminating resin, not finishing resin. Epoxy is not recommended because you are going to finish the repair with a layer of gelcoat, and gelcoat does not adhere as well to epoxy as to polyester.

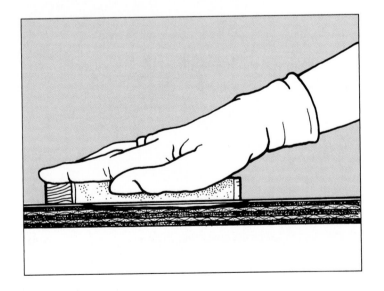

5 When the patch hardens, fill the remaining depression with gelcoat, overfilling slightly. Roll a piece of plastic into the repair and seal the edges with tape.

6 When the gelcoat cures, sand it flush with the surrounding surface and buff it with rubbing compound to restore the gloss.

CRAZING (ALLIGATORING)

Crazing, sometimes called alligatoring, is a random pattern of cracks that, at its worst, can cover the entire surface of a fiberglass boat—both deck and hull. There are two primary causes: flexing and excessively thick gelcoat. If flexing is the culprit, the crazing will be localized. For a repair to be successful, stiffening must be added to the deck in the area where the crazing has occurred.

Fortunately the more common cause of crazing is gelcoat thickness (or occasionally gelcoat formulation). As the hull heats and cools, it expands and contracts. A thin layer of gelcoat accommodates these changes, but thick gelcoat, not reinforced like the underlying laminates, tends to crack. In this case, the crazing is likely to be extensive. That's the bad news; the good news is that the repair doesn't require any structural alterations.

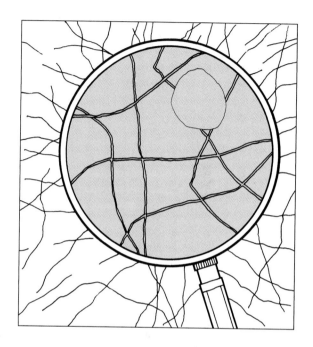

LOCALIZED CRAZING

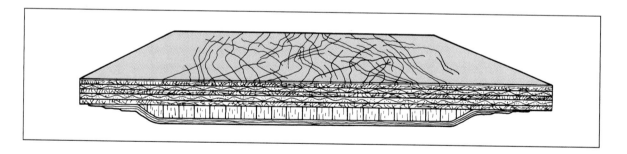

1 Stiffen the crazed area. See "Core Problems" for alternatives and step-by-step instructions.

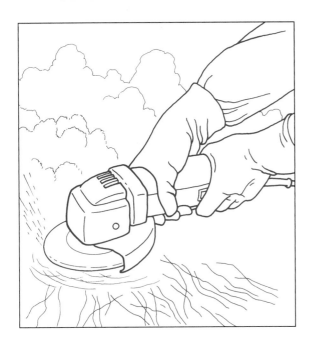

2 Trace each crack with the corner of a cabinet scraper, or if the pattern is too fine, grind the area with a 36-grit sanding disk. Stop when the disk begins to break through the gelcoat; don't grind all the gelcoat away.

3 Paint the cracks or ground area with color-matched gelcoat paste. Seal the surface to let the gelcoat cure.

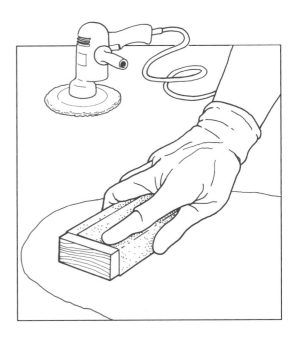

4 Fair the new gelcoat by block-sanding, then buff to a gloss.

WIDESPREAD CRAZING

Sanding and polishing surface-applied gelcoat is worthwhile when the new gelcoat area is relatively small and the rest of the gelcoat is in good condition, but when the majority of the original gelcoat is damaged, the labor intensive nature of gelcoat application suggests a different approach. The best alternative is painting the entire deck with a two-part polyurethane paint.

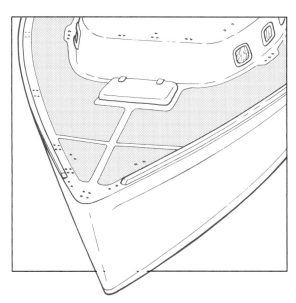

1 Remove as much deck hardware and trim as possible. The quality of your refinishing job is directly related to how much hardware you remove—how unobstructed the deck is when you apply the paint.

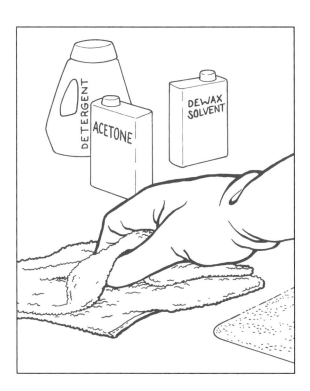

2 Clean, degrease, and dewax all the smooth surfaces of the deck. (Nonskid surfaces are restored in a separate process.)

3 Sand the gelcoat thoroughly with 120-grit sandpaper and wipe it dust-free with solvent.

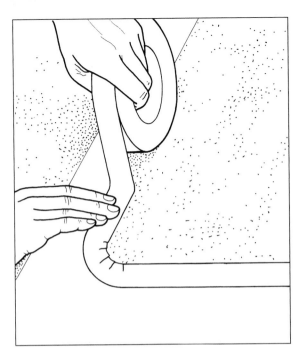

4   Mask nonskid surfaces and any hardware you have elected not to remove.

5   Paint the sanded gelcoat with a high-build epoxy primer. Apply the primer with a foam roller. Two coats are generally necessary to fill all crazing and porosity; machine sand each coat with 120-grit paper.

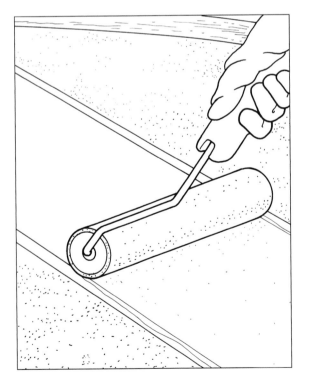

6   Paint the primed surfaces with two coats of two-part polyurethane, following the manufacturer's instructions for rolling and/or brushing the paint. For complete instructions on repainting decks—and all other boat surfaces—see *Sailboat Refinishing*.

RENEWING NONSKID

If you paint the smooth surfaces of the deck, you will probably want to refinish the nonskid surfaces as well. Painting nonskid surfaces tends to reduce their effectiveness. You can easily offset this by adding grit to the paint.

Always refinish the textured sections of the deck after the smooth portion. There are two reasons for this order. First, the nonskid surface is almost always a darker color than the smooth surfaces, and it is easier to cover a lighter color with a darker one than the other way around. Second, if the final masking is done on the textured surface, it will be hard to get a sharp line between the two. Prepare textured surfaces for refinishing before painting the other parts of the deck.

ENCAPSULATED GRIT

1 Scrub the nonskid thoroughly with a stiff brush, then use terry cloth—sections of old bath towels—to dewax the surface. The rough surface of the terry cloth penetrates the craggy nonskid.

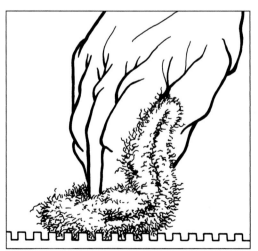

2 You can't sand the bottom surfaces of the nonskid, but abrade it with coarse bronze wool, using short, quick strokes. Fortunately most of the stress on the new paint will be on the top surface, which you can sand with 120-grit paper. Flood the surface and brush-scrub it again, then let it dry.

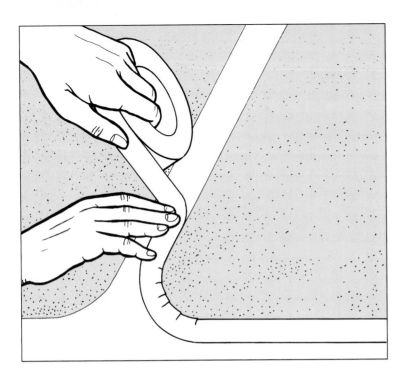

3 After the smooth surfaces are painted and dry, mask them at the mold line of the nonskid.

4 Mix a nonskid paint additive into the paint and roll it on with a medium-nap roller. (There is never any reason to "tip out" the paint on a nonskid surface.) This is the easy way to introduce grit into the paint, but because the additive—usually polymer beads—tends to settle to the bottom of the paint tray, dispersion of the grit on the painted surface can be irregular.

For a more aesthetically pleasing result, first coat the nonskid area with an epoxy primer and cover the wet epoxy with grit sifted from your fingers or a large shaker. When the epoxy kicks, gently sweep off the grit that didn't adhere (you can use it on another nonskid area), and encapsulate the grit that remains with two rolled-on coats of paint.

RUBBERIZED OVERLAY

For the best footing, you may want to consider a rubberized nonskid overlay, such as Treadmaster M or Vetus deck covering, also good choices for completely hiding old, worn-out nonskid textures. For overlay application, carry the paint ½ inch into the nonskid area when you paint the deck.

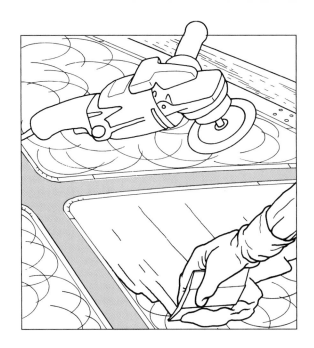

Preparing the surface.
Eliminate all molded texture. Most of it can be quickly taken off with a disk sander and a 36-grit disk. (A belt sander can also be used.) Be careful not to let the sander get outside the textured area. It is neither necessary nor desirable to *grind* away all the pattern. *Fill* the remaining depressions with epoxy putty. When the epoxy cures, sand the surface to fair it and prepare it for the adhesive.

Cutting patterns.

1. Make a pattern from kraft paper for each of the nonskid panels. Cut the paper oversize, then place it on deck to trace the exact outline. Tape across holes cut in the center of the paper to hold it in place. Use a flexible batten to draw curved edges, a can lid for uniform corners. For appearance and drainage, leave at least 1 inch between adjacent panels, at least twice that between the nonskid and rails, coamings, or cabin sides. Write "TOP" on the pattern to avoid confusion when you cut the overlay, and draw a line on it parallel to the centerline of the boat, with an arrow toward the bow.

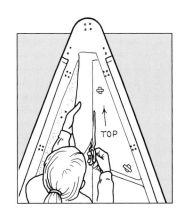

2. Do not cut patterns for only one side, expecting to reverse them for the opposite panels. Boats are almost never symmetrical, and hardware is certain to be in different locations. Cut a separate pattern for every panel. When all the patterns have been cut, tape them all in place and evaluate the overall effect before proceeding. Trace around each pattern with a pencil to outline the deck area to be coated with adhesive.

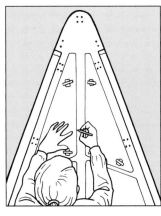

Cutting the overlay.

1 Place the patterns topside down on the back of the overlay material. Position all the patterns on your material to minimize the waste before making any cuts. Depending on the overlay you have chosen, it may be necessary to align the patterns; use the line you drew on each pattern for this purpose, aligning it parallel to the long edge of the sheet of material. Trace each pattern onto the overlay.

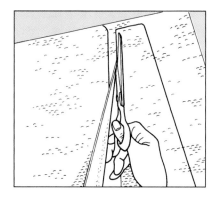

2 Cut out the pieces with tin snips or heavy scissors.

Applying the overlay.

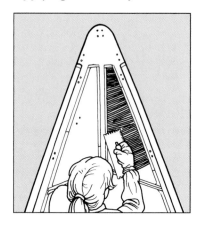 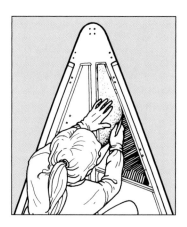 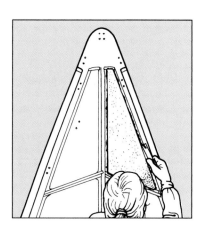

1 If the overlay manufacturer doesn't specify a different adhesive, glue the nonskid to the deck with thickened epoxy. Coat both the outlined deck area and the back of the nonskid with the adhesive, using a serrated trowel.

2 Position the nonskid on the deck and press it flat, beginning with pressure in the middle and working outward to all edges.

3 Pick up any squeeze-out with a putty knife, and clean away the residue with an acetone-dampened cloth. Continue applying each section in turn until all are installed.

CLEANING

Left untreated, good-quality teak would normally weather to an attractive ash gray, but the assault of modern-day air pollutants turns bare teak nearly black. Clean it with the mildest cleaner that does the job. Start with a 75/25 mixture of liquid detergent and chlorine bleach (no water), boosted with TSP. Apply this with a stiff brush, scrubbing lightly with the grain. Leave the mixture on the wood for several minutes to give the detergent time to suspend the dirt, and the bleach time to lighten the wood, then rinse thoroughly by flooding and brushing.

LIGHTENING

As good as chlorine is at bleaching cotton sweat-socks, it's not a very effective wood bleach. For that you need oxalic acid. You can get it by buying a commercial single-part teak cleaner—oxalic acid is the active ingredient in most—or for about one-tenth the price you can buy a can of Ajax household scouring powder. Whichever you select, brush the cleaner onto wet teak and give it time to work, then scrub the wood with Scotchbrite or bronze wool. (Never, ever, ever use steel wool aboard your boat—it will leave a trail of rust freckles that will be impossible to remove.) Oxalic acid dulls paint and fiberglass, so wet down surrounding surfaces before you start, and keep them free of the cleaner. Rinse the scrubbed wood thoroughly; brushing is essential.

For potential treatments for teak decks, see *Sailboat Refinishing*.

TWO-PART CLEANERS

Two-part teak cleaners are dramatically effective at restoring the color to soiled, stained, and neglected teak, but these formulations contain a strong acid—usually hydrochloric—and should only be used when all other cleaning methods have failed.

1 Wet the wood to be cleaned, then use a *nylon-bristle brush* to paint part 1 onto the wet wood, avoiding contact with adjoining surfaces. If you use a natural-bristle brush, the cleaner will dissolve the bristles; it is doing the same thing to your teak.

2 Scrub with the grain.

3 Part 2 neutralizes the acid in part 1 and usually has some cleaning properties. Paint sufficient part 2 onto the teak to get a uniform color change. Scrub lightly.

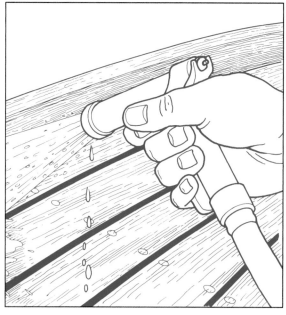

4 Flush away *all* traces of the cleaner and let the wood dry.

SURFACING

After a number of years, bare teak decks become rough and ridged. This unevenness traps dirt and harbors mildew, making the deck harder to clean and harder to keep clean. The solution is to resand the deck with a belt sander, using a 120-grit belt. Keep the sander moving at all times, and sand at about 15° to the grain.

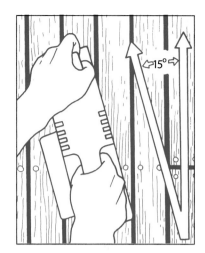

RECAULKING

The instructions that follow are for recaulking a section of a single seam, but the steps are the same for an entire deck.

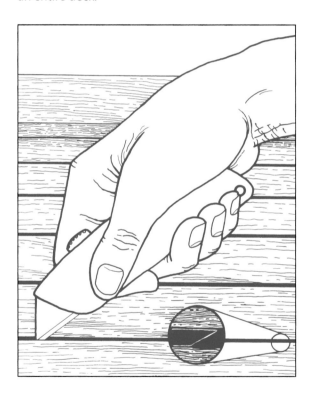

1 With a razor knife, cut the seam caulk at a diagonal a couple of inches beyond the bad section, then slice the section to be replaced free from the planks on either side, taking care not to nick the wood.

2 Dig out the old caulk. This is much easier with a rake made by heating the tail of a file and bending it about 90°. When every bit of the old caulk is off the planks, vacuum the scrapings out of the seam.

3 Use an acid brush or a Q-Tip to thoroughly prime both plank edges. Use the primer recommended for the caulk you are using. Two coats are generally required.

4 Mask the surface of the planks.

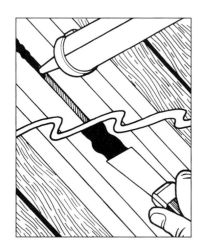

5 The "right" caulk for deck seams is two-part polysulfide. Mix the catalyst into the sealant per label instructions, taking care not to introduce bubbles, then fill an empty caulk tube with the mixture. (For limited repairs, a single-part polysulfide will also give good results and may be more convenient.) Cut the tip of the tube and fill the seam from the bottom. When the entire seam is slightly overfilled with sealant, compress it into the seam by dragging a putty knife over it firmly. The sealant will hump up slightly behind the knife, but it will shrink almost flush as it cures. Remove the masking carefully while the caulk is still tacky.

IDENTIFYING DECK CAULKING FAILURE

HOW DO YOU KNOW WHEN THE SEAM caulking on a teak deck has released its grip on the wood? The wood usually tells you. On a sunny day, scrub the deck, then keep it wet for half an hour or so before letting it dry. Areas along the seams that stay wet longer than the rest of the deck are suspect; spots that stay dark a lot longer definitely indicate caulk failure. Using the point of a knife, you will see that you can separate the caulk from the wood, and the edge of the plank will be wet. Repair all "flagged" seams before they result in bigger problems beneath the teak.

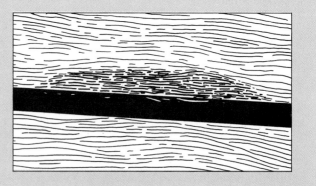

BUNG REPLACEMENT

The most common problem of teak decks is popped bungs. Years of scrubbing thins already-thin overlay planks until the grip of the bungs is insufficient to hold against flexing or expansion.

Just tapping a new bung in place will be a temporary repair at best. Deck overlay bungs require special procedures.

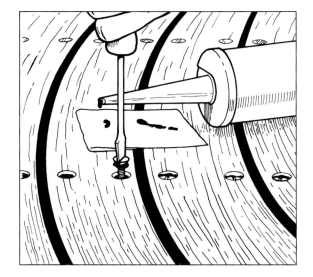

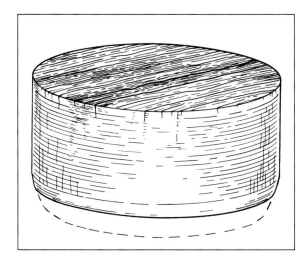

1 Remove and rebed the screw in polysulfide. Deck core problems often occur beneath teak overlay because the screws holding the overlay penetrate the top skin of the deck. *Always* rebed exposed screws. It is a good idea to check the core for sponginess with a piece of wire. (See "Core Problems.")

2 Reduce the plug bevel. In a shallow hole, you cannot afford the generous bevel found on most commercial teak plugs; sand the bottom of the plug to reduce it to the bare minimum.

3 Use a Q-Tip to wipe both the hole and the plug with acetone to remove surface oils. Wait 20 minutes to install the plug.

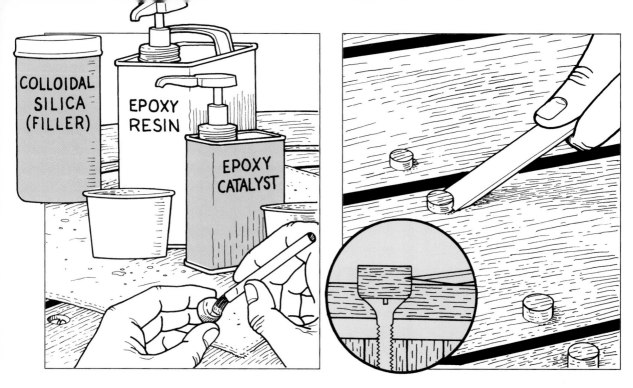

4 Mounting a plug permanently in a shallow hole requires the tenacious grip of epoxy glue. Paint the hole and sides of the bung with unthickened epoxy. Thicken the epoxy to catsup consistency with filler (colloidal silica) and coat the sides of the hole and plug. Tap the coated plug into the hole as far as it will go. Wipe up the excess glue.

5 After the epoxy is dry, place the point of a chisel—beveled side down—against the plug about $\frac{1}{8}$ inch above the surface of the plank and tap the chisel with a mallet. The top of the plug will split away.

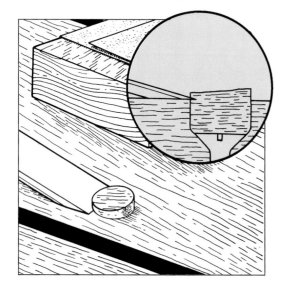

6 Working from the lowest edge of the trimmed plug, pare away the plug until it is nearly flush with the plank. Finish the job by block sanding the plug with 120-grit sandpaper.

PLANK REPLACEMENT

Occasionally a teak plank splits or is otherwise damaged and requires replacement. More often teak overlay problems have an underlying cause—usually a wet core—and to effect repair the teak must be removed. Since the cause of the leakage often turns out to be the screw holes, some boatowners elect not to replace the overlay, but most are unwilling to give up the beauty and footing of teak decks. A careful installation minimizes the risk to the core.

1   If you are replacing more than a single plank, number and crosshatch all the planks to be removed so you can put them back properly.

2   With bungs removed (carefully if you will be reusing the plank), extract the screws. Slice the plank free of the caulking all around, and pry the plank up from the bedding compound, using a block under your prying tool to protect the adjacent plank. If the plank is bedded in an organic compound, it should slowly pull free—like a gum-stuck heel. If it is bedded in polysulfide, you are likely to have to destroy the first plank to remove it. With side access, you should be able to separate the rest of the planks from the deck with a thin, sharpened putty knife. A length of steel leader wire connected to two lengths of dowel is sometimes effective in "cutting" deck planks free.

3 Scrape and sand away all old bedding compound.

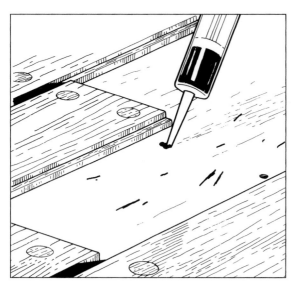

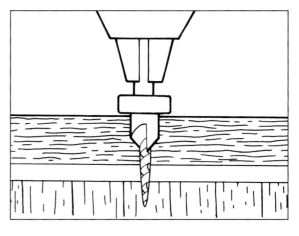

4 If the core is dry, protect it by injecting the hole full of epoxy. Give the epoxy a few minutes to saturate the edge of the core, then draw out the excess with a small brush or a stick. For greater security, drill each hole oversize and, after painting the sides with unthickened epoxy, fill each hole with epoxy thickened with colloidal silica. When the filler hardens, redrill the center for the screw.

5 If you are installing new planks, fill the old screw holes with epoxy putty, but don't redrill them. Wedge the new plank into position, then drill the plank and the deck. Counterbore the hole in the plank at least half the plank's thickness but not more than two-thirds. Epoxy the new holes in the deck in one of the two methods just detailed.

6 Wash the deck and the underside of the plank with acetone. For better adhesion, prime the teak. Coat the deck with black polysulfide (two-part preferred) and distribute it evenly with a saw-toothed spreader.

7 Hold or wedge the plank in position and screw it down. Select Phillips-head screws and you will be much less likely to damage the edge of the bung hole with the screwdriver.

8 Install bungs (with epoxy) and trim them. Caulk the seams. Belt sand the deck fair.

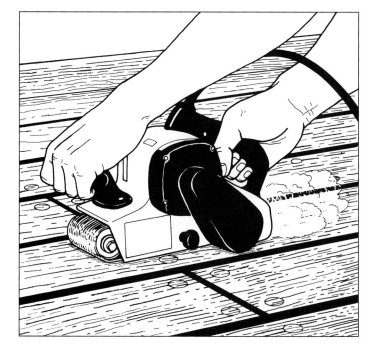

LAMINATE REPAIR

The hull and deck repairs described so far have either been cosmetic or leak related—problems that can be fixed with a proper topical application of one glop or another. But sometimes the problem is below the surface: the original laminate lacks the requisite stiffness; moisture has caused disintegration or delamination; or the glass fibers have been broken by impact. These problems require more extensive repair.

Fiberglass has become the predominant boatbuilding material because of its durability, but it is repairability that accounts for the near immortality of fiberglass boats. The most horrifying hole in a fiberglass hull is quickly healed with a bit of glass fabric, a can of resin, and equal parts skill and care. And the repair is less patch than graft—a new piece of skin indistinguishable from the old.

Fiberglass lay-up can hardly be simpler. It is nothing more than layers of glass fabric saturated with polyester (or epoxy) resin. With a paint brush, a cup of water, and a piece of old T-shirt, you can practice all the requisite skills for fiberglass lay-up.

Don't misunderstand: because of blocked access or complex shape, laminate repair cannot always be honestly characterized as easy, but such problems aren't what make most boatowners shy away from attempting a repair. It's the lay-up. Most boatowners imagine a self-applied laminate as only slightly more durable than a wet Band-Aid. That is a false concern. Follow a few simple rules—provided in this chapter—and your lay-up will be as good as or better than what you can expect a yard to do. And it will remain that way a decade down the road.

UNDERSTANDING POLYESTER RESIN

Polyester resin is the glue that binds glass fibers into the hard substance we call fiberglass. On the other side of the Atlantic, the same product is called GRP—glass-reinforced plastic. As usual, the British take more care with the language than we do; glass-reinforced plastic is *exactly* what it is.

Polyester resin, when catalyzed, hardens into plastic—not one of those tough plastics that deflects bullets or that you can use as a hinge for 100 years—but an amber-colored, rather brittle plastic that seems more like rock candy than boat-building material. But when polyester resin is combined with glass fibers, the sum is greater than the parts.

Polyester resins come in various formulations (see sidebar), although you can't always tell what kind a particular brand is from the label. Generally, you don't need to know. When polyester is appropriate for the repair (sometimes epoxy resin is a better choice), whatever laminating resin your supplier carries should prove satisfactory. Below-the-waterline repairs are the exception; avoid ortho resins if the repair will be continuously immersed.

LAMINATING VERSUS FINISHING

1 You do need to choose between laminating and finishing resin. Laminating resin is "air-inhibited," meaning that the resin will not fully cure while exposed to air. That may sound odd, but remember that polyester solidifies not by drying, like paint, but by a chemical reaction (called cross-linking) induced by adding a catalyst. Air interferes with this curing process.

For any job that requires the laminates to be applied in more than one operation, you need laminating resin. The fact that the surface remains tacky after the resin sets allows you to apply the subsequent laminates without any intermediate steps, and the new application will link chemically with the previous one to form a powerful chemical bond. For a tack-free surface on the final application, coat the resin with polyvinyl alcohol (PVA) or seal it with plastic wrap.

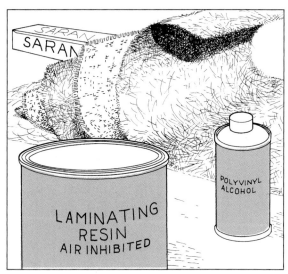

2 Finishing resin is identical to laminating resin, but with an additive that "floats" to the surface of the curing resin. This surfactant (once wax, but now usually a drying oil) seals the resin from the air, thus allowing the surface to fully cure to a tack-free, sandable state.

Use finishing resin for laminate jobs that can be done in a single operation. Finishing resin can also be used for the final layer of a multilayer lamination.

ORTHO, ISO, OR VINYLESTER?

FOR THE FIRST 30 YEARS OF FIBERGLASS BOAT MANUFACTURING, the only resin widely in use was *orthophthalic* resin. Ortho resin was cheap, easy to work with, and had no apparent failings—until fiberglass boats began to blister.

Isophthalic resin, slightly more expensive, has largely replaced ortho resin in boat manufacturing because it seems less prone to blistering, probably due to its higher solvent resistance. A packaged polyester resin sold for repair work, if it is good quality, will likely be iso resin.

Vinylester has long been used in performance boats because of its superior adhesion qualities and impact resistance, but its superiority as a moisture barrier has led to more widespread use. Many new boat manufacturers now use vinylester laminating resin and vinylester gelcoat in their quest to produce blister-resistant hulls. For repair work calling for polyester resin, vinylester's better adhesion makes it a good choice.

HOW MUCH CATALYST?

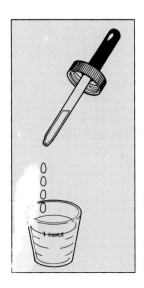

The catalyst for polyester resin is methyl ethyl ketone peroxide, or MEKP. Do not confuse MEKP with the common solvent MEK; they are *not* the same.

Polyester resin usually requires 1 to 2 percent of hardener by volume (follow the manufacturer's instructions). As a rule of thumb, four drops of hardener will catalyze 1 ounce of resin at 1 percent. Be certain to stir the catalyst in thoroughly or part of the resin will be undercured, weakening the lay-up.

You can adjust the cure time by adding more or less catalyst. Temperature, weather, and the thickness of the laminate all affect curing times. Some experimentation is generally required. The mix shouldn't kick (start to harden) in less than 30 minutes. Hardening in about two hours is probably ideal, but overnight is just as good unless the wait will hold you up. *Always err on the side of too little catalyst;* if you add too much, the resin will "cook," resulting in a weak lamination.

FIBERGLASS MATERIAL

Fiberglass material is exactly what it sounds like, a weave of glass fibers. For boat construction and repair, the glass comes in chopped-strand mat, roving, and cloth.

Chopped-strand mat.
Chopped-strand mat is made up of irregular lengths of glass strands glued together randomly. Generally speaking, *CSM* is the easiest fabric to shape, gives the best resin-to-glass ratio, yields the smoothest surface, is the most watertight, and is the least subject to delamination, but the short fibers do not provide the tensile strength of a woven material.

Mat is sold by the yard from a roll and comes in various weights designated in ounces per square *foot;* 1½-ounce mat is a good choice for general use.

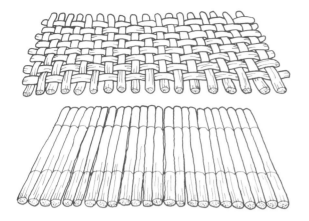

Roving.

Roving is parallel, flat bundles of continuous glass strands. In *unwoven roving* parallel bundles are cross-stitched together; *woven roving* assembles the bundles in two directions in a loose weave.

The straight, continuous strands in unwoven roving add excellent strength in the direction of the strands but little strength perpendicular to them. For hull and deck repairs, woven roving is usually a better choice because it provides full strength in two directions and good strength in all directions. (You can accomplish the same thing by rotating the orientation of alternating laminates of unwoven roving, but unless you need additional strength in a particular direction, using woven roving is simpler.)

Roving laminated to roving, either unwoven or woven, is unacceptably easy to peel apart. *Always* bind layers of roving together by using a layer of mat between each layer of roving.

For most repairs, select 18-ounce roving. That may sound heavy relative to 1½-ounce mat, but don't be confused. Weight designations for mat are per square foot, while for roving (and cloth) they are per square *yard*; 18-ounce roving weighs the same as 2-ounce mat.

Fiberglass cloth.

Fiberglass cloth looks like shiny canvas but not woven as tightly. Cloth is stronger for its weight than roving, less prone to pulling and unraveling in the laminating process, and the finished product looks better. While manufacturers generally use alternating layers of mat and roving, mat and cloth is a better choice for most repair work.

Cloth is commonly available in weights from 4 to 20 ounces. For any boat over 15 feet, there will be little, if any, fiberglass work that you cannot do with 1½-ounce mat and 10-ounce cloth. If you have a choice, buy 38-inch width.

OTHER MATERIALS

GLASS ISN'T THE ONLY MATERIAL THAT CAN be combined with resin. Increasingly, boatbuilders are using "exotic" materials to create composites with special characteristics—light weight, rigidity (or flexibility), impact resistance, tensile strength, or others. These materials include graphite (carbon fiber), Kevlar, polypropylene, xynole-polyester, Dynel, and ceramic. None of these is essential for the typical hull or deck repair. You should understand a material's strengths and weaknesses before you use it.

During the lay-up process, each application of resin links chemically with the previous application to form a solid structure—as though all the layers were saturated at once. The layer-cake look of fiberglass is deceiving; a better analogy is Jell-O salad—the fruit may be in layers, but the encapsulating Jell-O is solid. Chemical linking between resin layers occurs because each layer is applied before the previous one fully cures (the reason for using air-inhibited resin).

Unfortunately, no matter how strong the laminate-to-laminate bond, the initial bond of any *repair* is mechanical, not chemical. This need not weaken the repair as long as the surface is properly prepared. That means grinding.

1 Before grinding, always wash the area thoroughly with a dewaxing solvent. The original fiberglass will have traces of mold release on the outer surface and wax surfactant on the inner surface. If you fail to remove the wax first, grinding will drag it into the bottom of the surface scratches and weaken the bond.

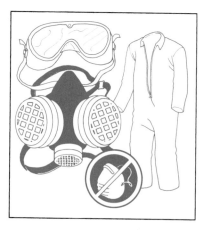

2 Protect your eyes with goggles and your lungs with a good dust mask. A paper mask is inadequate for all but the smallest grinding task. Long sleeves will reduce skin irritation.

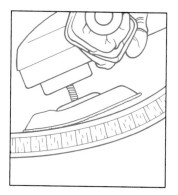

3 Outline the area of the bond and grind inside the outline with a disk sander loaded with a 36-grit disk. Tilt the sander so that only one side of the disk is touching the surface and the dust is thrown away from you.

4 Brush away the dust and wipe the area with an acetone-dampened rag. The surface should have a uniform dull look; if any areas remain glossy, make another pass over them with the sander.

THE BASICS OF FIBERGLASS LAY-UP

PREPARATION

1 Dewax and grind the surface the lay-up will be applied to. Specific types of repairs—detailed later—require additional surface prep.

2 Protect all surrounding surfaces by masking. Waxing below the repair area will make unanticipated runs easier to remove.

3 Cut the fiberglass pieces to the correct size and lay them out in the order you will be applying them. As a rule, apply the smallest piece first, the largest piece last. Always start and finish with mat.

APPLYING THE INITIAL LAYER

1 Catalyze the resin and mix it thoroughly.

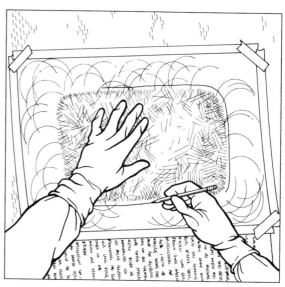

2 Hold the first layer of fiberglass in place and pencil a line around it. Use a throw-away brush to coat the outlined area with resin.

3 Apply the first layer of mat to the wetted surface. On a vertical surface, use masking tape to help hold the fabric in place. Use a squeegee to smooth the mat and press it into the resin.

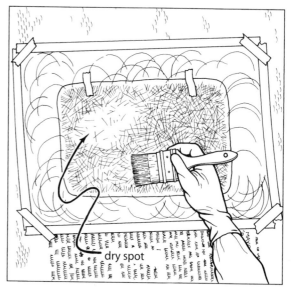

4 With a brush or a roller, wet the mat with resin until it is uniformly transparent. White areas are dry spots and require additional resin. Brush or roll gently to avoid moving the fabric or introducing bubbles.

ADDITIONAL LAYERS

1 Apply the next layer—cloth or roving—on top of the saturated mat. Smooth it against the mat with a squeegee.

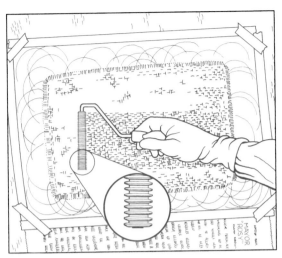

2 Wet out the cloth with resin. Use a squeegee or a grooved roller to compact the laminates and force any air bubbles to the surface. Remove excess resin with the squeegee.

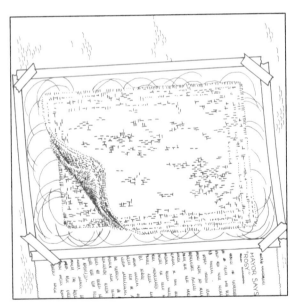

3 If the weather is cool or the repair area is small, you can apply up to two more layers without risk of the cure generating so much heat that it cooks the resin or warps the repair.

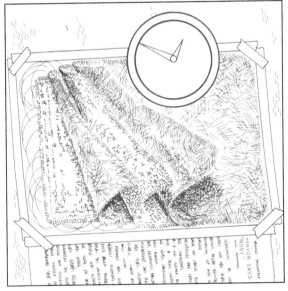

4 Allow the resin time to gel, then mix fresh resin and apply two (or more) additional layers, repeating this process until all the layers have been laminated.

FINISHING

1 For a smoother finish, roll an additional coat of resin over the final layer of material.

2 After the last coat of resin kicks, brush or spray on an unbroken coating of polyvinyl alcohol (PVA) to seal the surface so it will cure fully. This isn't necessary if you use finishing resin for the last coat.

WORKING OVERHEAD

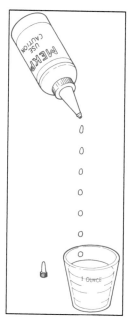

1 Alternative application techniques are required to laminate fiberglass overhead. Mix a small batch of resin, adding more catalyst than usual, and use it to wet the repair area.

2 For an overhead repair, always work with small pieces of fabric. Roll the first piece of mat onto a dowel or a cardboard tube, and wait for the resin to start to kick. When the surface feels tacky, carefully position the edge of the mat and unroll it, taking care to keep it smooth. The tacky resin will hold the mat in place while you saturate it with fresh resin. Use a roller or squeegee to distribute the resin.

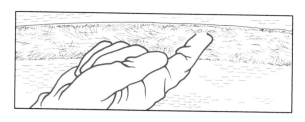

3 When the surface of the mat is tacky, you can unroll the next layer of fabric onto it, again taking care to keep it smooth. Saturate this layer with fresh resin. Repeat this step for each layer until all the laminates are in place.

WHEN TO USE EPOXY

Epoxy is almost always better than polyester resin for repair work because the mechanical bond it forms—the weakest link in any repair job—is stronger. Laminate made with epoxy is also superior— stronger and more durable—but because the cost of epoxy is more than twice that of polyester, manufacturers rarely use it for laminating. For repair work the additional expense is less significant, and the added strength is well worth the cost.

Do not use epoxy if the repair will be finished with gelcoat. While epoxy bonds tenaciously to polyester, the reverse is not true; the bond between polyester gelcoat and an underlying epoxy repair will not be strong. If the surface will be gelcoated, use polyester resin for the repair.

SELECTING EPOXY

Don't buy epoxy by the tube.

Select an epoxy formulated for boatbuilding. The two most common brands are West System (Gougeon Brothers) and System Three, but there are others. The main difference you are likely to notice between competing brands is the mix ratio, but metered pumps tend to make this difference of little consequence.

ADDITIVES

For saturating fiberglass laminates, use the epoxy as it comes—catalyzed, of course—but for bonding and filling, additives thicken the epoxy and give it specific characteristics. Three of these are especially useful for hull and deck repairs.

Fibers. Fibers added to epoxy will thicken it for filling and for bonding where there is a gap between the surfaces being bonded. You can snip glass cloth diagonally to generate short fibers for small putty needs, but for more than that buy packaged microfiber filler. Fiber fillers are easy to mix, provide good strength, and have excellent finish properties.

Microballoons. Microballoons are tiny hollow beads of plastic. Added to epoxy to produce a fairing compound, microballoons yield a putty that spreads and sands easily. Microballoons reduce the strength of the epoxy and should not be used for bonding or laminating. Also avoid using microballoons below the waterline because the resulting putty is porous and will absorb water.

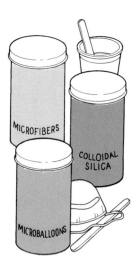

Colloidal silica. Silica is perhaps the most versatile of fillers. It provides better strength than microfibers and it doesn't affect the permeability of the cured epoxy. Silica-thickened putty cures with a rough texture and resists abrasion—including sanding.

MIXING

Metering pumps.
While polyester requires only a few drops of catalyst per ounce of resin to start the chemical reaction, the combination ratio for epoxy is much less one-sided. The resin-to-hardener ratio is typically at least five to one, but some formulations call for a two-to-one mix. Epoxy manufacturers typically have calibrated pumps available that will meter out the correct ratio—one pump of hardener to one pump of resin. Epoxy is very sensitive to mix ratio, so the purchase of metering pumps is strongly recommended. Stir the two parts together *thoroughly*, using a flat mixing stick to scrape the sides, bottom, and corners of the container.

Regulating cure time.
Unlike polyester, the cure time of epoxy cannot be adjusted by altering the amount of hardener. The specified proportion of hardener must always be used. However, epoxy manufacturers generally offer at least two hardeners—fast and slow—and they often have additional hardener formulations for special requirements, such as tropical use. Pot life varies with ambient temperature, but you will quickly learn how much time is available. Limit batch size to the amount of epoxy you can use in that amount of time. Epoxy cures faster in the pot, so the quicker you apply it, the longer you will have to work it.

Thickening.
Always add the thickening agent after the resin and hardener have been mixed. Stir in the thickener until the mixture reaches the desired consistency.

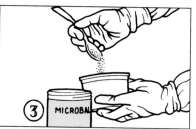

PRECAUTIONS

People in significant numbers develop a sensitivity to epoxy so that any exposure results in skin irritation and rash. Avoiding all skin contact is the safest course. Wear plastic gloves when working with epoxy. Goggles are recommended.

Avoid breathing the fumes of curing epoxy. Be sure you have good ventilation.

The heat generated by curing epoxy is sufficient to melt a plastic container and may even ignite into flames if you leave the mixture in the pot too long. If the mixture begins to heat up, put it outside—away from anything flammable—until it cools.

LAMINATING WITH EPOXY

1   Do *not* use chopped-strand mat when laminating with epoxy resin. The binder holding the strands together may react with the epoxy, affecting both the adhesion and the permeability of the epoxy. Epoxy is a strong enough adhesive to bind cloth to cloth without risk of delamination, and multiple layers of fiberglass cloth create an extremely strong laminate.

2   Prepare and wet the repair area as with polyester resin, but then thicken some epoxy to a catsup consistency with colloidal silica. Paint the repair area with the thickened epoxy. This serves much the same function as an initial layer of mat, filling voids and depressions and providing a good contact area for the initial layer of cloth.

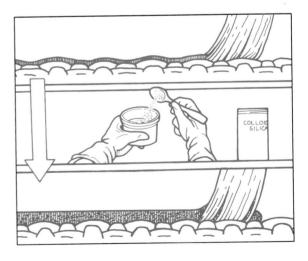

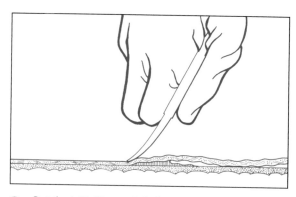

3   Put the initial layer of cloth in position and use the squeegee to smooth it. Wet it out thoroughly.

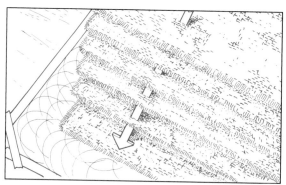

4   Place, wet, and smooth succeeding layers until you achieve the desired thickness. As long as the previous application has not reached a solid cure, which generally takes several hours, you can continue to add layers without any intermediate steps—cleaning, sanding, etc. Each application will chemically bond to the previous one. (If you let the epoxy reach solid cure, you must scrub then grind the surface before applying the next layer—so plan your repair accordingly.)

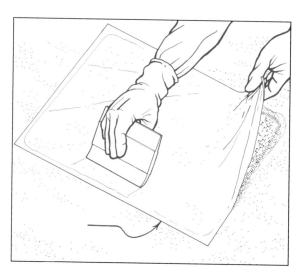

5   For smoothest results, cover the last layer with *peel ply*—a coated fabric epoxy will not adhere to—and use a squeegee to smooth and press the fabric. Scrape away excess epoxy.

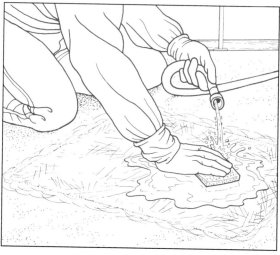

6   When the epoxy has cured thoroughly, remove the peel ply; the waxy amine blush that normally appears on the surface of cured epoxy will peel away on the fabric. If you haven't used peel ply, scrub the cured epoxy with a Scotchbrite pad and water before applying any coating (paint, etc.).

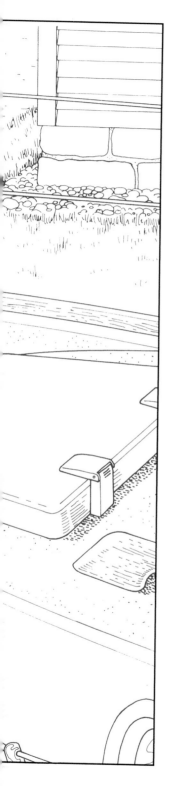

CORE PROBLEMS

Cored deck (or hull) is a sandwich construction of wood, plastic foam, or other material captured between two fiberglass skins. As long as the skins are attached to the core, this box-beam-like construction provides the desirable combination of stiffness and light weight; but if the bond between the skins and the core fails, the three components, none stiff individually, simply slide over each other as they flex—like leaf springs on an old car—and the stiffness is lost. Unfortunately the skin-to-core bond fails often.

This problem is made worse by moisture. Relaxed vigilance in maintaining the seal around deck-mounted hardware leads to water finding its way to the core. The core material, porous by design, absorbs the water like a sponge. The tenuous grip the resin had on dry core material is soon lost, not unlike a bandage releasing its grip under water.

It gets worse still. When water finds its way into the cavity between the two skins, it is captured as surely as if you had poured it into a capped jug. Once core gets wet, it is likely to stay wet until you take steps to dry it out.

The simplest of core problems is delamination, often signaled by cracking sounds underfoot when you walk on the deck. Sound also provides a clue to the more serious problem of wet core, but in this case the sound is a squish. Water may also squirt or weep from around hardware or a crack in the skin when you step on the wet area. Wet core should be attended to immediately. If left unattended until the deck feels spongy underfoot, the core is probably rotten and the repair job you face formidable.

The message here is simple: keep the deck well sealed and you won't need most of the information in this chapter. If it is already too late for this advice, then here are the instructions for dealing with core problems.

DELAMINATION

Sailboats rarely suffer from delamination except where core is involved. Between laminates of fiberglass, the bond is chemical (as long as the fabricator didn't delay too long between layers) and strong, but between the skins and the core the bond is mechanical and weak. Most often the outer skin separates from the core.

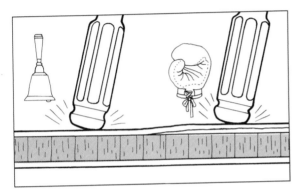

1 Map the area of delamination. Use a plastic mallet or the handle of a screwdriver to tap the area, listening for the telltale difference in sound. A void will have a dull, flat tone compared to the resonance of solid laminate.

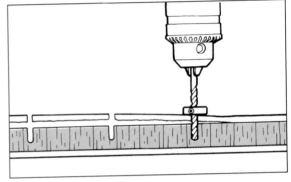

2 Drill several small holes (³⁄₁₆") just inside the outline. The holes should penetrate the outer skin and the core, but not the inner skin. Check the core material pulled out by the drill to make sure the core is dry. Poke at the core through the holes with a piece of wire to make sure it is solid. If the core is wet or spongy, additional steps are required—see the next two sections.

3 Identify the lowest hole in the pattern and mark it. With sheet metal screws, close all the other holes except one. Place the square-cut end of a piece of vinyl hose tightly over the marked hole and blow on the hose. Air should pass freely out the one open hole. Move one screw, closing the tested hole and opening another one, and check again for air flow. Check every hole. If any holes fail to pass air, drill a new hole 1 inch farther inside the outline and test it.

If any hole is more than 5 or 6 inches from another one, drill an intermediate hole to limit the between-hole distance to about 6 inches.

Remove the screws.

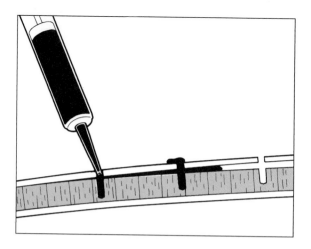

4 Mix an appropriate batch of epoxy and thicken it slightly—to catsup consistency—with colloidal silica. Cut the tip of an epoxy syringe (available from your epoxy supplier) at an angle and fill the syringe with the mix. Insert the tip tightly into the marked hole and inject the void with epoxy. As each hole begins to discharge epoxy, close it with tape. If you flow the epoxy in from the highest hole rather than injecting it from the lowest, you run the risk of trapping air resulting in an incomplete bond.

On a large void, you will need to inject a section at a time, using one of the outlet holes from the previous injection as the new fill hole. Keep flowing epoxy into the void until it flows out all the holes.

5 Weight (horizontal surface) or brace (vertical surface) the outer skin to compress it against the core. Take care not to deflect the skin out of shape. Use wax paper under the weights or braces, and pick up any excess epoxy that vents from the holes.

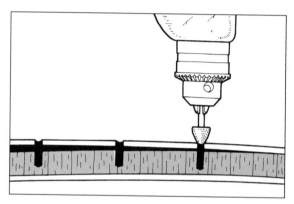

6 Repair the holes like any other surface damage. In this case, the underlying epoxy does not preclude the use of gelcoat to patch the holes as long as the epoxy is scrubbed clean of amine and the surface is dimpled and roughened with a drill-mounted grinding point.

SOLID LAMINATE DELAMINATION

DELAMINATION FOUND IN SOLID LAMINATE should be analyzed carefully. The cause is almost always excessive flex, which tears the bond between the laminates. Occasionally the lay-up schedule is too light—i.e., too few layers of glass—for the duty required of the laminate. In such a case, repair efforts must also include adding additional layers or perhaps other stiffening actions to prevent any recurrence.

More often the delamination is the result of an "incident," usually a collision with a solid object. Provided there is no indication of any substantive damage to the glass fabric, the repair detailed for delamination of the top skin from the core—the most common circumstance—can be used with equal success to treat delamination in solid lay-up.

WET CORE

If the drill bit brings out wet core material, it must be dried out before it can be rebonded to the skin.

SMALL AREA

Often the wet area is limited to the immediate proximity of the source of the moisture. Depending upon the core material and the extent of the saturation, one or all of the following drying methods may be applied.

Vacuum.
A shop vac will remove water from the cavity and extract some moisture from the core. Vacuum bagging using an air compressor and a vacuum generator will be more effective at drying the core. A refrigeration vacuum pump might also be adapted by threading a nipple into the skin.

Flushing.
Flooding the cavity with acetone can be effective. The acetone combines with water, carrying it away. Acetone left behind quickly evaporates, leaving dry core. Always keep in mind that acetone is extremely flammable.

Heat.
A hair dryer or a heat gun played over the wet area will effect some drying. (Be careful not to overheat the laminate; if it's too hot to touch, it's too hot.) The core must be sufficiently exposed for the heat-evaporated moisture to escape; otherwise the moisture simply rises to the underside of the skin and is reabsorbed by the core when the heat is removed. To expose the core, perforate the skin and the core with a pattern of holes drilled about every inch. Don't use a heat gun if you have flushed the core with acetone.

Dry air.
Simply leaving the core exposed will result in drying if the air is dry. Drill the pattern of holes in the wet core and leave the boat in a heated garage or other enclosed storage area for a few weeks, or tent the damaged area and leave a light bulb burning inside the tent to reduce the humidity.

LARGE AREA

If a large section of core is saturated, the only practical solution is to remove one of the skins to fully expose the core so it can be dried thoroughly.

Removing the inner skin.

Removing the inner skin is the preferable way of gaining access to saturated core because it leaves the glossy and the nonskid surfaces of the exterior hull or deck unmarked. Gaining access to the inner skin may require removal of furniture or an inner liner. If access will be very difficult, you are likely to be better off removing the outer skin instead.

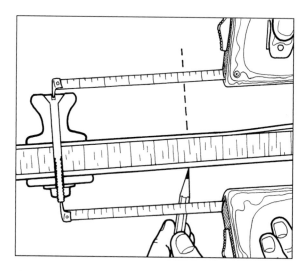

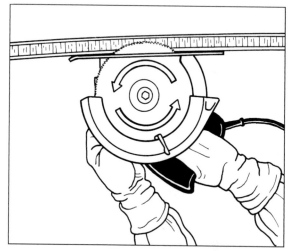

1 Outline the damaged area with straight lines and transfer this outline to the inner skin. This is easily done by making a paper pattern and measuring corner distances to some through-deck feature—a cleat-mounting bolt, for example.

2 Drill an exploratory hole to determine how far the underside of the outer skin is from the surface of the inner skin. Fit a circular saw with a carbide-tipped plywood bit and set the cutting depth to slightly less to allow for some variation in this dimension. Cut around the outline.

3 Finish the cut through the core with a razor knife. If the top-skin bond is completely broken, the cutout will drop out. If not, find a loose corner and pry down, then use a sharpened flexible putty knife as a chisel to free the rest of the core. Heat applied to the outer skin may help.

Removing the outer skin.
If access to the inner skin is difficult, removing the outer skin may be the better way
to expose a saturated core.

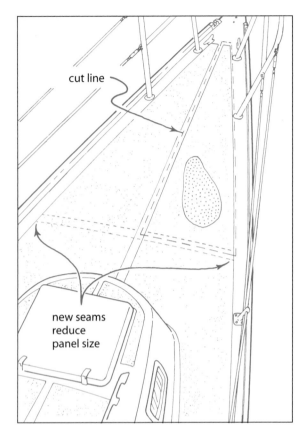

cut line

new seams
reduce
panel size

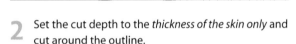

2 Set the cut depth to the *thickness of the skin only* and
cut around the outline.

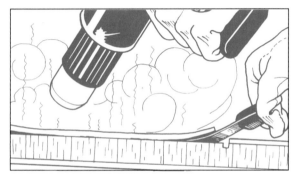

1 Plan your cut wisely. When you replace the skin, the
cut will be much easier to hide if it is in a smooth
section of the deck rather than across the nonskid.
On the other hand, if you are going to cover the
repair with a nonskid overlay, you will want to confine the cuts to the nonskid area. If the wet core is
only on one side of the foredeck, adding a smooth
seam to the nonskid on the centerline (when you
reinstall the skin) will allow you to cut away a
smaller section of deck.

3 If the skin is still partially bonded, pry up a free corner and use a sharpened flexible putty knife as a
chisel to free it completely. Heat applied to the skin
may help. Unless the skin is badly damaged, save it;
you will reinstall it when the core is dry.

Once you have exposed the core, you may discover that it has already begun to deteriorate. In that case, replacement is the only sensible course.

1 Chisel the damaged core from the inner skin. Or . . .

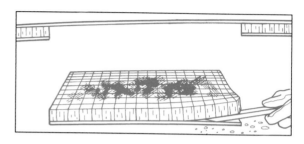

2 . . . Use a utility knife (for balsa or foam) or a saw (for plywood) to cut around the damaged area, taking care not to cut the inner skin. Remove the core with a chisel, shaving the inner skin completely clean.

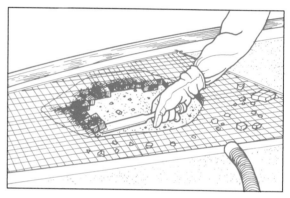

3 Make a paper pattern of the removed section and use it to cut a new piece of core. It is important to use core material the same as the original, both in type and thickness, if possible. Balsa and foam are available from specialty suppliers. If the core is plywood, use only marine-grade plywood for the repair. Sand the surface of the plywood and clean it with a solvent-dampened rag.

Dry-fit the core into the cavity, trimming as necessary. When you are satisfied with the fit, grind the inner surface of the skin.

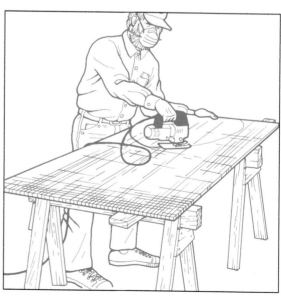

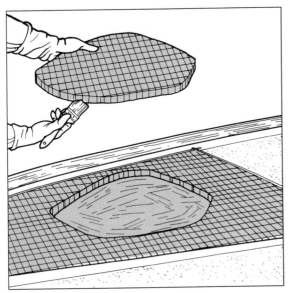

4 Wet out the surface of the skin, the appropriate surface of the new core, and all core edges (old and new).

5 Thicken the epoxy to mayonnaise consistency with colloidal silica, and coat all the bonding surfaces generously. Install the new core.

6 Brace the core in position. Or . . .

7 . . . Weight the core in position. Protect the weights (or braces) with plastic sheeting or wax paper. A sand-filled garbage bag makes an excellent weight for this purpose because it conforms to the shape of the deck. The core should be solidly bedded in the thickened epoxy, and epoxy should squeeze out the cut line all the way around the new section. Remove the squeeze-out, then let the epoxy cure fully before removing the weights.

If the old skin was in poor condition, you will have to lay up a new one with glass cloth and epoxy, but most of the time the old skin can be simply put back in place. Whether you have dried the old core or replaced it, reinstallation of the removed skin is the same.

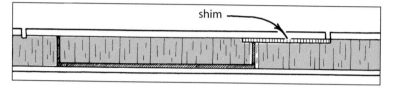

1 Dry fit the removed section. Grind or shim until the skin section realigns properly with the surrounding surfaces.

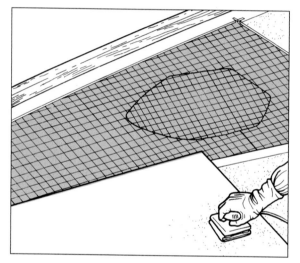

2 Sand the surface of the core and the underside of the skin. Clean with a solvent-dampened rag.

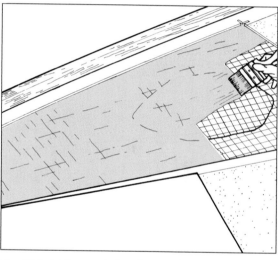

3 Wet out the sanded surfaces with epoxy.

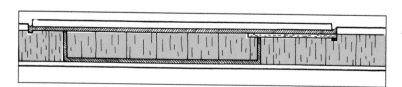

4 Thicken the epoxy to mayonnaise consistency with colloidal silica and coat both surfaces. Be sure to apply enough epoxy putty to solidly fill the space between the skin and the core.

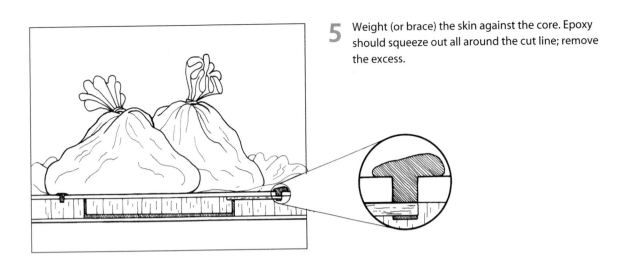

5 Weight (or brace) the skin against the core. Epoxy should squeeze out all around the cut line; remove the excess.

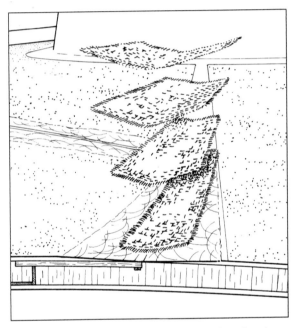

6 After the epoxy has cured thoroughly, bevel each side of the cut line at a 12-to-1 angle. If the skin is ¼-inch thick, for example, a 12-to-1 bevel would be 3 inches wide; i.e., you should have a shallow V-shaped depression 6 inches wide—3 inches on either side of the cut.

7 Cut fiberglass cloth into narrow strips (tape) and laminate them into the depression with epoxy resin. Each strip should be about 1 inch wider than the previous one. Remember not to use mat with epoxy. Sand the cured surface and paint it or cover it with nonskid overlay.

STRENGTHENING

Fiberglass boats sometimes flex alarmingly under pressure or exhibit a pattern of surface cracks around hardware, in corners, or at other stress points. These can both be signs of excessive weakness.

Fiberglass laminate is easily strengthened by adding additional layers. Strengthening layers are most often added to the inner surface of the hull or deck.

1 Outline the area to be strengthened. Dewax and grind the surface thoroughly to prepare it.

2 Cut multiple layers of fiberglass cloth, the first to the size of the outline, then each a little smaller than the previous. If you are reinforcing a large area, keep the cloth pieces small enough to handle—generally not much larger than 1 square yard if you're working alone. Overlap joints on an inside surface; butt them if you are adding laminates to the outside surface.

3 Follow the laminating procedures detailed in "Laminate Repair." Use epoxy resin. Epoxy is stronger than polyester resin, and strength is what you're after. Epoxy also binds the new laminates to the old more securely.

STIFFENING A SKIN

Glass-reinforced plastic is by nature flexible, and excessive flexing more often indicates inadequate stiffness rather than inadequate strength. Adding layers does stiffen the area as well, but when strengthening is not required, stiffening is usually better accomplished with a sandwich construction.

Doubling the thickness makes a panel eight times as stiff. This is the reason the manufacturer put core in the deck. You can add a layer of core and a thin inner skin to a panel to stiffen it, but often a reinforcing member or two will do the same job with less work and less weight.

Called "hat-shaped stiffeners," reinforcing members are rib- or stringer-like fiberglass constructions formed over a strip of wood or other material. Judiciously spaced, hat-shaped stiffeners are quite effective.

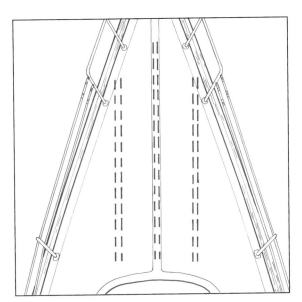

1 Decide where the stiffeners will go. Generally they should run parallel to the long dimension of the area you are stiffening. The number of stiffeners required will depend on the flexibility of the panel; add them one at a time until you are satisfied with the result.

2 Select a core material. Wood adds some strength, but most of the stiffness comes from the box construction, so an easier-to-form core material such as foam, hose, or cardboard may be a better choice. If you use wood, taper the ends to avoid creating a hard spot where the stiffener ends.

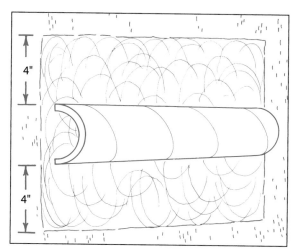

3 Dewax the panel where the first stiffener will be attached. Grind an area about 8 inches wider than the width of the core material.

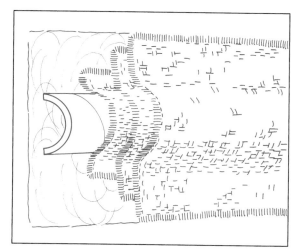

4 Cut a strip of 10-ounce cloth wide enough to extend out 2 inches on either side of the core. Cut a second strip 2 inches wider and a third 2 inches wider still. The recommended height-to-skin-thickness ratio is 30 to 1, so three layers of 10-ounce cloth (which yield a cured thickness of about 0.120 inch) are generally sufficient for stiffeners up to about 3½ inches high. If you want extra layers for added assurance, cut each strip 2 inches wider than the previous one. Be sure to grind a wider area.

5 Tack the core material in place with hot glue or quick-set epoxy. Since the glass cloth won't form into a sharp corner, it is good practice to put an epoxy-putty fillet along the edges of the core.

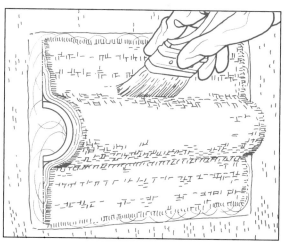

6 Apply the laminates over the core, wetting them out with epoxy resin. (Polyester resin is inferior for this use for reasons already mentioned, but if you use polyester, substitute mat for the odd-numbered layers.)

HULL REPAIRS

Fiberglass hulls are incredibly durable. They don't rot like wood or corrode like steel. They don't dry out and open seams. They don't get worms. In fact, after 35 years of production-line manufacture, the only insidious problem to surface in these boats is blistering, and even that affects only a small percentage of hulls.

If you keep the hull away from solid objects such as rocks, docks, and other boats, required repairs are likely to be limited to restoring the surface gloss. Unfortunately avoiding the occasional "kiss" sounds simpler than it really is. Boats aren't always where you think they are. Underwater obstructions aren't always charted. And rare is the skipper who hasn't watched in disbelief as his boat—a moment before in complete control—suddenly rushes sideways for the dock. Even impeccable navigation and iron-fisted control doesn't prevent another captain's lapse from leaving you with broken glass.

Because the hull is relatively featureless compared with the deck, hull repairs are generally less complicated. But they are more visible; a poor topsides repair can stand out like a shirt-pocket ink stain. You must take the time to fair the patch and match the color for the repair to be invisible.

While it is true that the hull is the part of the boat that "keeps the ocean out," there is no reason to approach hull repair with any greater trepidation than repairing the deck. Prepare the surface properly, which means little more than cleaning and grinding—always grinding—and follow the other steps carefully, and your patch will be just as strong as the surrounding hull, maybe stronger.

GOUGES

In "Restoring the Gloss," we looked at scratch repair, but sometimes an encounter with a sharp, solid object gouges into the underlying laminate. In this instance, the laminate must be repaired before the gelcoat is restored. How you make the repair depends on the extent of the damage.

REPAIRING A SHALLOW GOUGE

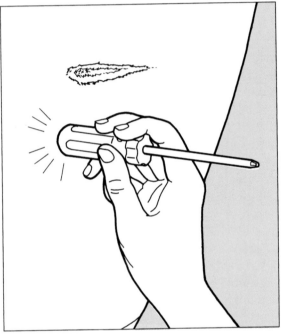

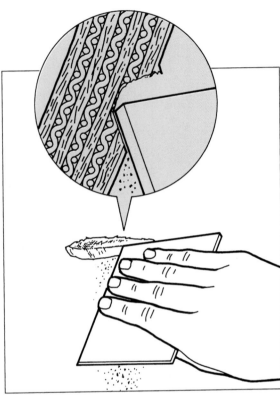

1 Sound the area for delamination. The impact that caused the gouge may have torn the underlying laminates. If the tapping sounds dead rather than resonant, repair the damage as if it were a deep gouge (see below).

2 Use the edge of a cabinet scraper to open the damage, putting a smooth chamfer on each side of the gouge.

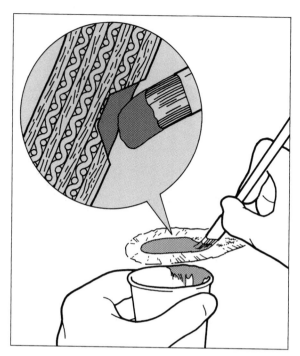

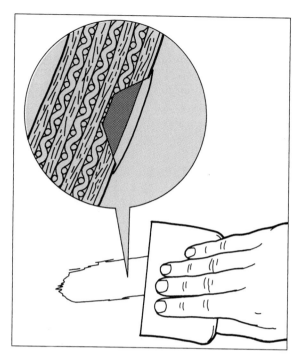

3 Catalyze a small quantity of polyester resin and thicken it with chopped glass. Wipe the V with styrene to reactivate the surface of the cured resin, then fill the V to the *bottom* of the gelcoat layer with the thickened resin.

4 When the resin kicks, fill the remaining depression with color-matched gelcoat paste, letting it bulge slightly above the surface. When the gelcoat begins to gel, seal its surface with plastic or a coat of PVA.

5 Allow the gelcoat to cure fully, then fair and polish the repair.

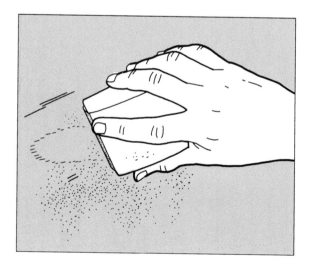

DEEP GOUGES

1 If the damage extends through more than the upper two or three laminates and the gouge is more than a couple of inches long, restoring hull integrity requires replacing the damaged fiberglass. Grind the damaged area into a depression with a 12-to-1 chamfer all around. Grind through all broken layers, using the first undamaged laminate as the bottom of the depression.

2 Cut alternating layers of mat and cloth, beginning with mat and making each layer larger than the previous one.

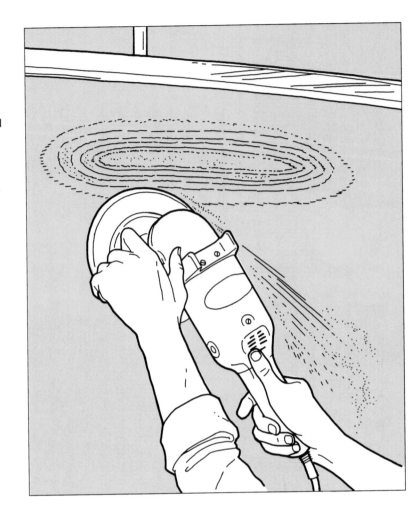

3 Wipe the depression with styrene, then coat it with polyester resin. Place the first layer of mat in the depression and wet it out. Position and wet out succeeding layers until the repair is even with the bottom of the gelcoat layer.

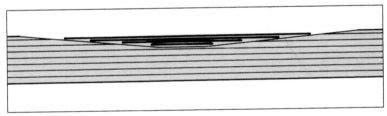

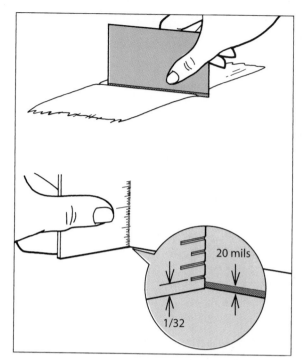

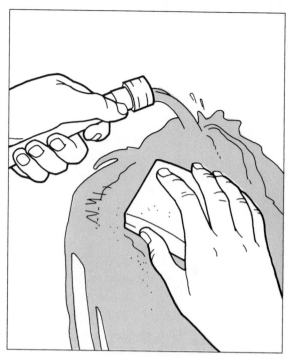

4 When the resin kicks, spray on several coats of color-matched gelcoat (see *Sailboat Refinishing*), or brush on at least 20 mils of gelcoat paste. Check the thickness by slicing the gelcoat with the edge of a piece of paper and comparing the height of the gelcoat on the paper to a 1/32-inch mark on a ruler, which is about 30 mils.

5 Allow the gelcoat to cure fully, then fair and polish the repair.

WHEN TO USE EPOXY

IF YOU PLAN TO PAINT THE REPAIR RATHER THAN finish it with gelcoat, repair the gouge with epoxy for a better bond. For a shallow gouge, wet the V first with unthickened epoxy, then fill it to the surface with the epoxy thickened with colloidal silica to peanut butter consistency. Try to get the surface as fair as possible before the epoxy kicks because the silica-thickened epoxy is hard to sand, especially without damaging the much softer gelcoat that surrounds it.

For deep gouges, use epoxy and 10-ounce cloth—no mat. Wet out the depression, then coat it with epoxy thickened with colloidal silica to catsup consistency. Apply the layers of cloth and saturate them with epoxy resin. Give the last layer two or three extra coats of resin to completely hide the weave of the cloth. Coating the surface with peel ply is recommended (see "Laminate Repair"). Fairing is likely to be required, but wait until the laminates have fully cured, then thicken some mixed epoxy to peanut butter consistency—use microballoons if the repair is above the waterline, colloidal silica if it is below—and fill all voids and depressions. Sand and paint.

BLISTERS

Fiberglass blisters occur because water passes through the gelcoat. Water-soluble chemicals inside the laminate exert an osmotic pull on water outside, and some water molecules find a way through. As more water is attracted into the enclosed space, internal pressure builds. The water molecules aren't squirted back out the way they came in because they have combined with the attracting chemicals into a solution with a larger molecular structure. Instead, the pressure pushes the covering laminate into a dome—a blister.

There has been a great deal of hysteria about blisters, but the reality is that the number of boats that develop *serious* blister problems is extremely small. An occasional blister or two is *not* a serious problem, any more than is an occasional gouge in the hull. Some boats seem to exhibit a greater propensity to blister, presumably due to the chemical components used and/or the lay-up schedule, but all boats are at some risk. Surveys suggest that about one boat in four develops blisters. Maybe the factory was training a new fiberglass crew the day your boat was built, or the humidity was abnormally high. Or maybe the factory did everything right but somewhere along the way someone sanded the gelcoat excessively, or even sandblasted it to prepare it for bottom paint. It is pointless to speculate. If your boat develops blisters, deal with them; if it doesn't, forget about it.

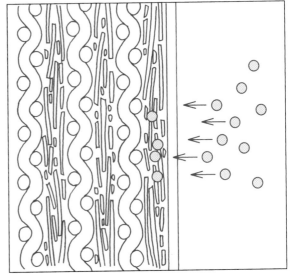

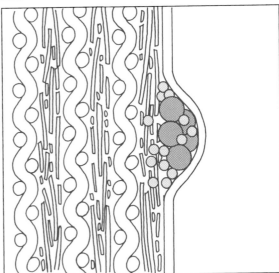

MINOR BLISTERING

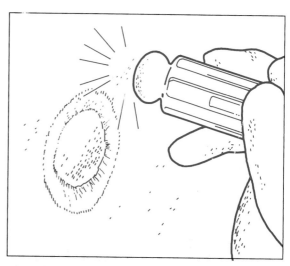

1 Open the blister. Wear eye protection; internal pressure can be double that of a champagne bottle, and the fluid that blasts out when you pop the dome is acid. Use a 36-grit disk to grind the blister into a shallow depression.

2 Sound around the blister to make sure there isn't any additional delamination.

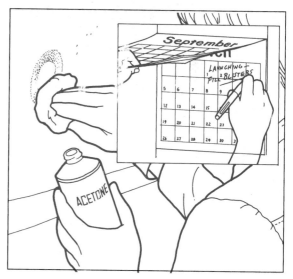

3 Flush the open blister with water, then scrub it with a TSP solution. Rinse thoroughly.

4 Allow the blister to dry for as long as practical. If you dry-store your boat for the winter, open blisters at haulout but don't fill them until launch time. Just before filling, wipe out each blister depression with a rag *dampened* with acetone.

5 Epoxy is the resin to use for blister repairs. It is less permeable than polyester and it forms a much stronger bond. Wet out the cavity with epoxy.

6 For small blisters, thicken epoxy to peanut butter consistency with colloidal silica and fill the cavity, using a squeegee to compress and fair the filler. Silica-thickened epoxy is hard to sand, so fair it well before it kicks. *Never* use microballons or any other hollow or absorbent (talc, for example) fairing compound to fill blisters.

7 Before the repair reaches full cure, paint it with at least two coats of unthickened epoxy.

BOAT POX

Boat pox is a much more serious condition, related to the occasional blister like acne to the occasional pimple. If the bottom of your boat is covered with blisters, filling them won't cure the problem. Pox is a systemic condition and requires remedial action.

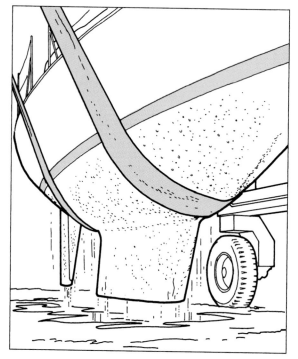

1 Examine the bottom as soon as your boat is lifted. Out of the water, blisters can shrink and even disappear altogether. If the bottom is covered with hundreds of blisters, your boat has pox, and the condition will only worsen unless you take the cure.

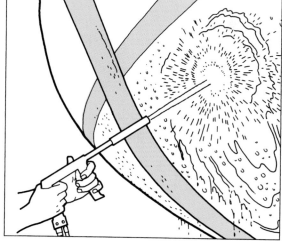

2 Scrub the hull to remove growth, oil, and all other contaminants.

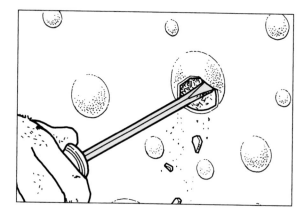

3 Open a few blisters to determine their location. Usually blisters occur between the gelcoat and the first layer of laminate. If they are deeper, see the sidebar on page 243.

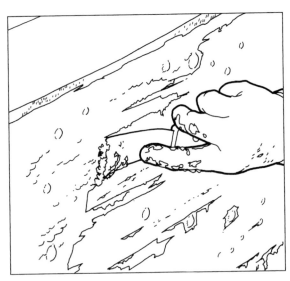

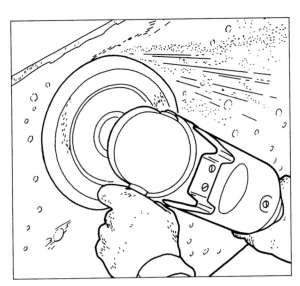

4 Unless you are having the hull machine peeled, chemically strip the bottom of all paint. Curing boat pox requires the removal of *all* the gelcoat below the waterline; but if you do not remove the paint first, gelcoat stripping will contaminate the underlying laminate with paint particles, weakening the bond of the barrier coat.

5 Grind away all the gelcoat below the waterline. You cannot just grind open the blisters because a hull with pox is saturated throughout and will not dry out unless the gelcoat is removed. Despite the time required, the best way to strip the gelcoat is with a lightweight disk sander and 24-grit disk on a foam pad. Boatyards prefer to sandblast the hull to remove the gelcoat, but this harsh treatment damages the underlying laminate. If you give in to the expediency of sandblasting, be sure the pressure is low and the sand is directed at the hull at a shallow angle—less than 30 degrees.

Some yards now have peelers that work like a power plane. Set to the appropriate thickness, they shave the gelcoat from the hull in a single pass without any damage to the laminate. If you have the hull peeled, run a 50-grit disk over the peeled surface to remove any ridges and to provide tooth for the barrier coat.

6 Wash the stripped surface with a stiff brush. It is imperative that all loose bits of gelcoat, paint, and grit are removed. Inspecting the surface with a magnifying glass is not overkill.

7 With the gelcoat removed and the laminate clean, allow the hull to dry out. This will take at least two weeks in hot temperatures and as long as six months in the cold. Tenting the hull and running fans or a heater will shorten the time.

Keep track of the drying process by taping 6-inch squares of plastic cut from heavy freezer bags to a dozen or more places on the hull—2 or 3 above the waterline. Seal the plastic all around with electrician's tape. Sun on the plastic will cause moisture in the hull to condense on the plastic. Open the plastic and wipe it and the hull dry every few days, then seal it back in place. When condensation ceases to form in any of the test panels on sunny days, the hull is sufficiently dry to reseal.

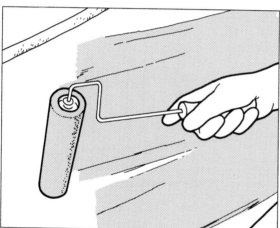

8 Select an epoxy barrier coat product such as InterProtect or West System epoxy and apply it to the recommended thickness—usually 20 mils—according to the manufacturer's instructions.

DEEPER BLISTERS

IT IS FAIRLY COMMON FOR BLISTERS TO OCCUR beneath the first laminate instead of in the laminate/gelcoat junction because of the all-too-common practice of getting the first layer applied to the wet gelcoat, then waiting a day to continue the lay-up. This makes the bond between the first and second laminate weak and susceptible to blistering. Blisters deeper in the laminate are thankfully much rarer, occurring only after less serious blisters have been long ignored.

If you discover that the blisters on your hull are beneath the initial layer of laminate, remove this layer along with the gelcoat. When the hull is dry, apply a replacement layer of 10-ounce cloth to the hull, working with manageable pieces and butt-joining (not overlapping) the sections. Wet each section with epoxy resin, then apply a layer of silica-thickened epoxy before positioning the cloth. Wet out the cloth and seal it with peel ply and a ply of plastic. Sand and fair the entire surface before applying the barrier coating.

ew things are more disheartening to the boat-owner than staring at the fuzzy edge of broken fiberglass. Most don't realize that the repair of impact damage is usually only a step or two more complicated than filling a gouge or a blister. You don't believe it? If you cut out the damaged area and bevel the edges, then close one side of the hole by laying up a single ply of fiberglass over it,

how is the resulting depression different from a deep gouge except in size? It isn't.

Sometimes, of course, damage is so extensive that a significant section of the hull or deck (or both) has to be rebuilt, but even then the lay-up process is the same. The only difficulty comes in getting the new laminates to take on the right shape.

CUTTING AWAY THE DAMAGED LAMINATE

1 Impact damage almost always has some associated delamination. Tap the area to determine the extent of the damage and map it. Enclose the marked area in a circular or oval trace.

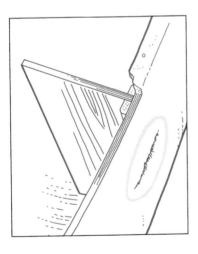

2 Go inside the boat and determine if anything will be in the way when you cut out the damaged section. Sometimes it is best to cut out an offending member; in other cases you may want to leave it intact, cutting the damaged skin free. If you don't have inside access, use a 3- or 4-inch hole saw to remove a circular plug from the hull so you can look and feel inside before making the full cutout.

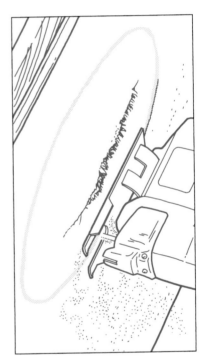

3 Saw around the oval trace. Never try to save damaged fiberglass; always cut it out and replace it with new laminate. You can make the cut with a circular saw fitted with a carbide blade or a cut-off wheel, or with a saber saw fitted with a blade for cutting fiberglass.

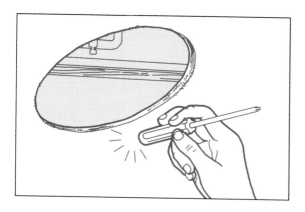

4 Check all the edges to make sure the laminate is solid, and tap again around the hole. Enlarge it if you find any additional delamination.

WORKING FROM THE INSIDE

There are two reasons you should make hull repairs from the inside whenever possible, especially when the damaged area is small. First, you are going to bevel the edge of the hole with a 12-to-1 chamfer. If you repair a 3-inch diameter hole through a ½-inch-thick hull from the outside, you end up with about 15 inches (diameter) of surface damage to refinish, but if you repair it from the inside, you have only a 3-inch hole to refinish.

The second reason is that if you back the hole on the outside with a polished surface, you can in effect create a mold that allows you to lay up the repair the same way the boat was built—gelcoat first—and very little finish work will be required.

1 Dewax the interior surface of the skin around the hole.

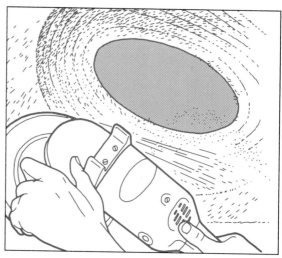

2 Grind the edge of the hole into a 12-to-1 bevel. Also grind a rectangular area of the inner surface a few inches beyond the hole to accommodate a finishing layer of cloth.

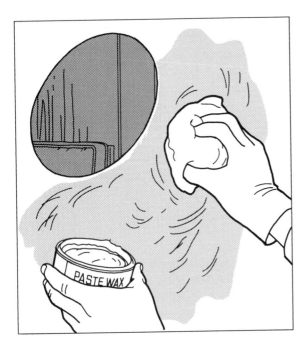

3 Give the exterior surface of the skin around the hole a heavy coat of paste wax, taking care not to get any wax on the edge or inside the hole. The purpose of the wax is to prevent any resin runs from adhering to the exterior surface; paint the wax with PVA to be sure. Mask the area below the hole.

4 Cut a scrap of smooth plastic laminate (Formica) or thin clear acrylic (Plexiglas) a foot larger than the hole. Wax this backer and paint it with PVA, and screw or tape it to the outer surface. If the hull is flat or curving in only one direction in the damage area, the backer will assume the correct curve—check

from inside to make sure it seats against the skin all around the hole. If the hull is spherical, i.e., curving in two directions, a sheet backer usually won't work. Where the compound curvature is slight, acrylic screwed to the hull will bend into the correct shape if warmed with a heat gun. Otherwise you will need to make a backer following the instructions in "Taking Off a Mold" below.

5 Cut the fiberglass material to fit the hole. Unless you have reason to follow a different schedule, begin with two layers of 1½- or 2-ounce mat, then alternate mat and 10-ounce cloth. The number of laminates will be determined by the thickness of the hull; you will need roughly one layer for every ¹⁄₃₂ inch. Cut the first layer of mat 1 inch larger than the hole, overlapping the bevel by ½ inch all around. Subsequent pieces should be ½ inch larger all around than the previous one.

6 From inside, spray or brush 20 mils of color-matched gelcoat onto the waxed backer. Check the gelcoat thickness with a toothpick—¹⁄₃₂ inch is about 30 mils.

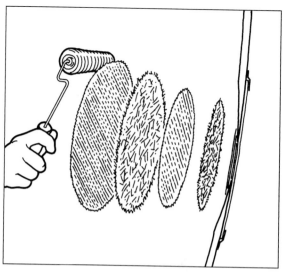

7　When the gelcoat kicks, wet it with polyester resin and lay up the first two layers of mat and one layer of cloth, compressing them against the gelcoat and working out all voids and bubbles with a resin roller and/or a squeegee.

8　Let the first three plies kick, then lay up four additional plies. Never lay up more than four plies at a time or the generated heat may "cook" and weaken the resin. Continue the lay-up four plies at a time until the repair is flush with the interior surface.

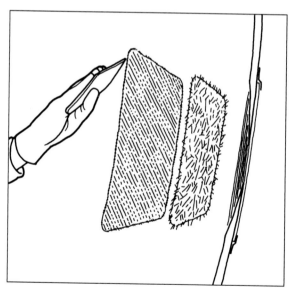

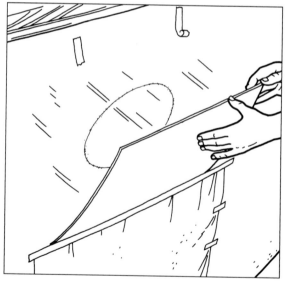

9　For a finished look, cut a rectangular piece of mat and one slightly larger of cloth and apply these over the patch, smoothing them with a squeegee. Seal this top layer with plastic or PVA to allow a full cure.

10　Remove the backer from the exterior surface. Fill any imperfections in the new gelcoat with gelcoat paste and allow it to cure fully. Clean the area around the patch, then sand—if necessary—and polish the repair area.

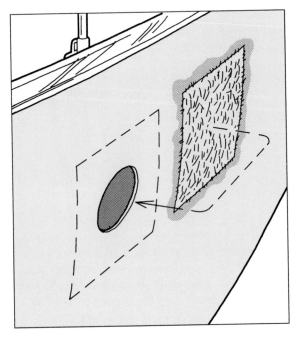

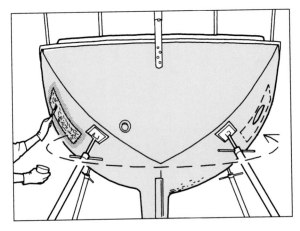

1 At its simplest, taking off a mold involves no more than waxing and release-coating (with PVA) a section of hull with approximately the same contour as the damaged area, usually adjacent to the damage. Coat the waxed area with resin, then lay up two plies of 2-ounce mat. When the lay-up cures, peel it from the hull, coat it with releasing agent, and tape in place over the hole to provide a contoured backer/mold for your repair.

2 For more extensive damage or damage in an area where the shape of the hull is rapidly changing, try taking a mold from the same spot on the other side of the hull. Reversed top to bottom, the molded piece should give you a close approximation of the correct contour. Transfer it while it is still "green," that is before full cure, and it should conform perfectly to the damaged side.

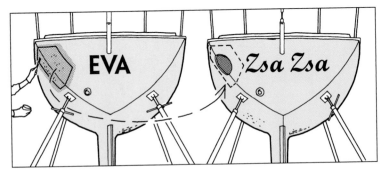

3 When damage is extensive or to an area of the hull with a feature, such as the intersection of the quarter and the transom, taking a mold from the opposite side may not give satisfactory results. If you can locate a sistership with a willing owner, you can lay up a perfect mold. If the mold is sizable, stiffen it with a few hat-shaped stiffeners. Be sure you know how to thoroughly coat a hull to assure release—meaning try it on your own hull first—before you paint someone else's hull with resin.

OUTSIDE REPAIR

If you are going to paint the repair rather than trying to match gelcoat, make the repair from the outside. Working outside is somewhat easier and a lot more comfortable—you're not engulfed in resin fumes or wedged into some impossible corner. If you're not going to finish the repair with gelcoat, you should also use epoxy for its superior bonding strength.

1 Dewax around the hole and grind the edge into a 12-to-1 bevel.

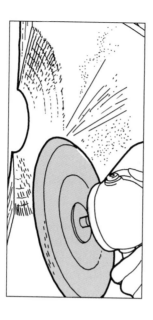

2 Wax the exterior surface of the skin around the hole, taking care not to get any wax on the bevel. Mask the area below the hole.

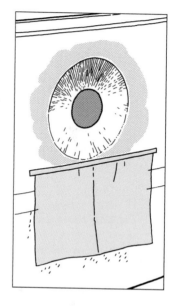

3 Wax and release-coat a scrape of smooth plastic laminate or thin acrylic and *brace* it tightly against the hole from inside. If the hull is flat or curving in only one direction in the damage area, the backer will assume the correct curve. If the hull is spherical, lay up a backer using an adjacent section of the hull as the mold.

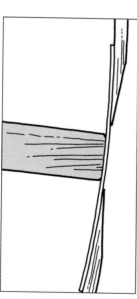

4 If you are using epoxy resin for the repair, cut all your repair pieces from 10-ounce cloth. Mix a batch of epoxy and wet out the first layer of cloth. Use a squeegee to smooth the cloth into position and to remove trapped air. Apply the second layer and wet it out. Squeegee. Repeat this process a layer at a time, mixing fresh epoxy as needed, until the repair is slightly below the surface.

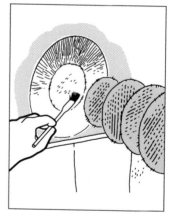

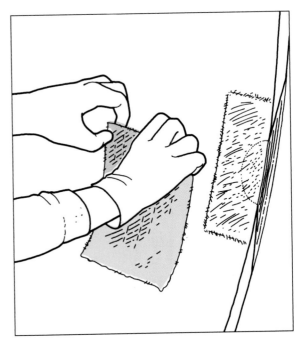

5 Give the final layer a coat or two of epoxy, then cover the surface with peel ply and a layer of plastic and smooth it with the squeegee. Wipe up any squeeze-out.

6 Remove the backer from the interior surface and grind the repair and a rectangular area around it. Cut a piece of fiberglass cloth to the size of the ground rectangle and laminate it in place to give the interior of the repair a finished look.

7 Fair the repair with epoxy thickened with micro-balloons (below the waterline, use colloidal silica) and paint.

NO INSIDE ACCESS

Often there is a liner or a tank or some other interior obstruction in the damage area that denies you access to the inside of the hull. Except for the need to take extra care when cutting out the damaged section and the effect working from the outside has on the size of the repair requiring finish work, lack of inside access isn't a very big problem.

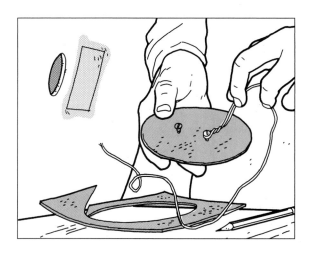

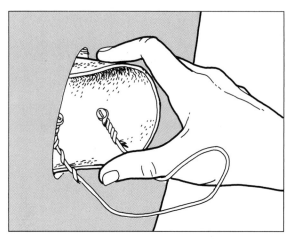

1. Using epoxy resin and two layers of 10-ounce cloth, lay up a backer piece on a waxed and release-coated section of the hull near the damage.

2. When the backer is thoroughly cured, peel it up and trim it to 1 inch larger than the hole. Screw two sheet-metal screws into the backer and twist the ends of a length of wire to the screws to provide a loop handle.

3. Dewax the inside of the skin around the hole by reaching through the hole with a solvent-soaked rag. Sand the dewaxed area with 50-grit paper, again by reaching through the hole. Scrub (with water) and sand the handled surface of the backer.

4. Bend the backer slightly and push it through the hole, holding on to the wire loop. No bending will be necessary if the hole is oval shaped.

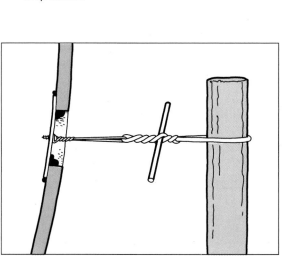

5. Thicken a small amount of epoxy to peanut butter consistency with colloidal silica, and butter it onto the perimeter of the backer. Center it and pull it tightly against the opening. Hold it in position with a string tied from the loop to some fixed object. Wipe up all the epoxy that squeezes out and let the bond cure completely.

6. Remove the screws and proceed with the repair as described above.

CORED HULL

Impact damage to a cored hull requires repair to the three components—inner skin, core, and outer skin—separately.

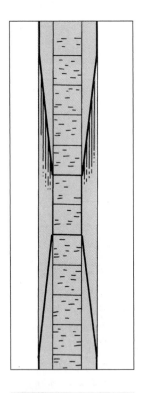

With inside access. Cut out the damage, then grind a 12-to-1 bevel on both skins. Bond a new section of core into the hole, then lay up new skins on either side.

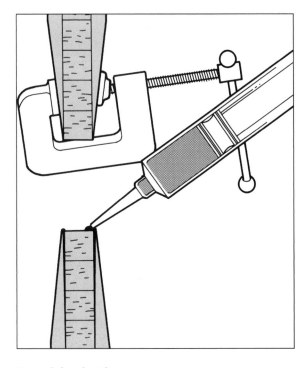

Core delamination. The flexing associated with an impact is likely to result in delamination beyond the area of skin damage. With edge access, inject the separation with epoxy and clamp it until it cures, then complete the repair.

Without inside access. Outline the damage and cut away the outer skin and the core with a router, taking care not to cut the inner skin. With the inner skin now exposed, cut out the damage to it. Bevel both the inner and outer skins, then lay up a new section of inner skin as previously detailed. Install new core on top of the new inner skin and lay up a new outer skin.

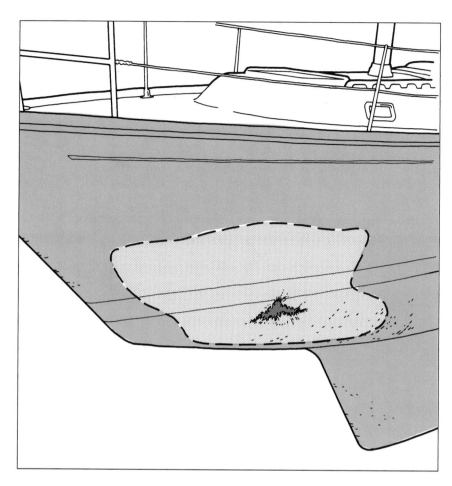

Wet core.

Impact damage below the waterline of a cored hull usually results in wet core. With inside access, determine the extent of the saturation by removing progressively larger sections of the inner skin. Let the core dry or replace it, then complete the repair normally.

Without interior access, it is the outer skin you will have to remove. If the damage to the outer skin is small but the area of saturation large—you should be able to tell by tapping the hull—you may do better to remove the large section of skin intact. While the core dries (if it hasn't been wet long, you will only need to replace the damaged portion), you can repair the damage to the panel of skin. Reglue the repaired skin to the core, then grind a 12-to-1 bevel around the cut line and bond the piece back in place.

KEEL AND RUDDER DAMAGE

Unless you are an extremely timid navigator, eventually you find yourself coming to a rude stop as you unexpectedly run out of water. In such events, it is generally the keel or the rudder that takes the brunt of the impact. When the bottom is ooze or sand, little if any harm is done, but fetching up against solid granite or jagged coral is likely to result in serious trauma.

Scrape and gouge repairs to a fiberglass keel and rudder are no different than on other parts of the hull, except that damage to the keel or rudder should make you suspicious. Because of the lever effect, even a modest impact near the bottom of an underwater appendage applies off-the-scale stresses at the attachment points; fin keels can break the hull like the pull ring on a pop-top can, and rudders can tear free of their stocks. Even an encapsulated full keel, less at risk at the bilge, may deform from the inertia and split, letting seawater into the ballast cavity. All repairs to keel and rudder should include a thorough inspection for collateral damage.

grounded boat lifted and dropped by even modest wave action hits the bottom with the force of a pile driver. If even a fist-size rock is under the hammering keel, the bottom laminate may be distorted enough to split. Such damage is likely to go unnoticed unless you look for it, or until the water intrusion causes iron ballast to swell and deform the keel.

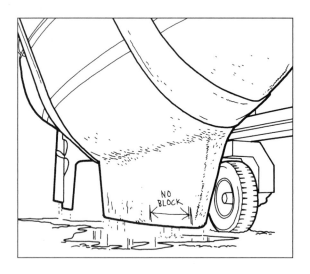

1 Examine the bottom of the keel while the boat is in the hoist and mark where you want yard workers to place the blocks so your access to any suspect areas won't be obstructed.

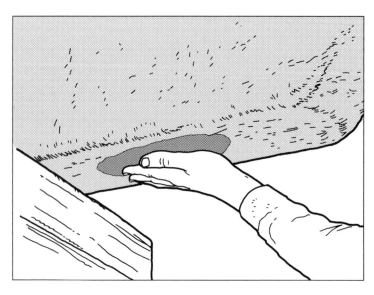

2 Scrape, scrub, and rinse the keel, and let it dry completely. Now examine it with eye and finger for any signs of lingering wetness. Weeping that persists for more than a day indicates a crack in the keel laminate.

3 Grind away the bottom paint in the wet area. The crack should become visible.

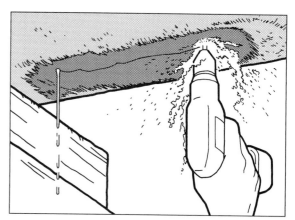

4 Find the ends of the crack and use a battery- or hand-powered drill to drill a 3/16-inch hole at each end. These holes mark the break, relieve stress that might lengthen the crack, and allow the cavity to drain. Don't use a plugged-in drill because water may pour out when you puncture the skin.

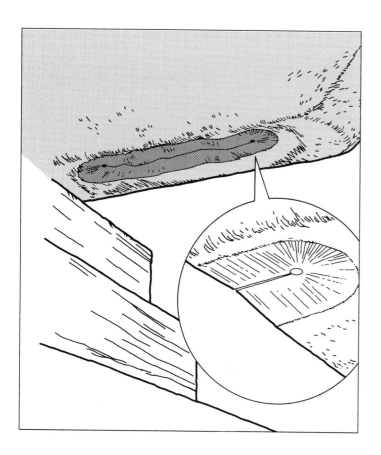

5 Grind a V along the crack line and beyond each end. The bottom of the V should reach the last layer of laminate, and the sides should have a 12-to-1 bevel.

6 Laminate the repair using epoxy resin for a better bond and better resilience to future groundings.

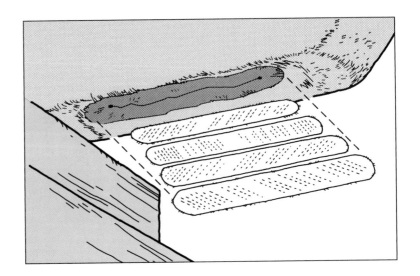

7 If a cracked keel is a recurring problem, grind the entire bottom of the keel and a few inches up the side, then add several additional laminates of glass cloth. You can also strengthen the keel by adding additional laminates from inside if you have interior access.

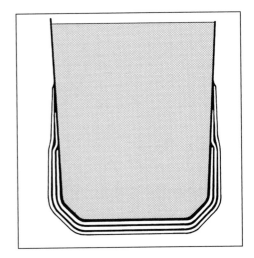

INTEGRAL FUEL TANKS

SOME OF THE SPACE INSIDE A MOLDED KEEL is often used for tankage. This is fine as long as there is actually a tank, but occasionally, to save money, designers or builders have opted for what is known as an integral tank— the designated space in the keel is simply partitioned off from the ballast area and given a fiberglass top. In such cases, a crack in the keel in the tank area may weep fuel.

Permanent repairs will not be possible without emptying the tank and removing all fuel residue from the fiberglass in the area around the crack. The best way of dealing with an integral tank is to replace it with a proper tank; the type will depend on the liquid it is to hold. Cut and grind away the top of the integral tank and steam clean the cavity, then take the dimensions to your tank builder. Meanwhile you can repair the crack in the skin.

KEEL/CENTERBOARD PIVOT PROBLEMS

In a keel/centerboard boat, the pivot pin usually passes through the stub keel, sealed on each end by a plug of mish-mash (a putty made from resin and chopped fiberglass). Leaks around the pivot only rarely get inside the boat because the space in the stub keel, presumably filled with ballast, is usually sealed off from the interior of the hull. A leaking pivot pin is nevertheless a serious problem, especially if the ballast is iron or steel. Rusting steel can expand with enough force to split the confining fiberglass. Even if the ballast is lead, water inside the ballast cavity can freeze during winter storage and rupture the hull.

How do you know if the pivot pin is leaking? If the area around the pin stays wet for days after the boat is hauled (check *inside* the trunk), water is weeping out of the keel and the pin is leaking.

1 Drill and chip out the putty covering both ends of the pivot pin. Take the weight off the pin by supporting the centerboard, and tap out of the keel stub. Remove the centerboard or shift it out of the way.

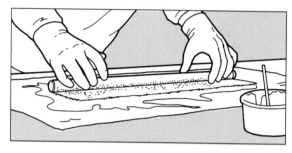

2 Because of hollows in the keel stub, drilling the hole oversize and filling it with epoxy is often impractical. Wax the pin *heavily*. Wet out a piece of light cloth with epoxy and roll it onto the pin to form a fiberglass tube. When the epoxy cures, slip the pin out of the tube.

3 Enlarge the hole in the keel stub to the outside diameter of the tube. This can be the most difficult part of the job if the hole is large and the ballast is iron.

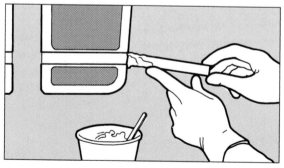

4 Cut the tube into two shorter pieces and epoxy them into the keel. Use epoxy thickened with colloidal silica, and take great care to get a good seal at each end of the tubes where they pass through the fiberglass. Reinstall the pin and seal each end with epoxy putty.

HULL DAMAGE AROUND FINS AND SKEGS

A bolted-on fin keel or skeg functions like a pry-bar when it hits something, deflecting the hull laminate into an S-shape as the front of the fin tries to tear away from the hull and the back tries to drive into the interior.

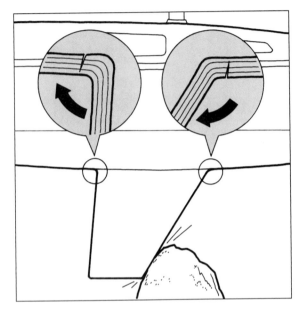

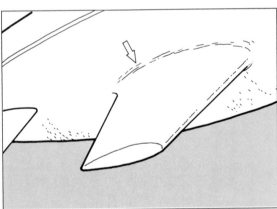

2 Don't confuse gelcoat cracks with laminate damage. Gelcoat often cracks around the fin or skeg because it is more brittle than the underlying laminate. Repair the gelcoat cracks to protect the laminate from water intrusion.

1 Check the hull, both inside and outside, all around the base of the fin. Expect ruptures to be in the outside laminates forward of the fin and in the inside laminates aft. Splits beside the fin can be inside or outside depending on how the fin was stressed.

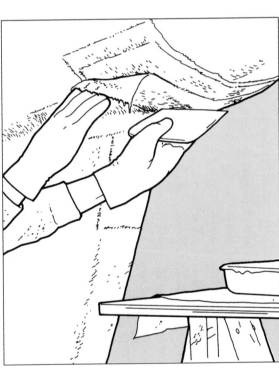

3 Hull damage around a fin almost always signals inadequate laminate strength. After you grind open and repair all damaged laminate, add additional layers of fiberglass to strengthen the hull in the affected area.

DAMAGED RUDDER

In order to neither float nor sink when the boat heels, a sailboat rudder needs to have nearly neutral buoyancy. That means fiberglass rudders are usually foam filled or hollow. Unfortunately, too many are also so lightly built that the slightest brush with anything more solid than a jellyfish breaks the skin. Weeping rudders are even more common than weeping keels, and water inside your rudder is almost certainly doing damage.

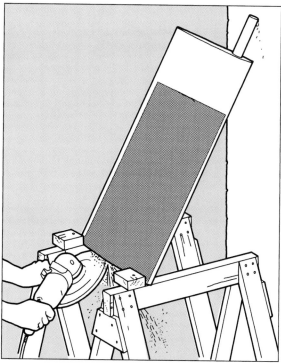

1 If you have a weep anywhere on your rudder, the entire rudder may be full of water, but it will only drain out to the level of the crack. It is almost always a good idea to grind a hole in the lowest part of the skin to allow complete drainage.

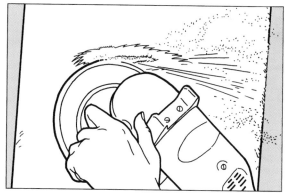

2 Grind the damaged area open to expose enough of the core to determine what it is and whether it is saturated.

3 If the core is saturated, you should have some success in drying it by removing the rudder and drilling a pattern of 3/16-inch holes all the way through it on about 6-inch centers. Put the rudder on sawhorses in an enclosed area and place a small electric heater beneath it. After a few days drill a couple of test holes to see if all the core is drying. If closer spaced holes seem necessary, removing one of the skins may be easier.

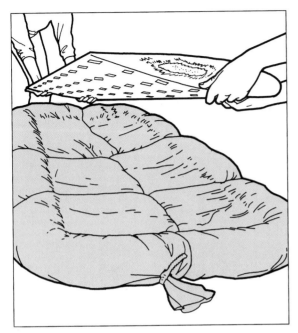

4 When the core is dry, tape the holes closed on one side. "Nestle" that side of the rudder into sand-filled garbage bags, then put it back on the horses, supported as close to the ends as possible to keep from compressing the skin against the core.

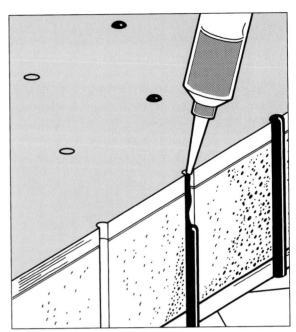

5 Mix epoxy to catsup consistency with colloidal silica and inject each hole until it refuses to accept more or until epoxy appears in the adjacent holes. Fill every hole, working quickly to fill all the voids before the epoxy begins to set. A slow hardener is helpful.

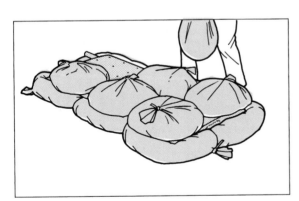

6 Position the rudder in the sandbag "nest" and weight the top surface with sandbags to compress the skins against the core.

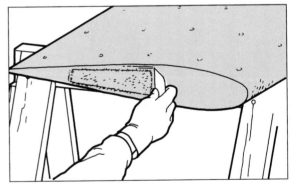

7 When the epoxy has fully cured, regrind the damaged area and the drain hole and repair both with lay-ups of fiberglass cloth and epoxy.

Resin doesn't attach to metal very well, so to keep a rudder from spinning on the stock, it is usually built around a metal framework welded to the stock. Done well, this provides a strong and trouble-free assembly, but too often the framework is little more than two or three metal straps or rods spot-welded to the stock. When (not if) these welds break, the rudder swings freely.

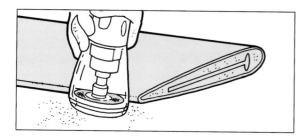

1 Fiberglass rudders are almost always built in two halves and glued together over the stock assembly and the core. Split the seam with a circular saw or rotary tool (Dremel) and separate the two halves. Making the cut to one side will make reassembly easier.

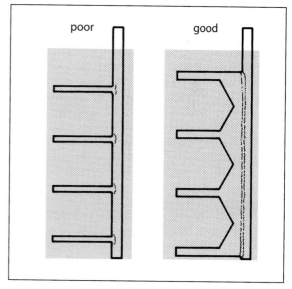

2 Remove the broken framework and have a new one constructed that attaches to the stock for almost the full length of the rudder.

3 Relieve the foam core to fit the new framework and join the two halves with epoxy thickened to mayonnaise consistency with colloidal silica. Clamp or weight the halves together until the epoxy cures fully, then grind a bevel on the cut line and laminate the two halves together.

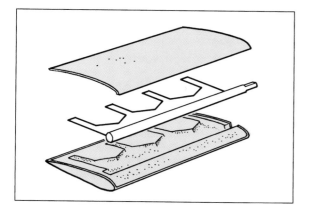

Grounding an external lead keel is less likely to damage the hull, but the keel may be deformed by the impact.

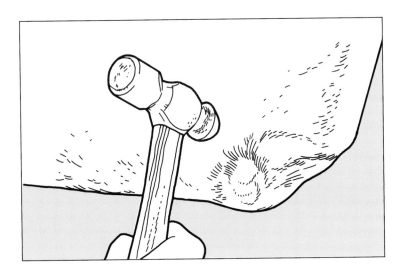

1 Use the round end of a ball-peen hammer to reshape the lead. You are trying to "push" the displaced lead back in shape; be careful not to shear the bulge.

2 Remove high spots with a body plane or a sharp block plane. Lubricate the lead with petroleum jelly before you plane it.

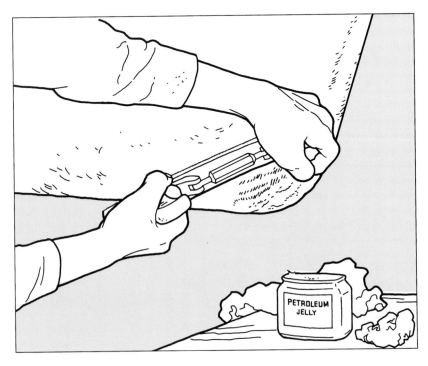

PETROLEUM JELLY

3 Fill low spots with epoxy and microballons. First remove the petroleum jelly and any other contaminants with acetone, and wire brush the lead. Wet the lead with epoxy, then wire brush it again to expose fresh lead to the epoxy without exposing it to the air. Thicken your epoxy to peanut butter consistency with microballoons (there is no blister risk here) and flush-fill the depressions.

4 Sand the entire area after the filler cures and coat it with unthickened epoxy, sanding the wet surface to expose fresh lead to the epoxy. Give the repair two additional coats of epoxy, then sand and paint.

"Of all the improvements
that can be made to a boat . . .
none will have a more dramatic
impact than refinishing.

EFINISHI

Sailboat
Refinishing

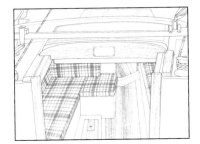

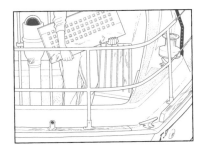

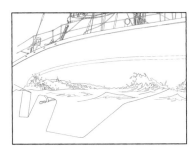

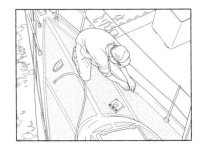

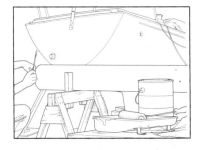

INTRODUCTION

Of all the improvements that can be made to a boat showing the effects of a few seasons of use, none will have a more dramatic impact than refinishing. And few boat tasks are easier. This is a combination forged in Valhalla.

Exposure to the wondrous powers of paint began for most of us with a yellow and green box of crayons. More recent experience is likely to involve rollers and walls. Almost everyone has some painting experience. Whether your training is extensive or limited, if you select the right product and take a deliberate and careful approach to applying it to your boat, you are almost certain to be happy with the results.

The most satisfying result of doing your own refinishing used to be the amount of money saved. Unfortunately the quality of most self-applied marine coatings was somewhat less satisfying— often characterized as "good enough." Today the savings are even more impressive, but the biggest change is in the quality of the finish. Significant technological advances in paints and varnishes in recent years have sharply reduced the craftsmanship required to achieve "professional" results. New products have been engineered for amateur application, and the best of these have flow characteristics that result in finishes that are nothing short of spectacular.

Today's boatowner-applied paint jobs look far better than yard-applied coatings of only a few years back. Of course the improvements in technology have benefited the professional painter as well, but the flow characteristics of this new generation of paints are to a great extent independent of the hand holding the brush, meaning that a motivated amateur can get results that are distinguishable from a professional job only in a close side-by-side comparison. From the dock there will be no discernible difference.

Advances in marine varnish have been less revolutionary but still significant. Flow characteristics have been improved to the point that the foot-deep look of professionally maintained brightwork can be duplicated by the amateur. Improved durability and the addition of sun-screening agents extend the life of exposed varnish and reduce the work required to maintain the coating.

Another technological advance that directly benefits the do-it-yourself boat painter is the expansion of CAD/CAM (Computer Assisted Design/Computer Assisted Manufacturing) technology into boat graphics and lettering. Computer-generated vinyl appliqués are widely available today at a fraction of the cost of having similar lettering and graphics painted on. Lettering the stern of a boat in virtually any style imaginable is hardly more difficult now than putting a peel-and-stick label on an envelope. And the equally uncomplicated application of colorful graphics to the sides of a hull can transform an ordinary boat into a real attention-getter.

Bottom paints have also changed in recent years, although not necessarily for the better. For almost two decades, tin-based bottom paints were king, but while their multi-year protection was good for boatowners, the toxins they contained were bad for the marine environment. In 1989, tin-based bottom paints were banned in the United States (except for use on aluminum hulls), and paint manufacturers simply dropped back to the less-effective copper products they had been manufacturing since the sixties. These provide good antifouling protection for a single season and, in areas where boats stay in the water year-round, the better bottom paints maintain a degree of protection into the second year. None, however, are true multi-year coatings. Some "permanent" antifouling treatments are marketed, but none of these technologies has yet matured, and none of the permanent treatments is effective against grassy growth.

While product improvements have made it much easier to get professional results, the sheer number of products now offered add a significant complication to most refinishing projects. Gone are the days when boat paint was synonymous with enamel, when the choice among two or three brand names depended mostly on the colors available, and when a can of mineral spirits was the only other item required, serving as thinner, surface wipe, and for clean-up. The paint shelf of the past has been replaced by a paint department. Today's chandleries stock hundreds of marine coatings and dozens of coating "systems." A catalog from a large mail-order marine supplier will have 50 or more pages of paints and related products.

Think of this book as a tool, a set of tools really—like a set of socket wrenches. The three sections that make up Chapter 1 are like the ratchet and handles and extensions—the parts of the set you need for every job. The rest of the book is the array of sockets; for now you may only need the one or two that fit the job at hand, but the time will come when you need the others. When you do, they will be close at hand.

Whether you are simply looking for the best way to restore that warm, golden glow to long-neglected teak trim or you plan to refinish the boat from truck to keel, the instructions assembled in this guide are certain to save you time, money, and perhaps grief.

THE BASICS

Good results depend as much on selecting the right product as on application technique. To help you choose wisely, this initial chapter contains use and application information for common marine coatings and systems. Also included is the life expectancy of the resulting finish and the safety precautions, if any, that are required.

Another essential ingredient in achieving the best possible finish is good tools. Good-quality tools almost always allow you to do the job better and get it done quicker as well. The cost difference between a poor-quality brush and a top-quality one is just a few dollars, and the difference between a cheap roller cover and a good one even less, so there is little reason to compromise. For a first-class finish, select only the best painting tools. The second part of this chapter shows you how to choose the right tools, how to use them, and how to maintain them.

The third requirement common to all refinishing jobs is good preparation. While different coatings call for different preparation schedules, many of the specific steps are the same. Labeling and detailing those steps in a single location saves a great deal of unnecessary repetition. This part of the chapter is, in effect, an illustrated glossary applicable to the refinishing projects individually detailed in the remainder of the guide.

No matter what refinishing project you have in mind, you need the information contained in this first chapter. Don't skip over it. Most of it will not be repeated, and a good grasp of the basics is essential to achieving satisfactory results.

UNDERSTANDING PAINTS AND OTHER MARINE COATINGS

Faced with hundreds of different products, each one claiming to be the best, how do you make a selection? The process is significantly simplified if you know the class of product most appropriate for the refinishing job you have in mind.

Marine coatings are invariably formulated for a specific purpose—e.g., providing a hard, clear protective coating for wood, giving a high-gloss finish to dull gelcoat, or discouraging growth on the underwater portions of a boat. Any product on the shelf intended for your purpose will do the job, but not all will do it equally well. Performance is often dependent upon a key ingredient—without chili pepper, it just ain't Mexican food.

It is this key ingredient that gives a coating its defining characteristics—long life, high gloss, abrasion resistance, ease of application, or whatever. Since every paint manufacturer starts with the same basic ingredients, all the products in the category defined by that ingredient exhibit similar qualities regardless of the manufacturer.

That is not to say there aren't differences between brands—there are—but a difference in the recipe doesn't stop it from being an enchilada. If you want the longest-life paint, every manufacturer will recommend their two-part linear polyurethane. Likewise, if you want to oil your teak without darkening it, you will hear tung oil mentioned repeatedly.

What follows is an illustrated list of the various classes of marine coatings and related products (such as thinners). With few exceptions, all the paints and varnishes and sealants on the chandlery shelves fall into one of these categories, and you should be able to determine whether or not a particular class of product—and, by extension, a specific product brand—will satisfy your refinishing requirements.

WHICH BRAND IS THE BEST?

Perhaps you're wondering why not just cut to the chase and recommend products by brand name. After all, if there are differences between brands, then one brand must be better than the others, right?

It depends on what you're evaluating. For example, one manufacturer may formulate a paint that outlasts its competitors by 20 percent, but perhaps the extra durability comes at the expense of flow characteristics. Which is more important to you, a glassy finish or an extra season of durability?

It gets worse. The paint or varnish that seems to have them all beat in Connecticut may well lose its composure under the relentless sun of South Florida. In fact, some products carrying the same brand name are formulated differently for use in different parts of the country. Even if the formula isn't supposed to be different, the actual product often varies from batch to batch—chemical suppliers change, machinery fails, operators drift off. It's paint, not pharmaceuticals.

Still, some brands are undoubtedly better than others, and consumer boating magazines regularly run comparative tests of marine coatings. Such evaluations can be helpful in selecting a particular brand, but don't be surprised if the results vary between publications, or if this year's test results differ from those of only a couple of years ago. There are just too many variables—surface preparation, application, geographic location, weather patterns, boat use, water salinity, even evaluation criteria.

Don't count on any selection help from newsstand boating magazines. You may encounter a product "roundup" in a commercial publication, but don't expect to find any "let-the-chips-fall" test results. Rare is the boating magazine that will risk alienating potential advertisers by publishing negative results.

LOCAL KNOWLEDGE

So how do you make a selection? Your best source will often be local knowledge. If you ask other boatowners in your area what bottom paint they use, one brand name is likely to come up more often than others. If you see an old boat with a topside finish you admire, find out what the finish is and if it was owner-applied. If you hear praise for several different varnishes, get each advocate to show you his brightwork and ask the hard questions: How long has it been on? Always exposed? How many coats? How long between coats? You will know quickly enough precisely which product to choose and what to expect from it.

PRODUCT GUIDE

Marine paints and other boat refinishing products are constantly changing. New technologies provide continuing opportunities for tougher, smoother coatings. Environmental pressures lead to the elimination of specific ingredients or entire products. Products from other arenas find their way into marine use. (An example of the latter is the widespread use in Europe of a diaper-rash cream containing zinc oxide in place of antifouling paint.) In spite of this flux, most of the refinishing products on chandlery shelves have been around for years, some for decades. You are likely to find yourself choosing products that have a long history of marine use. Having a basic understanding of each of these products by class will help you select the specific product best suited to your individual needs.

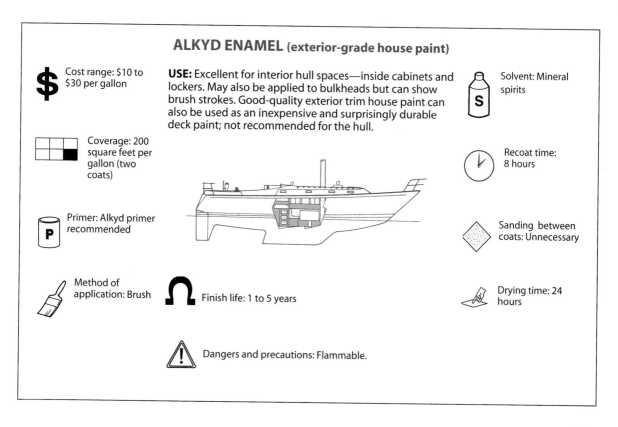

ALKYD ENAMEL (exterior-grade house paint)

$ Cost range: $10 to $30 per gallon

Coverage: 200 square feet per gallon (two coats)

P Primer: Alkyd primer recommended

Method of application: Brush

USE: Excellent for interior hull spaces—inside cabinets and lockers. May also be applied to bulkheads but can show brush strokes. Good-quality exterior trim house paint can also be used as an inexpensive and surprisingly durable deck paint; not recommended for the hull.

Finish life: 1 to 5 years

S Solvent: Mineral spirits

Recoat time: 8 hours

Sanding between coats: Unnecessary

Drying time: 24 hours

⚠ Dangers and precautions: Flammable.

TOPSIDE ENAMEL (marine alkyd enamel)

 Cost range: $12 to $20 per quart.

USE: The least expensive hull and deck coating. Can be applied to almost any above-the-waterline surface. Compatible with most old coatings. Better hiding characteristics than polyurethane, but lower gloss and much shorter life. Good choice for interior surfaces.

 Recommended solvent: Proprietary or mineral spirits.

 Coverage: 50 to 60 square feet per quart (two coats).

 Recoat time: 24 hours.

 Primer required: Alkyd or epoxy undercoat required.

 Sanding between coats: Recommended.

 Method of application: Brush, roller, or spray.

 Finish life: 2 to 3 years in exterior applications.

 Drying time: 24 hours.

 Dangers and precautions: Flammable.

BOOTTOP ENAMEL

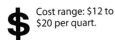 Cost range: $5 for 8 oz.

USE: Boottop and cove stripe. Commonly available in small cans. Any alkyd-based topside enamel will serve this function. Urethane paints may also be used for this purpose. For imitation gold leaf, use a bronze pigmented paint, such as Kemp's Permagild.

 Recommended solvent: proprietary or mineral spirits

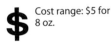 Coverage: 100 linear feet (2-inch-wide stripe, two coats).

 Recoat time: 24 hours.

 Primer required: per manufacturer.

 Sanding between coats: Recommended.

 Method of application: Brush or roller.

 Finish life: 2 to 3 years.

 Drying time: Overnight.

  Dangers and precautions: Flammable.

SINGLE-PART POLYURETHANE (urethane-modified alkyd)

 Cost range: $15 to $20 per quart.

USE: Hull and deck finish. High gloss and good durability. Easier to apply than two-part paints. Fewer compatibility problems with old paint.

 Recommended solvent: Proprietary or mineral spirits.

 Coverage: 50 to 60 square feet per quart (two coats).

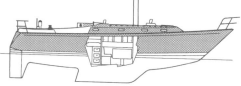

 Recoat time: Overnight.

 Primer required: Proprietary.

 Sanding between coats: Recommended.

 Method of application: Brush, roller, or spray.

 Finish life: 3 to 5 years, with some loss of gloss.

 Dangers and precautions: Flammable. Air-supplied respirator required for spray application.

 Drying time: 24 hours.

TWO-PART POLYURETHANE (linear polyurethane)

 Cost range: $35 to $95 per quart.

USE: The best hull and deck finish. Outstanding gloss and durability. Several brands formulated for amateur application. Not difficult to apply well, but intolerant of omissions and shortcuts. Done well, delivers a better-than-new finish.

 Recommended solvent: Proprietary.

 Coverage: 50 to 60 square feet per quart.

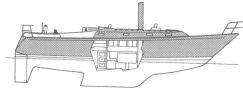

 Recoat time: 24 to 48 hours.

 Primer required: Proprietary.

 Sanding between coats: Recommended.

 Method of application: Foam roller, tipped with brush. Amateur spraying is strongly discouraged.

 Finish life: 5 to 7 years.

 Dangers and precautions: When roller- or brush-applied, hazards are similar to other paints—primarily those associated with exposure to solvent—but when atomized by spray equipment, linear polyurethane is highly toxic. Contains isocyanate: leaking methyl-isocyanate gas killed 3,300 people in Bhopal, India, in a 1984 industrial accident. Spraying requires a positive-pressure air-supplied respirator.

 Drying time: 48 to 168 hours.

LEMON OIL

 Cost range: $8 per pint.

USE: Unvarnished interior wood. Replaces natural oils and is poison to mildew.

 Recommended solvent: None.

 Coverage: Depends on the wood.

 Recoat time: Every 30 to 60 days.

 Sanding between coats: No.

Method of application: Rub into the grain with a cloth. Finish life: Perpetual.

 Drying time: Immediate.

LINSEED OIL

 Cost range: $10 to $15 per quart.

USE: Unvarnished exterior teak. Linseed is the primary oil in most teak-oil products. An excellent preservative but tends to darken the wood.

 Recommended solvent: None.

 Coverage: 150 to 200 square feet per quart (single application).

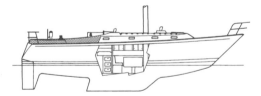

 Recoat time: Every 30 to 60 days.

 Sanding between coats: No.

 Method of application: Brush and/or cloth. Initial application usually calls for multiple coats. Finish life: Depends on location. To maintain the desired color in southern waters and the tropics, sun-carbonized oil will have to be scrubbed from the wood every 6 to 12 months.

 Drying time: Overnight.

TUNG OIL

Cost range: $12 to $17 per quart.

Coverage: 150 to 200 square feet per quart (single application).

Method of application: Brush and/or cloth. Initial application usually calls for multiple coats.

USE: Unvarnished exterior teak. Tung oil is the base for some teak-oil products. More water-resistant than linseed oil and does not turn the wood dark. More expensive than linseed: if a teak product contains tung oil, it will be prominently mentioned on the label.

Finish life: Depends on location. To maintain the desired color in southern waters and the tropics, sun-carbonized oil will have to be scrubbed from the wood every 6 to 12 months.

Recommended solvent: None.

Recoat time: Every 30 to 60 days.

Sanding between coats: No.

Drying time: Overnight

TEAK SEALER

Cost range: $10 to $20 per quart.

Coverage: 150 to 200 square feet per quart (single application).

Method of application: Brush. Initial application usually calls for multiple coats.

USE: Unvarnished exterior teak. Sealers are typically a mixture of oils and resins or polymers—kind of a cross between teak oil and varnish.

Finish life: The oil in teak sealers still carbonizes despite the shielding of the resin or polymer. Periodic stripping—as often as every 12 months—will be required in southern waters to maintain a light color. Some formulations are pigmented to counteract darkening.

Recommended solvent: None.

Recoat time: Every 60 to 90 days.

Sanding between coats: No.

Drying time: 1–2 days.

SPAR VARNISH

 Cost range: $10 to $30 per quart.

 Coverage: 90 to 125 square feet per quart (one coat).

 Primer required: Thinned varnish.

 Method of application: Brush. Minimum of five initial coats required, with the first two thinned as much as 50%.

USE: Clear finish for exterior and interior wood. Resin-based spar varnish is the least complicated wood finish and very long-lasting when properly maintained. Less abrasion-resistant than polyurethane but more flexible. Adds some color to the wood.

 Finish life: 3 to 5 years. To achieve this longevity, nicks and scratches must be sealed immediately and a fresh topcoat of varnish must be applied every 3 to 6 months. Covered varnish will last indefinitely.

 Dangers and precautions: Flammable.

 Recommended solvent: Proprietary or mineral spirits.

 Recoat time: Overnight.

 Sanding between coats: Required. It is possible to apply multiple coats without sanding by recoating as soon as the previous coat "skins."

 Drying time: Overnight.

POLYURETHANE VARNISH

 Cost range: $10 to $30 per quart.

 Coverage: 90 to 125 square feet per quart (one coat).

 Primer required: No.

 Method of application: Brush. Multiple initial coats required.

USE: Excellent finish for interior wood. Generally less satisfactory for exterior applications. Harder than spar varnish, but tends to lose adhesion when exposed to the sun, peeling off in plastic-wrap-like sheets. Excellent abrasion resistance for cabin sole applications. Water-clear finish adds no color. Polyurethane varnish should not be confused with clear two-part polyurethane, which is sometimes applied over epoxy-saturated wood to good effect.

 Finish life: 10 years on interior applications.

 Dangers and precautions: Flammable.

 Recommended solvent: Proprietary or mineral spirits.

 Recoat time: Overnight.

 Sanding between coats: Required. It is possible to apply multiple coats without sanding by recoating as soon as the previous coat "skins."

EPOXY

 Cost range: $75 to $95 per gallon.

 Coverage: 400 to 500 square feet per gallon.

USE: Primer/filler for porous and/or crazed gelcoat. Wood sealer under an overcoat of two-part polyurethane. Sheathing with lightweight fiberglass cloth for hard-wear surfaces. Barrier coat below the waterline for blister prevention. Extremely sun-sensitive; requires an overcoat with UV protection. Very difficult to remove if system fails.

 Recommended solvent: Acetone, cider vinegar (for cleanup only).

 Recoat time: Overnight.

 Sanding between coats: Required.

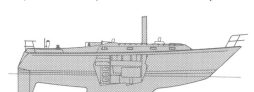

 Method of application: Brush, roller, or squeegee.

Finish life: Unlimited if protected from UV damage.

 Drying time: Overnight.

⚠ Dangers and precautions: Highly toxic. Contact can lead to allergic reaction and lifetime sensitity. Adequate ventilation and protective clothing (especially rubber gloves) required. Organic respirator recommended.

EPOXY BOTTOM PAINT (non-ablative)

 Cost range: $75 to $120 per gallon.

 Coverage: 150 to 200 square feet per gallon (two coats).

USE: Best choice for most boats left in the water year-round. Long-lasting hard coating that may be scrubbed to extend time between haulouts. Few compatibility problems with old coatings.

 Recommended solvent: Thinning not required. Proprietary solvent generally indicated for clean-up, but acetone will serve. Discard used rollers, brushes, and trays.

 Primer required: None.

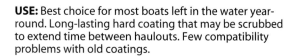

 Recoat time: 4 to 8 hours.

 Method of application: Roller or brush.

Finish life: 12 to 18 months. Some paints can be extended to 24 months by scrubbing.

 Drying time: Overnight.

⚠ Dangers and precautions: Toxic. Wear respirator when sanding old paint. Avoid contact with skin—paper coveralls and rubber gloves essential. Eye protection also recommended. Wash exposed skin immediately. Flammable.

VINYL BOTTOM PAINT (non-ablative)

 Cost range: $70 to $125 per gallon.

 Coverage: 125-150 square feet per gallon (two coats).

 Primer required: None.

 Method of application: Roller or brush.

USE: Preferred by racers because surface is smoother than epoxy-based paint and can be burnished for lower friction. May be scrubbed to extend time between haulouts. Incompatible with most other paints; apply over vinyl paint or bare gelcoat only.

Finish life: 12 to 18 months.

 Recommended solvent: Thinning not required. Proprietary solvent generally called for for clean-up, but MEK will serve. Discard used rollers, brushes, and trays.

 Recoat time: 1 to 6 hours.

 Drying time: Overnight.

Dangers and precautions: Toxic. Wear respirator when sanding old paint. Avoid contact with skin—paper coveralls and rubber gloves essential. Eye protection also recommended. Wash exposed skin immediately. Flammable.

COPOLYMER BOTTOM PAINT (ablative)

 Cost range: $100 to $150 per gallon.

 Coverage: 65-150 square feet per gallon (three coats).

 Primer required: None.

 Method of application: Roller or brush.

USE: The only choice for boats that spend time *out of* the water—unaffected by exposure to air. Antifouling properties more-or-less constant as long as some paint remains on hull. Ablative means the paint "washes" away, perpetually exposing a fresh surface. Life depends on number of coats. Scrubbing shortens time between hauling. Few compatibility problems.

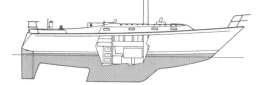

 Finish life: 18 to 24 months.

 Recommended solvent: Thinning not required. Proprietary solvent generally called for for clean-up. Discard used rollers, brushes, and trays.

 Recoat time: 1 to 16 hours.

 Drying time: Overnight.

Dangers and precautions: Toxic. Wear respirator when sanding old paint. Avoid contact with skin—paper coveralls and rubber gloves essential. Eye protection also recommended. Wash exposed skin immediately. Flammable.

OTHER BOTTOM PAINTS

SOFT BOTTOM PAINT

Use: A good choice for slow-moving boats that get seasonal use. An ablative paint, but much softer and quicker to erode than copolymer. Inexpensive. Easy to sand and recoat. Scrubbing not recommended.

Cost range: $40 to $70 per gallon.

Coverage: 150 to 200 square feet per gallon (two coats).

THIN-FILM TEFLON

Use: Preferred by some racers for its low-friction surface. A thin, hard coating with some similarities to vinyl paint, but incorporating Teflon to reduce drag. Incompatible with some other paints. May be burnished.

Cost range: $100 to $130 per gallon.

Coverage: 100 square feet per gallon (three coats).

TIN-BASED PAINTS

Use: Generally banned in the United States except through special permit for aluminum hulls. Does not contribute to galvanic corrosion.

Cost range: $15 to $20 for 12 ounces.

Coverage: 1 square foot per ounce.

ZINC-OXIDE BASED PAINTS

Use: A relatively new formulation in the United States. Shows promise.

RACING ENAMEL

Use: No antifouling properties. Buffable slick finish for dry-stored racing boats.

Cost range: $50 to $70 per gallon.

Coverage: 400 square feet per gallon (two coats).

CUPROUS RESIN

 Cost range: $200 to $500 per gallon ($1 to $10 per square foot).

USE: "Permanent" antifouling bottom coating. Effective for hard growth but generally ineffective for grass. Periodic scrubbing required.

 Recommended solvent: Proprietary or acetone.

 Coverage: 50 to 200 square feet per gallon.

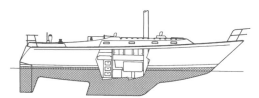

 Method of application: Roller and brush.

 Finish life: 7 to 20 years.

 Drying time: Overnight.

⚠ Dangers and precautions: Same as epoxy.

GELCOAT RESIN

Cost range: $15 to $35 per quart.

USE: Repairs to damaged gelcoat.

Recommended solvent: Acetone.

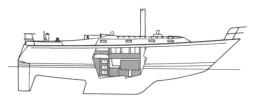

Recoat time: ½ to 2 hours.

Sanding between coats: No.

Method of application: Brush, spray, or squeegee.

Finish life: 10 to 20 years.

Drying time: 1 to 24 hours (adjustable by catalyst).

Dangers and precautions: The usual catalyst, MEKP (methyl ethyl ketone peroxide), is an irritant, especially to the eyes.

CONTACT CEMENT

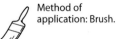
Cost range: $10 per quart.

USE: Adhesive for plastic laminates, wood veneer, vinyl headliners.

Recommended solvent: Acetone or toluene.

Coverage: 60 square feet per quart.

Method of application: Brush.

Drying time: 5 to 10 minutes.

Dangers and precautions: Toxic fumes. Extremely flammable. Use only with adequate ventilation.

SILICONE SEALANT

 Cost range: $6 to $10 per 10-ounce cartridge.

USE: Gaskets. Portlight bedding. Insulation between dissimilar metals. Not for use below the waterline.

 Cleanup: Trim and "roll" off excess after cure.

Cure time: 1 to 7 days.

 Method of application: Snug joint, then tighten after cure.

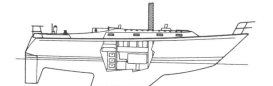

Seal life: 10 to 20 years.

POLYURETHANE SEALANT

 Cost range: $7 to $15 per 10-ounce cartridge.

USE: A permanent sealant for through-hull fittings and hull-to-deck joints. High adhesive strength makes disassembly very difficult. May attack plastics—not recommended for portlights.

 Cleanup: Mineral spirits or kerosene before cure.

Cure time: 2 to 7 days.

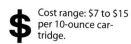 Method of application: Bead between parts to be assembled.

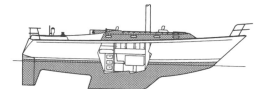

Seal life: 5 to 10 years.

POLYSULFIDE SEALANT

 Cost range: $9 to $13 per 10-ounce cartridge.

USE: All-purpose sealant for bedding deck hardware, through-hull fittings, wood trim, etc. Caulking compound for teak decks. Good flexibility and allows for easier removal of bedded parts. May attack plastics—not recommended for portlights.

 Cleanup: Trim and peel excess after cure.

Cure time: 2 to 7 days.

 Method of application: Snug joint, then tighten after cure.

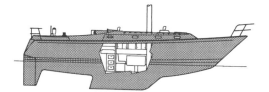

Seal life: 2 to 5 years.

ACETONE

$ Cost range: $6 to $10 per gallon.

USE: Multipurpose solvent. Cleans epoxy, polyester, vinyl, lacquer, polyurethane paints and sealants, and contact cement and other adhesives.

 Dangers and precautions: Avoid skin contact and excessive exposure to vapors. Extremely flammable.

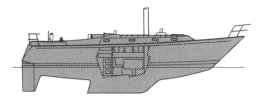

MINERAL SPIRITS

$ Cost range: $4 to $5 per gallon.

USE: Multipurpose thinner and solvent. Can be used to thin most oil-based paints. Good brush cleaner.

 Dangers and precautions: Avoid skin contact. Flammable.

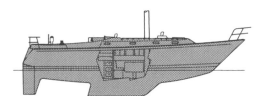

MEK

 Cost range: $8 to $12 per gallon.

USE: Similar uses to acetone, but takes ⅓ longer to evaporate.

 Dangers and precautions: Same as acetone—avoid skin contact and excessive exposure to vapors. Flammable.

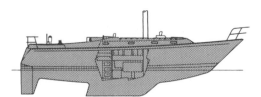

TOLUENE

$ Cost range: $8 to $12 per gallon.

USE: Lacquer thinner. Toluene is also the primary ingredient in brush cleaner. Excellent solvent for resin cleanup. Cleans stains from unpainted surfaces.

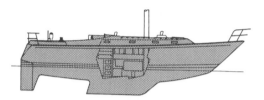

Dangers and precautions: Avoid skin contact and excessive exposure to vapors. Flammable.

CHEMICAL STRIPPER

$ Cost range: $20 to $50 per gallon ($0.75 to $1.50 per square foot).

USE: Dissolves old paint and varnish for easier removal.

Coverage: 30 to 50 square feet per gallon.

Exposure time: 5 minutes to 48 hours.

Method of application: Brush or roller.

Dangers and precautions: Strippers containing methylene chloride pose severe health hazards—skin irritant, carcinogen, increased cardiac risk—and should be avoided. They also attack and damage gelcoat. Select instead a stripper that does not contain methylene chloride. Use hand and eye protection, and have good ventilation.

GOOD RESULTS FROM GOOD TOOLS

Good tools don't necessarily indicate craftsmanship, but craftsmanship always indicates quality tools. Whatever the refinishing job you are planning, do yourself a favor and select only the best-quality tools. Saving $10 on a second-rate brush may well cost you a second-rate finish—don't even consider it.

Not that throw-away brushes and 99-cent roller covers don't belong aboard your boat. *Au contraire*, many of the refinishing jobs aboard, especially prime coats or undercoats, are handled most effectively, economically, and ecologically (thinner is the villain) with toss-away brushes and rollers.

Even cheap brushes vary in quality, and cost is no indicator. Look for brushes dense with well-groomed bristles, then try to pull a few out. A brush that sheds like a St. Bernard in July is no good—period. Throw-away brushes that don't shed are a treasure; if you find some, buy a couple of dozen and hoard them (but paint with one before you invest).

JUDGING BRUSH QUALITY

To evaluate a brush, first examine the bristles. They should all be smooth and straight and flagged at the ends.

Press the bristles against the palm of your hand with a slight twisting motion. They should fan out evenly—not separate into clumps—then spring back into shape when you release them.

Part the bristles to see how they are set into the base. A plug is okay—the space it creates may enable the brush to carry more paint—but the plug should be no more than half the thickness of the base. Make sure the ferrule is solidly attached to the handle.

Remove any loose bristles—all new brushes have a few—by slapping the brush across the heel of your hand. Now give a few single bristles a tug. If any pull out, pick a different brush.

Finally, look for a brush that feels balanced and comfortable in your hand. A glossy coating on the handle will be easier to clean and have a better feel.

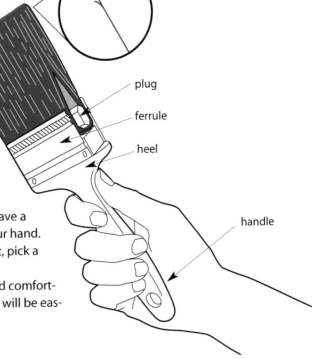

flagged bristle tip

plug

ferrule

heel

handle

THE RIGHT BRUSH FOR THE JOB

Paint-brush bristle is either natural or synthetic. Synthetic bristle—usually nylon or polyester—is favored by house painters because it is less affected by the water-based latex paints they use, but synthetic-bristle brushes have little to recommend them for most of the finishing jobs on a boat.

Most natural-bristle brushes are made from hog bristle, also called China (or Chinese) bristle because China is the largest hog-bristle supplier. Natural bristle is tapered, giving the tip of the brush a light touch that reduces the likelihood of leaving behind visible brush strokes in the finish. For fine finishwork, select a brush that is trimmed to a point or half-oval at the tip—called a "chisel" trim; this gives half the bristles the same "just touching" contact pressure on each stroke.

A good-quality China-bristle brush is adequate for all but the most demanding finishing jobs on a boat. For jobs requiring something better, an ox-hair brush, usually a blend of ox and hog bristle, is not a bad choice, but the best brushes are those made from badger hair. A badger-hair brush is the brush of choice for tipping-out polyurethane or applying the last coat or two of varnish.

Brush width depends on the intended use. Select a 3-inch brush for tipping-out topside paint; a wider brush is more difficult to control and tends to contact the surface of the paint unevenly due to the curvature of the hull. For varnishing handrails and caprails, a 1½-inch brush is about right; accent trim may require a narrower brush, cabin sides and bulkheads a wider one. Your brush should never be wider than the surface you are painting.

Foam brushes have developed a dedicated following, especially for applying varnish, but most find that foam brushes don't deliver the same quality finish as a badger-hair brush. For small jobs the difference in the finish may be less significant than their convenience (no clean-up) and economy (1/20th the cost of badger hair), but don't start a large job with a foam brush without first comparing the results to a badger-hair brush for yourself. If you want to give foam a try, get a Jen polyfoam brush; they have distinctive, varnished handles, and the black foam heads are glued in place.

CLEANING TECHNIQUE

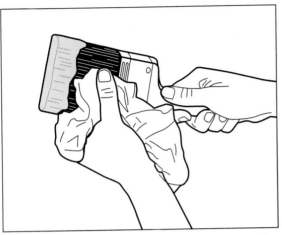

1 Pull the brush through a rag to remove any remaining paint.

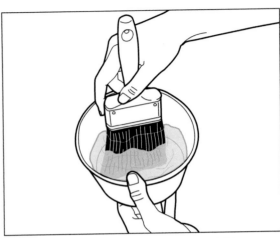

2 Press the brush into a small amount of thinner, twisting the brush slightly to spread the bristles.

3 Brush cleaning is much easier with a brush spinner—available for under $20 from most housepaint suppliers. Rinse and spin the brush several times, the final time in fresh thinner, to get it completely clean.

4 Comb the brush—any kind of comb will do—before you wrap the bristles.

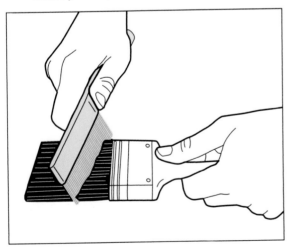

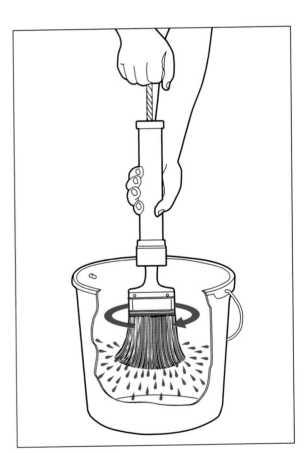

REUSE THE THINNER

WRAPPING THE BRISTLES

A strip of paper grocery bag is ideal for wrapping a paintbrush. Pre-crease the paper down the middle, then place the tip of the brush just shy of the crease. A rubber band around the wrap at the ferrule will hold it in place and preserve the shape of the bristles. Throw-away brushes cleaned for reuse can be wrapped adequately in a folded paper towel.

ROLLER COVERS

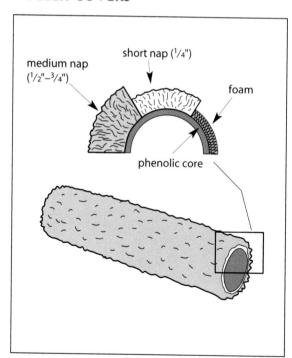

medium nap ($1/2$"–$3/4$")

short nap ($1/4$")

foam

phenolic core

Roller covers come in an array of quality, sizes, and nap lengths. For boat work, select only short nap (for antifouling bottom paint) or foam (for everything else). The one exception is molded-in nonskid, where a medium-nap roller may prove more effective. (A medium-nap roller might also be useful for coating roving-textured bilge and locker spaces, but brush application may be better.)

Cheap roller covers are adequate for bottom paint—you are not going to reuse them. Just be sure the nap is dense enough to hold paint and that it is firmly attached to the core.

For topside paint and other finishing uses, select the best foam rollers you can find. The aggressive solvents in polyurethane paints will dissolve standard foam roller covers; special covers with *phenolic cores* are required. To avoid unexpected disasters, make these the only kind of foam rollers aboard. Choose the 9-inch length for painting the hull; for the deck, 7-inch rollers may be handier.

CAGE-TYPE ROLLER HANDLE

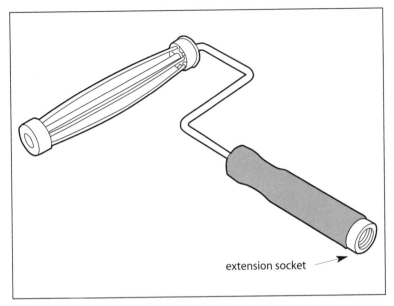

extension socket

Bird-cage-type frames make changing covers easier, and the frame gives the cover needed support in the middle. Three-inch frames are available for trim work.

CUTTING ROLLER COVERS FOR SPECIFIC NEEDS

For small areas such as boottops and narrow sections of the deck, shorter roller covers can be easier to control and do a better job. Cut standard 9-inch covers with a hacksaw to any required size. A 3-inch frame can be used with covers of various lengths.

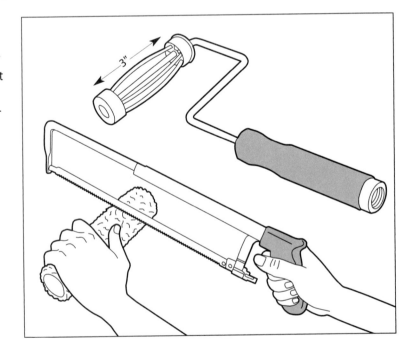

3"

SANDPAPER TYPES AND USES

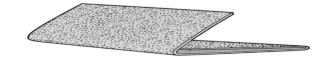

TYPE OF PAPER	IDENTIFYING COLOR	USES	SUGGESTED GRITS/COMMENTS	
Aluminum oxide	Tan or brown	Good all-around sandpaper	60D—rough sanding and paint removal; 120C—surface preparation for painting; 220A—between-coat sanding	The most useful paper; have plenty aboard
Emery cloth	Black	None	None	Except to prepare aluminum for paint, has no refinishing use; good for polishing metal and sharpening plane irons
Flint	Light beige or light gray	None	None	Dime-store sandpaper; use-less—never buy flint paper
Garnet	Red	Hand sanding fine woodwork	None	Expensive and will not stand up to machine sanding; leave to the cabinetmakers
Silicon carbide (open coat)	White	Fine finishing paper; the best choice for sanding disks	180A—between-coat sanding; 400A—pre-polish sanding	Cuts well and relatively long-lasting; good choice for fine sanding
Silicon carbide (closed coat)	Black	Waterproof paper for wet sanding	340A—wet sanding between coats of polyurethane; 600A—pre-polish wet sanding	Called wet-or-dry sandpaper; wet sanding yields the finest finish

Grit numbers roughly represent the number of grains of grit per square inch—the higher the number the smaller the grains must be, so the higher the grit, the finer the finish.

The letter code following the grit designation—i.e., 60D or 400A—indicates the weight of the paper. A is the lightest and F is the heaviest (D is the heaviest commonly available for typical boat applications).

Sandpaper is available in four common grades—cabinet, production, premium, and industrial. Production paper—the grade most general suppliers carry—is adequate for all boat-refinishing jobs.

"Closed-coat" paper has the entire surface covered with abrasive; "open-coat" leaves the paper about 40% uncoated to reduce loading—clogging. Closed-coat is fine for wood and for hand sanding, but for reasonable paper life when power sanding, especially for sanding paints and varnish, select an open-coat paper.

Sandpaper is much cheaper if you buy it by the sleeve (50 or 100 sheets, depending on the grit) from a supply house. Per sheet price will be about half the individual sheet price at hardware stores.

DISK SANDER

A high-speed disk sander can make short work of paint removal. The disk sander has traditionally been used to quickly sand boat bottoms for their annual application of antifouling paint, but more stringent pollution requirements have already outlawed this method of bottom-paint removal in many parts of the country.

Do not try to substitute an electric drill with a polishing/sanding disk; a sander runs five times as fast and is designed for the continuous use and side loading associated with sanding. In the hands of a skillful operator, a disk sander is capable of extremely fine work in an amazingly short amount of time, but in less skilled hands it can just as quickly do a great deal of damage. A foam-padded disk allows the paper to adapt to a boat's curved surfaces and makes the sander more forgiving. If you can't find a padded disk sander, a glued-on pad will work fine. Using a disk sander well requires practice and concentration.

SANDING BLOCK

Almost all refinishing jobs require some hand sanding. To ensure a uniform surface, the sandpaper should be backed by some type of block, not the irregular tips of fingers. For flat surfaces a wooden block works well; for curved surfaces choose a rubber block or a flexible float. Attach the sandpaper to the blocks with disk adhesive.

ORBITAL SANDER

Unlike the disk sander, the orbital sander is almost risk free. No matter how inexperienced the operator, the only danger to the surface is perhaps sanding the finish off sharp edges. Despite its benign character, the orbital sander is the boat refinisher's greatest boon, saving hours on surface preparation.

Orbital sanders, also called finishing sanders, come in half-sheet and quarter-sheet models. A half-sheet sander may allow for the sanding of large areas a bit faster, but the quarter-sheet model (pictured), known as a *palm sander*, is more versatile and easier on the operator (you!). A finishing sander is an essential tool for all but the smallest refinishing projects. If you don't already own an orbital sander, buy one, and select a palm sander when you do.

FOLDING SANDPAPER FOR HAND SANDING

Some finger-backed sanding is likely. Fold the sandpaper as shown to keep the paper from sanding itself and to provide three fresh faces from each piece of paper. Wearing cloth garden gloves—the kind with the hard dots—will save the tips of your fingers.

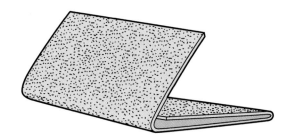

TIP: For heavy removal, such as bottom preparation, consider a random-bit sander. This useful tool combines the operations of both disk and orbital sanders.

SCRAPERS

When you repaint the bottom, scraping the old antifouling paint (with or without the application of a chemical paint remover) can be quicker than sanding and far easier on the lungs—yours and everybody else's.

For this particular task, use a 2½- or 3-inch hook scraper. If you aren't painting the bottom, leave hook scrapers at home with the latex paint and the synthetic-bristle brushes. The appropriate scrapers for all other boat refinishing are cabinet scrapers.

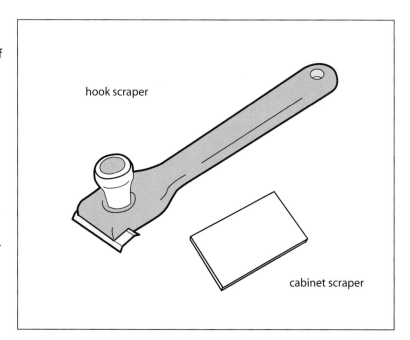

hook scraper

cabinet scraper

Learning to use a cabinet scraper effectively can save you a great deal of sanding (with expensive paper) and give you a much smoother surface. Scrapers are especially effective on wood surfaces prior to varnishing.

Hold the cabinet scraper tilted slightly toward you—at about 75° with the surface—and draw the scraper toward you. The blade should produce very fine shavings; if not, it needs to be sharpened.

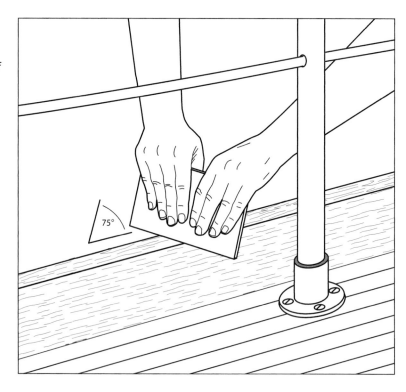

75°

SHARPENING A SCRAPER

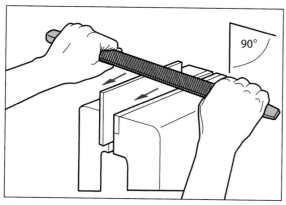

1 Draw a mill file across the edge to square it.

2 Whet each edge on an oil stone. If you are sharpening a hook-scraper blade, stop right here; never burnish the blade of a hook scraper.

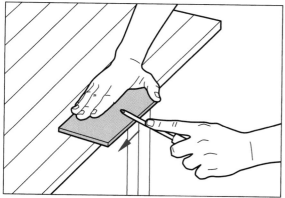

3 Burnish the sides of a cabinet scraper flat with a burnishing tool or the round shank of a Phillips screwdriver.

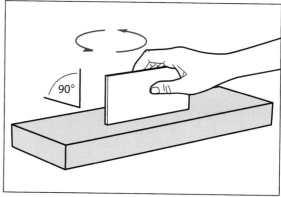

4 With heavy pressure, burnish the edges at 90°.

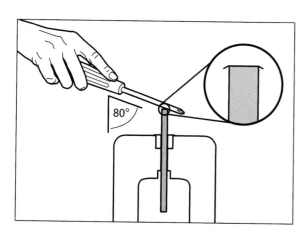

5 Tilt the shank about 10° and burnish one corner of the edge to 80°. Tilt the shank the other way and burnish the opposite edge. When you have burnished the entire perimeter, you will have eight fresh cutting edges.

RAGS

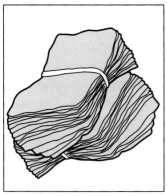

For any finishing project, you can never have too many rags. The best rags are cotton diapers—very absorbent and completely dye free. Marine suppliers and boatyard stores sell them by the pound.

DISPOSABLE COVERALLS AND CAP

Old clothes are the usual painting uniform, but for less than $10 you can buy a paper-like coverall that will provide better dust (and fiberglass) protection. A painter's cap will protect your hair and/or scalp.

GLOVES, GOGGLES, AND RESPIRATOR

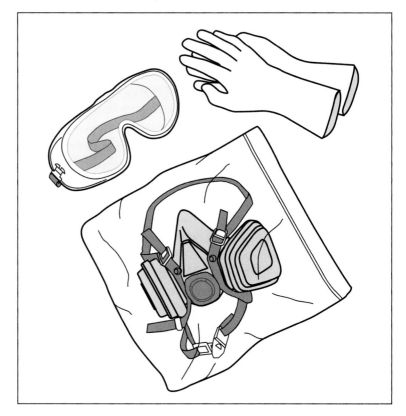

Some paints, especially bottom paints and two-part polyurethanes, require a higher degree of protection than mere coveralls. Avoid skin, eye, and lung exposure to their chemical components or their fumes. Be sure the gloves you buy are unaffected by the solvents you will be using.

A paper dust mask is inadequate protection from toxic bottom-paint dust—buy a comfortable respirator. None of the coatings you will be using are especially dangerous (assuming you are not spraying polyurethane), but as long as you have a respirator, use it—you'll need those lungs when you're 80. Replace the cartridges in your respirator if they aren't fresh, and replace them again as soon as you smell fumes (organic cartridges) or breathing requires any noticeable effort (dust/mist filters). Keep your organic respirator in a sealed plastic bag when you aren't using it.

PREPARATION

Genius is one percent inspiration and ninety-nine percent perspiration.
—Thomas Alva Edison

Brilliance is one percent application and ninety-nine percent preparation. Most people seem to think that a coat or two of paint will cover—meaning hide— all but the most serious surface flaws. Perhaps the source of this fiction is experience with interior wall paints—thick, rubbery coatings that dry to a flat (nonreflective) finish. Closer inspection will reveal that even these don't hide gouges and depressions, they merely camouflage them with uniform color.

It is not just color but gloss that we prize in a boat finish. The paints and varnishes used on a boat, with the exception of bottom paint, are formulated to provide that gem-like brilliance. Such high-gloss finishes accentuate every underlying surface flaw.

The bad news, then, is that your finish can never be better than the surface it is applied to; but there is good news. Because the gelcoat was originally sprayed into a highly polished mold, surface flaws on fiberglass boats are usually limited and easy to correct. As for brightwork, sanding the wood to a perfectly smooth surface—all that is required for that perfect varnish coating— is not difficult, but because the varnish is essentially clear, the wood must also have a uniform color. This second part presents more of a challenge.

When you prepare the surface, a lick and a promise will not be good enough. It will have to be mirror-smooth before you coat it if you want it to be mirror-smooth afterward. Every extra little bit you put into surface preparation will pay dividends in how the final finish looks, so don't cut corners. But don't get crazy either: it's a boat, not a Steinway.

REMOVING TRIM AND HARDWARE

Removing as much hardware and trim as practical from the surface to be painted makes painting much easier—you can roll right over the spot where the bow cleats are mounted rather than carefully painting around them with a brush. The quality of the finish will also be enhanced since it is much harder to get a stroke-free finish from paint applied with a brush than from rolled-on paint lightly tipped with a brush.

Removing hardware and trim also eliminates many "edges" where the paint stops. Paint failure usually begins at these edges, so having the paint skin extend under bedded hardware is best.

Bungs—wooden plugs—in a piece of trim mean it is screwed in place. If the bungs were set dry or with varnish, you can remove them by drilling a small-diameter hole in the center and running a screw through it; when the point stops against the underlying screw head, continuing to turn the screw lifts the bung. Unfortunately this can also lift the wood around the hole. A safer method is to use a bit just slightly smaller than the bung to drill out most of it, then collapse the remaining ring of plug with a small chisel.

Deck-mounted handrails are often bolted in place from inside the cabin. Sometimes the bolts are hidden by trim, matching interior handrails, or a removable headliner. If the handrails are mounted with screws, replace them with bolts when you reinstall the handrails.

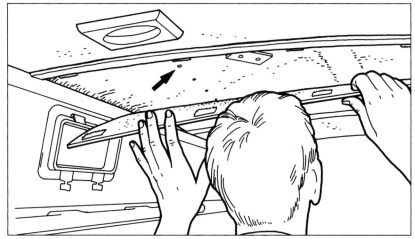

While painting the deck is a good time to replace crazed portlights and to service and re-bed opening portholes. Frames are usually through-bolted, but if the mounting screws thread into the frame, expect some difficulty in removing them without damaging the threaded socket. Drilling and through-bolting may be necessary to re-install the frame (see *Sailboat Hull and Deck Repair* for more information).

TIP: Interior wood trim is often attached to plywood or formica with finishing nails. Inspection may reveal where the holes are patched. To release the trim drive the nails all the way through it with a nail set. Glued trim can be lifted with a sharpened drywall knife driven under the trim. Lift both sides of a corner molding before trying to remove the piece.

Cleats and stanchion bases should be through-bolted. Make sure the screwdriver is the correct size for the slot. To run less risk of damaging the slot, release the fastener by loosening the nut underneath, not by turning the bolt with the screwdriver. An open-end wrench on the square shank of the screwdriver can make holding it against the torque of the wrench on the nut easier.

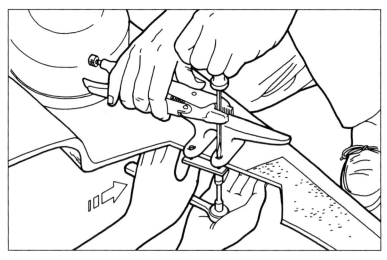

CLEANING

Preparation always begins with cleaning the surface. Use liquid laundry detergent (like Wisk) for most of your cleaning jobs. For better results, boost your detergent solution with trisodium phosphate (TSP), available in any hardware store. If the surface has any mildew, add a cup of chlorine bleach (Clorox) per gallon of water to the mix, and let the surface stand wet for about 30 minutes, then wash it again without the bleach. Be sure you rinse the surface completely free of all detergent residue.

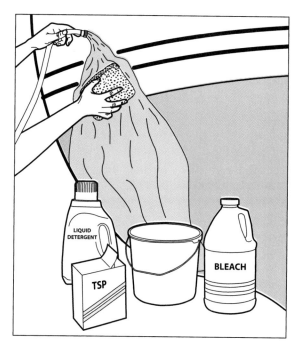

DEGREASING

Oil or grease on the surface will ruin the finish, and soap solutions may fail to remove these. Use a rag soaked with MEK to degrease the surface. (Acetone can also be used, but MEK evaporates more slowly to hold the contaminants in suspension longer. For wiping bare wood, the quick-flashing acetone will be less likely to raise the grain.)

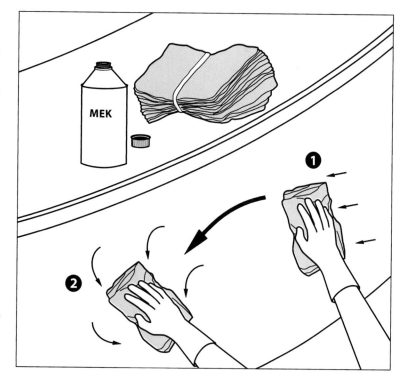

Wet the surface thoroughly with the solvent-soaked rag, then "sweep" the rag in one direction—like sweeping crumbs from a counter—to pick up the suspended contaminants. Turn the folded rag often, taking care not to reuse any areas. Change the rag when all areas have been used.

REMOVING ANY TRACE OF SILICONE

Silicone on the surface is just as ruinous as grease, and almost all boat waxes and polishes for the last 20 years have contained silicone. Even if the surface has never been waxed, the mold was, and the gelcoat almost certainly still retains traces of the mold release wax. Always dewax the surface *before* any sanding; otherwise the sandpaper drags the silicone into the scratches and it becomes very difficult to remove.

Silicone is resistant to detergents and many solvents—that's what makes it such a popular wax additive. *All* bare fiberglass, and all painted surfaces if there is any possibility that they may have been waxed, must be wiped down with a silicone-removing solvent—called wash, prep, or dewaxer by various manufacturers.

Soak a folded cloth with the wax remover and wipe it slowly across the surface in a single direction, again in a sweeping pattern. Change the contact surface of the cloth regularly.

CHECKING THE OLD PAINT WITH SOLVENT

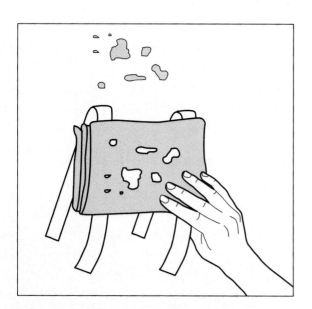

Check previously painted surfaces for compatibility by applying a rag soaked with the solvent for the new paint to the surface and leaving it for 10 minutes. If it lifts the surface, the old paint will have to be removed or sealed with a conversion coat—a paint or primer with a less aggressive solvent system. Perform this test in an inconspicuous spot.

CHECKING THE OLD PAINT WITH TAPE

No matter how tenaciously your new paint adheres to the old, if the old paint has lost its grip, early failure is guaranteed. If your old paint fails this test, it all has to come off. On the bright side, it may not be all that hard to remove.

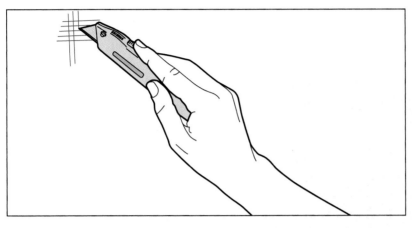

1 Score the old paint.

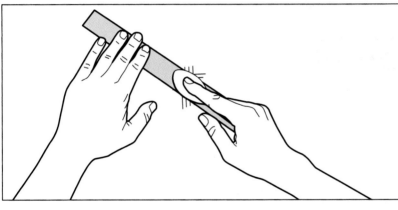

2 Buff down a strip of cellophane tape.

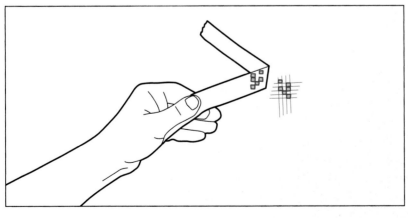

3 Peel the tape up with a jerk.

USING CHEMICAL STRIPPER

Gelcoat and paint are chemically similar, so many paint strippers also attack gelcoat. Select a stripper specifically labeled for use on fiberglass, and do not leave it on the surface longer than recommended.

Most strippers contain methylene chloride—read the label. Methylene chloride is extremely hazardous—a known carcinogen with a rogues' gallery of other serious effects on the heart, lungs, liver, and nervous system. Protect yourself with gloves, goggles, and an organic respirator.

1 Coat only as much surface area as you can scrape in five minutes.

2 Wait the specified time—usually 5 to 10 minutes.

3 Remove lifted paint with a putty knife or a hook scraper.

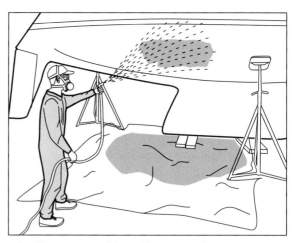

4 Rinse away residue with water or the recommended proprietary wash.

POWER SANDING WITH A DISK SANDER

No sanding tool removes material faster than the disk sander. A disk with a foam pad will make the sander much more effective for the rounded surfaces of boats. For bottom-paint removal, select 80-grit open-coat aluminum-oxide sanding disks. For finer work, use 180- or 220-grit open-coat paper. The disk sander is not recommended for stripping old varnish because of the risk to the wood.

Always tilt the disk slightly so that only one side is in contact with the surface. Use only light pressure; the disk sander gets its effectiveness from speed, not force. Moving the sander rapidly across the surface is generally the best technique, i.e., several quick passes rather than a single slow one. Care and concentration are required to prevent damage to the surface. Letting the spinning disk linger too long in one spot also heats the finish, making it soften and tend to load the paper.

A random-orbit sander can be a good compromise—slower, but safer. Hold the disk of a random-orbit sander flat against the surface.

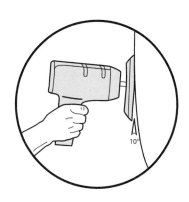

"SAFE" STRIPPER—A BETTER ALTERNATIVE

A NEW TYPE OF CHEMICAL STRIPPER—the so-called "safe stripper"—is a less hazardous alternative. Safe strippers contain no methylene chloride. They are not Evian, of course—they still contain toxic chemicals—but the health hazard for these products is typically classified as only moderate compared to severe for any product containing methylene chloride.

The most effective safe strippers rely on N-methyl-2-pyrolidone. This type of stripper is actually more effective at removing paint than methylene chloride and has no effect on gelcoat. The only drawback to these strippers is that they take much longer to do the job. They must be left on the surface as long as 48 hours. Cost range for these products is $.50 to $1.00 per square foot.

USING A PALM SANDER

No precautions are required to use an orbital palm sander. Material removal is deliberate and smooth. This is the best tool for preparing a surface for paint or varnish, and it makes short work of between-coat sanding.

As a general rule, preparing a surface for an initial coat of paint or varnish calls for 120-grit paper. The scratches left by this grit are fine enough not to show through the finish while still providing adequate "tooth" for the paint or varnish. For wood in poor condition, start with 60-grit, then 80-grit, and finally 120-grit. This will be smooth enough for teak or mahogany, but harder woods like walnut and oak may benefit from an additional sanding pass with 180- or even 220-grit.

You can make the job go faster if you load the sander with three or four sheets of paper at a time. When the surface layer stops creating dust, slice it away with a knife to reveal fresh paper.

Use 180- or 220-grit paper for between-coat sanding of both varnish and paint. The exception to this is two-part polyurethane, which needs to be wet sanded with 340-grit wet-or-dry paper between coats. NEVER WET SAND WITH AN ELECTRIC SANDER. However, the same effect can be achieved by misting the surface with a spritzer bottle and running the sander over the misted area. But keep in mind that water and electricity are a deadly combination, so take care to keep the sander dry. Rubber gloves are recommended as a precaution.

The high speeds of palm sanders—about 14,000 rpm—can result in an ear-damaging shriek. Ear plugs are available from any drugstore for about a buck; buy a pair and use them. Not only will they save your hearing, but by eliminating the fatigue that accompanies such an assault on the senses, they actually make the job much easier.

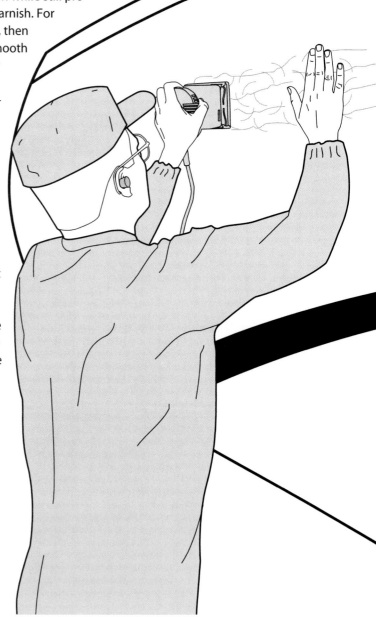

HAND SANDING

1 Machine sanding is not always possible: access may be restricted, the shape of the surface may be irregular, or the job may simply be a small one. When hand sanding wood in preparation for any kind of coating, always sand with the grain; cross-grain sanding will leave visible scratches.

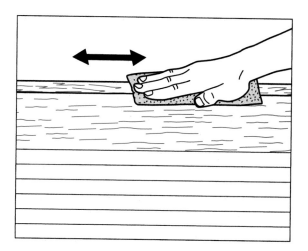

2 Sanding slightly across the grain with a float can be effective for fairing wood with ridges or "wows" (depressions). Starting with 80-grit paper, limit the angle off the grain line to no more than 30˚. Sand diagonally across the grain from both directions before finishing with the grain, using 100- and 120-grit paper.

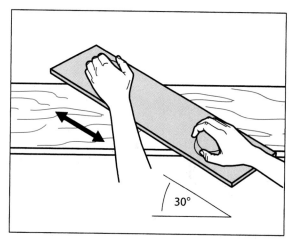

3 For hand sanding gelcoat and painted surfaces, direction is not important. The main concerns are to avoid introducing wows into the surface—a rubber sanding block is usually a good idea—and to select a grit fine enough not to leave scratches that will show through the coating. Use 120-grit paper if you are applying an undercoat, 220 if the coat will be the top one.

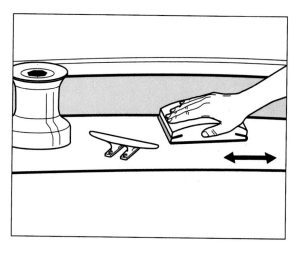

CLEANING RAW WOOD AFTER SANDING

1 The most effective way to remove dust from raw wood is with a vacuum cleaner and a brush attachment.

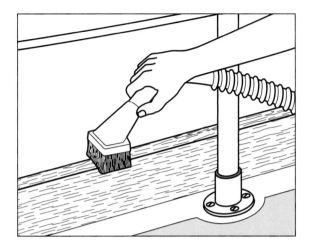

2 If that is unavailable, use a vigorous motion with a dense (and clean) paintbrush or shopbrush to sweep the dust out of the grain.

3 Finally, wipe the wood in a single direction with a cloth soaked with the thinner for the coating you are about to apply; using a commercial tack cloth can introduce substances incompatible with some coatings.

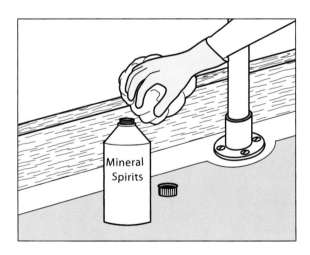

CLEANING FINISHED SURFACES

Flushing with water is the best way to remove dust from painted and varnished surfaces. Use a clean cloth to scrub the surface while flooding with a hose. When the surface is completely dry—watch out for water collecting in cracks, crevices, and joints—wipe it a final time with a solvent-soaked cloth before applying the coating.

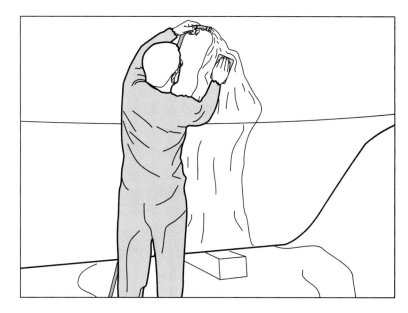

WETTING DOWN AROUND THE PAINT AREA

To keep the dust down, it is almost always a good idea to wet down the immediate area before varnishing or painting. Below decks, misting cushions, counters, and cabin soles with a fine spray from a spritzer can help give fresh varnish a chance to skin dust-free.

One caution: when applying two-part polyurethane, be careful about wetting the area on a hot, still day. The water may "steam," raising the humidity around the boat, and causing you problems with this moisture-sensitive paint. Any breeze—the reason you need to wet the ground anyway—should prevent any localized increase in humidity.

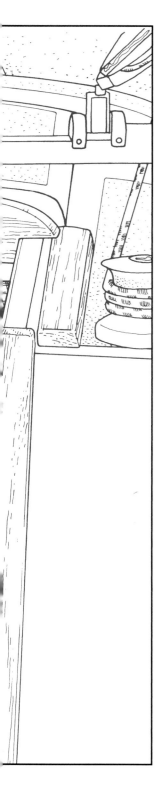

INSIDE THE CABIN

If you have limited experience applying paint or varnish, start your project in the interior of your boat. You will find plenty of surfaces that will benefit from a fresh coat of paint no matter how lubberly the application. For example, the area beneath bunk and settee cushions, often dirty, water-stained, or mildewed, presents a convenient surface to work on your roller and brush techniques. The fresh paint will protect the wood regardless of how it is applied, and any mistakes you make will be hidden by the cushions.

The interior of lockers and cabinets also provide risk-free surfaces for getting comfortable with the process and tools of refinishing. Brighten raw fiberglass lockers with a coat of paint. White is a good choice, but selecting a pastel can add an unexpected bit of cheer. To make the most of this effect, paint the inside of the doors and the underside of the access hatches.

Choose *alkyd* enamel for interior refinishing. Select low-luster exterior trim house paint; it is tough, washable, less expensive than marine paints, and available in an infinite selection of colors. It is perfect for lockers, bilges, and under-cushion furniture. Many boatowners like it for bulkheads as well.

For bulkheads covered with a plastic laminate, a roller-applied coating of single-part polyurethane—there is little need for the extra durability of two-part paint—can yield a surface that is indistinguishable in appearance from new laminate. Adding a little flattener generally produces a more pleasing effect.

Wood trim below decks may be maintained oiled or varnished with equal success. For oiling, choose *lemon oil* (not lemon polish or lemon wax). It won't stand up to the rigors of exterior exposure—you need linseed oil or tung oil for that—but lemon oil is wonderful below. It feeds the wood, replacing natural oils, it is poison to mildew, and it smells good.

If you plan to varnish the interior wood, choose polyurethane varnish often called urethane). Urethane varnish generally doesn't do well on exterior wood, but for interior use it is superior to spar varnish. It provides a harder, more durable surface; protected from the sun it can last indefinitely. Polyurethane's toughness makes it the best choice for a varnished sole, and the polyurethane is not as slick as oil-based varnish when it gets wet.

Remove trim or protect it with tape. Check compatibility of old paint with a thinner-soaked rag. Scrub the surface and bleach if mildew is present. (Adding bleach to the cleaning solution is almost always a good idea on a boat.) Set hatches, drawers, and doors aside to paint separately. Sand with 120-grit paper and wipe the surface dust-free with mineral spirits (if you are painting with alkyd enamel).

POURING PAINT AND RESEALING THE CONTAINER

1 Opening a paint or varnish can with a screwdriver will distort it and can prevent it from resealing; always use a paint-can opener. If you stir varnish at all, do it slowly and carefully to avoid introducing bubbles. Paint, on the other hand, can be stirred vigorously and must be stirred until there is no difference between the paint pulled up by the bottom of your stirrer and that at the top.

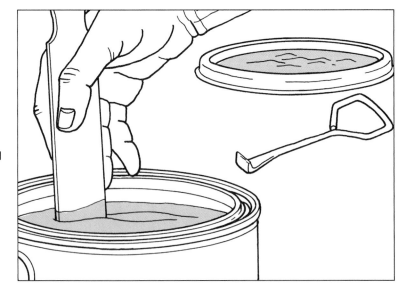

2 Never paint out of the can the paint comes in; that causes the paint to thicken from extended air exposure, and you introduce contaminants—loose bristles, dried paint, dust, and insects—to all your paint. Pour up as much as you will use in an hour or so into a convenient-size container—a clean discard from the kitchen or galley will do, or for a few cents buy one of the plastic paint buckets commercially available.

3 Close the container as soon as you have poured your paint. To make sure the can seals properly and that you can get it open next time, always clean the paint out of the can rim before replacing the lid. A ½-inch throw-away brush makes short work of this essential task, and it can be kept soft in a little thinner until the job is done. Press the lid closed with your thumbs—**do not hammer it closed** unless you are using a rubber mallet.

may compromise lid seal

USING A PAINT FILTER

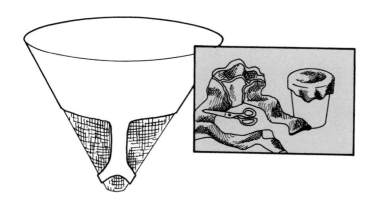

Even sealed paint can "skin," and broken bits of this semi-dried paint will ruin your finish. Filter all paint and varnish before you use it. Cone-shaped mesh filters can be purchased for 15 or 20 cents, or you can accomplish the same thing for free by stretching a section of discarded pantyhose over your bucket before pouring the paint into it.

THINNING

Thinning is the secret. If your paint is thinned perfectly, any numskull can get a great finish. A little off, and you can compensate some with good brush and roller technique. Get too wide of the mark and you may be driven to cut off an ear.

It needn't come to that. Proper thinning just requires patience.

If the brush or roller drags, the paint needs thinning. Too little thinner will prevent the paint from leveling, showing every brush stroke. Add too much thinner and the paint sags and runs, and much of the gloss will be lost. The trick is to sneak up on the perfect viscosity by adding a little thinner at a time and testing the results. Thin only the paint you are using, never your supply.

Thinner evaporates quickly, so the flow characteristics of your paint can change as you use it, particularly on a hot day. If that begins to happen, stir a few drops of thinner into your batch periodically, but remember that the less paint you have left, the less thinner it will take to achieve the desired effect. Go s-l-o-w-l-y.

With fresh paint, never add more than a capful of thinner at a time. You will spill far less thinner if you pour it with the spout up. Stir the thinner in thoroughly, then try the new mix on a test surface—a piece of glass is ideal. Keep adding a capful, mixing, and testing until the paint flows out the way you want. If it starts to sag or run (your test surface must be vertical), you have added too much thinner. Correct this by adding paint, but keep in mind that it will take a cupful of paint to offset the effects of a capful of thinner.

PAINTING

BRUSHING TECHNIQUES

1 Dip the *tip* of the brush into the paint—never deeper than ⅓ the bristle length.

2 Unload one side by dragging the brush over an edge.

For small jobs, the side of the bucket will serve; for larger painting projects, a piece of stiff wire (coat-hanger wire is perfect) installed across the bucket through a pair of punched holes will prevent the paint from finding its way to the outside of the bucket. A straight wire also introduces fewer bubbles into varnish.

3 Apply the paint—loaded side first—just beyond the wet edge. Use several straight back-and-forth strokes to join the paint to the previously painted area and to spread it evenly. You can brush enamel as much as you like, but when applying varnish, limit your strokes to the absolute minimum required. A good varnisher will try to use only three or four—one to apply, one or two to spread, and one to finish.

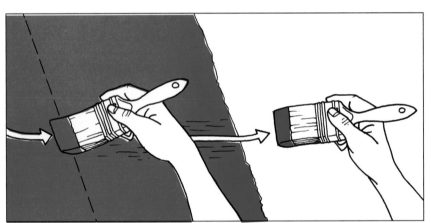

4 Finish by blending the new paint into the previous brush load. The usual method is to brush into the previously painted area, lifting the brush while the stroke is still in motion, but the best finish is achieved if the final stroke is outward. Start this stroke 6 inches behind the old wet edge, but don't let the bristles actually touch the paint until a couple of inches behind it. Think of landing an airplane—very softly. Continue this light stroke to the new wet edge. The advantage of this outward stroke is it pushes excess paint forward rather than back onto the previous application.

USING A PAINT ROLLER

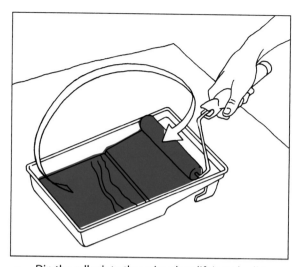

1 Dip the roller into the paint, then lift it and roll it **down** the slope to even the load and unload any excess paint. To avoid end tracks, unload the ends by tilting the roller and rolling each end down the slope with heavy pressure.

2 Apply the paint initially with a W or M motion, then continue to roll the surface until the coverage is complete and uniform. The direction of your strokes is not important—whatever is most convenient.

TIPPING FOR A SMOOTHER FINISH

Rolling leaves most paints with a slight orange-peel-like texture. This texture, similar to that found on many plastic laminates, can give an attractive, light-diffusing surface particularly suitable for bulkheads. For a smoother finish, such as a hull application, tip the rolled-on paint immediately with a first-quality brush. Tipping involves no more than dragging the tip of a dry brush—meaning not dipped in paint—over the surface immediately after the paint has been rolled on.

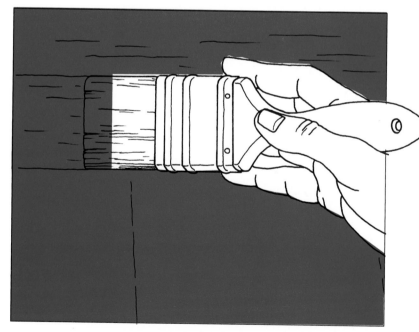

One or two strokes using the lightest touch will turn the surface to glass. Touch and lift with the stroke in motion to keep from introducing stroke marks.

KEEPING TOOLS AND PAINT FRESH

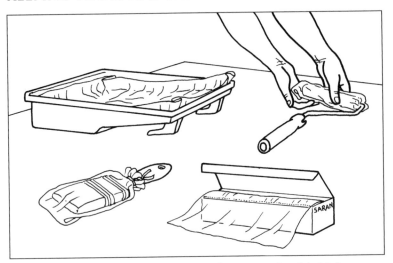

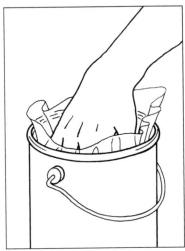

1 When you need a break, wrap your roller cover or brush in kitchen wrap—don't bind the nap or bristles tightly, just seal out the air. Keep the paint in your tray or bucket fresh by pressing a piece of plastic wrap onto the surface.

2 A piece of plastic wrap on the surface of leftover paint and pressed against the sides of the can will insulate the paint from air in the can and greatly extend its shelf life. Peel the plastic from the surface, and filter the paint to use it.

PREPARING PLASTIC LAMINATE FOR PAINTING

A HUGE NUMBER OF BOATS have been delivered with bulkheads covered with plastic laminate. Too often that laminate has been in a woodgrain pattern. Too much wood already tends to make boat cabins cave-dark anyway, and then for it to lack the warmth, texture, and smell of real wood is barely tolerable. If this sounds like elitist drivel to you, for your next wedding anniversary try giving a bouquet of plastic long-stem roses. You will quickly change your view on the importance of aesthetics.

The one good characteristic of woodgrain plastic laminate—of all plastic laminate, for that matter—is that it makes an excellent substratum for paint. The surface of plastic laminate is melamine resin (over a photograph of real wood, in case you wondered). Melamine resin is a tough, heat-resistant plastic. It is also slippery—the quality that gives it its legendary stain-resistance.

For paint to get a good grip on melamine, that slippery surface has to be roughened. Load your palm sander with 80-grit paper and thoroughly sand all the laminate to be painted to a uniform dullness, changing to fresh paper whenever the sander quits generating white plastic dust. Switch to 120-grit paper and sand the entire surface again to provide a final surface with adequate tooth, but with scratches fine enough to be completely hidden by the paint.

Select a single-part polyurethane paint—white is the traditional color for painted bulkheads—and roll it on with a foam roller. If you are painting with white, or any light color, the roller will leave a slightly textured finish; tipping with a brush will be unnecessary, and perhaps even undesirable. Practice on a scrap of laminate or the laminate surface of a discarded kitchen cabinet or piece of furniture.

PLASTIC LAMINATES

Decorative plastic laminate (often called Formica after the best-known brand name) provides an excellent "coating" for flat (and some curved) surfaces, and it is used extensively in boats of all types and price ranges. It is a tough, durable material with a life-span measured not in years but decades. Plastic laminate is usually replaced or re-covered not because it has worn out (though it does fade) but because the owner wants a different color or pattern.

The long life of plastic laminate offers a challenge in its selection. Trendy patterns may look great this year and next, but in five years they will date your boat. Similarly, a countertop that just matches the fuchsia in your settee cushions may quickly lose its appeal when it comes time to reupholster. This is not to say you should always select neutral colors—five years of pizzazz beats twenty years of blah hands down—but make your selection with the knowledge that if you select wisely, you will do this only once.

There are other countertop materials—tile, stainless steel, Corian—but the durability, simplicity, and light weight of plastic laminate, combined with a nearly unlimited selection of colors and patterns, have made it the default choice for most galley counters. The laminate was originally applied to an underlay of plywood when your boat was constructed, and if you are building a counter from scratch, that is how you should do it. Most boatowners, however, will not be changing the counter, just the surface, and in this instance the new laminate is installed right over the old—the procedure detailed here.

Decorative laminate typically comes in horizontal grade ($1/16$-inch thick), tough enough to shrug off the hard use of countertops, and in vertical grade ($1/32$-inch), ideal for cabinet faces and bulkheads. A standard sheet is 4 feet by 8 feet, but 10-foot sheets are commonly available, and even larger sizes can be obtained. The sheet size you need is determined by the size of the counter—avoid any seams in the top if at all possible.

Plastic laminate on bulkheads is far more durable than paint. The traditional color for yacht bulkheads has long been white. The main reason for this is probably that white bulkheads give the confines of a cramped cabin a more spacious appearance. It also makes a tremendous difference in how light the cabin is, both in the daytime and with the cabin lights on at night. Because these benefits are so desirable, white bulkheads have never gone out of style. White bulkheads are hard to fault, and accented with wood trim, they give the interior of almost any boat the classic look of a fine yacht.

TOOLS

LAMINATE WORK requires a few special tools. Special saber-saw blades without any set to the teeth minimize chipping. A router fitted with a laminate-trimming bit makes short work of edge trimming. Use a file to trim edges with limited access. Tin snips will cut vertical grade laminate. Rough cut horizontal grade by scoring and breaking. A rubber roller helps ensure a secure bond.

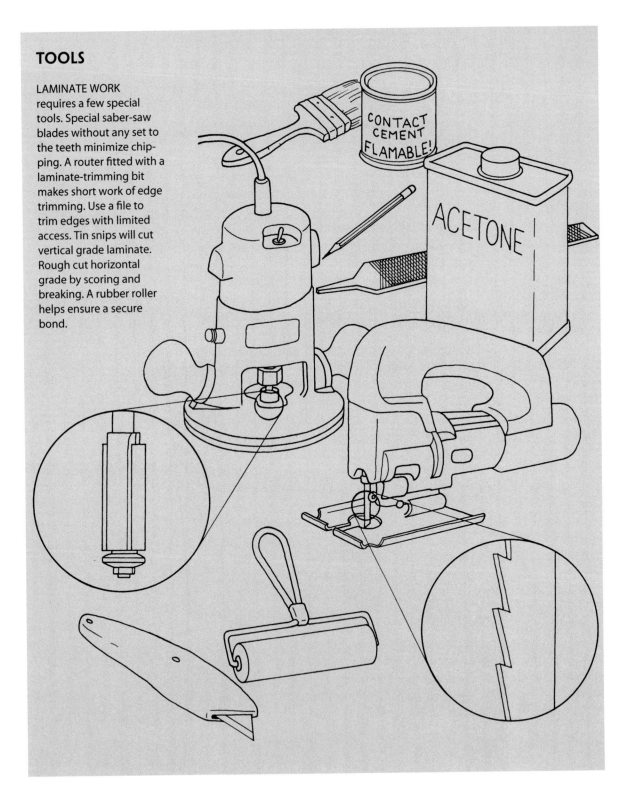

CHECKING FOR ADHESION OF THE OLD LAMINATE

The only precaution for installing new laminate over old is to make sure the bond between the old laminate and the plywood beneath it is still good.

This is rarely a problem, but if you find bond failure, the old laminate must be removed.

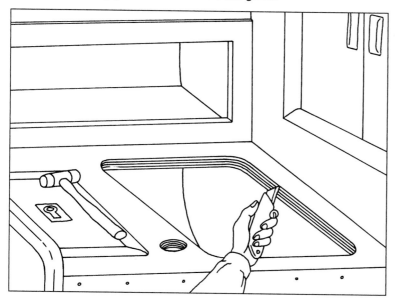

A sharpened drywall knife worked carefully between the laminate and the wood will usually lift the laminate with minimal damage to the wood. A heat gun can help anyplace the adhesion is still good.

If the surface looks okay, tap it with a plastic mallet or the handle of a screwdriver and listen for any sound differences that indicate bond failure. A bubble under the old laminate is an obvious failure. Check edges exposed by the removal of appliances or trim with the tip of a knife, but be careful not to chip the laminate; you are just checking to see if it is loose, not trying to loosen it.

DISK SANDING THE SURFACE

To give the new laminate a good bonding surface, thoroughly sand the old surface with 80-grit paper. This is one of the few instances in the curved environment of a boat where a belt sander can be used to advantage, but a disk sander will do the job just as well and is probably easier to handle.

Keep the sander moving in order not to introduce highs and lows. The *entire* surface must be uniformly dull: hand sand inside corners and any other areas inaccessible to the power sander. Fill any holes or surface damage with an epoxy filler, and sand the repairs smooth. Don't expect the laminate (especially vertical grade) to bridge voids; any significant underlying flaw will eventually print through.

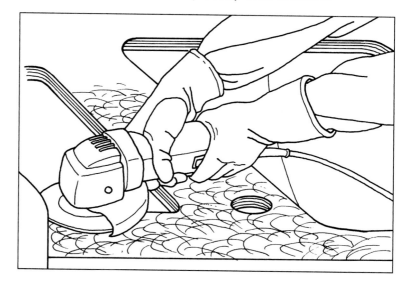

MAKING A PAPER PATTERN

New laminate can be cut from measurements, but with the irregular lines and angles of boat surfaces, the most foolproof method of sizing the laminate is with a paper pattern.

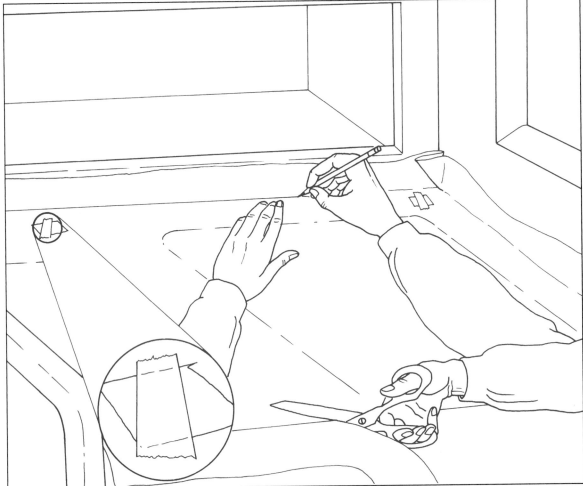

1 Lay the paper on the surface and carefully crease the paper into the intersections with other surfaces and over outside corners. It is usually a good idea to cut four holes in your pattern near the outside corners and run tape across these holes to hold the paper in position.

2 When the outline is complete, cut the paper on the lines, then check the cut pattern again for fit. Make any needed adjustments. Pattern shortages can be corrected by adding a piece of paper tape and trimming the tape to the correct shape. Once the pattern is perfect, write TOP on its surface while it is still in place to prevent any confusion later when you cut the laminate.

CUTTING THE NEW LAMINATE

It is a very good idea to practice cutting laminate on a scrap before you attempt to cut the pieces for installation. Cut horizontal grade with a saber saw fitted with a special laminate or plastics blade. Some laminates will cut perfectly while others will exhibit a tendency to chip. If you are using a variable-speed saw, try cutting at different speeds until you find the speed that leaves the cleanest edge. Always cut from the backside.

Vertical grade laminate can be cut with tin snips or heavy-duty scissors, but the laminate may tend to tear. Technique can usually avoid this, or at least force the tears into the cut-off side of the cut; practicing on a scrap is essential.

A quick way to rough-cut laminate is to score it on the good side with a special laminate-scoring tool or a razor knife, then break it like glass over a sharp edge. Again, practice is the key.

If all the edges of your laminate will be covered with trim, a chipped cut-line won't matter, and you can cut the piece the same size as your pattern. Where an edge of the laminate will show, that edge must be given extra width to allow for trim. Cutting ⅛ inch outside the pattern line is usually sufficient, but measure the depth of the largest chips on your test cut and allow more material if necessary.

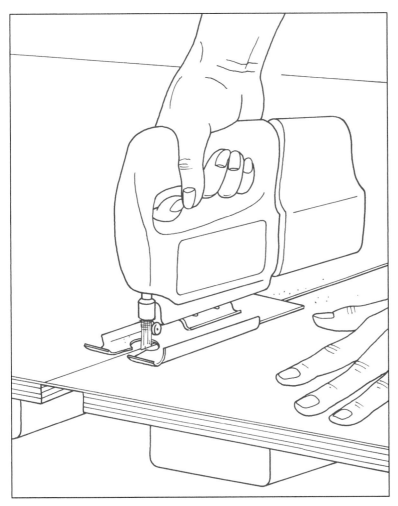

Finished edges that cannot be trimmed after the laminate is installed—where the back of the counter butts against a cabinet, for example—will need to be finished before (see below). You can often avoid the need to do this by placing this edge of your pattern along an edge of the full sheet.

Mark the visible edges and the hidden edges (covered with trim) on your pattern, then place the visible edges along the finished edges of the sheet or allow extra material for trimming. Remember to orient the pattern correctly—you will be marking the backside of the laminate, so the TOP you wrote on the pattern should not be visible when you trace the pattern onto the laminate.

Always dry-fit the laminate to check the fit before applying any adhesive. If alignment will be required, align the piece now and put pencil guidemarks on the laminate and adjoining surfaces.

APPLYING THE CONTACT CEMENT

Glue plastic laminate in place with contact cement. Contact cement attaches to almost any surface when it is wet, but only to itself when it is dry. Use a throw-away brush to completely coat both the surface being covered and the back of the new laminate, then let the glue dry. One coat is usually sufficient, but if you are laminating over bare wood, a second coat may be required. The dry glue should leave the surface with a slight sheen. It is dry when no longer sticky to the touch (be sure you don't have glue on your finger).

For the marine environment, always select petroleum-based adhesive, never water-based. The right contact cement will have "Flammable" printed prominently on the label—and it is. Very! So be sure everything that might generate a spark or flame is off. Light a cigarette while using this stuff in the cabin, and at least you won't be a lung-cancer statistic.

Contact cement is also quite toxic, so apply it to the new laminate on deck. When coating surfaces that can't be taken on deck, be sure you have lots of ventilation, and as soon as you get the surface coated, get out of there until the glue dries. If you have an organic respirator—you're going to need one to paint the bottom—this is another good use for it.

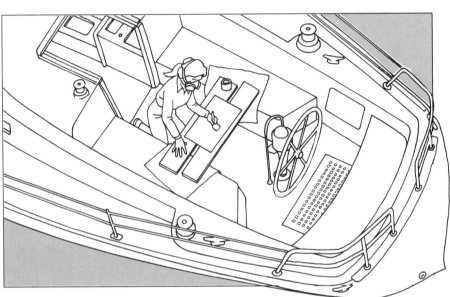

KEEPING THE GLUE-COATED SURFACES APART WHILE POSITIONING

Get two cement-coated surfaces too close and one will latch onto the other like a frog snapping up a fly—with the same opportunity for a second chance. Contact cement allows for zero adjustment once the surfaces touch. Avoid this potential disaster by covering one surface entirely with waxed paper—safe stix, so to speak.

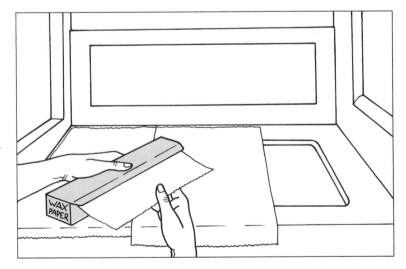

REMOVING THE SEPARATOR

With the help of the pencil marks you made when you did your dry-fit, position the new laminate on top of the paper. Holding the laminate in position with one hand, slide one of the end strips of paper out an inch or so. Press the laminate lightly in the area the paper uncovered (you can't see it, but you will know where it is) to fix the laminate in place. Now slide each of the other paper strips slightly; you just want to make sure you don't have any of them pinched behind the edge of the laminate while you can still lift it to free them.

If the papers are all free, check your alignment one more time. Working from the corner where the two pieces are already glued, extract the strips of paper one at a time and press the laminate down by sliding your hand across the top, always smoothing toward the area still separated by paper.

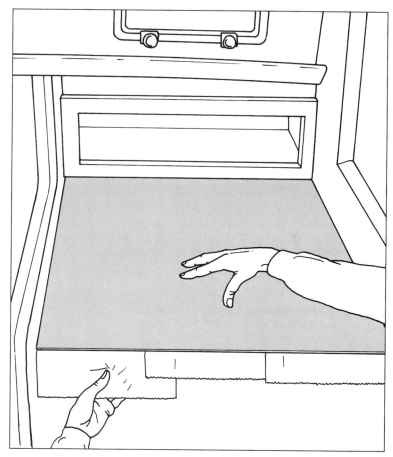

ROLLING A GOOD BOND

When all the paper separators are out, roll the surface firmly with a rubber roller to ensure full contact. Roll initially in a single direction to force any air pockets to the edge.

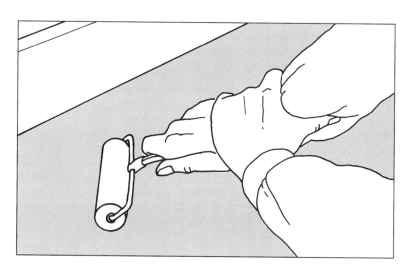

TRIMMING WITH A ROUTER OR A FILE

All the necessary trimming of a typical galley counter will take about two minutes with a router, so if you don't have one, buy or borrow one for this job. It makes it s-o-o-o easy.

If you need a finished edge before you install the laminate—the back edge of the counter, for example—clamp the laminate with a slight overhang to a straight piece of wood and run the router guide (the roller on the bottom of the bit) against the board. To have space at the ends for your clamps, rout the straight edge on the laminate before you cut out the piece.

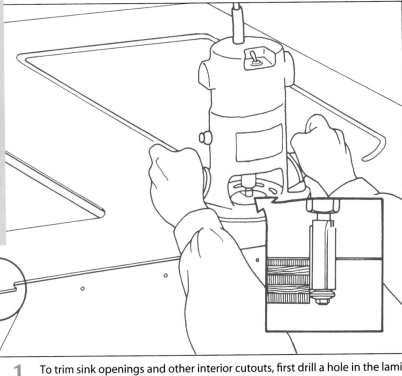

1 To trim sink openings and other interior cutouts, first drill a hole in the laminate over the counter opening large enough for the router bit. There is no need to saw out the opening; the router will cut out and trim in the same operation.

2 Use a file to trim where the router fails to reach. Lay the flat side of the file on the edge at a slight angle and use the edge of the file in a sawing motion to trim the laminate. If a router is unavailable, a file can be used for all the trimming.

REPLACING THE TRIM

If you want to be able to take the trim off easily in the future, rein-stall it with finishing nails. Glue is more secure but infinitely harder to remove later without damage.

Since you drove the old nails through the trim, they are proba-bly still in the furniture or bulk-head. Even if you pulled them out, the hole is still there; any nails used in these locations will have to be a size larger than the ones taken out. A better alternative is smaller nails in new holes.

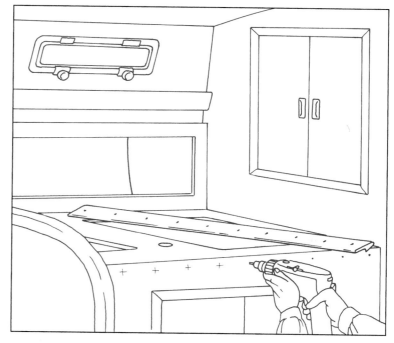

1 Nails will usually penetrate vertical-grade laminate without difficulty, but pilot holes may be needed to get a slender finishing nail through horizontal grade. If you cannot find a bit smaller than the nails you are using, give each nail a good rap to mark its location on the laminate, then set the trim aside and drill *through the laminate only* at the marked locations.

2 Set the nails below the surface with a nail set, then fill the holes—new and old—with a little wood putty.

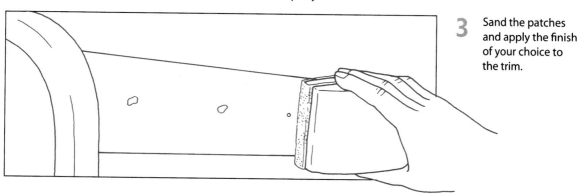

3 Sand the patches and apply the finish of your choice to the trim.

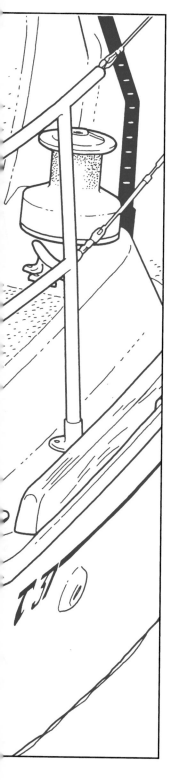

WOOD FINISHES

On modern fiberglass pleasure boats, exposed wood is there primarily to enhance the boat's appearance. Of course, teak handrails do serve the necessary function of providing a secure handhold, but we could accomplish the same thing with stainless steel rails and eliminate most maintenance in the bargain. So why don't we see more sailboats with stainless handrails? Because we want that warm, traditional look that only wood can provide.

We also like the look of wood in the cabin, at the very least as accent trim to give the interior a yachty look. Below deck almost any attractive wood will serve, although teak is by far the most popular. Teak reigns on the deck as well.

The second most common trim wood is mahogany, prized for its tight grain, classic color, and spectacular beauty when covered with a dozen coats of carefully applied varnish. To survive, mahogany must be protected from the elements.

Teak, on the other hand, can be left untreated for years, even decades, without losing integrity, which makes this wood consistent with the low maintenance nature of fiberglass boats. High oil content makes good quality teak virtually impervious to the marine environment, but while its integrity may survive neglect, its appearance is certain to suffer.

It is true that good teak left untreated should weather to an attractive ash gray, but the assault of modern-day air pollutants soon turn neglected teak nearly black. Scrubbing tends to leave behind an unattractive mottled look, neither golden nor gray. Most boatowners eventually find themselves unhappy with either look and decide that some treatment is essential. Some simply paint all exposed wood brown, an eminently pragmatic course, but if you want the natural beauty of the wood to show, you must apply a clear coating. For mahogany (and almost all other woods), varnish is the only practical choice. For teak the choices are oil, sealer, or varnish.

OILING WOOD TRIM

The application of oil has long been a common method of bringing out the natural beauty of wood. Oil intensifies the colors and grain patterns of wood, and gives the wood a rich, warm appearance. Because it simply enhances the inherent beauty of the wood—more like salt than sauce—oiling is arguably the most attractive of all wood finishes.

Virtually any uncoated wood surface can be oiled, but if the wood will be exposed to the elements, oiling is likely to prove unsatisfactory. Oil is the least durable common wood finish, and only naturally oily woods will tolerate the minimal pro-tection of oiling. Aboard a boat, that means teak.

Oiling teak on boats is a time-honored tradition, and oiling does restore some of the teak's natural oils and resins. However, the benefit of oiling exterior teak is extremely transitory. The irritating truth is that teak will last just as long if you don't oil it—longer really, since repeated between-coat scrubbing wears the wood away. But oiling teak isn't about protecting the wood; it's about recovering and maintaining that golden glow that made us want teak on the boat in the first place. You can set a party table with tarnished silver, too, but it's not so attractive.

SCRUBBING TEAK

Before teak can be oiled (or given any other coating, for that matter), it must be completely clean. Use the mildest cleaner that does the job. Start with a 75/25 mixture of liquid detergent and chlorine bleach (no water), boosted with TSP. Apply with a stiff brush, scrubbing lightly with the grain. Leave the mixture on the wood for several minutes to give the detergent time to suspend the dirt, and the bleach time to lighten the wood, then rinse thoroughly by flooding and brushing.

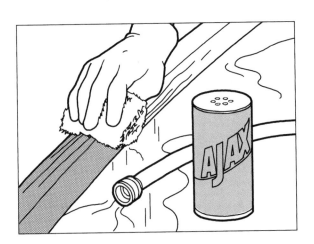

LIGHTENING THE COLOR

If the scrubbed teak is dark or stained when it dries, a cleaner with oxalic acid is required. This is the active ingredient in most single-part teak cleaners. It is also the bleaching agent in Ajax scouring powder—that ubiquitous blue can under the kitchen sink. Expect teak cleaner targeted for boat use to cost 10 times the price of lowly Ajax (biting the hand that feeds); judge for yourself if it is 10 times better. Whichever you select, brush the cleaner onto wet teak and give it time to work, then scrub the wood with Scotchbrite or bronze wool. (Never, ever, *ever* use steel wool aboard your boat—it will leave a trail of rust freckles that will be impossible to remove.) Oxalic acid will dull paint and fiberglass, so wet down surrounding surfaces before you start and keep them free of the cleaner. Rinse the scrubbed wood thoroughly—brushing is required—and let it dry completely.

USING A TWO-PART TEAK CLEANER

Two-part teak cleaners are dramatically effective at restoring the color to soiled, stained, and neglected teak, but these formulations contain a strong acid—usually hydrochloric—and should only be used when all other cleaning methods have failed.

Use a nylon-bristle brush to apply two-part cleaner. If you use a natural-bristle brush, the cleaner will dissolve the bristles; it is doing the same thing to your teak.

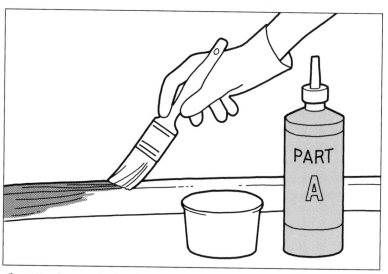

1 Wet the wood to be cleaned, then paint part 1 (or A) onto the wet wood, avoiding contact with adjoining surfaces.

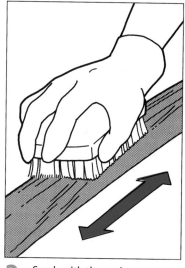

2 Scrub with the grain.

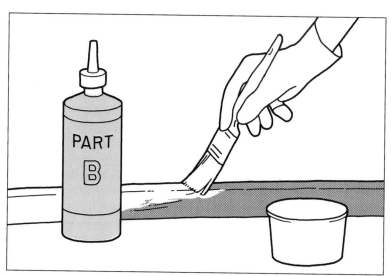

3 Part 2 (or B) neutralizes the acid in part 1 and usually has some cleaning properties. Paint sufficient part 2 onto the teak to get a uniform color change. Scrub lightly.

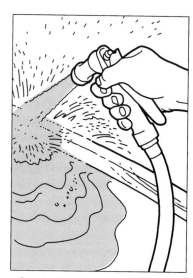

4 Flush away *all* traces of the cleaner and let the wood dry.

APPLYING TEAK OIL

Teak oils are primarily either linseed oil or tung oil, bolstered by resins to make them more durable. Linseed oil tends to darken the teak, but it is significantly cheaper. Tung oil doesn't darken the wood, and it is more water-resistant than linseed oil—a notable advantage for boat use. However, a month or two after application, it may be hard to discern that much difference since both oils carbonize in the sun and turn dark. Proprietary teak oils address this problem with various additives, including pigments, UV filters, and mildew retardants. Some that perform admirably in one climate are reviled in another. If you are going to oil your teak, make your teak-oil selection based on the recommendations of other boatowners in your area.

The best way to apply teak oil is to brush it on. Thinning the first coat about 20 percent with mineral spirits or turpentine will encourage the oil to penetrate the wood more deeply. *Immediately* wipe away (with a spirits-dampened cloth) any drips or runs on fiberglass or painted surfaces; otherwise the resins the oil contains will leave dark, nearly-impossible-to-remove stains. Watch out for sneaky runs below the rail.

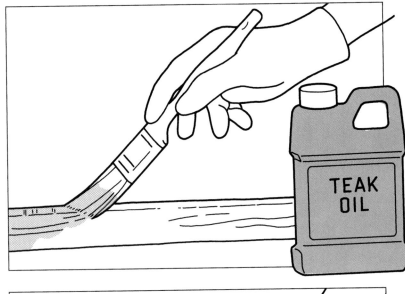

Oiling requires multiple coats. The teak will initially "drink" the oil, but by the third coat, oil will begin to stand in some areas. Wipe up excess oil with a cloth. Continue to brush on the oil, and wipe away any excess until the wood is saturated. The wood should have a matte finish without any shiny spots.

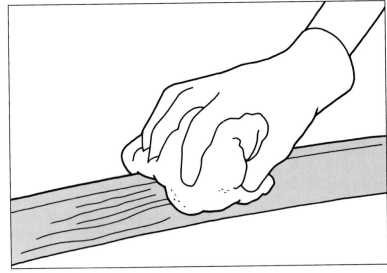

WIPING INTERIOR WOOD SURFACES WITH LEMON OIL

1 Wash unvarnished interior wood surfaces with 1 cup of *liquid* household laundry detergent and 1 cup of chlorine bleach in 1 gallon of water. Use a towel—not too wet or you will raise the grain—and leave the solution on the wood for 30 minutes to kill mildew spores. Rinse thoroughly with fresh water and a clean towel. If the grain is raised, sand the wood with 120-grit sandpaper on an orbital sander, then remove all surface dust with a mineral-spirits-*dampened* cloth. (Raised grain should happen only once; after you oil the wood, the oil will shield the wood from water penetration the next time you wash it.)

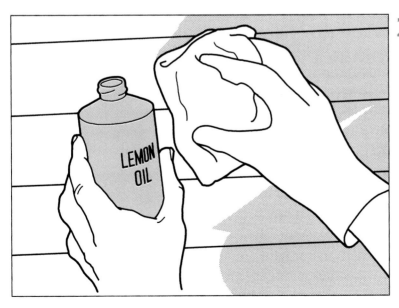

2 Use lemon oil on interior woods; it feeds the wood, is waxy rather than sticky when it dries, and is poison to mildew. Rub the oil into the grain of uncoated interior wood surfaces with a soft cloth. After a week, give the wood a second application, then oil it every two or three months after that, or as the wood needs it.

SEALERS

Sealers are another approach to achieving the natural look. Sealers don't feed the wood but, as the name suggests, they seal in natural oils and resins, seal out moisture and dirt. You can concoct an effective sealer by thinning spar varnish 50 percent with mineral spirits. Sealers work fine on new wood—if the seal is maintained by regularly applying a fresh coat—but on old wood the oils and resins you are trying to seal in have, like Elvis, already left the premises.

Some commercial teak products blend oil and sealer in an effort to combine the rejuvenating characteristics of the one with the durability of the other. These products are often called "dressings" or "treatments," and some enjoy substantial popularity.

PREPARING OLD WOOD

The first step toward applying a sealer on old wood is the same as for any finish—thoroughly clean the wood and brighten (bleach) it to a uniform color. Next, lost oils must be restored by oiling the wood until it refuses to accept more. Then take a break—*for a couple of weeks.* The resins need to dry before you apply the sealer.

When you return, wash the wood; the fresh oil has been snagging grime for a fortnight. When the wood is dry, wipe it heavily with a rag soaked in acetone to remove all oil from the surface. Yes, you did just put that oil on there, but the sealer needs an oil-free surface to get a grip. The oil the wood has absorbed is unaffected by this quick-flashing solvent.

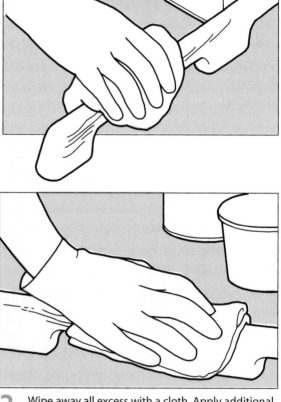

APPLYING A SEALER

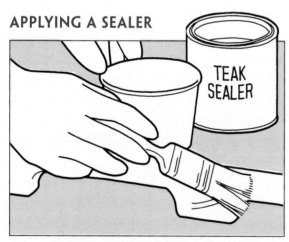

1 Apply sealer exactly like oil. A throwaway brush is adequate for the job, and brushing technique is not a concern.

2 Wipe away all excess with a cloth. Apply additional coats—wet on wet—until the wiped surface shows a uniform matte finish.

VARNISHING: PREPARATION

Varnish has long been the brightwork finish of choice among the yachting set. A mirror-like coating of varnish on tight-grained mahogany attracts universal admiration—for the boat and, by extension, for her owner. Skillfully applied and properly maintained, varnish is second only to high-gloss hull coatings in its ability to transform a boat from peasant to queen.

Aside from its much-admired appearance, varnish offers genuine protection for the wood. Wood coated with varnish will not dry out and split, will not absorb moisture and rot, is unaffected by dirt and pollution, and will be untouched, thus unstained, by oily or greasy spills. Protected from the sun, varnish will last indefinitely; even with direct sun exposure, varnish will outlast oils and sealers by at least a factor of five.

For exterior application, select spar varnish, not urethane varnish. Urethane varnish provides a harder, more abrasion-resistant surface, which makes it an excellent choice for interior woodwork, but it tends to lose its grip on the wood when subjected to continuous sun exposure. Because the finish is a thin layer of plastic, it may be that it is susceptible to a "greenhouse" effect, condensing moisture on its underside, which hydraulically lifts the coating. Whatever the cause, the adhesion of urethane varnish applied on exterior wood is almost certain to fail sooner rather than later, and the varnish will peel away in plastic-wrap-like sheets.

The absence of pigment in varnish means it does not shield the underlying surface the way paint does. The sun penetrates the coating and carbonizes the oils in the wood, causing the wood to darken *beneath* the varnish. To minimize this effect, varnish makers add ultraviolet inhibitors—sun screens—to their products. For exterior brightwork, select a quality spar varnish heavily fortified with UV inhibitors. As always, get local recommendations from other boatowners before selecting a specific varnish.

If the wood you intend to varnish has been previously varnished, and the old varnish is in bad shape, you will have to strip it. (If the varnish is in good condition— fat chance—skip to "'Laying On' the Finish Coats.") Sanding away the old varnish can be frustrating because the friction-heated varnish tends to soften and gum up the paper. The cleanest, safest, and sometimes the easiest way to strip old varnish is with a cabinet scraper. If you develop your skill with a cabinet scraper, you will be amazed at how smooth it leaves the wood.

STRIPPING OLD VARNISH

1 Hold a sharpened 4- or 5-inch cabinet scraper (see "Sharpening a Scraper" on page 297) tilted toward you at about 75° to the wood and draw it toward you. The microscopic burr on the edge of the scraper will finely plane the surface. Keep drawing the scraper across the wood until all the varnish has been planed off.

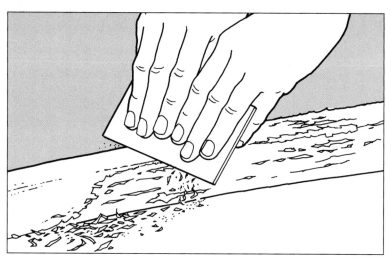

2 A chemical stripper can take much of the work out of removing old varnish, but the stripper will also lift paint, and many can damage gelcoat. Mask all surrounding surfaces, using sheet plastic, not newspaper. Select the thickest stripper you can find—so it will stay where you want it.

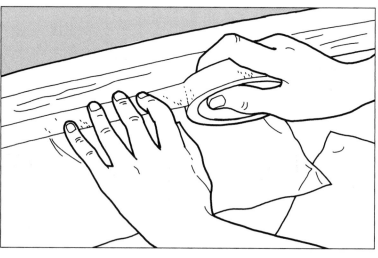

3 Pour a little into a small open container, not directly onto the wood. Dip a throw-away brush into the stripper, but do not unload it. Apply *with a single stroke*, probably not longer than 4 inches. Dip and apply the next 4 inches, and so on. Vapors from the stripper do the work, and if you brush back and forth, you release them into the air and reduce the effectiveness of the stripper by *as much as 80 percent*! Direct sun also reduces the stripper's effectiveness by drying it prematurely .

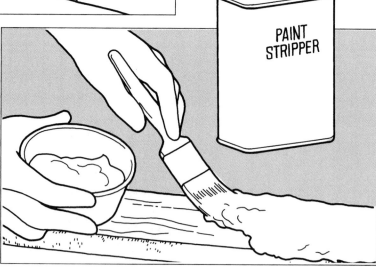

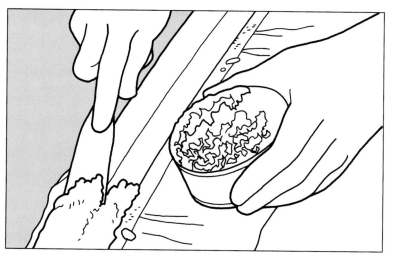

4 Leave the stripper on the varnish for about 30 minutes, then use a wide putty knife to scrape off the softened varnish. Be careful not to gouge the wood or raise a splinter. Don't let any of the curls fall onto painted or gel-coated surfaces. Wipe the toxic scrapings into an empty paint bucket for later disposal.

5 Scrub the wood with bronze wool to remove the varnish in curved or irregular areas and to clear the grain. If some varnish remains, apply the stripper a second time. After the second application has been scraped and scrubbed, use a cabinet scraper to remove any varnish "islands" and to fair the surface.

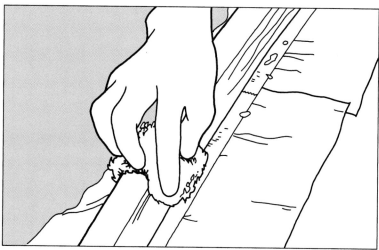

6 Wipe away all traces of stripper and varnish residue with a cloth soaked in denatured alcohol or lacquer thinner.

METHYLENE CHLORIDE

MOST EFFECTIVE PAINT and varnish strippers contain methylene chloride. Not only is this compound dangerously toxic, it has been cited by various government agencies as a demonstrated carcinogen. The list of health problems it may cause (read the warning label) doesn't leave out any important internal organs, and the EPA considers methylene chloride a hazardous air pollutant. This is a chemical with an attitude.

Protect your hands and eyes with gloves and goggles. A respirator is a good precaution—an essential one if you aren't in open air. You can significantly reduce your exposure—and everyone else's—by applying the stripper without brushing; the aggressive vapors remain captured, focused on dissolving paint rather than neurons or bronchioles.

BLEACHING RAW WOOD

For varnishing to succeed, the underlying wood must have a uniform color. Where old varnish has been gouged and split or allowed to peel, the wood will have taken on multi-hues. Chemical stripping is almost certain to leave the wood mottled. Scraping and sanding may restore uniform color, but only if a substantial amount of wood is removed. Unvarnished wood will also show a patchwork of discolorations from stains and mildew.

Mild discoloration may respond to scrubbing with a powdered cleaner—Ajax or your favorite single-part teak cleaner. (Note that most two-part cleaners cannot be used on woods other than teak.) After you scrub the wood, if it still shows stains or multiple shades, it will need to be bleached.

For this bleaching, you need oxalic acid, which you can buy in crystal form at your local hardware store. Also buy a box of soda ash or borax to use as a neutralizer.

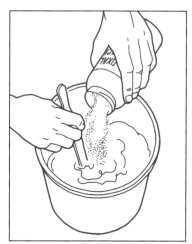

1 To make the bleach solution, stir oxalic-acid crystals into warm water until they stop dissolving. A strong solution requires about 16 ounces of oxalic acid to a gallon of water.

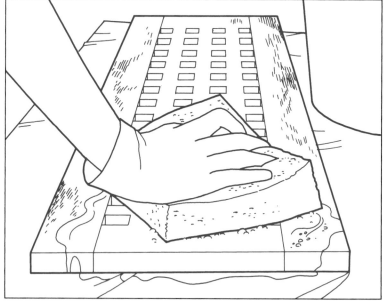

2 Paint or sponge this solution onto the wood, taking great care not to get it onto any other surface—it will etch paint and gelcoat.

3 Let it dry completely, then vacuum away the powder that remains, or brush it carefully into a dustpan.

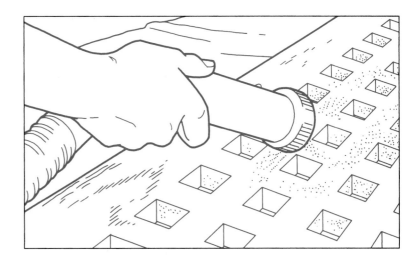

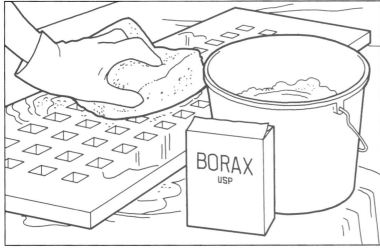

4 Mix a cup of soda ash or borax into a 2½-gallon bucket of water and wet the bleached wood generously with this solution.

5 Hose the wood and surrounding surfaces thoroughly, scrubbing the wood with a soft brush.

6 Treat the wood a second time with the neutralizing solution, then energetically flood and scrub again.

The wood should dry to a uniform color. Remaining dark spots can be retreated, but it may be difficult to achieve consistency by spot-bleaching.

SURFACE PREPARATION

Before you varnish, you want the wood surface to be as smooth as possible. Previously unvarnished wood is likely to be quite rough. Bleached wood may also have a ridged surface because the acid eats away the softer wood cells. Regardless of whether the wood is weathered, bleach-damaged, or new, sanding is required.

Scrub and perhaps bleach the wood first to remove dirt and other contaminants from the grain and to brighten the color of the wood.

Sand rough wood with an orbital sander loaded with 80- or 100-grit aluminum-oxide paper.

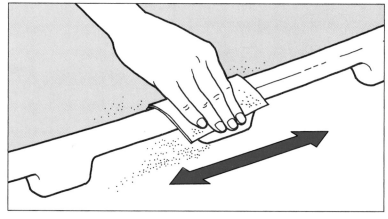

Anywhere you have to hand sand, be sure to sand with the grain; scratches across the grain will show through the varnish.

If the wood has been bleached, the sanding dust may still harbor some acid, so hose the wood after sanding to thoroughly rinse it away. This may raise the grain again, which will require another application of sandpaper.

Unless the wood is teak, switch to a finer grit for the final pass. The oiliness of teak makes it difficult for the varnish to adhere, so finish sanding with 100-grit paper provides a better "tooth" and con-tributes to a longer-lasting finish. On other woods—mahogany, for example—150-grit paper will yield a slightly better finish. Use an even finer grit on interior furniture—120-grit for teak and 220-grit for other woods.

After sanding, use a rag dampened with mineral spirits, turning it often, to wipe away all the sanding dust. When the wood is ivory smooth and dust free, you are ready to varnish.

VARNISHING: THE INITIAL COATS

To achieve its mirror-like finish, varnish must fill the grain of the wood, requiring the varnish to be relatively viscous. This is a desirable characteristic in later coats, but initially this viscosity prevents the varnish from penetrating the wood. The varnish bridges the pores of the wood, trapping air and finish-lifting moisture in the tiny voids.

To avoid this situation, thin the first two or three coats with mineral spirits, turpentine, or the thinner recommended by the varnish manufacturer. The first coat should be thinned by 50 percent, i.e., ½ ounce of thinner for every ounce of varnish. Thinning allows the varnish to fully penetrate the wood, effectively converting the varnish into a sealer. Applying a sealer other than thinned varnish as a base coat is not a good idea since these products often give the varnish an off color.

WHEN TO VARNISH

Although less so than they used to be, today's marine varnishes are still sensitive to moisture and temperature, especially in the first two hours after application. You will have to wait until the morning dew evaporates (oddly enough, hosing dew-soaked wood will cause it to dry sooner), and you want to finish well before the moisture settles again in the evening. Don't varnish on a day when the humidity meter is pegged at 100 percent. If rain is threatening or conditions are right for fog, put this job off for another day.

The varnish flows better if it is warm, so on a cool day, place the can in the sun or in a pan of warm water (open the can lid slightly). On the other hand, cool varnish will give you more time to brush it out, so chilling it on a hot day can be just as beneficial. Generally a warm surface is desirable, but too much sun can cook the varnish—if you need shade, so does the varnish.

A sudden temperature change during the critical two hours will cloud the varnish, so check the weather map for approaching fronts before you start. Red sky in the morning, varnisher take warning.

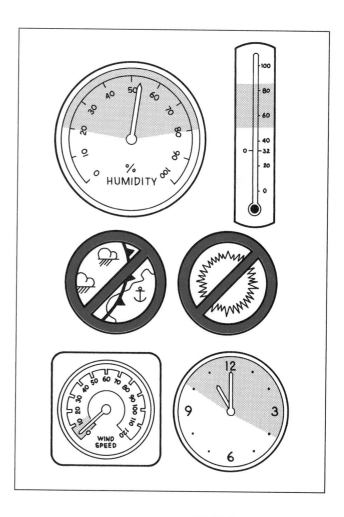

BUBBLES—THE NEMESIS

1 Varnish should always be applied with as few brush strokes as possible to minimize the number of bubbles introduced into the finish. For the same reason, never shake varnish, and if stirring is necessary—to add thinner, for example—stir slowly and gently.

2 Always pour varnish through a fine-mesh paint filter (or a double layer of pantyhose) before you use it, even if the can is new. Never apply varnish directly from its can; decant the amount you will be using into a clean container. Cleaning the rim with your brush and wiping the varnish back into the can introduces bubbles and bits of dried varnish; use a rag or paper towel to clean the rim, and reseal the can immediately.

paint filter

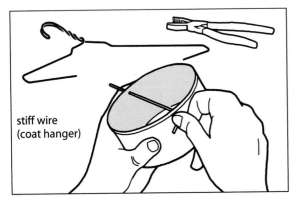

stiff wire (coat hanger)

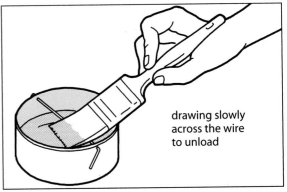

drawing slowly across the wire to unload

3 A tuna-can-size container limits the air exposure of the varnish before it is applied. Unload your brush on a wire rather than the curved rim of the container to minimize bubbles.

4 Dip the brush tip —not more than ⅓ of the bristles—long enough to become saturated. If not fully saturated, the brush will lay on bubbles rather than varnish. Unload one side of the brush.

TIP: Wipe both sides of the brush on a second can *after* each varnish application to expel particles, loose bristles, and dust .

BRUSHING TECHNIQUE

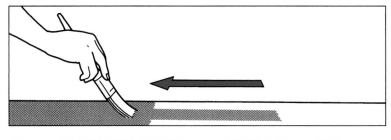

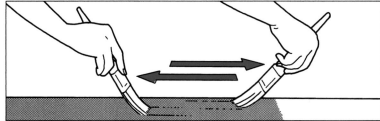

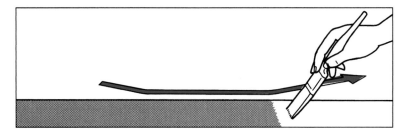

Six or more coats will be necessary to achieve the foot-deep finish potential of varnish. Apply the first coats quickly and without fuss. A throw-away brush—as long as it shows no tendency to shed bristles—is adequate for the first three or four coats. A foam brush can also be used with thinned varnish. Some find that for later coats foam brushes hold too little unthinned varnish, but foam brushes NEVER leave a bristle in the finish and they can lay down a stroke-free finish.

The wood will change color when you apply the first coat, but most of the varnish will be absorbed. As soon as the initial coat is dry to the touch, apply a second coat thinned about 25 percent. Allow both coats to dry overnight.

SANDING BETWEEN COATS

It is possible to apply multiple coats of varnish without sanding between coats. As long as you apply each coat within the recoat time specified on the can, the solvent in the varnish softens the previous coat and allows for a molecular bond. But for the smoothest finish, sanding between coats is required.

After the initial coats, sand each coat with 180-grit paper (220-grit for interior furniture). Use an orbital sander on large areas, keeping the sander moving to avoid softening the varnish. Small areas can be hand sanded, using a block if the surface is flat. Sanding not only removes all surface roughness and blemishes, it also provides essential tooth for the next coat. Never apply varnish (or paint, for that matter) to a glossy surface unless you are within the recoat time.

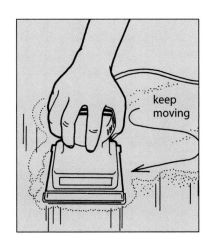

keep moving

KEEPING THE SURFACE DUST-FREE

Remove all dust from the varnished surface after sanding by wiping the surface with a spirits-dampened cloth or a tack rag (see sidebar). Preventing dust and other contaminants from spoiling the surface *after* you apply the coat is somewhat more challenging.

Wash the dust from all surrounding surfaces if you can do so without wetting the wood; otherwise wipe up the dust with a wet towel. Apply varnish on a still day. Applying it at anchor well away from shore has much to recommend it. In a slip, wet the dock and proximate shore to hold down dust. If the boat is on land, wet the ground around it.

Below deck, remove cushions and all other dust generators. Damp-wipe all interior surfaces, and mist—with a spritzer bottle—any fabric surfaces you cannot remove. Also mist your clothes.

TACK RAG

TACK RAGS ARE READILY available from hardware and paint stores, but for varnish work they can sometimes introduce contaminants. Make your own with a clean cotton cloth soaked in warm water and wrung out. Sprinkle the cloth with turpentine, followed with about a spoonful of your varnish. Wring the cloth again to distribute the varnish. Store it in a Ziploc bag between uses.

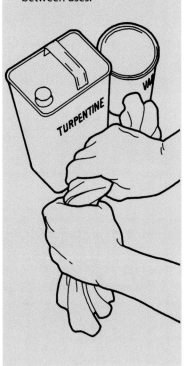

THE THIRD AND FOURTH COATS

For the third coat, thin the varnish just 10 percent, and apply this coat, like the first two, with minimal ado. Allow it to dry overnight, then sand the surface.

The fourth coat is the first one you apply without thinning the varnish and the last of the preparatory coats. Consider all coats after the fourth as finish coats, and take greater care in their application.

1 Applying the finish coats of varnish should be more like writing than painting. You do not want to worry the varnish with a lot of brush strokes. Think more of old-fashioned ink pens, the kind you have to dip in the ink. When you apply the nib to the paper, if you move it too slow, the ink stains the paper in ugly blobs; if you move it too fast, the line thins and skips. When you get the right speed and the right pressure, the pen rewards you with a sharp, crisp, perfect line. And the varnish brush correctly drawn rewards you with a flawless, glassy finish.

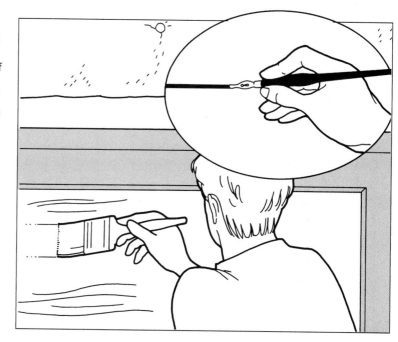

2 For the fifth coat, dip the tip of the brush in fresh unthinned varnish. This is the time to get out your good badger-hair or ox-hair brush. Unload one side on the wire, then apply the varnish with a single stroke, loaded side of the brush against the wood. Use another stroke or two—touching the surface lightly and drawing the brush slowly—to distribute the varnish. Apply each brush-load a few inches in front of the previous application, drawing the inital stroke back into the wet edge.

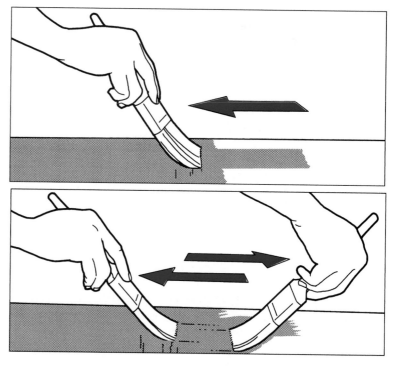

3 Finish with a single long stroke, or parallel strokes if the area is wider than your brush. Begin this final stroke just inside the old "wet edge," which is where the previous brush-load of varnish ended, and draw evenly beyond the new wet edge—where the varnish you just applied ends. If you brush back into the previous application, the technique usually recommended, excess varnish is pushed back into the previous application, causing a ridge or a wave in the finish; brushing out of the previous application moves excess varnish forward. In order not to mark the varnish where you start your final stroke, start the forward motion of your brush well before where you want the stroke to begin, and with the lightest of touches, "land" the brush—like landing an airplane—just behind the edge of your latest application.

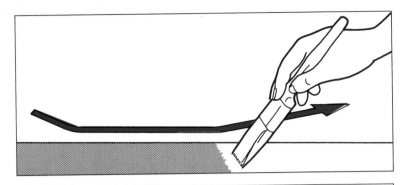

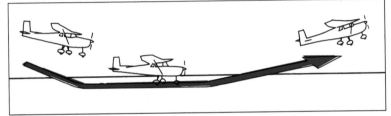

And so on, and so on. Before you return the brush to the varnish, wipe both sides on the edge of an empty can to remove contaminants. Dip the tip and apply the next brush load, beginning just at the wet edge. Distribute with a stroke or two, and finish with a light stroke from old wet edge to new. Continue, working quickly but drawing the brush slowly, until the surface is fully coated.

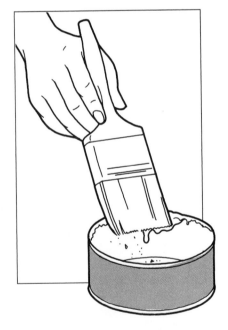

THE LAST COAT

The sixth coat is probably the final one. After the fifth coat is dry (at least overnight), sand it to remove any mistakes—runs, sags, or brush marks—and to provide smooth, uniform surface for the last coat. Some craftsmen elect not to use sandpaper before the last coat, scuffing the surface with fine bronze wool instead. Wipe the wood and all surrounding surfaces absolutely dust-free, and take all precautions against airborne dust—including waiting for another day if the wind is blowing. For the best possible finish, open a new can of varnish for the final coat.

Apply the sixth coat exactly like the previous one, only without the mistakes.

MAINTAINING A
VARNISHED SURFACE

1 Before you put away the varnish, obtain a nail polish or a paste bottle—a bottle with a brush built into the lid—and after thoroughly cleaning it, funnel it full of fresh varnish. Tear a half-sheet of 220-grit sandpaper into six squares and rubber band them to the bottle. This is your first-aid kit. Keep it handy, and use it to immediately repair any nicks and scratches.

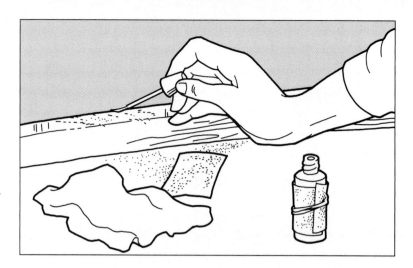

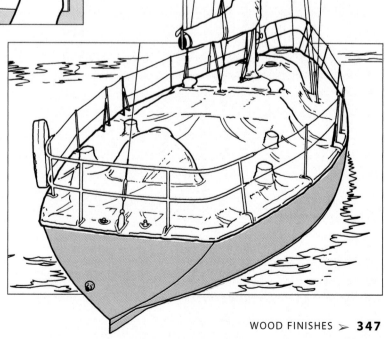

2 If you maintain the seal, varnish can last indefinitely. Besides avoiding moisture penetration at nicks and scratches, you must protect against surface erosion by periodically applying a fresh top coat. Exposed exterior varnish should be recoated at least annually in northern climes, every six months in the tropics. Scrub the varnish to remove all traces of grease and dirt, then sand the surface with 180-grit paper (or scuff it with bronze wool) and lay on a new finish coat.

3 The bond of the varnish is also damaged by the sun, and while the periodic addition of a fresh coat renews the UV protection of the varnish, the best protection is to cover the varnish; varnish kept mostly covered will last a decade or more.

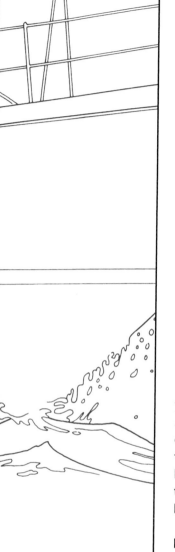

BELOW THE WATERLINE

About half the exterior surface of the typical sailboat is under water. In many ways it is this underwater portion that faces the worst assault. Scores of organisms that live in the water find the broad, smooth expanse of a boat's bottom irresistible for setting up housekeeping. Left unprotected, the bottom soon becomes, at best, a carpet of grass or, at worst, a boat-shaped living reef. Neither condition is conducive to sparkling sailing performance.

The universal solution is to paint the underwater surfaces with antifouling bottom paint. The type of bottom paint you should use depends on whether your boat goes fast or slow, whether it is kept in the water or out, whether it stays in the water year-round or only for a few months, whether you race or cruise, what material your hull is constructed of, and perhaps your environmental leanings. The brand of paint that will give the best results depends on what kind of critters lurk in your local waters. Consult the "Understanding Paints" section beginning on page 274 to determine the best type. To select the best brand, consult other boatowners in your area to determine the local favorite.

Unfortunately it isn't just the critters in the water that are attracted to your hull; it can be the water itself. Some fiberglass boats left in the water for a long period of time absorb significant amounts of water. Besides making the boat heavier, the water can combine with chemicals left over from the layup process to produce blisters and to form a destructive acidic solution.

The treatment is to let the hull dry out, then to replace or reinforce the gelcoat with a more water-impermeable barrier. A number of specialized coatings have come on the market in the last few years specifically for this purpose.

How much barrier coating or bottom paint do you need? Calculate a rough estimate of a boat's wetted area by multiplying the length times the beam times 0.90. The label will specify the coverage per gallon.

PREPARING THE BOTTOM FOR RECOATING

1 Assuming you are painting the bottom in a boatyard, the yard will pressure wash the hull for you immediately after it comes out of the water. This is usually included in the haul-out fee, but even if it isn't, be sure this happens. Most of the slime and vegetation will wash right off while still moist, but if they are allowed to dry, it will take a chisel to remove them—no exaggeration. Most yards also quickly scrape off barnacle encrustations as a part of the pressure-cleaning process.

2 If the old coat of bottom paint is in good condition and compatible with the new, all that is required is surface preparation. The safest and most environmentally friendly way to do this is to scrape it. Scraping peels away the old, dead paint without raising any dust, and the scrapings can easily be caught on plastic spread on the ground beneath the work area. Use a 2- or 3-inch hook scraper—any wider will bridge the curvature of the hull—and draw it toward you with sufficient pressure to peel the surface of the paint. Scraping is especially effective on softer bottom paints. Sharpen the scraper blade by drawing a mill file across the edge and chasing the edge with a whetstone; do not burnish a burr onto the edge of a hook scraper.

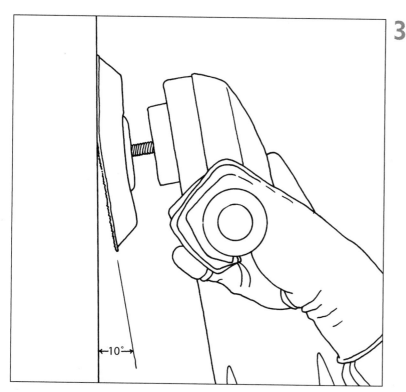

3 If scraping proves ineffective, as it may on hard bottom paints, sanding will be the next choice. A disk sander fitted with a foam pad and 80-grit paper will quickly and efficiently prepare a bottom for recoating. Tilt the sander about 10° so that only one side of the spinning disk is in contact with the surface. The direction of the tilt will depend on where you want the dust to fly. This dust is highly toxic, so wear a tight-fitting respirator—not a bandanna or a paper mask. There is no reason to sand the old paint away; sand it just enough to give you a clean, smooth surface for the new paint.

←—10°—→

4 If the old paint needs to be removed entirely for reasons of compatibility, thickness, or loss of adhesion, sanding it all off is an arduous and messy job, and the cloud of toxic dust you will generate is probably illegal under the 1990 *Clean Air Act.* Your boatyard is likely to prohibit heavy sanding. They may suggest sandblasting. *Never* allow the hull of a fiberglass boat to be sandblasted, no matter how convincing the yard's argument. Sandblasting will make your gelcoat porous, virtually guaranteeing hull blisters later on, and if the operator is only slightly inattentive, the underlying laminate will also be damaged. If you have a steel hull, sandblast it all you want, but never on a plastic hull.

USING PEEL-TYPE STRIPPER

The easiest way to entirely strip old paint is with a chemical stripper, but great caution is required. The health hazards have already been mentioned. In addition, there is very little chemical difference between paint and gelcoat, meaning that most strippers will also attack the gelcoat beneath the paint. Those specifically formulated for use on fiberglass can be used with significantly less risk to the underlying gelcoat, *provided they are not left on the surface any longer than the recommended time—usually 15 minutes or less.* Lose track of the time—easy to do—and your gelcoat will suffer damage.

A better alternative is a so-called "safe stripper." These products contain no methylene chloride. They are just as effective as other strippers, but may require much longer to do the job. Peel Away, for example, should be left on the surface as long as 48 hours. Magi-Sol, another methylene-chlorideless stripper, requires at least two hours to work.

1 Paint the stripper onto the bottom paint. If you are using a methylene-chloride stripper, set a timer to make sure you can remove the stripper within the recommended exposure time.

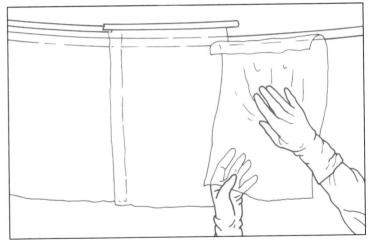

2 Strippers that call for extended exposure times can benefit from covering them to prevent the stripper from drying out and to trap all vapors against the paint. If covering sheets aren't provided, use plastic wrap or cut sections of plastic drop-cloth material.

3 Scrape away the lifted paint with a hook scraper, capturing the scrapings for proper disposal on a drop cloth spread under the work area. For methylene-chloride strippers, *immediately* wash the stripped area. (To avoid diluting the stripper, be sure the next area of application is a dry portion of the hull.)

FAIRING AND MINOR BLISTER REPAIR

Before you paint, repair any scratches, gouges, or hollows in the hull to make the surface fair. A few blisters in the gelcoat is no cause for alarm, but all blisters should be repaired as soon as they are discovered. Instructions for repairing more extensive hull damage can be found in *Sailboat Hull and Deck Repair*.

1 Open the blister completely with a sharp tool and let it drain. A countersink bit on a power drill is an easy-to-control tool for opening blisters. Wear eye protection—the pressure beneath the blister can be more than twice that in a champagne bottle. Wipe it out with a rag soaked in **brush cleaner**—a water-soluble toluene-based product available at any hardware store.

2 Use a 36-grit disk on your disk sander to grind the blister into a shallow depression. The hollow should be 20 times as wide as it is deep, and it should be only as deep as required to remove any damaged laminate beneath the gelcoat. Grind scratches or gouges into a uniform V–shaped depression.

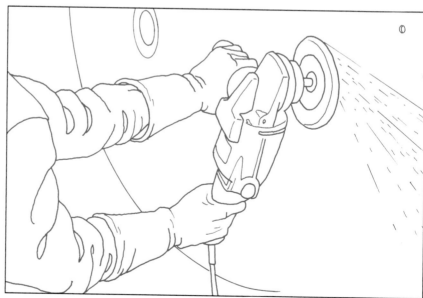

3 Scrub the depression squeaky clean with a hot TSP solution and a brush. Rinse fervently, then allow the spot to dry for a couple of days.

4 Paint the blister with unthickened epoxy, then fill it, if it is shallow, with epoxy resin thickened with colloidal silica to peanut butter consistency. Fill gouges and other surface damage the same way.

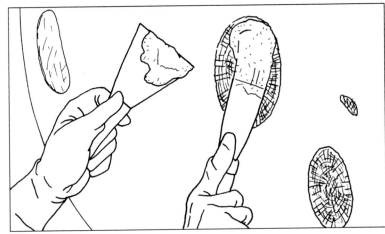

5 Deep depressions require layup of cloth disks of increasing diameter (never use mat with epoxy). Mask the hull, then paint the cavity with catalyzed epoxy. Saturate the first four disks and press each into place. Use the brush to compact them and remove excess resin. After the resin kicks—that is, begins to harden—apply additional layers (if needed) in exactly the same manner. For best results, use a squeegee or a short roller to make sure all the bubbles are forced from the laminates. Stop the layup at the bottom surface of the old gelcoat.

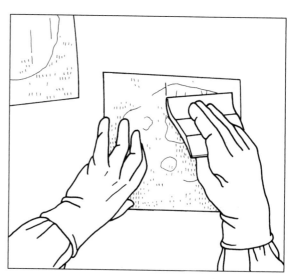

6 When the resin has kicked, finish filling the depression with silica-thickened epoxy. Take pains to get the surface as fair as possible, because the cured filler will resist sanding.

7 For smoother results, squeegee peel ply—a coated fabric epoxy does not adhere to—over the repair. The waxy amine blush will peel away with the peel ply when the epoxy has cured. If you don't use peel ply, scrub the epoxy surface with Scotchbrite and water before painting.

MIXING BOTTOM PAINT

Because the copper tends to settle into a solid lump in the bottom of the can, bottom paints generally require vigorous mixing. To allow stirring with the requisite zeal without sloshing the expensive paint from the can, pour half into another container. Stir the remaining half with a flat paddle, dredging the copper up from the bottom, until the bottom is clean and the copper is distributed throughout the paint. Still stirring, slowly pour the extracted portion back, mixing it in until all the paint is a uniform color and consistency.

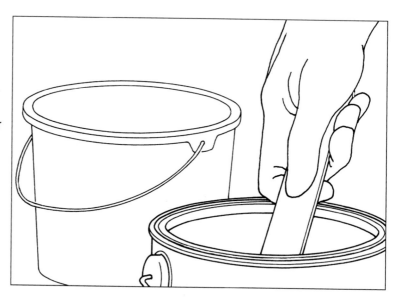

ROLLER APPLICATION

The easiest way to apply bottom paint is with a roller. Select a short-nap throw-away roller cover for this job. Use the paint as it comes from the can, without thinning. (On hot, windy days, some thinning may be necessary to get the paint to flow out.) An extension on the roller handle will keep you clear of droplets the roller may sling and will minimize the contortions required to paint hard-to-reach portions of the bottom.

For longer-lasting protection, apply two coats. This can usually be done in a continuous operation; i.e., by the time you finish rolling on the first coat, the paint in the area where you started will be dry enough to recoat. If you apply only one coat, at least give the hull a second coat at the waterline, where the scrubbing action of the surface tends to remove the paint more quickly.

Ablative paints—copolymers—require multiple coats to deliver satisfactory performance. It is a good idea to make the first coat a different color from the top coats. When the base-coat color begins to show, it will be time to repaint the bottom.

Mask the waterline or bootstripe before you begin. If you are painting bare gelcoat, wipe it thoroughly with a dewaxing solvent.

Pour a small amount of paint into the basin of the paint tray, stirring the paint each time you refill the tray. Roll the bottom paint onto the hull as quickly as you can. It is generally easier to roll up and down, that is, from waterline to keel. Save a bit of paint for the bottom of the keel and for the areas under the screw pads or wedges, to be applied when the boatyard workers relocate the poppets or when the boat is back in the slings.

TAPE

TRYING TO SAVE A COUPLE OF BUCKS by buying cheap masking tape is false economy. Almost any masking tape works fairly well when the paint is sprayed on, but when it is rolled or brushed on, the paint wicks under paper masking tape.

For crisp, sharp color separation, use *only* plastic "Fine Line" tape. Wider tape will tend to hold a straighter line. Save the paper tape for attaching masking paper to the hull—but not as a paint edge. Paper tape is also adequate to protecting surrounding fiberglass from varnish drops or runs.

Most masking tapes become difficult to remove with direct sun exposure of only a few hours, so remove the tape as soon as the paint is sufficiently dry to allow the tape to be peeled away without drawing out "strings" of paint. Peel masking tape by pulling it back on itself and slightly away from the painted edge.

RACING APPLICATION

Racing sailors may be concerned with the small paint ridges that sometimes form where the strokes overlap. These tiny ridges have no noticeable effect on normal boat performance, but for competition and for powerboat applications, rolling the paint from bow to stern may be preferable.

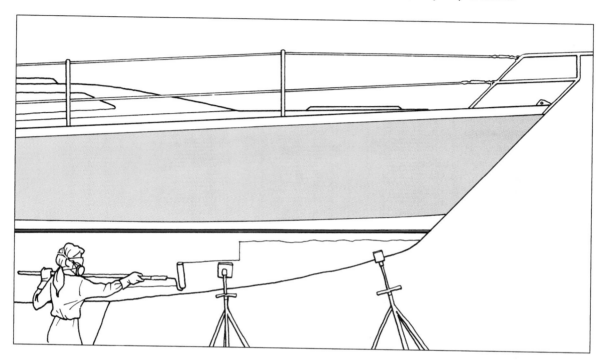

BURNISHING ANTIFOULING COATINGS

For an even smoother bottom, select a vinyl bottom paint, and after it is completely dry, burnish the surface with bronze wool or wet-sand it with 220-grit paper (or finer) on a foam block. Epoxy and copolymer bottom paints may also be burnished. For dry-stored boats, special buffable alkyd enamels are available. These have no antifouling properties and should be applied with the same roll/tip method recommended for topside enamels.

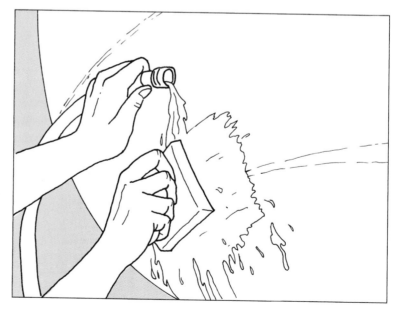

APPLYING CUPROUS RESIN

Bottom paints are, unfortunately, not environ-mentally friendly. Bottom coatings that do not leach out biocides into the water are available. While these seem to be effective against hard growth—barnacles, mussels, and the like—they are susceptible to the attachment of grass. These so-called permanent bottom coatings require periodic scrubbing (with a brush, not with a scraper) to keep them clean of grass, but if they last a number of years—test results are still early—periodic scrubbing may well represent less work and less expense than annual painting. An occasional brushing, not unlike washing your car, seems a small price to pay to eliminate the release of poisons into the water—and into the air and your lungs when sanding for a fresh application.

1 Permanent coatings are basically copper-loaded resins, either epoxy or vinylester. For application, the hull must first be stripped of all bottom paint. Even if your boat is decades old, expect the gelcoat to harbor traces of mold-release wax; wipe the bare gelcoat with a dewaxing solvent, turning and changing rags often. Sand the wax-free gelcoat lightly with 100-grit paper to smooth the surface and provide tooth for the coating.

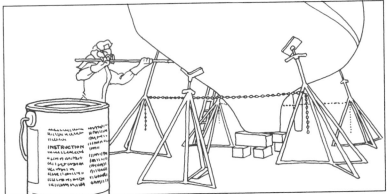

2 Apply the coating per the manufacturer's instructions, which usually involves rolling the resin on with a foam roller, perhaps smoothing the application with a foam brush. In the case of vinylester-based products, a wash coat of polyvinyl alcohol (PVA) may be required to seal the resin from the air.

3 When the resin is fully cured, remove the PVA with water and "activate" the coating—if required—by wet-abrading the surface with a scrubbing pad (Scotchbrite). If the boat is used seasonally, the cuprous resin coating will need to be activated each spring just before launch.

PROPS, ZINCS, AND TRANSDUCERS

Props may be left unpainted if the boat gets regular use; the rotation will keep the prop clean. If the boat sees less-frequent use, expect an unprotected prop to foul. Regular copper- or copper-oxide-based bottom paints will not stay on a bronze prop, and may contribute to galvanic action before they release. Special antifouling paints compatible with underwater metal are available, but they can require as many as four prime coats (eight hours apart) before two finish coats (24 hours apart). Most boatowners choose to simply polish the prop with emery cloth and give it a heavy application of wax, expecting to scrub the prop underwater if it fouls.

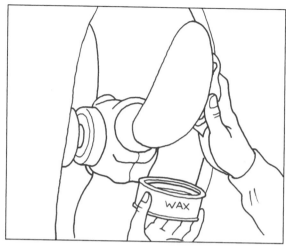

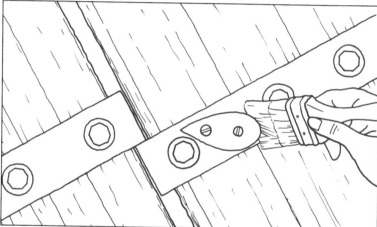

Underwater zinc anodes must never be painted. If they are removed when the bottom is painted, be careful not to paint any metal surface the mounted zinc will contact.

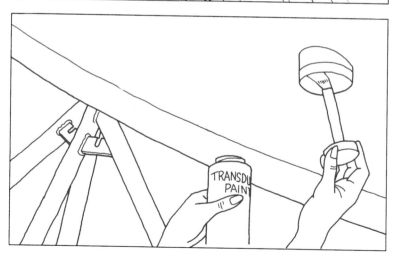

If not given an antifouling coating, depthsounder transducers will foul, causing false readings. The aggressive solvents in vinyls can attack the face of the transducer; other types are less likely to cause damage. If you are applying a vinyl bottom paint, protect the transducer with a primer coat of epoxy or apply a less aggressive paint (special transducer paints are available in small containers).

BOOTSTRIPE

The bootstripe is that narrow stripe of paint that separates the topsides from the bottom and gives your bottom paint a finished look. Usually black or an accent color, a bootstripe can be easily applied with bootstripe tape. This durable product is available in multi-stripe effects as well as a variety of widths and a rainbow of colors. Bootstripe tape is perfect for the slab sides of powerboats, but in order for the bootstripe to appear to have a uniform width on a sailboat, it must actually widen as the hull surface becomes less vertical. Conversely, uniform-width tape will appear to narrow where the hull is less vertical. If you want the width of the stripe to appear uniform, you will have to paint it.

FINDING THE WATERLINE

Check the waterline on a glass-calm morning. Be sure the trim of the boat is correct, redistributing equipment and supplies if necessary to get the correct bow attitude and eliminate any list. From the water or a dinghy, score the actual waterline on the hull at the bow and at both corners of the transom.

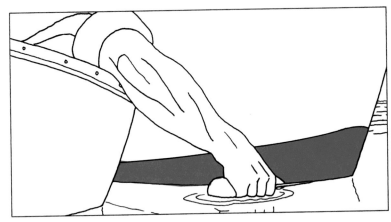

POSITIONING THE BOOTSTRIPE

1   If the existing bootstripe appears to be in the right location relative to the score marks, use it as the guide for your new stripe. If it needs to be raised or realigned, try to get the yard workers to level your boat to the score marks. You can make this easier by taking a carpenter's level aboard and finding two surfaces—one fore and aft, and one athwartship—that are level when the boat is floating on her waterline. If the yard blocks the boat up to make these two surfaces level, the three score marks will also be level.

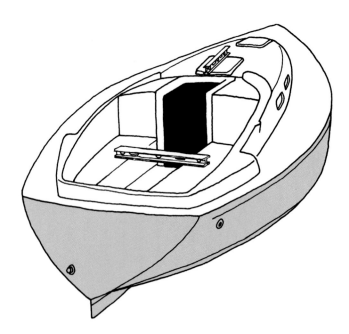

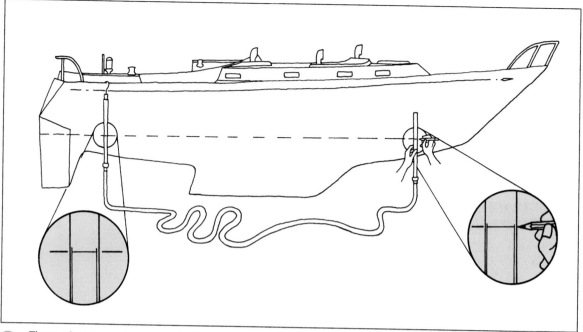

2 The modern way to locate the line joining the score marks is with a laser transit, but not all yards have this equipment. The poor man's solution is the water-filled hose. Put hose fittings (one male, one female) on the ends of a 3-foot section of clear ³/₄-inch vinyl hose, then cut the hose in half. Screw the pieces tightly to either end of a garden hose about half again as long as your waterline length. With wire or tape, hang one end from the rail with the bow score mark near the center of the clear section. Hang the other end with the top of the clear section at the stern score mark. Fill the hose from the high end until water runs out the low end. Now raise the low end 8 or 9 inches. The water level will remain even with the score mark, and if the boat is level, the water level at the other end will also be level with the score mark there.

You can walk around the boat with one end of the hose and mark as many points as you like for the waterline by holding the hose against the hull and making a pencil mark at the water level. Because the hose is flexible, the internal volume may vary, so a second person adding or spilling water as necessary to keep the level at the control point is recommended. Dewax the hull in the bootstripe area before you begin marking its location, then mark the hull every foot, more often if the hull is changing shape quickly.

3 Don't locate the bootstripe at the true waterline. It should be at least an inch above the water to prevent the stripe from fouling as a result of wave action or the boat being slightly out of trim. Mark the location of the stripe—bottom and top—at the control score mark, then add water to the hose to raise the level to these stripe locations. Use the other end of the hose to mark the hull all around. The stripe will vary in width, but the top will be a uniform distance higher than the bottom.

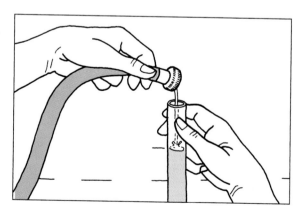

MASKING THE STRIPE

1 Use wide Fine Line tape to smoothly join the pencil marks on the hull. Tape above the lower-edge marks first to mask the top edge of the bottom paint. Let the bottom paint dry overnight.

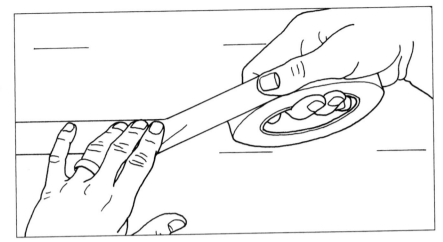

2 Apply a second strip of tape below and abutting the first strip, then remove the first strip.

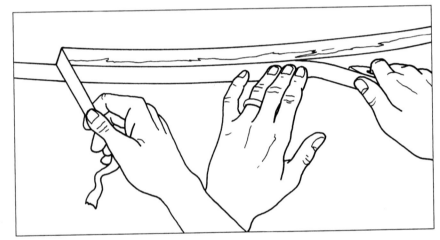

3 Apply a third strip above the upper-edge marks to mask the top edge of the bootstripe. Step away and check all taped lines for fairness; correct any hills or valleys. Burnish the inside edges of the tape with the bowl of a plastic spoon to press them tightly against the surface; this gives a sharper edge when you paint. Do not burnish the full width of the tape.

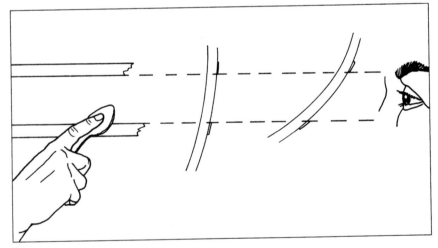

PAINTING THE BOOTSTRIPE

1 Sand the surface with 120-grit paper, taking care not to damage the edges of the tape. Wipe away all dust with a spirits-dampened cloth.

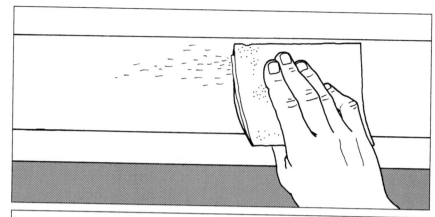

2 Cut a foam roller cover into sections slightly longer than the stripe width, and load a section onto a similarly shortened handle. (Handles with 3-inch roller cages are readily available.) Use alkyd enamel, one-part polyurethane, or bottom paint in a contrasting color. Apply it with your shortened roller, tipping it with a dry brush for a smoother finish, if you like. As soon as the paint is dry to the touch, apply a second coat. If paint is available, giving the stripe a third coat will extend its life.

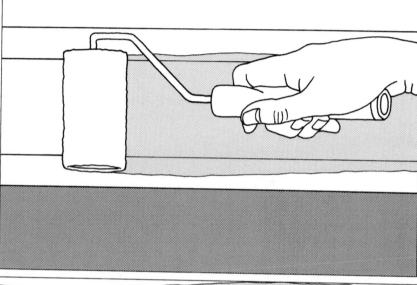

3 When the paint is dry, remove the tape by pulling it slowly back on itself and slightly away from the painted surface.

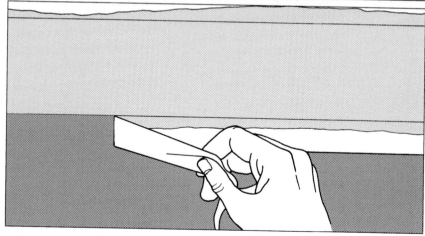

ANTI-BLISTER COATING

Hull blistering—boat pox—is the fiberglass boatowner's anathema. A single blister brings dread more appropriate to the discovery of a subcutaneous lump under an arm. Fiberglass boats can die of boat pox, but it is exceedingly rare. Still, the discovery of blisters suggests some action should be taken. What may be appropriate is difficult to determine.

In the best case, a single blister or two can be treated like pimples, not pox. You can easily deal with such pimples yourself—see "Fairing and Minor Blister Repair." In the worst (repairable) case, the gelcoat and usually the first layer of laminate are precision peeled and replaced—usually with a sprayed mixture of vinylester and chopped-strand glass covered with a 20-mil barrier coat of filled epoxy. This is a process requiring specialized equipment and expertise, and the cost of this cure is likely to be around $300 per foot of boat length.

WHAT CAUSES BLISTERS?

Gelcoat, once thought to be impermeable, does in fact allow water molecules to penetrate. This wouldn't be such a big problem were it not for various water-soluble materials generally contained in the underlying laminates. These attract water like a dry sponge, setting up an osmotic flow through the gelcoat and potentially through the layers of laminate. As more water is absorbed, the "sponge" swells, causing internal pressures that become gelcoat blisters if the bond between the gelcoat and the first layer of laminate is weak. Because of layup procedures, the weakest bond is just as often between the first and second layers of fiberglass, meaning the blister will be located beneath the primary laminate. If you are wondering why the water under pressure doesn't just pass back out the way it got in, this is because the relatively small water molecules have combined with the water-soluble material into much larger molecules that cannot pass through the gelcoat.

Less than 20 percent of the time do blisters form deeper in the laminate than the first layer. This suggests that 80 percent of the time, blisters are a cosmetic rather than structural problem. This would be true except that the laminate may also contain water-soluble acids that, combined with water, can begin a chemical reaction that weakens the surrounding chemical bond.

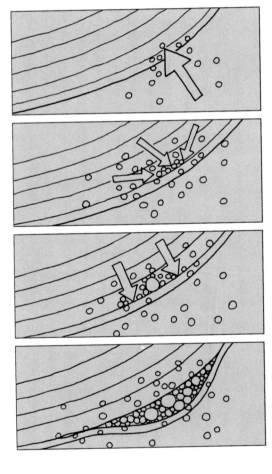

DETERMINING THE APPROPRIATE TREATMENT

What to do? If you have an older boat with no sign of blisters, the answer is do nothing. If you have a first-time blister, or a handful of blisters, the answer is to repair them and keep a close eye on the hull for further indication that a problem may be developing. If your hull has broken out with an undeniable case of pox, having the gelcoat peeled (and the first layer of laminate if the blisters are beneath it) may well be your only long-term solution. You could grind out and repair each blister, but the number of blisters suggests that the water that has penetrated the gelcoat is finding an ample supply of water-soluble materials in the laminate. That water is trapped inside the laminate, and can be dried out only by removing the gelcoat.

DRYING OUT

Of course, you may not want to do a $9,000 repair on a $6,000 boat. In that case, strip the hull of all bottom paint. Dewax the bare gelcoat. Locate, and grind open all the blisters. Scrub out the blisters with a warm TSP solution, then wash the entire hull with fresh water (hot if available). Let the hull dry for as long as possible. If you are planning to do this over a northern winter, tenting the boat will be essential. A catalytic heater in the tent can speed the process. Even in the South, the hull will need a couple of months out of the water if the humidity level is above 50 percent.

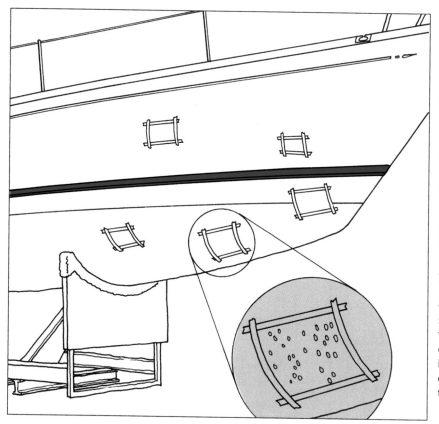

There are moisture meters around that supposedly measure the moisture content of the hull, but such readings are almost always suspect. A series of readings with the same meter might be useful for determining how the drying is progressing, but don't expect a moisture meter to tell you how wet your hull is (and don't take expensive corrective action based on such readings). The easiest way to check your hull is to tape squares of plastic—all edges sealed with electrical tape—over several spots on the hull, then check them after a couple of sunny days; if the inside of the plastic is damp, the hull needs more drying time. Dry the hull and the plastic and seal it back.

FILLING BLISTERS

Before apping an epoxy barrier coat to inhibit hull saturation, all existing blisters need to be ground open, drained, and scrubbed as detailed earlier. For more extensive instructions for repairing and preventing blisters, see *Sailboat Hull and Deck Repair*.

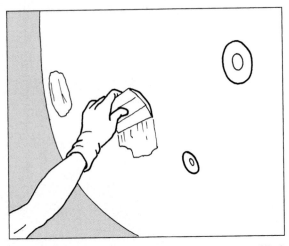

1 Paint the clean and dry depressions with an unfilled epoxy resin, such as West System #105, then thicken the same resin with collodial silica (West System #406) to a peanut-butter consistency and fill each of the ground depressions.

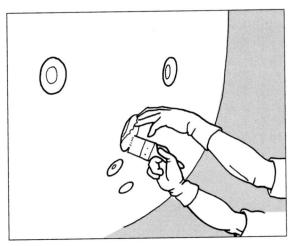

2 Deeper depressions should be laid up with epoxy-saturated layers of cloth (never use mat with epoxy). Fill the blisters flush with the surrounding hull surface.

3 When the epoxy has cured, scrub it with Scotchbrite and water to remove the surface amine.

4 Fair all the blister repairs with the palm sander, and fill any voids with additional epoxy putty. Scrub and sand again to fair all repairs, then sand the entire bare hull with 80-grit paper. Wipe the surface clean with acetone or other recommended solvent.

APPLYING AN EPOXY BARRIER COAT

Barrier coatings are generally special formulations of epoxy resin that exhibit less permeability than gelcoat. The most effective formulations have microscopic flakes of impermeable material that act like roof shingles to prevent penetration. All barrier coatings depend on adequate thickness to work. A thickness of about 20 mils is generally specified by the manufacturer. Even if less is suggested, bringing the thickness up to 20 mils will improve the performance of the product.

Expect to apply a half-dozen coats or more of barrier coat to achieve the recommended dry film thickness (DFT). Use a foam roller to apply the barrier coating. Subsequent coats generally can be applied without sanding as long as you do not exceed the maximum recoat interval. To avoid weakening the barrier by sanding the coating, apply an epoxy-based bottom paint within a few hours of applying the last barrier coat—the coating manufacturer will provide exact times for varying curing conditions.

PROTECTING A NEW BOAT

SHOULD YOU PUT A preventive barrier coating on the hull of a new boat? The answer is no.

Applying a barrier coating requires sanding the gelcoat, which will automatically void the manufacturer's warranty. Don't even sand the bottom for that first coat of bottom paint without checking with the boat manufacturer; some require that you prepare the surface with "no-sand" etching process to avoid breaching the surface of the gelcoat.

Warranty issues aside, the negative impact of early blistering has led most boat manufacturers to review their hull construction. New materials are being used by many boat manufacturers that provide the same protection as a barrier coating. Some companies warrant their hulls for as long as 10 years against blistering. Wait until the warranty is nearly expired to add this extra level of protection.

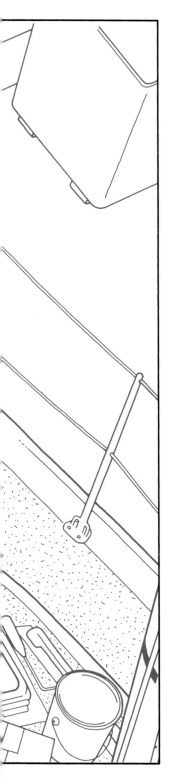

TOPSIDES AND DECK

While gelcoat is much like paint, being polyester-resin based gives it an advantage as a boat surface: when the hull laminates are originally applied to the layer of gelcoat in the mold, the two form a strong chemical bond. This applies only to layup; the bond between a long-cured hull and gelcoat brushed or sprayed on to cover a ding or scratch is strictly mechanical—just like paint. (Wiping the surface with styrene just prior to coating *can* partially reactivate the old gelcoat and result in some chemical crosslinking, but as a practical matter this step is often omitted.)

Where gelcoat differs from paint is in its thickness. The recommended film thickness of paint is likely to be about 2 mils; the range for gelcoat is 15 to 20 mils. That makes it stand up to wear and abuse much longer than paint. Scratches are less visible since they don't cut through to some different color base. And the thick coating can tolerate repeated polishing to restore its gloss.

The main disadvantage of gelcoat is that it has poor flow characteristics. Its original gloss comes from being sprayed onto the highly polished surface of a mold. When it is applied like paint to an external surface, the result is a rough, irregular surface, a far cry from the incredibly smooth and glossy finish of, for example, polyurethane paint.

Still, when the surrounding gelcoat is in good condition, surface damage repairs should generally be made with gelcoat. Even though the gelcoat application may initially be rough, it can be sanded smooth and polished to blend imperceptibly with the rest of the hull.

GELCOAT REPAIR

Gelcoat is essentially polyester resin with pigment added. As such, it can be applied in much the same manner as polyester, used as a surface coating, or thickened into a filler.

OPENING A SCRATCH FOR REPAIR

A scratch typically cannot be successfully repaired by painting over it with gelcoat. The gelcoat is too thin to fill the scratch, and if it is thickened to make a gelcoat putty, the putty bridges the scratch rather than filling it. To get a permanent repair, draw the corner of a scraper down the scratch to open it and put a chamfer on both sides, then fill the groove with gelcoat putty.

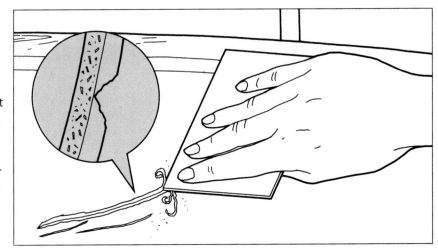

GOUGES AND OTHER DAMAGE REPAIRS

1 Damage to the underlying laminate must be repaired before applying the gelcoat. Shallow damage and drilled holes (where hardware has been removed) can be repaired with polyester resin thickened with chopped-strand glass. Epoxy resin must not be used for repairs that will be gelcoated because gelcoat does not adhere well to epoxy; stick with polyester resin for these repairs. Repair more extensive damage with a layer (or layers) of resin-saturated fiberglass fabric. "Fairing and Minor Blister Repair" in Chapter 4 provides more detail, but with polyester, use alternating layers of mat and cloth.

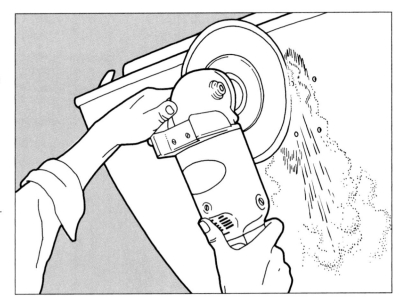

2 Use a polyester fairing compound—you can make your own by adding microballoons to the resin—to fair the repair prior to gelcoating.

3 Be sure the finished repair is below the surface or grind it below the surface with a disk sander and 100-grit paper. Otherwise you will cut through the new gelcoat when you later attempt to sand it flush with the surrounding surface. Vacuum or brush away all dust and loose fibers, and wipe the area thoroughly with acetone.

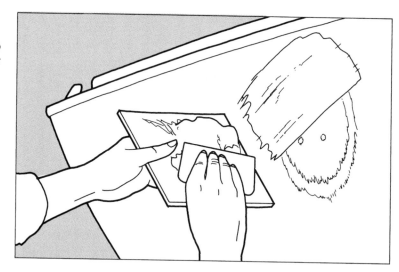

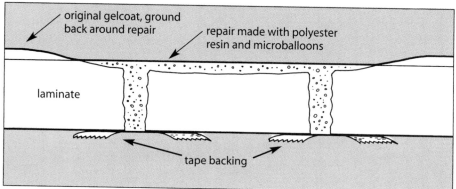

GELCOAT CHOICES

You will find gelcoat available as both a resin and in a thicker putty form called paste. The paste is what you want if you are repairing a scratch; repair kits containing a small amount of gelcoat paste and hardener along with a selection of pigments can be purchased for less than $20. For larger areas choose plain gelcoat, sold by the quart. You will also need coloring agents to tint it to the color you need.

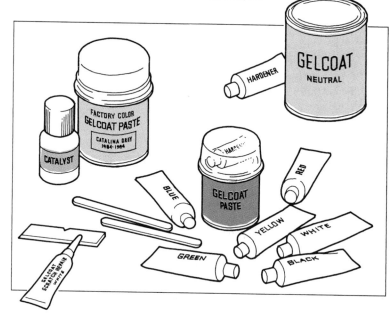

COLOR MATCHING

Gelcoat is also available in "factory" colors, but you are likely to have a difficult time finding one that is a perfect match for a hull that has been exposed to the fading rays of the sun for a few years. You will do as well buying pigments and tinting the gelcoat yourself.

1 What colors do you need? Go to a paint store and find a color-sample card close to the color of your hull. Show the card to the store clerk and ask what the formula is—the store custom mixes this color by adding pigments to a white base. If he tells you the mix calls for four units of blue and one of yellow, you need blue and yellow tints—and white. Sometimes the formula will call for half a dozen different tints. At least half of those, the ones called for in the least amount, are added to tweak the color to just the right shade. For gelcoat matching, the two or three primary tints should get you close enough.

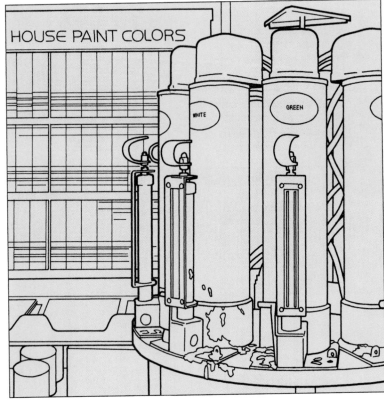

2 Be sure the coloring agents you buy are intended for use with polyester resin. Start with exactly 1 ounce of gelcoat, and add pigment a drop at a time, stirring between drops. Keep track of the number of drops. When the color looks close in the cup, put a drop of the mix on the gelcoat for a better comparison, then make any needed adjustments. When you're satisfied—don't expect perfection—write down the per-ounce formula to get the right color. Always tint the resin *before* you add the hardener.

CATALYZING

The hardener for gelcoat is the same as for any polyester resin—methyl ethyl ketone peroxide, or MEKP. Most gelcoat will require one to two percent of hardener (by volume). As a general rule, four drops of hardener will catalyze 1 ounce of resin at one percent.

Follow the manufacturer's instructions for catalyzing the gelcoat. It should not kick in less than 30 minutes. Hardening in about two hours is probably ideal, but overnight is just as good unless the wait will hold you up. Always err on the side of too little hardener. Also be certain to stir in the hardener thoroughly; if you fail to catalyze every bit of the resin, parts of the repair will be under-cured.

SPREADING GELCOAT PASTE

Gelcoat paste is applied like any other putty—with a plastic spreader. If you are filling a crack, the putty may bulge a little behind the spreader. This is okay: polyester resin shrinks slightly as it cures, and you are going to sand the patch anyway. Just don't let it bulge too much or you'll make extra work for yourself. Scrape up any excess beyond the patch area.

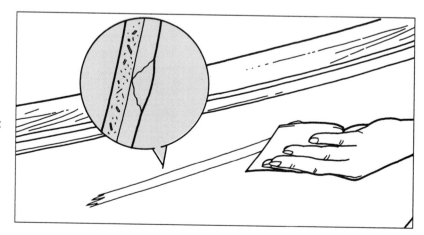

APPLYING GELCOAT WITH SPRAY

You can apply gelcoat over larger areas by brush, roller, or spray. Spraying can give the best initial finish, but it is also the most demanding way of applying the gelcoat. Gelcoat applied by brush or roller is likely to need a bit more sanding to achieve a polishable surface, but in the end you will be unable to determine how the gelcoat was applied. If you are comfortable spraying it on, do it that way; otherwise use a brush or a foam roller.

Getting gelcoat through a sprayer nozzle requires thinning the resin with styrene or toluene. Use a small gun with light to medium air pressure. If you don't have a spray gun, you can still spray the gelcoat with a Preval-type sprayer that uses a can of compressed air as the propellant. These are available for under $5.

Mask around the repair area to avoid getting gelcoat on any surrounding surfaces. Spray on the gelcoat with long, overlapping strokes. When the surface is coated, immediately apply a second coat with a spray pattern running diagonally across the first. Because the thinner flashes off very quickly, the gelcoat should show no tendency to run or sag with immediate recoating. Follow the second coat with a third one applied in another direction. Three sprayed coats should give you a skin thickness of about 15 mils. Giving the surface a fourth coat will give you extra gelcoat to work with—not a bad idea if this is your first experience with it.

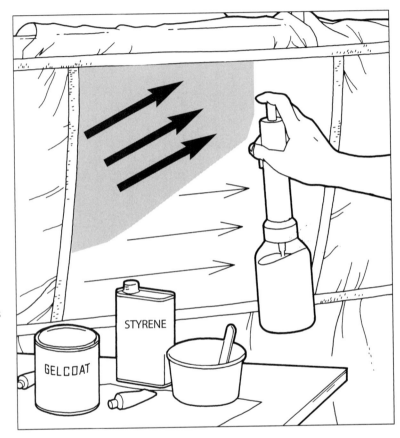

COVERING THE REPAIR

GELCOAT WILL NOT FULLY CURE in air. Regardless of how you apply the gelcoat, coat it with polyvinyl alcohol by brushing or spraying the PVA on after the gelcoat kicks.

APPLYING GELCOAT WITH BRUSH

For brush application, use the tinted and catalyzed gelcoat without thinning.

Because the gelcoat in the cup and the gelcoat on the surface are curing at about the same speed, you can't wait for the first application to kick and then apply a second layer without mixing up fresh gelcoat. The solution to this if the layer is too thin is to add a thickening agent to the gelcoat so that the first application is 20 mils thick. The usual thickening agent for gelcoat is dehydrated talcum, available in small quantities from your resin supplier. Add only enough to give a test stroke a 20-mil thickness. Be sure your test stroke doesn't exhibit a tendency to sag; if it does, stiffen the mixture by adding more thickener.

1 Lay the resin on in steady, slow strokes, much like a finish coat of varnish.

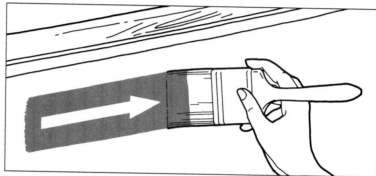

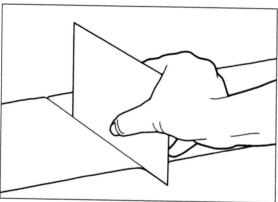

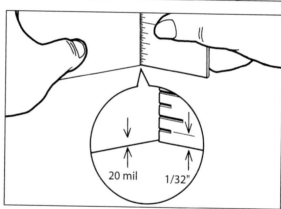

2 Check the thickness by "slicing" the test stroke with the edge of a piece of paper and comparing the height of the gelcoat on the paper to a 1/32" mark on a ruler, which is about 30 mils.

APPLYING GELCOAT WITH ROLLER

Roller application of gelcoat can give a more uniform thickness and a smoother surface. As with brush application, some thickening may be required to achieve the appropriate thickness with a single application. Use a foam roller cover cut to the appropriate width for the repair. Make a test application to check the thickness and thicken as necessary. Apply the gelcoat to the surface with a well-saturated roller, rolling in two directions.

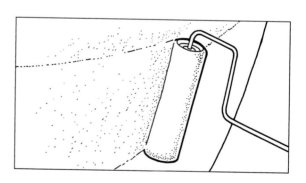

SANDING AND POLISHING GELCOAT REPAIRS

Wash off the PVA—it comes off with just water. The amount of sanding required depends on how smoothly you applied the gelcoat. If the gelcoat is a perfect spray application, light wet sanding may be all that is required, but for purposes of instruction, let's assume your repair resembles discarded chewing gum. Skip the steps your own repair doesn't require.

1. It is possible to use a power sander to remove a lot of extra gelcoat, but this requires great caution. A much safer approach to a lumpy gelcoat patch is to do the initial sanding with 120- or 150-grit paper on a sanding block. Use short strokes, taking care that the paper is sanding only the patch and not the surrounding surface. Keep in mind that the hull shape is probably convex in the repair area, so don't sand the gelcoat flat.

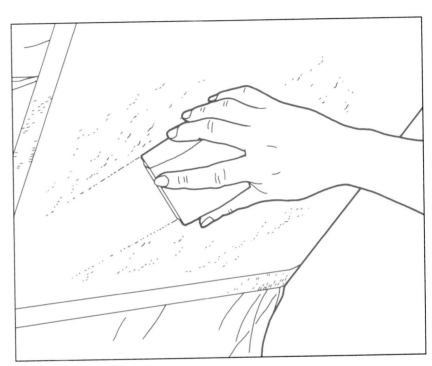

2. For a scratch repair, the edge of a 5½-inch length of 1 x 2 makes a convenient sanding block. Never do this initial sanding without a block backing the paper.

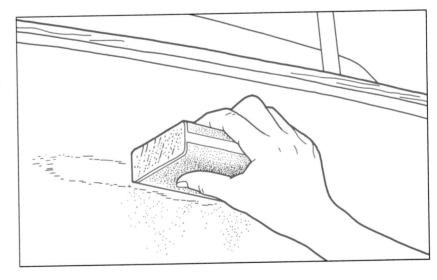

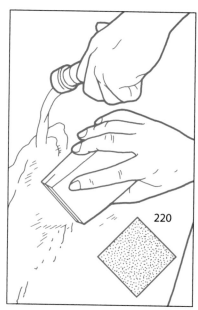

220

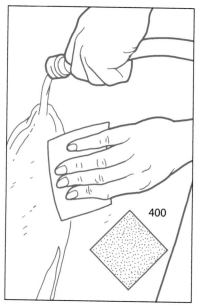

400

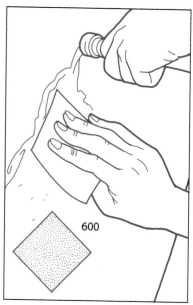

600

3 When the new gelcoat is flush, put 220-grit wet-or-dry paper on your block and wet sand the repair, feathering it into the old gelcoat until you can detect no ridge with your fingertips.

Switch to 400-grit wet-or-dry, abandoning the block, and wet sand the surface until it has a uniform appearance.

Follow this with 600-grit wet-or-dry.

4 Dry the area and use a buffing compound to give the gelcoat a high gloss. On small repairs, you can buff the gel-coat up to a gloss by hand. If the area is large, or if you want to buff the entire hull, buy or rent an orbital pol-isher. Either way, the process is the same. Apply the buffing com-pound to the surface, then buff it with a circu-lar motion, using heavy pressure at first, then progressively less pres-sure until the surface is glassy. If your color match is reasonably good, the repair will be virtually undetectable.

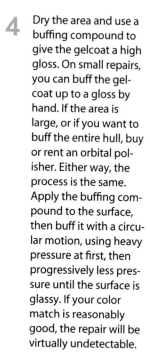

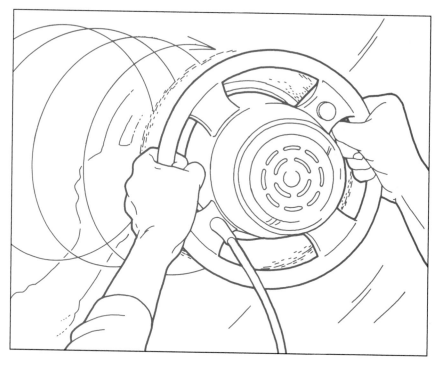

There may be valid reasons to use enamel or single-part polyurethanes (which are actually modified enamels) to paint the deck of a boat, but there is not a single reason to use anything but two-part linear polyurethane on a fiberglass hull. On deck, the limited working time the two-part paint affords can cause problems as you try to paint around hardware, portholes, or sections of nonskid, but the uninterrupted expanse of the hull is the ideal surface for applying polyurethane. The appearance and durability of two-part polyurethane is likely to be worth the extra effort of removing hardware and carefully mapping the sequence of application to use it on the deck, but electing to follow an easier course also has merit. However, the fact that two-part polyurethane is not appreciably more difficult to apply to an uninterrupted surface than any other paint makes all other choices for refinishing the hull significantly inferior.

PREPARING THE SURFACE

If your hull is in good condition, all that is required to prepare it for painting is dewaxing and sanding. A heat gun will make short work of removing any registration numbers or other vinyl graphics or stripes, but be sure not to heat the fiberglass enough to damage it. If it's too hot to touch, it's too hot. If the hull has been previously painted or is wood or metal, a conversion coat or a special primer will be required; follow the paint manufacturer's instructions.

1 No matter how old it is, every fiberglass hull must be solvent-wiped to remove all traces of wax, silicone, or mold-release agents. Dewax before sanding or the sandpaper will drag the wax into the scratches, making it far more difficult to remove. Soak your cloth with dewaxing solvent and wipe the hull in a single direction, as though sweeping a surface clear of sawdust. Turn the cloth often, and change it when you run out of fresh sides; otherwise you will spread the wax rather than remove it.

2 Sand the entire hull with 120-grit paper. If you will be sanding away the old bootstripe (a good idea), be sure to score the hull before you start so you can locate the waterline later.

CHECKING FOR POROSITY

Two-part polyurethane paints can be applied directly onto fiberglass in good condition. However, by the time most hulls need to be painted, the gelcoat has developed some porosity that will cause the paint to crater. Check the surface for porosity by applying paint of any kind—bootstripe enamel is perfect—to a test area on the hull. Examine the paint carefully for any sign of cratering, then wipe it from the hull with a solvent-soaked cloth. The paint may also form "fish eyes" (you'll know one when you see it), which indicate you need to do a better job of removing wax or silicone from the hull.

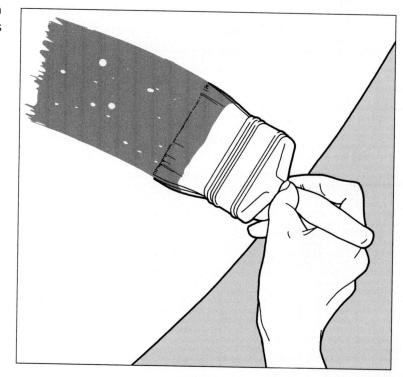

SURFACE CRAZING

In addition to porosity, old gelcoat may exhibit crazing—a pattern of tiny cracks in the surface similar to a cracked eggshell. Don't confuse surface crazing, which usually appears over a wide expanse, with stress crack associated with hardware mounting or molded corners. See *Sailboat Hull and Deck Repair* for stress-crack repair.

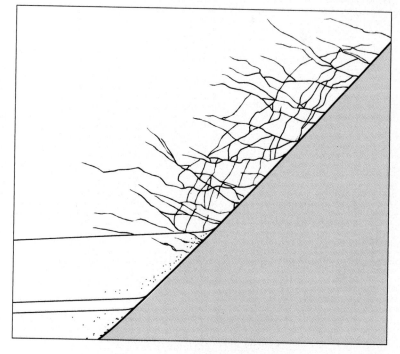

EPOXY PRIMER

The solution for both porosity and surface crazing is the same—a coat or two of epoxy primer. You may also need to apply epoxy primer as a conversion coating if the fiberglass has been previously painted. Check for compatability by wetting a cloth with the thinner for your linear polyurethane and taping it against the painted surface (in an inconspicuous spot) for about 10 minutes. If it softens or lifts the old paint, a conversion coating is required. Follow the instructions from the polyurethane manufacturer.

1 Mix the epoxy primer according to the label instructions and roll it onto the hull with a foam roller, without fuss. Allow it to cure overnight, and sand the surface with 120-grit paper. One coat will generally be adequate to correct porosity, but a second prime coat may be required for crazing.

TIP: Often it is very hard to see where you have sanded, especially on a white hull on a bright day. The solution to this is to *lightly* mist the surface with a can of dark **spray lacquer** (light on a dark hull). The lacquer dries instantly, and it comes away easily as you sand, making the sanded areas distinct from those not sanded. The spray pattern will also help prevent your eyes from losing focus on the otherwise featureless expanse of hull—a common and disconcerting occurrence.

2 Surface flaws that the primer obviously will not cover can be filled with fairing compound. After the first prime coat, apply this creamy epoxy filler to each spot with a small spreader. It will be dry enough to block sand in a few minutes. The second prime coat should give you a flawless surface.

SPRAYING POLYURETHANE PAINT

WHEN APPLIED BY BRUSH OR ROLLER, polyurethane paint is hardly more hazardous than oil-based enamel, but atomize polyurethane with a paint sprayer and it becomes potentially lethal. A component of this paint is isocyanate. If that sounds to you like it might be related to cyanide, you're paying attention. In aerosol form, this stuff is poison—pure and simple. Spraying polyurethane without an air-supplied respirator is not just foolhardy, it is stupid. You can get as good a finish—often better—by rolling and tipping this amazing paint, but if you are set on having your boat sprayed with polyurethane, don't be *dead* set on it. Pay to have it done by a professional with the required safety equipment.

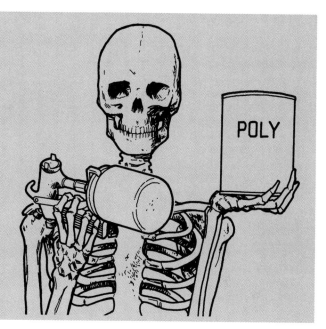

MIXING AND THINNING POLYURETHANE PAINT

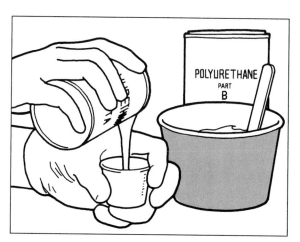

1 Mixing two-part paint is straightforward—put the designated amount of part A into the desired amount of part B and stir.

2 Thinning is not so well defined, and getting just the right amount of thinner in the paint is the key to getting a perfect finish. The trick is to sneak up on proper mix. The paint manufacturer's recommended ratio is no more than a starting point. In cool, dry weather, you will need less thinner; in hot, humid weather, more. Start with slightly less than called for and test the paint for flow.

TESTING FLOW-OUT

A scrap piece of window glass provides a perfectly smooth test surface for determining the flow characteristics of your mix. Set the glass vertically, and paint an area, using a throw-away brush and vertical strokes. Tip the test horizontally with your good brush. If the brush strokes fail to disappear entirely in a couple of minutes, you need more thinner. Add a capful to your mix and test again. Keep thinning a capful at a time until the brush strokes just disappear. If the paint runs or sags, you've added too much. Recover by adding a couple of additional ounces of paint to the mix. (Set a little mixed paint aside just for this purpose.) When the paint seems right, pour some into your tray, and roll and tip a test spot on the glass to make sure it is right for the film thickness you will be getting from the roller.

TIP: Getting the thinner right is the only difficult part to using two-part paint. You can greatly improve the likelihood of a perfect finish on your boat if you get familiar with the paint by first painting a dinghy or other small surface. Otherwise, paint just the transom of your boat first, mixing only enough paint for this limited area. Learning errors will be easy to sand out.

ROLLING POLYURETHANE (LIGHT COLORS ONLY)

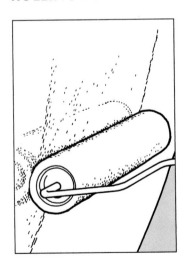

If you are applying white polyurethane (or any light color), you can get a very nice finish without ever touching a brush to the hull. Simply roll the paint on the hull with a solvent-resistant foam roller, taking care not to let the ends of the roller leave tracks. The rolled-on paint will dry to a high gloss with a very slight orange-peel texture, similar to a just-less-than-perfect spray finish. This is the easiest way to apply polyurethane, and you should try a test surface (the transom, for example) before deciding to roll and tip a light color. Dark colors will not flow out as well and require tipping with a brush.

KEEPING THE SURFACE CLEAN

THE WET GLOSS FINISH OF polyurethane will not only emphasize every underlying surface flaw, it will show dust contamination like a pimple on Elle MacPherson's face. Just before mixing the paint, always thoroughly wipe the surface you plan to paint with a solvent-dampened cloth, following with a clean, dry cloth.

The quick-skinning nature of two-part polyurethanes make them less susceptible to airborne dust contamination. Nevertheless, wetting the ground all around the boat with a mist spray from a garden-hose nozzle before you paint will help hold down dust that might otherwise find its way to the wet surface of your paint or into your paint tray.

THE ROLL-AND-TIP METHOD (ALL COLORS)

Done properly, tipping rolled-on polyurethane with a "dry" brush results in a finish that can only be described as stunning. Although one person can both roll and tip, the process is far easier with less opportunity for disaster if two people are involved.

Beginning at one end of the hull, the roller applies a uniform coat of paint to an 18- to 24-inch section of the hull, depending on the freeboard. If the freeboard is such that a roller load of paint will not cover at least 18 linear inches of the hull, you will have to apply the paint in over-and-under blocks, working with two wet edges.

The tipper follows behind the roller with a top-quality (badger or ox-hair) brush, tipping the surface of the paint lightly with a series of deliberate, parallel strokes toward the new wet edge. The tipper begins each stroke well back, gently "landing" the brush just behind the old wet edge and drawing it just beyond the new wet edge (see "'Laying

On' the Finish Coats" in the varnish section). The tipper's brush is never dipped in paint except that already applied to the hull.

While the last application is being tipped, the roller reloads the foam roller from the tray, rolling out all excess. When the tipper is finished, the roller is ready to coat the next section of the hull, just overlapping the wet edge. The tipper follows. Tip/load. Roll. Tip/load. Roll. Continue the process without pause or hesitation from one end of the hull to the other.

It is possible to continue right on around the bow or stern to the other side, painting the hull in one continuous session, but this is rarely done because one side of the hull is likely to be in the sun, and painting in the sun inhibits the flow of the paint. If you are continuing around to the other side, pause long enough to let the tipper clean his brush in solvent and dry it.

Painting with two-part paint is a sprint. Never go back and try to brush out a flaw; you will only make it worse. All problems with the first coat can be sanded out before the top coat is applied. With two people working together, expect the job to take less than a minute per foot. If it is taking you longer than that, your pace is too slow.

WET SANDING BETWEEN COATS

Let the first coat dry overnight, then wet sand it with 340-grit wet-or-dry paper. Never wet sand with an electric sander. However, to make the sanding go much faster, you can use a finishing sander on a surface moistened with water from a trigger sprayer if you are very careful to keep the moisture out of the tool. Thick rubber gloves are recommended as a precaution—as good as this finish will be, it's not to die for. Sand out any sags, runs, or other surface flaws. This is another good time to mist the surface with a contrasting spray of lacquer.

REMOVING SANDING SCUM

Sanding urethane produces a scum that is more tenacious than ordinary sanding dust. Flush the sanded hull with water, scrubbing as necessary. When the surface is dry, wipe it with a solvent-dampened cloth.

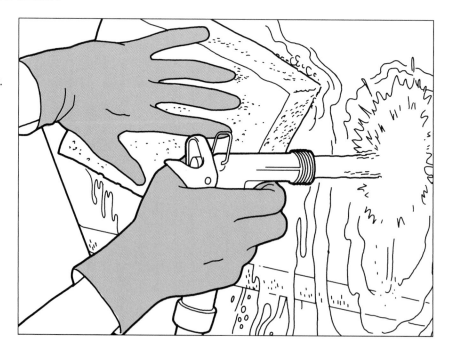

GETTING A MIRROR FINISH

The only thing different about the second coat is that you now know exactly what should and shouldn't happen. Thin the paint carefully to get it exactly right, then lay it on the hull in a nearly continuous flow. The results will be spectacular.

Two coats are generally adequate, but if you are dissatisfied with the results of your second coat, the cost of a third coat is nominal, and you begin it with twice the experience level you had on the previous coat. Stop at three—you aren't likely to get better. Besides, the improvement will be so dramatic that no one but you will ever notice the little flaws. Soon enough you won't notice them either.

COVE STRIPE

MOST FIBERGLASS HULLS HAVE A MOLDED-IN indentation for a cove stripe. Like the bootstripe, a cove stripe can be painted on or applied with tape. Regardless of how you intend to renew this stripe, you must strip and clean the indentation at the same time you are preparing the rest of the hull—before applying any primer or paint.

The molded-in recess generally simplifies painting. Mask the stripe with Fine Line tape laid to the edge of the recess. Use boottop enamel, and apply two or three coats with a brush. Two-part polyurethane is not a good choice for cove-stripe paint because it tends to wick under the masking tape. If the edge of the indentation is sharp, you may get as good or better results painting the stripe freehand, using a solvent-dampened rag as you go to clean away any paint that gets outside the recess.

The uniform width of a cove stripe makes it well suited for a tape application rather than paint. Stripe tape is available in myriad colors and widths from both marine chandleries and automotive stores. It is a simple matter to apply the tape, trimming the ends to match the recess contour. Solvent-wipe the recess before applying stripe tape.

Using an alkyd enamel or a single-part polyurethane on the deck will give you more time to work the paint around obstacles and still tip the paint out to a flawless finish. Your ability to get a perfect finish on deck with two-part polyurethane will be vastly improved if you remove as much deck-mounted hardware (including handrails) as practical. The extra work is repaid by the longer life of the polyurethane. Actually, removing hardware before painting will improve the job no matter what paint you choose because it eliminates edges where paint failure begins—the paint extends under the hardware. Besides, if the deck needs painting, the hardware likely needs rebedding anyway.

DEALING WITH NONSKID

Fiberglass decks generally have a pattern of molded-in nonskid. Painting nonskid surfaces reduces their effectiveness. To offset this effect, use a nonskid additive on those areas of the deck, even if the molded-in pattern is deep and well defined.

You may also want the nonskid portions of the deck a different color from the rest of the deck. In either case, refinishing the deck usually requires painting the smooth portions of the deck separately from the textured portions.

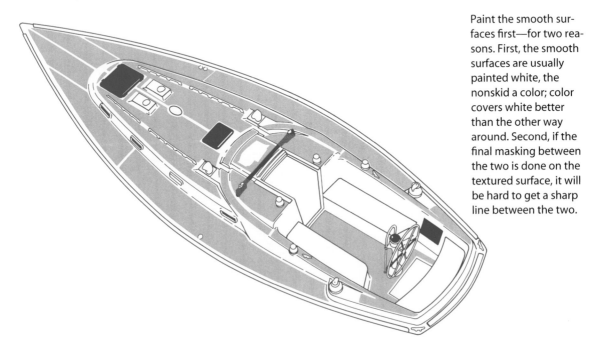

Paint the smooth surfaces first—for two reasons. First, the smooth surfaces are usually painted white, the nonskid a color; color covers white better than the other way around. Second, if the final masking between the two is done on the textured surface, it will be hard to get a sharp line between the two.

SURFACE PREPARATION

Preparing the smooth portions of the deck for paint is identical to preparing the hull. The textured nonskid sections require a little different approach.

1 Use terry cloth—sections of old bath towels—to dewax the non-skid. The rough surface of the terry cloth penetrates the craggy nonskid.

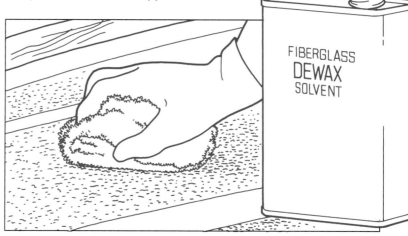

2 Sanding the bottom surfaces of the nonskid is not possible, but abrade the surface with coarse bronze wool, using short, quick strokes. Fortunately most of the stress on the new paint will be on the top surface, which you can sand. Machine sand the non-skid surface with 120-grit paper. Scrub the surface thoroughly with a brush and a hose, and let the surface dry completely before proceeding.

3 Mask all nonskid surfaces, applying the tape just inside the mold line. If the gelcoat is porous or crazed, remember to use an epoxy primer before applying the finish paint.

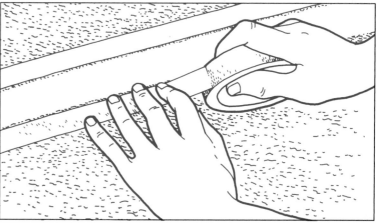

LIMITING WET EDGES TO ONE

1 Where the smooth part of the deck branches to divide or encircle sections of nonskid, you will find yourself dealing with two wet edges. If the branch branches again, you have three, maybe even four wet edges. And so on. Dealing with more than one wet edge is sure disaster with polyurethane and likely to cause problems with any kind of paint.

2 Avoid this by "mapping" the deck into manageable sections and masking off branches. For example, you might mask off all athwartship sections, then paint the deck between the nonskid and the rail all the way around the boat. When that is dry, move the tape to the other side of the paint lines (i.e., mask the section just painted) and paint the athwartship sections individually. Lines between sections will hardly be noticeable—a feature of the deck—and you avoid the disastrous problems of multiple wet edges.

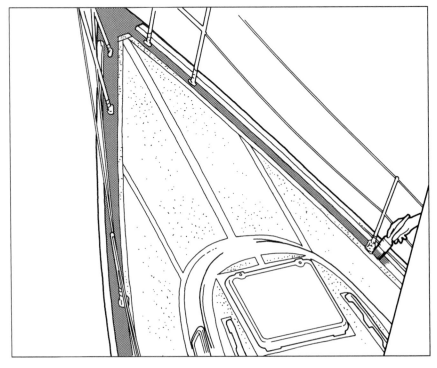

PAINTING MOLDED NONSKID SURFACES

1 After the smooth surfaces are dry, mask them and paint the nonskid sections. Instead of a foam roller cover, one with a longer nap may do a better job of getting paint into the bottom of the molded pattern. Give the new coating nonskid characteristics by introducing grit into the paint. This can be done in two ways.

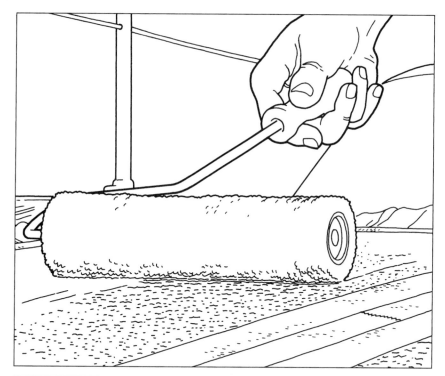

2 Paint manufacturers generally offer a nonskid additive—usually polymer beads—to be mixed into the paint before you apply it. Adding grit to the paint is easy and gives the rolled coating—there is no reason to tip paint on nonskid surfaces—a rough texture. Unfortunately the beads settle almost immediately to the bottom of the paint tray, resulting in irregular dispersion of the grit on the painted surface.

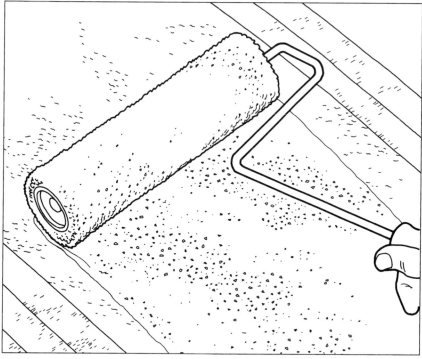

3 An alternative method providing a more aesthetically pleasing result is to first coat the nonskid area with an epoxy primer, and while the epoxy is wet, cover the entire surface with grit sifted from your fingers or a large shaker.

4 When the epoxy kicks, gently sweep off the grit that didn't adhere (you can use it on another nonskid area), and encapsulate the grit that remains with two rolled-on coats of paint. This results in a nonskid finish that few will find unattractive.

NONSKID OVERLAY

For the best footing, you might want to consider a rubberized nonskid overlay, such as Treadmaster M or Vetus deck covering. These are far more expensive than paint, but they do enhance security, and they can improve the boat's appearance as well, hiding old, worn-out nonskid textures. If you will be applying overlay, carry the paint ½ inch into the nonskid area when you paint the deck.

PREPARING THE SURFACE

Before the overlay can be applied, any molded-in texture must be removed. Most of the texture can be quickly taken off with a disk sander and a 36-grit disk. (A belt sander can also be used.) Be careful not to let the sander get outside the textured area. It is neither necessary nor desirable to grind away all the pattern. Fill the remaining depressions with epoxy putty. When the epoxy cures, sand the surface to fair it and prepare it for the adhesive.

CUTTING PATTERNS

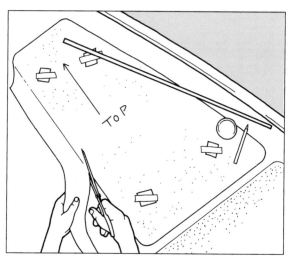

1 Make a pattern from heavy kraft paper for each of the nonskid panels. Cut the paper oversize, then place it on deck to trace the exact outline. Tape across holes cut in the center of the paper to hold it in place. Use a flexible batten to draw curved edges, a can lid for uniform corners. For appearance and drainage, leave at least 1 inch between adjacent panels, at least twice that between the nonskid and rails, coamings, or cabin sides. Write TOP on the pattern to avoid confusion when you cut the overlay, and draw a line on it parallel to the centerline of the boat, with an arrow toward the bow.

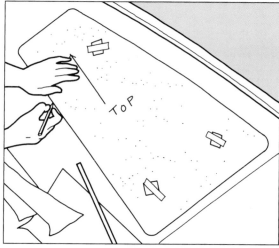

2 Do not cut patterns for only one side, expecting to reverse them for the opposite panels. Boats are almost never symmetrical, and hardware is certain to be in different locations. Cut a separate pattern for every panel. When all the patterns have been cut, tape them all in place and evaluate the overall effect before proceeding. Trace around each pattern with a pencil to outline the deck area to be coated with adhesive.

CUTTING THE OVERLAY

1 Place the patterns top-side down on the back of the overlay material. Depending on the overlay you have chosen, it may be necessary to align the patterns; use the line you drew on each pattern for this purpose, aligning it parallel to the long edge of the sheet of material.

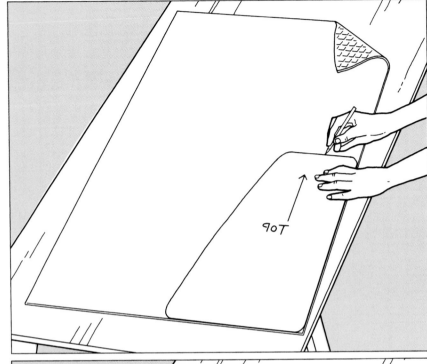

2 Position all the patterns on your material to minimize the waste before making any cuts. Trace each pattern onto the overlay, then cut out the pieces with tin snips or heavy scissors.

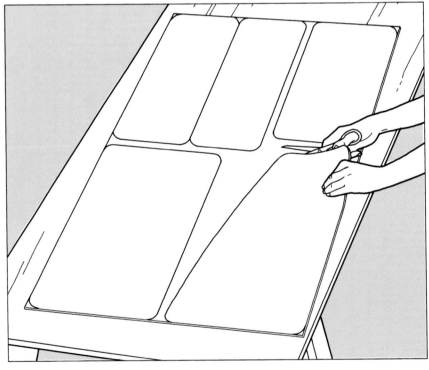

APPLYING THE OVERLAY

If the overlay manufacturer doesn't specify a different adhesive, glue the non-skid to the deck with thickened epoxy.

1 Coat both the outlined deck area and the back of the nonskid with the adhesive, using a serrated trowel.

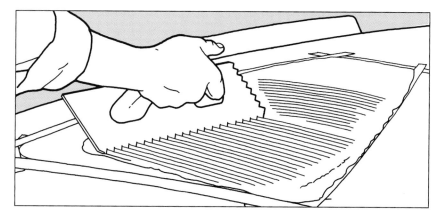

2 Position the nonskid on the deck and press it flat, beginning with pressure in the middle and working outward to all edges.

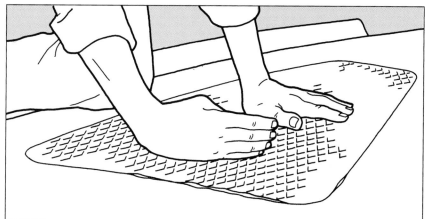

3 Pick up any squeeze-out with a putty knife, and clean away the residue with an acetone-dampened cloth. Continue applying each section in turn until all are installed.

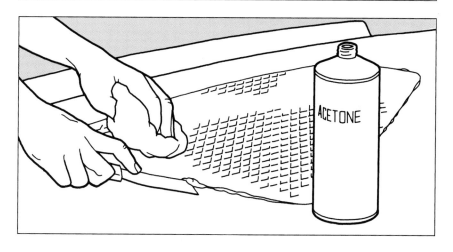

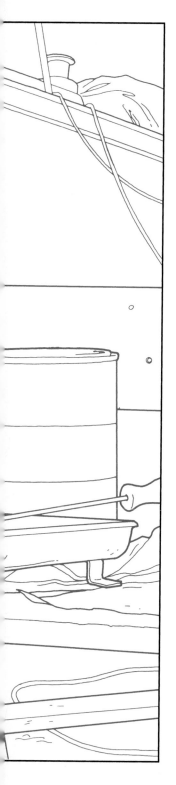

FINISHING TOUCHES

Masts used to come out of the boat every year to be checked for splits and rot, then get a fresh coat or two of varnish in the spring before being re-stepped. Today most masts are extruded aluminum, anodized against corrosion, and they may remain upright for a decade or more without *any* maintenance other than checking points of attachment for spreaders, tangs, and other hardware. That doesn't mean they don't show their age: A mast that has seen a decade or two of service is usually streaked with oxide and crosshatched with halyard scars. With fresh gloss on hull and deck, now is the time to spruce up that stick.

Your refinishing also can't be considered complete until the boat's name is back on the stern or the quarter. Unless you were satisfied with stick-on block letters, this used to be the domain of the professional signpainter. No more. With inexpensive computer-generated graphics, you can apply the name in virtually any configuration imaginable. And if your taste runs to eye-catching hull graphics, you have reached the fun part.

A couple of decades ago traditional wood rubrails began to be replaced with aluminum, then with vinyl. Aluminum and vinyl promised lower maintenance than wood, but, after a few years of exposure and a few encounters with fixed objects, aluminum rails typically look scarred and shabby, and vinyl rails harden, break, and fall off. It is possible to partially restore an aluminum rail by polishing it if it isn't badly damaged, but vinyl rails must be replaced. This can be a major undertaking if the boat manufacturer is out of business. Fortunately vinyl extrusions are used for thousands of other applications, so take a piece of your rail to a plastic extrusion supplier and you are likely to find something that will work and complement your new paint.

By the time a fiberglass boat needs refinishing, the plastic windows, especially the fixed deadlights in the main cabin, are likely to be fogged or crazed. Although not strictly refinishing, replacing portlights makes a striking difference in a boat's appearance. Detailed instructions for their replacement can be found in *Sailboat Hull and Deck Repair*.

The final touch should be bright, new canvas—sailcovers, a dodger, cockpit cushions. Find the instructions to make all these items and many others in *Canvaswork and Sail Repair*.

REFINISHING THE MAST

Having a mast reanodized is fairly expensive, not to mention the difficulty of getting a long spar to the treatment facility. Painting is justifiably the more popular solution. Forget about trying to protect your mast by spraying it with some kind of clear coat; by fall your deck will be aflutter with cellophane leaves. The best coating for your mast is the same as for your hull—two-part polyurethane.

1 Support the unstepped mast on sawhorses and remove as much hardware as you can. Wipe the mast with a cloth soaked in acetone or other solvent recommended by the paint manufacturer. Sand the entire mast with medium-grit emery cloth to remove oxidation and to give tooth to the surface of the mast.

    In order to allow the uninterrupted coating of the full circumference, suspend the mast above the horses with supports in the ends of the mast and metal rods through mounting holes in the center. The sail track should be facing up. Rewipe the suspended mast with solvent.

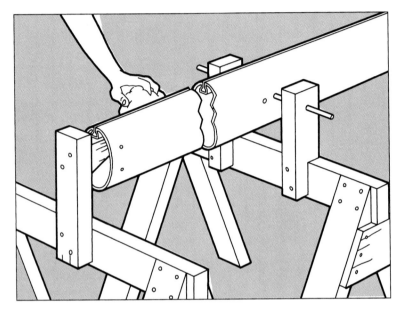

2 The key to a long-lasting finish is the prime coat. The specified undercoat for aluminum will probably be an acid-type primer that etches the metal to provide a better grip for the paint. Apply the primer per label instructions. Spray or roll it on to avoid introducing brush strokes. Acid primers are not sanded.

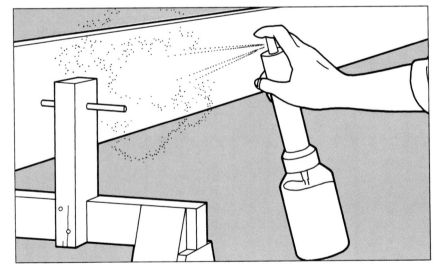

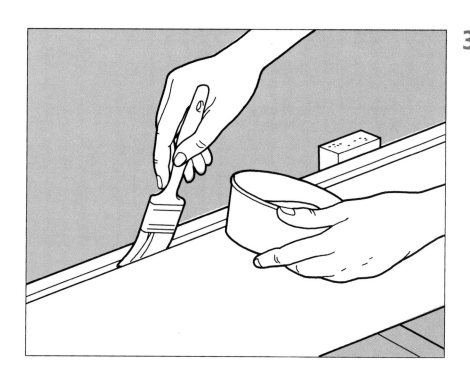

3 The most popular color for the finish coat is white, but black and buff are also common. Of course, you can paint your mast any color you like. Whatever the color, apply the urethane with a roller. Tipping is not likely to be necessary. Let the first finish coat dry overnight, and wet sand it with 340-grit paper before applying the top coat.

You will need a brush to cut the paint around any hardware you failed to remove and to get paint into the sail track.

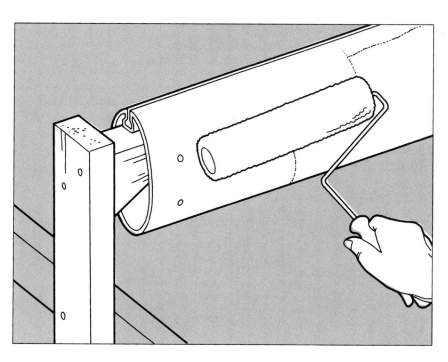

4 Start at the top end of the mast, painting 2 feet of the track with the brush, then running the lightly loaded roller all around the mast to coat the surface. Paint the mast in 2-foot sections, maintaining a single encircling wet edge. If you have problems early on, don't fret; they will be well out of sight, and by the time you get to the deck end of the mast, you will have found a rhythm and technique that gives you the quality finish you want.

GRAPHICS

It isn't that difficult to do a workman-like job of painting the name on your boat with spray mask, an X-acto knife, and can of spray enamel. One color. Block letters. Ho hum.

For a little more money and a lot less work, you can kick some stern. There seems to be no limit to what is now possible with computer-generated boat graphics. A graphics supplier can convert your most imaginative idea for your transom into an electronic image—allowing you to evaluate it on a computer screen and make appropriate modifications—then give it to you as a vinyl appliqué contoured and sized to precisely fit your boat. For the hull sides, eye-catching graphics in a rainbow of colors can be created and applied with similar ease.

DESIGNING CUSTOM GRAPHICS

For a boat name, the designer will provide you with examples of available fonts, examples of special effects—outline, shadow, arch, etc.—and a selection of solid and metallic colors. All you have to do is measure the area where the name will be applied and determine curvature of the hull—the designer will tell you exactly how. Hull curvature will affect how the applied graphic appears and must be accounted for to get the appearance you envision. You also pick a font, a letter size, a style, and a color or colors. A local supplier can show you the combined effect of your selections on a computer monitor and make instant alterations until you are satisfied. A distant supplier will send or fax a printed image for your approval.

For custom graphics, you will need to work directly with the designer.

LAYING OUT VINYL GRAPHICS

When you receive the appliqué, it will come as a single sheet to allow you to position it properly on the hull. The sheet will have both a centerline and a baseline printed on it.

Begin the layout by cleaning the area of the hull where the graphic will be applied. Locate the center-line of the area; on the stern, for example, measure from side to side. Draw the center-line on the hull with a pencil, making sure the line is long enough to extend beyond the appliqué at both the top and the bottom.

Position the graphic on the centerline and move it up and down until you locate the

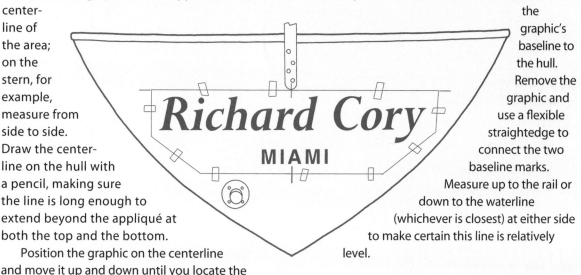

right position. Tape it in place and step back from the boat to evaluate the location. You may need to ascend a stepladder to get the proper on-the-water perspective. If a hailing port will be included, now is also the time to position it.

Once you are satisfied with the location, transfer the graphic's baseline to the hull. Remove the graphic and use a flexible straightedge to connect the two baseline marks. Measure up to the rail or down to the waterline (whichever is closest) at either side to make certain this line is relatively level.

DEALING WITH A LARGE APPLIQUÉ

One you have it aligned, you may find it easier to work with a sizable graphic if you cut it into smaller pieces. The actual decal is sandwiched between the decal backing and a transparent sheet of application tape. Make your cuts between words or letters. If you make these cuts in a gentle S-curve rather than straight, the pieces will only fit together one way when put on the hull. The alternative is to put a couple of inch-long horizontal alignment marks on the back of the tape where you will be cutting the graphic, then cut them in half when you scissor the appliqué.

APPLYING VINYL GRAPHICS

1 *Never* try to apply vinyl graphics on a windy day. Remember the last time you tore off a 3-inch strip of cellophane tape and it immediately folded back on itself? Once you peel away the backing from your decal, you are dealing with a sheet of sticky-faced tape measured not in inches but in square feet. If the wind flips one corner back on itself, either your boat will have a shorter name or you will be paying for a new graphic. Even on a still day, an extra pair of hands will cut down on adrenaline production.

2 Put the graphic on a flat surface, tape-side down, and carefully peel the paper backing. If the decal starts to come away with the backing, use a knife to gently separate the two, then hold the graphic against the tape with the flat of the blade while you continue peeling the backing. If you are applying the graphic in sections, peel the backing from the center section first.

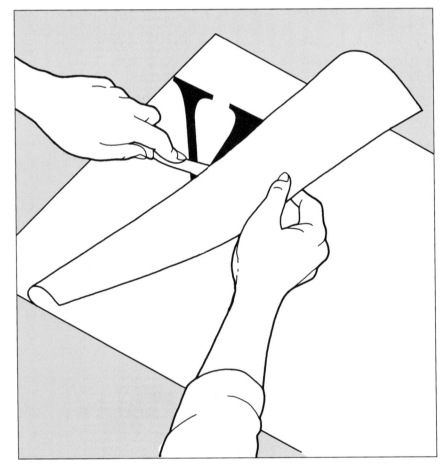

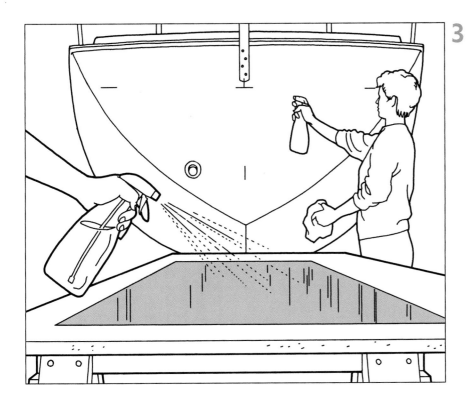

3 Spray the adhesive side of the graphic with window cleaner (Windex). Also spray the hull where the graphic goes, using a cleaner-soaked sponge to make sure the entire surface is wet. Be careful not to wash off your alignment marks.

4 Position the decal on the hull. The window cleaner allows you to slide the decal into the exact position—aligned with both the centerline and the baseline—but try to get close to start.

5 Making sure the graphic doesn't move, squeeze the moisture out from under it with a plastic squeegee. Start at the center and work toward the edges. If the graphic is in pieces, apply each piece in turn, working out from the center piece. Give the decal's adhesive at least 15 minutes to grab the hull—longer if the weather is cold—before the next step.

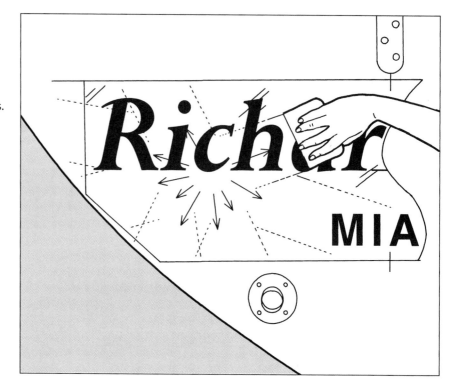

6 Spray the application tape heavily with the window cleaner, then use the squeegee with heavy pressure on the wet application tape to rub down the letters and graphics against the hull.

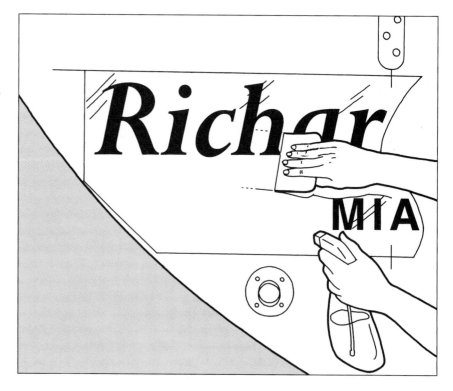

7 *Slowly* peel away the application tape. If the decal shows any tendency to come up with the tape, stop; you haven't waited long enough. Smooth the tape back down, rerub the lifted section of decal, and wait another 10 or 15 minutes before removing the tape.

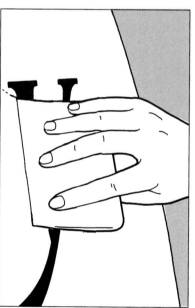

8 Burnish the installed decal with a cloth to remove any trapped air. Prick any bubbles at one edge with a pin to let the air escape, then burnish the bubble flat with the squeegee. (Small bubbles will disappear on their own in a few days.) Now back away. Could a pro have done any better? Give the decal a day to set, then wash all the alignment marks and glue residue off with soapy water.

That's it. There is just one thing left to do. Wad up those paint-stained coveralls and don your sailing hat. It's time to paint a wake on the bay.

BOAT EL

"Most of us find electricity as incomprehensible as the tax code."

Sailboat
Electrics
Simplified

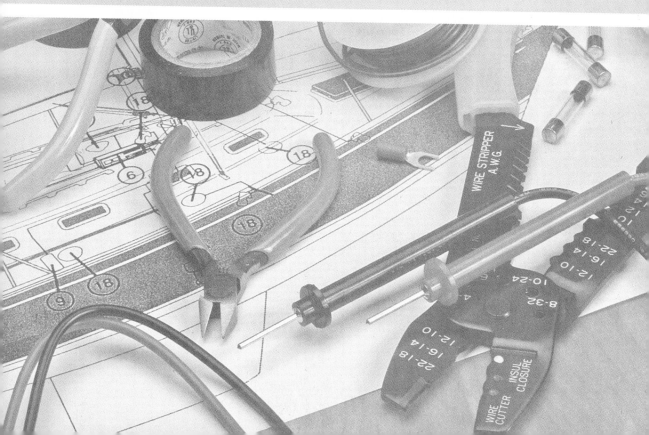

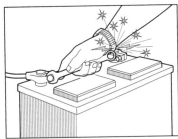

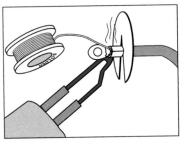

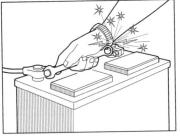

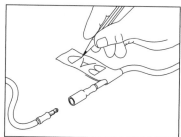

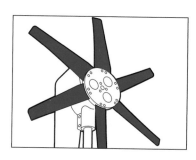

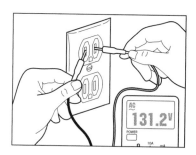

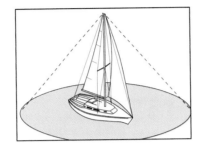

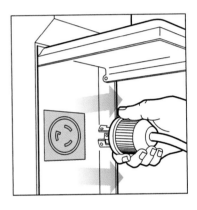

INTRODUCTION

I admire those hard cases who, before setting off around the globe, lever the engine out of the bilge and tilt it over the rail, deep-sixing a whole passel of woes. The time not spent doing maintenance can effectively add weeks to a cruise. Maybe the engineless do miss a few destinations with difficult approaches, but they also avoid languishing in some overdeveloped and under-flushed harbor awaiting the arrival of transmission parts. They never spill fuel, smudge the transom with soot, or besmirch profound silence with the clatter of reciprocating iron. Discarding the engine also rules out mechanical refrigeration, you won't find a watermaker aboard, and the absence of an engine-driven alternator necessarily simplifies the boat's electrical system.

I am personally OK with ice for uncomplicated refrigeration, and to me catching water actually seems preferable to "making" it, but when I contemplate kerosene lighting, the simplicity of "pure" sail loses all appeal. Kerosene illumination bright enough to read by will add at least 20 degrees to the cabin temperature. That may be nice when it is 40°F outside, but when it's 85°F—well, you do the math.

On my boat I want bright and cool electric lights. While that doesn't necessarily require an alternator powered by a 500-pound diesel engine—a couple of solar panels can provide enough electricity for cabin lights—I also want fans. And a radio transmitter. And a good sound system. When the anchorages get deep, I could use the help of an electric windlass. And speaking of hauling, resupplying the cooler with ice gets to be a drag quicker than I like to admit.

This, of course, is how electrical systems on boats evolve. Production sailboats come with a few lights, a freshwater pump, and the expectation that the purchaser will add a depth sounder and a VHF radio. The alternator, the battery, even the wiring are designed for these modest demands. The owner, however, is rarely of a mind with the manufacturer.

Maybe it starts with adding a reading light over a bunk. While a new lamp for home comes with a plug we simply insert into any unoccupied wall outlet, a lamp for the boat brings only a few inches of wire lead. Now what? Far too often the answer is a length of lamp cord twisted to the bare leads on one end and wrapped on the other around the terminal screws of the nearest cabin light.

What is wrong with that? Just about everything.

Adding appliances to your boat's existing electrical system is neither difficult nor complicated, but it is exacting if the modification is to be safe and trouble free. Sometimes sailors use the wrong wire because it is handy, but more often they simply don't know any better. If you're connecting a lamp, what can be wrong with using lamp cord? And if it is adequate for a 100-watt table lamp, how can it be inadequate for a 10-watt reading lamp? Fair questions, both, and their answers are provided in Chapter 4.

Most of us find electricity as incomprehensible as the tax code. Who really understands the basis for subtracting line 8 from line 5, then multiplying by 0.25 to get line 9, "but do not enter more than line 6"? So we pay someone to do our taxes. Or we buy Turbo Tax to tell us—without the bureaucratic doublespeak—exactly what to write on each line of the tax form and not trouble us with the why unless we ask. The underlying concept for this book is much the same—Turbo Wiring, if you will.

The objective of this book is to show you exactly how to service and modify the electrical system on your boat. Assuming that the less theory I throw at you, the happier you're going to be, I have included electrical arcana only where it is absolutely essential. But here's the deal: if I try to keep this dead simple for the masses, the eggheads in the bunch can't take me to task for taking liberties. I'm not teaching electricity here. I'm just trying to show you how to make a safe, durable connection.

OK, that isn't quite all there is to it. The connection I am really trying to help you make is the one between you and the electrical system aboard your boat—figuratively speaking, of course. For example, if you understand amp-hours the way you understand gallons, determining how long your batteries will run all the boat's electrical equipment is as easy as calculating how far you can expect to motor on a tank of fuel.

So when I describe amps in the following pages, it is for practical use, not scientific—something like introducing European tourists to mph. It isn't necessary to know that a mile is 1,609 meters when speedometers, maps, and road signs are all in mph. Likewise, you can read amps directly from a meter and make the necessary correlations without any understanding of the underlying science.

You will find practical information here about batteries—gel cells versus the flooded variety, cranking batteries versus deep cycle. You will learn how to select the "right" wire and how to make "good" connections. You will learn to calculate how quickly your electrical equipment will deplete your batteries, and how to counteract that drain with both traditional and alternative power sources.

Besides a handful of electrical terms, I will expose you to a few symbols that let you "map" your boat's electrical system, taking a lot of guesswork out of troubleshooting. You will see how to isolate problems quickly using a multimeter—where to connect the test probes and exactly what specific readings mean. (An adequate digital multimeter today costs less than this book and every boatowner should have one!)

You will find enough information about marine electronics to let you install new gear, enough about alternating current to avoid or correct the most common shore-power problems, and enough about lightning to let you maximize your level of protection from this unpredictable menace.

So put aside your preconceptions and turn the page. I promise explanations and instructions as uncomplicated as I can make them. There is nothing here that should put you at risk. To the contrary, understanding the wiring on your boat should only make you safer. The only shock you are likely to experience is how easy this stuff really is.

SAFETY FIRST

A lot of people are of the opinion that messing around with electricity is just asking for it. Touch the wrong wire and it's off to Fiddler's Green. Respect for the dangers of electricity is a good thing—not something I want to talk you out of. But the bulk of this book concerns battery-powered electrical systems that operate on what is called *direct current* or DC. DC voltage has to get up around 600 volts to represent a serious shock risk. Working on your boat's 12-volt electrical system has the same shock potential as changing the batteries in a portable lantern—none.

Alternating current (AC) is another matter, whether provided by an outlet on the dock, an onboard generator, or even an inverter. The pulsating nature of AC can interfere with your heart's natural rhythm, and a fatal disruption is possible with as little as 60 volts AC. Since onboard AC circuits carry at least 110 volts, you must take all necessary precautions to make sure you don't accidentally touch the wrong wire. As long as you disconnect the power supply first, it is possible to work on AC circuits in complete safety, but that means *all* power supplies. Keep in mind that an inverter energizes the AC circuits even when the boat is unplugged. If you are at all unsure, leave AC circuits to someone else.

Twelve-volt circuits won't shock you no matter which wires you touch, but that doesn't mean you can dispense with caution. There are other safety issues you should keep in mind.

BATTERY ACID

The liquid (electrolyte) inside a battery is a sulfuric acid solution. Spill it on yourself and it will eat clothes and burn skin. Never peer closely into the cells to check the water level; a popping bubble can spray enough acid in your eyes to cause permanent impairment, even blindness. Wear eye protection when working around batteries. If you do splash battery acid, flush it immediately with freshwater (*not* seawater, which gives off deadly chlorine gas when combined with battery acid). Neutralize the spill with baking soda.

CONTAINMENT

Mount batteries in an acid-proof box. Cracked battery cases are not unknown, and in such an event a box eliminates or minimizes collateral damage. You can purchase polypropylene battery boxes or construct your own using plywood sheathed in fiberglass.

Should a heavy battery come adrift, it can cause serious damage and injury. It is imperative to secure all batteries with strong straps or restraining rods.

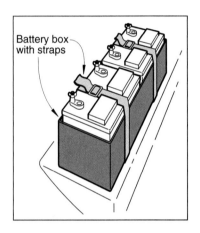

Battery box with straps

SPARK

If you have ever attached jumper cables, you have no doubt seen the sparking potential of a 12-volt battery. Electrical arcs—the basis for arc welding—generate tremendous heat. Accidentally touch a wrench to both terminals of a charged battery and the current will cut a notch in the wrench—and maybe in your hand. Remove all metal jewelry before working on battery connections.

Small wires can also spark, but with much less consequence because the current is limited by wire size and probably a fuse. However, any spark is dangerous in the presence of explosive fumes. Be sure the bilge is clear of propane or gasoline fumes before working on your electrical system.

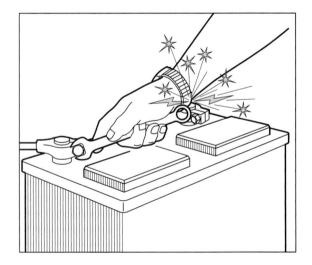

EXPLOSIVE GAS

When charging, batteries produce both hydrogen and oxygen—a volatile cocktail. Both gases are lighter than air, so they don't settle into the bilge, but they can accumulate in the battery compartment. Effective ventilation is a battery-compartment essential.

Never work on the electrical system while the battery is charging. Even if the batteries are well ventilated, the "head" of the cells is full of hydrogen and oxygen.

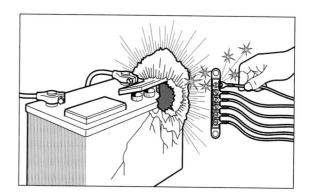

FIRE

Fire is far and away the most common consequence of inadequate or careless wiring. Resistance causes a conductor to get hot—the principle behind the burner coils on an electric range. Wire too small for the job, poor connections, and corrosion can all result in excessive and dangerous resistance. Hot wiring is most dangerous when it is in contact with flammables like paper or cloth, but a hot wire directly igniting polyester resin (fiberglass) is not unknown.

Protect against electrical fire by using large enough wire (tables are provided in Chapter 4). Tin-plated ("tinned") wire is much more corrosion resistant than bare copper. Terminals should likewise be tinned copper, never aluminum. Use only copper or brass washers on screw terminals, not steel or aluminum.

CORROSIVE FUMES

Charging batteries give off corrosive fumes. These are especially harmful to electronics, so never store or mount electronic equipment inside or even near the battery compartment. This is not so much a safety concern as an economic one.

FUSE

Normally adequate wiring can become a fire hazard if it becomes overloaded. Dampness and motion make boat wiring especially susceptible to unexpected "shorts" that result in just such an overload. A fuse or breaker acts to prevent this by disconnecting the wire if the current passing through it exceeds a safe level.

Every circuit aboard your boat must have a fuse or breaker in the "hot" wire leg. (The *only* exception *might* be the circuit supplying power to the engine starter motor.) The fuse protects the wire, not the appliances the wire supplies. Fuses and breakers should always be as close to the battery as practical.

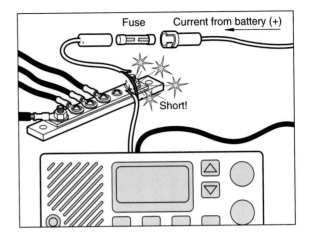

UNDERSTANDING THE BASICS

How many sailors does it take to screw in a light bulb? If you don't want to be the butt of this disparagement, you have to abandon the attitude that everything about electricity is just *too* complicated. *Baseball is complicated.* Compared to the infield fly, the balk, or the ground-rule double, the rules that govern electricity are (invoking a bit of irony here) child's play.

Electricity and baseball have at least one thing in common: nothing worthwhile happens until a runner completes the circuit around the bases. Whether a baseball player is at bat or has managed to advance all the way to third, he is only a *potential* run. We use potential to mean the same thing in electricity. The runner has to return to home plate to score. Electrons are the runners in the electricity game, and until they make the complete circuit, no numbers go up on the scoreboard.

Baseball has its own vocabulary—foul, fly, bunt, double play, pinch hit—but few of us have any difficulty grasping these terms, not even strike, which normally means "to hit sharply," but inexplicably means just the opposite in baseball. A few specialized terms are likewise required to follow the action in the electricity field, but too few to get excited about. Adding a half-dozen new words to your vocabulary will likely be sufficient.

This chapter is essentially the "official rules." In addition to defining terms, it shows how to play the game—including league differences (the electrical equivalent of the designated hitter)—and how to keep score. Nobody likes to read rules, but with electricity you don't get away with a breach just because the umpire misses it. When you break a rule, whether out of ignorance or indifference, there are *always* consequences. Conversely, if you know the rules and follow them, expect a happy outcome.

TERMINOLOGY

Most of the terms you need to work on your boat's wiring will come in context, but before we begin building that understanding, we need to lay the four cornerstones. These are the basic concepts of electricity, all named for 18th-century scientists.

AMP

Amp, short for ampere, is a measurement of electrical *current*. Just as the Department of Transportation measures traffic flow by counting how many vehicles per hour cross a sensor laid across the highway, we measure the flow of electricity in a wire by counting the number of electrons per second that pass a sensor.

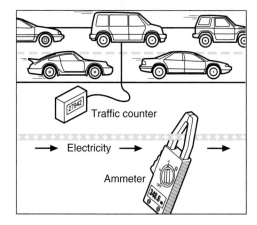

VOLT

Volt is a measurement of *potential*. Potential is not how many cars are on the road, but how many people own cars. The more drivers in downtown office buildings at 4:59, the greater the potential for the traffic flow to be heavier (or last longer) when we flip the switch at 5:00. Likewise, higher voltage forces a greater flow of electrons.

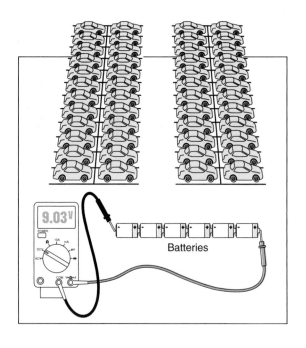

OHM

Ohm is a measurement of *resistance*. A six-lane highway is a good *conductor* of rush-hour traffic, but funnel that down to one lane and traffic nearly stops. Or change the road from straight, smooth asphalt to winding, rutted dirt and the rate of travel drops to a crawl. The flow of electrons is similarly conducted or resisted based on the size and composition of conductors.

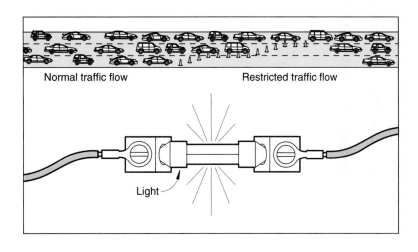

Normal traffic flow   Restricted traffic flow

Light

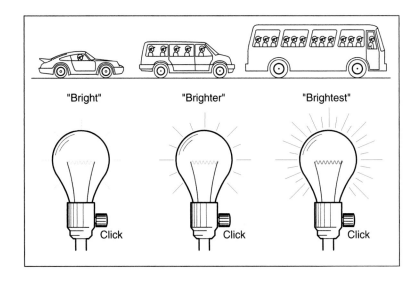

"Bright"   "Brighter"   "Brightest"

Click   Click   Click

WATT

Watt is a measurement of *power*. It is the rate at which work gets done. For example, consider how many people the road system transports from their offices to their homes between 5:00 and 6:00 P.M. Assuming the roads have sufficient capacity, we can increase that rate of "work" by putting more cars on the road or by putting more people in each car. Increasing either volts (force) or amps (current) increases electrical power.

THREE-PART HARMONY

Buy a roll of one hundred 37-cent postage stamps and the cost will be $37. Expressing this everyday calculation as the equation E = N x P (expenditure = number x price) doesn't make it any more complicated. Change the letters and this very same equation expresses how the electrical measurements defined above are related. If you can compute the cost of a book of stamps, you have all the math skill necessary to do electrical calculations.

OHM'S LAW

Understanding the relationship between current, voltage (potential), and resistance is essential to almost every electrical problem or project you might take on. Fortunately, this relationship is dead simple: an increase in voltage increases current; an increase in resistance decreases current. To be specific, *current is directly proportional to voltage and inversely proportional to resistance.* This is Ohm's Law.

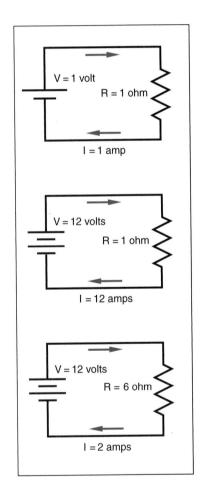

If this sounds confusing to you, it isn't. An identical law governs your personal economics—namely, the amount of anything you can buy is directly proportional to how much money you have available and inversely proportional to price. Our postage-stamp equation shows this relationship more clearly rewritten as N = E / P. Doubling the expenditure (E) doubles the number (N) of stamps you buy. Doubling the price (P) cuts N in half.

The equivalent equation for Ohm's Law is I = V / R, where I stands for current, V for voltage, and R for resistance. (We don't use C for current because I is the conventional abbreviation.) To use Ohm's Law, current must always be in amps, abbreviated as A; voltage always in volts, abbreviated as V; and resistance always in ohms, abbreviated as Ω.

If we apply 1 volt to a circuit having 1 ohm of resistance, 1 amp of current will flow (1 V / 1 Ω = 1 A). Increase the voltage to 12 volts, and the current increases proportionally to 12 amps (12 V / 1 Ω = 12 A). Raise the resistance to 6 ohms, and the current flow in the circuit is reduced to 2 amps (12 V / 6 Ω = 2 A).

When we want to calculate resistance rather than current, we rearrange the equation to R = V / I. For voltage calculations, the form becomes V = I x R, or simply V = IR. This latter is the easiest to commit to memory.

POWER

Power is the rate of doing work. The more powerful an engine is, for example, the more work it can do (i.e., push a larger boat or push a boat faster). The unit of measurement for mechanical power is usually *horsepower*, but for electricity we use the *watt*. The higher the wattage of a light bulb, the more light we expect from it.

Electrical power is derived by multiplying voltage times current. The shorthand for this relationship is P = V x I, where P stands for power, V for voltage, and I for current. If we want the power in watts—and we always do—then the voltage has to be in volts and the current in amps.

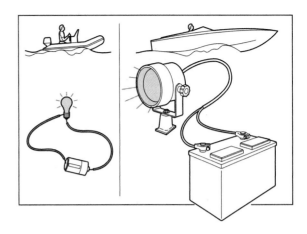

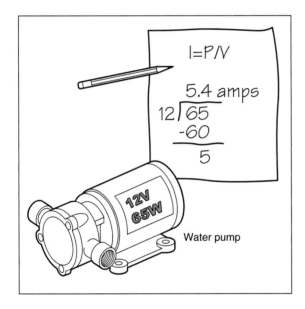

Water pump

As with Ohm's Law, we can write the power equation three ways, depending on what we want to calculate:

$$P = V\,I$$
$$V = P\,/\,I$$
$$I = P\,/\,V$$

The first form is the easiest to remember, but the last is the one you will use most often. Light bulbs and most other electrical equipment are rated in watts, but as you will soon see, we are more often concerned with how much current an appliance draws. To determine that, we simply divide the specified wattage by the electrical system voltage. A 25-watt cabin lamp in a 12-volt system will draw a little more than 2 amps when it is on (25 W / 12 V = 2.08 A).

LOAD CALCULATIONS

Now is a good time to calculate the current draw of every electrical item aboard. You will need this to determine appropriate battery capacity, alternator size, or solar panel benefit. Sometimes current requirements are specified, but more often the rating is in watts. List every appliance aboard, then divide its rated wattage by 12 to get its average current draw.

Note that some high-draw components are rated in kilowatts (kW). A kilowatt is 1,000 watts. So a starter motor shown in your engine manual as 1.8 kW has a current draw of 150 amps (1,800 W / 12 V). Electric windlasses have similar current demands.

Enter the loads into a chart similar to the one shown. We will return to this chart in Chapter 3. The loads depicted in the illustration are typical and may be used to approximate the load of any appliance for which you are unable to locate actual specifications.

TYPICAL 12-VOLT POWER CONSUMPTION			
Device	Amps	Device	Amps
Anchor light	0.8	Radar	4.0
Anchor windlass	150.0	Reading light	
Autopilot (above deck)	0.7	—halogen (10w)	0.8
Bilge blower	6.5	Refrigerator	5.0
Cabin fan (efficient)	0.2	Running lights	2.5
Cabin fan (oscillating)	1.2	Running lights	
Cabin light		—Tricolor	0.8
—fluorescent (8w)	0.7	Spotlight	10.0
Cabin light		Tape deck	1.0
—incandescent (25w)	2.1	Television (13-inch)	3.5
Chart light (10w)	0.8	Toilet	40.0
Compass light	0.1	Speed log	0.1
Deck lights	6.0	SSB (receive)	2.5
Depth sounder	0.2	SSB (transmit)	30.0
Gas detector	0.3	Starter	
GPS	0.5	—diesel (1,800w)	150.0
Ham radio (receive)	2.5	Strobe	1.0
Ham radio (transmit)	30.0	VCR	2.0
Inverter—standby	0.2	VHF (receive)	0.5
Microwave (600w)	100.0	VHF (transmit)	5.0
Pump—bilge	15.0	Waste treatment	45.0
Pump—freshwater	6.0	Weatherfax	1.0
Pump—shower sump	2.0	Wind indicator	0.1
Pump—washdown	6.0		

DESERT ALGEBRA

If your knowledge of algebra has been buried by the sands of time, you can rely on these two pyramids to keep the equations straight. Putting your finger over the variable you are trying find will reveal the arithmetic required. For example, cover I in the Ohm's Law pyramid and what remains is V over R: $I = V / R$. Cover P in the power pyramid and you are left with V I: $P = V \times I$. If these work for you, don't be reluctant to rely on them.

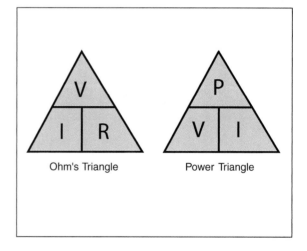

Ohm's Triangle   Power Triangle

CIRCUITS

It is no coincidence that batteries have two terminals and appliances have two leads. Connecting one lead to the battery's positive terminal and one to the negative provides the closed loop necessary for electrons to flow. This loop is called a circuit.

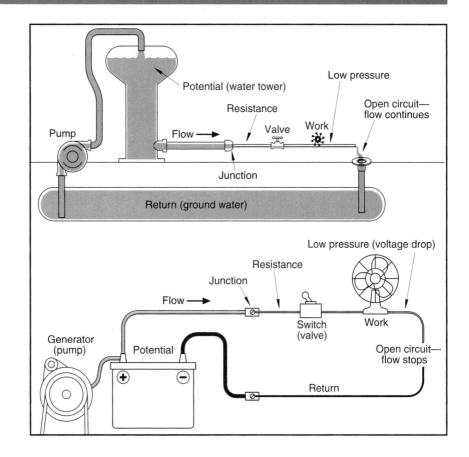

NOT LIKE WATER

Plumbing offers some useful insights into the invisible flow of electricity. You can see what makes a water wheel spin. The impact of wire size is clearer when likened to pipes. The concept of voltage can be easier to grasp when thought of as the electrical equivalent of water pressure. In fact, as long as we keep the plumbing system closed, water works pretty well as an analogy. But as soon as we open the circuit, we discover a major difference between the flow of water and the flow of electricity. As every homeowner knows, water flows out of an open pipe until we shut off or exhaust the supply. In contrast, when we open an electrical circuit, the flow of electricity stops. Not a single electron drips out of the end of the wire.

BOYS WILL BE BOYS

Teenagers offer a better analogy. A high-school gymnasium full of teenage boys at one end, girls at the other, separated by a partition, is essentially a battery. Because the boys are naturally attracted to the girls, we have potential—voltage—but nothing will happen unless the boys can find a path to the girls' side of the "battery." Give the gym an outside corridor connecting both ends—a circuit—and the boys will race from their end of the gym to the girls' end. Unless a chaperone breaks the circuit by closing the corridor door, this "current" continues until the battery is dead, i.e., until the boys' side is empty and the girls' side is full of couples.

POLARITY

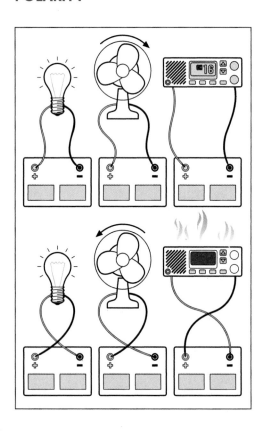

By convention we think of an electrical current as flowing from positive to negative, but the flow of electrons is actually from the negative or ground terminal to the battery's positive terminal. Either way, reversing connections to a circuit reverses the direction of the current flow. While lighting and heating appliances generally operate the same when polarity is reversed, most 12-volt motors run backwards, and electronics will, at best, simply fail to operate and may be damaged or destroyed. For 12-volt components to operate as designed, the lead marked with a "+" must always be connected to the positive side of the circuit.

OPEN AND CLOSED

An electrical circuit provides a continuous path from the positive terminal of a power source to its negative terminal. By this narrow definition, when we break that path we no longer have a circuit. Fortunately, circuit has come to mean any configuration of electrically connected components. A circuit that allows the flow of current is designated as a *closed circuit*. When a break in the circuit interrupts the flow of current, the circuit is *open*.

SERIES

When the entire current flow must pass through every component in a circuit, the components are all connected *in series*. Components in a series circuit are connected end-to-end like railroad cars.

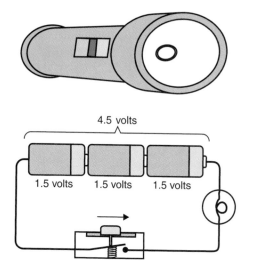

For power sources connected in series—dry cells dropped into the barrel of a flashlight, for example—the total voltage is the sum of the individual voltages. Each dry cell has a voltage of 1.5 volts, so a three-cell flashlight is operating at 4.5 volts.

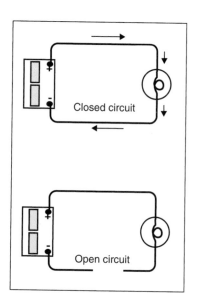

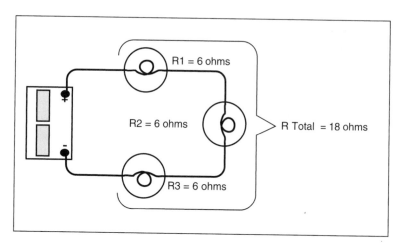

Similarly, the total resistance of loads connected in series is the sum of the individual loads. We calculated earlier that a 12-volt, 25-watt incandescent bulb draws about 2 amps, so by Ohm's Law the bulb's resistance is 6 ohms (12 V / 2 A). If we connect three bulbs in series, the total resistance is 18 ohms.

PARALLEL

When a component is connected in such a way that there is an alternative path for the current to follow, that component is connected *in parallel*. Parallel connections, in their simplest configuration, look like ladder rungs.

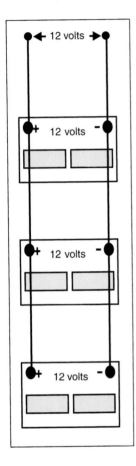

Source voltages don't aggregate in parallel. Connecting batteries in parallel—which you do every time you switch your battery-selector switch to BOTH—simply creates a "bigger" 12-volt battery, one with a capacity (detailed in the next chapter) equal to the sum of the individual battery ratings.

The total resistance of loads connected in parallel is a combination of their individual resistances, but not a direct sum. Rather, the reciprocal of the total resistance is equal to the sum of the reciprocals of the resistance in each branch. This sounds infinitely more complicated than it is. For once, the equation is clearer:

$$\frac{1}{R_T} = \frac{1}{R_1} + \frac{1}{R_2} + \frac{1}{R_3}$$

The reciprocal of total resistance of our three light bulbs connected in parallel is $^1/_6 + ^1/_6 + ^1/_6$, or $^1/_2$, so the total resistance is 2 ohms. *The resistance of loads in parallel is always less than the resistance of the smallest load.*

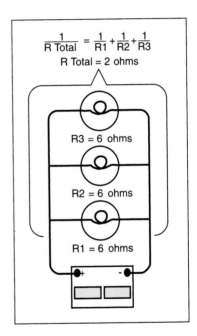

EXTRA CREDIT

WE HAVE ALREADY CALCULATED that a 25-watt, 12-volt cabin lamp draws about 2 amps and has a resistance of about 6 ohms. Three such lamps wired in series would have a combined resistance of 18 ohms. From Ohm's Law, a circuit with 18 ohms resistance connected to a 12-volt battery will draw 0.67 amps (12 V / 18 Ω). Since the definition of a series circuit is that the entire current passes through every component, only 0.67 amps passes through the bulbs—probably insufficient to make them light. It is generally a bad idea to put more than one load in series. We do put switches and fuses in series with the load because we want them to open the circuit.

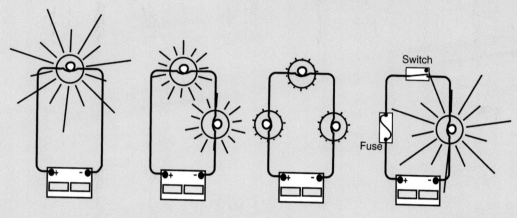

Multiple loads on a circuit are almost always connected in parallel. Connected this way, our three lights will each burn brightly. Since each is drawing 2 amps, the total current must be 6 amps. We calculated the total resistance of three 6-ohm bulbs in parallel as 2 ohms. Ohm's Law—I = V / R—confirms that a 12-volt circuit with 2 ohms total resistance does indeed have a 6-amp current flow (12 V / 2 Ω). The more parallel loads we put on the same circuit, the more current the wires, switches, and fuses must carry. Note that switch A turns off all the lights; switch B affects only one light. Also note that even though each lamp is rated at only 2 amps, we can't use a 2-amp breaker to protect the circuit.

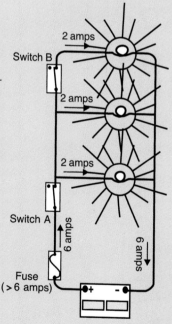

AC/DC

This book is mostly about 12-volt DC, but most modern boats also have AC (alternating current) circuits, whether powered by a cord from a dock outlet, an inverter wired to the ship's battery, or an onboard AC generator. Alternators also generate alternating current. Most of the rules that govern direct current, including Ohm's Law, are equally applicable to alternating current, but the AC league plays the game a little differently.

MAGNETISM AND CURRENT

Electric current and magnetism are related. Much like moving steel shavings on top of a piece of paper by passing a magnet underneath, electrons inside a wire can be induced to move by passing a magnet near the wire. This is exactly how all generators "create" electricity. Coils of wire surround a magnet, and when the magnet spins, it induces a current flow in the wire.

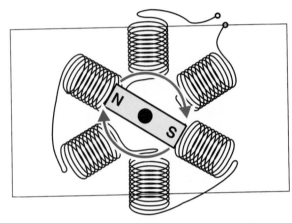

CURRENT

A charged battery has excess electrons in one side and a shortage of electrons in the other. Connect the two sides and electrons flow through the circuit in one direction—like water through a hose. Direct current is, by definition, a one-way flow of electrons.

In an AC circuit electrons don't flow; they do the two-step. Close an AC circuit, and for an instant the electrons start through the circuit just like DC. But back at the generator the positive pole of the spinning magnet is followed by the negative pole, which induces the electrons to flow in the opposite direction. This has the same effect as reversing the battery connections in a DC circuit. And just as the current starts to flow in the new direction, along comes the positive pole in the generator and reverses the direction again.

Alternating current, by definition, reverses direction at regular intervals. Electricity generated by U.S. power companies reverses direction 120 times *per second*.

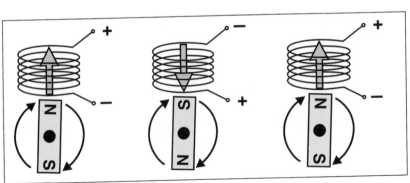

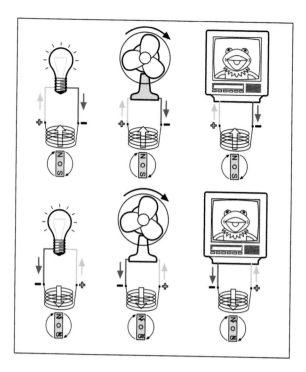

POLARITY

Since current is flowing one direction then the other through AC circuits, the function of AC components, in contrast to their DC counterparts, is unaffected by reversing connections. But while AC components are oblivious to polarity, this emphatically does not mean you can be, too. To the contrary, reversed AC polarity is extremely dangerous, particularly aboard a boat, and must always be avoided (see Chapter 8).

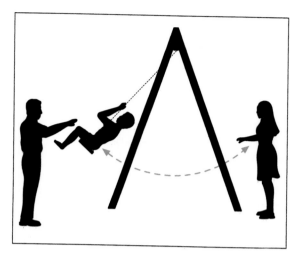

LOADS

How, you might wonder, does alternating current do any work if the electrons are more or less jogging in place? Consider a light bulb illuminated by connecting it to a battery: if you reverse the connections, the bulb still lights. In an AC circuit this reversal happens too fast for the eye to see anything more than perhaps a flicker as the light goes off and back on 120 times per second. In fact, if the bulb is incandescent, the white-hot filament doesn't have time to cool during the "off" times, so the bulb glows steadily even though current is only flowing through the filament intermittently—not unlike propelling a play yard swing with intermittent shoves. And as with the swing, the shove can be in either direction.

VOLTAGE

Ohm's Law tells us that in a circuit with a resistance of 1 ohm, voltage in volts will be equal to current in amps ($V = I \times 1$ or $V = I$). So if the current is alternating, the voltage must be also. Yet an AC voltmeter will register a steady voltage of somewhere between 115 and 125 volts when its probes are inserted into a 120-volt outlet. What's going on?

Since both positive and negative voltages (relative to ground) induce a current to flow, and AC circuits don't care which way the current flows, the AC voltmeter ignores polarity and registers all voltage as positive, which henceforth we shall do also. The meter also averages the voltage which, to yield a mean reading of 120 volts, is oscillating between 0 and a peak of about 170 volts. Fortunately we don't need to be concerned with these oscillations; average voltage (and current) satisfies our needs.

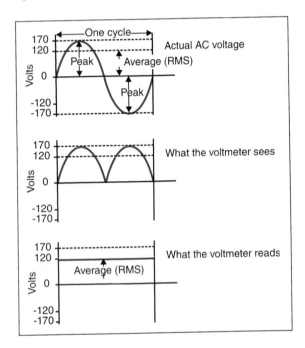

POWER FACTOR

The oscillating voltage of AC power does require one consolation. Some components in a circuit, most notably coils, oppose any *change* in current. This isn't resistance as defined earlier—it is called *reactance*—but it alters the relationship between voltage and current in AC circuits. Voltage times current gives us power in watts (P = V x I) for a DC circuit, but an AC component of a specified wattage may draw more current to compensate for the added load imposed by reactance. For AC, the power in watts is equal to volts times amps times a power factor (PF). In equation form this is P = V x I x PF, or more often I = P / (V x PF). PF is 1 when all loads are resistive—which is why we ignore it in DC circuits—but less than 1 when the circuit includes reactive loads. We won't do power factor calculations in this book, but you need to know that applying the DC power equation (PF = 1) to the rated wattage of AC appliances can substantially understate actual power consumption.

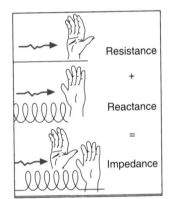

SAFETY REVISITED

Hand-to-hand resistance through the human body is usually at least 1,000 ohms (check yours by holding the two probes of an ohm meter with wet fingers). Applying Ohm's Law—I = V / R—we can see that should you touch both terminals of a 12-volt battery, body resistance limits current flow to 12 milliamps (0.012 amp)—insufficient to pose a serious risk. If, however, you get across an AC circuit, 120 volts will push 0.12 amp through your body. Combined with the pulsating nature of AC current, this is more than twice the level needed to interfere dangerously—even fatally—with heart rhythm. *Work on AC circuits requires extreme caution.*

BATTERY

A storage battery is like a fuel tank. As long as you keep it topped up, the electrical system should keep humming, but let it run out of juice and the system dies.

We don't much care what is going on inside a battery, only that it keeps our electrics running. Unfortunately, where batteries are concerned, ignorance is almost never bliss. About 99.99% of all 12-volt batteries are intended for automobiles, where they are required to give a half-second burst of power several times a day—after which they are immediately and fully replenished by the alternator. A sailboat battery doesn't get such prima donna treatment. We want it to supply all our electrical needs for 24 to 48 hours, then we want to fully replace that 2-day drain with a few minutes of charging time. Such treatment literally murders an automotive battery.

No battery lasts as long or recharges as quickly as we would like, but those designed specifically for periodic as opposed to continuous recharging come the closest. What identifies such batteries? "Marine" on the label is no assurance; many so-called marine batteries are simply relabeled automotive batteries, maybe with the addition of wing-nut terminals and a lifting handle. This might be unscrupulous except that the requirements for a powerboat's starting battery aren't that different from a car battery.

Gel batteries have been increasingly touted as the ideal marine battery, but claims about these should be viewed with some skepticism. Gel cells do have some desirable characteristics, but they are *not* next-generation technology.

The best way to pick a battery to suit your needs is to compare. This chapter explains physical and performance differences among various battery types, and shows how to interpret various battery ratings. It also provides standards for installation and maintenance.

Taking the time to select the right battery, install it well, and maintain it properly is simply good seamanship.

THE BASIC CELL

Batteries are made up of cells connected in series to achieve the desired voltage. For example, a 12-volt automotive or marine battery has 6 cells, each with a fully charged potential of a bit more than 2 volts. Cells convert chemical energy to electrical energy and, in the case of *storage cells*, vice versa.

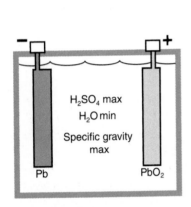

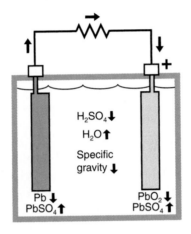

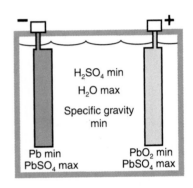

FULLY CHARGED

A cell consists of two dissimilar electrodes immersed in a conductive medium. In a *lead-acid* cell—the kind of cell in automotive and marine batteries—the negative electrode is lead (Pb), the positive electrode is lead dioxide (PbO_2), and the *electrolyte* is sulfuric acid and water ($H_2SO_4 + H_2O$).

DISCHARGING

Free electrons flowing from the lead to the lead dioxide through an external circuit unbalance the chemistry inside the battery, causing the acid to separate into hydrogen (H) and sulfate (SO_4) ions. An ion is a molecule with either extra or missing electrons—the link between chemical energy and electrical energy. Some of the sulfate ions combine with the lead electrode to form lead sulfate ($PbSO_4$). Other sulfate ions displace oxygen from the lead-dioxide electrode and combine with the free lead, also as lead sulfate. The displaced oxygen pairs up with the hydrogen ions to form water (H_2O).

FULLY DISCHARGED

As both electrodes are converted to lead sulfate, they are no longer dissimilar, and the potential between them declines to zero. Or the cell may run out of sulfate ions, leaving the electrodes immersed in pure water, which is not an electrolyte.

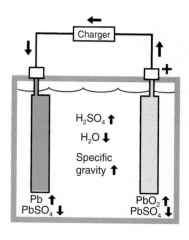

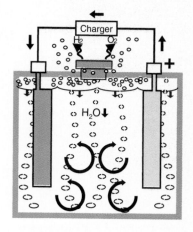

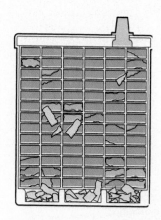

CHARGING

Placing a voltage across the electrodes of the discharged cell reverses the chemical reaction. The water separates into oxygen and hydrogen ions. The sulfate ions separate from the lead and recombine with the hydrogen into sulfuric acid. At the positive electrode, free oxygen recombines with the lead.

GASSING

When the charging current is too strong, some of the hydrogen and oxygen molecules from the decomposing water are released as gases, causing the charging cell to percolate. The rising bubbles have the desirable effect of improving the cell's acceptance of charging current by mixing the electrolyte—which tends to stratify—but as they escape into the air, they lower the water level in the cell. It is essential to closely monitor the fluid level in wet cells, especially when they are deeply discharged and/or rapidly charging.

SHEDDING

Because lead, lead dioxide, and lead sulfate have different densities, the transformation from one to the other and back again causes the plates to expand and contract. In much the same way that heat and cold erode the face of a stone cliff, the surfaces of the plates shed some active material with each discharge cycle. The battery loses the use of this disconnected material, resulting in slightly reduced capacity with each discharge cycle.

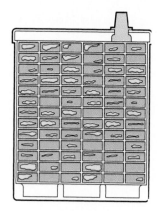

PLATE SULFATION

Sulfates that form on the plates during discharge are initially soft and readily separated from the lead with a charging current. In the absence of a charging current, sulfates begin to crystallize (harden) in a matter of hours. Sulfate crystals are not easily reconverted, and the battery suffers a permanent loss of capacity. Sulfation occurs when a battery is left in a discharged state—even partially discharged. It is analogous to rust forming on idle machinery. Even a small charging current inhibits plate sulfation.

INEFFICIENCIES

Drain 10 gallons from a full, 10-gallon fuel tank and it takes exactly 10 gallons to refill it. "Refilling" a storage cell is not so straightforward. The chemical reaction during discharge is the natural one, like water flowing down-hill. Charging is an "uphill" flow, and energy is lost to overcoming opposition. On average, expect to put back about 20 percent more energy than you take out.

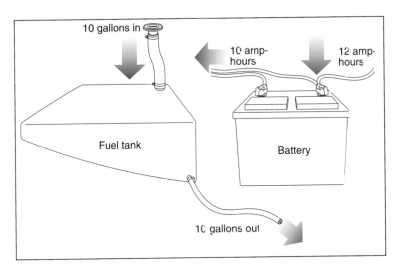

10 gallons in

10 amp-hours

12 amp-hours

Fuel tank

Battery

10 gallons out

BATTERIES

Batteries are technically a series of cells, although we ignore that distinction when we refer to a single dry cell as a flashlight battery.

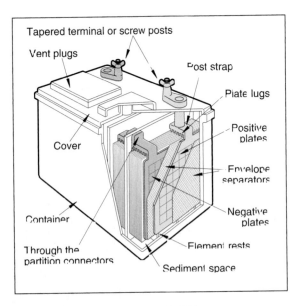

Tapered terminal or screw posts

Vent plugs

Post strap

Plate lugs

Positive plates

Cover

Envelope separators

Container

Negative plates

Through the partition connectors

Element rests

Sediment space

INTERNAL CONSTRUCTION

Voltage depends on the nature of the chemical reaction, so all lead-acid cells have fully charged potential of about 2.1 volts. Amperage, on the other hand, depends on how much chemical reaction is going on, which is mostly dependent upon the amount of electrode material. In lead-acid batteries, the electrodes are constructed as rectangular plates, each reinforced with a conductive grid. Lead and lead-dioxide plates are interleaved, like shuffled cards, and electrically insulated from each other with porous separators. All the positive (lead-dioxide) plates are connected electrically, as are all the negative (lead) plates. Individual cells—six of them in a 12-volt battery—are electrically connected in series, either internally or on top of the battery.

PLATE THICKNESS

All lead-acid batteries shed plate material with each discharge cycle. Naturally, thicker plates last longer. When thick, dense plates shed, it exposes inner plate surfaces the electrolyte previously did not reach, so that early in the battery's life the capacity does not decline and may even increase. For deep-cycling, you want thick plates.

But thick plates also react more slowly with the electrolyte, making thin plates better at delivering a lot of current at once. Likewise, thin plates accept a faster charge.

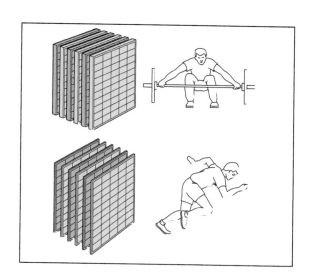

SPONGY LEAD

The lead used in lead-acid batteries is less like a slab and more like a sponge. Porosity facilitates chemical reaction by giving the lead more surface contact with the electrolyte. Low-density lead helps a battery deliver large currents, but it is also fragile and, by definition, there is less active material. High-density lead is more durable and less susceptible to shedding. The denser the lead, the more discharge cycles a battery will tolerate. A sure sign of lead density is relative battery weight.

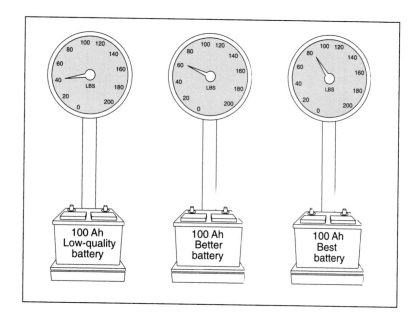

SELF-DISCHARGE

Wet-cell plate grids are lead but alloyed with a small amount of antimony to strengthen them. The dissimilarity between the lead and antimony sets up small internal currents which allow the battery to self-discharge. In warm weather an idle wet cell will lose as much as 1 percent of its charge per day, and more in the tropics. This means even a fully charged wet cell will be 30-percent discharged if idle for a summer month. A battery in this state—discharged and idle—will lose capacity to sulfation.

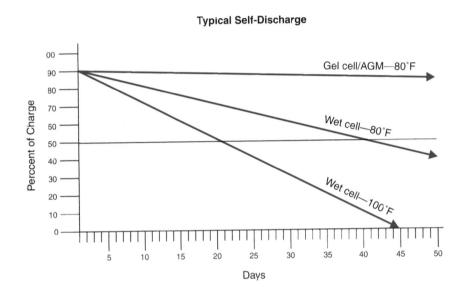

Typical Self-Discharge

Because gel and AGM batteries (see pages 436 and 437) do not contain antimony, their self-discharge rates are much lower—typically around 0.1 percent per day.

STARTING OR HOUSE?

BOAT BATTERIES can be categorized by how they will be used. A starting battery performs similarly to an automotive battery, providing a burst of current immediately countered by an input current sufficient to restore the battery to full charge. Starting batteries are sometimes selected for other high-current requirements such as powering a windlass, but such a choice assumes that the engine will be running when the battery is under load.

A house battery is expected to provide on-demand power to lights, pumps, fans, and electronics, delivering lower current levels but over a much longer time period. House batteries are routinely discharged to about half of capacity before being recharged.

Boats often have both starting and house batteries aboard. A house battery can be used as a starting battery without consequence (provided it is up to the task), but most starting batteries will not fully recover from even a single deep discharge as a house battery.

BATTERY CHOICES

Twelve-volt batteries are not all the same. Which will be your best choice depends entirely on what you expect from it.

AUTOMOTIVE—CONVENTIONAL FLOODED

Standard automotive batteries—what every garage and auto-supply house sells—are conventional flooded batteries. So are marine batteries designated as "starting" batteries. They have thin plates and low-density lead to maximize momentary output, and they are all designed to operate at at least 95 percent of full charge.

A boat's motion will literally shake the lead out of the internal grids in a cheap automotive battery, but there is no reason that a good-quality battery designed to start your car cannot provide the same function in your boat. However, if you deeply discharge an automotive battery—either accidentally or by design, you shorten its life. A conventional flooded battery may fail completely after as few as 20 discharge cycles, making this type unsuitable as a house battery—even occasionally. And because automotive batteries typically have high self-discharge rates, they are a poor choice even as a starting battery for a boat used infrequently.

MAINTENANCE-FREE

A maintenance-free battery is essentially a conventional flooded battery in a sealed case. As long as the rate of charge is kept low, the generated free oxygen and hydrogen are trapped inside the battery to recombine into water rather than escape as gasses. A safety valve allows excess pressure to escape, and maintenance-free batteries are given extra electrolyte to offset occasional venting. Maintenance-free batteries work well in cars where the charge voltage is relatively low (typically about 13.8 volts), but the voltage of almost all boat charging systems will cause maintenance-free batteries to vent and lose water. Since they have no fill caps—an identifying characteristic—water cannot be added, so these batteries are likely to have a short life. It is rarely feasible to lower charge voltage to accommodate a maintenance-free starting battery, since this would result in chronic undercharging of the house batteries. Maintenance-free batteries are simply unsuitable for a boat.

No fill caps

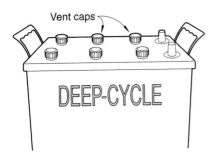

Vent caps

DEEP-CYCLE

No spill—can be used on its side

GEL

No fill caps

GEL CELL

The electrolyte in gel cells has the consistency of butter. Coated plates and separators are compressed tightly together like a multilayered sandwich. Because the electrolyte is a semisolid, it is unable to diffuse through thick, dense plates, so gel cell plates are thin and less dense. Tight lamination of plates and separators makes the assembly sufficiently rigid that grids can be pure lead or lead-calcium, eliminating antimony and thereby reducing self-discharge to less than 0.1 percent. Such a minuscule self-discharge rate means gel cells can be left idle for weeks or even months with no adverse effect.

Like a conventional flooded battery, gel cells can deliver a lot of current quickly, so they are suitable for starting or for powering high-current appliances (windlass, inverter, etc.). As a house battery, a gel cell has about $1/4$ the life *expectancy* of a similar quality deep-cycle battery, but a good-quality gel cell will deliver its 500 or so half cycles (to the 50% discharge level) without any care. Because a gel cell accepts a charge more quickly than a deep-cycle battery, it will be at a higher charge state for a given amount of charging time. Unless the deep-cycle battery gets additional charging time, the resulting sulfation can reduce its *actual* life to fewer cycles than the gel cell delivers.

Other advantages of the gel cell for a sailboat are that the battery is sealed so it cannot spill acid even if inverted, and it can survive submersion. The most significant fault is intolerance of overcharging. Charging voltage above 14.1 volts will cause a gel cell to gas, which it must not do. A not-uncommon regulator failure can quickly destroy gel cells, much like a failed shroud results in a broken mast.

DEEP CYCLE

True deep-cycle batteries have thick, high-density plates. Pound-for-pound they won't deliver as much instantaneous current as a conventional battery, but they are tolerant of repeated deep discharge. Top quality deep-cycle batteries are capable of being discharged to half their rated capacity more than a thousand times.

Most deep-cycle batteries are intended for golf carts and fork lifts. On a boat they are the top choice for house batteries *provided they are properly charged and maintained*. Because the plates are thick and dense, it takes a while for the electrolyte to diffuse into the interior of the plates, so deep-cycle batteries are painfully slow to reach full charge. But full charge is essential to prevent sulfation and allow the battery to achieve its potential.

Deep-cycle batteries typically gas vigorously during charging, which helps diffuse the electrolyte but also means the lost water must be replaced. Gassing can also be corrosive to nearby metals.

SCALES DON'T LIE

Ignore "deep-cycle" labels. Check the weight. There is a direct relationship between relative battery weight and potential battery life; the heavier a battery is (relative to others with the same case dimensions), the more discharge cycles you can expect it to deliver.

ABSORBED GLASS MAT

The absorbed-glass-mat battery (AGM) is a variation of gel-cell technology. The plates sandwich glass-mat separators that have been saturated with electrolyte. As with the gel cell, this type of battery requires thin plates compressed tightly against the wet mat. AGM batteries are extremely efficient and have low self-discharge rates, but they operate even closer to the edge than gel batteries. Overcharging will dry out the mat separators and destroy an AGM battery in short order.

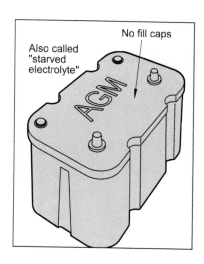

SELECTION CHART

Any 12-volt battery can power your electrical system—for a time. The generalizations in this chart should help you select the best type for your specific requirements.

BATTERY SELECTION CHART						
Type	**Automotive**	**Maintenance-Free**	**Deep-Cycle Marine**	**Golf Cart**	**Gel**	**AGM**
Initial Cost	Low	Low	High	Low	High	High
Amp-Hours	85 (Group 27)	85 (Group 27)	105 (Group 27) 225 (8D)	220 (T-105)	85 (Group 27)	95 (Group 27)
Deep Cycles	20	20	400 to 2,000	700	400 to 1,000	400 to 1,000
Cranking Capacity	Good	Good	Fair	Fair	Good	Good
Durability	Variable	Variable	Very good	Very good	Excellent	Excellent
Neglect Tolerance	Poor	Fair	Poor	Poor	Good	Good
Overcharge Tolerance	Good	Poor	Good	Good	Poor	Poor
Long-Term Cost	High	High	Low	Lowest	Low	Low
Best Use	Starting	None	House-Cruising boat	House-Cruising boat	Starting Inverter Windlass House-Weekend boat	Starting Inverter Windlass House-Weekend boat

CAPACITY

After you decide on the type of battery, you need to determine what size you need. Unfortunately, battery ratings seem designed to mislead.

AMP-HOURS

For house batteries, the only useful rating is amp-hours (Ah), which is a measurement of current flow over time. One amp flowing for one hour is 1 amp-hour. One amp flowing for two hours is 2 Ah. Two amps flowing for one hour is also 2 Ah. Amps times hours gives you amp-hours.

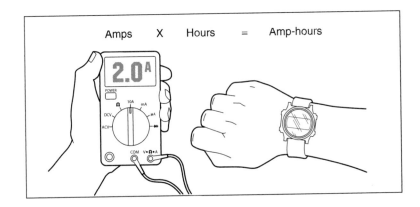

Amps   X   Hours   =   Amp-hours

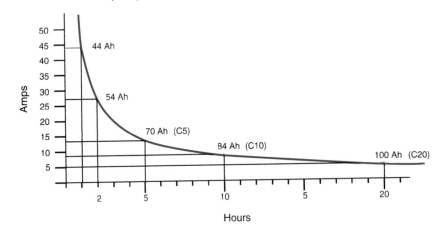

Capacity of 100 Ah (C20) Battery at Other Discharge Rates

44 Ah

54 Ah

70 Ah (C5)

84 Ah (C10)

100 Ah (C20)

Amps

Hours

A 5-gallon jug holds 5 gallons, but battery capacity isn't as exact. The faster you "pour" energy from a battery, the less of it you can get. For example, a battery capable of delivering 5 amps for 20 hours will deliver 50 amps for no more than an hour. In the first instance its capacity is 100 Ah, in the second, only 50. Conversely, slow the discharge rate to 2 amps and you might get 120 amp-hours or more from this battery.

Batteries in the U.S. are almost always rated for a 20-hour discharge—specifically, the current the battery should be capable of supplying over a 20-hour period before the cell voltage falls from 2.1 volts (fully charged) to 1.75 volts (dead). This is called a C20 rate. Batteries manufactured in other countries are often rated for a 10-hour discharge (C10 rate) and some deep-cycle batteries are rated for 5 hours (C5). The good news is that if you purchase a battery thinking the rate is C20 but it is actually one of the other ratings, the battery will have more capacity than you expected, not less.

Actual capacity also depends on temperature. U.S. ratings normally specify 80°F (27°C). As the temperature of a battery declines, so does its capacity. At freezing, battery capacity is reduced by about a third; i.e., a 100-Ah-rated battery will deliver only about 65 Ah of current at 32°F (0°C).

CYCLE LIFE

After amp-hours, the most valuable specification for a house battery is cycle life. It is also the most misleading. A battery completes one cycle when it is completely discharged then fully recharged. With each cycle, a battery loses some capacity. Manufacturers determine a battery's tolerance of deep discharge by counting the cycles until the capacity of the tested battery has declined to half its rating. A cell voltage of 1.75 volts is the standard for fully discharged, and this is the discharge depth manufacturers should use. Some do, but others discharge their batteries to only 50 percent. This has the (not unexpected) effect of approximately doubling the rated cycle life. When comparing batteries be sure you know the testing methods for both.

Lest you think that rating cycle life using the 50-percent-discharge method is more accurate anyway because that is the usual target discharge level for house batteries, note that the "life" of the test battery extends until capacity has halved. In practice, a battery that falls to even 75 percent of rated capacity will fail to meet power requirements and will need replacement. This optimism is somewhat offset by the life-shortening effect of deeper cycles, so cycle life determined by the full-discharge method is likely to better estimate real-world results. Limiting the depth of discharge dramatically extends the life of a battery.

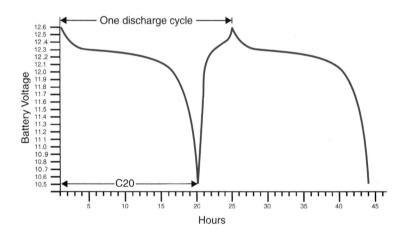

COLD-CRANKING AMPS

Cold-cranking amps (CCA) is the number of amps a battery at 0°F (–18°C) can sustain for 30 seconds without the cell voltage dropping below 1.2 volts. Unfortunately, this rating is also misleading. Even under starter load you don't really want to draw battery voltage down to 7.2 volts (1.2 V per cell). Use cold-cranking amps rating primarily to compare batteries; the higher the CCA, the heavier the starter loads the battery can handle.

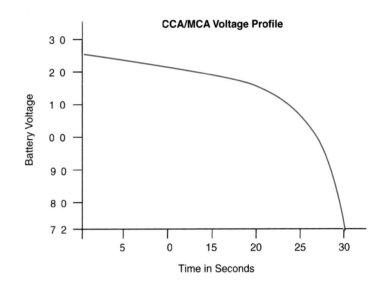

MARINE-CRANKING AMPS

Marine-cranking amps (MCA) is determined in exactly the same way as cold-cranking amps, except that the temperature is 32°F (0°C). Some see MCA as a more meaningful rating because pleasure boats are mostly used in warm conditions. More cynical types see it as a marketing ploy to inflate the CCA by about 25 percent. Either way, it adds confusion to a rating package that is already bewildering. When comparing batteries, be sure you compare MCA numbers only to other MCAs.

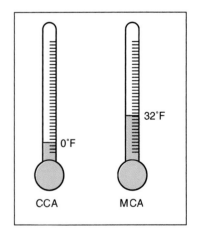

RESERVE MINUTES

Automotive batteries are not expected (by the maker) to supply power for hours, so their labels appropriately show reserve minutes rather than amp-hours. The idea behind reserve minutes—also called reserve capacity—is how long a fully charged battery will keep the engine running and the lights on if the alternator fails, or how long it will power emergency flashers if you break down. The rating is the number of minutes a battery can sustain a constant load—usually 25 amps (called R25)—at 80°F (27°C) before cell voltage falls from 2.1 volts to 1.75 volts. The reserve minutes rating can be helpful for evaluating a battery to be dedicated to a high-load use, such as powering an inverter or a long-range transmitter.

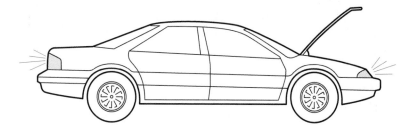

SIZING BATTERIES

How big should your batteries be?

LOAD CALCULATION REDUX

The required capacity for house batteries depends entirely on how much electrical gear you have aboard, how much power each item requires, and how much you use them. In the last chapter you should have listed the current requirements of every item aboard. Now we want to expand that to daily amp-hour requirements by factoring in the time each item is in operation. For example, if you have an incandescent light in the main salon that draws 2.1 amps and it is usually illuminated from 7 to 11 P.M., the average daily consumption is 8.4 amp-hours (2.1 A x 4 hours).

Picking another example, if your freshwater pump delivers 3 gallons per minute, and you never use more than 6 gallons per day, run time is around 2 minutes per day. That makes the daily consumption of a 6-amp pump about 0.2 amp-hours (6 A x 1/30 hour).

Calculate daily amp-hours for all your 12-volt appliances, then add them to estimate your total daily amp-hour requirement.

TYPICAL 12-VOLT POWER CONSUMPTION

Device	Amps	Hours of Use	Daily amp-hours
Anchor light	0.8	12	9.6
Anchor windlass	150.0	0.2	30.0
Autopilot (above deck)	0.7	8	5.6
Bilge blower	6.5	0.2	1.3
Cabin fan (2)	0.2	48	9.6
Cabin light—fluorescent (3)	0.7	12	8.4
Cabin light—incandescent (head)	2.1	1	2.1
Chart light (10 W)	0.8	0.5	0.4
Compass light	0.1	0	0
Deck lights	6.0	0.5	3.0
Depth sounder	0.2	8	1.6
Gas detector	0.3	24	7.2
GPS	0.5	8	4.0
Ham radio (receive)	2.5	1	2.5
Ham radio (transmit)	30.0	0.2	6.0
Inverter—standby	0.2	2	0.4
Microwave (600 W)	100.0	0.1	10.0
Pump—bilge	15.0	0	0
Pump—freshwater	6.0	0.03	0.2
Pump—shower sump	2.0	0.05	0.1
Pump—washdown	6.0	0.2	1.2
Radar	4.0	4	16.0
Reading light—halogen (2)	0.8	4	3.2
Refrigerator	5.0	12	60.0
Running lights	2.5	0	0
Running lights—tricolor	0.8	0	0
Spotlight	10.0	0	0
Tape deck	1.0	2	2.0
Television (13-inch)	3.5	2	7.0
Toilet	40.0	0.3	12.0
Speed log	0.1	8	0.8
SSB (receive)	2.5	1	2.5
SSB (transmit)	30.0	0.2	6.0
Starter—diesel (1,800 W)	150.0	0.02	3.0
Strobe	1.0	0	0
VCR	2.0	2	4.0
VHF (receive)	0.5	4	2.0
VHF (transmit)	5.0	0.2	1.0
Waste treatment	45.0	0.05	2.2
Weatherfax	1.0	0.1	0.1
Wind indicator	0.1	8	0.8

Total Daily Consumption   225.8

Note that some loads preclude others; i.e., when the anchor light is in use, the running lights are not.

THE ALTERNATIVE TO BIGGER BATTERIES

HALVING CONSUMPTION HAS THE SAME EFFECT AS DOUBLING CAPACITY, and it need not reduce comfort or convenience. Consider refrigeration, often the most voracious electrical item aboard. A change in the thickness of the insulation around the box has a nearly direct reciprocal effect on power consumption; i.e., doubling the thickness of the insulation halves the amp-hours the compressor requires. An additional 3 inches (7.62 cm) of foam insulation might easily reduce daily load by 30 or 40 amp-hours, reducing needed battery capacity by 100 amp hours. And foam is much lighter than lead.

How about your interior lighting? Factory-installed incandescent fixtures provide about 13 lumens (a measurement of light output) per watt. Halogen lights are somewhat more efficient at about 20 lumens per watt. Fluorescent lights raise the bar to 50 lumens per watt. Compact fluorescents (called PL tubes) are even more efficient, providing about 65 lumens per watt. Replace a 45-watt incandescent fixture with an Alpenglow 9-watt compact fluorescent unit and you get the same amount of light while reducing power consumption by a startling 80%.

Fans offer a similar opportunity to economize. A standard 12-volt oscillating fan draws about 1.2 amps, but Hella offers energy-efficient fans that move almost as much air, yet draw only 0.2 amps. This reduces the daily drain on the battery by as much as 24 amp-hours (per fan) in hot weather.

Taking economy to the ultimate, foot pumps completely eliminate the 6-amp draw of the freshwater pump, but a look at your consumption chart will show that this probably saves less than 0.5 amp-hours daily. Foot pumps are a good idea on a boat not because they save power but because they save water, also in short supply.

Before you add battery capacity, evaluate your electrical equipment. Efficient appliances don't just save the cost of bigger batteries, they also save—over and over again—with reduced loads on your charging system.

Lowering Battery Capacity Requirements

		Daily Load Reduction	Capacity Savings
Refrigerator	Refrigerator with added insulation	40 amp-hours	100 amp-hours
Incandescent light	Compact fluorescent light (PL tubes)	12 amp-hours (each fixture-4 hours use)	30 amp-hours
Inefficient fan	Efficient fan	24 amp-hours	60 amp-hours
Electric pump	Manual pump	0.5 amp-hours	1.2 amp-hours

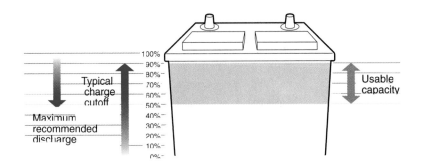

HOUSE BANK

If you limit discharge to about 50% of capacity, you need 2 Ah of capacity for every 1 Ah of consumption between charges. But that assumes you fully recharge the battery after each discharge, which, as you will see in Chapter 7, probably isn't going to happen. A 90% charge level is more likely, so consumption should equate to the battery capacity between a 50% charge level and a 90% level. We can restate this: As a general rule, house battery capacity should be about $2^1/_2$ times consumption, in amp-hours, between charges. The consumption level in the table requires more than 550 amp-hours of battery capacity.

STARTING BATTERY

The minimum capacity for a starting battery depends on the current requirement of the starter. This is usually specified in the engine manual, but if not, allow about 2 amps per cubic inch of diesel engine displacement; about half that for gasoline engines. An engine in good condition shouldn't crank more than a few seconds, so we are not interested in amp-hours here, just amps. Since charging systems do fail, we want to be able to crank the engine several times without recharging, not just once. A CCA rating of about four times the starter load will give you a dozen normal starts or let you crank a recalcitrant engine for close to two minutes.

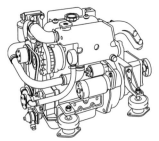

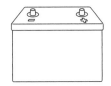

Engine displacement x 2 (cubic inches x 2)   =   Approximate cranking amps
Approximate cranking amps x 4   =   Recommended CCA rating

POWERING INVERTERS

Inverters for powering 120-volt appliances—microwave ovens, VCRs, bread makers, etc.—have become increasingly popular. The current demand of an inverter is similar to that of a starter motor, but you might operate an inverter for minutes or even hours rather than seconds. Solving the power equation for current (I = P / V), we can see that a 1,000-watt inverter (a relatively modest unit) draws 83 amps under full load, and since most inverters are only about 85 percent efficient, the actual draw is closer to 100 amps.

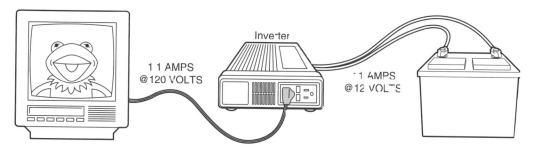

To determine the actual load your inverter imposes, calculate the amperage at 12 volts for each AC appliance plugged into it. For lighting and heating appliances do this the normal way—by dividing rated watts by 12 (volts). For other appliances the equation needs to include the power factor (see Chapter 2). (If you don't know the actual power factor, use 0.6 for microwave ovens, 0.5 for motorized appliances.) A 600-watt microwave places an 83-amp load on the battery (600 W / [12 V X 0.6]) plus about 15% due to inverter inefficiency.

When the appliance is rated in amps, this is amps at 120 volts, so you must first convert to watts—the amp rating times 120—then reconvert watts to amps at 12 volts by dividing by 12. Those with a bent toward math will see immediately that multiplying AC amps by 10 gives the same result. A TV labeled 1.1 amps will cause your inverter to draw 11 amps from the battery (plus efficiency losses).

Multiply current draw by daily use to get daily consumption. If the micro-wave above averages 6 minutes of use daily—typical for heating leftovers—it consumes less power than an hour of television. For those 6 minutes, though, it requires a battery capable of continuously supplying close to 100 amps.

Some deep-cycle batteries cannot maintain acceptable voltage at such high discharge levels. A conventional flooded battery can, but it will be damaged by the depth of the discharge if the inverter is in use for very long. Catch-22. This is where gel and AGM batteries excel. But regardless of battery type, using an inverter without the engine running requires lots of battery capacity.

INSTALLATION

Batteries on a sailboat should always be contained in an acid-proof box and secured in such a way that they will stay put even if the boat rolls 360 degrees. Flooded batteries require efficient ventilation to allow the escape of explosive hydrogen gas. Generated oxygen is especially corrosive to nearby electronics.

SERIES

Connecting batteries in series combines their voltages. It is a common practice to use two 6-volt batteries connected in series to provide a 12-volt power source. Besides keeping battery weight manageable, deep-cycle 6-volt batteries are an incredible value (see sidebar).

The rules for series installation are simple: batteries in series must be the same make, model and age to avoid a weaker battery drawing power from a stronger one—to the detriment of both. For the same reason, always replace both batteries at the same time even if only one is bad.

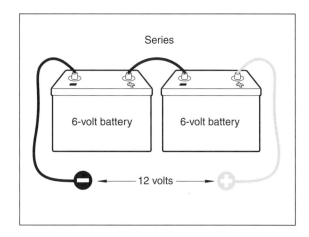

GOLF-CART BATTERIES

GOLF-CART BATTERIES are of interest to sailors because they are designed to be discharged all day, then given a charge to prepare them for the next day's gaggle of duffers—a use pattern remarkably similar to what a sailboat's house battery experiences. Good-quality golf-cart batteries last three or four years in this service.

What makes golf-cart batteries particularly notable is that they are readily available at very attractive discount prices. The well-respected Trojan T-105, for example, can be purchased for as little as $60. That makes the cost of a 12-volt, 225-amp-hour bank $120. A marine-quality deep-cycle 8D battery of equivalent capacity will run more than twice that amount. An 8D *might* deliver more cycles, but probably not twice as many (the T-105 is independently rated at a more-than-respectable 750 full discharge cycles). This makes a good-quality golf-cart battery the best value in terms of amp-hours for the dollar over the life of the battery, with the not-to-be-dismissed advantage that if some life-ending misfortune befalls your batteries—you forget to keep the water level up, an unnoticed regulator failure boils them dry, a stuck bilge-pump float submerges them—replacement cost is far more palatable.

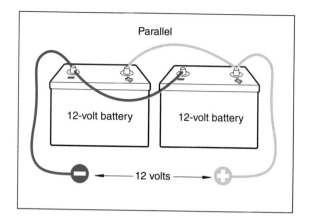

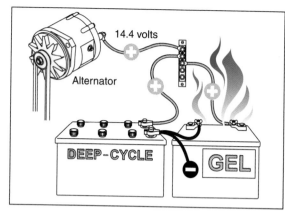

PARALLEL

Connecting batteries in parallel has no effect on voltage, but amperage is combined. Turning the battery-selector switch in your boat to BOTH connects battery (or bank) 1 in parallel with battery (or bank) 2. Many skippers select this setting for engine starting to double the current that would be available to the starter from one battery alone.

Wiring two or more house batteries in parallel to increase amp-hour capacity is also a common practice. Two 100-Ah 12-volt batteries connected in parallel in effect become a 200-Ah 12-volt battery; four provide 400 Ah of capacity.

For starting or other high-amperage use, you can parallel batteries with differing capacities (but not different voltages!) temporarily—through a selector switch—without harm, but the rules for hard-wiring two batteries in parallel are the same as for connecting them in series: batteries in parallel must be the same make, model, and age.

MATCHING

Batteries connected together permanently—in series or parallel—must be identical twins, but what about having a gel battery for starting and a deep-cycle flooded battery for house use? Generally speaking, it is a bad idea. Each requires a different charging regimen. The charge voltage needed to quickly revive a flooded battery—around 14.4 volts—will cook a gel cell, but if you lower charge voltage to 13.8 volts to accommodate the gel cell, the flooded battery will be destroyed by undercharging. Mixing battery types requires the ability to charge them at different levels—a considerable complication and expense. It almost always makes more sense to pick one type—either flooded or gel (or AGM)—and stick with it.

NEGATIVE GROUND

The negative post of all batteries should be connected to "ground" to hold it at 0 potential—relative to earth. This is normally accomplished with a cable between the negative battery post and a bolt on the engine block, which connects the battery to earth through the propeller shaft. We refer to the bolt on the engine as the "grounding lug." Multiple connections to ground should be made to a bus connected to the grounding lug. This is *the main grounding bus.*

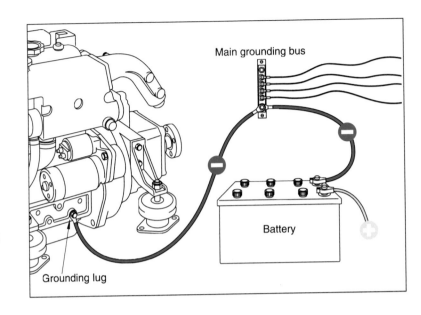

Main grounding bus

Battery

Grounding lug

TEMPERATURE

Charging, especially fast charging, raises the internal temperature of a battery. If the temperature exceeds 120°F (48.4°C), battery life will be shortened. To avoid this, it is essential to mount batteries in a relatively cool location so they can dissipate generated heat. As a general rule, batteries should not be mounted in the engine compartment.

MAINTENANCE

There is no such thing as a no-maintenance battery. All batteries require care if they are to last.

DISCHARGE

The deeper batteries are discharged, the more active material the plates shed, which reduces capacity and shortens the life of the battery. The generally accepted rule of thumb is that the best trade-off between battery capacity and battery life is achieved by limiting discharge to about 50% of capacity. In other words, don't drain more than 50 amp hours from a 100-amp-hour battery before recharging it.

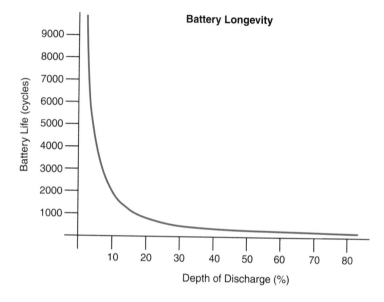

On the other hand, batteries accept higher charging currents at deeper levels of discharge. It takes a lot less charging time to bring a battery from 70% discharged to 50% discharged than from 20% discharged to fully charged, even though the number of amp-hours required is identical. Because the cycle-life curve is relatively flat beyond 50%—meaning that deeper discharges have a decreasing impact on battery life—it can make sense in some circumstances to trade shorter battery life for fewer engine hours or longer intervals between charges.

Under no circumstances should you discharge a battery beyond 80% of capacity or draw the no-load voltage below about 12 volts (2 volts per cell). At discharge levels greater than 80%, cell voltage drops precipitously, and as voltage approaches 0, stronger cells will reverse the polarity of weaker ones, doing irreparable damage to the battery.

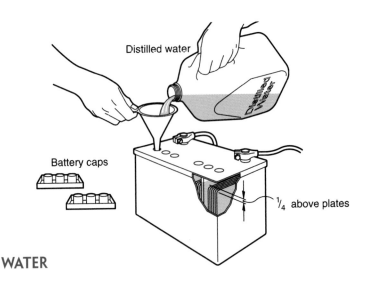

Distilled water

Battery caps

$\frac{1}{4}$ above plates

RECHARGING

Leaving a battery in a discharged state—even partially
discharged—leads to sulfation
and attendant loss of capacity. A
good charging regimen will add
years of life to a house battery.
Battery recharging is covered in
detail in Chapter 7.

WATER

Water may be lost to gassing during charging, especially in warm
conditions. If the electrolyte level is ever allowed to fall below the top
of the plates, all exposed plate area will oxidize and be forever lost to
use. Maintain the water level about $\frac{1}{4}$ inch above the plates.

To maximize battery life, use only distilled water for topping up;
trace minerals and/or chlorine will shorten battery life. Fill cells *after*
charging. If you fill them before, expansion during charging can
pump electrolyte out on top of the battery, causing a corrosive mess
and reducing the acid level inside the battery.

CLEAN AND DRY

Dampness, dirt, or acid on the battery case can
create a circuit between the terminals that will
drain the battery. Keep the top of the case clean
and dry.

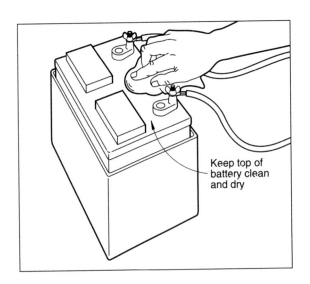

Keep top of
battery clean
and dry

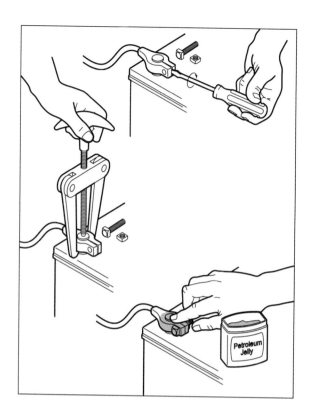

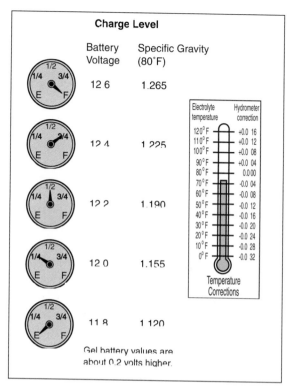

	Charge Level	
	Battery Voltage	Specific Gravity (80°F)
	12 6	1.265
	12 4	1 225
	12 2	1.190
	12 0	1.155
	11 8	1 120

Electrolyte temperature	Hydrometer correction
120°F	+0.0 16
110°F	+0.0 12
100°F	+0.0 08
90°F	+0.0 04
80°F	0.0 00
70°F	-0.0 04
60°F	-0.0 08
50°F	-0.0 12
40°F	-0.0 16
30°F	-0.0 20
20°F	-0.0 24
10°F	-0.0 28
0°F	-0.0 32

Temperature Corrections

Gel battery values are about 0.2 volts higher.

TERMINAL CORROSION

An inordinate number of electrical system problems stem from corroded battery terminals. If terminals and cable clamps are not bright, remove the clamps by releasing the bolt and spreading the clamp by twisting a screwdriver blade between the jaws. The clamp should slip off. If not, you need a battery-clamp puller. Never pry a cable clamp from a terminal; you risk ruining the battery. The puller is much cheaper.

Always remove the negative cable first and reconnect it last. If the terminals and clamps are heavily corroded, clean them with a wire brush. Polish off light corrosion with a baking-soda paste, then rinse the parts and thoroughly dry them. After they are reassembled, coat both the terminal and the clamp with petroleum jelly (not grease) to prevent future corrosion.

VOLTAGE

With a digital voltmeter you can assess the charge status of a battery by checking the open-circuit voltage. (An analog meter won't do because the difference between fully charged and half charged in a 12-volt battery is less than half a volt.) But don't expect a voltmeter to work like a fuel gauge. Battery voltage continues to rise after charging stops, so an immediate voltage reading will understate the charge status by as much as 0.1 volt—the equivalent of about one eighth of a tank. Similarly, after a heavy discharge battery voltage will "recover" over a period of several hours. Accurate readings are possible only after the battery has rested for 24 hours. In practice, letting the battery stabilize for about 2 hours will usually suffice.

Always test the battery isolated or with all circuits off.

SPECIFIC GRAVITY

Specific gravity (SG) is a better way of testing the level of charge because it tells you the condition of each individual cell. Using a battery hydrometer, squeeze the bulb, insert the rubber tip into the cell, and slowly release the bulb to draw just enough electrolyte into the tube to float the glass float. Do not remove the tip from the cell. Where the surface of the liquid crosses the graduated scale in the float is the specific gravity of the electrolyte in this cell. When you have a reading, squeeze the bulb to return the electrolyte to the tested cell. Test each cell in turn.

As with voltage, SG measurements are most accurate if the battery has rested for 24 hours, but most stabilization takes place in the first few hours. If the battery has rested for 2 hours, the SG reading will be within about 0.005 of the 24-hour value.

In a healthy battery, cell-to-cell readings will be uniform. Over time some disparity can appear, which usually can be corrected by overcharging the battery. If the fully charged SG varies 50 points (0.050) between cells, replace the battery.

KEEP RECORDS

Charge new batteries, then check and log the specific gravity of each cell—after an appropriate rest—to establish the "full charge" mark. A record of future SG readings will track the condition of the battery and let you avoid unexpected failure.

WIRE

Like a rode connects boat to anchor, every wire connects appliance to power source. The appropriate size for anchor chain depends on the anticipated load; likewise with the size of wire. And if you link chain to anchor with the wrong shackle, or you fail to safety-wire the pin, whose fault is it when the boat goes up on the rocks? In wiring, the same rules apply.

A wire could hardly find a more hostile environment than aboard a boat. To start with, there is a possibility—make that likelihood—that the wire will get wet. And even if it is never splashed or submerged, long-term exposure to moisture- and salt-laden sea air eventually has the same effect.

On a boat that gets use, the poor wire is always on watch, tossed around just like the rest of the crew. If long runs between attachment points let the wire flex with every dip and swoop, who can blame it when it succumbs to fatigue?

Then there is the problem of harmonics—the vibration that makes the cotter rings on your turnbuckles dance when the engine is running. A flexible wire just boogies to the beat, but if the wire is stiff or held captive, vibrations can cause it to work harden and fracture.

But the worst enemy of wire pressed into marine service is usually the installer. Either out of ignorance or parsimony, both yard workers and boatowners tend to choose wire too small for the job. They subject the wire to sharp edges, hot metal, and the crush at the bottom of lockers. They install the wrong terminals because that's what they have on hand. They entrust essential connections to a bargain-counter crimping tool.

No wonder electrical failures are common on boats, but they shouldn't be. All it takes to install wiring that will give decades of trouble-free service is the right wire, the right terminals, the right tools, and the right priority.

Every wire used aboard your boat needs to be the right type to withstand flexing and vibration, the right size to match current-carrying requirements, and appropriately insulated to resist moisture, petroleum products, and sunlight.

CONSTRUCTION

Boat wiring must be copper, but not all copper wiring is the same.

STRANDED

Never use solid wire on a boat, no matter how much you have left from a home wiring project. Wave- or motor-induced oscillations eventually fracture solid wire. Boat wiring must have the flexibility stranding provides. While boatbuilders may save a few dollars using type 2 wire, it is false economy for you to buy anything but type 3. Only type 3, the most flexible type, is appropriate for every use. A spool of type 3 aboard means always having the right wire at hand.

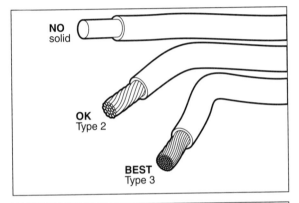

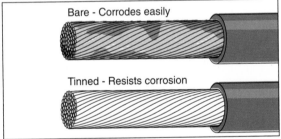

TINNED

Copper wire corrodes in the marine environment, reducing conductivity, especially at terminals and connections. Plating each strand with a thin coat of tin—called tinning—dramatically improves corrosion resistance. The additional cost of tinned wire is nominal, the benefits substantial. Under normal circumstances use only tinned wire.

DUPLEX

Stranded single-conductor wire is called hook-up or primary wire. Since most after-construction wiring requires two wires, duplex wire is more convenient and provides the added safety of a second layer of insulation. The best choice for most wiring projects is duplex safety wire, where the twin conductors are red (positive) and yellow (ground). Making the ground wire yellow rather than black reduces the chances of confusing a DC ground wire with an AC hot wire—also black.

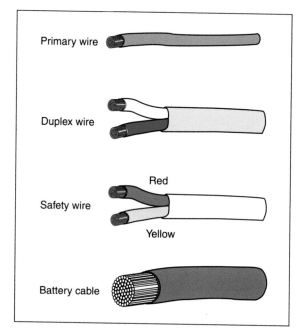

SIZE

As with water through a hose, electricity flows more easily through larger wire. It is essential to size wire for the maximum current flow you expect it to carry.

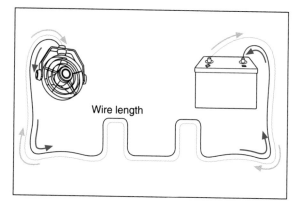

Wire length

LENGTH

All sizing formulas and tables use wire length from the power source to the appliance(s) *and back to the power source*. Doubling the straight line distance to the battery is not adequate. You must determine the actual length of the wire by measuring along the path it will follow—up, over, and around. It is not unusual for a wire run to be more than twice the straight-line distance.

Each wire should be a single continuous run between terminals. Always cut wire a foot or two longer than your measurement. The obvious reason for this precaution is that you can easily shorten the wire after it is installed, but lengthening it requires a highly undesirable splice. Less obvious, "relaxed" wire is less likely to abrade or suffer from harmonic vibration than wire put under strain because it was cut a tad too short. A loop of extra wire (called a *service loop*) also facilitates maintenance.

- 18

- 16

- 14

- 12

- 10

- 8

- 6

- 4

- 2

- 1

- 0 (1/0)

- 00 (2/0)

- 000 (3/0)

- 0000 (4/0)

GAUGE

Electrical wire appropriate for marine use carries a gauge designation printed on the insulation. The smaller the gauge number, the larger the wire diameter. Aside from *that* cockeyed logic (life could be *so* much easier), wiring sold by marine outlets almost always carries an AWG (American Wire Gauge) rating, while the published selection tables—including those appearing here—are for SAE (Society of Automotive Engineers) rating. In the sizes you are likely to use, AWG wire is about 10% larger than SAE of the same gauge, so you are safe using the tables for either designation.

The minimum gauge for boat wiring is 16 AWG. An exception could be made for circuits drawing less than 1 amp, but remember that the smaller the wire, the more fragile it is, and fragile has no place on a boat.

CURRENT CAPACITY

The first step in wire sizing is determining how much current the wire must carry. A circuit with a single 25-watt light needs to carry only 2 amps (25 W / 12 V), but if six lights are on the circuit, the wiring must be capable of carrying at least 12 amps. Drawing more current through a wire than it can handle heats it up. How much heating a wire can tolerate before becoming a fire hazard depends on the insulation. The table shows the current capacity for various kinds of insulation.

From the table you can see that boat cable in the smallest recommended size—16 gauge—can safely carry 25 amps (21.3 amps inside an engine space because of the higher ambient temperature). Since few boat circuits exceed this, you generally need to consider current capacity only for charging circuits and when wiring high-draw equipment such as windlasses and inverters.

VOLTAGE DROP

Just because it isn't overloaded by current draw doesn't mean you can use 16-gauge wire for all your circuits. The smaller the wire, the greater its resistance—as the table at right shows—and voltage is used up pushing current through this resistance. Suppose, for example, the round-trip distance from the battery to a deckwash pump at the bow is 100 feet (30 m). The table shows that the resistance of 100 feet of 16-gauge wire will be 0.41 ohms, and we know from the pump specifications that the current draw is 10 amps. We can use Ohm's Law ($V = IR$) to find that it takes 4.1 volts (10A x 0.41Ω) just to get the current to the pump. This is called *voltage drop*. If the battery voltage is 12.6 volts and we lose 4.1 volts to resistance in the wire, we have only 8.5 volts at the pump—probably too little voltage to run it.

The formula allows you determine what size wire is required to deliver adequate voltage to the other end. CM is the circular mil area of the conductor, which allows you to enter the table to determine gauge. I is the current, L is the round-trip length of the wire, and 10.75 is the resistivity of copper. E is the allowable voltage drop, which is normally 0.36 volts—3% of lowest battery voltage. For the example pump, the formula gives us a CM value of 29,861. From the chart, we find that this is larger than 6 gauge, so the appropriate wire size is 4 gauge.

ALLOWABLE AMPERAGE

Wire Type	TW	THW, HWN, THWN	MTW, XHHW	AWM, BC5W2, UL1426 Boat Cable
Temperature Rating	60°C (140°F)	75°C (167°F)	90°C (194°F)	105°C (221°F)
Wire Gauge (AWG)	Outside/Inside Engine Space	Outside/Inside Engine Space	Outside/Inside Engine Space	Outside/Inside Engine Space
18	10 / 5.8	10 / 7.5	20 / 16.4	20 / 17.0
16	15 / 8.7	15 / 11.3	25 / 20.5	25 / 21.3
14	20 / 11.6	20 / 15.0	30 / 24.6	35 / 29.8
12	25 / 14.5	25 / 18.8	40 / 32.8	45 / 38.3
10	40 / 23.2	40 / 30.0	55 / 45.1	60 / 51.0
8	55 / 31.9	65 / 48.8	70 / 57.4	80 / 68.0
6	80 / 46.4	95 / 71.3	100 / 82.0	120 / 102
4	105 / 60.9	125 / 93.8	135 / 110	160 / 136
2	140 / 81.2	170 / 127	180 / 147	210 / 178
1	165 / 95.7	195 / 146	210 / 172	245 / 208
0	195 / 113	230 / 172	245 / 200	285 / 242
00	225 / 130	265 / 198	285 / 233	330 / 280
000	260 / 150	310 / 232	330 / 270	385 / 327
0000	300 / 174	380 / 270	385 / 315	445 / 378

WIRE SIZE FORMULA

$$CM = \frac{I \times L \times 10.75}{E}$$

CM	=	Wire size in circular mils
I	=	Current
L	=	Length of wire (round trip)
E	=	Allowable voltage drop—generally 0.36

WIRE RESISTANCE

Circular Mils (CM)	Wire Gauge (AWG)	Ohms per 100 Feet (@ 77°F)
1,620	18	.654
2,580	16	.409
4,110	14	.258
6,530	12	.162
10,380	10	.102
16,510	8	.064
26,240	6	.040
41,740	4	.025
66,360	2	.016
83,690	1	.013
105,600	0	.010
133,100	00	.008
167,800	000	.006
211,600	0000	.005

Note: Circular mils are calculated by squaring the wire diameter in mils (thousandths of an inch)

KEY TO WIRE CODES

BC	=	Boat cable
H	=	Heat resistant (75°C rating)
HH	=	High heat resistant (90°C rating)
N	=	Nylon jacket
M	=	Oil resistant
T	=	Thermoplastic
W	=	Moisture resistant
X	=	Cross-linked polymer

10% DROP

MOST TEXTS also provide a 10% drop table, but a drop greater than 3% is not allowed (by American Boat and Yacht Council standards) for essential electrical items such as bilge blowers, running lights, and navigation equipment. While some items, such as cabin lights, can tolerate lower voltage, it is almost never a good idea to use the smaller-gauge wire. The cost savings is inconsequential compared to the potential problems inadequate wiring can spawn. Reduced weight is a desirable benefit for wiring leading to the masthead, but aside from the essential nature of most mast-mounted electrics, mast wiring also receives the most punishment—a poor argument for using less robust wire.

3% TABLE

I find the formula easier to use, but you may prefer using this table to determine appropriate wire size. Use the current draw to select the row, the round-trip wire length to select the column. The number where these two intersect is the recommended wire gauge.

ROUND-TRIP LENGTH OF CONDUCTOR (FEET)									
Current (Amps)	10	20	30	40	60	80	100	120	140
				Minimum Wire Size (AWG)					
1	16*	16*	16*	16*	16	14	14	14	12
2	16*	16*	16	14	14	12	10	10	8
5	16*	14	12	10	10	8	6	6	6
10	14	10	10	8	6	6	4	4	2
15	12	10	8	6	6	4	2	2	1
20	10	8	6	6	4	2	2	1	0
25	10	6	6	4	2	2	1	0	2/0
30	10	6	4	4	2	1	0	2/0	3/0
40	8	6	4	2	1	0	2/0	3/0	4/0
50	6	4	2	2	0	2/0	3/0	4/0	
60	6	4	2	1	2/0	3/0	4/0		
70	6	2	1	0	3/0	4/0			
80	6	2	1	0	3/0	4/0			
90	4	2	0	2/0	4/0				
100	4	2	0	2/0	4/0				

*18-gauge wire has adequate current capacity but is too fragile for boat use.

24 VOLTS

LARGER BOATS AND MULTIHULLS, because of long wire runs, may find it advantageous to adopt a 24-volt system. Our 120-watt (10A x 12V) deckwash pump in the previous example (page 456) would draw only 5 amps in a 24-volt version (120W / 24V). Also, a 3% voltage drop in a 24-volt system is 0.72 volts. Using these new values in the voltage drop formula, CM = 5A x 100' x 10.75 / 0.72V, or 7,465. From the chart, we find that 10 gauge wire has a CM of 9,343, more than enough to handle this load. Aside from the significant difference in size and weight, smaller wires are far easier to work with. Purchasing 100 feet (30 m) of 10 AWG wire rather than 4 AWG also results in a cost savings of more than $150 for this circuit alone!

INSULATION

Insulation prevents unwanted contact between the wire and other components of the boat—including crew. It also protects the wire from the elements.

DESIGNATION

Wire appropriate for boat use will have a designation code printed on the insulation or jacket. The keys shown here let you interpret most common codes. For example, THWN has thermoplastic insulation, a heat rating of 75°C, is suitable for wet locations, and it has an abrasion-resistant nylon jacket. XHHW designates a wire with a crossed-linked polymer insulation (stronger than PVC), a high heat rating of 90°C, and suitable for wet locations.

The break-down voltage of the insulation—typically 600 volts—should also be printed on the wire jacket, along with the gauge of the enclosed conductor.

KEY TO WIRE CODES		
BC	=	Boat cable
H	=	Heat resistant (75°C rating)
HH	=	High heat resistant (90°C rating)
N	=	Nylon jacket
M	=	Oil resistant
T	=	Thermoplastic
W	=	Moisture resistant
X	=	Cross-linked polymer

BOAT CABLE

In recent years wire meeting stringent standards set by Underwriters Laboratories—called UL 1426—has become widely available to boatowners. Specifically designed for the marine environment, this wire is known as boat cable. Typical jacket designation is BC5W2, where the two numbers designate dry and wet environment heat ratings respectively. It is type 3 for maximum flexibility, and while not specified in the standard, the best boat cable has each strand tinned for maximum corrosion resistance. When available, tinned boat cable from a reputable supplier is your best choice for all wiring needs.

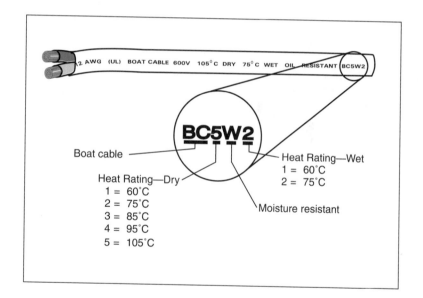

COLOR

This chart is included mostly for reference. While color coding is nice, it is rarely practical. However, you should use red wires for DC positive conductors only, and make all DC negative conductors yellow. Existing negative leads on your boat are likely to be black, but as previously mentioned, yellow has replaced black as the standard to distinguish DC negative conductors from the hot side of AC circuits.

ABYC RECOMMENDED WIRING COLORS	
COLOR	**USE**
Red	General DC positive conductor
Yellow	Preferred DC negative conductor
Black	Alternative DC negative conductor
Green or green with yellow stripe	General DC grounding conductor
Dark blue	Cabin and instrument lights
Dark gray	Navigation lights, tachometer
Brown	Pumps, alternator charge light
Brown with yellow stripe	Bilge blower
Orange	Accessory feed
Purple	Ignition, instrument feed
Yellow with red stripe	Starting circuit
Light blue	Oil pressure
Tan	Water temperature
Pink	Fuel gauge

ROUTING

Attempts to wire a new circuit sometimes reveal unanticipated barriers to a suitable route for the wire. It is prudent to run the wiring before you mount a new electrical item in case routing realities dictate an alternative location.

HIGH AND DRY

Wire and water is always a bad combination. Route wires as far above the bilge as possible. Dead space under side decks is ideal.

RACEWAYS

Running wire inside raceways has the dual benefits of protecting the wire and giving continuous support (for horizontal runs). Wooden raceways can masquerade as cabin trim.

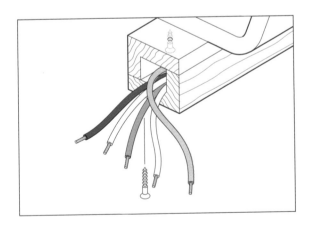

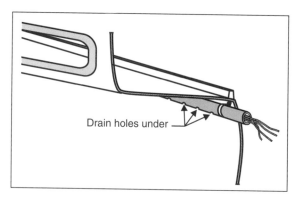

Drain holes under

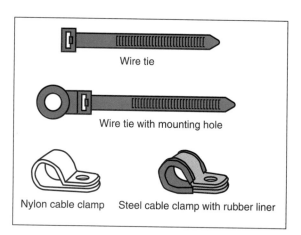

Wire tie

Wire tie with mounting hole

Nylon cable clamp   Steel cable clamp with rubber liner

CONDUIT

Rigid PVC conduit makes perfect lightweight raceways for out-of-view locations. Mount conduit under the side deck or as high as possible in locker spaces. Drill drain holes in low spots (before the wire is installed!) to prevent the conduit from trapping water. Do not use PVC conduit in engine spaces.

SUPPORT

Wires not continuously supported in raceways must be supported at least every 18 inches (45 cm). Cable clamps and wire ties simplify this requirement. Use metal clamps where loss of support could result in a hazard.

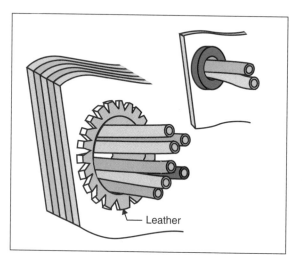

Leather

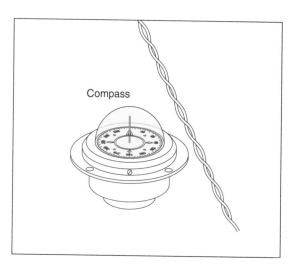

Compass

GROMMETS

Where wires pass through holes in panel boxes, masts, bulkheads, and other components, the hole must be lined to protect the wire from chafe.

TWISTED PAIRS

Direct current flowing through a wire produces a magnetic field that can interfere with the compass. Twisting positive and negative leads causes opposing fields to cancel. All wiring (other than coax) within 2 feet (0.6 m) of the steering or autopilot compass must be twisted in pairs.

CONNECTIONS

Other than chafe or lying against hot metal, wires rarely experience failures in the middle of a wire run. Almost all wiring problems occur at the terminal connections.

CRIMP CONNECTORS

You will minimize wiring problems if you terminate all wire ends with a crimp connector.

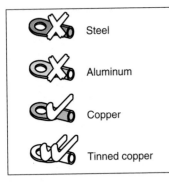

Steel

Aluminum

Copper

Tinned copper

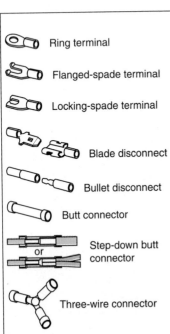

Ring terminal

Flanged-spade terminal

Locking-spade terminal

Blade disconnect

Bullet disconnect

Butt connector

Step-down butt connector

or

Three-wire connector

MATERIAL

Terminals used on a boat must always be copper, never steel or aluminum. Terminals should be tin-plated to resist corrosion.

SIZE

Selecting the proper connector requires that you match it to the wire gauge *and* to the size of the terminal screw.

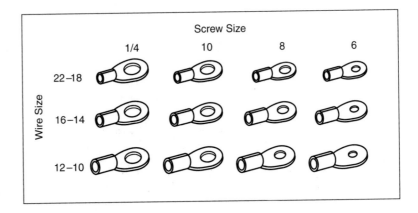

TYPE

Ring terminals are the best choice for all connectors unless the terminal screw is captive. In that case, use flanged spade connectors. Use butt connectors for appliances supplied with wire leads instead of terminals. Step-down butt connectors let you connect heavy supply wires to lighter leads. To simplify servicing, it can be a good idea to make the connection with blade or snap connectors instead of butt connectors. Three-way connectors are useful for tapping into an existing circuit.

CRIMPING

You simply cannot make dependable crimp connections with a rigging knife and a pair of pliers. Plan to add a wire stripper and a good-quality crimper to your tool collection.

STRIPPING

Remove only enough insulation for the wire to reach the end of the barrel of the terminal. Because SAE wire is smaller, most hardware store and auto supply wire strippers will cut into AWG wire. Nicks in the wire lead to corrosion, especially on a boat. Using the hole labeled for larger wire works for some sizes but is less satisfactory than buying a stripper for AWG wire.

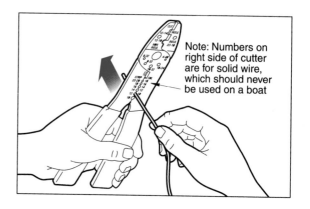

Note: Numbers on right side of cutter are for solid wire, which should never be used on a boat

MAKING THE CRIMP

Grip the terminal in the correct die in the crimper, fully insert the wire into the terminal, and squeeze. If the barrel has a seam, the crimp indent should be opposite.

In the hands of an amateur, only a ratchet crimper will give consistent crimps. Unfortunately, ratchet crimpers are far easier to use on a workbench than in the awkward work positions boat wiring can require. Many find the less-expensive pliers-style crimper better suited for onboard wiring. With practice you can make perfect crimps with a pliers-style crimper.

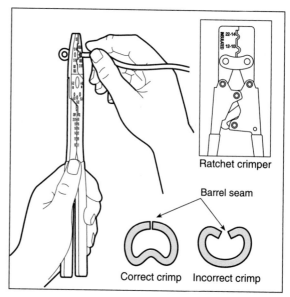

Ratchet crimper

Barrel seam

Correct crimp   Incorrect crimp

DOUBLE CRIMP

Better terminals feature a brass sleeve that can be crimped over the insulated wire to add mechanical strength. This type of terminal is usually installed with a double crimp tool.

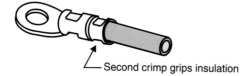

Second crimp grips insulation

PULL

There is only one accepted field test for a crimp terminal—pull on it. Test *every* crimp terminal this way. Without using any tool, grip the terminal and the wire and try to separate them. If they come apart, the crimp was bad.

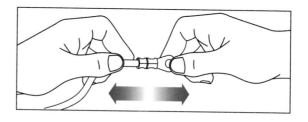

SOLDERING

If you use tinned wire and tinned terminals, most experts agree that soldering is not required. However, if you do it well, soldering improves the electrical connection between wire and terminal, especially as the connection ages. The potential for circuit-breaking corrosion makes soldering essential if either the wire or the terminal is untinned.

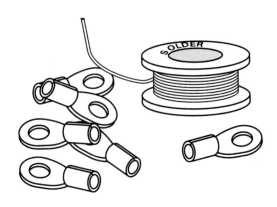

UNINSULATED TERMINALS

If you want to solder, use uninsulated terminals. Crimp the terminal to the stripped wire before soldering. Never depend on solder to provide the mechanical connection; a faulty connection can generate enough heat to melt the solder and let the wire drop out of the terminal.

ALUMINUM-CAN HEAT SINK

Melting the wire's insulation releases chemicals that are corrosive to the wire. To avoid this, slip a split 2-inch (5 cm) disk cut from an aluminum can over the bare wire where it enters the terminal to dissipate the heat before it reaches the insulation.

TINNING THE SOLDERING IRON

A SOLDERING IRON will not heat the joint properly unless it is properly tinned. Start by cleaning the tip of the cold iron with emery cloth to remove old flux and solder. Next, heat the tip and dip it in soldering paste. Coat the tip with solder, then wipe off the excess with a damp cloth. The hot tip should be completely silvered and shiny.

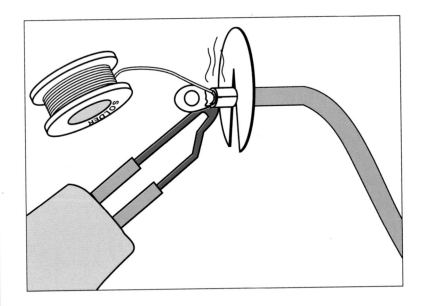

HEAT THE WIRE

Heat the barrel of the terminal with a well-tinned soldering iron until solder touched to the ends of the wire melts. Keeping the tip against the terminal, flow enough solder into the wire to just fill the barrel. Withdraw the solder and the heat and leave the joint undisturbed for a minute. A proper joint will be smooth and shiny, not dull or lumpy.

SOLDERED = SOLID

The only drawback to soldering crimp terminals—other than the effort it requires—is that the solder in effect converts the stranded wire to solid. This is of no consequence unless the solder wicks beyond the barrel of the terminal, where it causes a hard spot that can be susceptible to fracturing from vibration. Use a heat-shield at the barrel entrance and limit the amount of solder to avoid this problem.

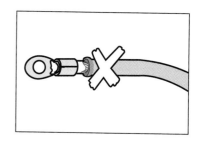

HEAT-SHRINK

Unlike electrical tape, which too often falls off or becomes a gooey mess, heat-shrink tubing is as durable as the insulation on the wire. Heat-shrink is often touted as waterproof, of dubious value except for butt connectors (which can be entirely enclosed). The real value of heat-shrink is to provide reliable insulation. If the heat-shrink is adhesive lined, it also relieves some of the strain on the wire connection.

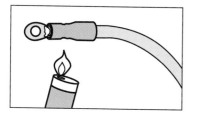

Slide heat-shrink tubing onto the wire before installing connectors. If a connector will be soldered, be sure the tubing is far enough from the end to remain cool. After the joint is crimped (and soldered), slide the tubing over it and heat the tubing by playing a flame under it, or shrink it with a heat gun.

BARE WIRES

Wrapping a bare wire around a terminal screw damages the wire when the screw is tightened. This type of electrical connection should be avoided. Set-screws are also damaging when they bear directly on the wire. Twisted-bare-wire connections don't damage the wire, but lack the tight contact and strain resistance of crimp connections. If you find yourself without an alternative, soldering a twisted-wire connection perfects the electrical connection, and if the joint is well sealed in heat-shrink tubing, it should be trouble-free.

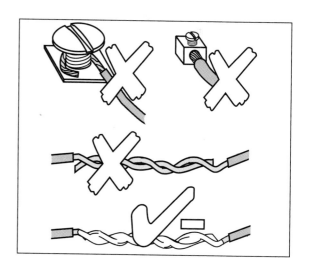

WIRE NUTS

Wire nuts are NEVER an acceptable means of making electrical connections on a boat.

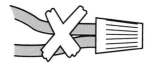

OVERLOAD PROTECTION

Excess current can turn a wire into a heating element capable of igniting anything flammable. Any wire aboard that is not overload protected represents a grave and unacceptable danger to boat and crew.

FUSES

The principle behind a fuse is simple; too much current melts the conductor and opens the circuit. Fuses are cheap, foolproof, and less convenient than breakers only when they blow—which will be almost never if the wiring is done well.

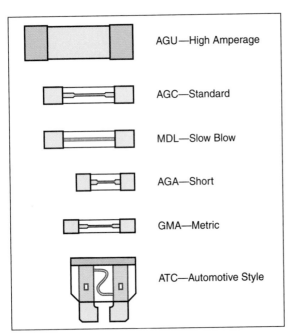

AGU—High Amperage

AGC—Standard

MDL—Slow Blow

AGA—Short

GMA—Metric

ATC—Automotive Style

CIRCUIT BREAKERS

Circuit breakers don't protect a circuit any better than a fuse, but since breakers can be reset over and over, they do simplify troubleshooting the faulty circuit. Breakers also do double duty as a switch to de-energize the circuit.

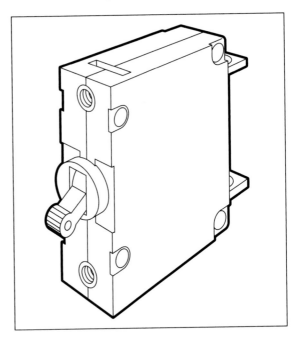

SIZING

The size of the fuse or breaker is determined by the sum of all the loads on the circuit OR by the current-carrying capacity of the smallest wire in the circuit, *whichever is smaller.* For example, 12 AWG boat cable to the masthead tricolor is adequately protected by a 50-amp breaker—marine standards allow the breaker threshold to be up to 150% of the wire rating (45 amps for 12 AWG). But since the normal load on this circuit should never exceed 2 amps, a 5-amp breaker will detect a problem sooner.

INSTALLING

Fuses and breakers are always installed in series in the positive conductor of a circuit. Locate them as close to the power source as possible. In practice, they are typically installed in a panel board located near the batteries.

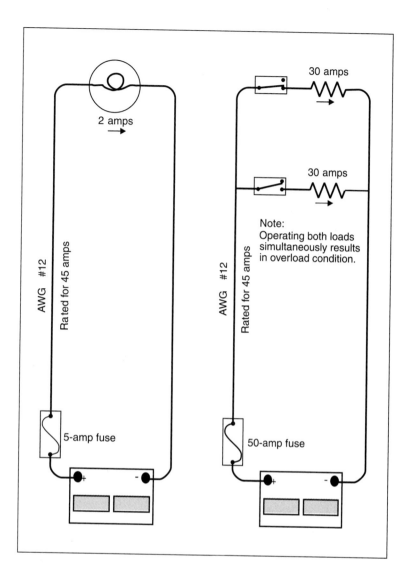

SUPPLY SIDE

Hundreds of thousands of boats have been wired with no overload protection for the supply cable to the electrical panel, and more than a few of those boats have been destroyed by a resulting fire. Today high-amperage fuses and/or breakers capable of carrying starter loads are available at nominal cost. The main positive cable from the battery should be overload protected *at the battery*, and the main lead from the battery selector switch to the distribution panel should also be protected. Also make sure the wiring to the engine panel is fuse-protected. If you do not have these safeguards, they are the first modifications you should make to your electrical system.

Size any fuse in the starting circuit as large as the capacity of the cable allows; you want protection from a dead short, but you do not want the fuse to interfere with starting the engine. In the feeder line to the distribution panel, the size of the fuse or breaker must not exceed the rated capacity of the feeder wire or the load capacity of the panel.

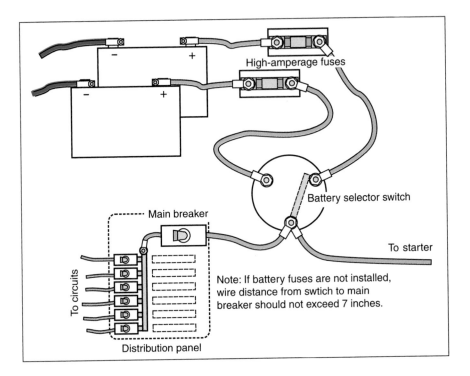

High-amperage fuses

Battery selector switch

Main breaker

To starter

To circuits

Note: If battery fuses are not installed, wire distance from swtich to main breaker should not exceed 7 inches.

Distribution panel

EQUIPMENT PROTECTION

The breakers in the panel are to protect the wiring from overload. Protecting an individual piece of equipment requires an additional fuse, either built in to the equipment or series installed in the positive lead with an in-line holder or a fuse block.

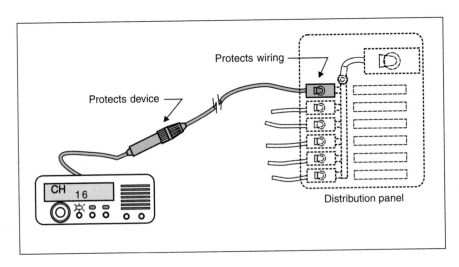

Protects wiring

Protects device

CH 16

Distribution panel

SWITCHES

Switches allow you to interrupt the flow of current. Like fuses and breakers, switches are installed in series in the positive conductor.

SPST

The simple ON/OFF switch is a single pole, single throw (SPST) switch. The switch has two terminals that are connected in the ON position, not connected in the OFF position.

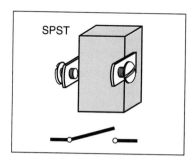

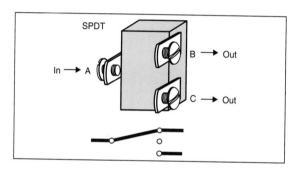

DT

Three terminals usually indicates a double-throw (DT) switch. Moving the toggle in one direction connects terminals A and B. "Throwing" the toggle the other way connects A and C. In the middle position, none of the terminals are connected.

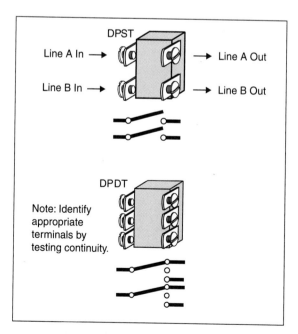

DP

Double-pole (DP) switches let you connect and disconnect two conductors simultaneously. Installed in both the positive and negative sides of a circuit, a DP switch completely isolates all components beyond the switch. Although double-pole breakers are rarely seen in 12-volt circuits, they are superior to single-pole breakers because they completely disconnect the circuit rather than just open it.

Double pole switches can also be double throw (DPDT).

BATTERY SELECTOR

The typical battery selector is a rotary switch allowing the boat's electrical system to be connected to battery 1, both batteries, battery 2, or disconnected from any power source. A better alternative is detailed in Chapter 7.

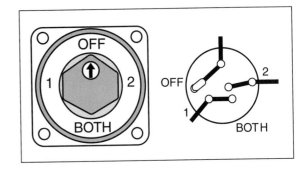

NEATNESS COUNTS

After using the right components and making good connections, the third essential to a trouble-free electrical system is neatness.

LABELING

It is just common sense to label both ends of a wire run, yet this step is often overlooked. The consequence is wasted time later when you need to work on this circuit. In an emergency, the absence of labeling can be dangerous.

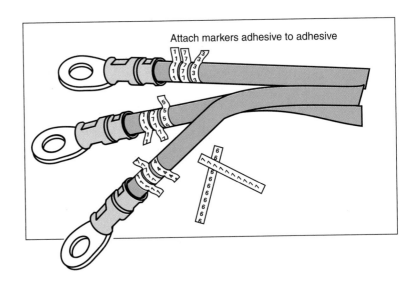

Attach markers adhesive to adhesive

WIRE MARKERS

Electrical suppliers sell books, sheets, or rolls of adhesive wire markers that are easily applied to the insulation near the terminals at each end. You can simply give the wire a number, which you will record on a drawing of your boat's wiring (see Chapter 6), or you can use a code, for example, "GL" for galley lights.

CLEAR SHRINK TUBING

Covering wire markers with clear shrink tubing ensures that they will never come unglued. You can also write your own markers on paper and capture it with shrink tubing. Labels written on tape flags are better than nothing, but tape soon falls off in the wet environment of a boat.

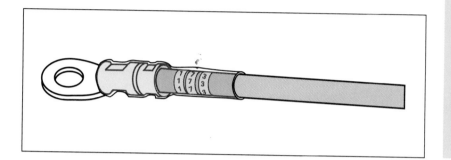

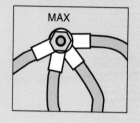
TERMINAL STRIPS

Terminal strips are superior to three-way connectors for wiring several appliances to the same circuit. A terminal strip/fuse block combination allows you to protect each appliance independently and have all fuses in an accessible location. Set-screw style terminals should have an internal shoe to keep the end of the screw from damaging the wire.

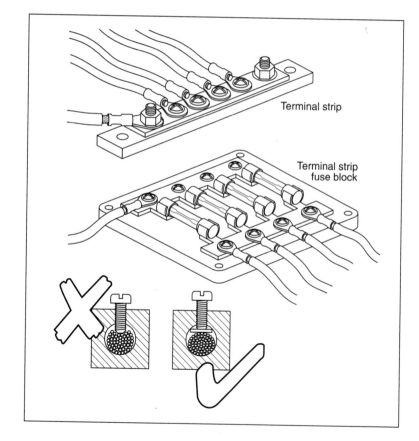

Terminal strip

Terminal strip fuse block

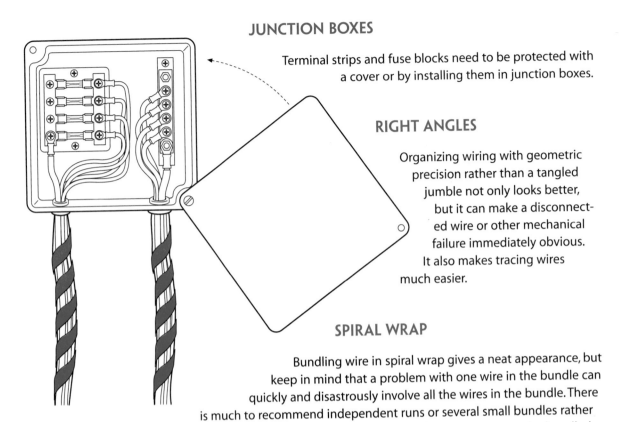

JUNCTION BOXES

Terminal strips and fuse blocks need to be protected with a cover or by installing them in junction boxes.

RIGHT ANGLES

Organizing wiring with geometric precision rather than a tangled jumble not only looks better, but it can make a disconnected wire or other mechanical failure immediately obvious. It also makes tracing wires much easier.

SPIRAL WRAP

Bundling wire in spiral wrap gives a neat appearance, but keep in mind that a problem with one wire in the bundle can quickly and disastrously involve all the wires in the bundle. There is much to recommend independent runs or several small bundles rather than a harness containing every wire running fore and aft. AC and DC conductors must never be bundled together.

PANEL LOCATION

Factory-installed electrical panels, particularly in older and/or smaller boats, are too often installed beneath the companionway and/or through the engine-compartment bulkhead. Wiring should not lead through the engine compartment unless it is engine wiring, and the electrical panel should be mounted where a dousing with rain, spray, or green water will be unlikely.

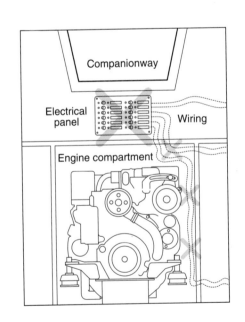

COAX

Antenna connections on a boat must be made with a special kind of cable that incorporates a surrounding wire braid. This is called coaxial cable, or simply coax. The signal travels on the outside of the core conductor and the inside of the braid, essentially trapped inside the cable.

SIZE

Bigger is better—period. Anything other than RG-213/U or RG-8/U will cut your transmitting power *at the antenna* by about 1% per foot—costly economy to save a few bucks on cable. For short runs, you might use RG-8X, called mini 8. Never use RG-58/U. And never use TV coax, no matter how big it is; it has incorrect impedance for marine radio use.

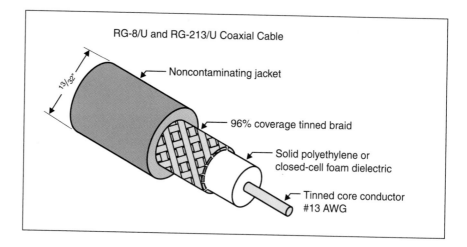

RG-8/U and RG-213/U Coaxial Cable

13/32"

— Noncontaminating jacket

— 96% coverage tinned braid

— Solid polyethylene or closed-cell foam dielectric

— Tinned core conductor #13 AWG

CONSTRUCTION

Both RG-213/U and RG-8/U are the same size, but the more durable jacket on RG-213/U gives a life expectancy of 20 years or more. For marine use the jacket should carry the "noncontaminating" designation. As with electrical wiring, tinned conductors—both the core and the braid—make the coax much more resistant to corrosion. To avoid signal leakage, the braid should be tightly woven, providing at least 96% shielding. A foam dielectric reduces power losses, but a solid polyethylene dielectric is better for marine use unless you are sure the foam is closed cell.

CONNECTIONS

Crimp-on connectors rarely last more than a couple of years before resistance caused by internal corrosion degrades radio performance. All coax connectors need to be soldered. The connector for both RG-213/U and RG-8/U is designated PL-259, and the same connector goes on both ends of the cable.

Manicure scissors are perfect for cleanly trimming the braid.

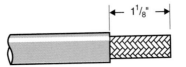

Cut end square and remove $1\frac{1}{8}"$ of jacket without nicking braid.

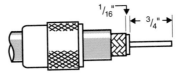

Bare $\frac{3}{4}"$ of center core, taking care not to nick it. Trim braid back $\frac{1}{16}"$ and tin it. Slide coupling ring onto cable.

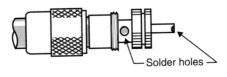

Screw plug assembly onto cable and solder it sparingly to both core and braid through solder holes. Screw coupling ring to plug assembly. Touch ohmmeter probes to center contact and plug body to check for a short.

Solder holes

WEATHERPROOFING

Join two PL-259 connectors by threading them onto a barrel connector, called a PL-258. To avoid moisture intrusion, this entire assembly must be encased in adhesive-lined heat-shrink tubing. A drip loop will prevent guttering.

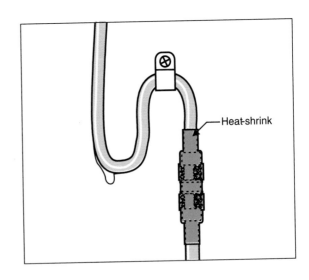

Heat-shrink

BACKSTAY CONNECTION

An insulated backstay often doubles as the SSB or ham radio antenna. Note that on a fiberglass boat, a lower insulator is unnecessary as long as the backstay chain plate is not bonded to the boat's grounding system. During transmission, the energized antenna can burn you, so insulate the bottom 6 feet (1.8 m) of the stay with rubber hose.

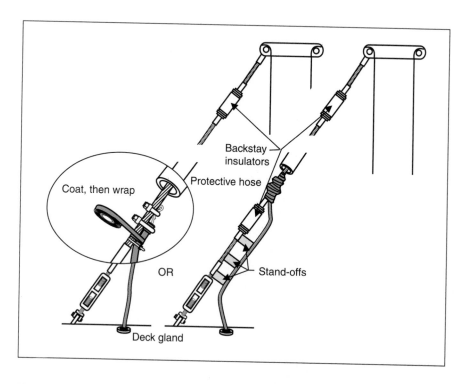

The connection to the stay is made as shown, using stainless steel cable clamps. The wire is typically antenna lead-in, held clear of the stay with stand-offs (as shown), but if you elect to use coax instead, be sure only the center conductor is in contact with the stay, not the braid. The entire connection should be protected from the weather by coating it with electrician's putty (Coax Seal), then wrapping it *from bottom to top* with self-amalgamating tape.

COPPER RIBBON

Ground connections for high-frequency radios—SSB and ham—should be made with copper foil ribbon rather than wire. Radio frequency (RF) current travels on the surface of the conductor, so the more surface, the better the ground connection. That directly translates into longer-range, clearer radio transmission.

Three-inch-wide (7.6 cm) copper foil is a good choice for RF grounding. The thickness of the foil is not important other than for durability. We take a closer look at how to make a good RF ground connection in Chapter 9.

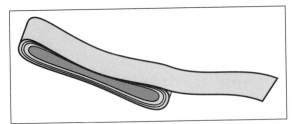

CIRCUITS

Back in Chapter 2 we defined circuit as a configuration of electrically connected components. For a circuit to allow the flow of electricity, it must be *closed*, i.e., one end of the circuit must be connected to the positive side of the power source and the other to the negative side. Any break in continuity *opens* the circuit and interrupts the flow of current.

Circuits can be as simple (and spectacular) as a steel wrench across battery terminals—called a *short circuit*—or as complex as the innards of a super computer. The electrical circuits found on pleasure boats are at the simple end of this spectrum.

Circuits are like the petals of a penciled daisy, each a loop starting and ending at the flower's center. Aboard a boat, the center of this electrical bloom is the distribution panel.

The various circuits on a boat are not identical. One may feed a single pump, while another branches through several lights. One may include fuses and switches and diodes, while another is protected and regulated only by the panel breaker. One circuit may require 6 gauge wire while 16 gauge is adequate for another. But despite such differences, all supply circuits on a boat are similar enough that understanding one circuit is tantamount to understanding them all.

Circuits are easier to understand when we draw them. A diagram of how the various components are connected is called a schematic. It works much like a map, with electrical components substituting for towns and wire for roads. Schematics don't just help you visualize the circuit; they show where to look and—just as valuable—where *not* to look when the current traveling these wires suffers a breakdown.

SYMBOLS

Labeled boxes or circles can represent the various components, but a handful of symbols makes circuit diagrams easier to draw and easier to read. Electrical symbols are not entirely standardized, so you may encounter alternative representations of the same component.

CONDUCTOR

The solid lines on a schematic represent the wire (or sometimes copper ribbon or copper terminal strips) that connect the various components.

TERMINAL OR CONNECTION

A dot or small circle indicates a connection. When lines cross without a dot, the represented wires are not connected. Sometimes a hump is used at line intersections to make it clear that no junction is indicated, but this adds unnecessary complexity.

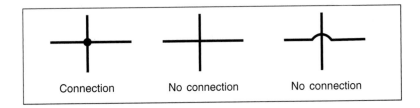

BATTERY

For 12-volt circuits, the battery is both the beginning and the end of the circuit. Use the battery symbol or a pair of terminal symbols marked with a + and a −.

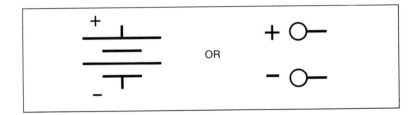

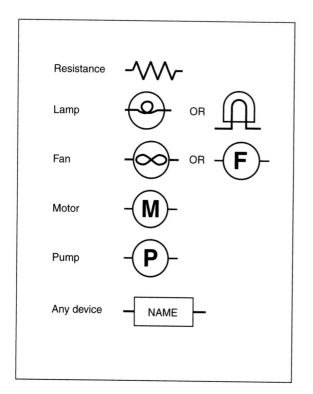

LOADS

You can show all loads with the zigzag resistance symbol, but schematics tell more at a glance if the symbol is more specific.

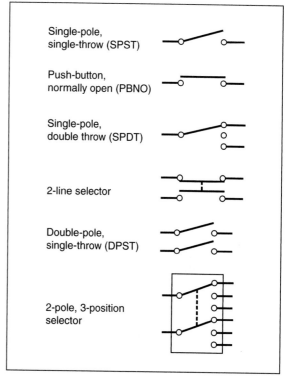

SWITCHES

The simplest switch symbol depicts a hinged conductor between two terminals. The symbols for specialized or more complicated switches are equally intuitive.

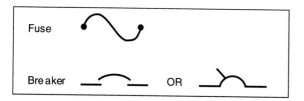

FUSES AND BREAKERS

You can use the fuse symbol for all load-protection devices, or distinguish between fuses and breakers.

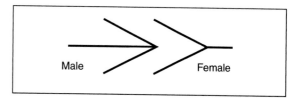

CONNECTOR

For ease of servicing, it is often a good idea to use pull-apart plugs to connect an appliance to the power circuit.

MORE ABOUT GROUND

WIRING DIAGRAMS for automobiles often show a ground symbol on the negative side of loads rather than a return wire because cars use a single-wire system, grounding the negative side of loads to the chassis. Proper boat wiring is a two-wire system—called insulated return—with the negative side of the load ultimately connected to the negative terminal of the battery (or other power source). A ground symbol appears on a boat wiring diagram only where the negative terminal of the battery is grounded, usually by connecting it to the engine and thus to the water through the shaft and prop. Typically the alternator is similarly grounded, as are engine-mounted electrics that use the engine for the return side of the circuit.

On a boat, the ground symbol is used more often in diagrams of bonding systems intended to reduce corrosion and/or reduce the potential for lightning-strike damage (see Chapter 9). Some electronics, particularly high-frequency radios, also require a connection to ground.

GROUND

The ground symbol indicates a connection to earth—in the case of a boat, a connection to the water the boat is floating in, usually through engine, shaft, and prop or through an externally mounted (and submerged) grounding plate.

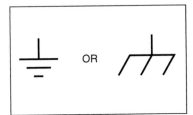

DIODES

Diodes are primarily used as check valves, passing current one way, but blocking the flow the other way. Light-emitting diodes (LEDs) are used today for almost all panel lights. Because of their astoundingly low current draw, LEDs are on their way to replacing 12-volt incandescent lamps.

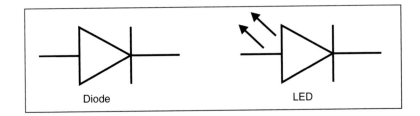

Diode   LED

ALTERNATOR

The engine-driven alternator is the main source of charging current on most boats. A generator performs the same function.

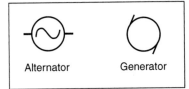

Alternator   Generator

METERS

Smart sailors are more and more including integral meters in various circuits to show immediate current flow or voltage level.

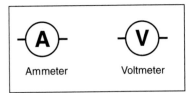

Ammeter   Voltmeter

A circuit requires only three components: a power source, a load, and conductors connecting the two.

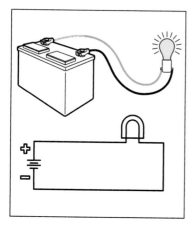 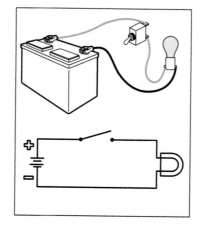 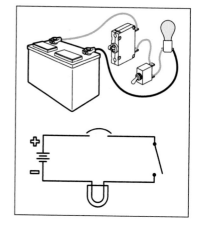

CLOSED CIRCUIT

Connecting the wire leads from a lamp to the terminals of a battery closes the circuit and, if the battery has a charge, illuminates the light.

OPEN CIRCUIT

We can stop the flow of current by disconnecting one of the wires, but adding a switch to the circuit makes extinguishing the light more convenient. Switches are always installed in the positive side of the circuit.

OVERLOAD PROTECTION

To avoid the dangers of a short, every circuit must also include a fuse or breaker in the positive side, as close to the power source as possible.

SERIES

Controlling components like switches, fuses, and diodes are always wired in series with the load.

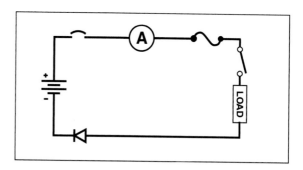

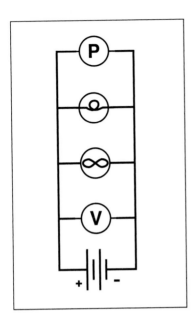

PARALLEL

When a circuit supplies more than one load, the loads are almost always connected in parallel. Parallel circuits all enjoy the same voltage.

REAL WORLD

A typical real-world circuit may have both series and parallel components, and some *branches* of the circuit may be open concurrent with others being closed.

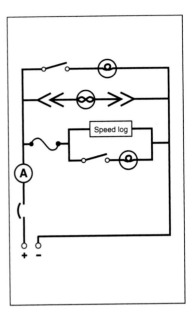

MAPPING YOUR OWN BOAT

Few boats are provided with factory schematics. Taking a few hours to work up a diagram of the wiring of your boat will pay sizable dividends: an accurate wiring diagram makes electrical problems much easier to diagnose; the process of tracing the wiring will familiarize you with your boat's all-important and otherwise-hidden electrical system, and will serve as an electrical survey to uncover shortcomings and potential problems; and the hands-on experience is sure to bolster your confidence as an electrician.

AC CAUTION

Before you start tracing wires, be sure that your boat is disconnected from shore power, and DISCONNECT YOUR INVERTER FROM THE BATTERY. It is far too easy to confuse 12-volt wiring with 120-volt wiring, and if the AC system is energized, such a mistake could be deadly.

Mapping AC wiring is a good idea, often leading to the discovery of serious deficiencies such as exposed connections, the absence of an AC circuit breaker, or reversed polarity. If you want to map your boat's AC system now while you are tracing the 12-volt system, read Chapter 8 first so you will know what kinds of problems you should be watching for.

WYSIWYG*

The best way to create a wiring diagram is to start with a layout of your boat and draw in every appliance, outlet, and remote switch more or less where they are actually located. This is usually an eye-opener as to how many electrical items are aboard.

The larger the sheet of paper, the less congested this drawing will become. Labeled boxes and circles will be adequate symbols.

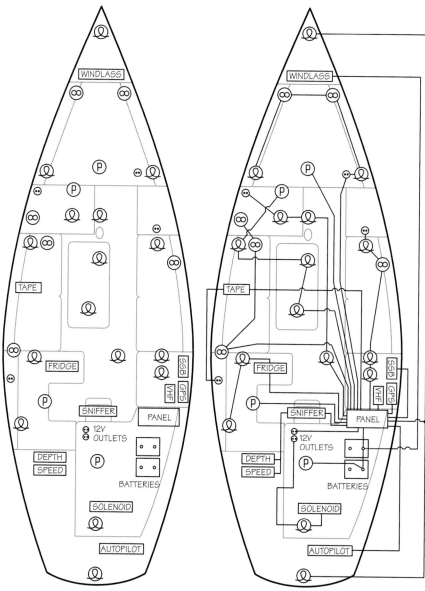

Once you have all the components on the drawing, convert it to a single-line wiring diagram by connecting the items on each circuit. With everything switched on, you can identify which items are on the same circuit by throwing the breaker and observing what goes off. Some circuits may not originate at the breaker panel; automatic bilge pumps, for example, are often connected directly to the battery so they will remain operational even with the main battery switch off.

The point of this step is to establish which components are interconnected. If you end up with some components on your drawing unconnected, just leave them for the moment. When you start tracing wiring, how they are connected into the system will become clear.

*WYSIWYG = What You See Is What You Get.

CIRCUIT DIAGRAMS

The basic sailboat electrical system typically has a main circuit—connecting the batteries to both the starter and the distribution panel—and at least six (usually more) branch circuits supplying power to lights, pumps, and other electrical items. In addition, there are charging circuits, which we haven't yet covered (Chapter 7), but which you can still diagram; and dedicated circuits connected directly to the battery for such items as bilge pumps and SSB radios.

Diagramming circuits will be easier if you do each circuit on a separate page. Where a wire is identified by a label, a color, or even the printed designation on the jacket, noting this information on your drawing can help you find the other end. Note, however, that factory "electricians" are notorious for grabbing any color available when the last spool empties, so a wire that leaves the panel blue might be pink when it reaches the appliance, perhaps with a butt splice behind the headliner.

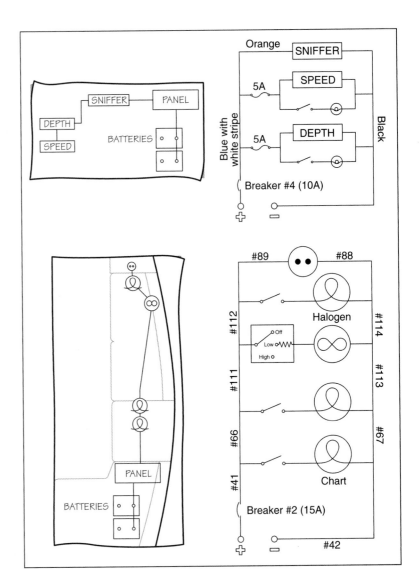

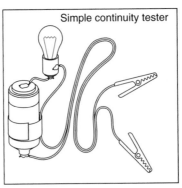

Simple continuity tester

For accurate circuit diagrams you will have to trace every wire. Wiring that disappears behind interior liners can be traced with a meter or a simple continuity tester. Be sure one end of the wire run is disconnected when checking for continuity.

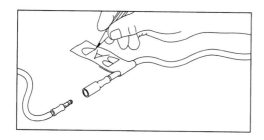

While you are tracing, pay attention to the condition of the wires and especially the connections. Tighten any that are loose and flag any that show signs of corrosion, also noting the problem on your drawing. You will come back later and take corrective measures.

MASTER DIAGRAM

The individual circuit drawings are perfectly adequate, but a master drawing will be more convenient. If you have access to a computer, a simple drawing program makes neat, legible wiring diagrams a snap, and it allows for later additions and corrections. A nearby copy center will print the diagram on a chart-size sheet of paper for a modest fee.

(If you are a Luddite, the back side of an old chart is ideal for accomplishing the same thing with pen and straightedge.)

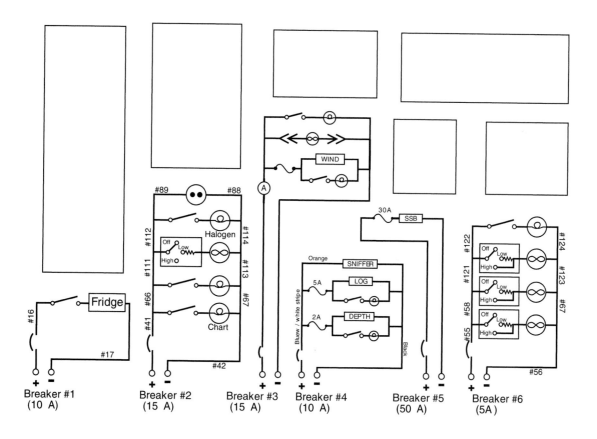

LAYOUT SCHEMATIC

An alternative to the simple circuit diagram is a layout schematic—essentially a combination of the component layout and the master wiring diagram. This has the advantage of showing not just the electrical path but also approximately how every electrical component in the boat is physically connected. Again, this type of drawing is easier to do on the computer.

SIGNAL WIRES

Signal wires connect transducer to depth sounder, radio to antenna, GPS to autopilot. Treat signal wires separately from power wires, mapping them on a separate drawing.

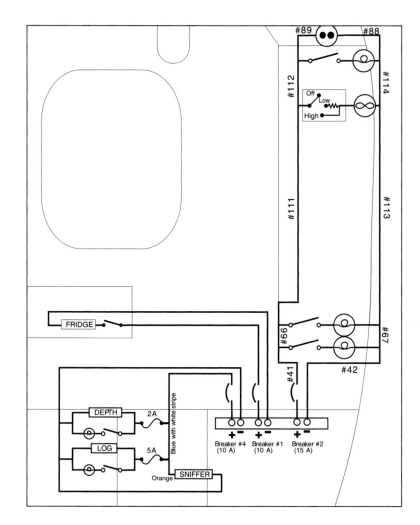

TROUBLESHOOTING

"Is it plugged in?"

It is the obvious question and, along with changing a light bulb, usually exhausts the electrical troubleshooting repertoire of most of us. Fortunately nearly all troubleshooting of 12-volt circuits is essentially determining if everything is "plugged in."

When you are familiar with the components of a circuit, it is a very short step to being able to assess the health of that circuit. Since we have just worked our way through circuits, now is the time to take that step.

Toss away visions of oscilloscopes and pocket protectors. When you squeeze the trigger on the nozzle of your garden hose and no water comes out, you look back down the hose for a kink, check that the faucet is open. The process of determining why current fails to flow through a wire is just as logical and hardly more complicated.

Of course, it is even less complicated to dial up your electrician, but always selecting that option can cost you more than just money. Electrical problems don't occur only at the dock, and an electrician can be hard to come by at sea. You might muddle through a crippling electrical problem on your first try, but a bit of prior troubleshooting experience certainly improves the odds.

Spend a little time running tests on your boat's electrics. They might be revealing. At the very least you will be developing a skill that could turn out to be more valuable than you imagine.

Finding electrical problems sometimes requires just being observant.

HOUSE OF CARDS

IF DIM LIGHTS are caused by a corroded or loose connection, cleaning and tightening that connection may be all the corrective measures required. But if you determine that the problem is a low charge on the battery, simply recharging the battery may be inadequate. Why is the battery low? Maybe you just haven't run the engine. Maybe the battery is dying. Maybe the anchor light has been left on. Maybe a short is draining the battery. Maybe a leaking stuffing box is causing the bilge pump to run. Maybe the alternator belt is loose. Maybe the alternator is defective; maybe the regulator. The interconnected nature of a boat's electrical system makes it imperative to determine what *caused* a problem and to correct that condition as well.

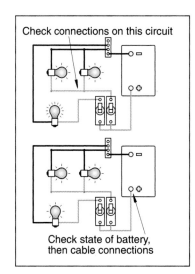

Check connections on this circuit

Check state of battery, then cable connections

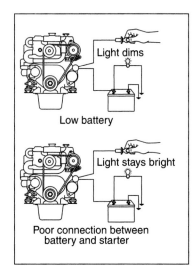

Light dims

Low battery

Light stays bright

Poor connection between battery and starter

DIMMING

Dim lights result from low voltage. Low voltage also slows fans and pumps and causes electronics to "crash." If only a single light or the lights on a single circuit are dim, the likely cause is a bad connection or inadequate wire size. When all lights are dim, suspect a low charge on the battery. Less likely is a poor connection between the battery and the distribution panel.

SLUGGISH STARTING

An anemic groan or just the click of the solenoid when you hit the starter button is the classic indicator of a "dead" battery, but a poor connection can exhibit the same symptoms. Observe an illuminated cabin lamp when the starter is engaged. Some dimming is normal, especially if the battery is a deep-cycle type, but if the lamp goes out, the battery is almost certainly low. If the lamp remains bright, look for a loose or corroded connection somewhere between the battery and the starter.

A defective starter motor is a less likely possibility.

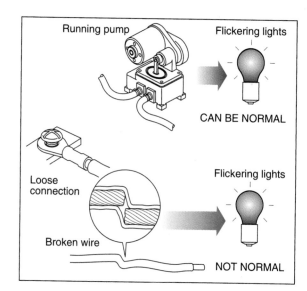

Running pump

Flickering lights

CAN BE NORMAL

Loose connection

Broken wire

Flickering lights

NOT NORMAL

FLICKERING

Flickering can be "normal" when it is caused by load variation—such as the cycling of a pump. Flickering that is not concurrent with the operation of some other appliance almost always indicates a loose or corroded connection or a broken wire.

BLOWN FUSE

When the lights go out you *know* you have an electrical problem. But a blown fuse is only a symptom. It means the circuit was overloaded. To avoid a recurrence, it is imperative to determine the cause of the overload and correct it.

If the overload is due to adding an appliance or upgrading to a component with higher wattage, substituting a larger fuse might be an acceptable solution, but only if all the wire in the circuit is capable of carrying the higher current. The inevitability of upgrading is reason enough to install wiring a size larger than immediate requirements.

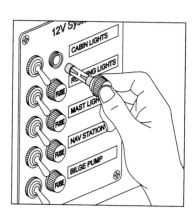

GROUND RETURN

THE ELECTRICAL ITEMS ON A MARINE ENGINE almost always use a ground-return circuit. That means the engine, rather than an insulated wire back to the battery, serves as the ground side of the circuit. Because components are electrically connected to the ground circuit by their mounting bolts, you must consider these mounts when you suspect a poor connection. A buildup of rust between mating surfaces can open the circuit as effectively as a disconnected battery cable. And speaking of battery cables, the ground-return circuit is typically completed through a cable connecting the engine block to the negative battery terminal. Be sure to check the connection of this cable to the engine.

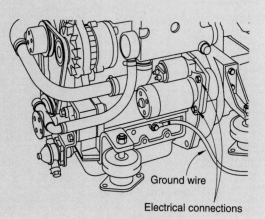

Ground wire

Electrical connections

HEAT

Wire too small for its load generates heat. If the wire gets hot enough, it can start a fire. Melted insulation is an all-too-common sign of less-disastrous wire heating. Treat such a discovery like chest pains—a fortunate warning you may not get again.

Wire the right size should not even get warm. As a matter of fact, heating usually occurs at junctions where a poor connection introduces resistance. It is a good idea to get in the habit of touching wires and connectors (12-volt only, PLEASE). If they are warm to the touch, they need attention. Aside from the danger (the problem will only get worse), resistance in the wiring means full voltage is not reaching the appliances in the circuit.

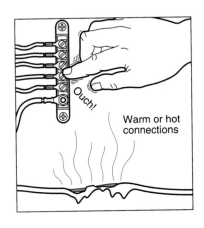

Warm or hot connections

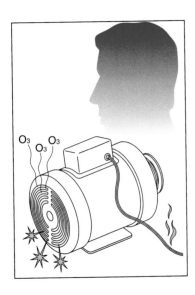

ODOR

The smell of hot insulation should lead you into a full-court press to find the source. Whether the insulation is burning due to a hot wire or contact with a hot engine, for example, is immaterial. Both circumstances place your boat at risk.

Another odor that should get your attention is ozone—that electric razor smell caused by electrical arcing. It is not uncommon for motors and generators to arc at their brushes, but equipment intended for marine use should be ignition protected—meaning either it should not produce sparks, or the arcing must be hermetically contained so it cannot be an ignition source. In the presence of propane that has leaked into the bilge, a spark is the equivalent of lighting a match. If you smell ozone, find the source and repair or replace the offending gear.

HEAT LOSS

IN CHAPTER 4 WE SAW that 100 feet (30 m) of 16-gauge wire has a resistance of 0.41 ohms, and if we push 10 amps through that resistance, we get a voltage drop of 4.1 volts (10A x 0.41Ω). What happened to that voltage? It was converted from electrical energy to heat energy. We can express this conversion in terms of power by multiplying the voltage drop times the current (P = V x I). In this case, we have 41 watts (4.1V x 10A) of power given up to heat. Spread over 100 feet of wire, this heat dissipates harmlessly, but what if the resistance is not due to small wire but rather a poor connection? Now we have 41 watts of power concentrated at a single point. The connection tries to become a light-bulb filament, until something melts.

If you are interested, you can reduce the two steps for calculating power loss to one: P = V x I, but since V = I x R, P = I x I x R or I^2R. Power lost as heat is often called I^2R loss.

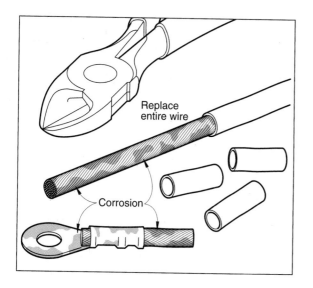

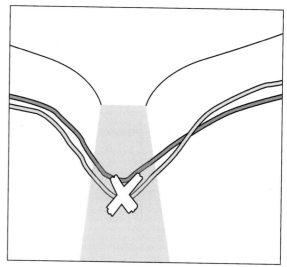

CORROSION

Electrical connections should be clean and bright. Clean away corrosion with a wire brush or bronze wool and coat the reassembled connection with petroleum jelly. Corrosion between wire and terminal requires cutting off the terminal and attaching a new one, but in this case you will often find that the wire inside the insulation is also corroded. If you cannot expose bright, unblemished wire, replace it.

WET WIRING

Any wire that is wet to the touch should be rerouted. Water and electrical wiring are a poor combination. Do not let wires lie in water or subject them to drips or drenchings.

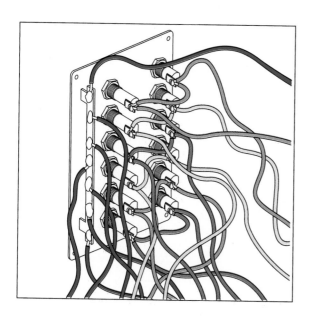

RAT'S NEST

Wiring that is a tangled jumble is a bad sign. If previous "electricians" had no appreciation for the importance of neat and orderly wire runs, suspect that they also cut corners with regard to the type of wire and terminals used. A sloppy end product always suggests slipshod workmanship.

You can diagnose a surprising number of common electrical problems by checking the circuit with a simple test light. This is essentially the same as checking a suspect outlet at home by plugging a lamp into it. If the lamp works, the outlet is fine.

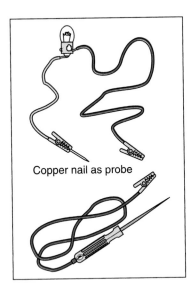

Copper nail as probe

MAKE OR BUY

A test light is easy enough to make by soldering leads to a 12-volt automotive bulb. Alligator clips on the leads let you clip one while you probe with the other—a nail in the gator's mouth makes a perfectly good test probe. But if you can't salvage the clips and bulb from your junk box, it will probably be cheaper to buy a ready-made tester. Appropriate 12-volt test lights—usually in the form of a probe with a light in the handle and a single clip-fitted wire lead—can be purchased for a couple of dollars at automotive supply stores.

USING A TEST LIGHT

ISOLATE THE FAULT

Connect one side of your test light to the negative side of the power source—in this case the battery—and methodically check the circuit by touching the probe to every junction. When the lamp fails to light, you have found the component or section of the circuit that is faulty. In this example, we find no power on the output side of the switch even though it is in the on position. The switch (or its connection) is faulty.

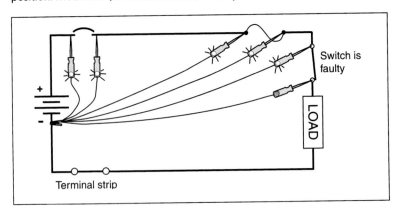

Switch is faulty

LOAD

Terminal strip

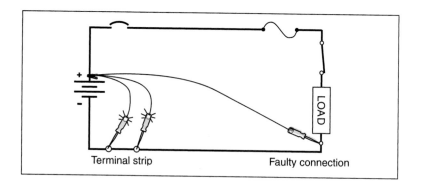

Terminal strip · · · Faulty connection

CHECK THE RETURN SIDE

What if you clipped the tester to the negative battery terminal and found voltage with every probe, all the way to the nonfunctioning appliance? Move the clip to the positive battery terminal and test the return side of the circuit.

FIND AN OPEN CIRCUIT

Because the bulb filament has higher resistance than hook-up wire, we wouldn't expect the test lamp to light if connected in parallel to one leg of a circuit. But if the circuit is open between the test probes, the lamp is now in series and should glow. Note that it may be dim because it is sharing the available voltage with other components in the circuit. If the tester lights when connected around a fuse holder, the fuse is bad. Connected around a switch, the tester should come on when the switch is in the off position, and it should go off when the switch is turned on.

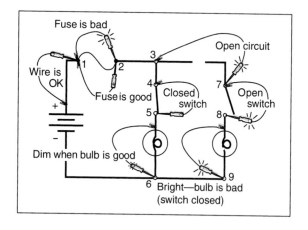

NARROW THE POSSIBILITIES

We have tested much more of this circuit than we needed to. If the 20-watt light works, it is a hard-wired test light, confirming power at junctions 3 and 6. We can clip our test light to junction 3 and test only the branch of the circuit supplying the 9-watt light. If neither light works, we should look for the problem on the battery side of junctions 3 and 6.

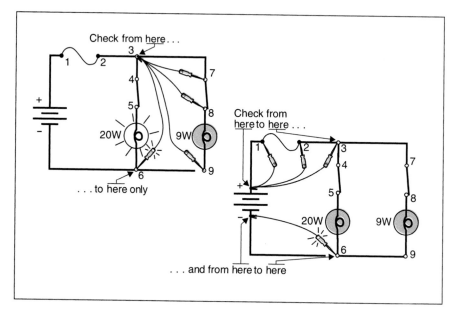

On today's sailboats, a multimeter is as essential as a rigging knife or an oil-filter wrench. Once you exceed the limited capabilities of a test light, you simply cannot troubleshoot electrical circuits effectively without a meter. A basic meter capable of measuring volts, ohms, and milliamps can be purchased for under $25 and is adequate for most tests you are likely to perform. If your budget allows it, a meter that allows direct current measurements up to 10 amps may eventually prove more versatile.

DIGITAL VS. ANALOG

Analog meters—meters with a needle—have served previous generations well, but like computers versus typewriters, modern digital meters are far superior. They are notably more accurate and much easier to use, especially for the novice. In addition, analog meters often alter the tested circuit—called meter loading—because they add a parallel circuit. This results in erroneous readings. Digital meters are connected the same way, but extremely high internal resistance makes the connection virtually invisible to the circuit. If you have an analog meter, donate it to a school and buy yourself a digital meter.

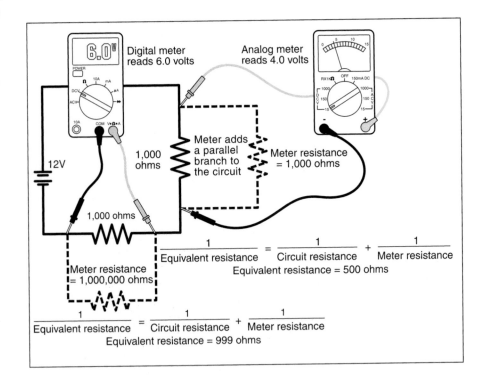

Digital meter reads 6.0 volts

Analog meter reads 4.0 volts

Meter adds a parallel branch to the circuit

Meter resistance = 1,000 ohms

1,000 ohms

12V

1,000 ohms

Meter resistance = 1,000,000 ohms

$$\frac{1}{\text{Equivalent resistance}} = \frac{1}{\text{Circuit resistance}} + \frac{1}{\text{Meter resistance}}$$

Equivalent resistance = 500 ohms

$$\frac{1}{\text{Equivalent resistance}} = \frac{1}{\text{Circuit resistance}} + \frac{1}{\text{Meter resistance}}$$

Equivalent resistance = 999 ohms

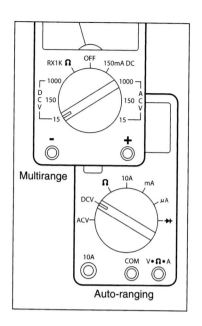

Multirange

Auto-ranging

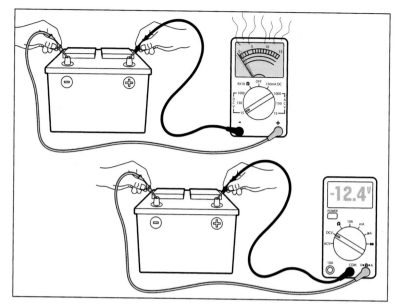

AUTO-RANGING

Since you don't always know what reading to expect, standard practice has always been to select the highest range setting, then "tap" the probes to make sure the reading isn't still going to "peg" the meter. If not, you switch down in range until reach the one appropriate for the reading. With an auto-ranging meter, you simply select what you want to measure—volts, amps, or ohms—and the meter does the rest. This is not only convenient, it greatly reduces the likelihood of meter damage. If you are buying a meter, get one that auto-ranges.

POLARITY

Another reason for tapping probes is to make sure the needle deflects in the right direction. If not, polarity is reversed and you need to reverse the probes. Nearly all digital meters have automatic polarity, measuring voltage or current with the probes connected either way. Polarity is typically indicated on these meters with a + or – in the display.

CLAMP-ON METERS

A multimeter that measures currents up to about 10 amps—the usual limit—more than satisfies the requirements of most boatowners, but if you want to measure starting currents, charging currents, or current flows to high-demand devices like inverters and windlasses, you need a clamp-on meter. Through magic known as Hall effect, this type of meter measures the current flowing through any wire passing through the center of the clamp. Clamp-on meters measure currents of 1,000 amps or more with the not insignificant advantage that they don't have to be connected into the circuit. They are less accurate for low currents.

METER FUNDAMENTALS

Your particular meter should have a user's manual, but here are the basics of connecting a multimeter to the circuit.

CONNECTING TEST LEADS

If the test leads are removable, the black lead is always plugged into the jack labeled COM—*common* to all tests. For voltage and resistance tests, the red lead goes into the jack labeled V/Ω. For current measurements, plug the red lead into the jack marked A or 10A. Some meters have a separate jack labeled mA for measuring smaller currents.

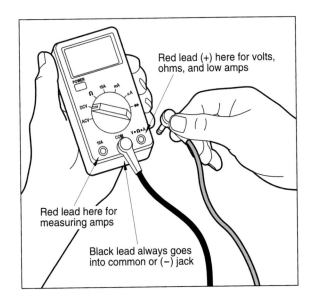

Red lead (+) here for volts, ohms, and low amps

Red lead here for measuring amps

Black lead always goes into common or (−) jack

MEASURING VOLTAGE

The voltmeter functions like the test light except that it tells you exactly how much voltage is present. Set the selector switch to V or DC V and touch the leads to any two points in the circuit. If there is a difference in potential between the two points, the meter will display it in volts.

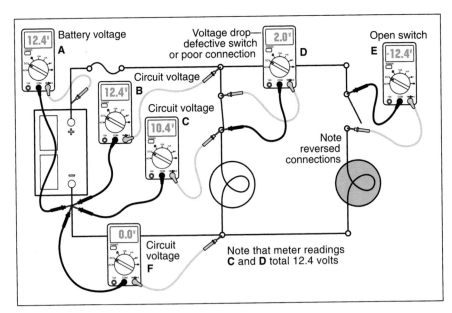

12.4ᵛ Battery voltage **A**

12.4ᵛ B

Circuit voltage

Circuit voltage

10.4ᵛ C

0.0ᵛ Circuit voltage **F**

Voltage drop— defective switch or poor connection

2.0ᵛ D

Open switch

E **-12.4ᵛ**

Note reversed connections

Note that meter readings **C** and **D** total 12.4 volts

MEASURING CURRENT

The ammeter must be connected in series with a conductor to measure current flow. That means you have to break the circuit and insert the ammeter at the break. Check the size of the breaker or fuse in the circuit to make certain expected amperage does not exceed the capacity of your meter.

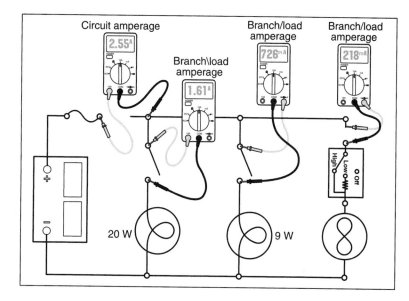

Even when the breaker is a 15-amp unit, you can often test the circuit with a 10-amp meter provided you operate only one appliance on the circuit at a time. Do not use a 10-amp meter to test starter motor or windlass circuits, or any other load that might exceed 10 amps.

MEASURING RESISTANCE (OR LACK THEREOF)

The ohmmeter measures resistance, and the component you are testing *must be disconnected from the circuit.* Otherwise, the meter is also measuring the resistance around the rest of the circuit. The meter can also be damaged if there is power in the circuit. When making resistance measurements, always turn off the circuit.

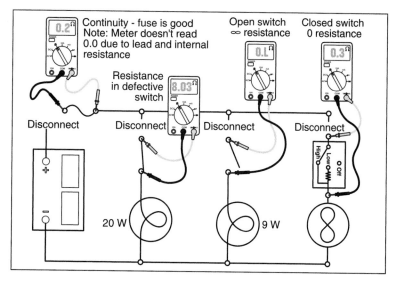

The safest practice is to confirm that the circuit is open with your voltmeter before doing resistance tests. If the circuit branches, disconnect one end of the component you are testing to isolate it.

Often you will use the ohmmeter to test for continuity rather than resistance. An unrestricted conductor will read near zero on the ohmmeter. An open circuit reads ∞ or O.L (overload).

The boatowner adept with a multimeter can quickly identify and pinpoint almost any electrical problem likely to occur on a boat. The following provides visual guidance.

Caution: Always double-check meter setting and test-lead connections before you attempt any tests. Modern meters are better protected against operator error, but you will still blow the meter's internal fuse if, for example, you intend to check battery voltage but have the meter set to check current. Verify the setting.

MULTIMETER CONNECTIONS

Voltmeter—Parallel

Ammeter—Series

Ohmmeter—Isolated

VOLTMETER TESTS

BATTERY VOLTAGE

With all circuits off *and the battery rested*, touching the probes to the battery terminals yields battery voltage. If you are using a digital voltmeter, this test can provide a fair assessment of the state of charge—if you know the fully charged rest voltage of the tested battery. The rule of thumb is that every 0.01 volts below the fully charged voltage equals a 1.25% discharge.

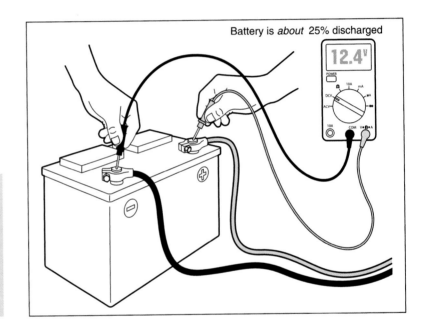

Battery is *about* 25% discharged

ZERO ADJUST

ANALOG METERS have an *Ohms Adjust* knob that allows you to set the meter to zero resistance when the probes are crossed. Digital meters rarely incorporate this adjustment, so always cross the probes of a digital meter first before taking a resistance measurement to determine the internal resistance caused by the leads and fuse. It is normally tiny, on the order of 0.4 ohms, but it will prevent a zero ohms reading even on a perfect conductor.

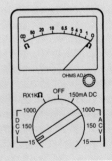

CHECKING YOUR HYDROMETER

IN CHAPTER 3, I pointed out that cell voltage is equal to the specific gravity plus 0.84. Check this for yourself by measuring the specific gravity for each cell, converting each reading to volts (V = SG + 0.84), adding the cell voltages together, and comparing them to your meter reading. Some disparity can be expected due to minor inaccuracies in hydrometer readings, but if the two voltages disagree by as much as 0.10 volts, try a different hydrometer. Poor calibration is common.

CIRCUIT VOLTAGE

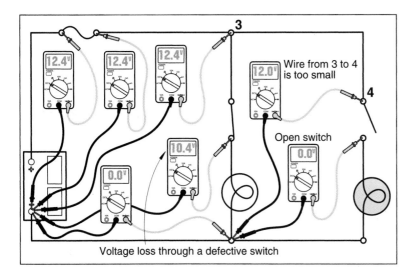

Wire from 3 to 4 is too small

Open switch

Voltage loss through a defective switch

With the black probe attached to the negative battery post, you can verify the voltage at every junction in the circuit. Remember that we don't want the total voltage drop between battery and appliance to exceed 3 percent. If battery voltage is 12.4 volts and we read 12 volts at the appliance, there is excessive resistance in the circuit.

VOLTAGE DROP

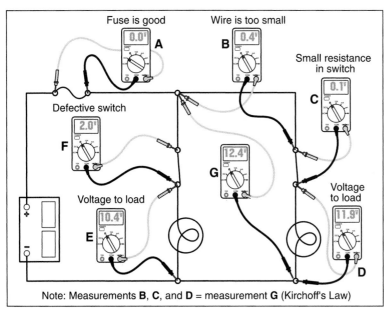

Fuse is good — A
Wire is too small — B
Small resistance in switch — C
Defective switch
F
Voltage to load — E
G
Voltage to load — D

Note: Measurements **B**, **C**, and **D** = measurement **G** (Kirchoff's Law)

Rather than calculate voltage drop across some section or component of the circuit, we can measure it directly by bridging it with the multimeter. Remember that voltage drop is directly proportional to current (V = I x R), so measure it with the circuit under maximum load.

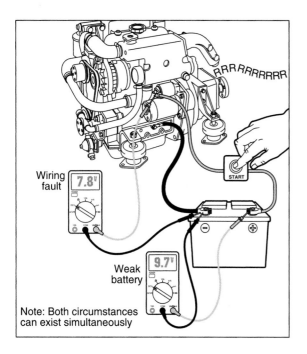

Wiring fault **7.8ᵛ**

Weak battery **9.7ᵛ**

Note: Both circumstances can exist simultaneously

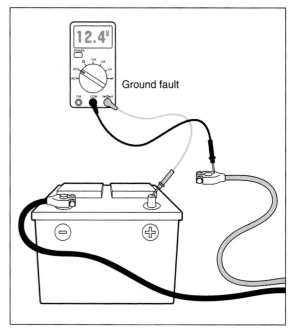

12.4ᵛ

Ground fault

LOAD VOLTAGE

Heavy starter current commonly pulls battery voltage down, but if voltage measured at the battery posts when the starter is engaged declines below 10 volts, need for a bigger battery is indicated. If voltage at the battery remains high, but falls at the load, the trouble is in the wiring.

A 0.1-ohm resistance will show up as a 0.2-volt drop if the circuit has a 2-amp load ($V = I \times R$)—seemingly not a problem in a cabin-light circuit. But if this small resistance is between the battery post and cable clamp, and we hit the starter button, drawing 150 amps, the voltage drop leaps to 15 volts—effectively an open circuit since we have only 12 volts available.

GROUND FAULT

Any current flowing to "earth" discharges batteries and may result in destructive corrosion. Such short circuits—called ground faults—are easy to detect. With all circuits off, a voltmeter connected between the positive battery post and the disconnected cable reads zero if no electrical path exists to ground. A voltage reading indicates a ground fault. Leaks are most often caused by moisture, faulty insulation, poor wiring, or defective switches. Trace the leak with the ammeter setting (see below).

EXTENDING YOUR REACH

TO MAKE VOLTMETER USE more convenient, make up a test-lead extension—a 20-foot (6 m) length of flexible (type 3) #16 wire with alligator clips on both ends. Clip one end to the "ground" point for the circuit—usually the negative battery post or the negative bus bar in the distribution panel—and clip the other end to the meter's common (black) probe. If you are measuring circuit voltage, be sure your reference voltage is with the extension in use.

KIRCHOFF'S LAW

NOTE THAT WHEN we check the battery voltage of an energized circuit, we are also measuring the voltage drop through the entire circuit. The total of the voltage drops in a circuit is always equal to the source voltage. This is called *Kirchoff's Law*, and it explains the detriment of voltage drops. If a defective switch uses 2 volts, we only have 10.4 volts left to supply a load designed to operate on 12 volts. Turning this around, if you measure a 10.4-volt drop across the load but 12.4 volts at the battery, somewhere in the circuit you will find additional voltage drops totaling 2 volts. It is just sums, and it tells you a lot about what you are looking for when you troubleshoot a circuit.

OHMMETER TESTS

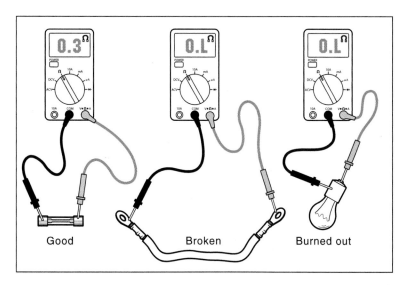

Good   Broken   Burned out

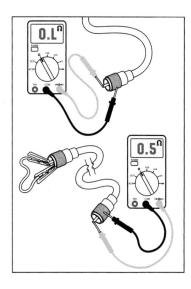

CHECKING CONDUCTANCE

Touching the probes to the ends of an isolated conductor shows you its resistance. A good wire or fuse will have little or no measurable resistance. An O.L (overload) or ∞ reading indicates a broken wire, blown fuse, or some other type of open circuit.

TESTING COAX

Disconnect the coax at both ends and touch the meter probes to the center pin and the body of one of the connectors. O.L is the only allowable meter reading. Clip a jumper wire between the pin and the body of this connector, then do the same test at the opposite end. Now the meter should read near zero, confirming unbroken conductors and uncorroded plug connections.

MASTHEAD LIGHTS

TEST THE NORMAL RESISTANCE of masthead light circuits by disconnecting (or unplugging) the wires at the deck and measuring the resistance of the circuit. Record the meter reading. When the light later fails, you can determine from the deck if the problem is an open circuit, probably a burned-out bulb (meter reads O.L), a corroded connection (meter reads more than normal but less than O.L), a short in the wiring (meter reads near zero), or a short to the mast (meter reads less than O.L when one probe is across both wires and the other touches the mast). In this last instance, be sure your fingers aren't touching the metal portion of the probes, or the "short circuit" resistance you will be measuring will actually be your body resistance.

If the meter reads O.L, twist the wires together before you go to the top of the mast. At the top, remove the bulb and check it with your meter; O.L means the bulb is burned out. Also test the resistance across the socket; with the wires twisted together at the bottom the reading should be near the wire resistance. For example, the resistance of #12 wire is about 0.16 ohms per 100 feet (30 m) (see Chapter 4), so on a 40-foot (12 m) stick wired with #12 wire, the ohmmeter reading should be near 0.13 ohms (0.8 x 0.16). With a crossed-probe resistance of 0.4 ohms, the meter reading for good wires should be around 0.5 ohms. Higher resistance suggests corrosion. O.L indicates a broken wire or a faulty connection.

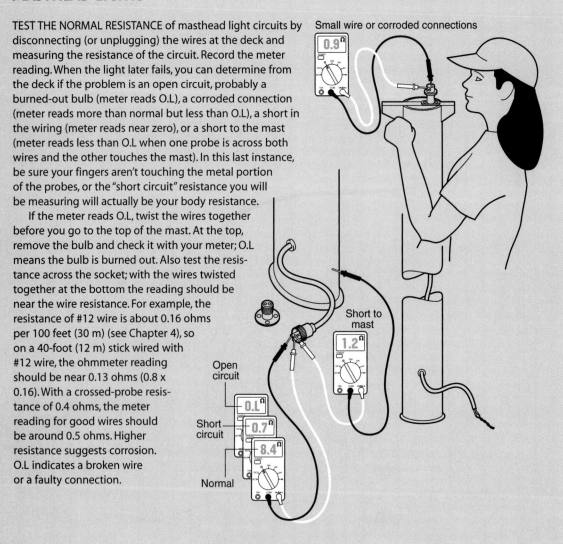

Small wire or corroded connections

0.9 Ω

Short to mast

1.2 Ω

Open circuit 0.L Ω

Short circuit 0.7 Ω

Normal 8.4 Ω

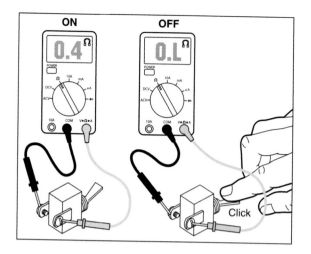

TESTING SWITCHES

With the probes in contact with the switch terminals, the ohmmeter should read O.L with the switch off, zero when you turn the switch on. All other readings suggest replacement.

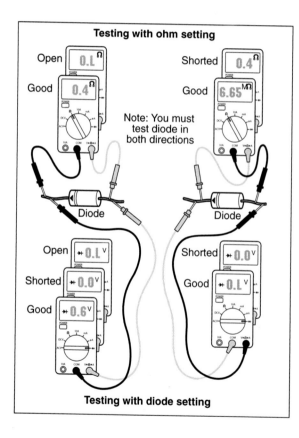

Testing with ohm setting

Open

Good

Shorted

Good

Note: You must test diode in both directions

Diode

Diode

Open

Shorted

Good

Shorted

Good

Testing with diode setting

DIODE TESTING

Diodes are electrical check-valves, passing current in one direction but resisting the flow in the opposite direction. A functioning diode will register low resistance when tested in one direction, high resistance when the probes are reversed. If the meter reads near the same in both directions—whether high or low—the diode is defective.

FINDING SHORT CIRCUITS

A blown fuse or burned wire indicates an overload, often caused by a "short" in the circuit that lets current bypass the load. Note that damage from a short often occurs away from the fault, in the most resistive part of the circuit.

First remove the load component and test it. A near-zero reading across the terminals of an appliance usually indicates an internal short. If the appliance is good, the short is in the circuit.

Shorts are easier to diagnose when the expected resistance is O.L, so leave the load out of the circuit and connect the meter in its place. Be sure the battery is also disconnected. The meter should read O.L; any other reading indicates a short. Opening and reclosing the circuit methodically will pinpoint the location of the short. When a break in the circuit has no effect on the meter reading, the short is on the meter side of the opening; if the meter reading jumps to O.L, the short is on the other side.

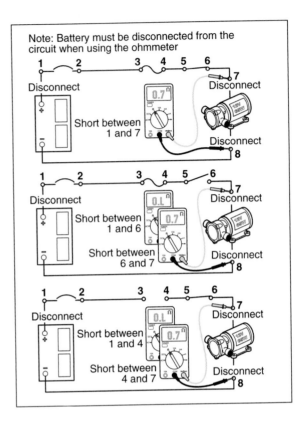

EVALUATING A GROUND FAULT

If you found a ground fault when you connected the voltmeter between the positive battery post and its disconnected cable, you can determine how serious that leak is by connecting the ohmmeter between the disconnected positive *cable* and the *negative* battery post. This measures the resistance of the ground fault.

If the meter reads less than 10 ohms, your "leak" is probably a piece of gear you failed to turn off for this test. Otherwise, the lower the reading, the more serious the leak. But even though battery drain may be negligible with a high resistance fault ($I = V / R$), even a tiny current leaking to ground through some metal component of the boat can cause destructive corrosion. Use your ammeter to locate (as described below) any ground fault less than 10,000 ohms.

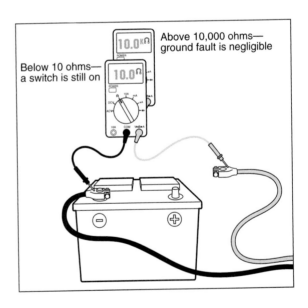

CHANGING RESISTANCE

YOU CAN USE OHM'S LAW to calculate the ohmmeter reading you might expect when you touch the meter probes to the terminals or contacts of an appliance. However, Ohm's Law calculates operating resistance; "cold" resistance can be much lower. Incandescent bulbs in particular show a fraction of calculated resistance when they are not illuminated. Likewise, electric motors may give a lower reading than expected. Before assuming an internal short, compare your reading to one taken on a similar appliance that you know is good.

ESTIMATING CIRCUIT CURRENT

With the circuit disconnected from power, connect the ohmmeter to the battery ends of the circuit to measure its total resistance. Be sure all breakers and switches are on. Divide the meter reading into battery voltage (12.6 V) to determine the expected current in the circuit—and whether you can safely use your ammeter in this circuit.

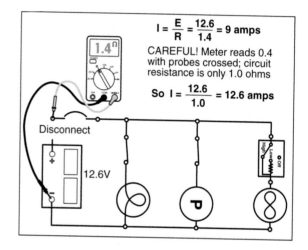

$$I = \frac{E}{R} = \frac{12.6}{1.4} = 9 \text{ amps}$$

CAREFUL! Meter reads 0.4 with probes crossed; circuit resistance is only 1.0 ohms

$$\text{So } I = \frac{12.6}{1.0} = 12.6 \text{ amps}$$

AMMETER TESTS

POWER CONSUMPTION

Manufacturers are sometimes "optimistic" in rating the current requirements of their equipment. By inserting an ammeter in the circuit, you can measure the actual current draw. It is a good exercise to update your load-calculation chart (Chapter 3) with actual measurements.

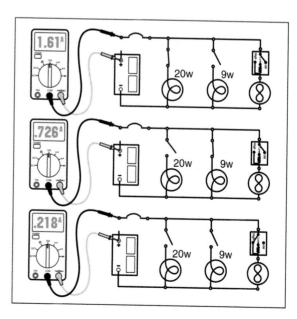

TRACING GROUND FAULTS

The sensitivity of an ammeter makes it ideal for tracing the tiny currents that often leak, sometimes with dire consequences, from boat wiring. With all breakers off, connect the meter between the positive battery post and the disconnected positive cable. One at a time, disconnect any circuits connected directly to the cable clamp or otherwise unfused. If the leak disappears, it is on the just-disconnected circuit. If the leak persists, check each breaker with your ohmmeter. It should read O.L when the breaker is open.

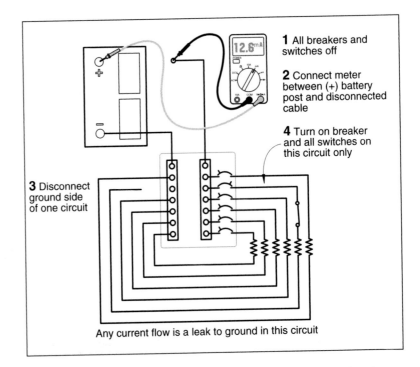

1 All breakers and switches off

2 Connect meter between (+) battery post and disconnected cable

4 Turn on breaker and all switches on this circuit only

3 Disconnect ground side of one circuit

Any current flow is a leak to ground in this circuit

Testing the wiring beyond the breakers—which is most of the boat's wiring—requires disconnecting the ground side of each individual circuit one at a time. With the ammeter between the positive post and the disconnected cable, and with all other breakers off, turn on the breaker and all switches in the ungrounded circuit. If any current flows, it is leaking from this circuit into one of the ones still connected to ground. If the leak is to a metal through-hull fitting—a common occurrence—and finding its way back to ground outside the boat, it is doing more than draining your battery. This is called stray current, and It is destroying the involved through-hull. It is essential to track down and eliminate any stray currents that exceed 5 milliamps.

CHARGING SYSTEMS

As soon as your boat is beyond the reach of an extension cord, the only way to replace power you drain from your batteries is by generating it. For more than half a century that has meant a belt-driven generator/alternator combined with a mechanical/electronic regulator, both borrowed virtually unchanged from the automobile industry. Only in the last decade have we begun to see charging equipment designed specifically for the unique requirements of sailboat electrical systems.

Because the primary propulsion of a sailboat is the wind (sadly, today this is a disputable proclamation), a sailboat's engine may not run enough performing its chief function for the engine-driven alternator to satisfy the vessel's electrical needs. The traditional solutions to this shortfall have been to motor rather than sail—contrary to the reasons for owning a sailboat—and/or resort to the equally distasteful practice of running the engine with the boat anchored. This latter option not only rends tranquility with the clatter of a reciprocating iron, in the long run it is damaging to the diesel engine.

A partial solution is the marine regulator, designed to charge batteries at their maximum acceptance level. Where battery capacity merits, this regulator can be combined with a more powerful alternator. One or both of these enhancements reduces charging times, sometimes dramatically.

For those wanting to pare engine time even more, perhaps eliminate it altogether, alternative energy sources are available that can partially or fully meet a sailboat's typical electrical requirements. Of these, solar power is perhaps the most attractive because solar panels have no moving parts. However, wind generators offer higher capacity from a smaller package. And even the smallest water-powered generator will usually satisfy all charging requirements of a boat on passage.

This chapter will show you how to configure an effective charging system, how to connect it, and how to keep it operating at peak efficiency.

ALTERNATORS

The engine-powered alternator remains the primary charging source on most sailboats.

OUTPUT

Alternators are often rated at about 6,000 rpm rotor speed, but most sailboat charging is done with the engine at idle speed, around 800 rpm. With a 2-to-1 pulley ratio (see sidebar), that translates into a rotor speed of 1,600 rpm. Most alternators will put out less than 30% of rated output at this speed. Heat also decreases output by as much as 25%. To determine the actual output of your existing alternator you will have to measure it (using a high-capacity ammeter, **NOT** your 10-amp multimeter) with the batteries deeply discharged so the regulator allows maximum output.

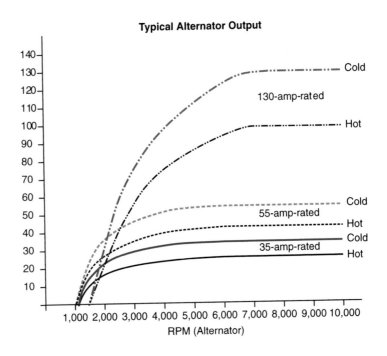

Typical Alternator Output

If you are buying an alternator, be sure you find out the hot rating (200°F or 93°C) for the rotor speed that corresponds to your charging pattern. As a general rule alternators should not run continuously at more than about 75% of their rated maximum.

PULLEY RATIO

WHERE THE ALTERNATOR PULLEY is 2½ inches (6.4 cm) in diameter and the one on the engine is 5 inches (12.7 cm), the pulley ratio is 2 (5 ÷ 2.5). That means the alternator rotor makes 2 revolutions for each engine revolution. At 800 engine rpm, the alternator is turning 1,600 rpm.

It is relatively simple to fit the alternator with a smaller pulley or the engine with a larger one to increase rotor speed. The limiting factor is the maximum safe rpm for the alternator, usually 10,000 rpm. Dividing maximum rotor rpm by maximum engine rpm provides the largest safe pulley ratio. For an engine rated at 3,600 rpm, that ratio is 2.78 (10,000 ÷ 3,600).

Multiply the alternator pulley by this ratio or divide the drive pulley by it, depending on which you want to change. For example, 2.78 times 2½ gives us an engine-pulley size of 6.95, so a 7-inch (18 cm) pulley will be the optimum size for getting the highest output at idle without overspinning the alternator at higher engine speeds. Rotor speed increases to 2,224 rpm at 800 engine rpm, which more than doubles alternator output.

Drive Pulley Selection

Drive Pulley	Alternator Pulley	Ratio	Engine RPM	Alternator RPM
5-inch	2½-inch	2	1,000	2,000
			3,600	7,200
6-inch		2.4	1,000	2,400
			3,600	8,640
7-inch		2.8	1,000	2,800
			3,600	10,080
8-inch		3.2	1,000	3,200
			3,600	11,520

SIZING

Batteries should not be charged at a rate that much exceeds 25% of capacity. So if your boat's total battery capacity is, say, 200 Ah, an alternator capable of putting out about 50 amps provides all the charging capacity you can use.

To get 50 amps with the alternator hot and the engine at idle speed, you may have to buy an alternator rated at 70 or 80 amps. Beyond that, more charging capacity is wasted—unless you are running other electrical equipment while charging. In that case increase the alternator size by the current requirements of the equipment.

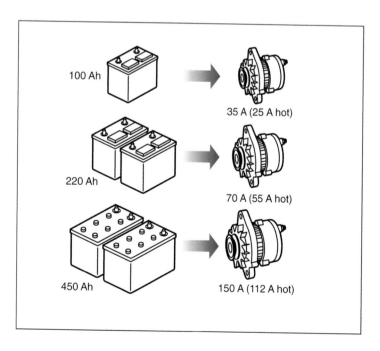

100 Ah → 35 A (25 A hot)

220 Ah → 70 A (55 A hot)

450 Ah → 150 A (112 A hot)

IGNITION PROTECTION

If you have a gasoline engine or LPG (propane) appliances, the alternator should be ignition protected. Automotive alternators are not ignition protected.

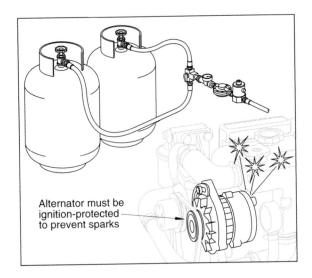

Alternator must be ignition-protected to prevent sparks

EXPECTING TOO MUCH

Because conventional batteries safely accept a 25% charge for only a short period of time, installing a larger alternator may reduce charging times less than you expect. Let's consider the replacement of a 50-amp alternator with one rated at 100 amps to charge a 400 Ah bank. If you discharge the batteries to 50% or more before charging, the big alternator will turn out maximum amperage for perhaps 10 minutes before the regulator starts cutting it back to a level compatible with declining battery acceptance. At the end of the first hour, the large alternator will have replaced perhaps 70 amp-hours. It takes the small alternator about 25 minutes longer to reach this charge level. For the remainder of the charge, the outputs from both alternators are essentially the same. The large alternator takes $3\frac{1}{2}$ hours to reach the 90% charge level, the small one gets there in 3 hours and 55 minutes. That is less than an 11% improvement in charging times from a 100% increase in alternator capacity. AGM and gel batteries have a different acceptance profile, so for these batteries the benefits of a big alternator may be somewhat better.

Whatever the potential benefit, it is less when the batteries are not deeply discharged—a common scenario when the engine runs daily for mechanical refrigeration. At the 30% discharge level, the big alternator provides full amperage for less than 5 minutes before the regulator starts limiting it. The standard alternator, at half the peak output, takes 10 minutes to reach the same cut-back point. After that the charging profile for both units will be identical. Net reduction in total charging time: just 5 minutes.

One benefit not to be overlooked, however, is that for a given battery capacity, a larger alternator will operate at a lower percentage of capacity, potentially extending the life of the alternator. Some large alternators also provide higher amperage at engine idle speeds, but in general, low output alternators have more windings (because the wire can be thinner), so they give better low-RPM performance. If most charging is done at anchor, this is a significant consideration.

REGULATORS

The rate of charge should be high when the batteries are low but less as they approach full charge. Adjusting alternator output to match need is the job of the regulator.

Back in Chapter 2, I told you that a generator consists of a spinning magnet that induces electron flow in surrounding wire coils. The magnet in a marine alternator is an electromagnet. When the alternator is spinning, it doesn't generate electricity unless this magnet is energized. The regulator simply controls the current to this magnet, allowing us to turn the alternator off without disconnecting the drive belt or stopping the engine. The current that energizes the magnet is called the *field current*.

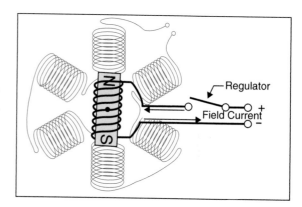

STANDARD REGULATOR

The basic regulator—manufactured by the millions for the automobile industry—is simple and trouble free. It is nothing more than an electronic switch that works like a spring-loaded magnetic switch. Closed, the switch provides current to the alternator's magnet, thus inducing alternator output. When voltage rises to a preset level, the switch opens, turning off the alternator. This causes output voltage to fall, but when it drops below the regulator's set voltage, the switch closes again. This all happens very rapidly—hundreds of times per second. The net effect is a rippling constant voltage and a pulsating current. As battery voltage rises, it takes less time for the alternator to elevate charging-circuit voltage to the cutout level, shortening "on" time. Voltage remains fixed, but shorter current pulses reduce the average current output.

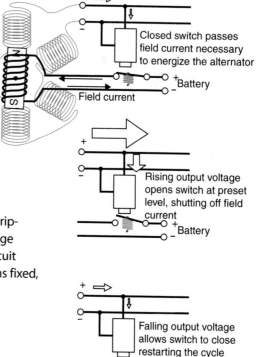

Closed switch passes field current necessary to energize the alternator

Rising output voltage opens switch at preset level, shutting off field current

Falling output voltage allows switch to close restarting the cycle

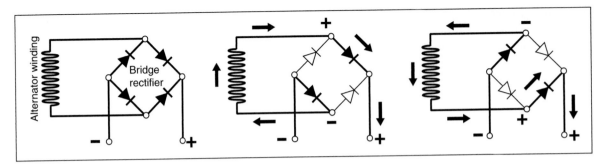

Of course, alternator output is AC and we need DC to feed our batteries. This is elegantly accomplished by passing the current through a diode array called a bridge rectifier. Acting like one-way gates, the diodes redirect half the current pulses, converting the output to pulsating DC. And that is all we need to know about rectification.

REGULATOR VOLTAGE

Generally, the higher the regulator voltage, the quicker the charge, but if charging voltage rises above around 14.4 volts, the batteries will begin to gas vigorously, lose electrolyte, and overheat. So the usual regulator choice for efficient charging is one that maintains output voltage at 14.4 volts (at 25°C/77°F).

However, once the battery nears full charge, 14.4 volts is too high, gassing the batteries vigorously and causing the positive plate to oxidize (corrode). If you continue to run the engine—perhaps motoring—a charging voltage of around 13.2 volts is ideal for maintaining full charge without overcharging. For years automobile manufacturers compromised on 13.8 volts—high enough to replace the shallow discharge from starting without later resulting in serious overcharging. And anyway, regulators are temperature compensated to lower output about 0.01 volts per degree centigrade of ambient temperature, so if the engine compartment warms by 50°C (90°F), a 13.8-volt regulator actually holds the alternator output at 13.3 volts.

Using a 13.8-volt regulator in a sailboat charging system nearly eliminates any risk of overcharging (the engine compartment heats up enough to derate the regulator), but charging times with a 13.8-volt regulator will be twice that of a 14.4-volt unit. Unless you motor a lot, expect your batteries to be chronically undercharged, leading to sulfation and early battery failure. Most sailboats should be fitted with the higher-voltage regulator. You will have to deal with the risk of overcharging in some other manner.

FIELD DISCONNECT

The simplest method of preventing a standard regulator from overcharging is with a switch in the field wire. When the battery is fully charged but you are continuing to run the engine, flipping the switch opens the field circuit, turning off the alternator. Where there is no ready access to the field wire, a switch in the excite circuit (see below) will do the same thing, but this requires stopping the engine, then restarting it.

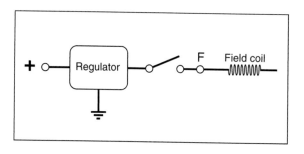

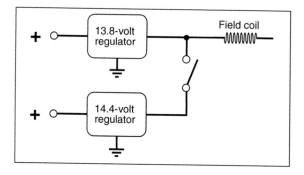

DUAL REGULATORS

Paralleling a 14.4-volt regulator with a 13.8-volt unit is only slightly more expensive—automotive regulators are dirt cheap—and this configuration lets the alternator continue to keep the battery in a fully charged state during long hours of motoring. When the switch is closed, the higher alternator output automatically shuts off the lower-voltage regulator. It is simple enough to put a timer switch in this circuit to make the voltage decrease semi-automatic.

FOOLING THE REGULATOR

As the engine room heats up, the output of a 14.4-volt regulator is likely to decline to around 13.9 volts—not ideal, but low enough not to hurt the batteries as long as you keep them supplied with water. But long engine hours are presumably the exception. It is more common for a sailor to want more output from the alternator, not less.

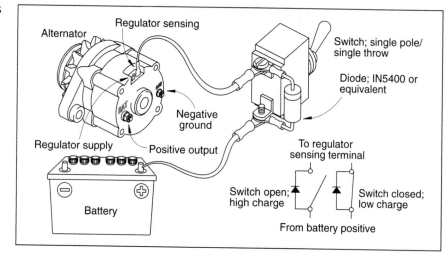

The voltage drop through a silicon diode is about 0.6 volt, so inserting a diode in the sensing wire fools the regulator into thinking battery voltage is lower than it really is. This causes the regulator to increase alternator output. Current in the sensing wire flows to the alternator, so be sure the cathode end of the diode—the marked end—is on the regulator/alternator side of the circuit.

This is a low-budget method of reducing charging time, and it requires some caution. Unless you know that your alternator is rated for continuous duty, be sure output doesn't rise above around 75% of its rated maximum for more than a few minutes. Monitor the batteries to make sure they do not get hot—above about 120°F. And you *must* remember to flip the switch to take the diode out of the circuit when the batteries start gassing vigorously. A timer minimizes the risk of costly forgetfulness.

MANUAL CONTROLLER

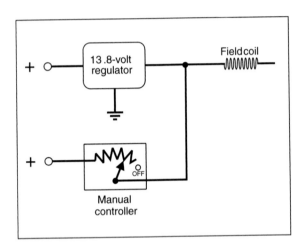

It is logical that the stronger the rotating magnet in an alternator, the more current flows, and vice versa. Since increasing the field current makes the electromagnet stronger, it also increases the alternator's output; reducing the field current reduces output. This provides another way to control alternator output. Rather than switching field current off and on, a manual controller adjusts the strength of the field current with a variable resistor—called a rheostat. This allows adjustment of alternator output exactly the same way you adjust light intensity with a dimmer switch. Unfortunately, forgetting that the current is cranked up, or even speeding up the engine without adjusting the controller (it is not actually "regulating" alternator output) can ruin the batteries, which happens with depressing regularity on boats fitted with manual controllers. Alternator control is best left to silicon instead of cerebrum.

THREE-STEP REGULATOR

A standard regulator is, in effect, a two-step regulator. It maximizes current output while letting the battery voltage rise to the set level, then it holds voltage constant and allows output current to decline. More sophisticated regulators charge the battery in three distinct phases.

BULK CHARGE

In the initial stage the alternator puts out maximum current until the battery voltage rises to around 14.4 volts. Assuming a 25% of battery amp-hour rating charge rate, the battery will be around 75% charged.

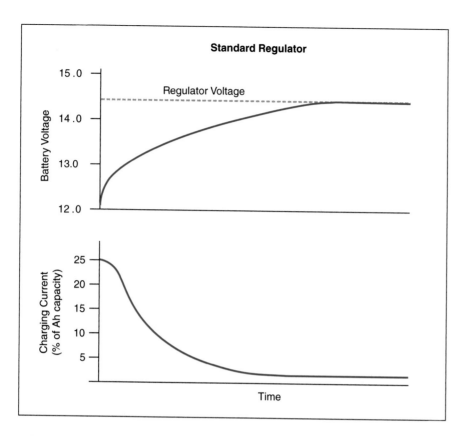

Standard Regulator

Battery Voltage

15.0

Regulator Voltage

14.0

13.0

12.0

Charging Current (% of Ah capacity)

25

20

15

10

5

Time

ABSORPTION CHARGE

When voltage reaches 14.4, the regulator holds it there and allows the current to decline according to what the battery can accept. Ideally, this continues until charging current declines to 2% or 1% of the battery's amp-hour rating, indicating a charge level of around 90% or 95% respectively. In practice, most three-step regulators terminate the absorption phase based on time rather than current level.

FLOAT CHARGE

Triggered by time or current level, the regulator cuts voltage back to around 13.2 volts, which allows the engine to continue to run without overcharging the batteries.

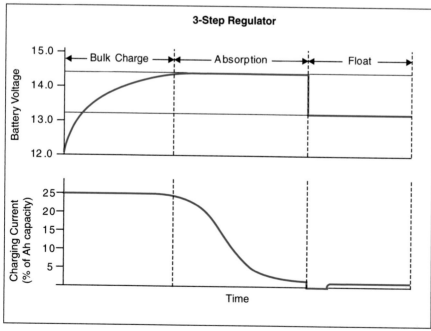

3-Step Regulator

Bulk Charge — Absorption — Float

Battery Voltage

15.0

14.0

13.0

12.0

Charging Current (% of Ah capacity)

25

20

15

10

5

Time

EQUALIZATION—THE FOURTH STEP

Some "smart" regulators have a fourth phase intended to restore batteries to full capacity by converting inevitable sulfate deposits in the plates back into active material. This is accomplished by feeding a fixed current of less than 4% of amp-hour capacity to the battery until battery voltage rises to its maximum natural level—around 16.2 volts. This normally takes several hours. Equalization is only appropriate for heavy-duty deep-cycle batteries. Gel cells and AGM batteries are *never* equalized, and the high voltage is likely to do more harm than good to thinner-plate wet cells.

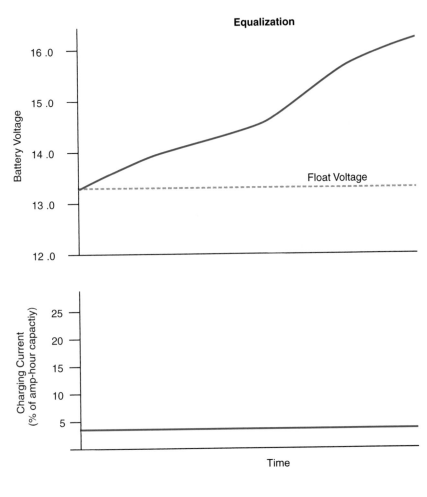

Equalize not more often than every 30 discharge cycles.

CHARGING GEL BATTERIES

WHILE SOME GEL BATTERIES purportedly can accept a bulk charge at current levels approaching 50% of battery amp-hour capacity, voltage cannot be allowed to exceed 14.1 volts. Taking advantage of a gel battery's high absorption requires a specialized regulator and usually a larger alternator.

ALTERNATOR AND REGULATOR WIRING

There are dozens, perhaps hundreds of different alternator and regulator combinations, so any help you find here is necessarily general in nature.

OUTPUT

The output terminal will be the largest terminal on the alternator and is nearly always labeled BAT, B+, or just +. You may find your alternator has two identical wires connected to the B+ terminal. Don't let this confuse you; for increased flexibility it is common to substitute parallel smaller wires for the large cable required for the high amperage of the alternator output.

ALTERNATOR TERMINAL DESIGNATIONS	
Output	B+, BAT, +
Negative	D−, E, GND, B−, −
Field	F, DF
Auxiliary	D+, 1, L, AUX, IND, 61
Tachometer	W, AC, R, STA, X, N, P
Sense	2, S

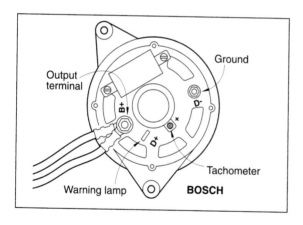

Output terminal

Ground

Tachometer

Warning lamp

BOSCH

INTERNAL REGULATION

The regulator may be incorporated into the alternator. In this case the alternator may have only one or two other terminals. The one labeled D+, L, AUX, or sometimes 61 is the warning-lamp connection. If there is a tachometer feed, it is usually labeled R, W, or AC. A ground terminal, labeled GND, E (earth), B−, D−, or just − may also be provided. The S terminal on this Hitachi alternator is for the battery sensing wire.

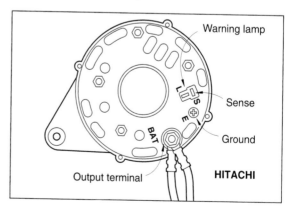

Warning lamp

Sense

Ground

Output terminal

HITACHI

ATTACHED REGULATOR

Many alternators have a matching regulator attached. Except that the wiring and terminals are typically located beneath the regulator and accessible only by removing the mounting screws, attached regulators are connected to the alternator in the same manner as an external regulator.

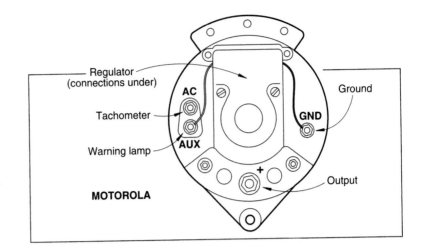

EXTERNAL REGULATION

Because they can be mounted off the engine, external regulators have the advantage of running cooler, and they simplify servicing. An alternator configured for an external regulator will have a field terminal labeled F or DF. The regulator's sensing wire is usually connected to either the D+ or the B+ terminal on the alternator (machine sensed), or to the positive terminal of the house battery (battery sensed).

This connection also supplies the power to most regulators. The R terminal on the alternator

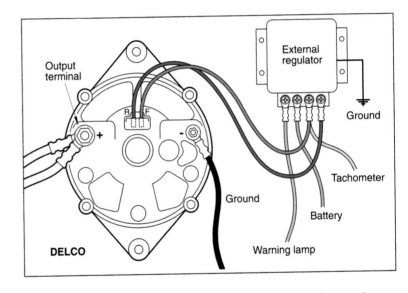

is unrectified output for the tachometer, and in this case it also disables the excite circuit when there is alternator output. Most external regulators also have a ground connection, which often is the housing.

POLARITY

Alternators generally fall into two types, P (positive) or N (negative), depending on which side of the field winding the regulator is located on. If the regulator is between the battery and the field winding, the alternator is a P-type. If the regulator is between the field winding and ground, it is an N-type alternator. Most externally regulated alternators are P-type; those with internal regulation are most often N-type.

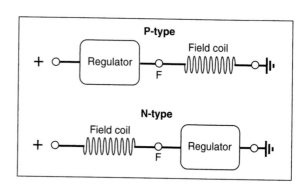

With the batteries switched off and the field wire disconnected, you can determine type by checking the resistance between the F terminal and the ground. Near-zero resistance suggests a P-type; high resistance means the alternator is an N-type. (There are exceptions.) You only need to know this if you are changing regulators—to a three-step, for example—or if you need to "excite" the alternator.

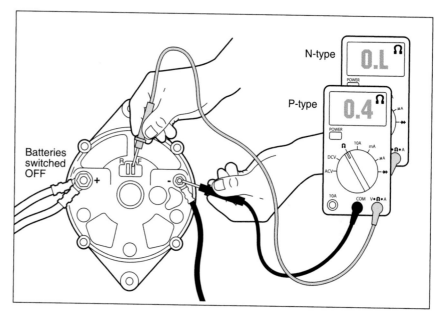

EXCITATION

Alternators don't operate until there is field current, but since most alternators supply their own field current, there isn't any until there is alternator output. This is something of a Catch-22. To overcome it, most alternators are "excited" with a temporary current

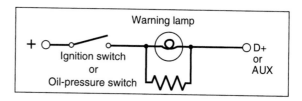

supplied by the battery, usually to the D+ terminal on the alternator. The engine-panel warning light is typically part of the excitation circuit. Once the alternator starts generating, the voltage on either side of the lamp is nearly the same, causing the lamp to go out. A resistor parallel to the lamp provides excitation current if the bulb burns out.

SURGE PROTECTION

The most common form of alternator failure is a direct result of opening the charge circuit while the alternator is running, usually due to mistakenly turning the battery-selector switch to OFF. This causes a high-voltage spike in the alternator windings that burns out some or all of the alternator's diodes. A surge protector such as Zap-Stop (Xantrex) shunts such a spike to ground and is especially recommended if the alternator is connected through a battery selector switch (see below).

Inadvertently reversing battery leads will also fry the diodes in your alternator.

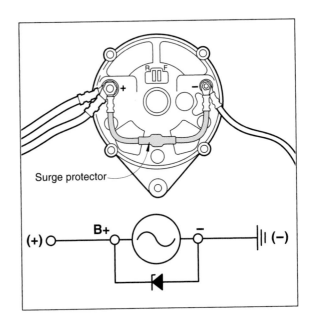

Surge protector

ALTERNATOR MAINTENANCE

BELTS

Make sure drive pulleys are aligned and drive belts are tight. Loosen (and retighten) both the pivot bolt and the tension-adjustment bolt. The best way to tighten a belt is with a tensioner fabricated from a turnbuckle; otherwise a dowel or wooden hammer handle to lever the alternator away from the engine will be less likely to cause damage than a metal tool. The rule of thumb is 10 pounds of pressure on the center of the belt's longest span should cause about ½ inch deflection.

A ⅜-inch belt is adequate for alternators up to around 70 amps. Up to about 130 amps, a single ½-inch belt should handle the load, although dual belts are preferable. Beyond 130 amps, dual ½-inch belts are essential to avoid belt slippage and/or excessive tension.

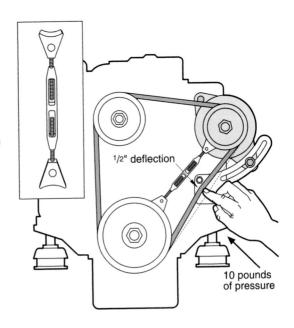

½" deflection

10 pounds of pressure

CONNECTIONS

High-frequency vibrations tend to loosen alternator connections and fatigue the wires. Check alternator wiring every 100 engine hours.

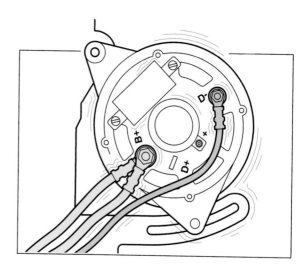

BEARINGS AND BRUSHES

You will avoid inopportune alternator failure if you have the bearings and brushes replaced every 3,000 engine hours.

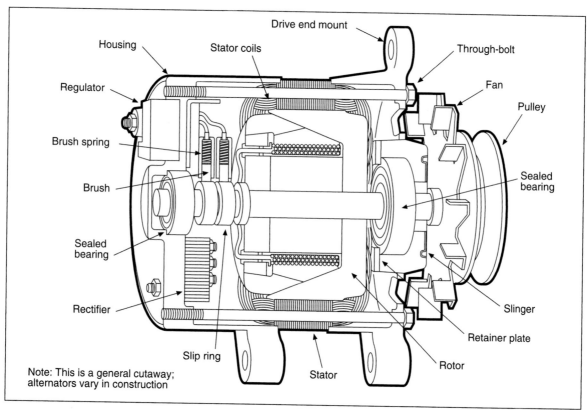

Note: This is a general cutaway; alternators vary in construction

TROUBLESHOOTING ALTERNATORS AND REGULATORS

Alternator repair is beyond the scope of this book, but a number of easy-to-correct problems can disable an otherwise healthy alternator. When regulation is external, it can be helpful to distinguish between regulator and alternator failure. In an emergency, it is possible to bypass the regulator. Remember: never disconnect the battery from a running alternator. Removing the load for even an instant will destroy the alternator's diodes.

ALTERNATOR OUTPUT

Measure terminal voltage at the battery, then start the engine. Voltage should increase by a volt or more. If not, check alternator output directly by touching voltmeter probes to the B+ terminal and the alternator case. CAUTION: WHEN TESTING ALTERNATOR OUTPUT, KEEP CLOTHES, HAIR, AND FINGERS CLEAR OF BELTS AND PULLEYS.

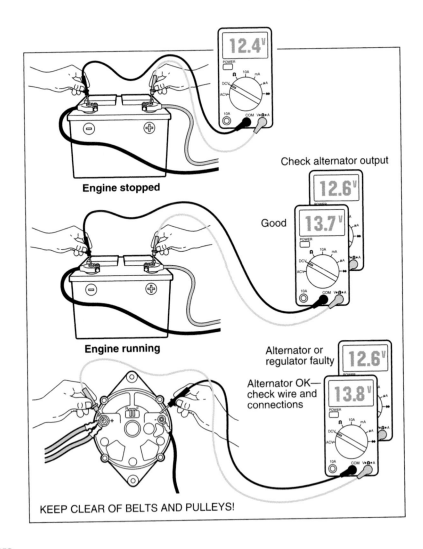

Engine stopped

Engine running

Check alternator output

Good

Alternator or regulator faulty

Alternator OK— check wire and connections

KEEP CLEAR OF BELTS AND PULLEYS!

With the battery near full charge—around 12.6 volts at rest—checking the alternator output at the B+ terminal after a few minutes of engine time will give you the output voltage set by the regulator. It will normally be 14.2 to 14.4 volts. Now check the voltage at the battery posts. Unless you run your engine a lot, anything less than 14 volts will result in chronic undercharging of your batteries. The problem is either resistance in the cables or a voltage drop caused by isolating diodes. (If you have a three-stage regulator, be sure it has not switched to float voltage.)

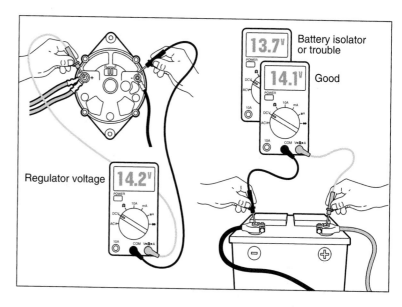

Discharge the battery by turning on all lights for a few minutes. Start the engine and immediately—while the alternator is at full load—measure the voltage between the alternator's B+ terminal and the positive battery post. Voltage drop should be less than 0.5 volts, not more than 1 volt if you have a battery isolator in the circuit. Do the same test between the alternator case (ground) and the negative battery post. Excessive voltage drop indicates corrosion, poor connections, or undersized wire. Undersized wire is a common cause of chronic undercharging.

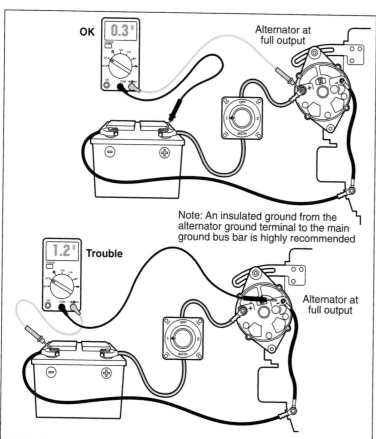

Note: An insulated ground from the alternator ground terminal to the main ground bus bar is highly recommended

REGULATOR FAULTS

If voltage measured at the B+ terminal is *above* 14.4 volts, the regulator is faulty. A likely cause is a loose or broken sensing wire. Also make sure any diodes in the sensing circuit are oriented to allow current to flow *toward* the regulator.

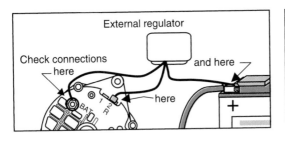

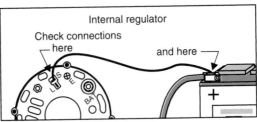

Battery voltage at B+ (or no voltage if you have isolating diodes in the charging circuit) means the alternator isn't charging, but the problem might still be the regulator. Check this with a test light fabricated from a 12-volt lamp of 10 to 15 watts. A common #93 automotive lamp is perfect.

Disconnect the regulator field wire from the F terminal on the alternator and protect it from shorting. Nearly all alternators with external regulators are P-type, so connect your lamp between the now-open F terminal and the positive post on the battery—or some other nearby source of battery power. (If the alternator output doesn't pass through external isolating diodes, you can use the B+ terminal.) This energizes the field circuit with the lamp limiting the current to around 1 amp. The lamp may or may not light. Start the engine. If you now measure the right voltage at B+, the likely problem is the regulator.

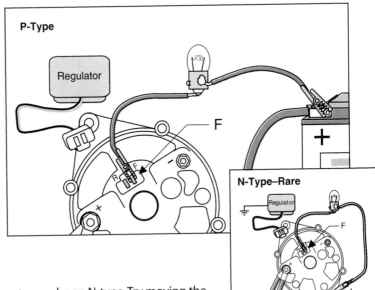

If the regulator is attached, removing it normally exposes the F terminal. If it isn't labeled, try your test light on all exposed terminals; you will not harm the alternator.

An alternator that still doesn't generate may be an N-type. Try moving the test lamp connection to ground and recheck B+ voltage. If the alternator generates, the regulator is defective.

If the test-light connection *to the battery* produced output, the alternator is a P-type and it generates. But before condemning the regulator, stop the engine and reconnect the field wire from the regulator. With the alternator running and one lead of the test lamp still connected to the positive post on the battery, touch the other momentarily to the F terminal. This is called *flashing the field*. If this starts the alternator and it keeps working, the problem is in the excitation circuit, and you can fix it.

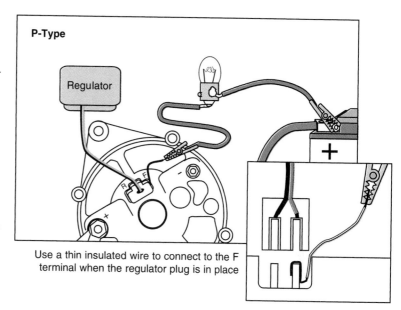

Use a thin insulated wire to connect to the F terminal when the regulator plug is in place

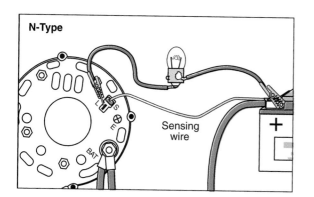

If none of the previous tests have produced output, reconnect the regulator wires and start the engine. With one side of the test lamp connected to the battery's positive post, touch the other side to the D+ terminal on the alternator. If the alternator is an N-type, this will flash the field and the alternator may start charging, indicating a problem with the excitation circuit.

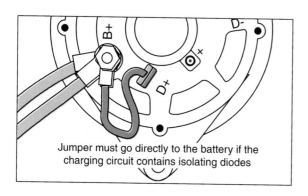

Jumper must go directly to the battery if the charging circuit contains isolating diodes

If the alternator starts charging when you touch the test lamp to the D+ terminal but quits when you remove it, the problem is the diode trio supplying current to the regulator. A jumper from the positive battery terminal to the D+ terminal will get the alternator running normally, but you must disconnect it when you stop the engine to prevent the battery from discharging through the regulator.

EXCITATION

If flashing the field started the alternator, you need to repair the excitation circuit. Excitation current usually comes from the ignition switch or the oil-pressure switch on the engine. It normally passes through an "idiot" light, but sometimes a diode is used instead. The excitation wire usually leads to the D+ or 1 terminal on the alternator, but may also go directly to the regulator.

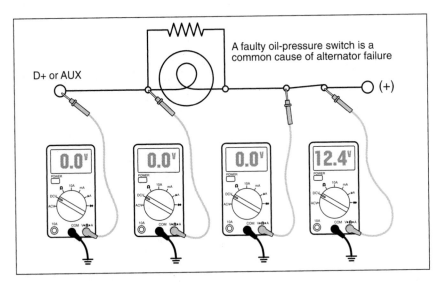

D+ or AUX

A faulty oil-pressure switch is a common cause of alternator failure

(+)

Trace the circuit with your meter. The usual problems are a defective switch or a poor connection. A burned-out warning lamp also will open the excitation circuit if it isn't paralleled with a resistor. In a pinch, use your test light to excite the alternator.

BYPASSING A FAULTY REGULATOR

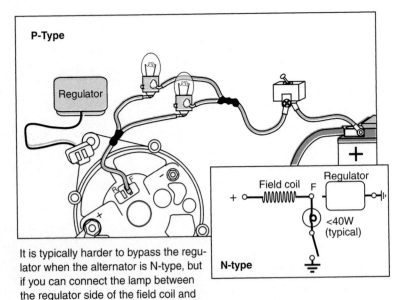

P-Type

Regulator

Field coil   F   Regulator

<40W (typical)

N-type

It is typically harder to bypass the regulator when the alternator is N-type, but if you can connect the lamp between the regulator side of the field coil and the ground, the same principle applies.

If the regulator fails and you don't have a spare, you can operate the alternator without it using your test light to supply the field current. If alternator output is too low, raise it by using a higher wattage bulb—up to about 40 watts—or by connecting a second bulb in parallel. Keep in mind that the alternator is unregulated, so you must make sure not to overload it. If the batteries get warm or start to gas vigorously, disconnect the bulb to turn off the alternator.

DIODES

If the alternator appears to be functioning normally but you are still having charging problems, the problem may be with the diodes.

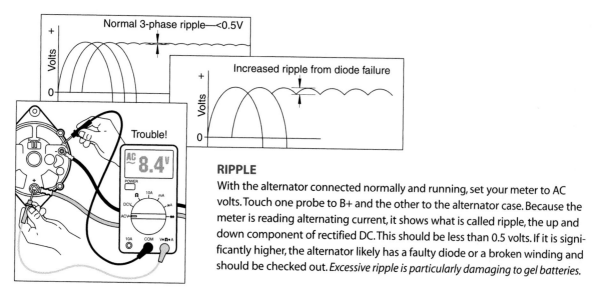

RIPPLE

With the alternator connected normally and running, set your meter to AC volts. Touch one probe to B+ and the other to the alternator case. Because the meter is reading alternating current, it shows what is called ripple, the up and down component of rectified DC. This should be less than 0.5 volts. If it is significantly higher, the alternator likely has a faulty diode or a broken winding and should be checked out. *Excessive ripple is particularly damaging to gel batteries.*

LEAKAGE

Leaking diodes can drain the battery when the alternator is stopped. With the engine not running and the battery switch in the OFF position, disconnect all wires connected to the B+ and the D+ terminals. Set your meter to measure amps and connect it between the positive battery post and B+. The meter will read leakage back through the rectifying diodes. More than a few milliamps means the alternator needs to be serviced. The same test to the D+ terminal shows leakage through the alternator's isolating diodes.

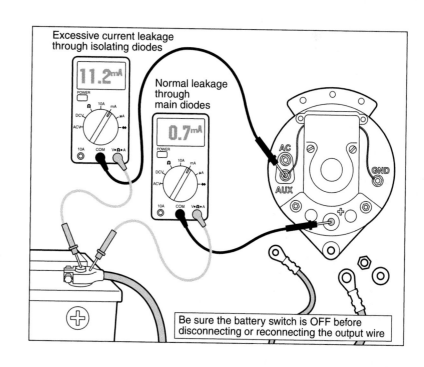

OPEN OR SHORTED

With the B+ and D+ wires still disconnected, set your meter to the diode-test function and touch the leads to D+ and the AC terminal, then reverse them. If the meter reads less than 1 volt in one direction, O.L in the other, the alternator's isolating diodes are good. Do the same test between B+ and GND to check the main diodes. A reading less than 2 volts in one direction is OK. Similar readings in both directions—either high or low—indicate faulty diodes.

You can also do this test with an ohmmeter, but some have insufficient forward voltage to cause the diode to conduct. If you get an infinite-ohms reading in both directions, try a different meter before condemning the diodes.

DON'T FORGET TO RECONNECT THE OUTPUT CABLE AFTER THESE TESTS!

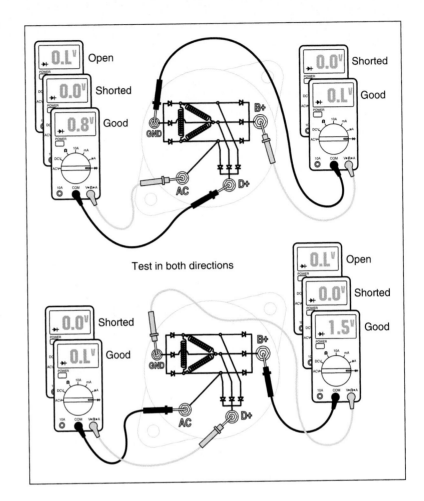

Test in both directions

BATTERY SWITCHING

With a single battery bank, you can wire the alternator output directly to the positive terminal on the battery. Dual battery banks require some method of isolating the banks so they can be used independently.

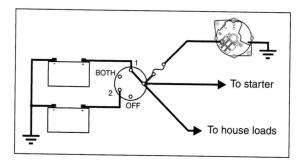

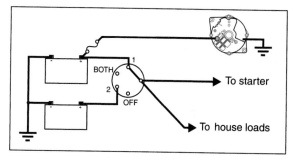

THE STANDARD WAY

Most sailboats are delivered with two batteries connected to a selector switch that allows them to be used independently. For charging, and sometimes for starting, the switch is turned to BOTH. This arrangement has two major flaws. First, if you forget to switch from BOTH when you stop the engine, the starting battery discharges along with the house battery. This is the most common cause of being unable to start the main engine. Second, rotating the switch the wrong way when changing battery selection moves it through OFF rather than BOTH, removing the load from the spinning alternator. This is the most common cause of alternator failure.

DIRECT ALTERNATOR CONNECTION

Connecting the alternator directly to the house battery, not through the selector switch, eliminates the risk of inadvertently removing the load from the alternator, but the switch must still be turned to BOTH to charge the starting battery.

FUSE

ANY WIRE CONNECTED directly to the positive battery terminal, even the output wire from the alternator, must be fused as close to the battery as possible. Otherwise, if the output wire vibrates loose from the B+ terminal on the alternator and comes in contact with the case, the engine, or any other ground, it creates a dead short with a high likelihood of a resultant fire.

ISOLATING DIODES

Inserting isolating diodes into the charging circuit eliminates the risk of alternator damage since the alternator is always connected—through the diodes—to the batteries. And it reduces the risk of leaving the batteries interconnected unless you set the switch to BOTH for starting. But you must still rotate the switch for engine starting, then remember to turn it back or house use will discharge and ultimately damage the starting battery. And unless you modify the charging system, the voltage drop caused by battery isolators will cause chronic undercharging of both batteries.

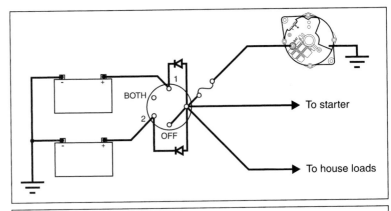

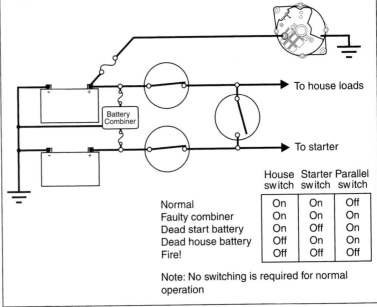

	House switch	Starter switch	Parallel switch
Normal	On	On	Off
Faulty combiner	On	On	On
Dead start battery	On	Off	On
Dead house battery	Off	On	On
Fire!	Off	Off	Off

Note: No switching is required for normal operation

A BETTER WAY

By keeping the starter/starter-battery circuit independent from the house circuit, you never have to change any switch settings while you are aboard. A separate paralleling switch allows the batteries to be combined or substituted in an emergency. The alternator is connected to the house bank. Starting battery charging is accomplished with a battery combiner that connects the batteries when it senses charging voltage—above around 13 volts. Battery combiners cost less than a single alternator repair.

SOLAR CELLS

Solar power is clean, quiet, infinitely renewable, and free—except for the cost of the solar panels. No other form of alternative energy has quite as much appeal. In just 15 minutes the sun bombards the earth with more energy than all of humanity consumes in a year, and the fraction that falls on the on the deck of a 35-foot (11 m) boat is the equivalent of about 600 amp-hours of 12-volt power. All we have to do is convert it from light to electricity.

CHOICES

All solar cells function on the same principle: light striking the top layer of the cell "knocks" electrons into the bottom layer. Connecting the two layers allows the displaced electrons to flow through the circuit and back "home."

CRYSTALLINE

The most efficient silicon-based solar cells are the single-crystal type, where each cell is a single hair-thin wafer sliced like bologna from a "grown" crystal. Polycrystalline cells combine smaller wafers—something like silicon chipboard. This type is only slightly less efficient in ideal light and sometimes better at lower sun angles. For the most output for a given panel size, buy only panels made of crystalline cells.

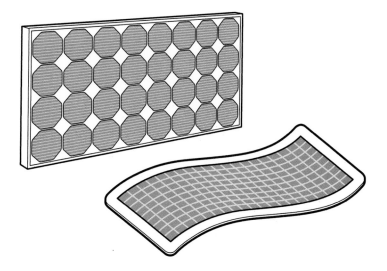

THIN FILM

Amorphous silicon, often called thin film, is like a silicon paint. Widely used in calculators, thin-film solar cells are less than half as efficient as crystalline units. Amorphous silicon can be applied to a flexible stratum to create a flexible panel.

OUTPUT

RATING

Crystalline photovoltaic cells have an open circuit voltage of around 0.5 volts no matter what size they are. Their current output is about 0.25 amps per square inch of cell area. The cells in a panel are connected in series, so their voltages are added together, but the total amperage for the panel is the same as for a single cell. A panel with 36 5-inch (12.7 cm) cells will put out about 5 amps (3.14 x 2.5 x 2.5 x 0.25) at around 18 volts (36 x 0.50). That gives the panel a rating of around 90 watts (18V x 5A).

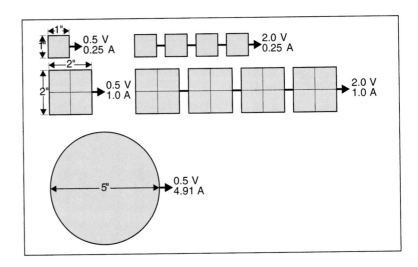

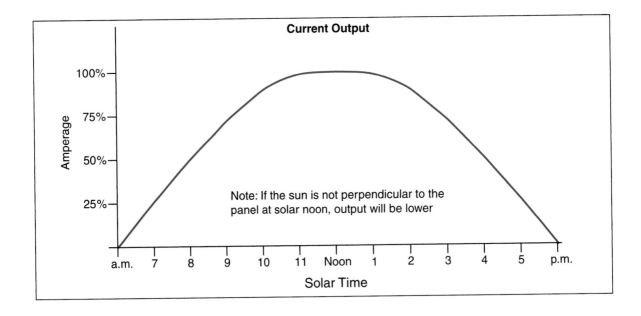

Note: If the sun is not perpendicular to the panel at solar noon, output will be lower

DAILY

Rated output only occurs at high noon; the rest of the time the panel puts out less current. The rule of thumb (for a horizontal panel) is to expect no more than the equivalent of 4 hours of rated output per day. A 5-amp panel should supply about 20 amp-hours daily—when the sun shines.

TEMPERATURE

Solar cells lose efficiency when they get hot. A 10°F (6°C) temperature increase decreases cell voltage about 3%. It is not unusual for cell temperature to exceed 125°F (52°C) in the tropics, reducing actual voltage to about 15% less than the panel's rating (at 77°F, 25°C).

SELF REGULATING

Self-regulating panels have fewer cells—typically 30 to 33—so that their output voltage will be low enough not to require additional regulation. Unfortunately, on a hot day the voltage of a 30-cell panel will fall below 13 volts—too low for appreciable battery charging. Unless you will limit use to a temperate climate, always select panels with more than 33 cells.

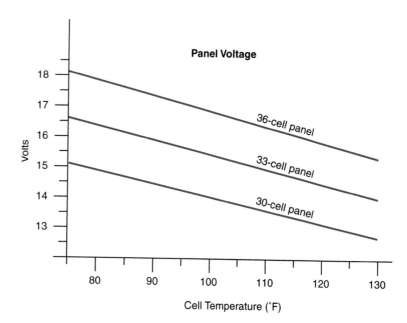

USES

Unrealistic expectations from the current state of solar technology can result in expensive disappointment.

BATTERY MAINTENANCE

If your boat—like most—sits idle for days or weeks, a small solar panel will keep your batteries at full charge and quadruple their life. And unlike a shore-power connection, the solar panel does not introduce any risk of stray-current corrosion (see Chapter 9). The output of a maintenance panel should be about 0.3% of the total battery capacity. For example, for a 220-amp-hour battery bank, you want a panel that puts out about 0.66 amps—close to what you would expect from a 10-watt panel (10W / 16V).

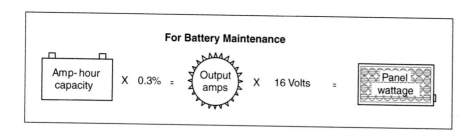

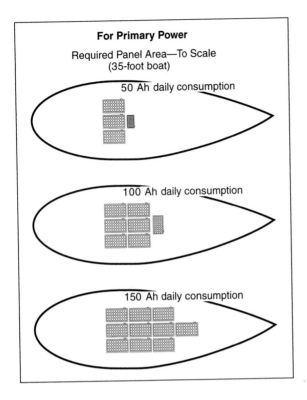

For Primary Power

Required Panel Area—To Scale
(35-foot boat)

50 Ah daily consumption

100 Ah daily consumption

150 Ah daily consumption

PRIMARY POWER SOURCE

With enough solar generating capacity, you could avoid running the engine for electrical power. Unfortunately, a square foot of crystalline solar-panel surface typically generates only about 3 amp-hours per day. In other words, replacing 80 amp-hours of daily consumption (plus 20% battery inefficiency) would require an array roughly the size of a full sheet of plywood. Expect such a solar array to cost more than $2,000. Any attempt to make the sun your primary source of electricity must necessarily be accompanied by a philosophy of power conservation.

INSTALLATION

ORIENTATION

Ashore, solar panels are usually angled toward the track of the sun, but random movement makes a horizontal mount give the best results on a boat not tied to a dock.

LOCATION

Some panels are so shade sensitive that even the thin shadow from a shroud can lower output voltage below battery voltage. Mount panels where they will not be shaded during the peak solar hours.

VENTILATION

It is essential to leave an inch or so of air space beneath panels to avoid output-robbing heat buildup.

TURNING THE PANEL OFF FOR INSTALLATION

Solar panels start generating as soon as they are exposed to sunlight. To avoid the risk of causing a short circuit, cover the panel during installation to turn it off.

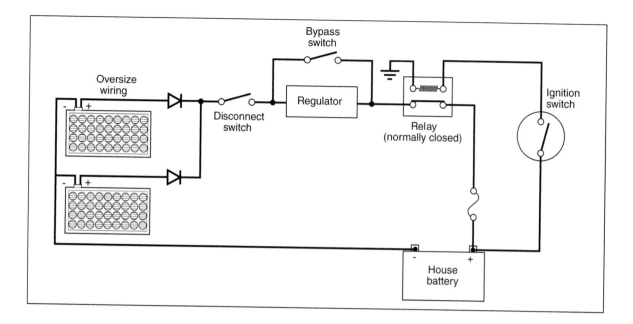

WIRE SIZE

Based on peak output current, connect the panel to the battery with wire one size larger than the formula or 3% table indicates (see Chapter 4). Given the cost of solar panels, you don't want to lose any output to undersize wiring.

COMBINING PANELS

Like batteries, multiple panels are wired in parallel to combine current output.

DIODE

A diode in the + wire lets the solar panel deliver current to the battery, but prevents current from flowing back through the panel at night. A diode for each panel has the added benefit of keep panels isolated in multipanel installations. Diodes do cause a drop in the voltage delivered to the battery—another reason to always select panels with more than 33 cells. Use low-loss Schottky diodes.

FUSE

As mentioned previously, any wire taken directly to the positive side of the battery must be fused as close to the battery as possible. Otherwise, a short in the wire represents a very real fire hazard.

REGULATOR

If the output of the panel exceeds 1% of battery capacity, a regulator is necessary to prevent battery damage. A regulator that disconnects the solar panel when it senses reverse current eliminates the need for a blocking diode.

BYPASS SWITCH

Because they put out a relatively constant current at elevated voltage, solar panels are ideal for equalizing batteries. If you have deep-cycle wet cells, install a bypass switch around the regulator so the full output of the panel can be delivered directly to the battery.

REGULATOR INTERACTION

With the batteries connected to solar panels, the regulator for the alternator may sense elevated voltage in the circuit and turn off the alternator even though the battery is less than fully charged. This can be handled with a manual switch in the + wire of the solar array, or automatically by taking the wire through a normally closed relay energized by the engine ignition switch.

TROUBLESHOOTING

Solar panels are generally trouble-free, another of their many appeals.

VOLTAGE

Check the open-circuit voltage of a new panel in bright sunlight and compare it to the panel's rating. Most manufacturers now warrant output to be within 10% of rating for at least 10 years. If output declines below this threshold, exercise your warranty rights.

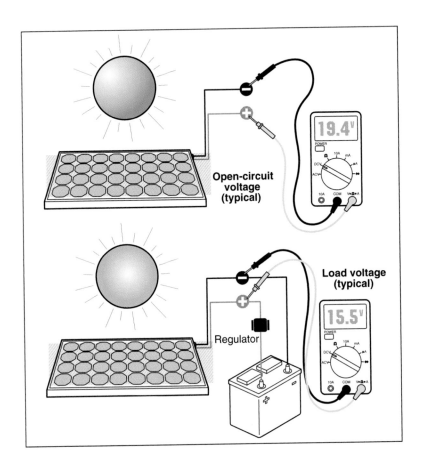

CONNECTIONS

Most solar-panel problems are related to corroded connections. If the panel has a junction box, it is advisable to fill it with silicone sealant after making the initial connections. All other connections should be made below deck.

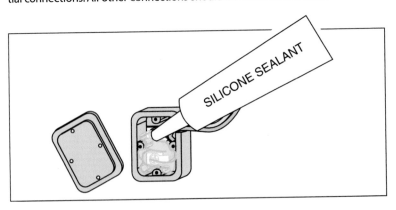

WIND GENERATORS

No charging system seems more compatible with a sailboat than one powered by the wind.

CHOICES

It is instructive to think of wind generators marketed to sailors as falling into one of two categories: the 5-foot-diameter (1.5 m) DC-motor type, and the less obtrusive and less powerful 3-foot-diameter (0.9 m) alternator type. There are, however, now some units that attempt to combine the best features of each type.

Large-diameter wind generators give higher output at all wind speeds, but they may not be left unattended. Sudden squalls have caused many to self-destruct, and even if yours doesn't fly apart, the high output current is likely to damage the generator, wiring, batteries, and other electrical gear. Large-diameter generators require constant vigilance.

Small-diameter wind generators provide less power, but they may be mounted permanently and more or less ignored. Alternator-type wind generators also require less maintenance. Four-foot (1.2 m) alternator types—providing higher output—are a relatively recent addition to the wind generator arena.

OUTPUT

Wind generator output is related to blade diameter squared and wind speed cubed. In other words, doubling blade diameter quadruples theoretical output (2 x 2); doubling wind speed increases it eight-fold (2 x 2 x 2). The number of blades has no effect on output, but additional blades do tend to reduce noise—a not-insignificant consideration.

RATED OUTPUT

Real output is often quite different from theoretical. The table shows the output you should expect from both 36-inch and 60-inch generators at pertinent wind speeds, regardless of more optimistic output claims from some manufacturers. No wind generator will start at less than 5 knots, and some need 6 or 7 knots of wind to start generating. Above 20 knots, large generators are likely to be shut down due to their high current levels. Some alternator types will also be shut down, switched off automatically to protect their windings from overheating. Given the protected nature of most anchorages, the most meaningful number for comparison is likely to be output at 10 knots of wind speed.

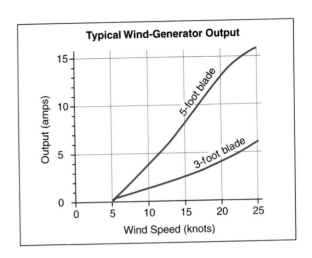

Typical Wind-Generator Output

DAILY OUTPUT

Assuming similar efficiencies, the rated output of a 36-inch wind generator will be about 36% of that of a 60-inch unit ($36^2 / 60^2$). But because of the risk of self destruction and damaging high currents, and because it is incredibly dangerous to physically turn an overspeeding generator away from the wind to shut it down, most owners routinely disable large-diameter generators at night and when they are off the boat. The total output of a large-diameter unit limited to 8 hours of daily operation would actually be less than that of an unattended small-diameter unit running around the clock. Where a small-diameter unit can fill daily power requirements, it will be safer and more convenient.

MOUNTING

To maximize output, wind generators must face directly into the wind, which requires a swivel mount. A fixed mount that depends on the weather-cocking nature of the boat will be significantly less efficient because boats tend to sail around their anchors and are influenced by currents. And underway, sailboats never sail directly into the wind.

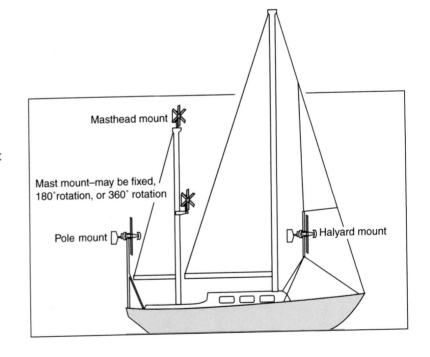

CONNECTIONS

Wind-generator connections are straightforward.

WIRE SIZE

Use the rated output (under load) of the generator to determine the appropriate wire size. Voltage drop should not exceed 3%.

FUSE

As with all direct battery connections, a fuse is required to avoid a fire risk. However, should this particular fuse blow, it unloads the wind generator, which may cause the machine to overspeed and self-destruct. Use the largest-capacity fuse that does not exceed the capacity of the wire. If this is not at least 50% above the maximum generator output, you will need to use larger wire to allow for the use of a higher-rated fuse.

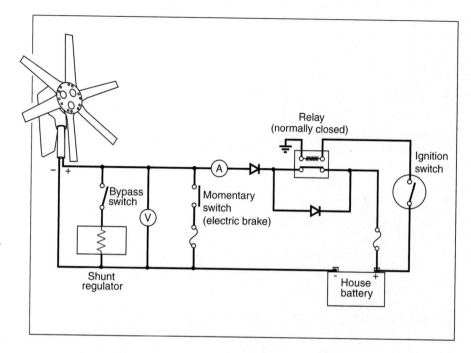

REGULATOR

All wind generators require regulation. Most can be controlled with a shunt-type regulator. This device, connected across the generator circuit rather than in series, diverts current through a resistive load as the voltage in the circuit rises toward a preset limit.

The only available regulation for a few wind generators is to monitor output and shut down the generator when battery voltage reaches 14.4 volts. In anything but light winds, that is likely to leave the battery undercharged.

BYPASS

Shunt regulators begin to divert current from the battery well before the voltage in the charging circuit rises to the preset limit. Output typically starts tapering off at around 13 volts. Disabling the regulator—by switching it out of the circuit—results in faster charging, but battery voltage must be monitored closely and not allowed to rise above 14.4 volts before returning the regulator to the circuit. Otherwise the batteries will suffer serious and permanent damage.

Taking the regulator out of the circuit also lets you use a wind generator to equalize deep-cycle wet cells, provided output from the generator does not exceed 4% of the amp-hour capacity of the batteries.

DIODE

A diode is always required between the generator and the battery. Sometimes the regulator incorporates the diode. This simplifies the connection to a single bank but complicates a dual-bank connection unless the regulator has dual isolated outputs. Make battery connections downstream of any existing isolation diodes to avoid detrimental voltage drop.

REGULATOR INTERACTION

As with solar power, elevated battery voltage due to a wind generator can cause the engine alternator to shut off even though the battery is less than fully charged. Disconnecting the wind generator is usually not an option because it can result in damaging overspeeding. Inserting an extra diode in the wind generator's charging circuit should reduce the generator-induced voltage sufficiently to eliminate interaction problems. Like the automatic disconnect for the solar panel, this can be handled automatically with a normally closed relay connected to the ignition switch.

MONITORING

A voltmeter and an ammeter wired into the charging circuit allows convenient performance monitoring.

TROUBLESHOOTING

Overcharging, under-charging, or a change in performance can lead you to suspect trouble. A few quick tests with your multimeter will diagnose most wind-generator problems.

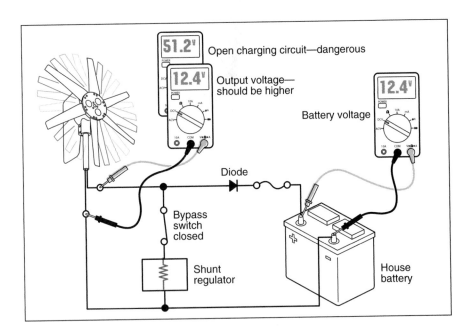

With a diode in the circuit, output voltage with the generator spinning in the wind should be around 0.5 volts above battery voltage. If it is higher, suspect a break in the charging circuit. Be more cautious than usual when checking wind-generator output; the open-circuit voltage of some units can well exceed 50 volts—enough to give you a nasty shock.

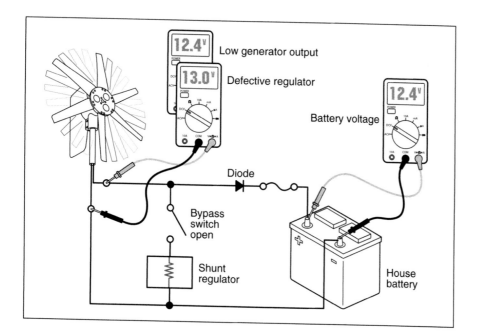

Low generator output

Defective regulator

Battery voltage

Diode

Bypass switch open

Shunt regulator

House battery

With generator output confirmed and the generator running, disable or disconnect the regulator and check charging-circuit voltage again. If it is now above battery voltage, the regulator is faulty.

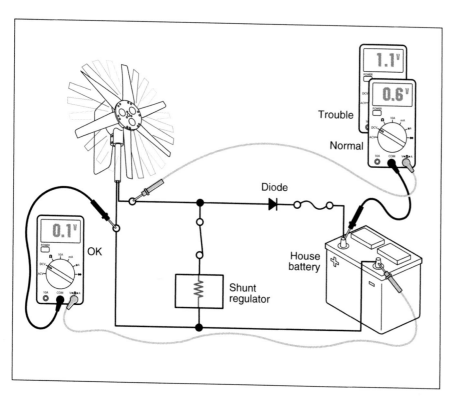

Trouble

Normal

OK

Diode

House battery

Shunt regulator

With the generator still running, check both positive and negative legs of the charging circuit for voltage drop. The diode in the positive leg will cause a drop of around 0.6 volts; more than that indicates unwanted resistance. Check for bad connections, broken wires, or blown fuses. Regulators often have an internal fuse.

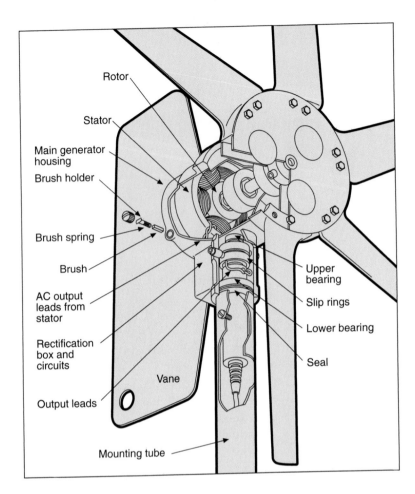

Rotor

Stator

Main generator housing

Brush holder

Brush spring

Brush

AC output leads from stator

Rectification box and circuits

Output leads

Vane

Mounting tube

Upper bearing

Slip rings

Lower bearing

Seal

If the closed-circuit voltage in your initial test was the same as battery voltage, open the charging circuit and check it again to confirm that the generator is not charging. The usual cause of zero output is worn or stuck brushes. Blown diodes are another possibility in alternator-type machines, as is failure of the thermal disconnect in the windings.

WATER GENERATORS

Water generators are essentially wind generators powered by a freewheeling prop as the boat moves through the water. Water's higher density means that water generators are capable of substantial output when a boat is underway. All of the information provided for connecting and testing a wind generator applies equally to water generators.

ALTERNATING CURRENT

No aspect of sailing is more inherently dangerous than pulling up to a dock and plugging in.

If yours is an older boat, the so-called "shore-power" system was probably just shy of criminal when the boat left the factory, and it hasn't improved with age. Even if your boat is relatively new and wired to the highest standards, the slightest fault—a bit of corrosion or an errant trickle—can put you in grave peril. And let's not overlook the possibility that the last electrician to work on the marina wiring might not have graduated at the top of his class.

Every schoolchild knows electricity and water are a deadly combination. So why would a sailor risk AC power in the wet environment of a boat? Originally, the idea was to take advantage of cheap (and silent) shore power to recharge batteries, provide better cabin illumination at the dock, and perhaps power a small, high-draw appliance like an iron or a coffee-maker. But soon enough boatowners wanted *all* their shoreside comforts and conveniences when they were plugged in. Today's sailors are becoming less willing to give up those conveniences even when they leave the dock.

In this chapter I will show how to wire an onboard AC system for maximum safety. If the AC system on your boat falls short of the standards outlined here, corrective measures are essential. With sufficient care you can make the required changes yourself; AC wiring is no more complicated than DC—only more dangerous. If you decide to take the more prudent course of leaving AC system repairs to a qualified marine electrician, you still should use your multimeter to check your existing AC wiring for the most egregious problems. When it comes to AC power, what you don't know definitely *can* hurt you.

ALTERNATING CURRENT KILLS!

I don't know how to say this any more clearly. It is not just the higher voltage, it is also the pulsating nature of the current. Even a small alternating current, if it passes through your chest, is capable of fatally disrupting heart rhythm. If you accidentally touch a hot AC wire and any part of your body is grounded, you become part of the circuit. If it is your elbow that is grounded, you may escape with nothing worse than a fright and a sore arm muscle, but if the ground connection is at your feet or your other hand, you will be extremely lucky to survive the event. Fortunately it is easy to avoid such a tragedy. Here are the rules:

Disconnect the AC system from all power sources. You may have to energize the wiring for testing, but never, ever work on the system hot.

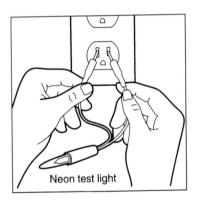

Neon test light

Check all wires with a voltage tester before touching. This practice is the electrician's version of "measure twice, cut once." Use your volt meter or a neon tester, and make sure there is no voltage between any two wires, or any wire and ground. Even if you unplugged the shore-power cord, you may have forgotten to disconnect the inverter.

Keep one hand in your pocket. Obviously you will need both hands occasionally, but the habit of working with one hand until you need the other reduces the risk of lethal shock.

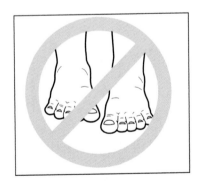

Wear rubber soles. Don't work on the AC system with bare feet. If your sole is damp, you may be electrically connected through a through-hull to ground.

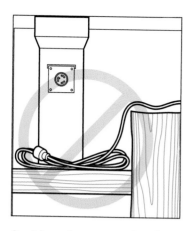

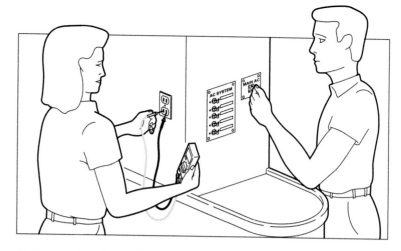

Don't leave the power cord on the dock. A helpful passer-by might plug it back in for you and send you to the next life.

Don't work alone. Especially if you are testing a live circuit, have someone close at hand who can shut off the power and/or provide assistance in case of a shock.

If you keep the danger solidly in mind, working on the AC system can actually be less risky than using it.

AC BASICS

Generators induce a current flow by passing a magnet near a wire coil. But the magnet is spinning, and its opposite pole follows almost immediately, reversing the direction of the induced current. And so it goes. This electron two-step is alternating current.

We can represent AC visually with a wavy line oscillating above and below zero. From peak plus to peak minus and back to peak plus is called a cycle. The frequency of the power is the number of cycles per second, measured in hertz (Hz). In the U.S., AC power has a frequency of 60 hertz.

FREQUENCY

Generated current builds, peaks, then declines as the magnet approaches the wire coil, passes near it, then swings away. As the opposite pole of the magnet passes the coil, current again builds, peaks, and declines, but in the opposite direction.

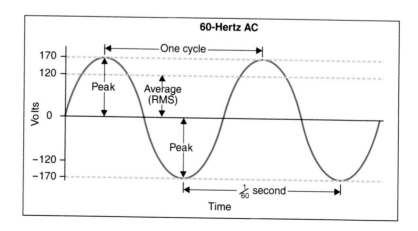

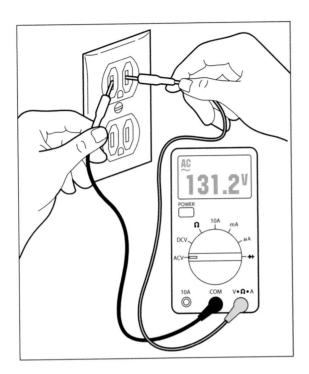

VOLTAGE

Since AC voltage is also oscillating, its designation is actually equivalent DC voltage, called RMS (root mean squared). Like battery voltage, it is subject to some variation.

120 VOLTS

The designation for "standard" household voltage varies from 110 to 125, and the range of actual voltages is even wider. I have adopted 120 volts as the wall-outlet standard in this book, primarily because at exactly ten times 12-volt battery voltage, it simplifies AC-to-DC calculations.

240 VOLTS

Our coverage of AC power does not extend to 240 volts. Two-forty will kill you twice as quickly as 120 volts. If your boat is large enough to require a 240-volt supply, your pockets are deep enough to hire a qualified electrician to work on it for you.

POWER FACTOR

Some components in a circuit, most notably coils, oppose *changes* in current. This isn't resistance as measured by an ohmmeter—it is called *reactance*—but it nevertheless causes many AC components to draw additional current. We account for this by including a *power factor* in AC power calculations, so that P = V x I becomes P = V x I x PF, where PF is always 1 or less.

You might expect a 120-volt AC appliance with a 1,200 watt rating to draw 10 amps, but if the PF is 0.5—a common power factor—the actual consumption is 20 amps (I = P ÷ [V x 0.5]). So the rated wattage of an AC appliance can substantially understate its actual power consumption—an important consideration when sizing wires, inverters, or generators. Sometimes the PF is shown on the faceplate.

THREE-WIRE SYSTEM

In a DC circuit, the wire carrying power from the source to the load is called positive, but with AC voltage switching between positive and negative (relative to ground), we call this side of an AC circuit *hot*. The hot wire in a 120-volt circuit is normally black, but sometimes red or blue.

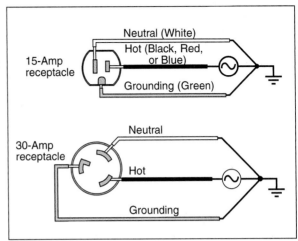

As with DC, we need a second wire to complete the circuit and provide a return path for the current. This side of the AC circuit we call *neutral*. At the power source, AND ONLY AT THE POWER SOURCE, the neutral side of the circuit is connected to a buried metal plate or bar to hold it at ground potential. The neutral wire is always white.

The third wire is called the *grounding* wire and it, too, is connected to ground *at the power source*. At its other end, the grounding wire is connected to all metal components, junction, and appliance housings and, through the third socket in 120-volt outlets, to the external cases of plug-in equipment. Ashore, the grounding wire is often bare, but in boat wiring it should be insulated and green.

THE GROUNDING WIRE

Since neutral also runs to ground, you might wonder why we need a second grounding wire. It is there to keep you alive. If, for example, wire insulation inside an appliance melts or abrades and the wire comes in contact with the case, it puts the case at the same potential as the hot wire. It doesn't blow a fuse because there is no circuit and thus no current flow. And depending on the fault, it probably doesn't have any effect on the normal operation of the appliance. All seems right with the world ... until you touch the case. Then your body completes the path to ground, and you get a nasty shock.

The grounding wire changes all that. A short to the case instantly becomes a short to ground, probably opening the breaker in the circuit. And even if the short is insufficient to kick the breaker, or if it occurs while you are holding the appliance, the grounding wire still protects you by providing a lower-resistance path to ground than your body does.

Anything that degrades or opens the grounding circuit, such as a corroded or missing ground prong, leaves you dangerously vulnerable. And even if your connections are perfect, marina outlets are far too often poorly grounded or not grounded at all. Before you plug in, check the ground (see Testing later in this chapter).

WIRE TYPE AND SIZE

As with DC wiring, use only flexible stranded wire, preferably tinned. In fact, all wiring guidance provided in Chapter 4 applies equally to AC circuits, except that it is primarily amperage capacity and not voltage drop that dictates wire size. If the circuits aboard are protected by 25-amp breakers, #16 AWG (boat cable) is indicated, but as a practical matter, the wire should be a size or two larger than the minimum.

BUNDLING

Gathering parallel wires into bundles is tidy, especially when contained in spiral wrap, but bundling can have unanticipated consequences. Think of too many people in an airless room. Bundled wires combine the heat each generates individually, and for this reason, a wire in a bundle of three should carry not more than 70% of its rated current, 60% in bundles of four to six, 50% in bundles up to 24. A #16-AWG wire in a bundle of eight other wires, for example, should never carry more than 12.5 amps (50% of 25 A).

ALLOWABLE AMPERAGE

Wire Type: AWM, BC5W2, UL1426 Boat Cable
Temperature Rating: 105°C (221°F)

Wire Gauge (AWG)	Outside Engine Space	Inside Engine Space
18	Not allowed *	
16	25	21.3
14	35	29.8
12	45	38.3
10	60	51.0
8	80	68.0
6	120	102

* ABYC guidlines allow limited use of #18 AWG wire inside the panel board, but in deference to human nature, boatowners should never buy wire smaller than #16 AWG.

DERATING FOR BUNDLED AC CABLES

Current-Carrying Conductors	Derating Factor
3	0.7
4 to 6	0.6
7 to 24	0.5
25+	0.4

AT THE DOCK

Like it or not, *your* AC system begins with the outlet on the dock.

PLUG TYPES

The standard wall outlet is rated at 15 amps. This type of receptacle, called 15-amp straight blade, accepts a common three-blade plug and is still seen at older and smaller marinas.

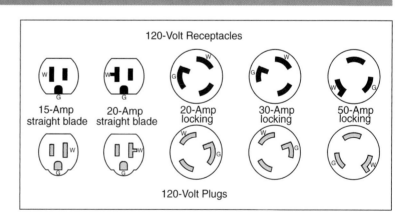

You can also plug a 15-amp plug into a 20-amp straight-blade receptacle, but not vice versa.

The 30-amp locking receptacle has become the norm at most marinas. Because of this, outfitting your boat to plug into a 30-amp receptacle, even if you don't need 30 amps, will make shore hookups simpler. A locking receptacle makes them more secure.

POLARITY

Since alternating current by definition flows in one direction then the other, reversing the connection has no effect on an AC appliance. But correct polarity is still an essential requirement in AC circuits. Why? When an overload trips the breaker, it disconnects the load from the power. But suppose connections to the dockside receptacle are reversed. That puts the breaker in the neutral side of the circuit, so the circuit is essentially unprotected. The same short now continues uninterrupted until the circuit burns open. If you are lucky, the breaker at the marina office will trip before flames break out, but don't count on it.

Shock risk is also increased. Turning off a breaker appears to remove power from the circuit because it turns off all appliances connected to that circuit. But with reversed polarity you have disconnected the appliance from ground, not from power. THE CIRCUIT IS STILL LIVE.

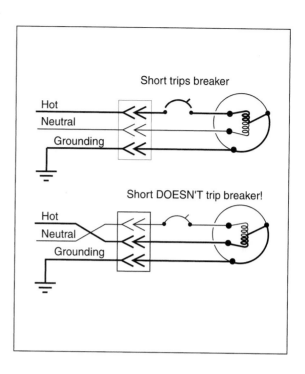

POLARITY TESTER

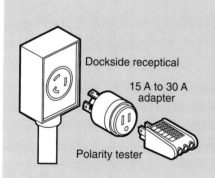

Dockside receptical

15 A to 30 A adapter

Polarity tester

A POLARITY TESTER hardwired into your AC switch panel (described below) is a good precaution, but if you have an existing circuit fault, damage can occur the instant you plug in. Using a plug-in polarity tester *before* you plug in your power cord is the best way of avoiding reversed polarity. Most also detect an open grounding wire and other dangerous conditions.

SHORE-POWER CONNECTION

The electrical connection between boat and dock is subject to weather, submersion, abrasion, and often strain. It needs to be up to the task.

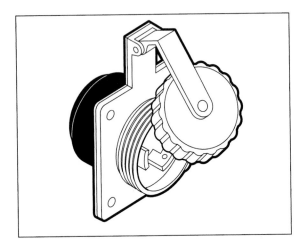

INLET FITTING

The inlet fitting on your boat should be weather tight when connected and when disconnected. Screw-on caps are more secure than those sealed with spring pressure. A high-quality bronze or stainless steel fitting costs only a few dollars more than the plastic variety, but should last the life of the boat.

Locate the inlet where it is convenient but safely out of the way. Mount it as high as possible. The backside of the inlet should be well ventilated and not at risk of mechanical damage.

POWER CORD

An extension cord from a builder's supply store, even one labeled "Heavy Duty," is not an appropriate shore-power cord. To stand up to the hard service of marine use, the cable should carry a hard-service rating—SO, ST, or STO. There must be no possibility of the cable pulling free of the plugs (dock cords sometimes become dock *lines*) or of the plugs pulling out of the receptacles. For 30-amp service, the conductors must be #10 AWG or larger.

SUPPLY WIRE

Since protection is somewhere back up the line, wire size to the main breaker is dictated by the type of inlet. A 30-amp inlet requires 10-gauge wire. Fourteen-gauge is adequate for a 15-amp inlet.

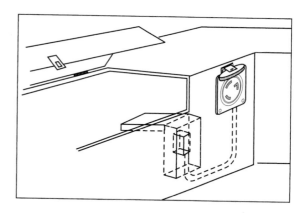

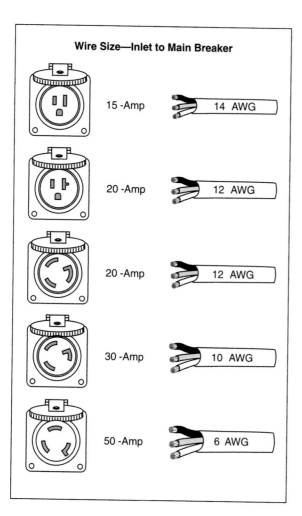

Wire Size—Inlet to Main Breaker

15 -Amp	14 AWG
20 -Amp	12 AWG
20 -Amp	12 AWG
30 -Amp	10 AWG
50 -Amp	6 AWG

MAIN BREAKER

Within 10 feet (3 m) (wire distance) of the inlet you must have a circuit breaker that protects both the hot and the neutral conductors. The breaker rating cannot exceed the service; i.e., if you have a 30-amp inlet, the main breaker cannot exceed 30 amps.

Despite the tendency of builders to incorporate the AC main breaker into the main switch panel, locating the breaker in a small (household) breaker box near the inlet fitting—typically high in a cockpit locker—gets it into the circuit sooner and is the preferable configuration. You will rarely, if ever, switch this breaker.

NEUTRAL AND GROUND

A look inside your breaker panel at home will reveal that neutral wires and grounding wires are all connected to the same bus bar. Connecting the neutral wire to the grounding wire on a boat makes the underwater hardware a current-carrying path to ground, an unhealthy circumstance for nearby swimmers. The potential for reversing polarity means appliance cases and wiring boxes might also become energized. On a boat plugged in to shore, the neutral (white) conductor and the grounding (green) conductor MUST NEVER BE DIRECTLY CONNECTED.

How many AC circuits you need depends on how much AC equipment you have aboard. Keep in mind that you are limited to 30 amps when connected to a 30-amp service.

SINGLE CIRCUIT

The AC requirements on many sailboats can be satisfied with a single circuit. Here, a single double-pole breaker feeds six outlets wired in parallel. Because the outlets are rated for 15 amps, the breaker must also be a 15-amp unit. A single circuit offers the benefit of simplicity, and if (as recommended above) the breaker is located in a dedicated box adjacent to the inlet, this configuration also maintains complete separation between the AC and DC system. No switch panel in the cabin is needed.

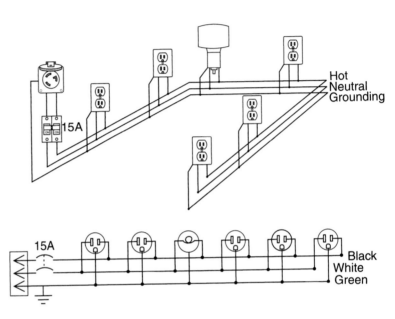

DUAL CIRCUIT

Dual 15-amp circuits let you take full advantage of a 30-amp service. The main breaker is 30 amps, the two circuit breakers 15 amps. All three breakers are located in a box near the power inlet. Here, one circuit supplies a hard-wired battery charger.

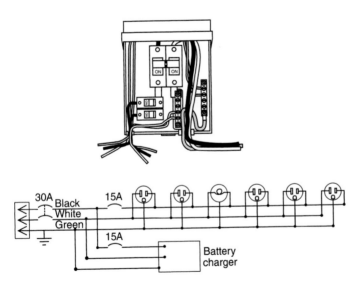

BREAKERS

Although single-pole breakers are commonly used for branch circuits, this is risky economy. Double-pole breakers, which open both sides of the circuit when tripped, fully protect the circuit even if polarity is reversed. Perhaps *you* will never forget to check polarity before plugging in, but *I'm* not that confident.

Breakers should be sized for the wire or for the load, whichever is smaller. For cabin outlet circuits (using at least #16 AWG wire) use 15-amp breakers. If you install 20-amp outlets, the breaker must likewise be 20 amp. For dedicated circuits, a smaller breaker provides some protection for the appliance, but be sure you know the load. This is where the power factor mentioned above comes in. Also, motors and incandescent lights require momentary start-up currents (called inrush) that can be as much as seven times operating currents. Breakers are time-delayed to handle momentary inrush without tripping, but since the delay is related to the percentage of overload, inrush can trip a breaker that is too small.

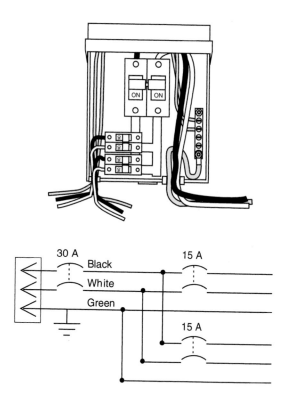

SWITCH PANEL

If you prefer a switch panel in the cabin, commercial units are available. Do not combine AC and DC in a single panel.

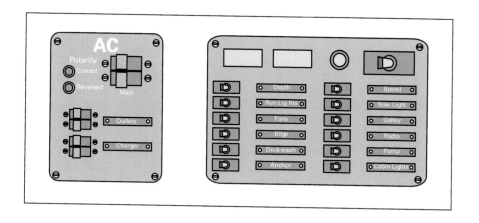

POLARITY TESTER

Your AC system must have a hard-wired reverse-polarity indicator if the circuits are protected with single-pole breakers, but even if you follow the more prudent course of using only double-pole breakers, do not omit this extra safeguard. Reversed polarity still puts ON-OFF switches on the wrong side of the circuit, leaving OFF appliances fully energized. You must know about reversed polarity, and you must correct it.

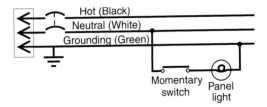

A light or buzzer connected across the white and green wires will not operate as long as the white wire is at 0 potential, but reversing the polarity puts the white wire at 120 volts, illuminating the light or sounding the buzzer. However, since the white and green wires on a boat must never be directly connected, a momentary switch is a required part of the circuit.

An alternative method of maintaining the required separation between white and green is to use a high-resistance indicator like a neon lamp. The circuit shown allows the indicators to operate without manual intervention, and with a resistance exceeding 25,000 Ω, the potential current is less than 5 mA, too little to cause any mischief. This type of polarity indicator is required if your AC circuits are protected by single-pole breakers.

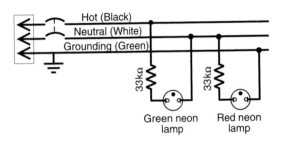

ROUTING AC WIRING

AC wiring should never be routed where it might be at risk of submersion. The best place for AC wiring is high in the boat—against the underside of the deck. Do not bundle AC wiring with DC wiring. There is considerable potential to confuse the black AC hot conductor with the DC negative —also black—so strive to keep the wiring separated and clearly labeled. (For new DC wiring, use yellow wire for the negative.) As with DC wiring, support the wire continuously with conduit, or at least every 18 inches (0.5 m) with cable clamps or wire ties. Protect the wiring from chafe.

JUNCTION BOXES

All AC connections must be protected by an enclosure. Wires should enter junction, outlet, and breaker boxes from the bottom so they cannot provide an entry path for water. Clamp the wire where it enters the box to avoid the risk of chafe from the motion of the boat. Leave enough extra wire (around 4 inches) in outlet boxes to allow the outlet to be connected outside the box. Fold the excess wire behind the outlet.

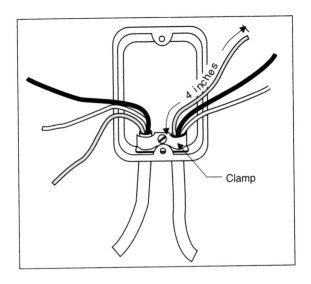

OUTLETS

"HI HO SILVER"

The Lone Ranger's famous call to his white horse has long provided the association necessary for me to remember which wire connects to which terminal on a polarized outlet. *White* goes to *silver*. The black wire connects to the opposite terminal, usually brass, but sometimes dark. The green terminal is for the green grounding wire.

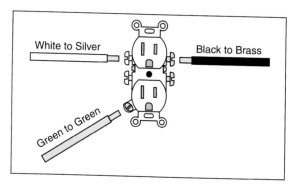

WIRE TERMINALS

Ashore, outlet terminal screws are simply tightened onto a loop of wire. This is inadequate on a boat both because the wire is stranded, not solid, and because boats introduce motion into the equation. As with all connections, those to outlets (and other terminal screws) require a proper terminal on the conductor. Where the terminal screws are captive, use locking spade terminals rather than ring terminals. You can connect wire directly to commercial-grade outlets that have screw-tightened wire clamps.

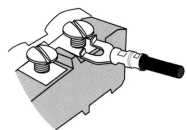

GROUND FAULT INTERRUPT

Regular circuit breakers are essentially fire-protection devices and offer no protection against electrical shock. A ground-fault circuit interrupter (GFCI), on the other hand, provides a high degree of shock protection. If you accidentally touch an energized wire or component and you are grounded, the GFCI disconnects the circuit in about $\frac{1}{40}$ of a second, too little time for the current to build to a dangerous level. In recognition of the increased risk of shock in damp environments, many municipal building codes mandate GFCIs in bathrooms and, increasingly, kitchens. Boats are damp environments, and every outlet on a boat should be protected by a GFCI.

It is possible to install a GFCI in the main panel to protect all circuits, but tiny current leaks that are inevitable in the marine environment can accumulate to the point of tripping the GFCI. And the tripped GFCI disables your entire AC system until you locate these nearly undetectable leaks. To minimize nuisance tripping, it is better to protect each circuit individually. Replacing the first outlet (counting from the distribution panel) with a GFCI outlet protects the rest of the downstream outlets in the circuit. Be sure the wires marked LINE are connected to the power source and those marked LOAD feed the remainder of the circuit.

THE GREEN-WIRE CONTROVERSY

Should any of the various metal cases enclosing your AC system become energized, the green wire provides a low-resistance path to ground. But what if the leak is into the DC wiring, caused, for example, by a crossed wire or a short in a dual-voltage appliance (charger, inverter, dual-voltage light fixtures)?

THE DANGER

Any AC that leaks into the DC system will seek ground, meaning it will automatically travel through the wiring to the ground connection on the engine and down the prop shaft to the water. (If you have a flexible shaft coupling, you need a shaft brush to make electrical contact with the shaft.) This is essentially the same as dropping a hot wire into the water. In freshwater, this poses a real risk of electrocution for anyone in the water nearby. The better conductivity of salt water (which tends to pass the current straight down to ground) reduces the risk of electrocution, but the current field can be (and has been) enough to paralyze muscles and cause a swimmer to drown.

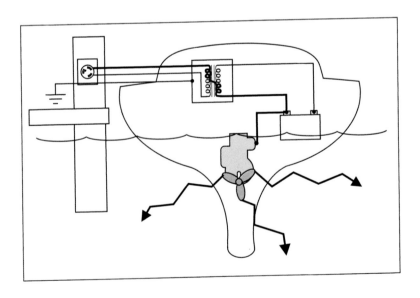

GROUNDING THE GREEN WIRE

To reduce the risk to swimmers, the green wire should be connected to the ground terminal on the engine. This gives AC leakage into the DC system a safe path to ground. But you must be aware that grounding the green wire is not without problems. Should the green wire have a fault somewhere between the power inlet and the buried grounding plate, ground-fault current will flow into the water—just what we are trying to prevent. So it is essential to test the ground *at the dock,* and to keep cords and plugs in good condition. Protecting all AC circuits with GFCIs virtually eliminates this risk.

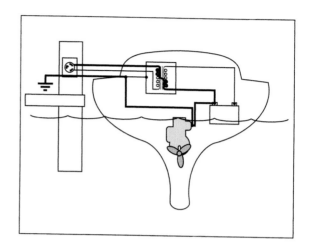

GALVANIC CORROSION

A more insidious problem is galvanic corrosion. Connecting the green wire to an underwater fitting completes the circuit between your boat and all other nearby boats with their own green wires grounded. With seawater as the electrolyte, every grounded fitting essentially becomes part of a big battery.

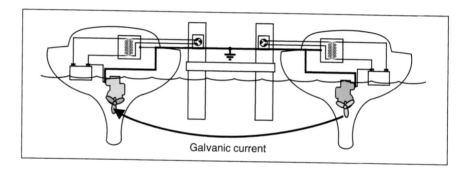

Galvanic current

If your fittings are less noble on the galvanic scale than your neighbors' (see Chapter 9), they are anodes and begin to erode. This can be bad news if you have an aluminum outdrive in the water and your neighbors' underwater fittings are bronze and stainless steel.

STRAY-CURRENT CORROSION

Even if your prop and shaft are similar to those around you and well protected with zinc, stray DC currents from a neighboring boat can seek ground through your green-wire connection, causing electrolysis. A serious stray-current leak can eat underwater components away in a matter of hours. Boats sink at the dock every year due to this condition.

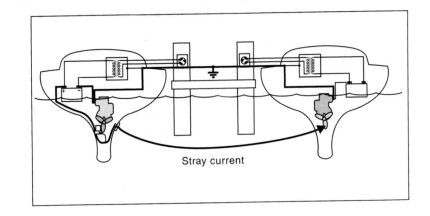

Stray current

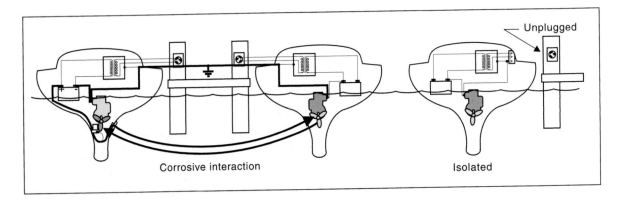

Corrosive interaction   Isolated

CUTTING THE GREEN WIRE

Disconnecting the green wire from the ground lug on the engine eliminates the risk of galvanic or stray-current caused by other boats. But it puts anyone in the water at risk while the boat is plugged in. Don't do it. There are safer solutions.

UNPLUG

Unplugging the boat breaks the grounding wire connection, minimizing or eliminating the risks of galvanic and stray-current corrosion caused by other boats. It also removes the risk to swimmers. Unplug when anyone is going in the water near the boat, and always leave the boat unplugged when you are not aboard. (A solar panel is better for your batteries than a battery charger anyway.)

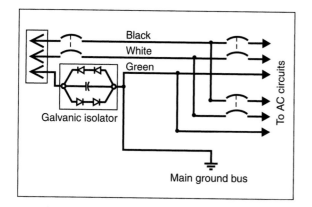

Galvanic isolator

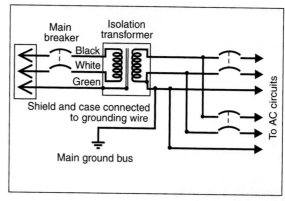

Shield and case connected to grounding wire

Main ground bus

GALVANIC ISOLATOR

The galvanic isolator is simply a pair of diodes connected in parallel to a second pair conducting in the opposite direction. Since it takes about 0.6 volts to "push the gate open" (i.e., cause a diode to become conductive), two diodes in series block all current flow unless the voltage exceeds about 1.2 volts. Galvanic voltages between underwater metals are lower than this, so no current flows. The voltage of most stray currents, by the time it reaches your boat through the water, will also be too low to cause the diodes to pass a current. Opposing pairs of diodes pass current in both directions, so both AC and DC flows freely through the isolator once the diodes become conductive. Galvanic isolators need hefty diodes able to carry short-circuit amperage—up to 3,000 amps in a 30-amp circuit—long enough for the circuit breaker to trip. Unfortunately, not all isolators have this capability. Some isolators parallel a capacitor—an electronic component that passes AC but not DC—so that a diode failure does not disconnect the grounding wire, a potentially hazardous condition.

Insert the galvanic isolator into the green wire as soon as it comes aboard to prevent unknown connections between the AC grounding wire and the DC system from allowing currents to bypass the isolator.

ISOLATION TRANSFORMER

Shore power flowing through one side of an isolation transformer induces AC power on the other side that energizes the boat's AC system, but there is no direct electrical connection between the boat's AC system and shore. The DC system is likewise isolated from shore, eliminating external galvanic and stray-current corrosion as effectively as unplugging. Isolation transformers also eliminate most polarity concerns, but because they are big, heavy (200 lb.), and expensive, they are rarely installed on modest sailboats.

TESTING

A few quick tests with your multimeter will help you assess the condition of your AC system.

POLARITY

We never think about polarity ashore, but its importance in the wet environment cannot be overemphasized. Not only must you verify the polarity of every dock connection, but if the polarity of any outlet is reversed, the shock risk of any appliance plugged into that outlet increases. Check all outlets for correct polarity, even those you didn't wire (perhaps especially those).

Check polarity with your voltmeter by measuring the voltage between the receptacle's long socket (neutral) and the roundish grounding socket. The meter should read zero. Checked across the short socket (hot) and the grounding socket, the voltage should be normal—around 120 volts. It is a good practice to confirm the neutral connection by also measuring the voltage between the short and long sockets. BE SURE YOU DO NOT TOUCH THE METAL PART OF THE METER PROBES WHEN MAKING THESE TESTS.

You can perform these same tests with a neon test lamp. When the lamp lights, it shows a voltage differential; when it fails to light, both sockets (or wires) are at the same potential. A plug-in polarity tester is the easiest of all to use: just plug it into each outlet.

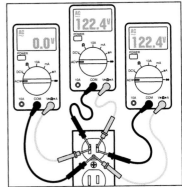

GROUNDING WIRE

If you have a generator or inverter, shut off the former, disconnect the latter, and switch both out of the AC circuit. Unplug your shore-power cord from the dock—but not from the boat—and take the plug into the cabin. If you have a galvanic isolator—or if you aren't sure—insert the stripped end of a short piece of insulated wire into the ground socket of a cabin outlet and touch the other end to the ground blade on the plug. This discharges the capacitor in the isolator (if it has one). Set your meter to measure resistance (Ω) and touch one probe to the ground blade on the plug and the other to the grounding socket of the outlet. If you don't get a near-zero reading, the ground is faulty and must be fixed. Check the ground connection of every onboard outlet this way.

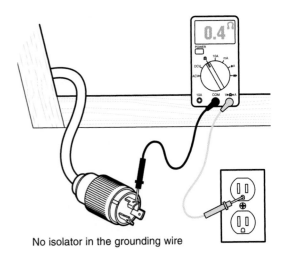

No isolator in the grounding wire

ISOLATED GROUND

In the previous test, a galvanic isolator in the circuit increases the resistance measured by the meter. The meter may take a few minutes to stabilize because the voltage from the meter is recharging the capacitor. When the meter settles, note the reading. Remove the meter and discharge the capacitor again by shorting the ground blade to a ground socket. With the meter connections reversed, recheck the resistance, again allowing time for the reading to stabilize. If both readings are about the same and above 50 ohms, the isolator checks out. If the meter reads O.L or near zero in either direction, the isolator is defective.

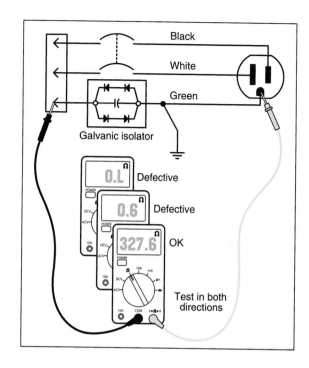

If your meter has a diode-test setting, the same test on this meter setting should give a reading of around 1.0 volt in both directions. A reading of around 0.5 volts indicates a shorted diode; 0.0 volts means tandem diodes are shorted. An O.L reading tells you the diodes are open. Shorted diodes render the isolator ineffective. Open diodes break the grounding connection, a dangerous condition that must not be allowed.

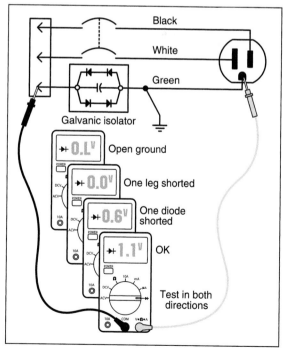

GREEN-WIRE CONNECTION

To verify a good green-wire connection, measure the resistance between the ground blade on the plug and the negative battery cable. It should be near zero (or whatever resistance your isolator exhibited in the previous test).

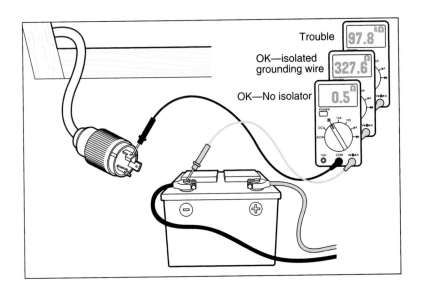

GROUND AND NEUTRAL SEPARATION

Make sure the shore-power cord is unplugged, generators and inverters are off *and* switched out of the AC circuit, and all AC breakers are in the ON position. Double-check for voltage in the system by inserting your voltmeter probes into the slots of any outlet. Check between hot and neutral, between hot and ground, and between neutral and ground. Now switch the meter to ohms (Ω) and measure the resistance between neutral and ground. The meter should read O.L if you do not have a hard-wired polarity tester in the system, above 25,000 ohms (25 kΩ) if you do. A low resistance reading means neutral and ground are tied together. This connection *must* be located and eliminated.

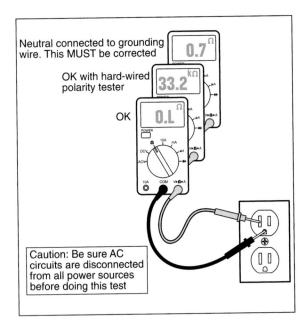

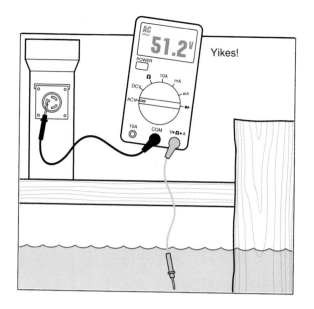

GROUND FAULT

Set your meter to AC volts and insert one probe into the grounding socket of the dockside outlet. WARNING: THE GROUNDING SOCKET IS EASY TO IDENTIFY IN 15-, 20-, AND 30-AMP RECEPTACLES, BUT LESS OBVIOUS IN 50-AMP RECEPTACLES. BE SURE YOU *KNOW* WHICH IS THE GROUNDING SOCKET. Dangle the other probe into the water. Any voltage reading indicates a serious grounding leak and condemns the outlet.

STRAY CURRENT

After checking for a grounding leak, reset the meter to the highest DC amp setting, and check for DC current between the grounding outlet and the water, switching down as necessary. Any reading above around 10 mA suggests stray current from nearby boats and you should not connect to this outlet unless your AC system is isolated.

LEAKAGE

With your shore-power cord plugged into the boat but not into the dock (generators and inverters off and disconnected), make sure there is no AC voltage between the grounding socket in the dock receptacle and the grounding blade on the cord plug. Set the meter to the highest DC amp setting, switching down as necessary. Any current that passes through the meter is leakage. If the current is flowing toward the boat (a + reading with the red probe to the receptacle, black to the plug), it is damaging your underwater fittings; if it flows the other way, the fittings on neighboring boats are suffering. A galvanic isolator in the grounding wire should block all galvanic current and your meter should read zero (although some isolators pass a few milliamps, which zinc anodes should easily handle). If the meter reads more than 15 mA, the isolator is not preventing corrosion.

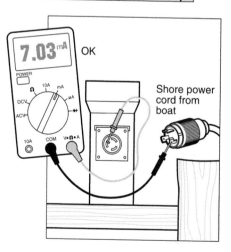

INVERTERS

An inverter, functioning like a battery charger in reverse, allows AC appliances to be powered by the ship's batteries. Advancing technologies have made inverters more efficient and more affordable. They have become an extremely popular add-on in recent years.

TYPES

Line-frequency inverters are usually bigger and always heavier than equivalent *high-frequency* inverters. In the past, line-frequency inverters enjoyed a lower failure rate, but today dependability is more a function of the quality of the inverter than of the number of electronic components it contains. The line-frequency inverter's primary advantage has long been its "reversibility," becoming a powerful battery charger, but small inverters (under 1,000 watts) nearly all use high-frequency switching. High-frequency switching is finding its way into high-power inverters, including inverter/charger models.

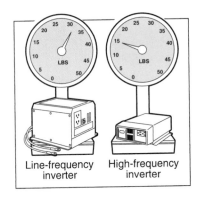

Line-frequency inverter   High-frequency inverter

WAVEFORM

Inverters that generate true sine-wave power are more expensive than those that have a square waveform, but the price difference is narrowing. The power from a sine-wave inverter is indistinguishable from shore power, so it will run any appliance. Most AC equipment will also run fine on square-wave AC, particularly the stepped square wave (called *modified sine wave*) inverters typically generate. But some appliances, notably microwaves, televisions, laser printers, variable-speed devices, and battery chargers (for ni-cads) can have problems with square-wave power and may even be damaged. Before you buy an inverter, know what you want it to power.

SIZING

Inverters are typically most efficient at about two-thirds rated capacity, so select an inverter with a continuous-output rating of about 50% more than the wattage of the appliances you want the inverter to power. Be sure it has adequate surge capacity to handle start-up loads.

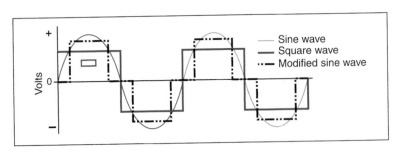

LOAD REALITIES

Often overlooked in selecting an inverter is the load it places on the ship's batteries. A 120-volt AC appliance draws 10 times the rated amps when it is running on 12 volts, plus additional amps to run the inverter. The actual draw is further affected by the PF of the appliance and the effect of the inverter's waveform.

For example, a microwave oven rated at 700 watts would seem to draw 5.8 amps, but with a PF of around 0.6, the actual draw is closer to 10 amps at 120 volts. In addition, microwave ovens don't much like square-wave power, so they are about 30% less efficient when powered by a square-wave (modified sine-wave) inverter. That means the inverter has to deliver 13 amps—1,500 watts—to power the oven. A 1,500-watt draw on a 12-volt battery results in 125-amp current. But the inverter is only about 85% efficient, so the actual draw is closer to 150 amps. This likely exceeds starter-motor draw, so if you run this microwave for 15 minutes, the effect is similar to cranking the engine for that long.

Small inverters are a marvelous convenience, but large inverters will quickly overwhelm your batteries unless their draw is offset by concurrent replenishment, meaning that you will normally need to run the engine while the inverter is under significant load.

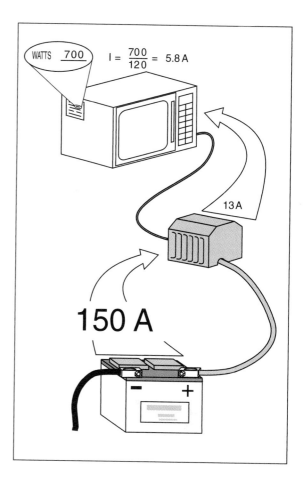

BATTERY CAPACITY

THE AMP-HOUR DRAW from a 1,500-watt inverter load for 15 minutes (plus inefficiency) is "only" 37.5 Ah, but you will recall from Chapter 4 that a high discharge rate severely reduces battery capacity. A discharge rate of 150 amps for 15 minutes will leave a 200 Ah battery (20-hour rating) close to 50% discharged. In all likelihood, such a heavy draw will pull battery voltage below 10.5 volts in less than 15 minutes and trip the inverter's low-voltage shutdown switch. The actual amount of battery capacity needed to support an inverter ultimately depends how much you use it between battery charges, but limiting inverter wattage to five times battery capacity is a good rule of thumb. In other words, don't expect a 100 Ah battery to power an inverter larger than 500 watts.

CONNECTIONS

PORTABLE

Small inverters have the AC outlet built into the unit, avoiding a direct connection to the AC system. Most are equipped with a cigarette-lighter plug, but with a current limit of 15 amps. Such plugs are inappropriate for inverters larger than 150 watts. Even then you must make sure that the wire from the battery to the socket is of adequate size. For example, a round-trip wire length of 20 feet (6 m) requires 10-gauge wire.

Unless you absolutely need the portability of a plug, remove it and wire even a small inverter directly to the battery or the distribution panel. WARNING: FEW INVERTERS ARE PROTECTED AGAINST REVERSE POLARITY. IF YOU REVERSE THE CONNECTIONS TO THE BATTERY, YOU WILL RUIN THE INVERTER. The center contact on the plug is positive, so be sure to label the wire when your remove the plug. As with all direct connections to the battery, a fuse in the positive line is an essential safeguard.

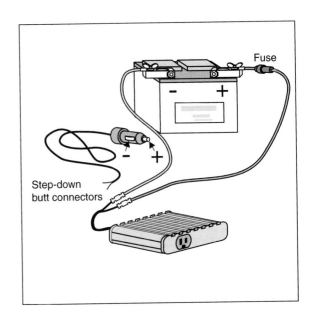

CONSOLE

Large inverters are always wired directly to the battery (or adjacent distribution posts). A slow-blow fuse must be included in the positive side of the DC connection. Wire size must be adequate (see Chapter 4); for example, a 2,500-watt inverter less than 5 feet (1.5 m) from the batteries requires size 1/0 cable.

Inverters without built-in AC receptacles nearly always include an internal transfer switch to prevent the inverter from being on line when the AC system is energized from another source. If you wire the inverter to outlets and appliances that are also connected to the shore-power inlet or a generator, and the inverter does not have a transfer switch, you must install one.

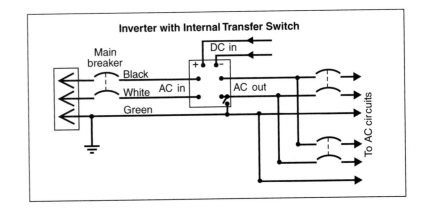

Inverter with Internal Transfer Switch

LOCATION

AN INVERTER SHOULD IDEALLY BE LOCATED adjacent to the batteries, but never inside the battery compartment. The mounting location must be dry, and since inverter efficiency declines as the temperature of the unit rises, good ventilation is another requirement. In the tropics a cooling fan will improve both output and reliability.

TRANSFER SWITCH

The transfer switch makes certain that only one source of AC power can be connected to your AC circuits at a time. A low-tech way of accomplishing this is to feed inverter (and generator) output to a cord that fits the shore-power inlet. Since only one cord can be plugged in at a time, the AC wiring can never be connected to more than one source. The transfer switch accomplishes the same thing, only more conveniently.

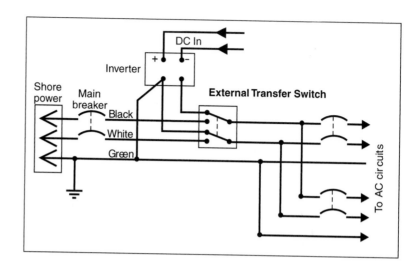

NEUTRAL AND GROUNDING CONNECTION

We saw earlier that the neutral and grounding wires are connected together only at the power source, never on the boat. In the case of shore power, the power source is the breaker panel servicing the dockside outlet. But what happens when the power source is an inverter or a generator on the boat? For shock protection it remains essential to have the neutral and grounding wires connected together at the power source. But whenever the power source is not on the boat, this connection must be broken. This is a second function of the transfer switch—to open the connection between neutral and ground when the boat is connected to shore power.

GENERATORS

For heavy or prolonged AC loads away from the dock, the only practical solution is a generator. Plugging the dock cord into the outlet of a portable generator is the easiest way to connect it to cabin outlets. Gensets installed below deck are sufficiently expensive and complicated that professional installation is usually prudent.

TRANSFER SWITCH

It must be impossible for the generator and shore power (or the inverter) to feed the AC circuits at the same time. This is commonly accomplished by running shore power through the inverter's internal transfer switch, with a second break-before-make transfer switch downstream to select the genset. A three-way transfer switch is another alternative.

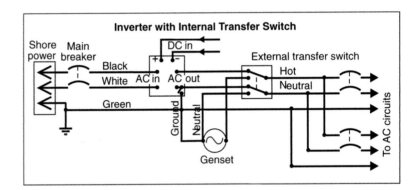

FREQUENCY

Generator output voltage should be within a few volts of 120, and frequency should be close to 60 Hz. You can measure voltage with your multimeter, but how do you monitor frequency? With a half-dozen components available from your local Radio Shack, you can make a simple frequency meter.

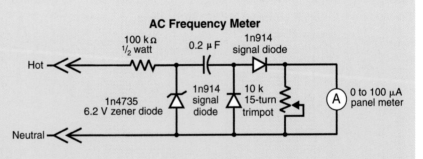

To calibrate it, connect it to shore power and adjust the trimpot until the ammeter reads exactly 60 µA. The meter reading will now correspond to the line frequency. (For a full explanation of how this circuit works, see *Boatowner's Illustrated Handbook of Wiring* by Charlie Wing.)

HEAVEN AND EARTH

There is an old joke about a man standing in the middle of a park blowing a single braying note on a beat-up trumpet. When the police arrive, they ask him what he is doing.

"Keeping the elephants away," the man says.

"But sir, there are no elephants within thousands of miles," the officer points out.

"See," replies the man.

Lightning protection is like that. If you take preventative measures and your boat never gets struck, at least you can say, "See." But there is an absence of scientific evidence that anything improves the odds of being spared a strike.

Don't flatter yourself that you can be a cosmic player: lightning doesn't know you exist, and it doesn't care. The trick to dealing with lightning is the same as with elephants: *stay out of the way*. On a sailboat, staying out of the way primarily means giving the lightning an unimpeded path to ground.

A good ground is also required by onboard radios to provide a counterpoise for long-distance transmissions. In this chapter we detail a grounding system that reduces the risk of damage and injury from a lightning strike and simultaneously serves as a radio counterpoise. Bonding, a second component of lightning protection, is also covered.

LIGHTNING PROTECTION

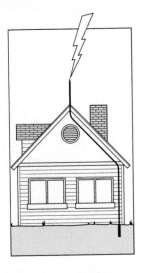

Despite the low risk, statistically, of being struck by lightning, getting caught out on the water in an electrical storm can be a frightening event. Fortunately, going below provides the crew substantial protection. It is the boat that is in greater peril. The best way to minimize the risk of damage is with a properly configured lightning-protection system.

LIGHTNING ROD

The lightning rod was conceived in 1752 by Ben Franklin to protect wooden structures from fire by attracting the lightning strike and conducting it safely to ground. Lightning that would otherwise strike nearby finds the rod and its ground cable a lower resistance path to ground than another 100 feet (30 m) of air or the roof of a wooden building.

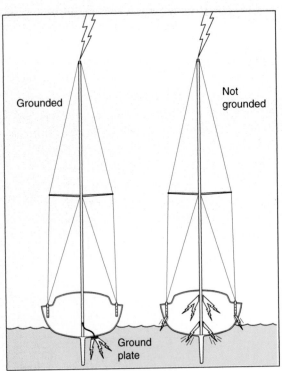

A sailboat with an aluminum mast already has a conductor sticking up in the air. The only thing necessary to make it a lightning rod is to give it a good ground, but the concept of *attracting* lightning makes some sailors reluctant to ground the mast. This logic is fundamentally flawed because, grounded or not, an aluminum mast is a better conductor than air and thus attractive to nearby lightning. When a hitchhiking strike reaches the bottom of an ungrounded mast, it generally fires through the hull to the water, often leaving holes big enough to sink an untended boat. It may also leap to other metal components in the boat, potentially passing through a crewmember.

There is compelling evidence that grounding the mast lowers the incidence of damage or injury from a lightning strike, and no evidence that it increases the likelihood of being struck.

STATIC DISSIPATOR

Some would have you believe that topping your mast with a pointed rod or a copper bottle brush will prevent a lightning strike. The theory is that the point or points of these static dissipators bleed off the charge from the grounded mast, thus lowering the voltage differential below what is required to "spark" lightning. Dissipators do bleed off static charge, but, to use a cliché, there is plenty more where that came from. Trying to bleed the ocean's charge into the air with a dissipator on your mast is like trying to lower the ocean's level with a soda straw. Ironically, because a dissipator ionizes the air around it, under some circumstances it could theoretically contribute to a lightning strike, although it is extremely doubtful that these units have any effect either way.

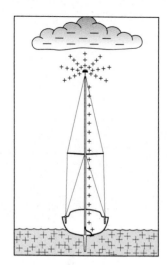

CONE OF PROTECTION

Intuitively, a mast sticking up would seem to put you at greater risk during an electrical storm, not unlike standing beneath the only tree on a golf course. However, powerboaters are statistically at much greater personal risk. If your mast is grounded, it is actually your savior. When the mast is closer than the ground, lightning tends to divert to it. This results in a cone-shaped area that is essentially protected from lightning. This area is known as the cone of protection. It has a height and radius approximately equal to the mast height.

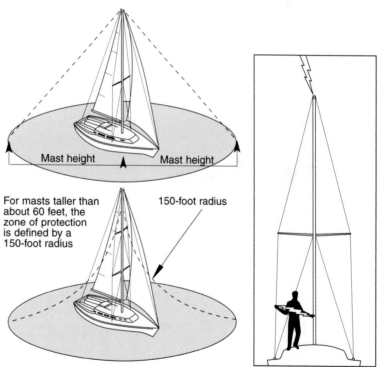

Mast height   Mast height

For masts taller than about 60 feet, the zone of protection is defined by a 150-foot radius

150-foot radius

As long as the boat is entirely within the cone, there is little risk of anyone aboard being struck directly. However, you are still at risk if you are touching metal, and especially if you are bridging two metal components—the wheel and a stanchion, for example. And if the mast is poorly grounded, *side flashes*—a leap from the mast to other parts of the boat—can also cause injury. Even with a good ground, it is wise to stay well away from the mast during an electrical storm.

WOODEN MASTS

IF YOUR BOAT has a wooden mast, you need a metal lightning rod extending above everything at the masthead by at least 6 inches (15 cm) and connected to ground with #4 AWG wire. Without the metal rod, wooden masts struck by lightning tend to blow apart as the high resistance generates enough heat to instantly convert moisture in the wood to steam. A pointed dissipator, called an *air terminal*, makes a fine lightning rod.

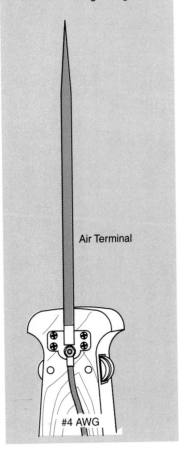

Air Terminal

#4 AWG

GROUND

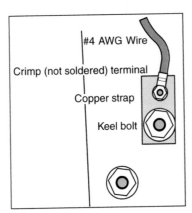

#4 AWG Wire

Crimp (not soldered) terminal

Copper strap

Keel bolt

A metal keel makes an excellent ground for a lightning protection system. Bottom paint does not act as a significant barrier to a strike that has gotten this far in its quest to reach the water.

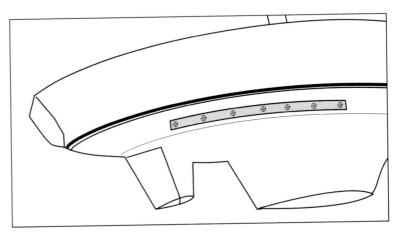

If your keel is encapsulated, a copper ground plate is needed. Lightning dissipates from the edge of the plate, so the perimeter of the plate should be at least 4 feet (1.2 m) if you sail in salt water. If there is any chance that you might sail in freshwater, the ground plate should have at least 24 feet (7.3 m) of sharp edge, usually accomplished by attaching a 12-foot (3.7 m) length of 1-inch (2.5 cm) copper strap fore and aft. Bronze bolts are preferred over stainless steel for bolting the plate to the hull and for cable attachment.

Sintered bronze plates designed for grounding radios are a poor choice for conducting lightning to ground. They are less effective than solid copper at dissipating the charge of a strike, and reportedly they tend to explode when heat from the strike turns trapped water to steam.

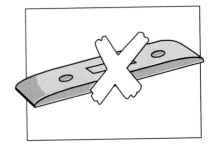

Do not route the strike through the engine. The propeller might have enough edge length to do the job in salt water, but passing such high voltage through the engine can damage the bearings. Likewise, never ground the mast to a sea cock. The lack of adequate conductivity is almost certain to generate enough heat to melt the fitting right out of the hull. And then where are you?

DIRECTING THE CHARGE

Connect the mast to the underwater ground with #4 AWG or larger cable. Because lightning travels on the surface of the conductor, solid copper strap is an even better choice. I like ½-inch copper tubing (water pipe), first radiused then flattened.

Lightning doesn't like to change direction, so conductors should lead as straight as possible to the ground. If a turn is required, give it a radius of 12 inches (30 cm) or more. Even if your mast sits directly on the keel, perfect the electrical connection with a copper strap from the mast to a keel bolt.

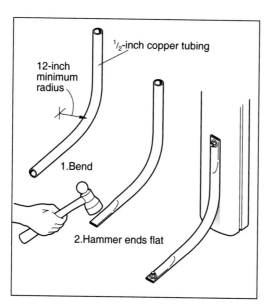

½-inch copper tubing

12-inch minimum radius

1. Bend

2. Hammer ends flat

CONNECTIONS

The electrical connections must be perfect. The current flow in a lightning strike ranges from around 20,000 to nearly 400,000 amps, so a 1-ohm resistance can cause a 400,000-volt difference (I x R) from one side of the connection to the other. The result is enough heat to vaporize metal, and the resistance may encourage dangerous side flashes.

Drill attachment holes in the ends of copper strap. Cable connections should be made with mechanically attached terminals—solder will melt. Be sure all connections are clean and tight, and use copper washers to increase the contact area—except use stainless steel washers on the mast connection to minimize corrosion. Coat the assembled connection with an anti-corrosion spray, and disassemble and clean it at least once a year to make sure it stays resistance-free. Periodically check the resistance from the mast to the ground plate with your ohmmeter.

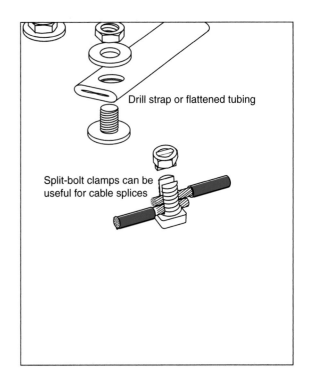

Drill strap or flattened tubing

Split-bolt clamps can be useful for cable splices

PARALLEL PATHS

Although an aluminum mast offers lower resistance than steel stays, a powerful strike may nevertheless induce current flow in stays and shrouds. To provide this current a safe path to ground, the chainplates should also be connected to the underwater ground. Here again, the route should be as direct as possible with only large radius changes of direction. You can use #6 AWG for these secondary grounding paths.

Salt water grounding plate

BONDING

The original idea behind bonding was to put all underwater fittings at the same potential to stop galvanic corrosion. Unfortunately, this type of bonding invites more-destructive stray-current corrosion. Bonding is still intended to put fittings at the same potential, but today the purpose is to prevent side flashes from voltage differences in the event of a lightning strike.

The rules for bonding are simple: bond all sizable metal components within 6 feet (1.8 m) of the mast or rigging to the mast ground, but do not bond any submerged metal (ground plate excepted).

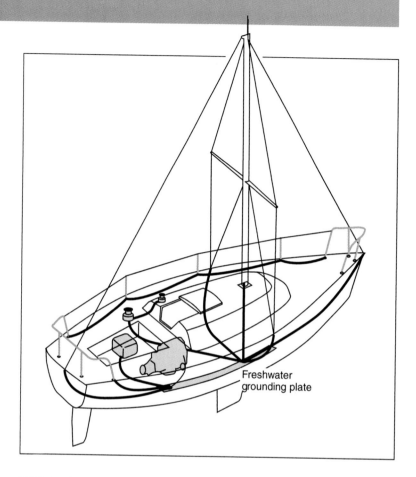

Freshwater grounding plate

FOR LIGHTNING PROTECTION

During a lightning strike, when the mast has a potential of 30,000 volts and other metal components inside the boat are essentially at 0 volts, there is some risk of the lightning jumping to the lower potential. This is called a *side flash* and it is extremely dangerous to anyone in its path. To minimize this risk, give the charge a lower-resistance path by connecting all significant metal masses (e.g., tanks, stove, lifelines) within 6 feet (1.8 m) of the mast or rigging to the ground plate. Use #6 AWG wire (or larger), and connect each component to the ground with a dedicated wire.

FOR CORROSION CONTROL

If underwater components are not galvanically identical, bonding them completes the circuit and *causes* corrosion (which must be controlled with zinc anodes). Bonding does protect underwater fittings from damage caused by onboard stray currents, but it invites damage from stray currents in the water, and "hot" marinas are today the rule rather than the exception. It is easy enough to avoid onboard stray currents with good wiring practices, but you have no control over stray currents in the water. *No good can come from bonding underwater metal components that are or could be otherwise isolated.*

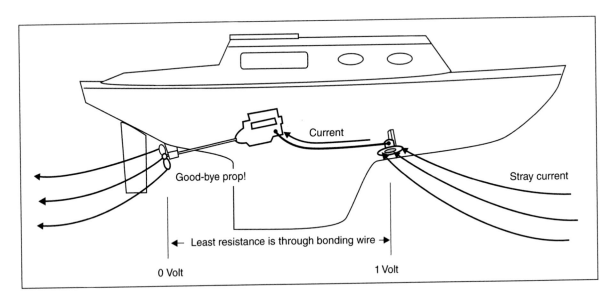

ISOLATING

Metal through-hulls connected to rubber hose are already isolated. Likewise, the rudder shaft and/or fittings are normally isolated, but be sure components are not grounded some other way. For example, the rudder might be connected to the boat's central ground through steering cables and pedestal wiring. A fuel tank connected to the engine with metal fuel line is likewise electrically connected to the DC ground. In this latter case, bonding the tank for lightning protection provides a path for stray current to enter your boat at the ground plate and pass out at the prop (or vice versa).

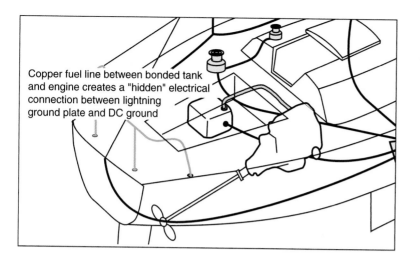

Copper fuel line between bonded tank and engine creates a "hidden" electrical connection between lightning ground plate and DC ground

Isolate bonded tanks by inserting a section of rubber hose in the fuel line. The propeller and shaft are easily isolated with a flexible coupling. (Note: A zinc collar is still required to protect the bronze prop if the shaft is steel.)

GROUNDING

The general rule for corrosion control is to bond to a single underwater component. This eliminates any possibility of providing a circuit for stray current, and it also eliminates galvanic currents except between dissimilar metals in contact. The preferred configuration is to isolate the propeller shaft from the engine so the prop doesn't provide a ground, then use the lightning grounding plate for all ground connections. If the engine is not isolated, the necessity for ground near the base of the mast means you will have two bonded components in the water. Copper and bronze are close enough on the galvanic scale that significant galvanic corrosion is not likely, but stray current corrosion is a risk. The solution in this case is to keep the lightning ground electrically separated from the engine ground (for the DC and AC circuits).

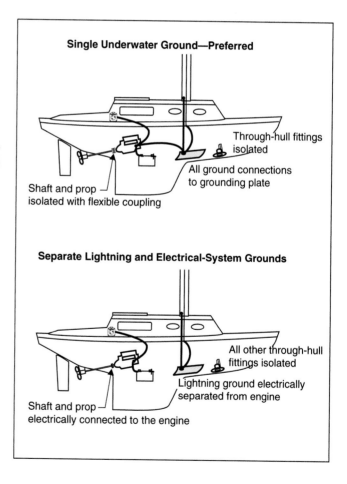

Single Underwater Ground—Preferred

Through-hull fittings isolated

All ground connections to grounding plate

Shaft and prop isolated with flexible coupling

Separate Lightning and Electrical-System Grounds

All other through-hull fittings isolated

Lightning ground electrically separated from engine

Shaft and prop electrically connected to the engine

TESTING FOR ISOLATION

Measure the resistance between the lightning ground terminal and the DC ground terminal. In salt water the meter should read around 200 kΩ per foot of underwater separation between the ground plate and the stern tube, about 2 MΩ per foot in freshwater. A low resistance reading reveals a connection between the two grounds. Disconnect one bonding cable at a time until the meter reading changes: the unwanted connection is through the just-disconnected component.

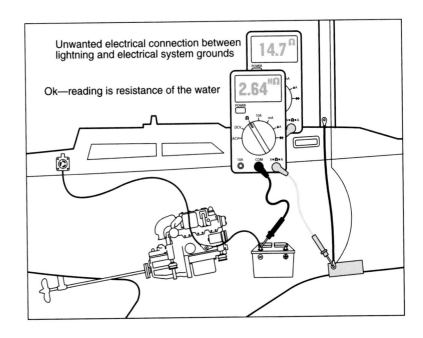

Unwanted electrical connection between lightning and electrical system grounds

14.7 Ω

Ok—reading is resistance of the water

2.64 MΩ

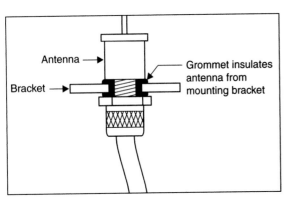

Antenna →

Bracket →

Grommet insulates antenna from mounting bracket

Often you will find that the connection is through the mast, usually due to contact between a masthead antenna bracket and the coax shield. You can break this connection by installing insulating grommets around the bracket mounting bolts or in the antenna-mount hole.

Radio equipment may also be grounded to the engine and other metal components in the boat. If it is also connected to the lightning ground plate—as it should be—this is another electrical connection between the lightning ground and the DC ground. We deal with this problem below.

RF GROUND

SB and ham radios need a good ground to provide the necessary counterpoise for transmission—like planting your feet to jump or throw. A good radio ground is a large mass of metal very close to but not necessarily touching seawater. This is usually accommodated by grounding the radio to the engine, other large metal components, and to the water through a ground plate. The lightning ground plate serves well.

RIBBON, NOT WIRE

Radio grounds should be made with copper foil ribbon, not wire, because the current we want the conductor to carry is RF (radio frequency), not DC. RF currents travel on the surface of the conductor (lightning is also an RF event), so the more surface, the less the conductor impedes the RF current. This essentially means less of your radio's power is wasted in the ground system, so more is radiated from your antenna. That translates into longer range and clearer signals.

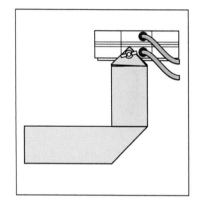

Use 3-inch-wide (7.6 cm) foil ribbon for the best RF ground connection. Fold the ends into a point for terminal attachment. Bend the foil around corners and obstacles as shown.

COPPER SCREEN

Today's automatic antenna tuners compensate for a less-than-perfect counterpoise, so few boats bother with "building" a counterpoise, relying instead on the metal masses already in the boat combined with a good "connection" to the ocean. Still, for the best radio installation, about 100 square feet (9.3 m²) of copper screening inside the hull can avoid a lot of transmission problems. Hardware stores sell copper screening for windows inexpensively, and it is easy to install in below-the-waterline lockers, covered with a layer of lightweight fiberglass cloth. However, because the wire in the screening is just woven together, corrosion may eventually degrade their electrical contact. Soldering two edges before installation avoids this problem. Join the various screen panels with 3-inch (7.6 cm) foil tape, also soldered.

STOPPING DIRECT CURRENT

Not only does the RF ground system not need to carry DC, but we don't want it to because that allows the flow of destructive stray current. This is easily prevented by cutting the foil ribbon leading to the ground plate and installing the ends on a double bus circuit block, leaving a gap of about $^1/_{16}$ inch. Now bridge the gap with a 0.15μF ceramic capacitor (available for under a buck from most electronics suppliers). You can solder the capacitor to the ribbon, or if the leads are long enough, simply capture them under an opposing pair of the terminal screws. The capacitor passes RF current but blocks DC.

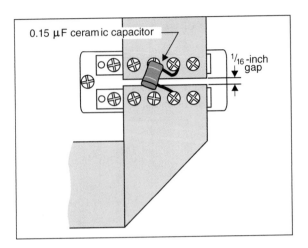

If other metal components bonded for lightning protection are also connected to the RF ground system, disconnect RF connections from the components to the radio and make them to the ground plate. Configured this way, a single capacitor will separate the DC ground from the RF ground. If your foil is thick enough—at least 9 mils (0.009 inches)—you can substitute the ribbon for the wire; otherwise connect the ribbon parallel to the #6 AWG bonding wire.

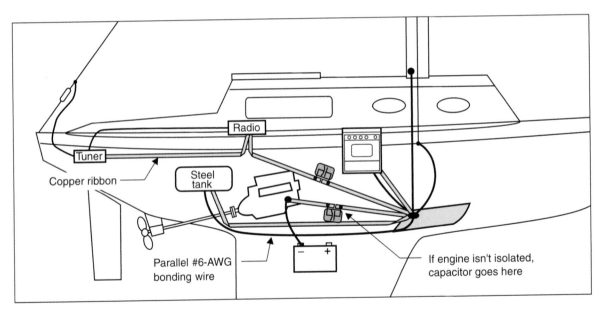

LIGHTNING AND ELECTRONICS

While a lightning-protection system can nearly eliminate personal risk and significantly reduce damage to the boat, it offers little if any protection for electronics. About half the boats struck by lightning experience damage to some or all of the electronics aboard.

THE FACTS

Like any moving current, lightning can induce current to flow in any conductor it passes near. Considering the enormous power of lightning, "near" might well be 100 yards or more. The closer and more powerful the strike, the more current that is induced. Such currents often exceed the capacity of the tiny, low-current components inside most electronics. Since electronics need not be connected to anything to be affected, disconnecting them does not prevent damage.

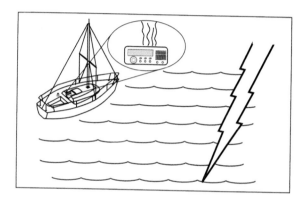

PROTECTIVE MEASURES

A surge protector in the supply line may provide protection for a limited range of lightning-induced power spikes. Twist all electronics power leads so induced currents will tend to cancel. All bonding wires should cross electrical wiring at 90 degrees to minimize the inductive effect of current flowing to ground. Grounding the chassis—the metal housing—protects internal circuits and components from directly induced currents. But despite every protective effort, if your boat is struck, your electronics have only one chance in two of not becoming toast. So the best protective measure is keeping your insurance paid up.

"The secret to a troublefree engine isn't knowing how to repair it, but knowing how to maintain it so you don't *have* to repair it."

DIESELS

Troubleshooting
Marine
Diesels

Peter Compton

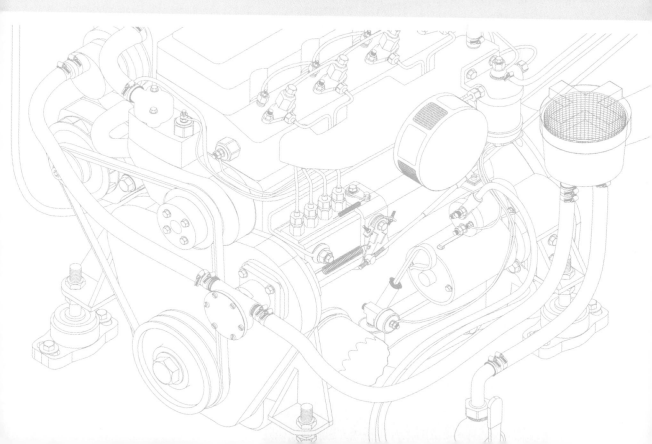

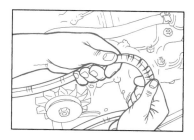
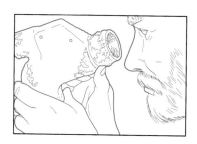
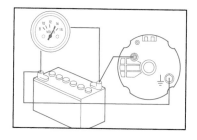

INTRODUCTION

"Knock! Knock!" says the owner as his head pops out of the engine bay.

"Who's there?" says I, playing the game.

"No! No! You bloody fool—the engine went 'knock knock,' then 'screech,' before it died!"

Down in the engine room, we find the crankshaft totally seized. The bilge is full of oil, and nothing shows on the dipstick. Thirty seconds later, we locate the culprit—the oil pipe to the engine-oil cooler had chafed through after months of rubbing against a rear engine mount. All the oil pumped into the bilge as the owner happily motored through the Virgin Islands. It probably happened so quickly that *anyone* would have been lucky to notice the drop in oil pressure on the gauge. Still, why didn't the low–oil-pressure switch set off the alarm bell? It finally comes out that there had been a short in the bell's wiring, and the owner disconnected the wires because the alarm was too noisy.

Like all such stories, this one has a moral.

If only the owner had fixed the wiring short, the alarm would have given him enough warning to shut down the engine before any serious damage occurred. A daily check on the engine might have spotted a drop in oil level on the dipstick or excess oil in the bilge. Certainly, a more thorough inspection would have picked up the chafed hose long before it failed. The consequences were expensive: a new engine, three weeks stuck in a marina waiting for the replacement to be shipped from the States, and another expensive week having it professionally installed.

The secret to a troublefree engine isn't knowing how to repair it, but knowing how to maintain it so you don't have *to repair it.*

This book offers a detailed approach to diesel maintenance from the owner's point of view. It doesn't delve into theory or look at overhauls and repairs that require special skills, tools, manuals, or a workshop.

Determining the cause of a problem can be a mind-boggling task. In many cases, the symptoms lead straight to the obvious cause. More often, though, a problem can stem from one of many faults and produce one or more symptoms. As in medicine, the diagnosis is not always straightforward. Frequently, there is insufficient evidence to confirm the cause at first glance; you may have to examine individual components or conduct further tests in a process of elimination.

The Troubleshooting Charts in Chapter 2, in combination with the System Fault Tables at the end of each chapter, cover most marine diesel problems and should make the diagnostic process easier.

The reality of diesel maintenance is far from the ideal workbench conditions most manuals show. Often you'll be hanging upside down, squeezed into an impossible position, trying to unscrew a drain plug you can feel only with the fingertips of your left hand. If you lose it, you know it's headed straight into the bilge. Space will always be at a premium in a sailboat, and difficult access can make it tempting to put off maintenance for another day. Make the effort—you'll

enjoy sailing much more knowing that the "Iron Genny" is always there when you need it.

If I've done my part well this book should soon be covered in oily fingerprints. It should save you big bucks—and probably put me out of a job.

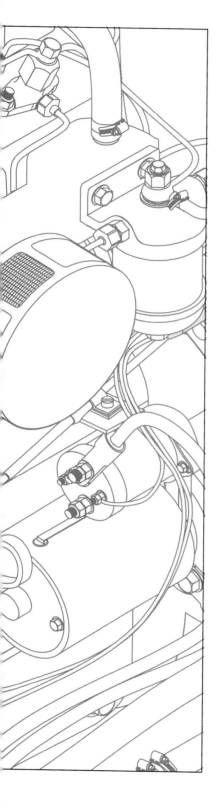

MAINTAINING YOUR DIESEL

MAINTENANCE TASK	FREQUENCY
Full System Inspection	seasonally
Mechanical System	
Check valve clearances	every 250* hours
Check cylinder head torque	after first 50 hours
Check engine alignment	every 250* hours
Oil System	
Check for leaks	daily
Check oil level	daily
Change oil	after first 50 hours & every 125* hours
Change oil filter	after first 50 hours & every 125* hours
Coolant Circuit	
Check coolant level	daily
Change coolant	every 250* hours
Check fan belt tension	daily
Raw-Water Circuit	
Check raw-water flow	daily
Check impeller	every 250* hours
Check heat exchangers & oil coolers	every 250* hours
Fuel System	
Check primary filter bowl	daily
Change primary fuel filter	every 125* hours
Change secondary fuel filter	every 250* hours
Test injectors	every 1,000 hours
Intake and Exhaust Systems	
Change paper and foam type intake filters	every 250* hours
Clean metal intake filters	every 250* hours
Electrical System	
Check battery fluid	after first 50 hours & every 125* hours
Transmissions	
Check fluid level	after first 50 hours & every 125* hours
Corrosion Protection	
Inspect and rectify as necessary	daily

* or seasonally, whichever comes first

A diesel engine, properly installed and maintained, will give thousands of hours of reliable service. Sadly, few marine diesels fitted to pleasure craft ever have the chance to wear out; poor maintenance condemns nearly all of them.

"If it ain't broke, don't fix it!" Like most sayings, this one contains an element of truth. Unfortunately, most boatowners—and quite a few professionals—treat it as gospel. How wrong they are!

Think safety for a moment. Visualize a so-called safe anchorage. A violent squall screams through in the wee hours, the wind veers, the hook trips, and suddenly the boat is beam-on, dragging toward concrete docks. You press the start button, but nothing happens.

Think money. Maintenance procedures are relatively inexpensive. Major repairs caused by poor maintenance are anything but.

Think time. Boating is about fun, relaxation, and leisure. A well-planned trip, whether it's a day sail, a weekend downriver, or that dream bluewater cruise, can quickly turn into an oily, stress-filled disaster, with more time spent stripping diesels than sipping sundowners.

"If it ain't broke, don't fix it" may appear to work in the short term, but each time you ignore your diesel, you notch up another IOU. One day you'll have to pay—big time.

A better maxim might be: "Look after your diesel and it will look after you." More than 99 percent of problems can be avoided with good maintenance. Whether you're mechanically minded or employ others to do the work, don't put yourself and your crew at risk with a poorly maintained, unreliable engine.

GOOD OPERATING PROCEDURE

A solid maintenance program includes operating a diesel within its designed limits:

- Keep the engine clean; layers of oil and dirt can hide many problems.
- Keep fuel clean and free of water.
- Keep engine free of corrosion.
- Inspect daily before starting.
- Check-start the engine well before departure.
- Allow the engine to reach operating temperature before heading out.
- Avoid prolonged idling.
- Avoid overloading the engine.
- Allow the engine to cool before shutting it down.

ROUTINE MAINTENANCE

Whether you call it routine, scheduled, or preventive maintenance, rare is the owner who habitually carries out the few tasks necessary to keep a diesel engine running reliably. Without regular trips to the engine bay, you miss the opportunity to look over the engine for unexpected problems and to correct them before they jeopardize your safety, time, and money.

Even an engine that is working well will slowly deteriorate with normal use. Regularly scheduled preventive maintenance tasks lessen the effects of such wear and tear before noticeably affecting performance and reliability. Inspect V-belts, fuel filters, and fluid levels daily. Take time to examine the engine for anything amiss. In addition to looking for loose and broken parts, check for leaks and belt dust—telltale signs of other problems. Always treat corrosion *before* it eats important and expensive components. Replace suspect hoses and clamps *before* they have a chance to fail. Follow your engine's maintenance schedule or, if you don't have a manual, follow the recommendations on page 589. Once every season, carry out a more thorough inspection of each engine system, as detailed in later chapters.

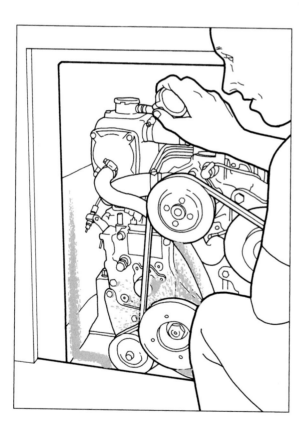

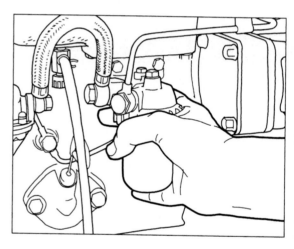

SURVEYING THE ENGINE: THE INITIAL INSPECTION

There are several occasions when you should survey the diesel's condition, even though it appears to be running well. Whether you're buying or selling a boat, getting ready for that once-in-a-lifetime bluewater cruise, or simply preparing for the coming season, performing a thorough engine survey will reduce the chances of an unexpected failure, and boost your peace of mind every time you need the diesel.

THE VISUAL INSPECTION

The engine compartment's general condition can indicate how well the diesel has been maintained. A clean, neatly painted engine suggests good care. On the other hand, a few layers of paint can hide a multitude of problems. Look in those awkward places where a brush or spray couldn't reach.

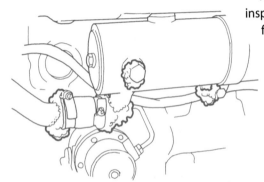

The following table lists each engine system and the items to inspect. The cross-reference column points to more detailed information elsewhere in the book.

Run methodically through each of these tasks, and you'll cover more than most mechanics do during a full engine survey.

COMPONENT	CHECK FOR	PAGE
Mechanical System (Chapter 3)		
Engine block	loose components, cracks, corrosion	—
Crankshaft	free rotation	606
Freeze plugs	leaks, corrosion	629
Cylinder-head gasket	leaks	630
Engine mounts	loose nuts, corrosion	634
Engine alignment	easy shaft rotation	635
Lubrication System (Chapter 4)		
System	external oil leaks	643
Oil	correct level, condition of oil, contamination	641
Oil cooler	leaks, corrosion	665

COMPONENT	CHECK FOR	PAGE
Raw-Water Circuit (Chapter 5)		
Through-hull fitting and valve	operation, leaks, corrosion	658
Raw-water strainer	debris, corrosion, leaks	658
Hoses, pipes, and clamps	deterioration, chafe, corrosion, tightness	670
Raw-water pump	external leaks, corrosion	659
Heat exchangers	external corrosion, leaks	665
Antisiphon valve	operation	669
Sacrificial anodes or "zincs"	condition	667
Coolant Circuit (Chapter 6)		
Coolant	level, condition	675
Pressure cap	good sealing, correct pressure rating	679
Expansion tank	level, coolant condition	679
V-belt	correct tension, condition	682
Circulating pump	bearing play, seal leakage	681
Header tank	leaks, corrosion, loose fittings	679
Fuel System (Chapter 7)		
Fuel tanks	fillers, vents, fittings, valves, hoses	689
Primary filter	water, dirt, algae growth	690
Lift pump	leaks, external corrosion	691
Secondary filter	external fuel leaks	693
Injector pump	attachment to block, external leaks	695
Injector pipes	leaks, good support, corrosion	—
Intake and Exhaust System (Chapter 8)		
Intake filter	cleanliness	710
Exhaust manifold	loose fittings, leaks, corrosion	711
Exhaust injection elbow	raw-water and exhaust gas leakage, loose attachment, internal restrictions	711
Exhaust hose and clamps	deterioration, corrosion	712
Lift box/muffler	corrosion, splitting, leaks	713
Turbocharger	cleanliness, free rotation	714
Intercooler	corrosion, external leakage	715
Electrical System (Chapter 9)		
Batteries	electrolyte level and specific gravity, voltage, condition of plates and casing	719
Battery switches	connections, corrosion	724
Starter	connections, corrosion	728
Alternator	connections, corrosion	725
Battery isolation diodes	connections, corrosion	—
Wiring	loose wiring, chafing, loose or corroded connections, burned or melted insulation	—
Controls and Instruments (Chapter 10)		
Throttle control	smooth operation, full travel	733
Gear-selector controls	smooth operation, full travel	735
Mechanical stop control	smooth operation, full travel	736
Electrical stop control	loose connections, corrosion	736
Control cables	smooth operation, external corrosion	737
Gauges	water temperature and oil pressure should zero when the ignition is switched on	739

SURVEYING THE ENGINE: THE STARTUP

You can't properly survey an engine without running it. If the boat is out of the water, run a water supply into a bucket with a separate hose connected to the raw-water pump inlet. Running the engine out of the water will not cover all the following checks, but it will give a good indication of engine condition.

Before you start the engine, check:

Throttle mechanism. Check for full and free throttle travel from stop to stop. Be sure to return the throttle arm to the idle stop.

Cable stop mechanism. Check for full and free travel. Ensure the lever returns to the run position.

Solenoid stop mechanism. Check that the wiring is good. In particular, push on connectors that often vibrate loose.

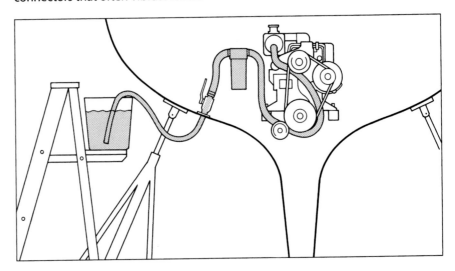

Start the engine and check:

Quick start. A good engine should start instantly, without needing several turns of the crankshaft. Cold-weather starting will take a little longer, since cold metal absorbs heat from the compressed air. If the engine starts slowly, shut it off and start it again. This time it should start immediately. Instant starting confirms that the compression, fuel delivery and atomization, battery, and starter are good. Avoid using starting fluid. If a diesel will not start without starting fluid, it needs repair. If the engine will not start or proves difficult to start, follow the Troubleshooting Charts in Chapter 2.

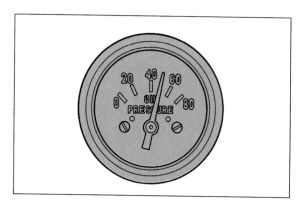

Oil pressure. If the gauge doesn't register oil pressure within 15 seconds of starting, shut down the engine. Pressures vary among engines, and will be higher when the engine is cold. Consistently low oil pressure suggests a worn engine. (Troubleshooting Chart 4)

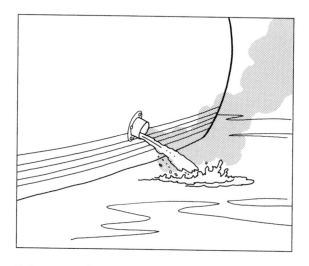

Exhaust smoke. Modern, environmentally friendly engines produce little smoke, but older engines—even those in good condition—may produce light smoke. It is normal to see smoke during and immediately after starting, but it should clear to almost nothing within the first few minutes. (Troubleshooting Chart 5)

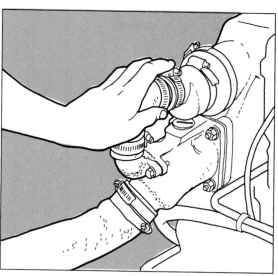

Raw-water circulation. Check that plenty of raw water is coming out of the exhaust outlet (top). The raw-water pipe feeding the exhaust injection elbow should feel warm, not hot or cold (above). (Chapter 8)

Noise and vibration. With the engine running, listen and feel for anything abnormal. (Troubleshooting Chart 7)

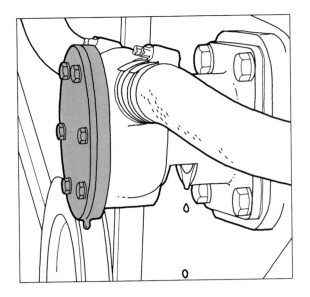

Leaks. Look for oil, coolant, and raw-water leaks. Check for fuel leaks around the injectors. Soot deposits in this area indicate poor gas sealing of the copper seat washers.

Water temperature. Allow the engine temperature to stabilize, and check that it is close to the thermostat rating. There should be little fluctuation. (Troubleshooting Chart 6)

Charging. Check the alternator output. The charging light should go out immediately after startup, although some installations require rpm to be increased above idle. An ammeter fitted in the circuit will show output as soon as the alternator starts charging. Standard alternators will initially charge at a high rate, but decrease rapidly as battery voltage increases. Voltage regulators typically control voltage at 14 to 14.5 volts. Measure voltage between the alternator's positive output terminal and casing ground to confirm output. (Troubleshooting Chart 9)

Transmission. Check for positive engagement in both forward and reverse.

No-load rpm. If a tachometer is fitted, briefly push the throttle to maximum and check the rpm.

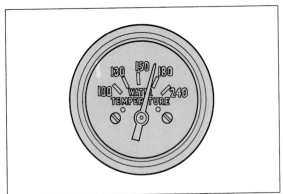

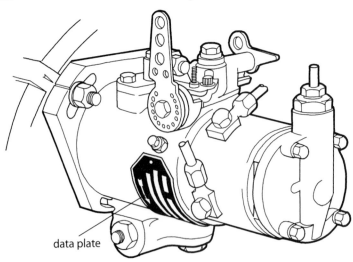

data plate

The engine should be within 10% of its rated rpm, which is usually stamped on the injector-pump data plate or can be listed in the engine specifications. Failure to reach rated no-load rpm could be due to a faulty tachometer, but more often suggests other problems. (Troubleshooting Chart 3)

SURVEYING THE ENGINE: THE SEA TRIAL

Take the boat out to a clear stretch of calm water and operate the engine at gradually increasing rpm. Visually inspect the engine while it is under load, and look for leaks and vibrating components. Note the oil pressure, water temperature, and any exhaust smoke.

Check maximum achievable rpm. Most small engine manufacturers define a **maximum intermittent rating** for their engines. Theoretically, with a correctly matched transmission and propeller, an engine should reach this rating at the same time as a displacement vessel reaches hull speed. Provided the engine is normally operated below 90% of this rpm, the engine should not be overloaded and will still have a little in reserve when needed. Cruising sailors and certainly commercial operators looking for maximum service from an engine should match the transmission and propeller to the manufacturer's **maximum continuous rating**. (Troubleshooting Chart 3)

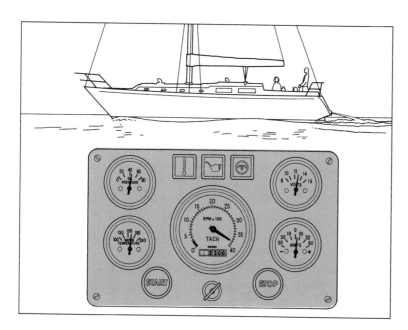

PREVENTING CORROSION

Corrosion is the natural deterioration of metals, due mostly to their surface reaction with oxygen. This reaction usually is chemical or electrochemical and is accelerated by the presence of water and heat. Electrochemical or electrolytic corrosion occurs through a reaction between dissimilar metals in the presence of water or chemicals that form an electrolyte.

Considering the combination of hot metal, hot exhaust gases, and sea-water to which they're exposed, it's not surprising that most engines head for the diesel graveyard long before they wear out. Corrosion is the marine diesel's number one enemy. During the life of the average diesel, owners will spend more money on corrosion-induced failures than any other cause.

Tell-tale signs of corrosion are:

Iron and steel: Brown or black staining, dust, or flakes.
Stainless steel: Black spots usually in areas starved of oxygen.
Aluminum: White powder or crystals of aluminum chloride.
Bronze, brass, and copper: Green staining or powder. Severe corrosion will
   dezincify base metal, leaving a copper-colored light pink.

With minimal forethought and regular maintenance, you can avoid nearly all corrosion problems. Just follow the two cardinal rules: Prevent water and chemicals from contacting bare metal; and keep dissimilar metals apart.

PAINT

The simplest way to protect metal surfaces is with a good layer of paint—a common practice with marine engines. Unfortunately, normal wear and tear and routine maintenance take a toll on paint finishes, exposing bare metal that will corrode rapidly. Don't rely on paint coverage alone.

CORROSION INHIBITORS

For additional protection, spray on a soft, protective, water-repellent layer of oils or waxes. There are several brands of inhibitors. Thinner oils provide good coverage for short-term protection; they're easy to apply and remove and are best suited to spotless engines with good paint coverage and no corrosion.

Thicker, heavy-duty corrosion inhibitors provide much more durable protection and can even be applied over corroded components. Good inhibitors remain soft and flexible but have the disadvantage of collecting dirt over time.

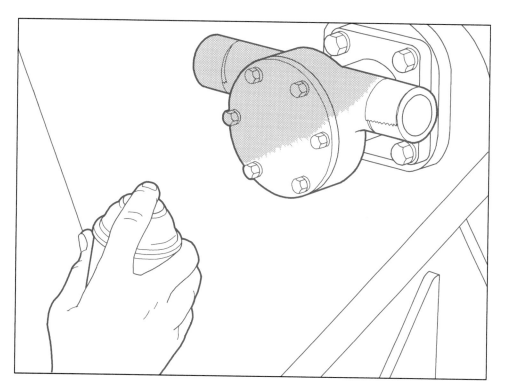

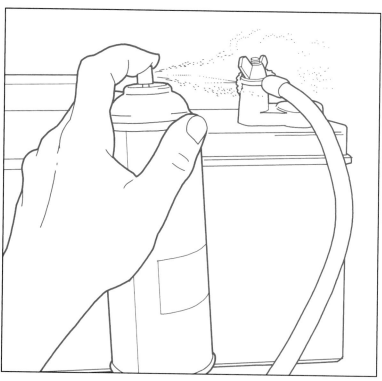

LAYING UP OR "WINTERIZING" A DIESEL

This procedure protects the engine inside and out against the elements and should be carried out whenever the engine will not be used for an extended period. The following steps are fairly standard regardless of climate:

1. Drain the coolant, opening all engine, heat-exchanger, and oil-cooler drains.
2. Replace the coolant with a clean, fresh, 50/50 mixture of water and antifreeze.
3. Replace the oil and oil filter. Normal combustion produces corrosive acids that are absorbed by the oil. Leaving dirty oil in the engine for an extended time allows these acids to attack and damage bearing surfaces.
4. Replace the fuel filter elements—draining any water from the filter bowls.
5. Bleed the fuel system of air.
6. Run the engine up to operating temperature.
7. Top off coolant and oil.
8. Close the raw-water inlet seacock.
9. Remove the raw-water pump impeller.
10. Backflush the raw-water circuit to remove corrosive salts by connecting a freshwater supply to the raw-water hose that feeds the exhaust injection elbow.
11. Drain the raw-water circuit thoroughly.
12. Fully charge the batteries. Disconnect all leads. Unattended, a battery naturally discharges over a period of several weeks. The electrolyte on a discharged battery can freeze at 20°F (–7°C), so keep the batteries fully charged or, better still, remove them to a warmer storage area. Small automatic trickle chargers work well.
13. Treat battery and cable terminals with petroleum jelly, silicone grease, or a heavy-duty corrosion inhibitor.
14. Protect external surfaces with a heavy-duty corrosion inhibitor.
15. Cover the engine with a waterproof sheet in case there are any leaks from above.

Points to remember:

- Filling the raw-water circuit with antifreeze will swell raw-water pump impellers and render them useless. Remove the impeller first if you are using antifreeze.
- Each time you visit the boat, additional protection can be achieved using the starter to turn the engine over and circulate oil to the bearings and cylinder walls. Remember to pull out the stop cable and keep turning until the low oil pressure light extinguishes or pressure registers on the gauge.

- Special inhibiting oils are available that provide greater protection. Use these to replace the standard engine oil; run the engine briefly to coat all surfaces, and then drain the oil. Protection remains good, provided the engine is not turned.
- If the engine cannot be fully winterized, replace oil, coolant, and all filters and run the engine up to operating temperatures monthly if possible.

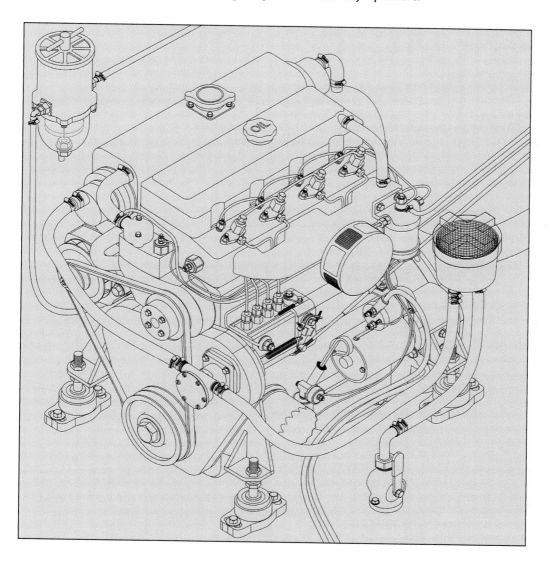

TROUBLESHOOTING MARINE DIESELS

Troubleshooting a sick diesel calls heavily on experience, a thorough knowledge of diesel operating principles, and most of all, the ability to think logically. Don't worry if you're missing the first two—that's where the troubleshooting charts below come in. Organize your thoughts as follows:

IDENTIFY THE SYMPTOMS

Ask yourself these few simple questions to get started.

- ❑ Did the problem occur suddenly or did it gradually worsen? Sudden problems are usually due to a blockage or component failure. Gradual worsening is most often caused by wear or slow degradation from contamination, corrosion, or dirt.
- ❑ Has anyone worked on the engine recently? Many problems are maintenance induced; perhaps a part was reassembled incorrectly.
- ❑ Was there excess smoke? Color and quantity of exhaust smoke is a helpful indicator. (See Chart 5.)
- ❑ Were there any unusual noises? Noise will often lead you to the problem, but keep an open mind: Noise in one area can be caused by

a problem elsewhere. (See Chart 7.)
- ❑ Was there any unusual vibration? Same as above.
- ❑ What was the rpm doing? A sudden racing, slowing, or dying means something. (See Chart 3.)
- ❑ Has the engine lost power? (See Chart 3.)
- ❑ Was the oil pressure normal? Loss of oil pressure can lead to serious mechanical problems. (See Chart 4.)
- ❑ Was the water temperature normal? (See Chart 6.)
- ❑ Did the alarm sound? Low oil pressure or high water temperature trigger the alarm circuit. (See Charts 4 and 6.)
- ❑ Will the engine restart? (See Chart 1.)

USING THE TROUBLESHOOTING CHARTS AND SYSTEM FAULT TABLES THROUGHOUT THIS BOOK

❑ The Troubleshooting Charts in this chapter are simple flow diagrams that lead from symptoms to a list of possible causes.

❑ The Fault Tables at the end of the system chapters look at each component and list its common modes of failure, causes, and possible symptoms.

Approach the charts and tables with common sense and treat them purely as tools to guide you in the right direction. They were compiled primarily for four-stroke, water-cooled diesels and cover the majority of problems you may encounter with these engines. Nevertheless, owners of air-cooled or two-stroke diesels should also find the charts valuable.

REMEMBER THE "HOW LIKELY" FACTOR

Use the following probability factors as a general guide in the Troubleshooting Charts and the System Fault Tables. Direct your initial investigation toward faults with a factor of 1, 2, or 3, until additional information points you elsewhere.

[1]	Very Common	Occurs very frequently; check this first.
[2]	Common	Occurs fairly frequently.
[3]	Possible	Does not occur too often.
[4]	Rare	May never occur in the life of the average diesel.
[5]	Very Rare	Theoretically possible, but few mechanics will ever see it. Don't waste too much time exploring this possibility unless you've tried everything else.

CHART

1

TROUBLESHOOTING MARINE DIESELS—START HERE

Diesel engine problems, at their most basic, usually fall into one of three categories: engine fails to start, engine not running correctly, or engine fails to stop. More specific symptoms flow from these three options. Always start here when troubleshooting a problem with your diesel.

ENGINE FAILS TO START

ENGINE DOES NOT TURN

1. **Confirm the engine turns over freely.** GO TO CHART **2**

2. **Confirm the starting system is working correctly.** GO TO CHART **8**

ENGINE TURNS SLOWLY

1. **Is the oil viscosity correct? Too heavy an oil will make the engine difficult to turn over, especially in cold weather.**  GO TO Chapter 4

2. **Confirm the engine will turn over freely.** GO TO CHART **2**

3. **Confirm the starting system is working correctly.** GO TO CHART **8**

ENGINE TURNS NORMALLY— BUT FAILS TO START

1. **Check fuel is reaching the injectors.** GO TO CHART **11**

2. **Check the intake and exhaust systems for restrictions.**  GO TO Chapter 8

3. **Check for good compression.** GO TO Chapter 4

4. **If you have not found a fault at this stage then your problems are becoming more serious. Before you take further action recheck the above systems thoroughly.**

ENGINE NOT RUNNING CORRECTLY

PERFORMANCE
PROBLEMS

STARTING SYSTEM
PROBLEMS

OIL PROBLEMS

CHARGING SYSTEM
PROBLEMS

SMOKE PROBLEMS

TURBOCHARGER
PROBLEMS

TEMPERATURE
PROBLEMS

FUEL PROBLEMS

NOISE AND VIBRATION
PROBLEMS

SHUT DOWN

ENGINE FAILS TO STOP

CHART 2

CHECK CRANKSHAFT TURNS FREELY

If you suspect a mechanical problem, turning the engine over slowly by hand will allow you to feel any abnormal resistance. Use a wrench on a convenient crankshaft bolt to turn the engine in its normal direction of rotation—clockwise when viewed from the front. If no crankshaft bolt is accessible, use the alternator pulley nut and apply pressure to the middle of the belt to stop slipping. You must turn the crankshaft of a four-stroke engine at least two full turns before you can be sure the pistons are not hitting anything they shouldn't!

NO MOVEMENT

A. Engine stopped suddenly
Probably due to overheating or lack of lubrication.

CAUSES:

- ❏ Piston seized in cylinder [3]
- ❏ Main bearings seized [4]
- ❏ Rod bearings seized [4]

B. Engine ran well when last used
Probably caused by corrosion.

CAUSES:

- ❏ Raw water in the cylinder head [2]
- ❏ Starter seized with the gear engaged [4]

TURNS SLIGHTLY IN EACH DIRECTION

Slight movement in both directions suggests the crankshaft is able to move but a component attached to the timing gears is broken or seized.

CAUSES:

- ❏ Gearbox seized [3]
- ❏ Gear-driven pump seized [4]
- ❏ Timing gears jammed or seized [4]
- ❏ Camshaft followers seized [4]
- ❏ Camshaft seized [5]

HOW LIKELY?   [1] Very common   [2] Common   [3] Possible   [4] Rare   [5] Very rare

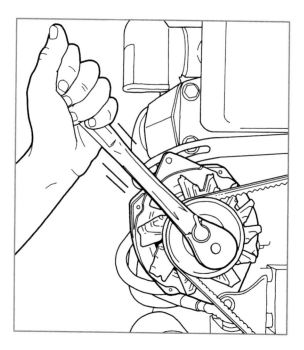

TIGHT AND DIFFICULT TO TURN

Before you strip the engine, remember that as each piston reaches the top of its compression stroke, considerably more effort is required to turn the engine over. This is normal. If you are not sure that compression is the reason it's tight, remove the injectors and turn the engine over again.

CAUSES:

❏ Normal compression   [2]
❏ Gearbox still selected   [2]
❏ Piston rings/cylinders scuffing   [4]
❏ Bearings binding   [4]
❏ Starter gear jammed in flywheel ring gear   [4]

TURNS BUT LOCKS UP IN BOTH DIRECTIONS

Easy movement during crankshaft rotation that stops solidly suggests a reciprocating component is broken or locking up. Before stripping the engine, remove the injectors to check for fluid—particularly water—in the cylinder.

CAUSES:

❏ Water, coolant, oil, or fuel in cylinder   [2]
❏ Connecting rod broken   [4]
❏ Valve dropped into cylinder   [4]
❏ Cam followers seized   [4]
❏ Crankshaft broken   [5]

PERFORMANCE PROBLEMS

A change in performance can be sudden or gradual. It covers everything from a slight drop in maximum rpm to the engine dying unexpectedly. Remember the basic rules: Sudden change suggests a defect or failure; gradual change suggests degradation from wear or contamination.

LOSS OF POWER

Check no-load rpm first—see Chapter 1.

If rpm is within 10% of governor setting, most likely cause of power loss is overloading. If rpm fails to get within 10% of setting, check fuel, air, and compression.

CAUSES:

A. Overloading (expect dark exhaust smoke)
- ❏ Propeller dirty [1]
- ❏ Boat bottom dirty [1]
- ❏ Transmission or prop shaft binding [2]
- ❏ Incorrect propeller [3]
- ❏ Incorrect transmission ratio [3]

B. Poor fuel supply
- ❏ Injector defective [1]
- ❏ Air in fuel system [1]
- ❏ Fuel filter contaminated [2]
- ❏ Water in fuel [2]
- ❏ Control cable travel restricted [3]
- ❏ Two sealing washers under injector [3]
- ❏ Injector pipes leaking [3]
- ❏ Lift pump defective [4]
- ❏ Injector pump contaminated [4]
- ❏ Fuel tank vent restricted [4]
- ❏ Governor sticking [4]
- ❏ Fuel grade incorrect [4]
- ❏ Incorrect timing [4]

C. Restricted air supply (expect dark exhaust smoke)
- ❏ Restricted air intake [2]
- ❏ Restricted exhaust [3]

D. Compression low
- ❏ Valve clearances incorrect [3]
- ❏ Valve seats worn [3]
- ❏ Piston rings worn or broken and cylinders worn [3]

E. Oil system
- ❏ Incorrect oil grade [4]

ENGINE DIES

Common cause is restricted primary filter. If so, engine usually restarts if left for a few minutes while the fuel filters through, but will shut down soon after.

CAUSES:

A. Restricted fuel supply
- ❏ Air in fuel system [1]
- ❏ Fuel filter clogged [1]
- ❏ Water in fuel [2]
- ❏ Fuel tank empty [3]
- ❏ Fuel tank vent restricted [3]
- ❏ Lift pump defective [4]
- ❏ Governor failure [5]

HOW LIKELY? [1] Very common [2] Common [3] Possible [4] Rare [5] Very rare

- Air in fuel system [2]
- Water in fuel [3]
- Injection timing incorrect [4]
- Governor linkage sticking [4]
- Governor defective [4]

B. Erratic compression

- Intake or exhaust valve sticking [4]

DECELERATION POOR

When the throttle setting is decreased, engine maintains rpm or is slow to decelerate.

CAUSES:

- Throttle-lever return spring tired or broken [3]
- Fuel rack sticking [4]

IDLE RPM INCORRECT

Idle rpm adjustment is the only setting on the fuel pump or governor that may be adjusted. When the idle rpm requires adjustment, it usually indicates a problem elsewhere. Make adjustments only when the engine is warm and working properly!

MAXIMUM RPM INCORRECT

Maximum rpm is factory set and should not be adjusted.

A. Maximum rpm high

CAUSES:

- Injector pump out of adjustment [4]
- Governor weights broken [5]

B. Maximum rpm low

- Follow procedure for loss of power, above.

B. Mechanical problems

- Engine seized [3]
- Debris around prop or shaft [2]
- Transmission seized [4]

ACCELERATION POOR

Poor acceleration is closely allied to loss of power, so check the problems under "Loss of Power" first.

CAUSES:

If the engine produces good power but acceleration is slow then it is possible that the acceleration limiter on the governor mechanism is incorrectly set. Not all governors have an acceleration-limiter adjustment, and those that do are usually factory set. Leave any adjustment to the experts.

MISFIRING OR SURGING

Misfiring or surging where engine rpm is erratic or the engine does not appear to be firing on all cylinders is mostly caused by inconsistent fuel supply.

CAUSES:

A. Erratic fuel delivery

- Injector(s) defective [1]
- Fuel filter clogged [2]

CHART 4

OIL PROBLEMS

A loss of oil pressure will seize the engine within seconds. Never run the engine if the oil system is suspect. If you don't have an oil gauge, consider installing one.

OIL CONTAMINATION

Oil contamination is covered in Chapter 4. Any contamination must be removed quickly, the cause rectified, and the system cleaned before you run the engine again.

A. Coolant in Oil

If the engine has recently been run, the oil and coolant will emulsify and appear milky. Left to settle, the water will have the same coloring as the engine coolant. Do not be fooled by clear water droplets on the oil filler cap—these are from condensed vapor that can originate from coolant, raw water, or natural condensation.

CAUSES:

- ❏ Coolant poured into oil filler [2]
- ❏ Cylinder-head gasket failed [3]
- ❏ Cylinder head cracked [4]
- ❏ Engine block cracked [4]
- ❏ Cylinder liner cracked [4]
- ❏ Liner seals defective [4]
- ❏ Cracked exhaust manifold [4]

B. Raw water

If the engine has recently been run, the oil and raw water will emulsify and appear milky. Left to settle, the water should appear clear. Often, saltwater crystals on the dipstick or components will help identification. Do not be fooled by clear water droplets on the oil filler cap—these are from condensed vapor that can originate from coolant, raw water, or natural condensation.

CAUSES:

- ❏ Gear-driven raw-water pumps—seal failure or in-adequate greasing on old style with solid body [2]
- ❏ Antisiphon valve stuck closed [2]
- ❏ Exhaust system—poor design [2]
- ❏ Engine oil cooler failed [3]
- ❏ Cylinder-head gasket failed—direct-cooled engines [3]
- ❏ Intercooler failed (if fitted) [3]
- ❏ Cracked exhaust manifold [4]

C. Fuel

Level may rise on dipstick. Oil will appear thin with a strong smell of diesel.

CAUSES:

- ❏ Lift pump diaphragm [4]
- ❏ Injector pump seals [4]

D. Metal

If metal is visible in the oil when drained, much more is in the bottom of the oil pan. Cut open the used oil-filter cartridge and remove the oil pan. Depending on the quantity, the problems could be very serious and mean a full engine strip. If you catch the cause early enough, you may save the engine. Can be almost any component whose bearing surface is lubricated by the oil system.

CAUSES:

- ❏ Piston rings/cylinders [3]
- ❏ Main bearings [4]
- ❏ Rod bearings [4]
- ❏ Valve gear [4]
- ❏ Timing gears [5]
- ❏ Oil pump [5]

HOW LIKELY?   [1] Very common   [2] Common   [3] Possible   [4] Rare   [5] Very rare

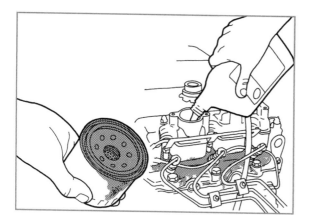

E. Oil dirty and black

If the oil is thin, dirty, and black, it is probably heavily contaminated with combustion products. Modern quality oils contain dispersants that prevent the contamination from forming a sludge.

CAUSES:

- ❏ Infrequent oil changes [1]
- ❏ Excessive combustion products [2]

OIL PRESSURE INCORRECT

A. High oil pressure

Oil consumption and blue exhaust smoke may increase with the denser crankcase oil mist. This is neither common nor a serious problem.

CAUSES:

- ❏ Defective gauge [3]
- ❏ Pump pressure-relief valve sticking closed [3]
- ❏ Incorrect grade of oil [4]

B. Low oil pressure

Low pressure can have serious consequences— always investigate.

CAUSES:

- ❏ Oil level low [1]
- ❏ Oil filter restricted [2]
- ❏ Oil temperature too high [2]
- ❏ Excessive wear on bearings [3]
- ❏ Defective gauge [3]
- ❏ Oil viscosity too low [4]
- ❏ Oil pump worn [4]
- ❏ Pressure-relief valve relieving low [4]
- ❏ Oil pump pickup tube defective [5]

EXTERNAL OIL LEAKS

To locate leaks, clean the engine first and then run at fast idle while looking for the source. A clean piece of paper or absorbent sheet under the engine will make leaks more apparent.

CAUSES:

- ❏ Valve-cover gasket [2]
- ❏ Flywheel seal [3]
- ❏ Crankshaft seal [3]
- ❏ Oil-pan gasket [3]
- ❏ Timing-cover gasket [3]
- ❏ External pipes connecting oil cooler [3]
- ❏ Oil in exhaust water—failed oil cooler [3]
- ❏ Lift pump gasket or pivot [3]

HIGH OIL CONSUMPTION

All engines burn oil to some extent. On new engines, the amount is not normally enough that oil has to be added between oil changes. As the engine starts to wear, expect to add oil occasionally. High oil consumption is not seriously detrimental to the engine provided the level is maintained.

CAUSES:

- ❏ External leaks [2]
- ❏ Cylinders/piston rings worn [3]
- ❏ Valve guides worn [3]
- ❏ Valve seals worn [3]
- ❏ Excessive oil [3]
- ❏ Incorrect oil grade [4]
- ❏ Engine-oil cooler leaking internally [4]

CHART
5

EXCESSIVE EXHAUST SMOKE

The color and quantity of exhaust smoke tells a great deal about the condition of a diesel. Most engines create some smoke, but if the diesel is in good condition the quantity will be almost invisible. Defects that affect the fuel, breathing, or compression will prevent correct combustion and lead to excessive exhaust smoke.

WHITE SMOKE

White exhaust smoke is unburned fuel that can be caused by excessive fuel or poor combustion.

CAUSES:

A. Poor atomization
- Injector nozzle stuck open   [1]
- Injector-nozzle seat worn   [1]
- Injector pressure low   [1]
- Low ambient temperature   [3]
- Low fuel grade   [4]
- Injection timing retarded   [4]

B. Poor compression
- Leaking inlet or exhaust valves   [3]
- Worn piston rings and cylinders   [3]
- Piston rings stuck in grooves   [3]

C. Water in fuel
Small quantities of water in the fuel will show as white exhaust smoke.

- Contaminated fuel   [2]
- Defective cylinder-head gasket   [3]

Note: Excessive periods at idle cause a buildup of unburned fuel within the exhaust system that burns off in the first few minutes the next time the engine is operated under normal power. This condition is normal for diesel engines and common in sailboats that idle for lengthy periods charging batteries or running freezers.

BLACK OR DARK SMOKE

Black smoke is caused by partially burned fuel. When the fuel/air mixture increases there is insufficient oxygen in the cylinders to complete combustion. Large quantities of carbon appear from the exhaust as minute, black soot particles.

CAUSES:

A. Engine overloaded

As load increases on the engine, the governor senses the slight decrease in rpm and adjusts the injector pump to deliver more fuel. If the engine becomes overloaded, the increase in fuel does not increase rpm and no extra air is sucked into the cylinders. Net result: soot.

- ❏ Propeller dirty or fouled   [1]
- ❏ Boat bottom dirty   [1]
- ❏ Engine alignment incorrect   [2]
- ❏ Transmission ratio incorrect   [3]
- ❏ Propeller incorrect   [3]

B. Insufficient air

- ❏ Air-intake filter clogged   [2]
- ❏ Air intake restricted   [3]
- ❏ Exhaust restricted   [3]
- ❏ Leaking inlet or exhaust valves   [4]
- ❏ Poor engine room ventilation   [4]

C. Excessive fuel

- ❏ Defective injector(s)   [1]
- ❏ Incorrect injector nozzle   [3]
- ❏ Two sealing washers under injector   [3]
- ❏ Injector pump incorrectly set   [4]
- ❏ Low fuel grade   [4]

STEAM

If you are not sure whether the white cloud from the exhaust is smoke or steam, watch how it dissipates. Steam or water vapor will rise and clear fairly quickly. Smoke tends to stay closer to the water and take longer to dilute with the local breezes.

CAUSES:

- ❏ Water vapor from condensing exhaust gases is normal in colder climates   [1]
- ❏ Insufficient raw-water flow   [2]
- ❏ Excessive exhaust-gas temperatures   [4]

BLUE SMOKE

More accurately, the smoke will appear white with a hint of blue. It often takes a trained eye to differentiate.

CAUSES:

- ❏ Valve seals defective   [3]
- ❏ Valve guides worn   [3]
- ❏ Piston rings/cylinders worn   [3]
- ❏ High crankcase pressure   [3]
- ❏ Oil leaking into the intake from defective gaskets   [4]

CHART
6

TEMPERATURE PROBLEMS

If your engine overheats, shut it down before any damage occurs. Running an engine at too high a temperature will cause severe damage in a very short time. Temperatures above 220°F (105°C) reduce the lubrication properties of the oil, and components will begin to fail. Always let the engine cool naturally. It may take several hours before the engine can be worked on. Be patient!

Never remove the filler cap or add cold water until the engine has cooled.

TEMPERATURE HIGH

Can mean a gradual degradation of the system caused by wear or a buildup of salts, marine growth, or corrosion. Sudden increases are caused by component failure or system blockage. A common cause, which can be difficult to diagnose, is a plastic bag or similar debris covering the raw-water inlet. Suction holds the bag in place while the engine is running, but as soon as it is shut down the bag disappears. In the meantime, the lack of water has probably destroyed the raw-water pump impeller.

ENGINES WITH FRESHWATER COOLING
A. Insufficient raw water

- ❏ Raw-water impeller defective [1]
- ❏ Restriction in raw-water inlet or strainer [1]
- ❏ Heat exchanger dirty [2]
- ❏ Oil cooler dirty [2]
- ❏ Exhaust injection elbow restricted [3]
- ❏ Leaking hose/filter gaskets before raw-water pump letting air into system (if above waterline) [3]
- ❏ Raw-water pump cam worn [3]
- ❏ Exhaust manifold restricted [4]

HOW LIKELY? [1] Very common   [2] Common   [3] Possible   [4] Rare   [5] Very rare

B. Insufficient coolant circulation
- ❏ Coolant level low   [2]
- ❏ V-belt broken or slipping   [2]
- ❏ Thermostat sticking closed   [2]
- ❏ Coolant circuit dirty or restricted   [2]

Note: Engines that incorporate a "by-pass" circuit in the cooling system will overheat if the thermostat sticks open or is removed.

ENGINES WITH RAW-WATER COOLING
A. Insufficient raw water
- ❏ Raw-water inlet or strainer blocked   [1]
- ❏ Raw-water impeller defective   [1]
- ❏ Thermostat stuck closed   [2]
- ❏ Exhaust injection manifold restricted   [2]
- ❏ Cylinder block dirty or restricted   [3]
- ❏ Exhaust manifold waterways restricted   [4]

ALL ENGINES
A. Inadequate lubrication
- ❏ Insufficient oil   [3]
- ❏ Contaminated oil   [3]

B. Engine generating excessive heat
- ❏ Fuel problems   [2]
- ❏ Overloading   [3]

C. False indication
- ❏ Defective gauge or sender   [4]

TEMPERATURE LOW

Engines with indirect cooling systems operate at 160–195°F (70–90°C). Direct-cooled engines operate at much lower temperatures: 120–140°F (50–60°C). An engine running at low temperatures will have reduced life due to buildup of acids on the cylinder wall, which cause wear. Both indirect and direct systems use a thermostat to control temperature. Low temperatures are nearly always due to problems with the thermostat.

CAUSES:
- ❏ Thermostat stuck open   [2]
- ❏ No thermostat fitted   [2]
- ❏ Incorrect thermostat   [4]
- ❏ Very low ambient temperatures   [4]

TEMPERATURE ERRATIC

The temperature gauge will fluctuate as though it is sticking. Temperatures will be higher and lower than normal.

CAUSES:
- ❏ Thermostat sticking   [2]
- ❏ False indication   [4]

CHART

7

NOISE AND VIBRATION PROBLEMS

Engine noise and vibration are excellent indicators of the onset of a problem. Although these symptoms are difficult to quantify, most owners hear or feel a change in the engine the second it occurs. Even if your experience is limited, trust these senses and investigate further.

If you're having trouble locating the source of a noise or vibration, try using a large screwdriver as a stethoscope by placing the sharp end on different parts of the engine and the rounded handle hard against your ear. A piece of wood can be equally effective.

NOISE

A. Knocking

Sounds like: Hammer hitting engine block. Hard mechanical sound with frequency proportional to engine rpm.

CAUSES:

❏ Defective injector	[2]
❏ Excessive fuel	[3]
❏ Worn connecting-rod bearing	[4]
❏ Connecting-rod bolt loose	[4]
❏ Piston hitting valve	[4]
❏ Injection timing too far advanced	[4]
❏ Flywheel loose	[5]

B. Rattling

Sounds like: One or a handful of nuts being shaken in an empty metal can.

CAUSES:

❏ Excessive valve clearances	[2]
❏ Loose accessories	[2]

C. Rumbling

Sounds like: Slow-speed, dull sound, like assorted rocks being turned in a large drum.

CAUSES:

❏ Propeller shaft out of balance	[2]
❏ Cutlass bearing worn	[2]
❏ Propeller out of balance	[2]
❏ Gearbox bearings worn	[4]
❏ Drive plate worn or loose	[4]

D. Squealing

Sounds like: Car tires during a racing start.

CAUSES:

❏ Fan belt slipping	[1]
❏ Lack of lubrication on piston	[3]
❏ Gasoline in fuel tank	[5]

E. Hissing air

Sounds like: Escaping gas. Occurs intermittently as a piston approaches the top of its compression stroke.

CAUSES:

❏ Leaking injector seating washer	[2]
❏ Leaking cylinder-head gasket	[3]
❏ Leaking inlet-valve seat	[4]

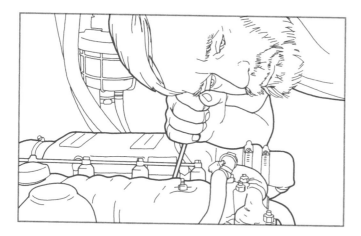

F. Clicking

Sounds like: Light metallic sound that can occur once or continuously.

CAUSES:

❏ Starter solenoid engaging—once is normal [2]
❏ Excessive valve clearances [3]

G. High-pitched whir

Sounds like: Very high-speed zing that rapidly increases in frequency.

CAUSES:

❏ Starter still energized or engaged [3]

VIBRATION

A. Low-frequency vibration

Components moving and turning at slower speeds.

CAUSES:

❏ Natural resonance—see note at right [1]
❏ Damaged or dirty propeller [2]
❏ Engine misfiring [3]
❏ Propeller-shaft coupling loose [3]
❏ Bent prop shaft [4]
❏ Flywheel loose [5]

B. Medium-frequency vibration

The majority of vibration at a frequency close to engine rpm.

CAUSES:

❏ Engine mounts loose [2]
❏ Engine misfiring [3]
❏ Flywheel loose [5]

C. High-frequency vibration

Components moving and turning at very high speeds.

CAUSES:

❏ Starter stuck/engaged [3]
❏ Alternator fan out of balance [3]

Note: Smaller engines with 1, 2, or 3 cylinders will often vibrate violently at slower rpm. This is particularly noticeable with lighter, alloy engines whose softer mounts are optimized for the smoothest running at operating rpm. All engines have rpm bands where the vibration is greater. Often the vibration is more pronounced because of poor installation.

CHART
8

STARTING SYSTEM PROBLEMS

Problems with the starting system account for a high percentage of diesel engine faults. Diesel engines ignite fuel by compressing air in the cylinders to generate heat. The speed at which a starter turns over the engine has a major effect on cylinder pressures. Keeping the starting system in top condition is even more important in cold weather, when much of the heat is robbed by cold cylinders and cylinder heads, batteries produce less power, and thicker oil creates increased drag.

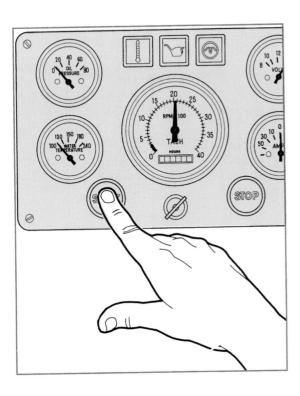

NOTHING HAPPENS WHEN THE IGNITION IS SWITCHED ON

No indication of power to the instrument panel. Water temperature and oil pressure gauges fail to "zero," no warning lights, and no buzzer.

CAUSES:

❑ Battery selector switched off [1]
❑ Battery-ground isolation switch off [1]
❑ Battery voltage very low [1]
❑ Loose or broken wiring [2]
❑ Defective ignition switch [2]

NO RESPONSE WHEN STARTER IS SELECTED

Water temperature and oil pressure gauges "zero," panel lights and buzzers work, but there is no response from the starter when selected.

CAUSES:

❑ Battery voltage low [1]
❑ Loose or corroded connections [2]
❑ Defective ignition/start switch [3]
❑ Poor ground connection on engine [3]
❑ Broken wiring [3]

STARTER TURNS SLOWLY OR JUST "CLICKS"

Power is evident at the instrument panel. Selecting "start" causes the starter to turn the engine over very slowly or the solenoid to energize and just "click."

A. Solenoid "clicks" once—battery voltage drops

The click indicates power has energized the starter solenoid. A voltage drop indicated by the voltmeter or dimming lights shows the starter is drawing high amperage.

CAUSES:

- ❑ Engine seized [3]
- ❑ Starter shorting internally [3]
- ❑ Starter jammed in flywheel ring gear [4]
- ❑ Starter seized [4]

B. Solenoid "clicks" once—battery voltage remains high

Power has energized the starter solenoid but is not getting to the starter motor.

CAUSES:

- ❑ Starter solenoid not making contact [2]
- ❑ Starter positive supply not connected or loose [3]
- ❑ Engine ground wire not connected or loose [3]

C. Solenoid "clicks" repeatedly

Power has energized the solenoid, but the voltage drop is so great when the starter is energized that the solenoid disengages. Voltage recovers and the solenoid energizes, and the cycle repeats, creating a rapid clicking sound.

CAUSES:

- ❑ Battery voltage low [1]
- ❑ Loose or corroded connections [2]

STARTER OVERSPEEDS OR REMAINS ENGAGED

When the starter is selected, the engine fails to turn over and is accompanied by a high-pitched whirring.

A. Starter overspeed occurs when "start" is selected

The starter is getting power, but the spinning gear is not engaging with the flywheel ring gear.

CAUSES:

- ❑ Clutch slipping [2]
- ❑ Dirt, wear, or corrosion on starter shaft preventing the gear from engaging [3]
- ❑ Bendix-type starter—Bendix defective [3]

B. Starter overspeed continues when not selected

The solenoid is jammed in the energized position with the starter gear not engaging.

CAUSES:

- ❑ Defective solenoid [2]
- ❑ Defective start switch [3]

Warning: This problem can be serious. You can only stop the starter from turning by disconnecting the power. If your starting system is well designed, the engine battery switch will kill power. Some systems have a ground-isolation switch that will have the same effect. If you have neither, the starter will spin until it has drained all the battery power. More likely, it will burn out the wiring or the starter will overheat and the commutator explode. Make sure your wiring is correct before this occurs and burns your boat to the waterline!

C. Starter continues engaged after the switch is deselected—see warning above

CAUSES:

- ❑ Defective solenoid [2]
- ❑ Defective start switch [3]
- ❑ Damaged starter gear or flywheel ring gear [4]

CHART 9

CHARGING SYSTEM PROBLEMS

As their name suggests, alternators produce alternating current which is rectified into the direct current that powers the boat's electrical equipment. Output is controlled by a voltage regulator, which senses battery voltage and varies the current fed to the rotor windings. Higher current increases rotor magnetism, which induces higher output from the stator windings. All alternators work on the same principle, although output will vary with size and regulator design.

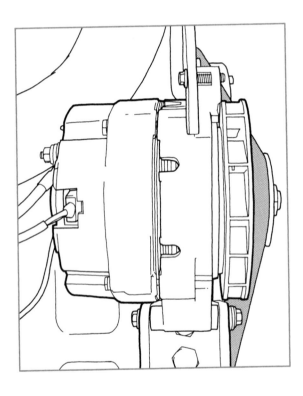

NO CHARGING

Indications of alternator not charging are:
- Ignition warning light fails to extinguish.
- No voltage increase at the alternator output terminal.
- No voltage increase at the battery terminal.
- Alternator does not get warm/hot.
- No indication on the ammeter.

CAUSES:
- ❏ V-belt slipping or broken [1]
- ❏ Output wire disconnected, broken, loose, or corroded [2]
- ❏ Ground connection poor [2]
- ❏ Regulator failed—open circuit [2]
- ❏ Stator or rotor coils defective [3]
- ❏ Rectifier defective [3]
- ❏ Brushes worn or broken [3]

HOW LIKELY?   [1] Very common   [2] Common   [3] Possible   [4] Rare   [5] Very rare

UNDERCHARGING

Indications of undercharging are:

- Minimal voltage increase on the engine panel voltmeter.
- Batteries fail to fully charge.

CAUSES:

- ❏ Insufficient charge time   [1]
- ❏ V-belt slipping   [1]
- ❏ Output connection loose or corroded   [2]
- ❏ Ground connection loose or corroded   [2]
- ❏ Brushes worn   [3]
- ❏ Slip rings contaminated or worn   [3]
- ❏ Stator or rotor coils defective   [3]
- ❏ Rectifier defective   [3]

OVERCHARGING

Indications of overcharging are:

- Battery very hot.
- Electrolyte boiling violently.
- Strong acid smell.
- Voltmeter reading over 14.5 volts.
- Low electrolyte level.

CAUSES:

- ❏ Battery-voltage sensing wire broken, loose, corroded, or disconnected   [2]
- ❏ Regulator failed—short circuit   [2]
- ❏ Battery defective   [2]

CHART
10

TURBOCHARGER PROBLEMS

These faults are applicable only to engines fitted with turbochargers and are in addition to faults covered in the other charts.

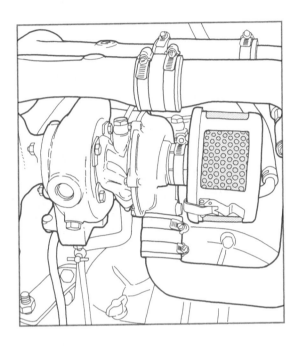

NOISE

A. Hissing air

The increased air pressure created by the turbocharger compressor is usually less than the 20 psi when the engine is running at maximum rpm. It is unlikely that escaping air can be heard over the noise of the engine and turbocharger.

CAUSES:

❏ Gaskets leaking between compressor outlet and inlet manifold [3]

B. Surging

Surging is the breakdown of airflow over the compressor blades during rapid acceleration. The result is a series of pressure surges as the intake air momentarily reverses direction. The noise created is difficult to describe but sounds like very fast popping or rasping.

CAUSES:

❏ Dirty turbocharger [2]
❏ Turbocharger binding [3]

EXCESSIVE SMOKE

A. Black/dark smoke
Dark smoke indicates partially burned fuel, usually caused by excessive fuel or a reduced air supply.

CAUSES:

- Restricted air filter [2]
- Compressor dirty [2]
- Intercooler dirty [2]
- Air leak from intake pipes downstream of compressor [3]
- Turbocharger binding [3]
- Restricted exhaust-gas flow [3]
- Exhaust-gas leak before turbocharger [3]
- Turbocharger seized [4]

B. Blue smoke
White exhaust smoke with a hint of blue indicates burned oil.

CAUSES:

- Turbocharger shaft seals leaking [2]
- Turbocharger oil-return pipe clogged [4]

PERFORMANCE PROBLEMS

Turbocharged engines produce more power for their size because the greater quantity of air in the cylinders allows more fuel to be burned. Any reduction in turbocharger efficiency can have a marked effect on performance.

CAUSES:

- Restricted air filter [2]
- Turbocharger dirty [2]
- Intercooler dirty [2]

- Turbocharger binding [3]
- Air leak from intake pipes downstream of turbocharger [3]
- Restricted exhaust-gas flow [3]
- Turbocharger seized [4]
- Exhaust-gas leak before turbocharger [4]

VIBRATION

A. Very high frequency
Turbochargers rotate at very high speeds—often close to 200,000 rpm. At this speed, the smallest of uneven forces will cause high-frequency vibrations that can be destructive.

CAUSES:

- Turbine/shaft/compressor assembly out of balance. Possible broken or damaged blades [3]
- Excessive bearing wear [3]
- Compressor or turbine making contact with casing [3]

B. Low frequency

CAUSES:

- Loose pipes and fittings [4]

CHART
11

FUEL SYSTEM FUNCTIONAL CHECK

The following procedure can be carried out by anyone with a few basic tools. If your engine will not start, is difficult to start, or dies soon after starting, this check will confirm whether the fuel system is the cause. It will also identify many other problems that can cause low power, rough running, and excessive smoke.

 START

Is the fuel turned off?
Is the stop cable pulled out? (very common)
Have you turned off any fuel supply or return valves?
Is the fuel tank empty?
Could there be air in the fuel?
Is starting difficult after carrying out maintenance on fuel system?

 Yes

Bleed the fuel system of air
The injector pump will not work with air in the fuel system. Although some pumps can self-bleed, all air should be removed from the system any time it is disturbed.
While operating the manual lever on the lift pump, bleed air from:
1. The bleed screw on the secondary filter.
2. All bleed screws on the injector pump.

No

Confirm fuel is reaching the injectors
The quickest method of checking the fuel system is to confirm fuel is reaching the injectors. Loosen all the injector supply lines at the injector. Turn the engine over using the starter.
Does a small shot of fuel spurt from each injector line?

Yes

The injector pump is suspect
The injector pump is not delivering high pressure fuel to the injectors, despite having a good supply of air-free fuel. If you have just serviced part of the fuel system, the most likely cause is air in the injector pump. Follow your service manual's instructions carefully on bleeding air out of the pump. If the pump still fails to deliver a shot of fuel at the injector-inlet connection, it is probable your injector pump is defective. Pump failure is not very common, so consider bleeding the system again before replacing a very expensive component.

Injector pumps can only be rebuilt by diesel shops that have the specialized test equipment. If defective, replace it with a new or reconditioned unit.

 No

Check the low-pressure fuel system
Unscrew the bleed screw from the secondary fuel filter. Turn the engine over using the starter.
Does airless fuel flow full-bore in spurts?

 Yes

 No

Check the lift pump and secondary filter
Disconnect the fuel supply line to the lift pump, and replace it with a hose with one end dipped in a container of clean fuel. Turn the engine over on the starter once more.
Does airless fuel flow full-bore in spurts?

Yes

The fuel supply to the engine is suspect
Fuel is not reaching the lift pump. The most common cause is a restricted element or poor sealing on the primary filter, which is letting air into the system. If the filter checks out okay then inspect the fuel hoses and connections. The fuel tank pickup tube or vent could be blocked.

 No

Check the lift pump
With the fuel supply still from a separate container, disconnect the fuel-outlet line from the lift pump. Turn the engine over on the starter once more.
Does airless fuel flow full-bore in spurts?

 Yes

The secondary fuel filter is suspect
Check that the secondary filter is not clogged and that hoses, pipes, and connections are good. A poor connection after the lift pump sees low pressure fuel and will leak fuel rather than suck in air.

 No

The lift pump is suspect
Before condemning the lift pump, remove it from the engine and operate the actuator lever. The pump should make rude noises as the diaphragm sucks in air and expels it past small non-return valves. A finger over the inlet and outlet should feel good suction and pressure, respectively. Some engines have an additional external valve on the pump inlet that is prone to sticking shut.

Confirm the injectors are good
Remove all the injectors from the cylinder head. Then refit each injector back into its fuel line so you can see the nozzle. Leave return lines disconnected during this procedure. Turn engine over using the starter and note the spray pattern from each injector nozzle.
Warning: High-pressure fuel can penetrate skin and cause infection. Be sure to keep clear of the spray.
Do all the injectors produce a finely atomized spray with no dripping from the nozzle?

 Yes

 No

 Yes

The injectors are suspect
Defective injectors must be replaced. Although an engine will run with worn or contaminated injectors, starting will become progressively more difficult with an accompanying increase of smoke from the exhaust. If a telltale rainbow slick of fuel is visible on the water surface by the exhaust, it's a sure sign that the injectors need servicing.

Although some service manuals show how injectors can be disassembled for cleaning, this task requires special test equipment to ensure injectors are "popping" at the correct pressure and are producing the correct pattern of finely atomized fuel.

Check that the cold-starting device is being used correctly
Some engines do not need the cold-starting device for starting in warm climates. Most diesels will not start without one in colder climates.
Warning: Never use ether starting aids with heater-type cold-starting devices. The consequences can be explosive!
Is the cold-starting device being used for the recommended time?

 No

Yes

Use the correct starting procedure
Usually preheat devices are operated for 30 seconds before the starter is engaged. If you are not sure of the correct procedure, check the operator's manual.

Check that the cold-starting device is working
Cold-starting devices vary among manufacturers. Confirm which type is fitted and then check that it is operating correctly.
Is the cold-starting device working?

Cold-starting device is suspect
Nearly all cold-starting devices use a sealed heating element that cannot be repaired and must be replaced if suspect.

No

Yes

The return line may be restricted
Depending on the engine, return lines carry surplus and aerated fuel back to the top of the fuel tank. On some injector pumps, a blocked or restricted return line will affect its performance. Although you may not have a problem if no fuel appears from the return line, it is a good idea to disconnect both ends to confirm there is no restriction.

 No

Check the injector return line is not restricted
Disconnect the return line close to the fuel tank. Place the line into a bucket and try running the engine.
Does fuel flow into the bucket?

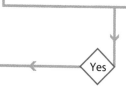 Yes

Fuel system appears to be functioning correctly
The checks you have carried out suggest there is no problem with the fuel system. You should have checked the following:
❏ Fuel is reaching the injectors.
❏ All the injectors are producing finely atomized fuel in a good spray pattern.
❏ The cold-starting device is working.
❏ The return line is not blocked.
There are several other reasons why the fuel system may not still be performing correctly, but they are less common and should be tackled only by an experienced mechanic.

CHART
12

ENGINE FAILS TO STOP

Before you press the start button, you should know how to shut down the engine. It's also advisable to know what type of shutdown mechanism is fitted and how to stop the engine if it fails.

EMERGENCY SHUTDOWN

If the engine fails to stop, identify the type of shutdown mechanism and check out the following methods first.

A. Cable/mechanical shutdown
1. Locate the engine end of the cable.
2. Operate the shutdown lever by hand.

B. Electrical solenoid "energized to run"
1. Locate the solenoid, which usually is fitted to the injector pump.
2. Disconnect the power-supply cable.

C. Electrical solenoid "energized to stop"
1. Locate the solenoid.
2. If shutdown lever is remotely mounted, operate by hand.
3. Otherwise, if solenoid is fitted to injector pump, use a lead to jump power from the positive supply on the starter or battery to the solenoid.

D. If all else fails
1. Stop the intake airflow by blocking the air intake. Be very careful not to let anything get sucked into the intake!
   OR
2. Loosen the injector supply lines.
   OR
3. Shut off the fuel supply. Remember: You will have to bleed the fuel system before the engine will start again.

MECHANICAL STOP LEVER

A push-pull cable operates a shutdown lever fitted to the injector pump or governor. Failures are mostly cable problems that can be overridden by operating the pump shutdown lever by hand.

CAUSES:
- ❑ Cable disconnected at engine   [2]
- ❑ Cable broken or seized   [3]
- ❑ Governor lever seized or binding   [3]

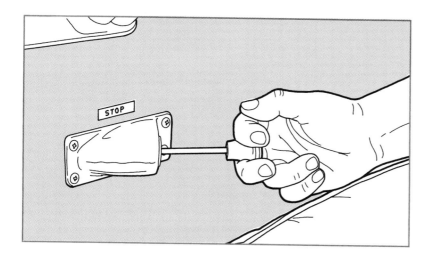

ELECTRICAL STOP BUTTON

Electrical shutdowns differ with engine design. The main types are:

- ❏ External solenoid that pulls a fuel shutoff lever on the injector pump or governor
- ❏ Integral solenoid fitted to the injector pump that controls the pump's fuel supply
- ❏ Integral solenoid fitted to in-line injector pumps that pulls the fuel rack to a shutoff position

A. "Energized to run" type

The solenoid is permanently energized while the engine runs. Power is cut off to stop the engine. Disconnecting the lead at the solenoid should shut down the engine. This method is mainly used on generators.

CAUSES:

❏ Solenoid sticking	[3]
❏ Injector-pump fuel rack sticking	[3]
❏ Shut down relay defective	[3]

B. "Energized to stop" type

This type of solenoid is energized only when the stop button is pressed. If the engine fails to stop, voltage is probably not reaching the solenoid. If it has an external solenoid, try operating the lever manually.

CAUSES:

❏ Voltage not reading solenoid	[1]
❏ Solenoid mechanical linkage disconnected	[2]
❏ Solenoid or linkage sticking	[3]
❏ Injector-pump fuel rack sticking	[3]
❏ Solenoid travel incorrectly set	[3]

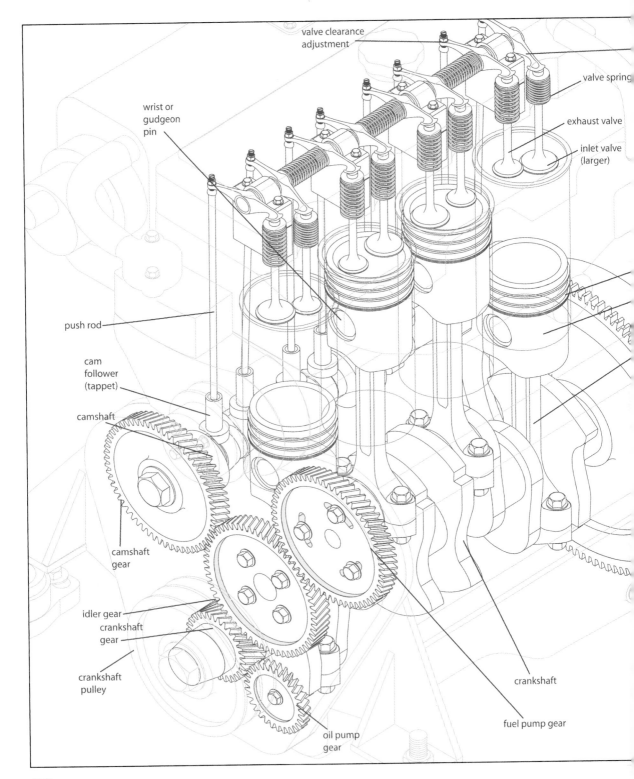

valve clearance
adjustment

valve spring

exhaust valve

inlet valve
(larger)

wrist or
gudgeon
pin

push rod

cam
follower
(tappet)

camshaft

camshaft
gear

idler gear

crankshaft
gear

crankshaft
pulley

oil pump
gear

crankshaft

fuel pump gear

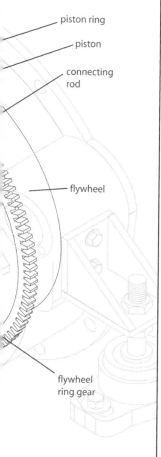

rocker arm

piston ring

piston

connecting
rod

flywheel

flywheel
ring gear

THE
MECHANICAL SYSTEM

The engine block, cylinder head, and a host of reciprocating and rotating components harness the force of the exploding diesel/air mixture and transmit combustion energy through the flywheel to the transmission. These components are extremely reliable, requiring no routine maintenance other than the occasional valve-clearance adjustment.

Mechanical problems can often be traced to failures in other systems—particularly the lubrication and exhaust systems—which can cause severe damage to bearing surfaces. Rectification often entails major work, but you can make many of these repairs yourself, without purchasing special tools or removing the engine. Even an experienced mechanic, however, will need a repair or shop manual that details the correct strip, inspection, and assembly procedures.

ENGINE BLOCK

The cylinder block of a diesel engine is machined from a complex casting that includes locations for the cylinder liners, crankshaft, camshaft, engine mounts, oil galleries, and waterways; it is designed to take the high loads and thermal stresses imposed by the moving components. The block requires no routine maintenance.

FREEZE PLUGS

Freeze plugs protect block and head castings in the event that the coolant freezes. They will normally last the life of an engine if the cooling system is well maintained. If not, these steel plugs will corrode; check them regularly. The

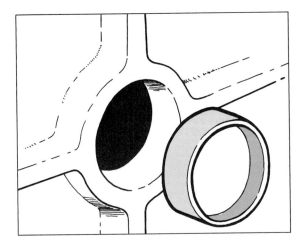

first sign of a problem will appear as a pinhole slowly weeping coolant. If one plug fails, replace all the freeze plugs.

CYLINDER HEAD

The cylinder head must fit tightly onto the engine block to maintain a good seal at the top of each cylinder. Uneven tightness leads to air, oil, and coolant leaks and may induce high stresses that can warp and crack the cylinder head. Most engines require the cylinder head bolts be retorqued after the first 50 hours of running to compensate for settling of the cylinder head gasket.

CYLINDER-HEAD GASKET

The first sign of head-gasket trouble is often a slight bubbling or fluid leak at the joint between the engine block and the cylinder head. More serious leakage can cause difficult starting, rough running, and loss of power. With severe leakage, the coolant pressure cap will vent coolant as combustion gases escape across the gasket into the coolant circuit.

Although retorquing the cylinder-head bolts will often stop small leaks, it's better to remove the cylinder head and replace the gasket. Leave this task to the more experienced with access to a

shop manual and torque wrench. Don't forget: Retorque the new gasket after 50 hours of operation.

CRANKSHAFT

The largest moving component in the engine, the crankshaft converts the reciprocating movement of the pistons into the rotary movement that drives the propeller shaft. Crankshafts are forged from high-quality steel to withstand high stresses.

The crankshaft requires no routine maintenance and will run for thousands of hours with minimal wear if you change the lubricating oil regularly.

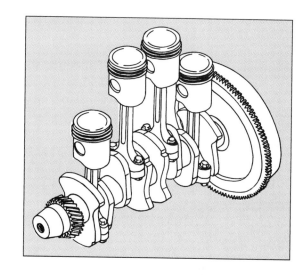

TIMING GEARS

Timing gears rotate the camshaft at half crankshaft speed and ensure that the inlet and exhaust valves open and close at the correct point in the four-stroke cycle. They also drive the high-pressure fuel pump. The engine manufacturer sets the timing at assembly by aligning the gears that connect the camshaft to the crankshaft. Unless the engine has been stripped and incorrectly reassembled, the timing will not change and needs no adjustment.

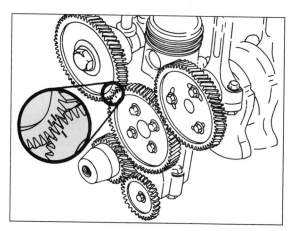

VALVES

Small clearances between the valve stems and rocker arms compensate for thermal expansion. These valve clearances change with normal wear and need occasional adjustment.

The engine shop manual—and sometimes the owner's manual—will list the correct clearance, which often differs between the inlet and exhaust valves. Adjustment is straightforward, unless the engine has an overhead camshaft in the cylinder head and uses special shims to alter clearances.

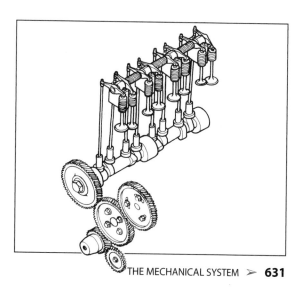

CHECKING AND ADJUSTING VALVE CLEARANCES

Adjust valve clearances with the engine cold and the valve fully closed, with its cam follower off the camshaft lobe. Placing the piston on or near top dead center (TDC) on the compression stroke ensures that both the inlet and exhaust valves are fully closed.

1. Place the #1 cylinder—usually the one nearest the front of the engine—at TDC on the compression stroke. On an engine with TDC alignment marks on the crankshaft pulley or flywheel, turn it slowly clockwise (as viewed from the front) until the marks align *just* after the intake valve for the #1 cylinder closes. On an engine with no alignment marks, turn it slowly until the #1-cylinder intake valve closes fully, then turn another 90°; this will place the camshaft in a good position.

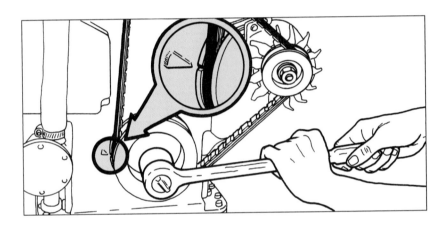

2. Measure the gap, or clearance, of the intake and exhaust valves with a feeler gauge. The gauge should just slip between the top of the valve stem and the rocker arm.

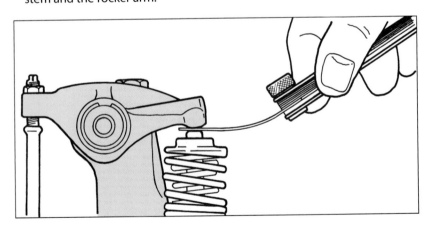

3. Adjusting the clearance almost requires three hands to hold the feeler gauge and adjustment screw while locking the nut. Always recheck the clearance after locking the nut.
4. Repeat for all cylinders. Continue rotating the crankshaft clockwise until the intake valve of the next cylinder fully closes; turn another 90° and then check that cylinder's valve clearance.

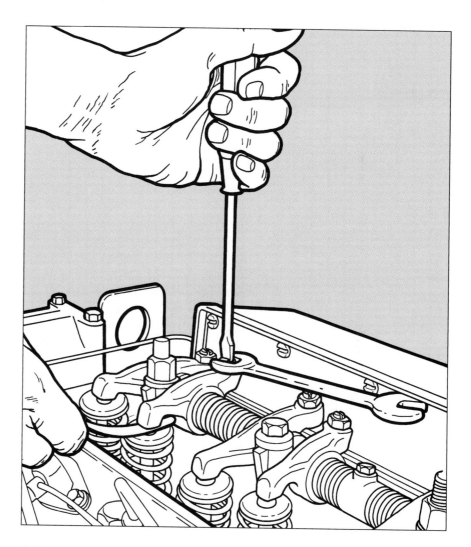

PISTONS AND CYLINDERS

Pistons and cylinders work extremely hard and therefore wear more than any other engine component. Fortunately, the process is gradual, and with frequent oil changes, a good intake-air filter, and well-maintained injectors, they will give thousands of hours of service before demanding attention.

Difficult starting, loss of power, and excessive smoking are typical symptoms of severe cylinder wear. But these symptoms might also signify that one cylinder's rings are stuck in the piston grooves, or perhaps that one of the inlet or exhaust valves is not seating well. Before condemning an engine or stripping it for a major overhaul, test its compression.

TESTING COMPRESSION

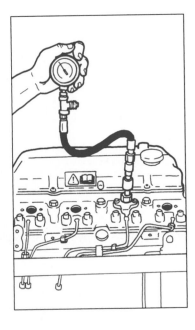

The compression tester consists of a dummy injector connected to a 0–600–psi gauge. A small non-return valve retains the maximum pressure. All the injectors are removed and each cylinder tested, using the starter motor to turn over the engine. Initially, the test is carried out "dry"; then a small amount of oil is added to each cylinder and the test repeated.

A comparison between cylinders will identify those with lower pressures. If the suspect cylinder increases pressure dramatically when tested "wet," the problem lies with worn piston rings and cylinders. No change when wet suggests leaking valve seats.

It sounds simple in theory, but in practice the volume of the dummy injector, hose, and gauge affects the indicated pressure, as do the state of the battery, condition of the starter, viscosity of the oil, and temperature. Compression should be carried out by a professional who has a good "feel" for the pressures an engine will produce with his or her test equipment. Compression testing tends to be comparative but is really effective in identifying problems in individual cylinders.

MAJOR OVERHAUL

Excessive wear on the piston rings and cylinder bores can mean costly repairs. Weigh carefully the many hours of labor to repair an older engine versus the cost of fitting a new one—especially if you lack the skills and are considering hiring a professional mechanic. Information on overhaul procedure is detailed in the manufacturer's repair or shop manual.

ENGINE MOUNTS

Most installations use flexible engine mounts to help absorb vibration. In ideal conditions, these mounts require no maintenance. Unfortunately, conditions are far from ideal below a leaky engine, close to the bilge.

INSPECTION

Check that all adjustment nuts are tight. Lower nuts tend to wind down. Black or rusty dust indicates loose mounts that are fretting. Check that the bolts holding the mounts to the engine bed are tight. Rubber should not be split or separating from the metal. Corroded mounts make engine alignment impossible and should be replaced. Treat all mounts regularly with a heavy-duty corrosion inhibitor.

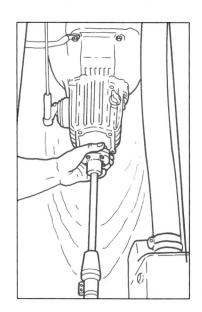

ENGINE ALIGNMENT

An engine out of alignment with its propeller shaft will cause excessive bearing friction, which can increase stern-gear noise and considerably reduce power. A large alignment error will bend the prop shaft on each revolution. Couplings will work loose, transmission bearings and seals will fail, and eventually the prop shaft itself will fatigue and break.

QUICK-AND-EASY CHECK

If you can turn the shaft by hand without feeling any tight spots, the alignment is probably close.

MEASURING AND CORRECTING ALIGNMENT ERRORS

Measuring alignment along the three major axes is straightforward, but correcting errors is not. Each adjustment on one axis affects the other two. Engine alignment is not complicated, but it may take several hours and try your patience.

Remove the coupling bolts; then turn the shaft several times to *just* separate the two halves of the coupling. If the length of prop shaft between the coupling and stern gland is substantial, support the shaft to keep it in position. If a flexible coupling is used, alignment procedures vary with coupling manufacturer. If in doubt, remove it.

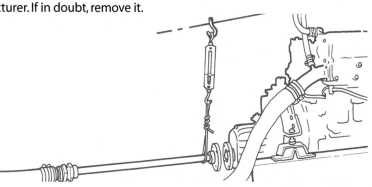

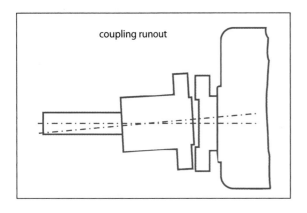

coupling runout

1. COUPLING RUNOUT

To determine the *coupling runout error,* measure the gap between the faces at the top and bottom with feeler gauges and subtract the smaller number to get the vertical error. (For example, 0.024 inches at the top and 0.013 inches at the bottom show a gap of 0.024 – 0.013 = 0.011 inches at the top.) Now, rotate only the shaft half of the coupling 90° and recheck. If the gap changes dramatically, the shaft coupling is incorrectly machined or fitted, or the shaft itself is bent.

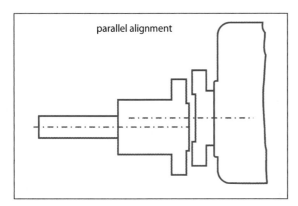

parallel alignment

2. PARALLEL ALIGNMENT

Measure *parallel alignment* by bringing the two halves of the coupling together and placing a straightedge across the top. Measure any gap beneath the straightedge with feeler gauges. Repeat at the bottom and sides of the couplings. Maximum permitted error is 0.005 inches for small couplings; correct any greater error by adjusting all the engine mounts evenly in the same direction.

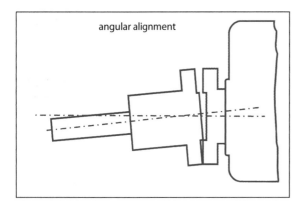

angular alignment

3. ANGULAR ALIGNMENT

For *angular alignment,* measure the top and bottom gap between the coupling faces and subtract the smaller number to get the vertical error. The maximum permitted error is 0.001 inches for each 1 inch of coupling diameter. In other words, a coupling measuring 5 inches diameter should have a gap of 0.005 inches or less. To close a gap at the top of the coupling, either raise the front mounts or lower the rear mounts. For a gap at the bottom, do the opposite. Repeat the measurement side to side to get the horizontal error. To close a gap on the port side, slide the aft mounts to starboard or the front mounts to port. For a gap on the starboard side, do the opposite.

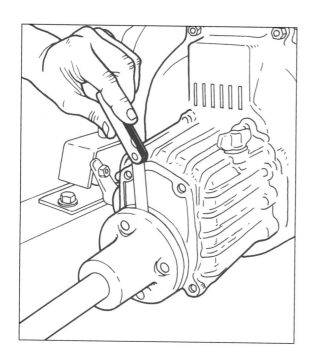

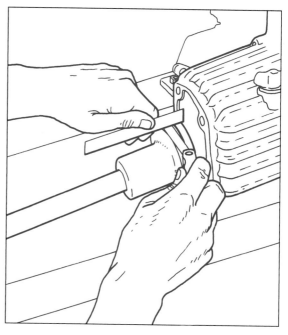

MECHANICAL SYSTEM FAULTS

Problem	Possible Cause	Possible Symptoms

CRANKSHAFT ASSEMBLY

Problem	Possible Cause	Possible Symptoms
Crankshaft broken	Fatigue [5]	Engine will not run and makes unusual noise
Flywheel loose	Poor assembly [4] Broken locking device [5]	Severe vibration; knocking
Connecting rod bent or broken	Water in cylinder [2] Broken valve [3] Incorrect timing [4]	Erratic rpm; loss of power; difficult starting; compression low
Rod bearing loose	Poor assembly [4] Broken bolt [4]	Hard mechanical knocking
Rod bearings worn	Excessive wear [3] Poor lubrication [3]	As above
Front pulley loose	Poor assembly [4] Broken locking device [5]	V-belt thrown; vibration

PISTONS AND CYLINDERS

Problem	Possible Cause	Possible Symptoms
Piston seized	Corrosion [2] Overheating [3] Poor lubrication [4]	Engine seized; water in cylinders
Piston knocking	Piston rings picking up on bore [4] Broken valve [4] Rod bearings worn [4] Incorrect valve timing [5]	Loud knocking, particularly at high rpm
Piston rings worn	Tired engine [3]	Poor compression; loss of power; high oil consumption; difficult starting; blue exhaust smoke
Cylinder liner cracked	Overheating [4] Corrosion [5]	Coolant in oil; coolant in cylinder
Cylinder liner scored	Poor intake-air filtration [2] Poor lubrication [3]	High oil consumption; blue exhaust smoke

HOW LIKELY?　[1] Very common　[2] Common　[3] Possible　[4] Rare　[5] Very rare

Problem	Possible Cause	Possible Symptoms

CYLINDER HEAD

Problem	Possible Cause	Possible Symptoms
Cracked	Overheating [3] Adding cold water to overheated engine [3] Incorrect torque on bolts [4]	Coolant in oil; oil in coolant; loss of power; difficult starting
Warped	Incorrect torque on head bolts [2] Overheating [3]	Leaking cylinder-head gasket—see below
Gasket leaking	Incorrect torque on head bolts [2] Warped head [4]	Coolant in oil; oil in coolant; loss of power; difficult starting; water in cylinders; slight bubbling from joint

VALVE GEAR

Problem	Possible Cause	Possible Symptoms
Valve stuck open	Valve stem contaminated with carbon [3] Corrosion [3] Valve bent [3] Poor lubrication [4]	Loss of compression; uneven running; poor starting; excessive exhaust smoke
Valve seat leaking	Seat damaged, eroded, or worn [2] Valve bent [3] Inadequate valve clearance [4]	Loss of compression; fuel mixture forced out of inlet manifold (inlet valve); excessive exhaust smoke
Valve guides worn	Tired engine [3]	High oil consumption; blue exhaust smoke
Valve spring broken	Fatigue—usually from operation at very high rpm [3]	Knocking; loss of power; difficult starting; excessive exhaust smoke
Excessive valve clearance	Normal wear on valve gear [1] Incorrect adjustment [2]	Rattling sound from the valve cover; slight loss in performance
Reduced valve clearance	Incorrect adjustment [2] Valve seat or face worn [3]	Loss of performance
Camshaft broken	Fatigue [5]	Engine fails to run; pistons hitting valves; engine running rough
Push rod bent	Incorrect valve clearances [3] Seized valve [3] Incorrect timing [5]	Loss of performance

ENGINE MOUNTS

Problem	Possible Cause	Possible Symptoms
Loose, broken, delaminated	Vibration [2] Poor assembly [2] Oil contamination [3]	Vibration; loss of power; prop shaft difficult to turn

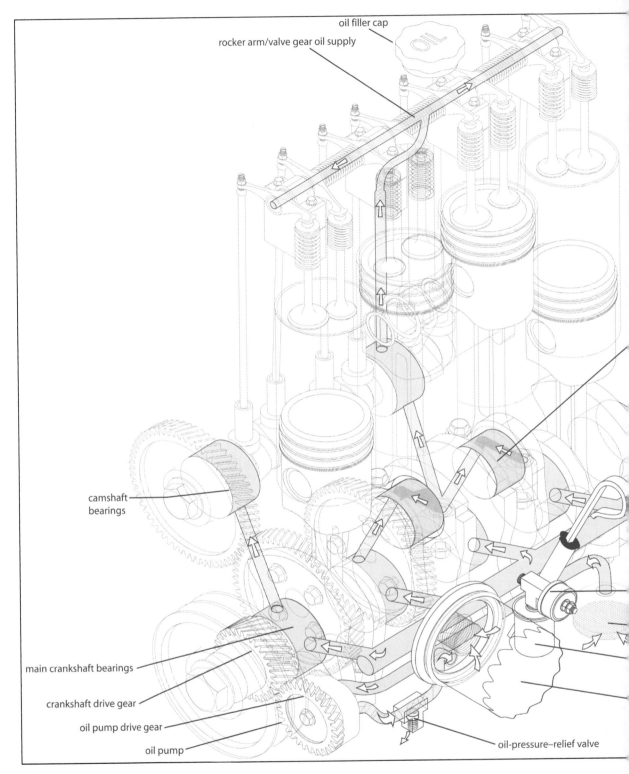

oil filler cap

rocker arm/valve gear oil supply

camshaft
bearings

main crankshaft bearings

crankshaft drive gear

oil pump drive gear

oil pump

oil-pressure–relief valve

THE LUBRICATION SYSTEM

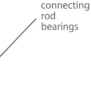

connecting
rod
bearings

main oil
gallery

dipstick

low–oil-pressure
warning switch

oil strainer

oil-pressure–gauge
sender

oil filter

To minimize friction and wear, a diesel engine's complex lubrication system maintains a thin film of oil on the contact surfaces of hundreds of moving metal parts. The oil system also plays an important role in removing excess heat from pistons and cylinder walls. Without oil, the heat of metal-to-metal contact would melt bearings and piston rings within seconds.

Maintaining the oil system is straightforward: Use a good-quality oil of the appropriate grade; monitor levels; and keep it clean by changing both oil and filter frequently. With normal use, oil loses its lubricating and cleaning properties as the level of contaminants rises. Replace the oil before it reaches that point.

Common lubrication system problems include minor leaks, which are usually just cosmetically objectionable; and oil contamination, which requires immediate action.

OIL

The quality of your oil and the frequency with which you change it are major determinants of your engine's life.

CHECKING THE LEVEL

Check the oil level before you start the engine. If you must check it after the engine has run, give the oil time to settle into the pan before pulling the dipstick. Wipe any splashed oil off the dipstick and reinsert it fully to get a reading. The level should be close to the high mark. Never run the engine if the oil level is outside the dipstick marks. Too little oil, and you risk seizing the

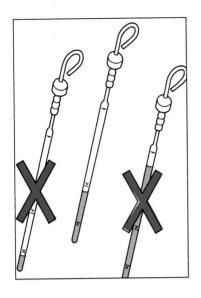

engine; too much, and the crankshaft will dip into the oil, causing aeration, overheating, and uncontrollable over-revvings. Black oil is normal for a diesel, but watch for sludge, milkiness, a thin quality, diesel smell, or particles in the oil.

WHICH GRADE?

Oil should meet the American Petroleum Industry (API) CF-4 or CG-4 requirements. These "C" grades indicate that the oil is designed for diesel engines. (Gasoline engines use "S" grade oils.) Many good oils will work in both diesel and gas engines, but always check both engine and oil specifications first.

WHICH VISCOSITY?

Stick with the engine manufacturer's recommendations. Temperature affects viscosity dramatically: A low ambient temperature calls for thin oil; a high ambient temperature calls for thick. Too thin, and lubrication qualities suffer; too thick, and components will drag, starting will be difficult, and again, lubricating properties will be poor.

Multigrade oils have proven more effective than single-grade oils at reducing engine wear, especially during cold startup; their lower viscosity creates less drag and allows oil to reach bearing surfaces more rapidly. Reduced deposits on the piston rings allow the rings to move more easily, with consequent better sealing. This results in less oil in the combustion chamber—reducing oil consumption and smoke.

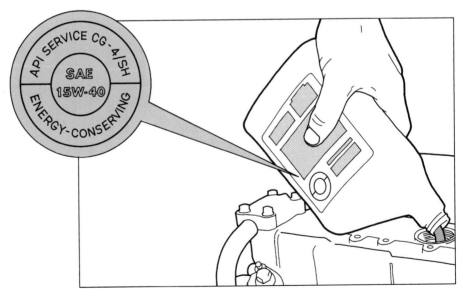

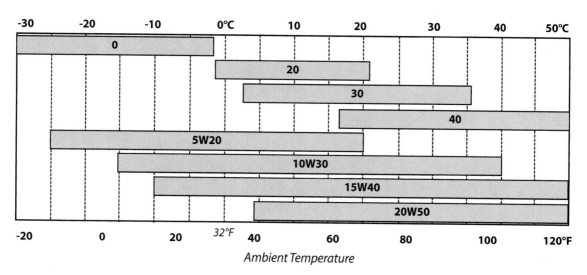

OIL ADDITIVES

Oil manufacturers use additives to improve the properties and extend the life of an oil. Today's oils combat soot, sludge, and varnish buildup, neutralize acids, and fight condensation—all while maintaining good viscosity. Antiwear and antiscuff additives extend engine life. After-market additives, however, have limited effect, and are not really cost effective. You'd do better to change the oil and filter more frequently.

OIL LEAKS

Nearly all engines leak oil to some extent from seals and openings. Early designs placed less emphasis on gaskets and seals, so expect more leakage in older engines. External leaks become more pronounced with age and use and can be a good indication of engine life and its quality of maintenance.

OIL CONSUMPTION

All diesels burn oil to some extent, but usually in such small quantities as to be barely noticeable between oil changes. Other than the

blue smoke it produces, oil consumption is not a problem and alone is seldom cause for rebuilding an engine.

OIL PRESSURE

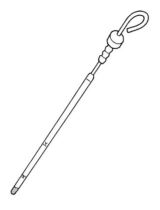

Many factors affect oil pressure, especially oil grade, age, and temperature. As bearings wear and clearances increase, the oil system must work harder to maintain pressure. Oil pressure can therefore be a very good indicator of engine condition. Pressures are typically 40–60 psi at idle on cold startup and must show within 15 seconds (if not, shut down the engine).

At high rpm, these pressures should be maintained but will drop as temperatures increase. When returned to idle, a hot engine may show pressures below 20 psi.

Low pressure throughout the rpm range may indicate a well-used engine, but check the specifications—some low-pressure/high-flow systems are rated as low as 8 psi!

CHANGING OIL

With automotive-engine manufacturers continually stretching the time between servicing, it becomes tempting to squeeze in an extra few hours between oil changes on your boat's diesel. Don't! Changing the oil often will prolong that expensive diesel's life. Follow the manufacturer's recommended oil-change frequencies *as a minimum*. In general, change oil every 125 hours or seasonally, whichever comes first.

If your fuel has a high sulfur content, you need a heavy-duty oil to handle the sulfur. Alternatively, double the frequency of oil changes.

DRAINING OIL

A little forethought can make the messy job of changing oil much easier—and the easier it is, the less likely you'll be to put it off. Place oil-absorbent pads beneath the filter and drain plug to catch wayward spills before they reach the bilge. Run the engine just before changing the oil to get all the contaminants off the bottom of the pan and suspended in the oil. Warm oil will drain more quickly than cold oil. With a good-sized container close by, remove the drain plug at the bottom of the pan. Inevitably, the plug will slip from your fingers and fall into the container, just as the warm oil gushes everywhere *except* the container. No wonder changing the oil is one of the most hated routine-maintenance tasks.

If you use an oil pump to suck oil out through the dipstick tube, be sure the pickup tube reaches the bottom of the sump. Many marine diesels have a manual oil pump connected to the pan drain plug, which makes oil changes much easier and cleaner.

If your engine has no pump, consider installing one. Simply replace the drain plug with a threaded hose barb. (Take care to match the threads of the barb to the pan; some manufacturers use threads other than the standard NPT.) Fix the pump in an accessible location, connect the barb and pump with an oil-resistant hose, and clamp them securely. Do not use the popular clear polyester braided hose; it will harden and crack within a season.

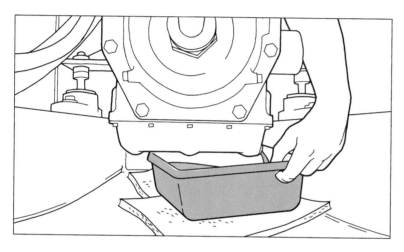

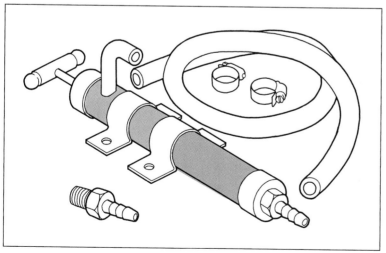

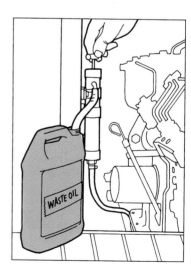

DISPOSING OF OIL

We are all aware of the effects of oil spills on our fragile environment. Always dispose of used oil responsibly. Many service stations offer a collection point for recycling. *Never* pump it over the side.

ADDING USED OIL TO THE FUEL

Operators of truck fleets sometimes dispose of large quantities of dirty oil in this way. It is technically possible to mix oil into diesel—as much as 17% by volume—but it requires filtration to remove contaminants and an expensive homogenization rig to mix the oil thoroughly. Clearly, this is not a practical proposition, even for the long-term cruiser.

OIL PUMP

Most oil pumps use an epicycloidal design, turning a multi-lobed rotor within a rotating body that has one more slot than the rotor has lobes. The pump sucks oil out of the oil pan, or sump, and pumps it through the oil filter and into internal galleries that feed the bearing surfaces. Oil pumps are maintenance free and rarely give problems.

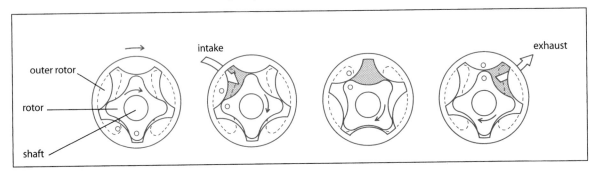

OIL PRESSURE–REGULATING VALVE

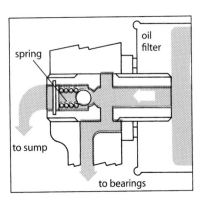

The pressure-regulating valve is a simple ball valve kept on a seat by a spring. When oil pressure reaches a preset value, the ball lifts off the seat and bleeds excess oil back to the oil pan. Pressure-regulating valves can be part of the oil pump, part of the oil-filter housing, or fitted separately. Like the oil pump, this component requires no maintenance and is relatively trouble free.

OIL FILTER

Disposable screw-on or spin-on filters are now almost universal. They are more effective than a simple sump gauze, and easier to replace than the old canister type with replaceable elements. Spin-on filters have an internal safety valve, which allows unfiltered oil to reach the bearings should the filter clog.

Always change the oil filter when you change the oil. Although the filter may have more life, it's pointless to fill the oil pan with clean oil, when a sludge-filled filter will contaminate it the next time you run the engine.

REMOVING THE FILTER

Removal is relatively simple, if somewhat messy—especially with filters mounted horizontally or upside down. Use oil-absorbent pads, rags, or a container to catch any spills. Various filter-wrench designs are available from automotive stores; the cloth-strap type works well over a wide range of filter sizes. If you don't have a wrench, punch a screwdriver midway through the old filter for better leverage.

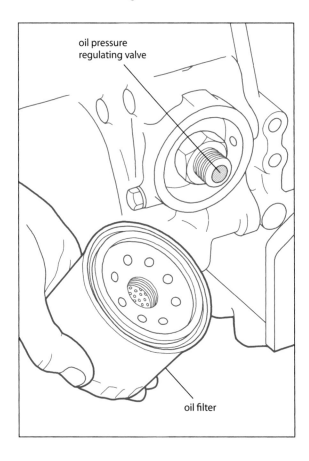

oil pressure regulating valve

oil filter

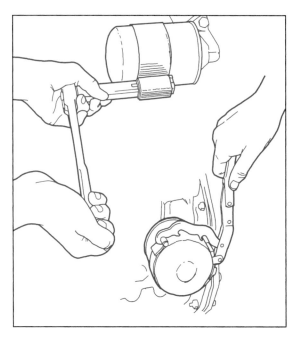

FITTING A NEW FILTER

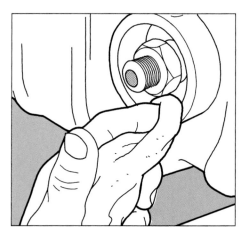

1. Wipe the contact sealing surfaces clean.

2. Lightly smear the filter seal with clean oil to improve sealing and ease removal for the next time.

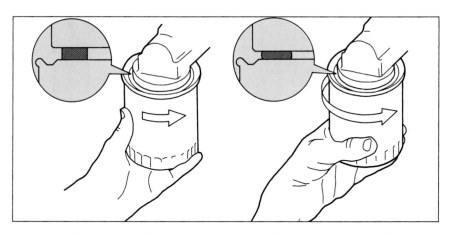

3. Spin on the filter until the seal makes contact, then tighten another three-quarter turn.

PRIMING THE OIL SYSTEM

Most engine wear occurs during the first few seconds after starting, before oil reaches the bearing surfaces. This is especially so after an oil and filter change, when the filter and oil galleries are empty; in that case, it may take 30 seconds for oil to reach the crankshaft. Larger commercial engines solve this problem with an electrical high-pressure priming pump that builds up oil pressure before the engine is started.

This type of pump is less common on smaller diesels, so it's a good idea to prime the oil system after an oil and filter change. Pull the stop cable or disconnect the run solenoid to prevent the engine from firing. Then, turn the engine over on the starter until the oil pressure light extinguishes, or oil pressure shows on the gauge. Let the starter rest; then repeat the exercise once more.

OIL CONTAMINATION

Running an engine with contaminated oil can seriously damage or even destroy it in a very short time. You may not notice oil contamination until the problem is severe, and then you may have to strip the engine completely to gauge the extent of the damage. It's best to find the contamination early, determine and rectify the cause, and then clean the system thoroughly as soon as possible. Check Chapter 2, Chart 4 (Oil Problems) for possible causes of contamination.

If bearing surfaces have been damaged, you may notice an increase in oil consumption, blue exhaust smoke, or difficult starting (piston rings and cylinders); screeching (rings and cylinders or other bearings); low oil pressure (main bearings); and hard mechanical knocking (rod bearings).

RAW WATER OR COOLANT IN THE OIL

Water will usually show on the dipstick as clear droplets in the oil, and the engine will appear to be "making oil" as the sump level increases. If the engine has been running, the oil will appear thick, gray, and milky; otherwise, the heavier water will separate and settle below the oil. If you can't see water in the oil, drain some oil into a glass container and let it settle overnight. Colored coolant will become quite visible if present.

Water—particularly salt water—can severely damage bearing surfaces, especially if it has been present for more than a few hours.

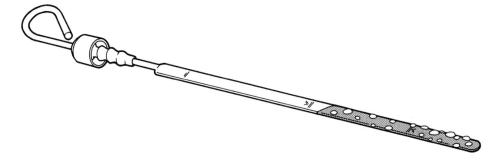

METAL IN THE OIL

Minute quantities of metal from bearing surfaces are produced in normal wear and usually remain invisible to the naked eye. If you do notice metal particles when the sump is drained, it pays to look further for the cause.

If you're concerned with the quantity or size of particles, cut open the oil filter with tin snips (a hacksaw will just deposit more metal) and wash the outside of the paper element with solvent into a container. Use a magnet to separate ferrous metals from the solution; then drain the remainder through a coffee filter to collect the debris.

Assessing the source of metal and degree of wear is not an easy task. As a rough guide, if the metal particles you collect from a small diesel fill more than $1/100$ of a teaspoon, or if individual particles are larger than a coarse grain of sand, call in expert help.

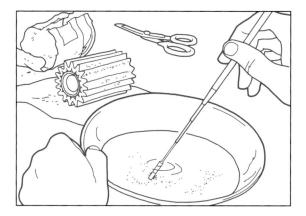

FUEL IN THE OIL

Diesel is not a good lubricant; running an engine for any length of time with fuel-diluted oil can seriously damage main and rod bearings. Look for thin oil with a strong diesel smell. The engine will appear to be "making oil," with the level on the dipstick slowly rising. A split or hole in the fuel lift-pump diaphragm is a common culprit.

SLUDGE IN THE OIL

If the oil is exceptionally thick and dark, it is most likely due to heavy contamination through infrequent changes or low-quality oil. Small quantities of antifreeze in the oil also cause sludge.

THIN OIL

If you don't smell diesel, the oil is probably well used and filled with contaminants affecting viscosity. Try replacing the oil more frequently, but continue to monitor the level, just in case there is diesel in the oil.

OIL ANALYSIS

If you suspect contamination but cannot identify the source, most oil manufacturers offer a spectromatic oil analysis service that will accurately measure the type and amount of contaminants in suspension. This service is intended more for larger operators monitoring the wear cycle of fleet engines, but is also available to the small diesel owner. Oil analysis is particularly effective in comparing samples from the same engine over time.

CLEANING A CONTAMINATED OIL SYSTEM

If you discover oil contamination, drain the oil, eliminate the source of contamination, and clean the system as soon as possible. Clean and run the engine promptly if you discover raw water or coolant in the oil, before any residue has a chance to corrode and seize rings in the cylinder bores.

    1. Close the seacock and remove the raw-water pump impeller.

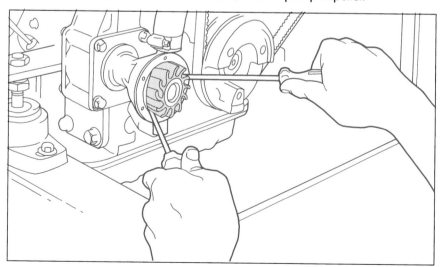

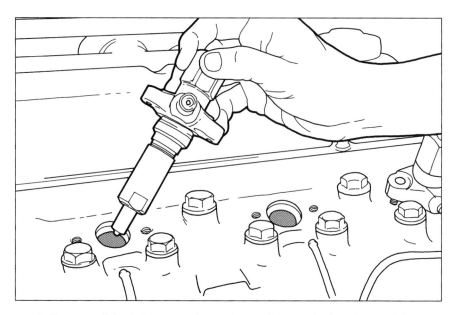

2. Remove all the injectors and turn the engine over by hand several times to expel any fluid from the cylinders.

3. Drain the sump. Replace the oil and oil filter.

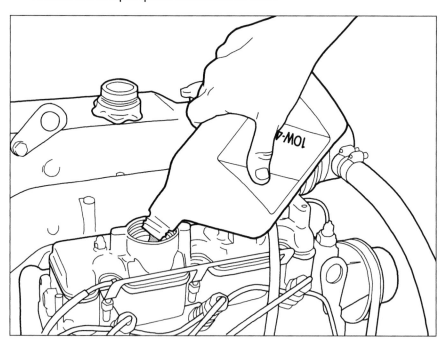

4. With the stop lever pulled out, or while pressing the stop button, turn the engine over using the starter until oil pressure shows on the gauge or the oil warning light goes out.
5. Repeat several times to circulate oil to all the components. Do not overload the starter—if it's too hot to touch, let it cool for 30 minutes.
6. Replace the oil and filter again, checking the color of the oil. If it's still contaminated, repeat steps 5 and 6 until the oil looks clean.
7. Refit the injectors and raw-water pump impeller. Open the seacock. Start the engine and run for five minutes.
8. Change the oil and replace the filter once more. Run the engine for 30 minutes to achieve operating temperature, then change the oil and filter once again.

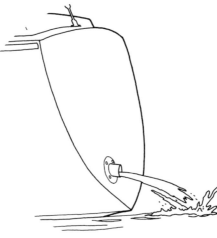

This process should remove all traces of contamination. With luck, there was minimal damage to the bearing surfaces. Double the frequency of the next two oil changes and monitor the oil gauge closely; low pressures indicating bearing damage.

LUBRICATION SYSTEM FAULTS

Problem	Possible Cause	Possible Symptoms
PICKUP TUBE		
Filter screen blocked	Oil contaminated [5]	Erratic, low, or no oil pressure
Tube defective	Seals defective [4] Tube loose [5]	As above
OIL PUMP		
Worn	Normal wear—high hours [4]	Low oil pressures
Drive loose	Poor assembly [5]	As above
PRESSURE-RELIEF VALVE		
Worn	Normal wear—high hours [4]	Low oil pressures
Sticking	Contamination [3] Wear [4]	Erratic pressures
Incorrect pressure	Incorrect setting [4] Spring worn or tired [4]	Stable pressures outside of limits
OIL FILTER		
External leaks	Filter loose [2] Seal dirty or damaged [2] Incorrect filter [3]	
OIL		
Level low	Poor maintenance [1] High consumption [2] External leaks [3]	Low or erratic oil pressures
Level high	Poor maintenance [1] Contamination with coolant, water, or fuel—see below	Increased external leakage; excessive exhaust smoke; engine over-revs out of control
Contaminated	See Troubleshooting Chart 4	
High consumption	Excessive wear [3]	Consistently low oil levels; excessive blue exhaust smoke

CRANKCASE PRESSURE

High

	Possible Cause	Possible Symptoms
	Blocked breather [3] Worn piston rings and cylinders [3]	High oil consumption; blue exhaust smoke; difficult starting; increased external leakage; engine over-revs out of control

CRANKSHAFT OIL SEALS

Leaking

	Possible Cause	Possible Symptoms
	High oil level [2]	Excessive crankcase pressure; possible blue exhaust smoke
	Worn or damaged seal [3]	External oil leak; oil will drip from flywheel housing if rear seal is defective
	Excessive crankcase pressure [3]	High oil mist from crankcase breather will cause blue exhaust smoke if breather connected to inlet
	Excessive wear on main bearings [4]	If bearings are worn enough to allow crankshaft to move, the engine is very tired and should be knocking from bottom end
	Scored or worn crankshaft [4]	External oil leak; oil will drip from flywheel housing if rear seal is defective

HOW LIKELY?   [1] Very common   [2] Common   [3] Possible   [4] Rare   [5] Very rare

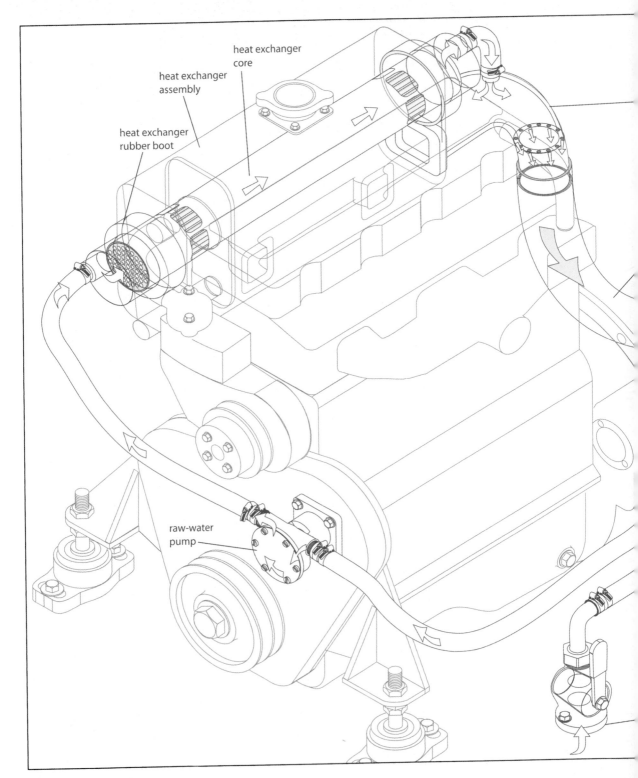

heat exchanger
core

heat exchanger
assembly

heat exchanger
rubber boot

raw-water
pump

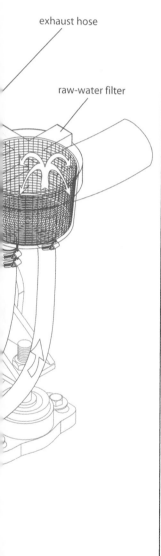

exhaust injection elbow

exhaust hose

raw-water filter

raw-water inlet
shutoff valve

THE RAW-WATER CIRCUIT

When diesel fuel is burned in the cylinders, roughly 30% of the heat energy is converted to usable power, 35% disappears with the exhaust gases, and 35% remains as excess heat that would melt the engine if it weren't quickly removed. The marine engine dissipates surplus heat into raw cooling water that is pumped through the engine and then overboard by way of the exhaust.

A marine diesel can be either direct cooled or indirect cooled.

On a direct-cooled engine, a raw-water pump circulates raw water through the engine block and cylinder head, out through the exhaust manifold, into the exhaust injection manifold, and overboard through the wet exhaust. A thermostat maintains engine temperature by controlling the amount of cooling water that bypasses the engine. Direct-cooled engines have lower-temperature thermostats to reduce salt formation.

The advantages of direct-cooled engines are their simplicity, lower cost, and reduced bulk. The disadvantage, though, is their vulnerability to corrosion—particularly with smaller, inexpensive automotive engines that have been marinized.

Indirect-cooled engines route the raw water through a heat exchanger, where it extracts surplus heat from the engine coolant. The raw water is then pumped into the injection elbow and overboard through the wet exhaust.

Because only the raw-water pump and heat exchanger come into contact with raw water, corrosion problems on indirect-cooled engines are reduced. This type of engine may cost more, but its longer life makes it worth every cent.

The raw-water circuit requires regular maintenance to keep the pump working and waterways clear of debris, salt deposits, and corrosion. Most overheating problems can be traced to poor maintenance of the cooling circuits.

THROUGH-HULL FITTING AND VALVE

INSPECTION

Check for leaks, corrosion, and good sealing. The valve must operate easily, but depending on type it may require a locking screw to be loosened first. Some composite valves require part of the body to be unscrewed before the valve will turn. Never force a tight valve while the boat is in the water.

RAW-WATER STRAINER

A raw-water strainer keeps debris from damaging the raw-water impeller or obstructing cooling-water flow. It must be an adequate size for the job.

INSPECTION

Close the seacock. Remove any debris from the basket. Check gaskets and seals for leaks. Check for corrosion, particularly on wing nuts that hold covers in place. Plastic strainers tend to be maintenance free, but hose connections are easily split by over-tightening the hose clamps. Remember to open the seacock on completion.

RECONDITIONING

1. Close seacock.
2. Disconnect the hoses and remove the filter from the boat.
3. Disassemble the filter.

4. Sandblast metal components if possible, or dip them in a 25% solution of muriatic acid. Dip for the minimum time; prolonged contact will damage brass or bronze. Muriatic acid works well on plastic bowls. (Do not scrape or use solvents on plastics.) Wash parts thoroughly with water to remove all traces of acid.

5. Replace the seals and gaskets. Replacement kits are available for most brands.

6. Reassemble and reinstall, checking the hoses and hose clamps.

7. Replace the anodes. (See page 667 for information on anodes.)

8. Spray all metal with a heavy-duty corrosion inhibitor.

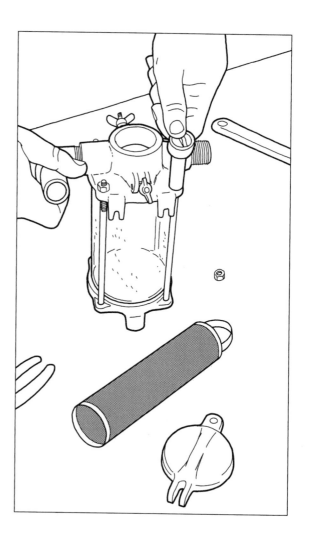

RAW-WATER PUMP

Raw-water pumps continuously suck cooling water from outside the boat and pump it through the engine. Nearly all small-diesel raw-water pumps contain rubber-vaned impellers. These self-priming pumps give good service if well installed and maintained, despite each vane's flexing more than a million times in every 10 engine hours. The weak point of these pumps is the vulnerability of the soft rubber impeller: hard debris or loss of lubricating water can destroy them in seconds. With an adequate water supply and a good strainer upstream, the average impeller should give a couple of seasons' service—provided it does not have to work against high suction or pressure.

INSPECTION

Check the front cover gasket for leaks. Corroded cover screws are common, often severe enough for heads to be missing. Check the pump body drain hole for raw water or oil, a sure sign of shaft seal failure. Water flow from the exhaust outlet will give a good indication of pump condition.

REMOVING THE IMPELLER

1. Remove the screws that retain the front cover and remove the cover plate and gasket.

2. Pry out the small rubber plug that protects the impeller splines, if fitted.

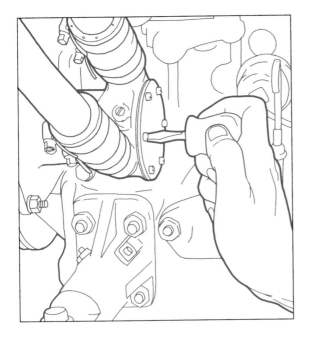

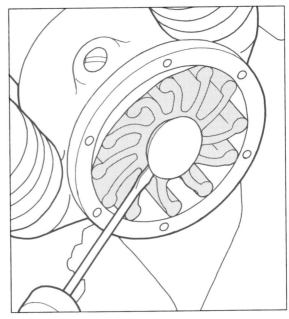

3. Check the way in which the impeller is attached to the pump shaft. Most pumps have splined impellers, but some have keyways and others have a through-bolt. Removing the splined impeller with pliers will usually tear the vanes; it's better to use two blunt screwdrivers as levers.

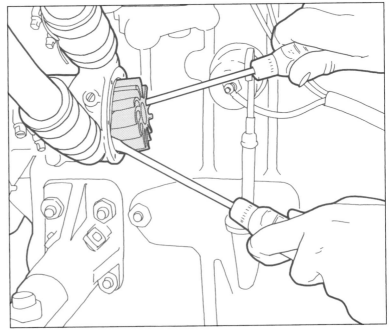

INSPECTING THE IMPELLER

Check for:

- Damaged or missing vanes. Missing vanes normally lodge themselves in the heat-exchanger inlet. Locate and remove them.
- Permanent set. New vanes are perpendicular to center. A slight set is acceptable.
- Worn vanes. The tips of new vanes have a symmetrical bead. Tips will wear on one side.
- Hardening of the rubber with age.
- Corrosion of the cover plate screws.
- Scoring of the cover plate, which dramatically reduces pump efficiency.

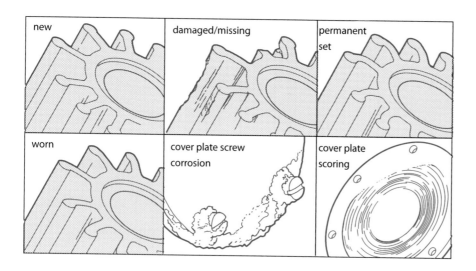

INSTALLING THE IMPELLER

- When refitting the impeller, lubricate it with lithium grease if you plan to run the pump soon; otherwise, use a silicone grease or prime with water. Don't forget the impeller plug, if fitted.
- Install used impellers with the same direction of rotation as before.
- Where an O-ring is used to seal the front cover, lightly grease the ring. O-rings can be reused if supple and not damaged.
- Where a paper gasket is used to seal the cover, clean the sealing faces with solvent to remove surplus grease. Always fit a new paper gasket. A flexible sealant works well here.

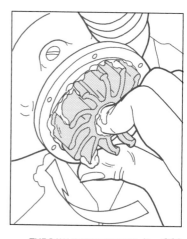

RECONDITIONING A RAW-WATER PUMP

Reconditioning a raw-water pump can be costly. Often the pump body, shaft, and drive gear are the only reuseable parts. Professional reconditioning may not be economical if the pump shaft needs replacing.

DISASSEMBLING THE PUMP

Pump designs vary widely—even within the same manufacturer's product line. The following instructions will work with most designs, but proceed with care in case your pump calls for special procedures.

1. Remove the front cover plate and the impeller (see above).

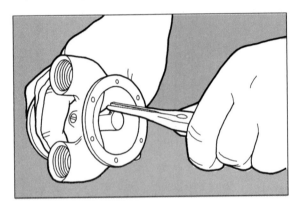

2. If the impeller is secured with a key, remove the key.

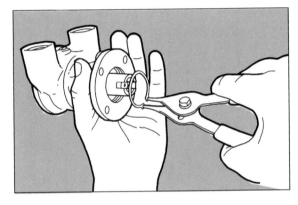

4. Remove the bearing-retaining snap ring(s), if fitted.

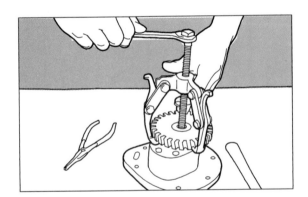

3. Remove the drive gear. Pumps with drive couplings can skip this step.

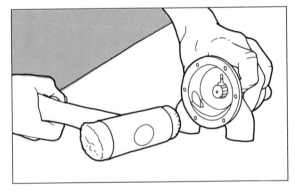

5. Tap the shaft and bearing assembly out of the pump body. Do not hammer on the shaft.

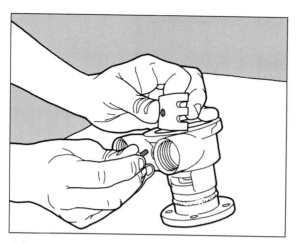

6. Remove the screw that holds the cam (if fitted). Remove the cam.

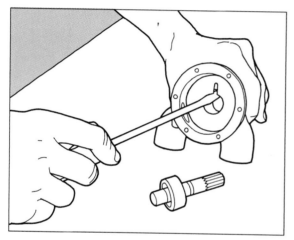

7. Remove the back plate carefully (if fitted) with a screwdriver. These thin plates can be difficult to remove without damaging them.

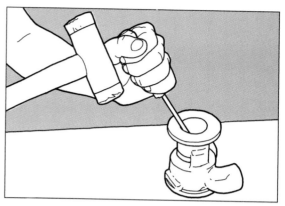

8. With a screwdriver and hammer, remove the shaft seals from the pump body. Disassembly will damage the seals—this is normal. Take care that the screwdriver blade picks up only the rear face of the seal and not the pump body, which can break.

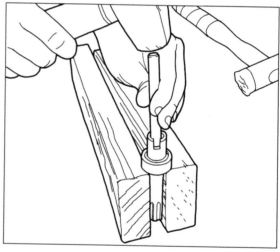

9. Remove the bearing(s) from the shaft with a puller or press. *Note:* If you must hammer on the shaft, use a soft-faced hammer or a block of wood to protect the soft stainless shaft, which distorts easily. Shafts are *very* expensive!

INSPECTING THE PUMP COMPONENTS

Pump body. If the impeller housing is deeply scored or pitted by corrosion, go no further: You need a new pump.

Cam. Check the cam for scoring and corrosion.

Shaft. Shaft scoring where the seals rub that is deep enough to be felt with a fingernail means replacement seals will have a short life. Replace the shaft.

Bearings. Bearings are usually self-lubricating, sealed-ball races; they should feel smooth and have no play. Bearings are relatively cheap; once you've stripped the pump this far, you may as well replace them.

Cover plate and back plate. Replace the cover plate and/or back plate if either shows significant scoring.

Screws. Cover plate and cam screws are particularly vulnerable to corrosion. If pink, replace. (See page 93 for more on pink corrosion.)

Seals. Replace.

Impeller. Replace.

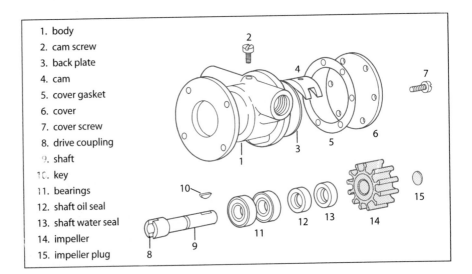

1. body
2. cam screw
3. back plate
4. cam
5. cover gasket
6. cover
7. cover screw
8. drive coupling
9. shaft
10. key
11. bearings
12. shaft oil seal
13. shaft water seal
14. impeller
15. impeller plug

REBUILDING

To reassemble the pump, reverse the order of the above procedure, noting the following points:

- Fit the seals squarely in the body, with the springs toward the fluid it is retaining: The oil-seal spring faces the bearings, and the water-seal spring faces the impeller.
- Liberally coat the seals, shaft, and bearings with grease. Don't forget to install the rubber-washer fluid slinger, if fitted.

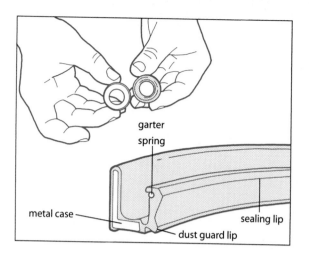

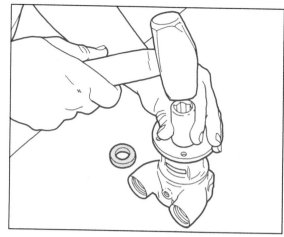

garter
spring

metal case

dust guard lip

sealing lip

HEAT EXCHANGERS AND OIL COOLERS

Heat exchangers and oil coolers remove surplus heat from the engine. Comparing the temperatures of the raw-water inlet and outlet pipes will give a good indication of heat transfer. The inlet pipe should be slightly above ambient water temperature, and the outlet should feel *warm*. If the outlet feels *hot,* too little water is passing through the heat exchanger; check the raw-water pump, strainer, and exhaust injection elbow. If the outlet feels *cold,* water flow is good but heat transfer is poor; check the internal cleanliness of the heat exchanger's raw-water and coolant passages.

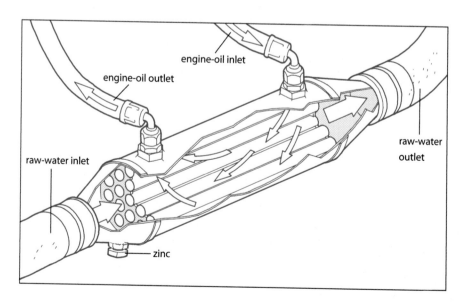

engine-oil inlet

engine-oil outlet

raw-water
outlet

raw-water inlet

zinc

Salt buildup can quickly clog the raw-water side of heat exchangers and oil coolers, especially in warmer climates. The coolant side will deteriorate equally quickly if the coolant lacks corrosion inhibitors. Salt buildup dramatically affects the transfer of heat between raw water and coolant, and is a major cause of engine overheating.

Note: Shutting down a hot engine that has been working hard can cause the raw water in the heat exchanger to boil and leave heavy salt deposits. Idle the engine for 15 minutes before shutting it down.

An internal leak in a heat exchanger will result in a loss of coolant or contaminate the coolant with salt water, depending upon system pressures. An internal leak in an oil cooler can be disastrous.

CLEANING

The best way to clean heat-exchanger and oil-cooler cores is to boil the whole assembly in a noncaustic solution. If you don't have access to this type of professional-grade equipment, you can use a 25% solution of muriatic acid. But, beware: Acid-cleaning will quickly weaken a cooler, opening small holes and cracks that salts and corrosion had sealed.

If you acid-clean a core, note the following points:

- Don't forget the protective gloves and glasses!
- Immerse the core for the minimum time (just until all contamination is gone), or the corrosive acid may eat into the metal and cause serious damage.
- Cores fitted with aluminum sleeves need the special attention of a non-caustic solution; muriatic acid quickly attacks aluminum.
- Acid will contaminate the oil system, so block off oil connections on oil coolers.
- Flush the cleaned core thoroughly with water to remove all traces of acid.
- Look over the core carefully. Corrosion will show as soft, crumbly, pink metal.
- Spray the core with a light corrosion inhibitor if it won't be installed immediately.

TESTING

Test a heat exchanger by pressurizing the raw-water side with air while the whole assembly is immersed in a large container of water. Bubbles will signal a leak. An oil cooler should be pressurized on its oil side. Test pressures should be approximately 25% above specified system pressure.

Take care not to overpressurize:

- Heat exchanger with 7-lb. pressure cap—test at 10 psi
- Heat exchanger with 15-lb. pressure cap—test at 20 psi
- Engine-oil coolers running at 60 psi—test at 75 psi

Repairs are not recommended unless you are an expert coppersmith! If in doubt, always replace.

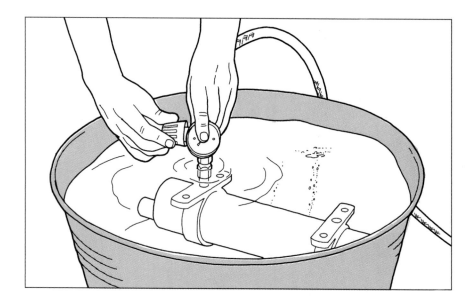

SACRIFICIAL ANODES, OR "ZINCS"

To reduce corrosion, sacrificial anodes—also called zincs—are often fitted to the raw-water side of engine components such as heat exchangers and oil coolers and to the base of most metal raw-water strainers. A direct-cooled engine will have a large zinc in the block itself.

Well-maintained zincs extend the life of the heat exchangers and oil coolers, saving your hard-earned dollars for better purposes. The frequency of zinc replacement depends on several factors, so check the zincs monthly at first to understand how long individual zincs last in your system.

CHECKING AND REPLACING

1. Remove *all* the old zinc. Pieces of old zincs can restrict heat exchangers and coolers.

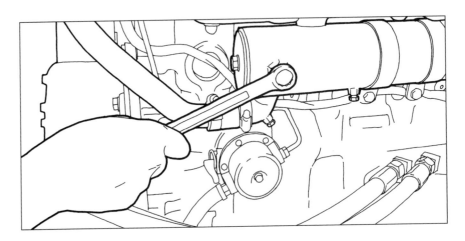

2. Knock off flaky oxides with a hammer.

3. If a zinc is less than half its original size, replace it. Tighten the new zinc well into the holder without shearing off the soft metal.

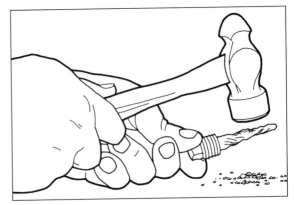

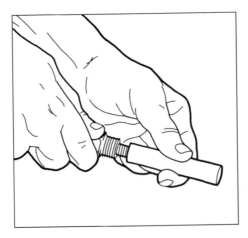

4. A flexible sealer on the plug threads will prevent leakage but still allow part of the thread to make electrical contact when tightened. Teflon tape will stop leakage, but may also prevent continuity. If in doubt, check it with a multimeter.

ANTISIPHON VALVE

The antisiphon valve prevents raw water from siphoning back into the exhaust manifold and filling the cylinders. It may be fitted between the raw-water pump and the heat exchanger or between the heat exchanger and the exhaust injection elbow. The antisiphon valve must be located at least 18 inches above the waterline to allow for heel. It may be excluded from the raw-water circuit only if the injection elbow is well above the waterline—again, under all sea conditions and angles of heel. Chapter 8 contains additional information on exhaust injection elbows.

CHECKING OPERATION

The antisiphon valve is a simple inverted U-tube with a non-return valve that prevents the pressurized raw water from escaping while the engine is running, but allows air to enter and break the siphon as soon as the engine is shut down. Check by removing the non-return valve and blowing through it in each direction. You can often resurrect defective valves by removing salt deposits with warm, soapy water.

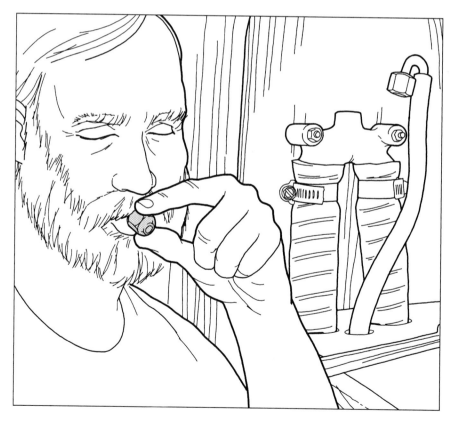

RAW-WATER HOSES

Raw-water hoses from the inlet through-hull to the strainer and on to the raw-water pump must be wire reinforced to prevent collapse under pump suction. The hoses beyond the pump are pressurized, so unreinforced hose will do the job unless a tight radius causes the hose to kink. Always use rubber hose; plastic hose does not withstand heat well.

HOSE CLAMPS

The average sailboat diesel uses dozens of hose clamps. There are many design variations, all based on a worm screw tightening a gear-cut band.

SELECTING THE CORRECT TYPE

Use only 100%–stainless hose clamps intended for marine applications. The lower grades of steel in many automotive clamps will corrode into a solid, unusable block in a very short time.

Of the quality stainless clamps available, solid bands are far superior to slotted bands. Not only are they stronger, but they will withstand considerably more corrosion before failing.

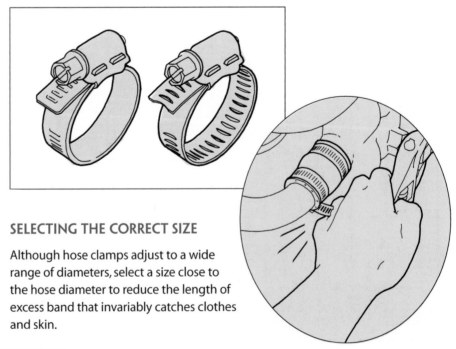

SELECTING THE CORRECT SIZE

Although hose clamps adjust to a wide range of diameters, select a size close to the hose diameter to reduce the length of excess band that invariably catches clothes and skin.

PROTECTING HOSE CLAMPS

Hose clamps are often hidden away in seldom-visited, damp corners and are often subject to extreme temperatures, humidity, and salt. Spraying each hose clamp—particularly the adjusting mechanism—with heavy-duty corrosion inhibitor will more than double its life. Repeat every time the clamp is disturbed.

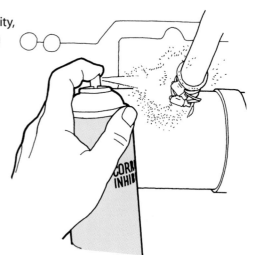

RAW-WATER THERMOSTATS

Thermostats in direct raw-water–cooled engines open at lower temperatures than those in indirect-cooled engines—usually 120°F–140°F (49°C–60°C). The instructions for inspecting and testing thermostats in Chapter 6 apply to thermostats in both direct- and indirect-cooled engines.

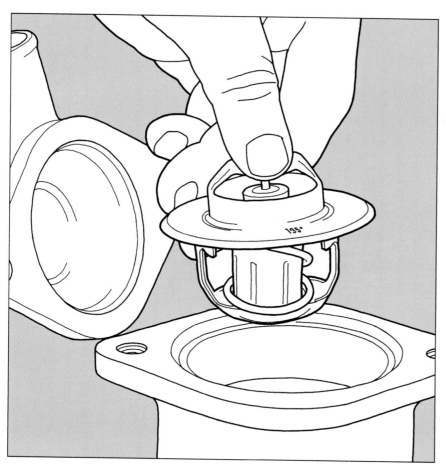

RAW-WATER CIRCUIT FAULTS

Problem	Possible Cause	Possible Symptoms

SYSTEM TEMPERATURE PROBLEMS—See Troubleshooting Chart 6, page 614

RAW-WATER STRAINER

Problem	Possible Cause	Possible Symptoms
Restricted	Contaminated with debris [2]	Insufficient raw-water flow; engine overheats
Leaking	Gaskets defective [2] Cover loose [2] Hose clamps loose [3]	External raw-water leaks; if strainer is above waterline, air will be sucked into cooling system; engine overheats

RAW-WATER PUMP

Problem	Possible Cause	Possible Symptoms
Cover plate leaking	Defective gasket [2] Screws not tight enough [3]	Visible raw-water leaks; corrosion and salt crystals are often the first sign
Water leak from pump body	Shaft water seal defective [2] Shaft worn [2]	As above
Oil leaking from pump body	Shaft oil seal defective [3] Shaft worn [3] Excessive crankcase pressure [4]	Visible oil leak
Pump body hot	No water flow [1] Through-hull closed [1] Strainer blocked [1] Air leak on inlet side of pump [3]	High operating temperature; engine overheats
Poor pumping	Defective impeller [1] Worn or rough body, cover plate, cam, or back plate [2] High exhaust backpressure [3] Excessive suction—pump too high above waterline [3] Inadequate water supply—see above	As above
Impeller torn	Debris passing through pump [1] Pump overloaded [3] High exhaust backpressure [3] Excessive suction—pump too high above waterline [3]	As above
Impellers failing often	Worn and rough body, cover plate, or back plate [2] Poor water supply [2] No lubrication on initial build [3] High exhaust backpressure [3] Excessive suction—pump too high above waterline [3]	As above

HEAT EXCHANGER/OIL COOLER

Problem	Possible Cause	Possible Symptoms
Corrosion	No zinc in raw-water side [1] Poor maintenance [1]	Metal "dezincified"; looks "pink," especially after cleaning
External leaks	Defective gaskets or seals [1] Loose hose clamps [2] Corroded housing or end caps [2]	Visible leaks
Internal leaks	Corrosion [2] Solder failure [4]	Heat Exchanger: Header tank "makes water"; loss of coolant Oil Cooler: See warning in chapter text.

EXHAUST INJECTION ELBOW—See Chapter 8

DIRECT-COOLING THERMOSTAT—See Chapter 6 (For coolant-system thermostat, the symptoms are the same.)

HOW LIKELY?   [1] Very common   [2] Common   [3] Possible   [4] Rare   [5] Very rare

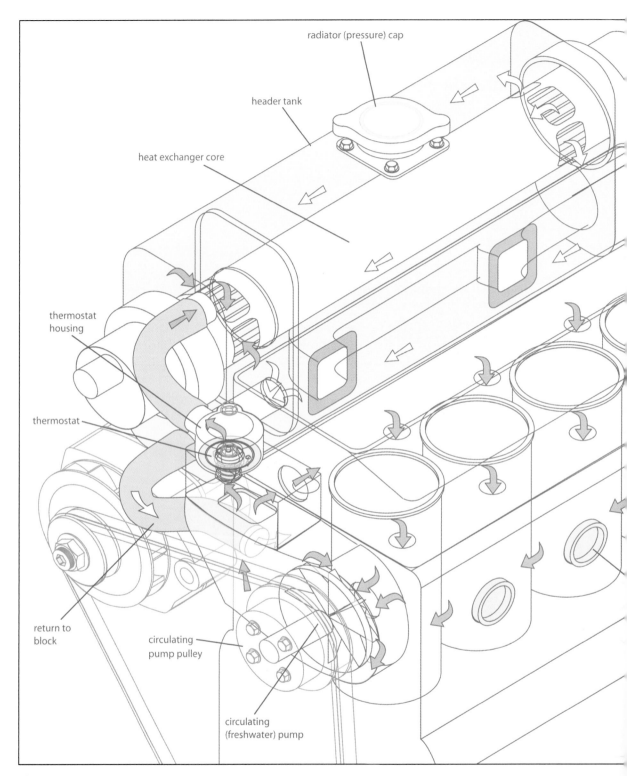

radiator (pressure) cap

header tank

heat exchanger core

thermostat
housing

thermostat

return to
block

circulating
pump pulley

circulating
(freshwater) pump

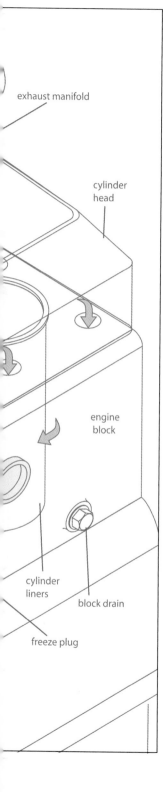

exhaust manifold

cylinder head

engine block

cylinder liners

block drain

freeze plug

THE COOLANT CIRCUIT

The majority of boats are equipped with indirect-cooled diesels, in which a freshwater or coolant circuit keeps corrosive raw water away from the main-engine components.

A dedicated, belt-driven centrifugal pump circulates coolant through the engine block and cylinder head to remove surplus heat. The hot coolant then passes through a heat exchanger, where the heat transfers to the raw-water circuit and is pumped overboard with the raw water through the exhaust. A thermostat maintains the temperature of the engine by controlling coolant flow through the block and cylinder head.

Coolant circuits require regular maintenance to keep the components clean and to ensure good heat transfer across the heat exchanger to the raw-water circuit. While most overheating problems can be traced to the raw-water side of the cooling system, thermostats and circulating pumps occasionally fail.

COOLANT

Keep the freshwater circuit clean. Good-quality coolant will help prevent buildup of scale and corrosion that can reduce heat transfer by as much as 95%.

Note: Never check the coolant while the engine is hot. Removing the pressure cap from a hot engine can spray scalding water over the engine bay. Always wait until the engine has cooled to below 120°F (48.9°C) or feels warm to the touch.

INSPECTION

Check the coolant level before you start the engine. The coolant should be visible. Where access is poor, you should be able to feel the level with your finger. An adequate mix will have a strong coolant-green/blue color. (Simple hydrometers are available to measure mixtures more accurately.) Internal corrosion and overheating are indicated by brown discoloration.

WHICH COOLANT?

Coolant added to water will lower the freezing point and raise the boiling point; and prevent corrosion. Most coolants are based on ethylene glycol (although the heavier-duty varieties use propylene glycol), and contain additives to reduce foaming, corrosion, and scale deposits. Good-quality coolants will give the best protection.

WHAT MIXTURE?

Mix coolant and water in a 50/50 solution. Any lower concentration of coolant will reduce both corrosion and freeze protection. A mixture of more than 70% coolant will gel and block waterways, causing overheating.

COOLANT MIXTURE VERSUS TEMPERATURE PROTECTION

Antifreeze Concentration By Volume (%)	Propylene Glycol	Ethylene Glycol
	Freeze Point (°F)	
0	32	32
20	19	16
30	10	4
40	-6	-12
50	-27	-34
60	-56	-62
80	-71	-57
100	-76	-5

DRAINING THE OLD COOLANT

The location of coolant drains differs with each engine.

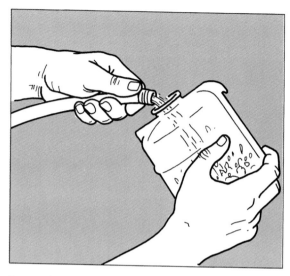

Engine block — usually aft, above the height of the crankshaft.

Expansion tank (if fitted) — remove the tank and wash it out.

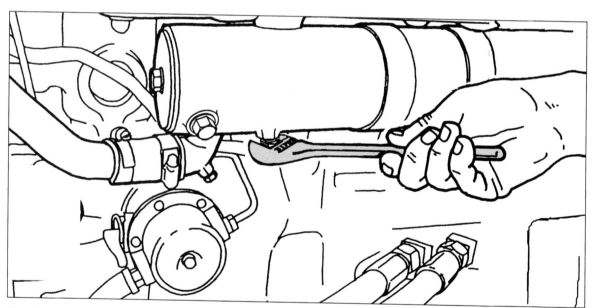

Header tank — probably will drain through the cylinder block, but some engines have separate drains.

Heat exchanger — at the lowest point.

CLEANING THE COOLANT CIRCUIT

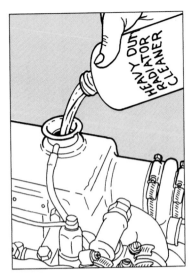

An acid-based solution will remove scale and corrosion. Acid will also find weak points, so if your heat exchanger or header tank has been neglected, acid-cleaning will find their faults.

Automotive stores carry several types of acid-based radiator cleaners; select the strongest one. These products are simple to use, but always follow the instructions on the bottle.

ADDING COOLANT

Premix the coolant to the proper concentration in a separate container. Pour the solution into the correct filler cap—it's not an unusual mistake to pour coolant into the oil filler. To ensure the thermostat has opened, run the engine at idle with the pressure cap off until the engine reaches operating temperature. Continue adding more solution until the header tank is full. Top off the expansion tank, if fitted.

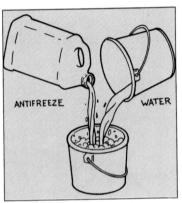

TESTING THE COOLANT CIRCUIT FOR LEAKS

If you suspect a leak in the coolant circuit or have just rebuilt any of the components, it's good practice to pressure-test the system. You'll need a coolant-pressure tester that fits on the header tank. If you don't own a tester, it may be worth borrowing one: A 10-minute check can save you the considerable time it would take to disassemble the entire system and test components individually.

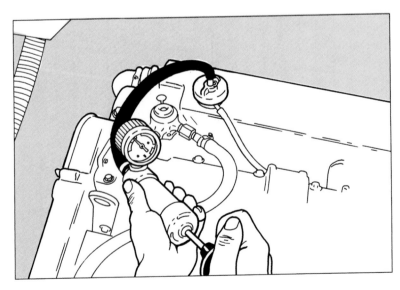

HEADER TANK

Many engines have a header tank that combines a water-cooled exhaust manifold and heat exchanger. The tank itself requires no scheduled maintenance; it is, however, usually made from cast aluminum, which is vulnerable to corrosion. White, powdery deposits under hoses and around joints are the signal to remove the header tank and treat the corrosion.

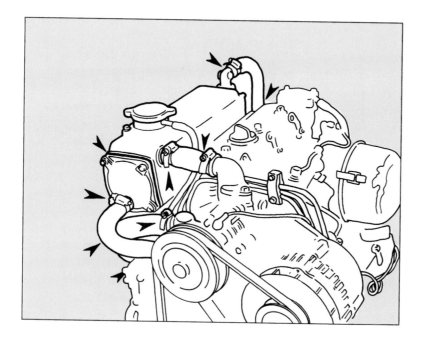

PRESSURE CAP

The pressure cap on the header tank is identical to an automotive radiator cap, and requires no scheduled maintenance. It's not unusual for corrosion to appear on the cap's external surface, but should it affect the spring or sealing surfaces, replace the cap. Replacements must have the correct pressure rating for the system—usually 7 or 15 psi.

EXPANSION TANK

Expansion, or overflow, tanks are common on automotive engines, and are sometimes found on marine engines. The tank collects the expanding coolant as the engine warms, and returns it as the engine cools, keeping the header tank full and the heat exchanger fully immersed in coolant at all times.

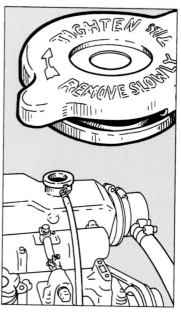

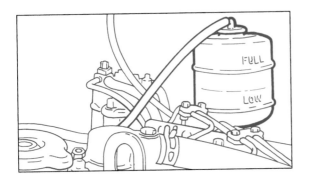

Design variations include simple expansion bottles or fully pressurized containers, which are usually constructed of translucent plastic to permit easy monitoring of the level.

Note: Don't rely on the expansion tank alone as an indicator of coolant level. Always check coolant level in the header tank. If the expansion-tank hose breaks its siphon, the header tank can show full with the engine out of water.

THERMOSTAT

The thermostat is a simple, temperature-sensitive valve that opens and closes to control coolant flow through the engine block and cylinder head.

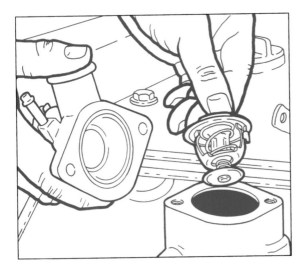

In operation, thermostats hover in the partially open position, sensing variations in coolant temperature caused by changing loads and ambient conditions. If a temperature gauge is fitted, the temperature should gradually rise from cold to operating temperature as the thermostat begins to control. A sticking thermostat will allow the temperature to rise well above operating temperature before it opens; or, if it is already stuck open, the engine may take a long time or never reach the correct temperature.

INSPECTION

Remove the thermostat from the engine. If it is contaminated, corroded, or shows score marks where it has been binding on its guide, replace it.

TESTING

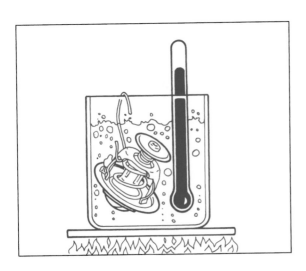

Check the rating stamped on the flange or body. At temperatures below this rating, the thermostat should be fully closed. Test by suspending it in a container of water and slowly bringing it to a boil. The thermostat should start to open at its rated temperature. If you don't have a thermometer, watch the thermostat open as the water approaches boiling point. It must be fully open by the time the water boils and fully closed once the water cools. If not, replace it.

CIRCULATING PUMP

Circulating pumps are mostly of the centrifugal type. Such pumps are simple in construction, with problems limited to seal leakage or bearing failure. They can often be reconditioned but usually require a hydraulic press to remove the pulley or bearings.

CHECKING SEALS

The face seals in a circulating pump keep the coolant from reaching sealed bearings. When a seal fails, coolant leaks from the pump-body drain. Leaks will be more noticeable if the engine is shut down at operating temperature, when the system is pressurized. Any leakage means that the pump should be replaced or reconditioned before the coolant causes bearing failure.

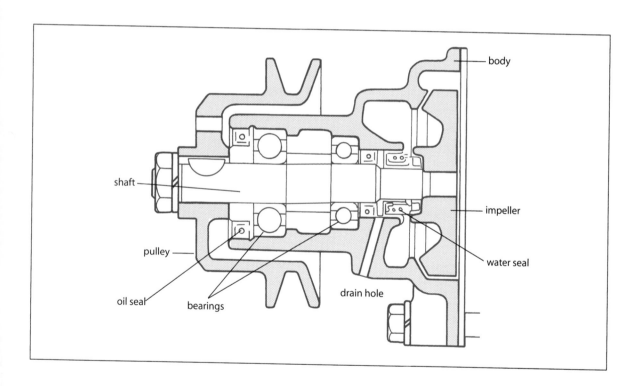

CHECKING BEARINGS

Circulating pumps usually have two self-lubricating and sealed ball race bearings. Check the bearings with the V-belt removed; they should feel smooth when rotated by hand. Grip the pulley firmly and try moving it side to side and fore and aft. Any more than negligible movement means that the bearings are close to failure; replace or recondition the pump.

V-BELT

The V-belt drives both the circulating pump and the alternator from the crankshaft pulley. If the belt fails, the circulating pump will not run, and the engine will overheat in minutes. Check the belt regularly as part of your startup routine, and always carry a spare.

INSPECTION

Check for excessive wear, cracking, and polished or sticky V surfaces. If in doubt, replace the belt. If you upgrade alternators, upgrade the belts and pulleys as well.

CORRECT TENSION

Belt tension is correct when firm thumb pressure applied midway along the longest belt run deflects the belt by about ½ inch. Insufficient tension allows the

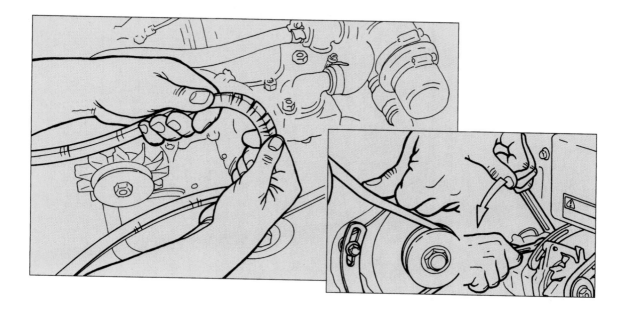

belt to slip; too much tension causes premature bearing failure in pumps and alternators. Adjust tension by repositioning the alternator.

COOLANT-CIRCUIT HOSES

Hoses used in the coolant circuit connect the circulating pump, heat exchanger, and oil cooler to the cylinder head and engine block.

INSPECTION

Coolant hoses suffer the effects of high temperature, pressure, and contact with coolant and oil. Rubber hoses should feel soft when squeezed. Check for bulging, splits, cracking, chafing, and stickiness caused by oil contamination.

COOLANT CIRCUIT FAULTS

Problem	Possible Cause	Possible Symptoms

SYSTEM TEMPERATURE PROBLEMS—See Troubleshooting Chart 6, page 614

HEADER TANK

Problem	Possible Cause	Possible Symptoms
Coolant low	Natural expansion [1] External leaks [3] Internal leaks [4]	Tank needs frequent filling
Coolant dirty	Not changed often enough [2] Overheating [3]	High temperature
"Making water"	Defective heat exchanger [3] Loose hose clamps on heat exchanger rubber boots [3]	Continuous flow of water from open pressure cap or through overflow tube
Oil in coolant	Cylinder-head gasket blown [3]	As above

PRESSURE CAP

Problem	Possible Cause	Possible Symptoms
Leaking	Defective seal [3]	Excessive leak as engine warms up and pressure builds
	Cylinder-head gasket blown [3]	Excess pressure in cooling system; coolant will be blown out of cap; loss of power; poor starting

CIRCULATING PUMP

Problem	Possible Cause	Possible Symptoms
Noise	Bearing failure; probably caused by seal failure or V-belt too tight [3]	Shaft seal leaking often indicates initial deterioration
Coolant leaking from pump body	Shaft seal failure [2]	External leak; coolant low in header tank

V-BELT

Problem	Possible Cause	Possible Symptoms
Slipping	Too loose [1]	First sign: polishing of contact surfaces; squealing; overheating; low alternator output; false reading on alternator-driven tachometers

Problem	Possible Cause	Possible Symptoms

V-BELT continued

Problem	Possible Cause	Possible Symptoms
Excessive wear	Too tight [2] Poor alignment of crankshaft, water pump, and alternator pulleys [2] Belt overstressed, often by upgrading alternator without increasing pulley and belt size [2]	Excessive wear on circulating pump and alternator bearings; large amounts of belt dust adjacent to belt track; thinning of belt
Thrown belt	Belt too loose [2] Pulleys not correctly aligned [2]	Engine overheats; alternator-driven tachometers will not work

THERMOSTAT

Problem	Possible Cause	Possible Symptoms
Stuck open	Wear [2] Contamination [2]	Normal circuit: Operating temperature remains low. Bypass-type circuit: Engine will overheat.
Stuck closed	Wear [2] Contamination [2]	Normal circuit: Operating temperature very high; engine overheats. Bypass-type circuit: Operating temperature remains low.
Thermostat not fitted	Someone tried to overcome system overheating problems incorrectly [2]	Normal circuit: Engine will not reach operating temperature. Bypass-type circuit: Engine will overheat.

HOW LIKELY?   [1] Very common   [2] Common   [3] Possible   [4] Rare   [5] Very rare

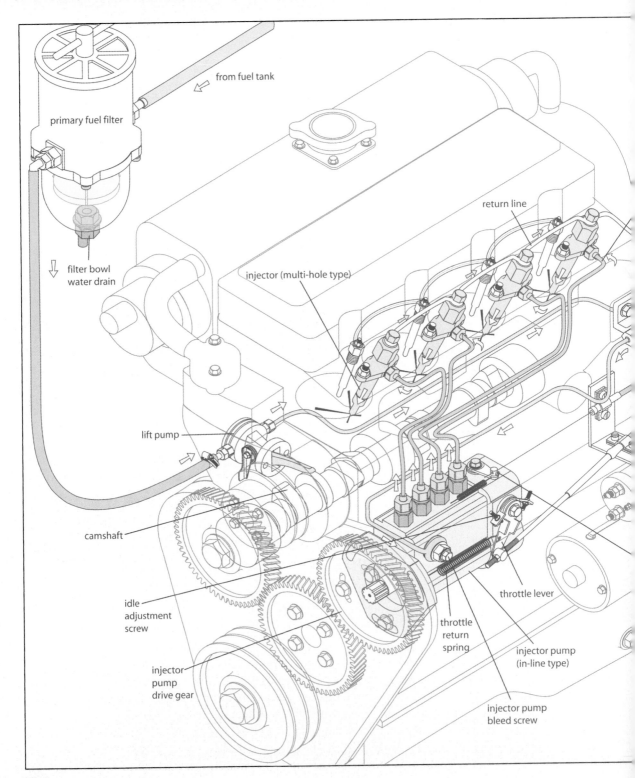

from fuel tank

primary fuel filter

filter bowl
water drain

return line

injector (multi-hole type)

lift pump

camshaft

idle
adjustment
screw

injector
pump
drive gear

throttle lever

throttle
return
spring

injector pump
(in-line type)

injector pump
bleed screw

THE FUEL SYSTEM

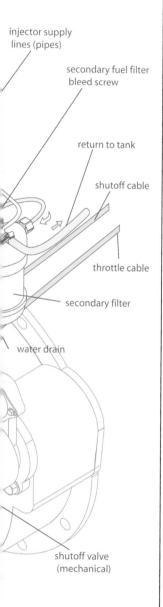

injector supply
lines (pipes)

secondary fuel filter
bleed screw

return to tank

shutoff cable

throttle cable

secondary filter

water drain

shutoff valve
(mechanical)

An efficient diesel engine requires a precise amount of fuel atomized into the combustion chamber at *exactly* the right time. Injecting these minute quantities of fuel accurately at high speed and pressure demands components with mirror-smooth surfaces and fits measured in ten-thousandths of an inch. Therein lies the weakness of the diesel engine: Even the smallest particle of dirt or water can seize or corrode components. For this reason, engine manufacturers design their fuel systems with good filtration and water separation to remove all contaminants *before* they reach the injector pump or injectors.

Fuel system cleanliness is essential to keeping a diesel engine running reliably. Keep the fuel free of dirt and water, and your fuel system will give years of reliable service: Injectors will continue to atomize, and the engine will start more easily, burn less fuel, and produce less smoke.

Replace filters regularly to prevent dirt and water from restricting delivery or contaminating the system. Injector nozzles gradually wear and need periodic testing to confirm they are atomizing the fuel correctly.

Surprisingly, a diesel will run even when a defective injection system is pouring uneven quantities of neat fuel into the engine. The lax owner may not even notice the deterioration in performance until the engine eventually fails to start.

After the starting system, the fuel system is the most likely to cause problems. Common faults can be traced to contamination with air, water, and dirt and the slow deterioration of injectors.

FUEL

The diesel fuel we pour into our tanks contains more energy, has a higher flash point (and is therefore safer), and is heavier than the gasoline we pour into our cars. A diesel engine burns less fuel and gives off fewer emissions than its gasoline counterpart.

All diesel fuel contains sulfur; the amount depends on the quality of the crude oil and the refining process. During combustion, sulfur converts to corro-

687

sive acids that are absorbed by the oil. New emission regulations reduce the allowable sulfur content to less than 0.3%, but if you buy diesel in countries with less-stringent regulations, change the oil more frequently (see Chapter 4).

CLEANLINESS

Even the smallest amount of debris will score and block the finely machined surfaces of fuel-system components; cleanliness is essential.

If you're unsure of fuel quality, filter the fuel to remove water and dirt before it goes into your tank. A good fueling filter can be fairly expensive—especially if it can handle the flow rate of a typical dockside delivery pump. Cost is relative, however: The price of a filter is low compared to that of replacing the injectors and injector pump destroyed by contamination.

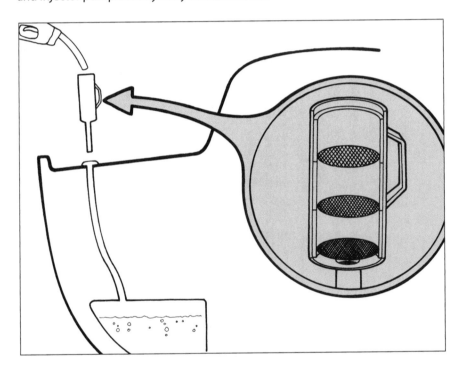

FUEL ADDITIVES

Oil companies put special additives in diesel fuel to reduce smoke, prevent pre-ignition, and mitigate the effects of low temperatures. In most cases, after-market additives have little effect, and those containing alcohol actually damage water-separator elements. There are a couple of exceptions.

Biocide. Certain types of algae and fungus survive on water in the fuel, appearing as a black, stringy sludge contaminating fuel tanks and blocking fuel lines and the primary filter. Fortunately, you can treat and even prevent such biological growth with one of several products readily available from marine-supply stores.

Fuel lubricants. Sulfur acts as a lubricant, prolonging the life of seals and O-rings. Modern fuels with reduced sulfur may be enhanced by the addition of a fuel lubricant.

FUEL TANKS

Fuel tanks come in all shapes, sizes, and materials, depending on the boatbuilder. Although they appear to be a maintenance-free component, the accumulation of water, dirt, and debris over the years causes major problems for fuel system components. Problems usually appear when rough seas stir up the debris at the bottom of the tank—just when you need the engine most.

INSPECTION

Tank. Periodic opening of the inspection cover (if fitted) to clean out accumulated water and sediment is advised; frequency depends on the quality of fuel used and the tank's age and material. Inspection cover seals must be made of fuel-resistant materials. Most seals deteriorate with age, and even the best materials will eventually break up and block fuel lines. Periodically unscrew the drain plug (if fitted) to remove any water and sediment.

Tank fittings. Check all fittings, hoses, and clamps for tightness; hoses that connect the filler to the tank are often forgotten. Pick-up tubes should reach the lowest point of the tank to prevent a buildup of water and sediment. Regularly inspect deck-mounted filler cap seals—they are a prime cause of water in the fuel. Shut-off valves should operate smoothly full travel.

PRIMARY FILTER

The primary filter provides the first and most important level of filtration. A well-designed filter will absorb considerable contamination. It *must* be capable of removing water and be of adequate size.

CHECKING THE BOWL

Inspect the filter bowl daily and drain any sediment and water. If the bowl requires draining more than once every 100 hours, the tank is dirty and needs cleaning.

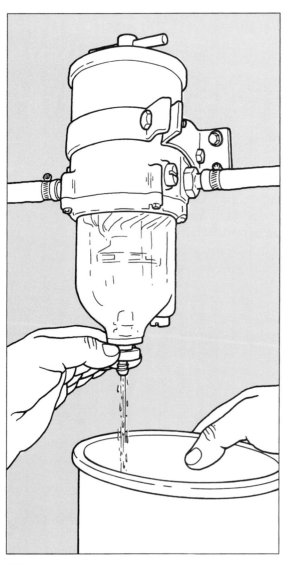

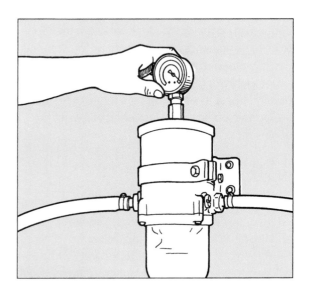

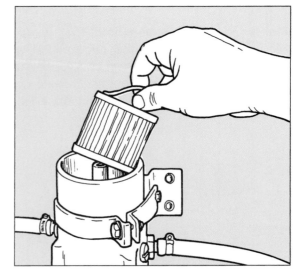

REPLACING THE ELEMENT

Replace elements at the first sign of discoloration. Always fit new seals. If replacement elements are available with different filtration rates, use the primary filter to remove the larger debris and let the secondary take care of what's left. Small engine primary filters use 10- or 20-micron elements. A vacuum gauge fitted to the outlet side of the filter can give an effective indication when the element is starting to restrict flow and needs to be replaced.

FUEL LIFT PUMP

The fuel lift pump supplies fuel under pressure to the injector pump. Most lift pumps are mechanically driven off a dedicated cam lobe on the engine camshaft. A reciprocating diaphragm sucks fuel from the fuel tank with flow controlled by two small internal non-return valves.

Lift pumps seldom have problems. Most lift pumps are sealed units that can't be repaired. Even if the pump can be stripped, repair kits can be difficult to locate; in most cases it is easier to replace the pump.

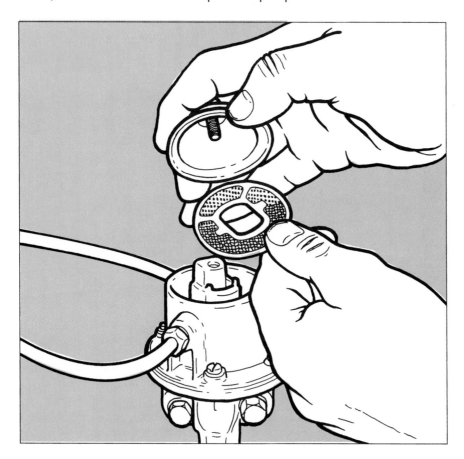

CLEANING THE PUMP FILTER SCREEN (IF ACCESSIBLE)

Clean the internal filter on fuel lift pumps annually. Remove the top cover, the seal, and the filter screen, and carefully wash the screen in a small container of diesel. Make sure the seals are good before reusing them.

CHECKING OPERATION

Disconnect the fuel outlet pipe from the pump and turn the engine over with the starter. The pump should produce full-bore flow in spurts. If it doesn't, check for supply problems by replacing the inlet pipe with a hose immersed in a container of clean diesel, and repeat the test.

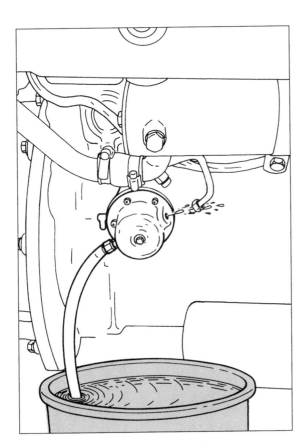
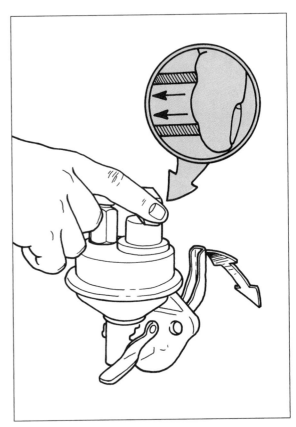

Remove a suspect pump from the engine and operate the cam lever. The pump should make a loud, sucking noise, and you should feel both suction and pressure when you place a finger over the inlet and outlet connections, respectively. (Although it's possible to test the pump on the engine using the priming lever, these levers commonly fail while the pump continues to function correctly.)

SECONDARY FUEL FILTER

The design of the secondary filter varies with engine and manufacturer. Replacement elements come in different shapes and sizes, with spin-on types becoming popular on newer engines. Each manufacturer specifies the level of filtration for their fuel system. Elements as fine as 2 microns are available that will stop particles larger than 0.002 mm (0.00008").

REPLACING THE ELEMENT

Although you don't have to replace secondary filters as often as primary filters, neglected secondary filters can still cause fuel supply problems. As a general rule, replace secondary-filter elements at every other primary-filter change.

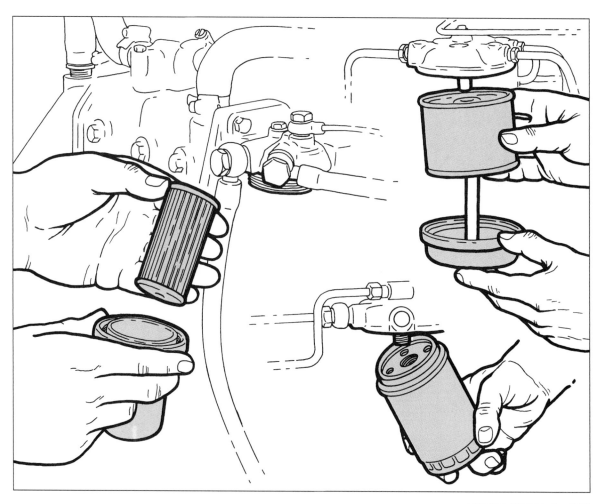

GOVERNOR

Governors are rpm–sensitive mechanisms that balance centrifuged flyweights against spring pressure to control the injector pump setting and maintain rpm under changing loads.

Governors, whether part of the engine or injector pump, require no maintenance. They may have external adjustments for maximum-rpm, acceleration, and idle-rpm settings, but only the idle-rpm setting can be altered. Maximum rpm and acceleration screws are factory set, and usually sealed; do not attempt to adjust them.

ADJUSTING IDLE RPM

Set idle rpm high enough that the engine is not laboring and shaking on its mounts, but low enough that boat speed is controllable. An incorrect idle rpm is most likely a sign of problems elsewhere. Before making adjustments, check that the injectors are atomizing well, the filters are clean, and the air supply is not restricted.

Adjust by turning the screw that sets the bottom stop of the throttle lever arm. With the engine running at operating temperature, loosen the locknut and slowly turn the stop screw in the required direction. Remember to tighten the locknut when you're satisfied with the setting.

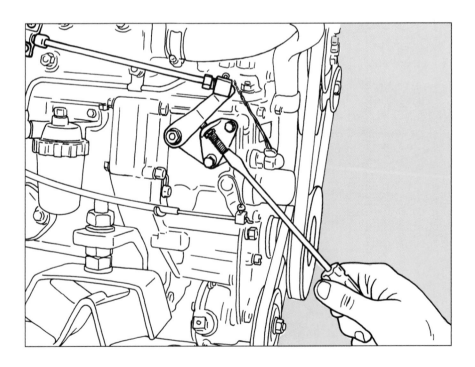

INJECTOR PUMP

The injector pump is the heart of the fuel system. This complex component receives low-pressure fuel from the lift pump, senses the engine's fuel requirement, and then, at exactly the right moment, pumps the correct amount of fuel to the injectors at very high pressure. Both in-line and distributor-type pumps are common on small diesels.

Injector pumps will provide years of reliable service if supplied with clean fuel. They are factory set and, for the most part, require no maintenance. A few models have their own oil sump and require regular oil changes. Failures are not common, and most problems are due to the presence of air.

CHECKING OPERATION

If you suspect a fault with the injector pump and have confirmed that the fuel supply to the pump is good and free of air and the shut-off mechanism is not operated:

1. Remove the injector lines from the pump.
2. Turn the engine over with the starter while looking closely at the injector-line connections. You should see a small shot of fuel from each connection as the piston reaches its injection point.
3. If you don't, bleed the pump of air thoroughly and repeat the test. If the pump still fails to supply fuel, call in a more experienced mechanic before condemning an expensive pump.

FUEL TIMING

Fuel timing determines when each injector receives its shot of fuel from the injector pump. It is set by the mesh of the timing gears and the position in which the injector pump is mounted on the engine.

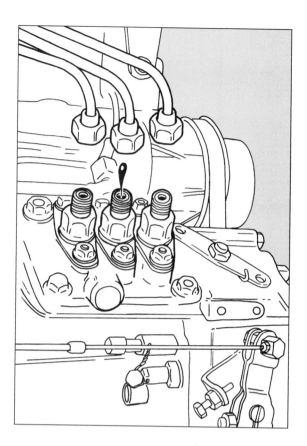

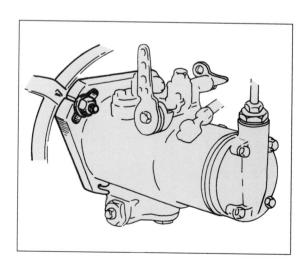

Timing varies with engine design and number of cylinders. Typically, a four-cylinder diesel will have a setting of 10° to 15° before top dead center (TDC). Timing is factory set and should not need adjustment unless the timing gears are disassembled or the injector pump disturbed. Rarely, the injector pump or timing-gear adjustment may work loose and affect the timing.

COLD-STARTING AIDS

Cold-starting aids help initial combustion by increasing combustion-air temperature and/or increasing the fuel/air ratio. Many engines will not start easily without a starting aid, even in tropical climates. The design of these devices varies.

In sub-zero temperatures, the paraffin wax in diesel fuel can separate and clog fuel lines. If you're crazy enough to play with boats in such conditions, look into purchasing heaters for the primary filter and oil sump.

THERMOSTARTS

A thermostart is an electrically heated coil that burns fuel in the intake manifold. To test, remove the intake-air filter and operate the preheat switch:

- The coil should glow.
- A flame should appear when the fuel valve opens.

If the coil doesn't heat, check power supply and grounding. If the coil glows but there is no flame, the valve may not be opening or fuel may not be reaching the device.

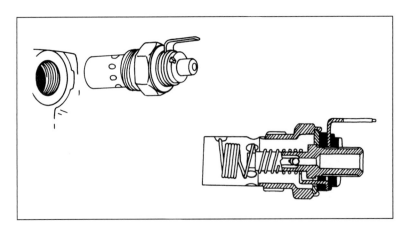

GLOW PLUGS

Glow plugs are electrically heated elements that heat the air/fuel mixture in the precombustion chamber. To test, operate the preheat switch:

- The panel ammeter or dimming lights will indicate high current flow. Glow plugs can draw as much as 40 amps of current; or
- The glow plugs will feel warm.

Before replacing suspect glow plugs, check the voltage at the plug itself and make sure the relay is functioning. Corrosion on the glow-plug body can prevent good grounding. A multimeter set to measure resistance should indicate continuity through the plug element.

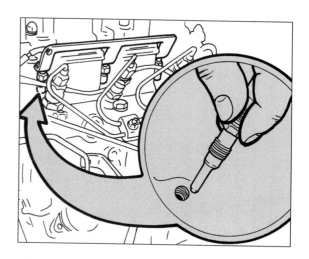

AIR HEATERS

Air heaters heat the air before it reaches the combustion chamber. Like glow plugs, they draw considerable current. The same tests as for glow plugs apply.

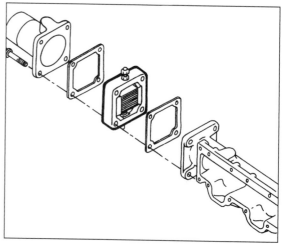

EXCESS-FUEL DEVICES

Excess-fuel devices are built into the injection pump or governor and provide extra fuel for starting—similar to a choke on a gasoline-engine carburetor. Excess-fuel devices are factory set and should not be adjusted.

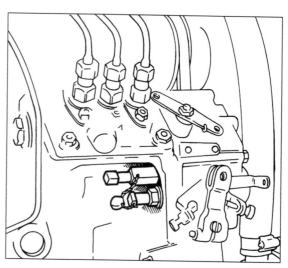

FUEL INJECTORS

Although relatively simple in construction, fuel injectors are the most critical components in the diesel engine. They atomize fuel into the combustion chamber at temperatures above 1,000°C and pressures approaching 20,000 psi. They withstand constant vibration, yet still must operate as many as 10 times a second.

Small marine diesels use two main types of injector. Each injector has a specific spray pattern. The number, size, and angle of the jets is determined by the design of the engine.

Engines with swirl or pre-combustion chambers use injectors with pintle nozzles.

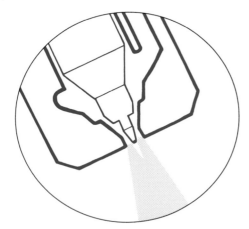

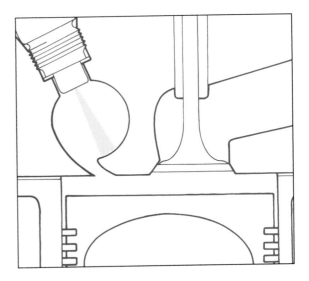

Direct-injection engines use injectors with multi-hole nozzles.

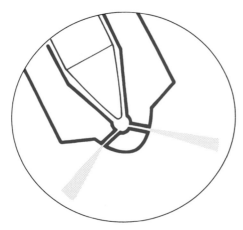

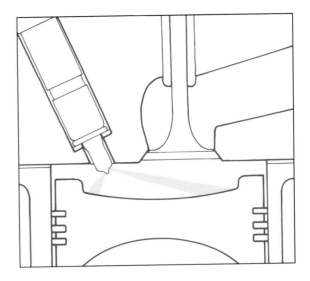

INJECTOR MAINTENANCE

Supplied with clean fuel, injectors require minimal maintenance and should give several thousand hours of reliable service. If nozzle holes and seats are worn, corroded, or contaminated, the injector will fail to atomize the fuel; raw fuel in the combustion chamber will not burn completely.

If your engine suffers from poor starting, loss of performance, erratic rpm, or excessive exhaust smoke, your problems are more likely due to defective injectors than to all the other causes combined.

Normal wear on injector nozzle seats can affect spray patterns as early as 1,000 hours. Severe wear or contamination will allow even more fuel to leak into the combustion chamber, causing damaging pre-ignition, or "knocking."

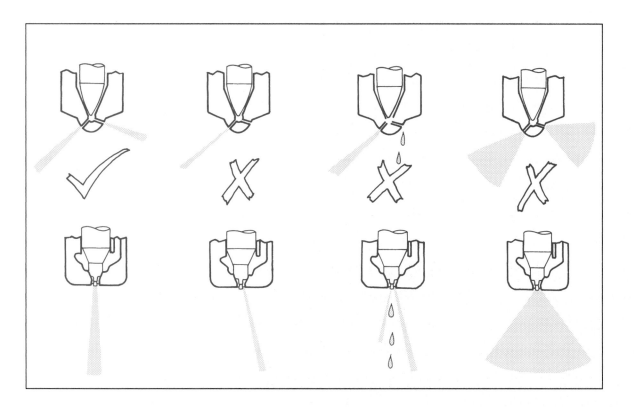

CHECKING OPERATION

The standard test to check a suspect injector is to run the engine at high idle and then momentarily loosen each injector supply line. No audible change in rpm identifies the problem injector. If an injector is causing knocking, the noise will disappear when its supply line is loosened. This test is very basic and

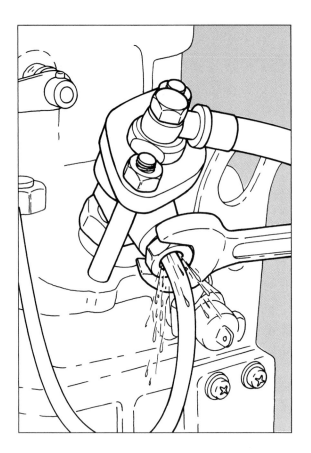

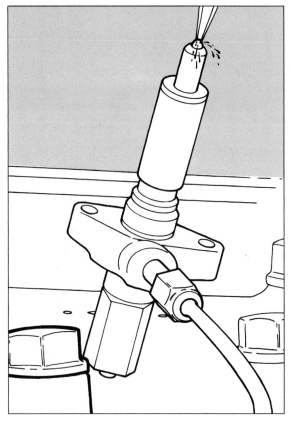

only confirms whether fuel is being delivered to the cylinder. It does not indicate whether the fuel is being correctly atomized.

A better test is to remove all injectors and reconnect them, inverted, to their supply lines. Turning the engine over with the starter will pump fuel through the injector; you can then examine the spray pattern. *Warning: Keep clear of atomized fuel. It is under high pressure and will penetrate skin and cause infection.*

If your injectors are defective, have them serviced by a qualified diesel shop.

REMOVING INJECTORS

Remove the supply and return fuel lines, taking care not to drop the sealing washers. If the injectors have not been regularly serviced, the combination of rust and carbon products can make them difficult to remove. If so, apply a good penetrating oil and rotate the injector side to side while lifting. For

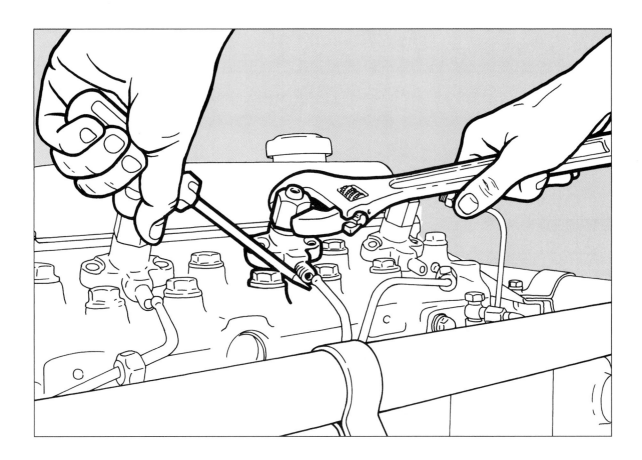

obstinate injectors, try loosening the retaining nuts slightly and using the cylinder's compression to eject them by turning the engine over on the starter.

REFITTING INJECTORS

Before refitting injectors, clean the injector holes of all carbon deposits. A wedge of paper towel jammed into the hole and turned with a large screwdriver is effective. To prevent leaks, replace all metal sealing washers—especially copper washers, which harden with age. In an emergency, you can soften copper washers by heating them to cherry red over the stove and then quenching them rapidly in water.

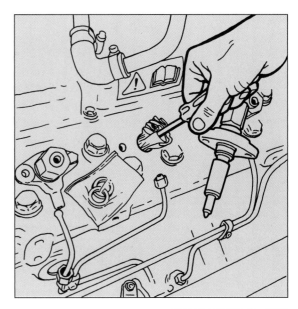

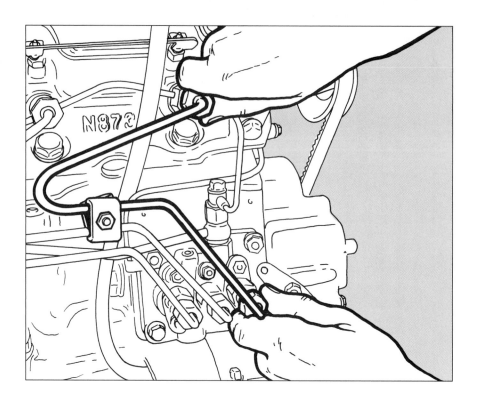

Take care not to pre-stress injector supply lines when refitting; this can lead to failure. You can correct a poor fit by removing the pipe completely and checking alignment at the injector pump and injector connections. If necessary, slightly bend the pipe to achieve a good fit before tightening the connections.

EMERGENCY REPAIRS

It is possible, in an emergency, to disassemble an injector for cleaning or even to replace a defective nozzle. Cleaning small nozzles, though, usually has only a temporary effect. If the injector uses shims for adjustment, the pressure setting should not drift too far when you reassemble the injector with the original parts. You can usually replace nozzles on injectors that use screw adjustment without disturbing the adjustment. Remember: Use this technique only in an emergency. It's better to carry a spare set of injectors aboard and have the problem injectors repaired at a diesel shop.

Carburetor cleaners will remove carbon and varnish buildup from nozzle valves; nevertheless, take great care to keep everything clean. These components are lapped to very smooth surfaces of close tolerance. Nozzle valves should slide easily.

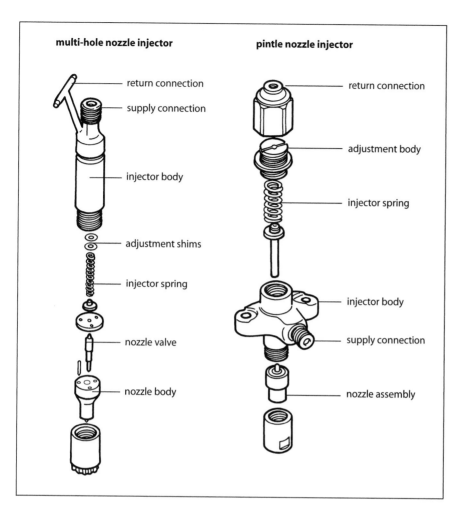

multi-hole nozzle injector

- return connection
- supply connection
- injector body
- adjustment shims
- injector spring
- nozzle valve
- nozzle body

pintle nozzle injector

- return connection
- adjustment body
- injector spring
- injector body
- supply connection
- nozzle assembly

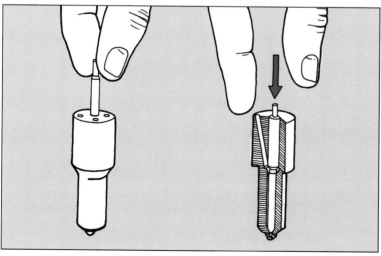

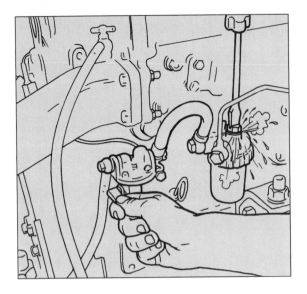

AIR IN THE FUEL SYSTEM

Air can find its way into the fuel system by several routes. It is normally sucked into the fuel supply through a poor seal upstream of the lift pump. Downstream of the lift pump the system is pressurized, and a faulty seal will result in an external fuel leak when the engine is running. *The most common cause of air in the fuel system is insufficient bleeding after a fuel-filter change.*

BLEEDING AIR FROM THE FUEL SYSTEM

Bleed the system in the following sequence:

1. Loosen the bleed screw at the top of the secondary filter. Operate the external lever on the fuel-lift pump. If the lever is only pumping at the bottom of the stroke, rotate the crankshaft one full turn to reposition the cam lobe. Continue pumping until air-free fuel flows from the screw, then tighten the bleed screw. If the primary-filter element has just been changed, it may take some time to clear all the air. If air remains, check the primary-filter seals and lift pump.

2. Loosen the bleed screw on the injector pump and continue operating the lift pump until the fuel is free of air. If the pump has more than one bleed screw, bleed the lower one first. Tighten the bleed screw(s).

3. Loosen all the injector supply lines at the injector. Turn the engine over with the starter until air-free fuel flows in spurts from each line. Retighten.

FUEL SYSTEM FAULTS

Problem	Possible Cause	Possible Symptoms
FUEL CONTAMINATION		
Water	Source suspect [1] Deck-plate filler leaking [3] Condensation [3]	White smoke; difficult starting; loss of power
Air	Poor sealing on primary filter [1] Leaking pipes, hoses, and connections [2] Fuel valves shut off [3] Lift pump defective [3] No fuel in tank [4] Tank pickup tube defective [5]	Difficult starting; erratic rpm; engine dies
Algae or fungus growth	Water in fuel [2]	Primary filter or fuel lines clogged with black, stringy debris; difficult starting; erratic rpm; engine dies
Incorrect grade	Source suspect [5]	Difficult starting; loss of power; black smoke
FUEL FILTERS		
Air in fuel	Defective sealing [1] Leaking pipes between tank and filter [3]	Difficult starting; erratic rpm; engine dies
Clogged	Filter not changed often enough [1] Tank dirty [3]	As above
LIFT PUMP		
Not pumping	Internal valves contaminated or broken [3] External non-return valve, if fitted, stuck closed [3] Diaphragm leaking [4]	As above Fuel in oil sump; engine appears to be "making oil"
INJECTOR PUMP		
Not pumping	Air in fuel system [1] Lift pump defective [3] Filters clogged [3] Injector pump defective [4]	Engine will not run; difficult starting; rough running; erratic rpm; engine dies

INJECTOR LINES

Problem	Possible Cause	Possible Symptoms
Cracked	Vibration [3] Inadequate pipe support [3] Pre-stressed on installation [3]	External fuel leaks; rough running; vibration; loss of power
Not sealing	Nut loose [2] Conical sealing surfaces damaged [2]	As above

INJECTORS

Problem	Possible Cause	Possible Symptoms
Nozzle stuck open	Contamination [2] Wear [2]	Knocking (pre-ignition); loss of power; white smoke; black smoke
Nozzle stuck closed	Contamination [2] Wear [2]	Uneven injection; rough running; loss of power; vibration; difficult starting
Nozzle eroded	Wear [2] Water in fuel [2]	Knocking (pre-ignition); loss of power; white smoke; difficult starting
Pressure high	Incorrect setting [3]	Difficult starting
Pressure low	Wear [2] Incorrect setting [3]	Difficult starting; white smoke; loss of power
Spring broken	Fatigue [5]	Difficult starting; low power; rough running
Two sealing washers under injector	Poor maintenance [3]	Black smoke; difficult starting

GOVERNOR

Problem	Possible Cause	Possible Symptoms
Sticking	Wear [4] Contamination [3]	Loss of power; erratic rpm
Weights defective	Governor components loose [5]	Low maximum rpm
Spring defective	Fatigue [4] Governor components loose [4]	High rpm; erratic rpm

COLD-STARTING AID

Problem	Possible Cause	Possible Symptoms
Not functioning	No electrical supply [2] No fuel supply [3] Poor grounding [3] Defective [3]	Difficult starting

TIMING

Advanced	Injector pump loose [3] Set incorrectly [4] Governor sticking [4]	Knocking; rough idle; difficult starting; black smoke
Retarded	As above	Loss of power; overheating; white smoke

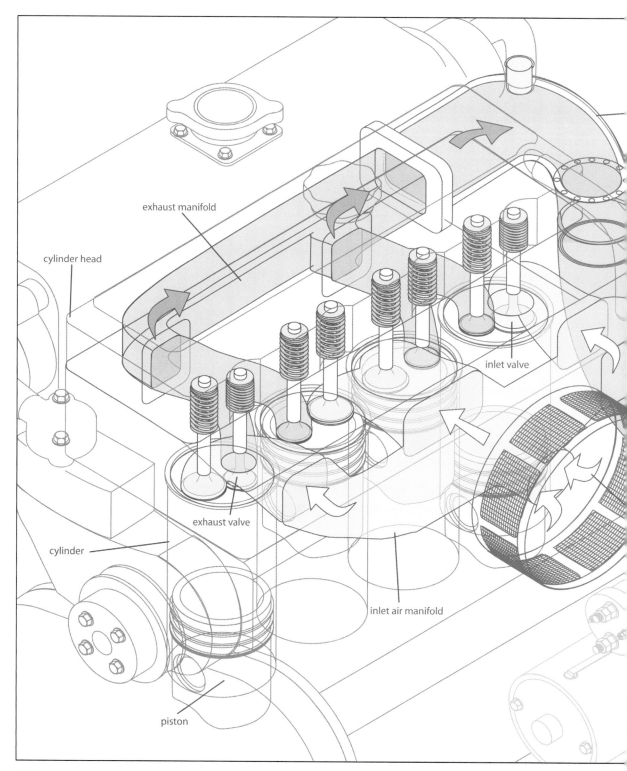

exhaust manifold

cylinder head

inlet valve

exhaust valve

cylinder

inlet air manifold

piston

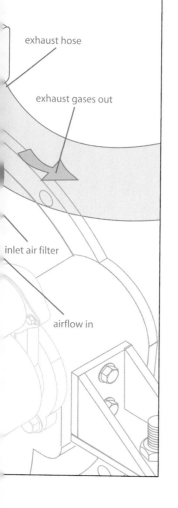

exhaust injection elbow

exhaust hose

exhaust gases out

inlet air filter

airflow in

THE INTAKE AND EXHAUST SYSTEM

A small four-cylinder engine running at high speed will typically consume more than 6,000 cubic feet of air per hour. Not all of it is necessary for combustion, but restrict the air flow and the burn will be incomplete, producing more carbon monoxide and black soot.

It is therefore critical that air flows unrestricted through the intake and exhaust system. Engine rooms must be well ventilated, and exhaust systems well designed.

The more air in the cylinders, the more fuel can be burned, which in turn means more power. With a trend toward small, light, high-power diesels, turbocharging offers an effective method of increasing the amount of air that can be packed into the cylinders, boosting output by as much as 50%.

Larger engines are often fitted with an intake-air cooler, or intercooler, to lower the air temperature. This increases the density of air, so even more can be packed into the cylinders.

The exhaust system not only removes harmful gases, it also carries away 50% of the engine's excess heat. In small marine engines, raw water is injected into the exhaust system to reduce the temperature of gases and hot exhaust pipes. Wet-exhaust systems operate at sufficiently low temperatures to allow the use of flexible-rubber exhaust hose and fiberglass mufflers.

Intake and exhaust systems require minimal maintenance. Periodic air-filter cleaning and a visual inspection will usually locate potential problems.

A badly designed exhaust system can restrict gas flow, which will cause difficult starting, loss of power, and premature engine wear. Correct muffler sizing and hose routing will prevent raw water from flowing back into the cylinders and destroying the engine.

AIR-INTAKE FILTER

The minimal dust and dirt in an engine compartment means marine air filters need not work quite as hard as their automotive counterparts. Still, an air-intake filter stops dirt from entering the engine and scoring the cylinder bores, and so improves oil consumption and extends engine life. A well-designed filter assembly can also reduce engine noise.

In many engines, coarse metal or plastic screens on the intake manifold stop larger debris from being sucked into the engine. Paper or foam elements improve filtration further, but require more frequent servicing to maintain good airflow. Water- or oil-soaked elements restrict airflow severely. Excessive oil on the filter or inside the intake manifold suggests that worn cylinders and/or piston rings are causing high crankcase pressure.

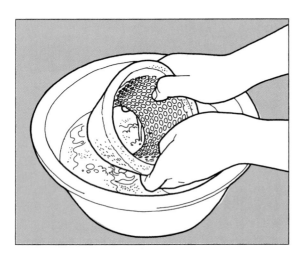

SERVICING FILTER ELEMENTS

Although maintenance is relatively simple, owners tend to ignore air filters and seldom service them properly.

- Tap paper elements on a flat surface to dislodge loose dirt particles. It's impossible to successfully wash paper elements. If the contamination is heavy or oily, they should be replaced.
- Wash foam elements with a mild detergent solution. Dry the element before refitting.
- Wash metal elements in solvent.

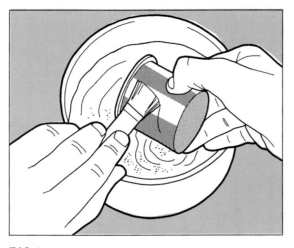

EXHAUST MANIFOLD

For the most part, exhaust manifolds are water cooled. Chapter 6 covers fresh-water– or coolant-cooled exhaust manifolds that incorporate the header tank and heat exchanger. Raw-water–cooled exhaust manifolds are prone to internal corrosion. Periodically remove hoses and covers to inspect for restricted water-ways. The same instructions apply as for cleaning the exhaust injection elbow, covered below.

EXHAUST INJECTION ELBOW

The exhaust injection elbow is the point at which cooling raw water is injected into the exhaust system to cool and silence the exhaust gases. Injection elbows come in all shapes and sizes and may be made of aluminum, cast iron, steel, stainless, and even bronze. Because no metal is totally resistant to the corrosive effects of sea water and hot exhaust gases, injection elbows have a heavy wall thickness.

INSPECTION

Salt or corrosion products indicate a leak caused by severe corrosion. The first indication usually is small, pin-prick–sized holes opposite the point where raw water is injected into the elbow. Soot deposits by the mounting flange indicate a loose joint or gasket failure. Check the tightness of attachment bolts, which loosen due to high temperatures and the settling of thick gaskets.

Exhaust injection elbows restrict easily with buildup of oily carbon and corrosion deposits, especially if the engine is run at low rpm for long periods to charge batteries. The elbow should be inspected internally every other

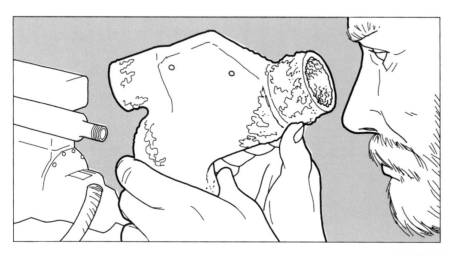

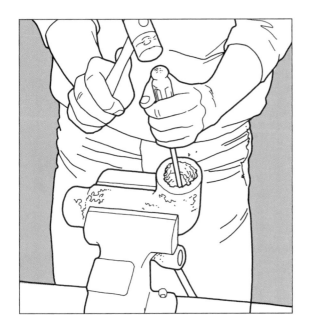

season. However, removal can be one of those tasks that's easier said than done, especially with stiff wire-reinforced exhaust hose, corrosion, and limited access!

CLEANING

The most effective cleaning method is sandblasting, but not everyone has access to this equipment. Dipping in acid is risky: It can eat too much base metal. Carburetor-choke cleaners are reasonably effective at removing soot deposits but work slowly. You can also chip with a hammer and screwdriver, but this can be time consuming.

Corrosion attacks elbows of cast iron more than those made of other metals—particularly if the engine runs infrequently. Thick flakes of iron will break off during chipping. If you're working on an older diesel, have a replacement handy before attacking severe corrosion.

EXHAUST HOSE

Because wet-exhaust systems run at relatively low temperatures, they pose little fire risk aboard a boat. Lower exhaust temperatures also mean that you can run lighter fiberglass tubing and flexible piping materials such as wire-reinforced rubber hose. Do not use plastic tubing: It increases the risk of fire if the raw-water supply is disrupted.

INSPECTION

Almost every small marine diesel exhaust system uses rubber hose reinforced with spiral-wound steel wire. The hose is maintenance free, but deteriorates with age; inspect it every 12 months for kinking, cracking, corroded wire, and delamination.

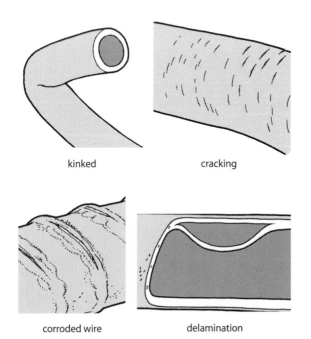

kinked   cracking

corroded wire   delamination

MUFFLERS AND LIFT BOXES

Wet-exhaust lift mufflers use exhaust pressure to lift pellets of raw water through the exhaust hose and overboard. A good installation requires only seasonal inspection, but a bad one can cause high exhaust backpressure or allow water to flow back into the cylinder head and destroy the engine. Questionable installations should be inspected by a professional.

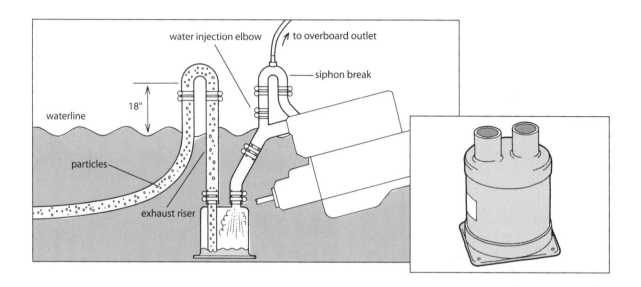

EXHAUST BACKPRESSURE

An unrestricted path for exhaust gases is equally important as a good supply of intake air. Resistance within the exhaust system will result in high backpressure, causing difficult starting, loss of power, and increased engine wear.

MEASURING BACKPRESSURE

Backpressure can be measured with a sensitive 0–5 psi gauge attached to a football inflator nozzle. Make a small hole in the exhaust hose close to the injection elbow with a sharp spike, and insert the nozzle. Take readings with the engine running at maximum rpm. Pressures on wet exhaust systems fluctuate as the lift box expels a pellet of water; take an average reading. As a general rule, backpressure should not exceed 2.0 psi (52 inches of water) on naturally aspirated engines, or 1.25 psi (32 inches of water) on turbocharged engines. Many manufacturers specify even lower limits.

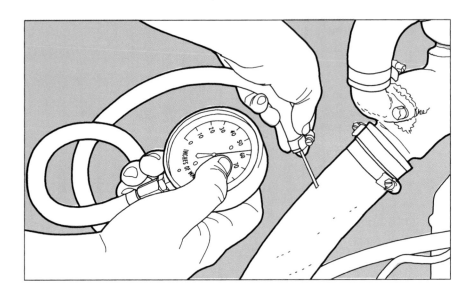

REDUCING BACKPRESSURE

Exhaust-hose diameter. Never reduce the hose below the size of the injection elbow.

Hose length. Minimize the length of exhaust hose. If the transom is far from the engine, exit through the side of the hull.

Hose routing. Raise the hose as high as possible immediately after the muffler to keep out following seas. The hose should drop gradually toward the outlet, with no dips to collect water.

Bends and elbows. Minimize elbows and sharp bends in the hose.

Lift box. The lift box must be of adequate size. Its volume should be at least twice (ideally, three times) the volume of the hose to the top of the first loop.

Exhaust through-hull. The through-hull must match the exhaust-hose size, and should offer no restrictions.

TURBOCHARGERS

Turbochargers increase an engine's output by harnessing the normally wasted energy from hot exhaust gases to pack more air into the cylinders.

Turbochargers are surprisingly reliable—especially when you consider that some of the smaller units spin at almost 200,000 rpm. There is little an amateur mechanic can do to service this high-speed air pump other than to inspect it regularly and clean the compressor. Replace a defective turbocharger.

INSPECTION

- Remove the air filter and check the compressor wheel for cleanliness. Excessive oil suggests seal failure. Wash the compressor if dirty (see below).
- Spin the shaft slowly by hand and check that there is no contact between either wheel and the housings.
- The bearings should feel smooth, with minimal shaft end float or radial play.

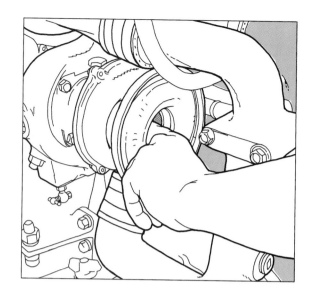

WASHING

Keep turbocharger compressor blades clean to maintain efficient airflow. Compressors can quickly become contaminated with an oil film that collects dirt and dust. Engine manufacturers specify how often to wash compressors, but intervals between cleanings depend on the cleanliness of the air in the engine room. To wash the compressor, run the engine up to high rpm and spray the manufacturer's recommended cleaning solution into the intake.

INTERCOOLERS

Intercoolers should be maintenance free; nevertheless, you should remove them periodically to clean and inspect. The small gaps between intercooler fins tend to collect dirt, especially if there is oil in the intake.

Pressure-test the unit if you find any corrosion. Remember: Most intercoolers use raw water to cool the intake air, so an internal failure can allow raw water to enter the cylinders and destroy the engine.

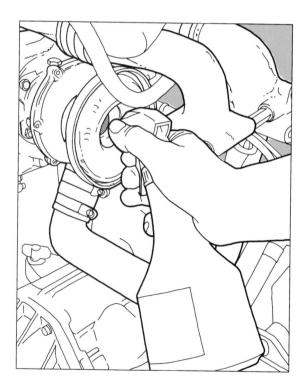

INTAKE AND EXHAUST SYSTEM FAULTS

Problem	Possible Cause	Possible Symptoms

INTAKE FILTER

Contaminated	Excessive oil from crankcase breather [2] Element wet [2] Environment dirty or dusty [4]	Loss of power; black/dark smoke; low maximum rpm

EXCESSIVE SMOKE—See Troubleshooting Chart 7, page 616

White smoke—water in fuel	Contaminated fuel [2] Defective cylinder-head gasket [3]	Misfiring; loss of power; poor starting
White smoke—unburned fuel	Defective injector [1] Insufficient compression [3] Low air temperature [3] Incorrect timing [4] Incorrect fuel grade [5]	As above
Blue smoke—burned oil	Oil overfilled [2] Worn valve guides [3] Worn piston rings/cylinders [3] Incorrect fuel grade [5]	High oil consumption
Black/dark smoke—partially burned fuel	Engine overloaded [2] Blocked air filter [2] Defective injectors [3] Incorrect timing [4]	Loss of power

HIGH BACKPRESSURE

	Poor design [1] Buildup of carbon at exhaust injection elbow [2] Collapsed exhaust hose [3]	Loss of power; poor starting; engine dies; low maximum rpm

EXHAUST TEMPERATURE HIGH

	Insufficient raw-water cooling [2] Engine overloaded [3]	Steam from exhaust; exhaust hose hot to touch

EXHAUST INJECTION ELBOW

Restricted	Excessive periods at idle [2] Corrosion [2] Oil contamination [3]	White/blue smoke; difficult starting; loss of power; low maximum rpm

TURBOCHARGER

Inefficient	Dirty compressor [2] Seized [3]	Reduced performance; dark exhaust smoke
Noisy	Bearings worn [3] Damaged compressor or turbine blades [3]	As above
Water leaks	Loose manifold nuts [3] Defective gasket [3] Corrosion [4]	Water in cylinder head; engine seized; external corrosion salts
Oil leaks	Worn or damaged seals [3] Oil drain blocked [3]	Blue exhaust smoke; high oil consumption

INTERCOOLER

Water leaks	Corrosion [3] Gasket failure [3]	Water in cylinder head; seized engine
Air leaks	Loose joints [2] Corrosion [3] Gasket failure [3]	Loss of performance

EXHAUST HOSE

Delaminating	Deterioration of bonding between layers, often due to excessive oil and fuel contact
Soft	External deterioration due to prolonged contact with fuel and oil, often from sitting in an oil-filled bilge
Rusting	Internal wire corrosion; water will seep along wire and destroy reinforcing, which will promote delamination
Kinked	Bends too sharp
Cracking	External rubber cracks with age

HOW LIKELY?   [1] Very common   [2] Common   [3] Possible   [4] Rare   [5] Very rare

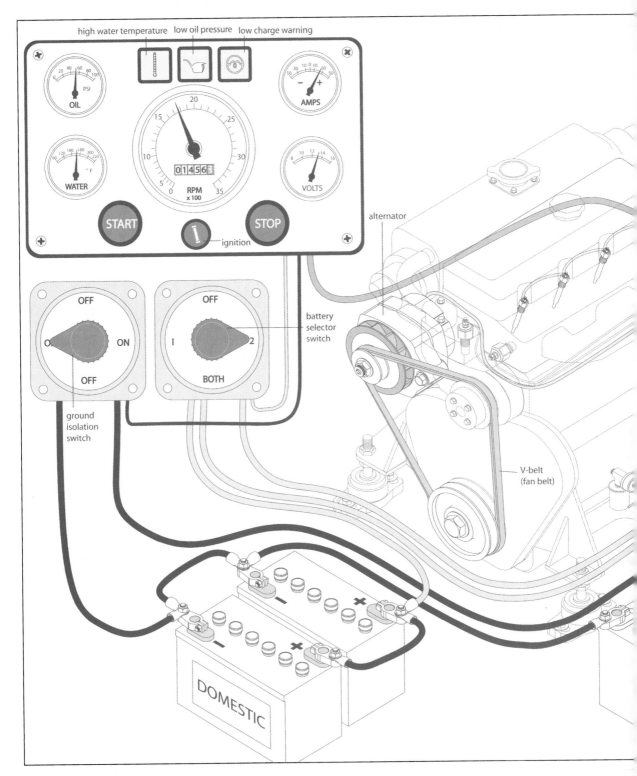

high water temperature low oil pressure low charge warning

OIL
PSI

WATER
°F

RPM
x 100

01456

AMPS

VOLTS

START STOP

ignition

OFF

ON

OFF

OFF

BOTH

battery selector switch

ground isolation switch

alternator

V-belt (fan belt)

DOMESTIC

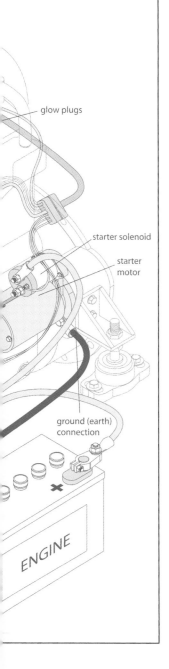

glow plugs

starter solenoid

starter
motor

ground (earth)
connection

ENGINE

THE ELECTRICAL SYSTEM

The typical sailboat diesel has two electrical circuits: one for engine starting, and one for charging. The starting circuit consists of a battery, a starter motor, and the wiring and switches to connect the two.

Starters themselves are generally reliable, unless they are overheated or soaked with water from the bilge or leaking wet-exhaust connections.

Starting-circuit problems are common, and usually due to low battery output or poor connections. Check these connections regularly for tightness and corrosion; in other respects, the starting circuit will look after itself.

The main component in the charging circuit is the alternator, which charges the battery banks and supplies power for the boat's electrical equipment.

Most faults with the charging circuit are caused by the alternator failing to charge the batteries, or overcharging caused by a defective or incorrectly modified voltage regulator.

Routine maintenance for the charging circuit involves monitoring the batteries and the V-belt that drives the alternator.

It is not within the scope of this book to cover wiring in detail, but whenever you inspect your engine, pay particular attention to the wiring. Wire must be correctly sized. The high resistance of a wire too small for the current it has to carry will create considerable heat that can lead to fire.

BATTERIES

There are three types of batteries used in marine applications: wet lead-acid, gel lead-acid, and occasionally, nickel-cadmium. Although the wet lead-acid type requires more maintenance than the other two, it is generally a better value for the money and by far the most popular.

Batteries come in all shapes and sizes. The standard internal configuration is six cells, each generating just over 2 volts. Batteries can be connected in parallel to increase capacity, or in series to increase voltage. Six-volt and 8-volt batteries are commonly combined to make up banks of 12, 24, and 32 volts.

WHICH BATTERY?

Engine-starting batteries must deliver high amperage in short bursts. The starter on a four-cylinder auxiliary diesel will typically draw more than 350 amps during start. Dedicated starting batteries should be the cranking type, designed with thinner, often porous, plates for rapid discharge; they must be large enough to provide adequate cranking power—especially for cold starting.

Although you must consider weight and size, it's better to have spare capacity than not enough. As a general rule, the battery should provide 2 to 3 cranking amps for each engine cubic inch. A 2-liter diesel, for example, would need at a minimum a battery capable of about 250 cranking amps.

The house, or domestic, batteries must be capable of handling all the

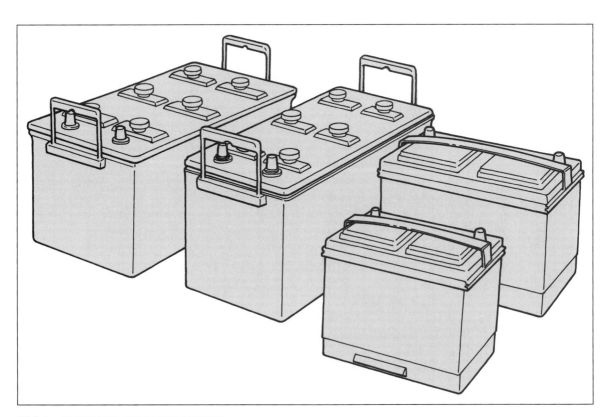

remaining demands of a boat's electrical system. House batteries should be of the deep-cycle type, which have thicker plates and separators to better handle deep discharge. Six-volt, deep-cycle golf-cart batteries are proving very successful in marine applications, exhibiting excellent capacity and long life. Deep-cycle batteries can be used as starting batteries, provided they are large enough to recover from high discharge rates.

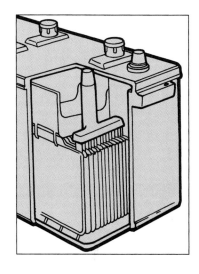

TESTING

To test a battery's charge level, measure the specific gravity of each cell's electrolyte with a hydrometer. A fully charged cell should read above 1.260 SG; adjust your readings for temperature according to the scale on the hydrometer.

% CHARGED	SPECIFIC GRAVITY	VOLTAGE
100%	1.265–1.275	12.6
75%	1.225–1.235	12.4
50%	1.190–1.200	12.2
25%	1.155–1.165	12.0
0%	1.120–1.130	11.7

Load testing is also an effective method of checking a battery's

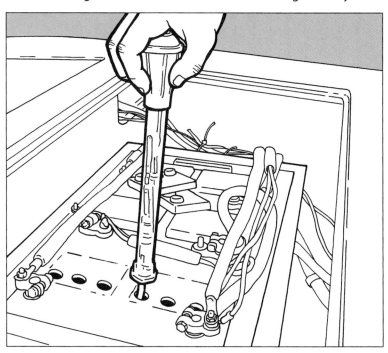

condition. Although commercial testers are available, measuring the voltage of the battery during the start cycle will produce similar results. To conduct the test, charge the battery fully and pull the stop cable so the engine won't start. Voltage must remain above 80% of the no-load voltage; a typical 12-volt battery, for example, must not drop below 9.5 volts. If the battery fails this test, replace it: It is either defective or too small for the job.

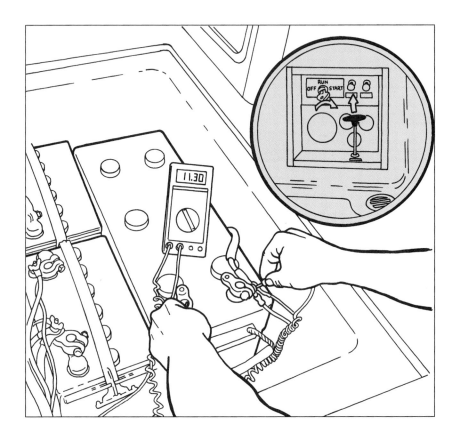

CHARGING

Battery-charging requires carefully controlled voltage. Alternator voltage regulators, which sense battery voltage and adjust alternator output accordingly, are usually preset between 14.2 and 14.4 volts. Above 13.8 volts, the electrolyte starts to gas and the water in the electrolyte begins to evaporate. Higher voltages cause the electrolyte to boil, and the cells will need constant filling. The heat of severe overcharging distorts the plates and will eventually destroy the battery. Do not charge gel cells over 14.1 volts.

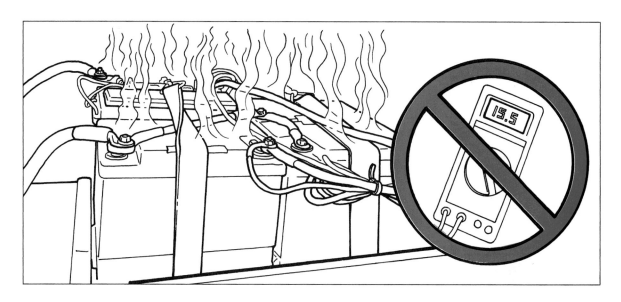

MAINTENANCE

Batteries don't like being deeply discharged; if left in that state for a period of time, capacity-reducing lead sulfate forms on the plates and can be difficult to remove. Keep the battery well charged, avoid discharging it below 50%, and maintain the correct electrolyte levels to ensure maximum life. Top off wet cells with distilled water; drinking water is acceptable, provided it is not high in mineral salts.

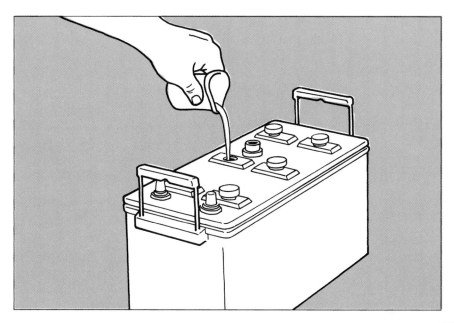

BATTERY SWITCHES

Battery switches select individual batteries, connect multiple batteries in parallel, and allow the batteries to be disconnected in an emergency or when not in use. Battery switches must be of adequate size for the current they conduct. Check occasionally for loose connections, and regularly apply a light spray of corrosion inhibitor.

Warning: Never disconnect batteries while the engine is running; it will cause a voltage surge in the alternator that can damage diodes and transistorized regulators.

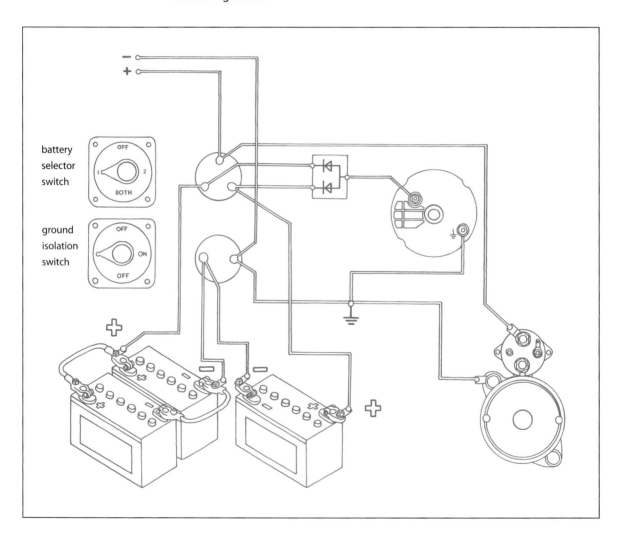

ALTERNATOR

An alternator operated without modification can last almost the life of the engine without maintenance.

INSPECTION

With the V-belt removed, an alternator should make little noise when spun by hand. There should be no contact between the rotor and the stator coils, the fan shouldn't rub, and the bearings should feel smooth. The alternator pulley width must match with the crankshaft and circulating pump pulleys and be correctly aligned. Refer to Chapter 6 for information on tensioning the V-belt.

TESTING

Check the output shown on the panel ammeter, if fitted. Measure output voltage with a voltmeter, touching one probe to the + output terminal and the other to the casing ground. Any reading above battery voltage indicates some level of charging. With a low battery, expect the voltage to be close to 13.0V, rising to 14.2V as the battery reaches full charge.

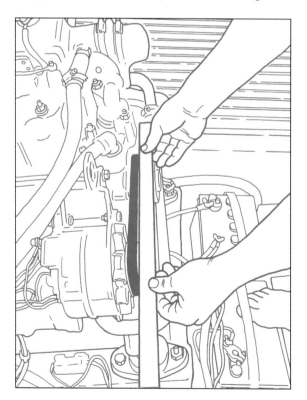
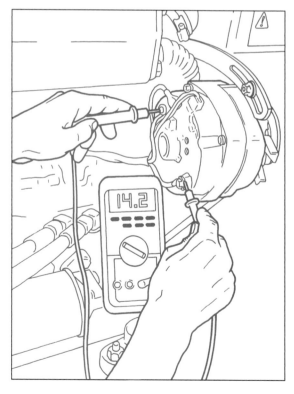

MAINTENANCE

Although testing and replacing internal regulators, rectifiers, and brushes is not particularly difficult, variations in alternator design make it impractical to adequately cover this topic here. Reconditioned alternators are inexpensive; carry a spare on board.

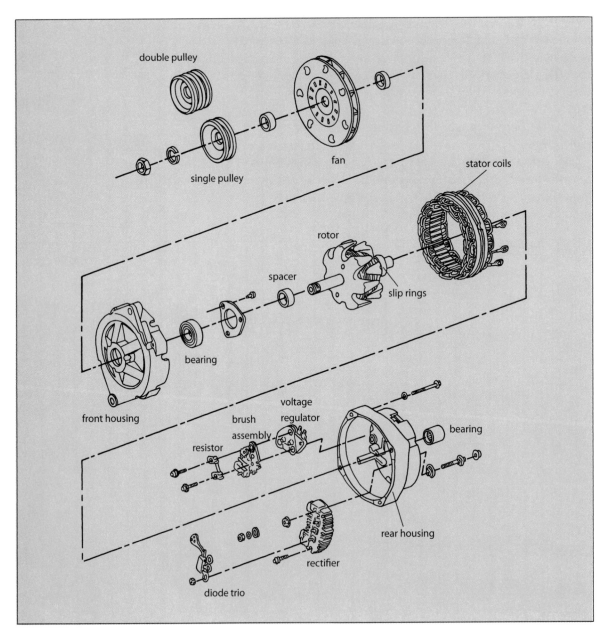

IMPROVING OUTPUT

Standard marine-engine alternators use automotive-type voltage regulators that allow charging at a relatively low rate after an initial high charge. This is fine for a vessel whose engine runs constantly, but a sailboat would have to idle its engine for hours every day to keep up with normal domestic electrical needs. Many owners replace the standard alternator with higher-output units whose computerized, step-charging regulators charge the batteries more efficiently. If you upgrade your alternator, be sure the pulley matches those on the crankshaft and circulating pump and that the V-belt can handle the job.

You can easily and cheaply increase the output of a standard alternator by reducing the voltage the regulator senses. Insert a diode of adequate size (IN5400 or larger) into the sensing circuit. It is not the diode's one-way flow that's important in this instance, but the nominal ¾-volt drop across the diode. This fools the voltage regulator into "thinking" that the battery voltage is lower than it really is, and the regulator increases the charge rate accordngly.

Use a switch to route the sensing circuit through the diode, and you will have the option of a high or low charge rate. More than a single diode in the circuit will further increase the charge rate, but you may burn out the alternator or overcharge the batteries.

This modification should also be applied to alternators that charge batteries through isolation diodes to compensate for the voltage drop.

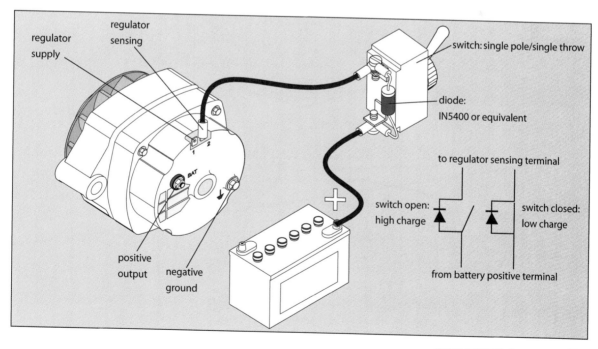

STARTER MOTOR

Starter motors are generally of two types. Pre-engaged starters use an external solenoid to engage the drive gear with the flywheel ring gear before the motor itself is energized. Inertia starters use centrifugal force on a helical slot to throw the drive gear into the flywheel when the motor is energized. This mechanism is commonly called a Bendix. Solenoids on inertia starters just switch the high current.

TESTING

Most starter problems are with the supply voltage rather than the starter motor. Voltage measured at the starter terminals during the start cycle should be higher than 80% of the battery voltage—more than 9.5 volts for a 12-volt system. Starters that pass this test but still fail to turn the engine over enough to start the engine either have a bad ground or are defective.

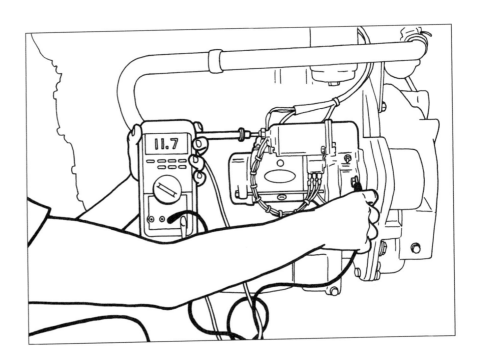

MAINTENANCE

Starters are generally maintenance free and should give years of service if kept clean, dry, and free of corrosion. Solenoids on pre-engaged starters tend to stick. You can replace these solenoids, as they're generally sold separately.

Inertia starters are prone to corrosion, dirt, or wear to the Bendix mechanism that prevents the gear from engaging. You can often solve the problem by removing the starter and cleaning and greasing the Bendix.

TYPICAL ENGINE-INSTALLATION CIRCUIT DIAGRAM

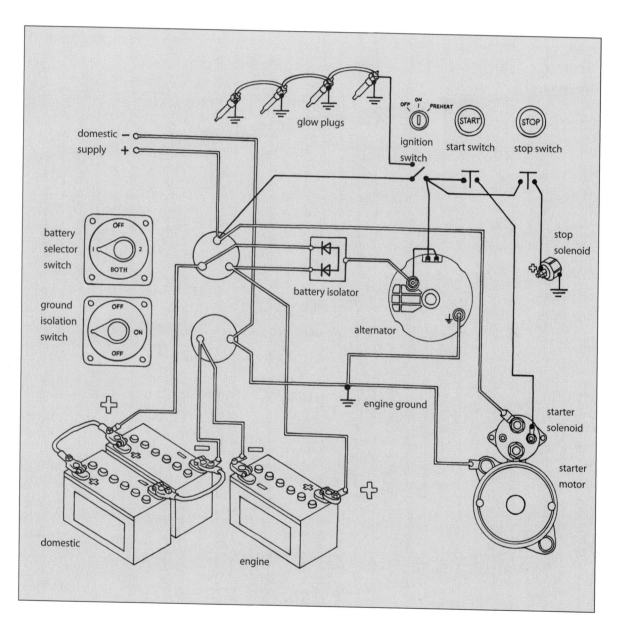

ELECTRICAL SYSTEM FAULTS

Problem	Possible Cause	Possible Symptoms

STARTING SYSTEM PROBLEMS—See Troubleshooting Chart 8, page 618

CHARGING SYSTEM PROBLEMS—See Troubleshooting Chart 9, page 620

START SWITCH

Problem	Possible Cause	Possible Symptoms
Open circuit	Defective switch [3] Loose terminals [3] Corroded terminals [3]	Starter fails to operate; no voltage at starter solenoid positive terminal when selected
Short circuit	Defective switch—mechanically jammed in selected position [3] Water contamination [3]	Starter engages as soon as battery isolator is switched on

STARTER MOTOR

Problem	Possible Cause	Possible Symptoms
Brushes worn	Normal wear [3] Commutator scored [3]	Starter fails to operate or turns slowly
Internal short circuit	Contaminated with water [2] Wiring chafed [3]	Starter fails to operate or turns slowly; starter draws high current when selected
Internal open circuit	Corrosion [3] Loose or broken wiring [4]	Starter fails to operate or has reduced power; starter draws low current when selected
Internal contamination	Water ingress from exhaust manifold or heat exchanger [3] Oil from defective flywheel oil seal [3] Water from bottom of flywheel sitting in high bilgewater [3]	As above
Drive gear defective	Bendix defective (inertia starters only) [2] Clutch mechanism jammed or broken [3]	Starter overspeeds and fails to turn the engine over

STARTER SOLENOID—Pre-Engaged Starters

Problem	Possible Cause	Possible Symptoms
Jammed in "off" position	Contamination [3] Wear [3]	Starter will not operate
Jammed in "on" position	Contamination [3] Wear [3]	Starter runs continuously, even when start switch is released; starter may overspeed
Corroded or eroded contacts	Normal wear [2] Contacts wet at some time [3]	Starter intermittent or slow-turning

BATTERY

Problem	Possible Cause	Possible Symptoms
Low output	Discharged [1] Low electrolyte [1] Sulfated [2] Distorted plates [2] Loose terminals [2] Corroded terminals [2]	Starter fails to operate; starter turns engine over slowly; starter solenoid only clicks; lights dim excessively when start selected
Will not hold charge	Low electrolyte [1] Sulfated [2] Distorted plates [2]	As above

ALTERNATOR

Problem	Possible Cause	Possible Symptoms
Overcharging	Voltage regulator defective [2] Battery sensing wire disconnected [3]	Electrolyte boils; smells of acid
Not charging	V-belt broken or slipping [2] Voltage regulator defective [2] Brushes worn or contaminated [3]	No increase in voltage when engine starts; charge light stays on
Undercharging	Inadequate charging time [1] V-belt slipping [2] Battery defective [2] Corroded or loose terminals [2]	Battery never reaches full charge

HOW LIKELY?   [1] Very common   [2] Common   [3] Possible   [4] Rare   [5] Very rare

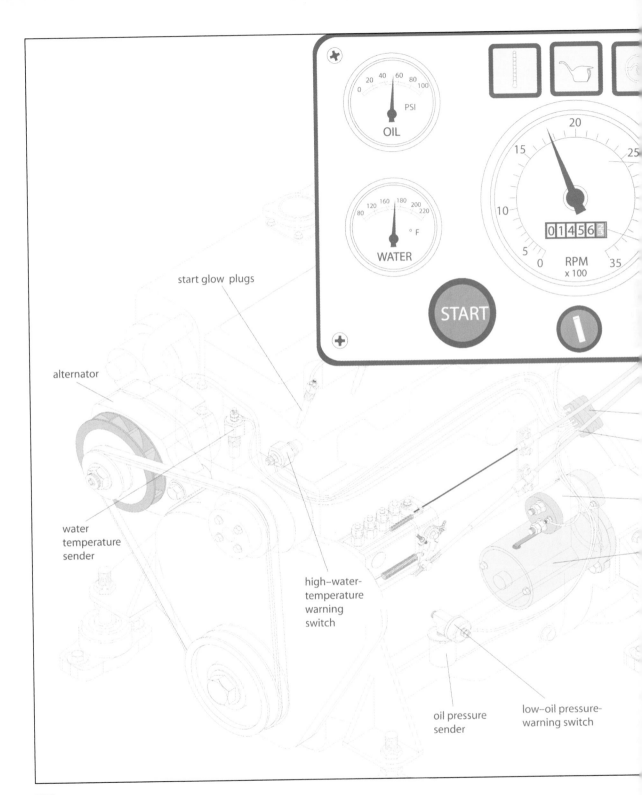

OIL

0 20 40 60 80 100

PSI

120 160 180 200
80 220

°F

WATER

15 20 25
10

5
0 35

RPM
x 100

0 1 4 5 6 2/4

START

start glow plugs

alternator

water
temperature
sender

high–water-
temperature
warning
switch

oil pressure
sender

low–oil pressure-
warning switch

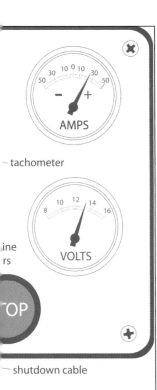

AMPS

— tachometer

VOLTS

ine
rs

OP

— shutdown cable

engine wiring loom connector

throttle (accelerator cable)

— starter solenoid

— starter motor

CONTROLS AND INSTRUMENTS

Whether attached to the binnacle or to the side of the cockpit, start, stop, throttle, and gear-selector controls should be within easy reach of the helmsman. These cable-operated remote controls usually are reliable and require little maintenance.

It's best to place instruments and warning lights in a visible location, sheltered from the elements. Every instrument panel should include a tachometer and warning lights connected to alarm circuits for low oil pressure and high coolant temperature. Oil-pressure and water-temperature gauges allow the helmsman to continuously monitor the condition of these two important systems.

THROTTLE CONTROLS

Engine idle and maximum rpm are set by stops on the governor or injector pump (see Chapter 7). The throttle lever must allow unrestricted movement between these stops.

CHECKING TRAVEL

To check the throttle controls, disconnect the end fitting from the throttle arm on the engine. Pull the control lever all the way back, and make sure the end fitting travels beyond the idle stop. With the engine arm against the maximum stop, push the control lever all the way forward and make sure the connector travels beyond its mounting hole. If it passes these two tests, reconnect the end fitting.

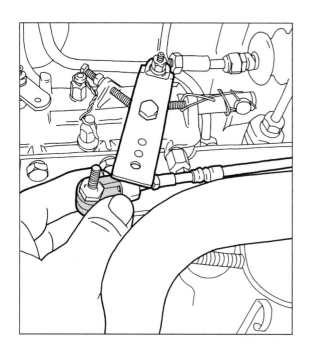
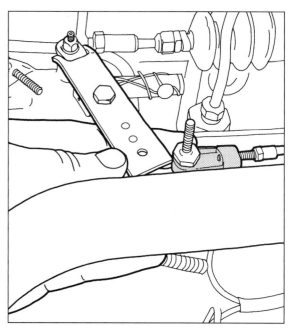

ADJUSTMENTS

To increase or decrease the amount of cable travel, move the end fitting into a lever-arm hole farther from or closer to the pivot. To bias the travel toward the idle or maximum stops, adjust the position of the end fitting on the cable, and remember to tighten the locknut or clamp screw when finished.

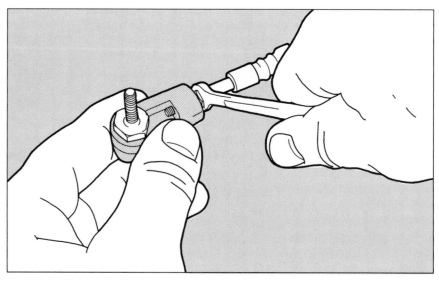

GEAR-SELECTOR CONTROLS

The gear-selector control doesn't have stops to define the limit of travel. You must, however, move the gearbox-selection lever fully into gear; partial selection is a major cause of gearbox failure.

CHECKING TRAVEL

Place the shift lever in neutral and disconnect the cable end fitting at the gearbox lever. The cable must approach the lever at a 90° angle.

Push the shift lever into the forward position and check that the cable end fitting at the gearbox travels beyond the position where the gearbox lever makes positive forward selection. Do the same test for reverse.

ADJUSTMENTS

If the cable does not approach the gear-selector lever at a 90° angle in neutral, reposition the clamp that holds the cable jacket. This setting must be correct before you make other adjustments. To adjust travel and range, follow the instructions for throttle-control adjustment above.

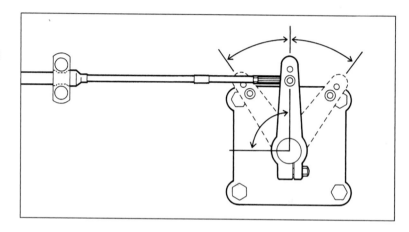

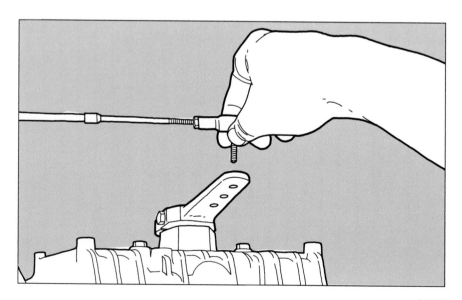

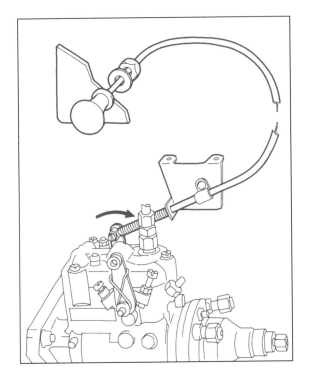

ENGINE-STOP CONTROLS

The engine-stop control cuts off the fuel supply to the injectors at the governor or injection pump and can be either mechanically or electrically operated.

Mechanical stop levers pull the shutdown arm with a cable. They require occasional lubrication, but provide reliable service and will function even when electrical power is lost.

Electrical stop controls can be either the energized-to-stop or the energized-to-run type. In energized-to-stop controls, a heavy-duty solenoid pulls the shutdown arm when the stop button is pressed. A spring returns the shutdown arm to the "run" position when power to the solenoid is cut off. If electrical power fails, it can be difficult to shut down the engine with an electrical control—particularly when the solenoid is built into the injector pump.

Many newer engines are equipped with an energized-to-run solenoid-operated valve built into the injector pump. These smaller solenoids are energized all the time the engine is running. If electrical power is cut off, the solenoid valve will close and shut down the engine fuel supply.

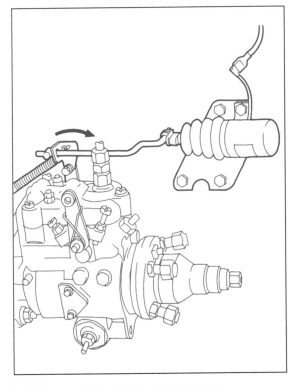

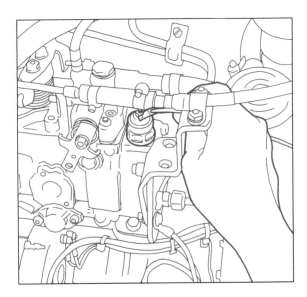

CONTROL CABLES

The control cables in throttle, gear-selector, and stop controls are normally the push-pull type with a solid stainless steel inner cable sheathed in a plastic-coated, flexible steel jacket. Such cables are very reliable, but tight turns and water ingress can lead to corrosion, splitting, and seizing.

MAINTENANCE

Lubricate the cables at the first sign of difficult movement.

If you have access to the cockpit end of the cable, disconnect the end fitting from the control lever. Rig a funnel to the jacket by attaching a small plastic bag with a strong elastic band. Fill the bag with lubricating oil and leave the cable suspended overnight. The oil will slowly work its way down the length of the cable. Operate the inner cable at full travel to speed up the process.

Alternatively, clamp a short length of hose to the jacket. Fill the hose with oil; then clamp the open end around the air hose of a bicycle pump—or better still, an electric tire-inflator pump. Gradually add air pressure to force the oil into the cable. Be careful, though: This method can be messy if you apply more pressure than your jury-rigged hose can handle.

TACHOMETERS

Mechanical tachometers are common on older engines and are very reliable. Periodically lubricate the drive cable using the method described above. Electrical tachometers are driven by signals taken from a dedicated flywheel sensor or from the alternator.

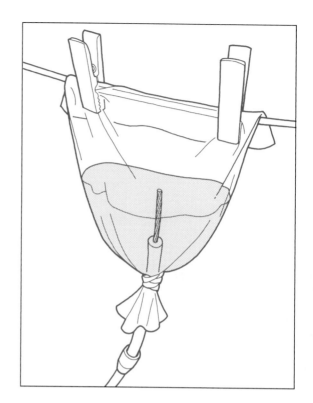

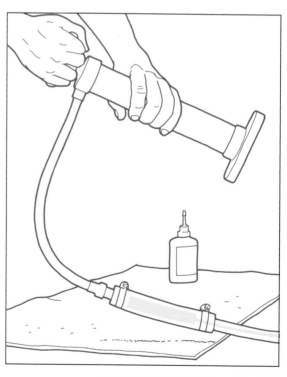

ALTERNATOR-DRIVEN TACHOMETER CONNECTIONS

Alternator-driven tachometers take their signal from the alternating current of the stator coils. Most alternators have a dedicated terminal for the tachometer output marked "R."

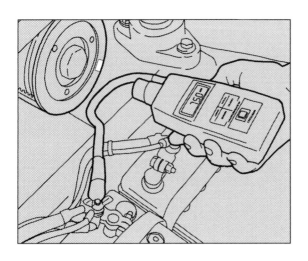

CALIBRATING TACHOMETERS

Tachometers are calibrated by the engine manufacturer and normally need no further adjustment. If you change the alternator or any of the drive pulleys, however, you must recalibrate the alternator-driven tachometer. Although this task is straightforward, you will need a phototachometer and calibration instructions for your particular tachometer; it may be easier to call in the expert for this adjustment.

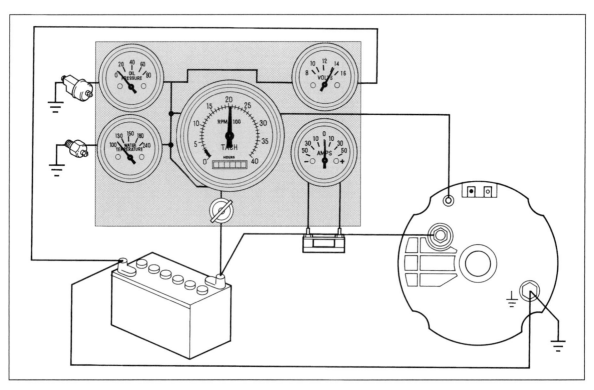

ENGINE-PANEL GAUGES

WATER TEMPERATURE

The sensor for the water-temperature gauge is usually fitted into the cylinder head close to the thermostat. On mechanical gauges, a sealed capillary tube connects a wax-filled sensor bulb to the gauge mechanism. These gauges require power only for illumination. On electrical gauges, a sender varies resistance as temperature increases.

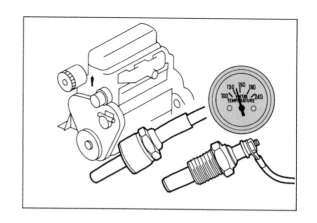

OIL PRESSURE

This gauge indicates the pressure of the lubricating oil. The pressure is usually measured just after the oil pump. Mechanical gauges use a small hose connected to the engine oil gallery. Electrical gauges use a sender fitted to the oil gallery; the sender varies resistance with changes in oil pressure.

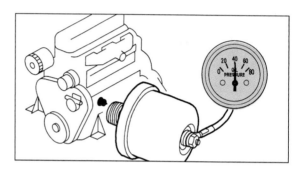

AMMETER

Control panel ammeters usually indicate alternator output. Some ammeters are connected in series and measure the current passing through the alternator output wire. Other, high-output alternators use a shunt to avoid routing heavy cables to the cockpit; this type of ammeter measures only a fraction of the current, but the gauge is calibrated to indicate the total current flow.

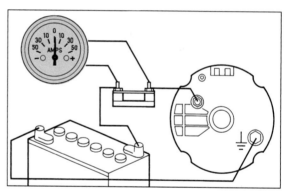

VOLTMETER

Voltmeters are connected in parallel to the circuit they measure. Most engine-panel voltmeters indicate the voltage supplied to the panel. With the ignition turned on, the meter shows the engine-starting battery voltage. Once the engine is running, the meter indicates alternator-output voltage.

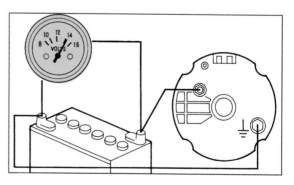

WARNING CIRCUITS

The soundproofing of a good engine installation can make it difficult to hear the onset of problems before they have caused serious and expensive damage. Oil-pressure and water-temperature gauges give excellent indication of the important engine functions but are not often installed in the most visible location. Warning circuits are an essential fail-safe that should be fitted to every marine diesel. Even the simplest design will give immediate warning of problems with oil pressure, water temperature, or charging system.

The warning circuit on a generator will automatically shut it down in the event of a problem. This may be good for the engine but could be disastrous for a boat. Warning circuits on propulsion engines should be just that—warning circuits. The decision to shut down the engine must be the helmsman's. Those extra few moments of engine power could save lives when you're heading into a rocky harbor entrance with dangerous following seas.

- A switch in the low–oil-pressure warning light circuit makes the circuit when the oil pressure drops below a preset figure. Most switches operate at around 5 psi, but such a low setting gives little time to shut down the engine before it seizes. Unless the engine normally operates at very low oil pressures, it's safer to fit a 15-psi switch that provides earlier warning.

- The high–water-temperature warning light connects to a temperature-sensitive switch in the cooling system. This switch makes the circuit when temperature rises above a preset point—usually 215°F (102°C).

- The charging warning light, commonly called the ignition light, extinguishes as soon as the alternator comes on line. The light's remaining on can be an early warning that the V-belt has failed and the engine is about to overheat.

- A warning alarm is an essential piece of equipment. While you might not instantly notice a light, an alarm will get your attention. Be sure it is loud enough to be heard above engine noise and howling rigging.

If your engine does not have an alarm, rig one: A warning circuit is inexpensive and easy to install.

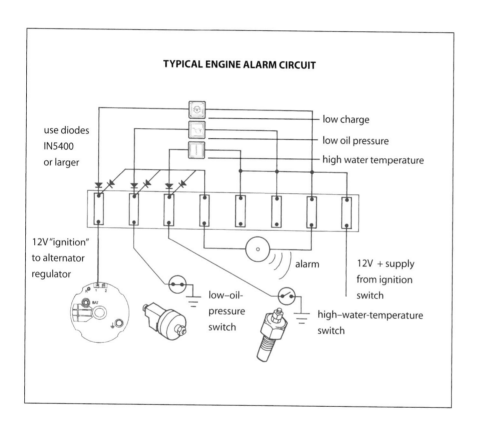

TYPICAL ENGINE ALARM CIRCUIT

use diodes
IN5400
or larger

low charge
low oil pressure
high water temperature

12V "ignition"
to alternator
regulator

alarm

12V + supply
from ignition
switch

low–oil–
pressure
switch

high–water–temperature
switch

CONTROL AND INSTRUMENT FAULTS

Problem	Possible Cause	Possible Symptoms

THROTTLE CONTROL LEVER

Seized or stiff	Cable seized [2] Lever mechanism seized [2]	
Limited travel	Incorrect adjustment [2]	High idle rpm; low maximum rpm

GEAR-SELECTOR LEVER

Seized or stiff	As above	
Limited or uneven travel	As above	Poor gear selection in either or both forward and reverse

MECHANICAL STOP CONTROL

Fails to shut down engine	Cable seized [2] Lever mechanism seized [2] Cable disconnected [3] Outer sheathing not clamped correctly [3] Cable broken [4]	

ELECTRICAL STOP CONTROL—Energized to Run

Engine fails to start	Solenoid defective [4]	
Fails to shut down engine	Wiring disconnected or broken [2] Switch defective [2] Solenoid defective [4]	

ELECTRICAL STOP CONTROL—Energized to Stop

Engine fails to start	Spring return defective [3]	
Fails to shut down engine	Wiring disconnected or broken [2] Switch defective [2] Mechanical link disconnected or loose [3] Solenoid defective [4]	

TACHOMETER

Problem	Possible Cause	Possible Symptoms
No reading	Alternator defective [3] V-belt broken or thrown[3] No voltage to tachometer[4]	
Readings erratic	V-belt slipping[2] Alternator defective [3] Loose wiring[3]	Loose belt may cause overheating
Incorrect reading	Incorrect calibration [2]	

WATER-TEMPERATURE AND OIL-PRESSURE GAUGES

Problem	Possible Cause
No reading	Wiring disconnected or broken[2] Gauge defective [3] Sender defective [3] Mechanical gauge: capillary or oil-supply pipe damaged [3]
Reads in reverse	Incorrect sender [2]
Incorrect reading	Incorrect sender [2] Mechanical gauge: capillary or oil-supply pipe damaged [3]

HOW LIKELY?   [1] Very common   [2] Common   [3] Possible   [4] Rare   [5] Very rare

APPENDIX
DIESEL ENGINE TOOLKIT

Y ou can't do much without a set of tools. You don't need to buy the most expensive, but do buy good-quality tools: They are a pleasure to work with and will last a lifetime if you take care of them. Cheap tools break easily, and inexpensive wrenches can stretch out of shape and damage the nuts and bolts on that expensive diesel. Like any metal aboard a boat, tools are vulnerable to corrosion—especially after a few dunkings in dirty bilgewater. Wipe down your tools with a light film of oil before storing them in the toolbox for another winter.

Plastic toolboxes, unlike metal boxes, are water- and corrosion-resistant, but the cheaper varieties have weak catches that break easily with the weight of a comprehensive set of tools. Try separating tools into smaller plastic boxes that are lighter and easier to stow.

Toolbags are not waterproof, but their soft material is less likely to mark interior surfaces. Make up small cloth bags with Velcro closures to hold loose wrenches and sockets. The cloth absorbs oily fingerprints and after a while the absorbed oil builds up a protective barrier against corrosion.

A typical toolbox should include:

MECHANICAL TOOLS

- Engine repair manual
- Set of combination wrenches, $\frac{1}{4}$" – $\frac{7}{8}$"
- Set of combination wrenches, 8mm – 19mm
- Set of feeler gauges, 0.0015" – 0.025" (Unprotected, they rust very quickly, so store in a small container of oil.)
- $\frac{3}{8}$"-drive socket set, with $\frac{3}{8}$"–1" and 10mm – 19mm sockets (Should include a ratchet handle, plus short and long extensions.)
- Set of slotted screwdrivers, including a stubby
- Set of Phillips-head screwdrivers, including a stubby
- 2- or 3-lb. lump (or machinist's) hammer (It may seem large but will reduce the effort when a real hammer is needed in a confined space.)
- 1-lb. ballpeen hammer
- Set of hex (Allen) keys, standard and metric sizes
- Large and small Channel-Lock pliers
- Pair of 7" side cutters

- Medium-sized locking pliers
- Medium-sized snap-ring pliers with internal and external capability
- Adjustable wrenches, 6" and 12"
- Utility knife with spare blades
- Gasket scraper—sharp old wood chisel

ELECTRICAL TOOLS

- Digital multimeter. Don't waste money on cheap analog meters—they're pretty useless.
- Cable terminal kit including a good crimping tool (Most steel-plate crimping tools produce ineffective crimps.)
- Set of instrument (or jeweler's) screwdrivers

CRUISING TOOLS

In addition to the tools above, a cruising boat will need the following to be self-sufficient in an out-of-reach anchorage:

- Torque wrench, 30 – 100 ft. lbs.
- 12-volt or propane soldering iron and cored electrical solder
- Hacksaws, large and small
- $\frac{1}{4}$"-drive socket set, with $\frac{3}{16}$"–$\frac{1}{2}$"

and 4mm –12mm sockets
- ½"-drive socket set, with ½"–1" (up to 1½" if budget permits) and 10mm – 19mm sockets
- 0–6" Vernier calipers for accurate measurements
- Small propane torch
- Small and large 2- or 3-legged pullers

SPARE PARTS LIST

ESSENTIAL SPARES

- Raw-water pump impeller
- Raw-water pump cover-plate gasket
- Cylinder-head gasket
- Valve-cover gasket
- Oil filter(s)
- Oil
- Primary fuel filter(s)
- Secondary fuel filter(s)
- Transmission fluid
- V-belt(s)
- Coolant
- Alternator (complete)
- Assorted hose clamps

CRUISING SPARES

If you are preparing a comprehensive kit for cruising, take into account the duration of the trip and availability of spares in the region you'll be cruising. Add the following to your list of essentials.

- Raw-water pump (complete, or full overhaul kit)
- Circulating pump (complete)
- Full engine gasket set
- Full set of engine hoses

- Alternator spares, including regulator, rectifier, diode pack, and brush assembly
- Fuel lift pump
- Set of spare injectors
- Set of injector sealing washers
- Set of spare injector nozzles

MATERIALS

SEALERS

- Oil-based instant gasket sealers, such as Permatex 2B, are excellent all-purpose sealers; they remain flexible for some time, but will harden after a few years. They are effective in just about any joint in contact with coolant, raw water, oil, or fuel.
- Silicone-based gasket sealers produce good gaskets that set quickly. Silicone is resistant to high temperatures; it tends to peel, however, and lower-quality sealers should not come in contact with fuel and oil.
- High-copper contact adhesive sprays help seal gaskets if surfaces are clean. These are useful for holding a gasket in position during assembly.
- Specialized gasket sealers such as Hylomar work well in applications requiring non-hardening properties. Hylomar is particularly effective on copper cylinder-head gaskets and resists fuel, oil, and water.

GREASES

- Silicone greases are effective on raw-water impellers, since they

do not attack rubber. They also provide good protection for battery terminals.
- Lithium-based greases are waterproof; they're ideal for stuffing boxes and bearings that come into contact with water.
- Use high-temperature greases on bearings in high-speed or heavy-load applications.

CORROSION PROTECTION

- Thin, oil-based products such as WD-40 are good, all-purpose corrosion inhibitors.
- Heavy-duty corrosion inhibitors such as CRC SP350 and CRC SP400 are application-specific. The latter gives effective long-term protection.

MISCELLANEOUS

- Thread-locking adhesives such as Loctite offer levels of locking according to the job.
- Antiseize compounds protect threaded components for years yet allow them to come apart when necessary.
- Penetrating fluids such as Blaster can be invaluable when you're trying to release corroded components.
- Abrasive papers should be the wet-and-dry type that will work with water and oil. Carry several grades, ranging from 100 grit to 400 grit. If any grade feels too coarse for a particular application, try rubbing it against itself to reduce its bite.

CANVAS

"The skills required
to do stellar canvaswork
are astonishingly few."

Canvaswork
& Sail
Repair

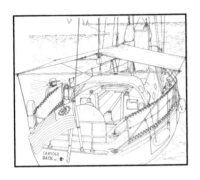

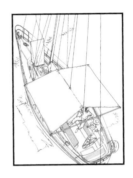

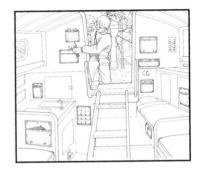

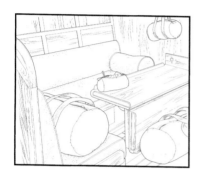

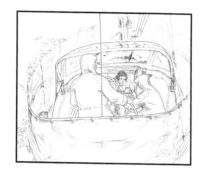

INTRODUCTION

The ozone layer—the BIG awning—is apparently getting threadbare. The amount of ultraviolet (UV) radiation passing through it and reaching the earth's surface is on the rise. These heavier doses of UV are destroying our Dacron sails, chalking our fiberglass decks, carbonizing our teak oil, and lifting our varnish. And they're giving some of us skin cancer at a rate that has doubled in the last two decades.

The long-term solution to the problems with the BIG awning is both complex and uncertain. The short-term solution is simple and efficacious: *Stay in the shade.* Of course, natural shade can be hard to come by out on the water. You can slap on a John Deere cap to protect your pate and your fine Roman nose, but that doesn't do anything for your sails or your varnish, which need the protection just as badly as that aquiline beak.

The most effective way to keep the sun off your boat and your body is with canvas covers and awnings. This isn't news; virtually every sailboat in your marina will be fitted with a canvas sailcover, and a substantial number will sport a fixed-frame awning known universally as a Bimini top. Sailcovers are standard equipment because they extend the life of expensive sails about tenfold. The popularity of the Bimini is no mystery if you've ever sailed a summer in the Torrid Zone.

But if a canvas cover adds life to your sail, wouldn't similar protection for other parts of your boat be a good idea? And if the patch of shade cast by a Bimini makes all the difference between *enduring* and *enjoying* a summer sail, couldn't the expansive shade of a good harbor awning be equally beneficial? The answers are yes and yes. Canvas's

potential to protect your boat and enhance your enjoyment of it is practically limitless.

This book is about taking advantage of the myriad uses fabric has aboard a boat—all fabrics, not just canvas. Canvaswork, in marine usage, has come to describe anything aboard made of cloth. Sails, flags, ditty bags, and cushion covers are all canvaswork.

Why do your own canvaswork? Because you'll save a bunch of money. It's true that generic sailcovers and Bimini awnings aren't terribly expensive, but they rarely fit well either. If you want canvaswork to fit, it has to be custom tailored for your boat, and much of the essential canvas—interior upholstery, for example—is unavailable any other way. Canvaswork is not difficult, but it takes time. Every hour a sailmaker spends traveling, designing, measuring, sewing, fitting, adjusting, and installing adds dollars to the cost—lots of dollars—that you can eliminate by doing the job yourself.

A second reason for doing your own canvaswork is to get exactly what you want. Your sailmaker can keep fiddling with your project until it matches your vision, but with the meter running, that seldom happens. A week after your new weather cloths are installed, you say, "Gee, I wish I'd had her put in a pocket for a chart, and one for sun block," but fulfilling that wish is defeated by the cost or the hassle. However, if *you* made the weather cloths, by the next weekend they'd have pockets, probably at zero additional cost.

There is a third reason to do your own canvaswork: It is pleasurable. There is satisfaction in doing other jobs on the boat, but few of us will find much pleasure in barking our knuckles on the engine, grinding fiberglass, or sanding bottom paint. Canvaswork is different. It is clean, safe, and risk free; gratification is almost immediate; and you can generally work in a comfortable environment. Canvaswork can also be satisfying on a creative level, unlike changing the oil or bedding the stanchions.

The skills required to do stellar canvaswork are astonishingly few. The sewing machine does all the hard work. Your part is to cut the fabric to the required dimensions and guide the pieces through the machine. If a seam doesn't come out quite right, simply pull out the stitches and do it again. Try that with a carpentry project!

This book is designed to give you all the information you need to tackle virtually any canvaswork project you can conceive, but it takes a crawl-before-you-walk approach. Unless you are already comfortable machine-sewing heavy fabric, do not turn to page 832 and start reupholstering your boat's settee as a first project. Take the time to read at least the first two chapters and to make one or two of the items detailed in "Flat Sheet Projects."

"What You Need" is a canvaswork primer. Here you will find a description of the tools you need (including practical selection advice for those of you that don't already have a sewing machine). You will find information about all the most common marine fabrics. You will find out what size needle you need and what kind of thread works best. And you will learn how to set up a sewing machine and how to get it to stitch well.

"Flat-Sheet Projects" provides you with the opportunity to apply what you learned in the first chapter. All the projects are essentially flat sheets,

hardly more complex than a handkerchief—just bigger. These projects require hems at their edges; some require seams; and some require reinforcing, grommets, or other special features.

By the end of "Flat-Sheet Projects," you should have stitching, hemming, and seaming down pat. Subsequent chapters essentially detail canvas items a single step more complicated than those in the previous chapter. For example, in "The Pocket" we fold the flat sheet and seam two sides to form the basic envelope shape of the several illustrated projects. In "The Bag" we modify the envelope to make bag-like projects, and in the next chapter we put a lid on the bag to form the box-like structure of, for example, cushion covers. This evolution concludes with a chapter illustrating custom canvas items such as boat covers and dodgers—seemingly complicated projects, but by now you know better.

The final chapter is a bonus. Its initial focus is on emergency sail repairs—dealing with split seams and torn cloth—but once you have become comfortable sewing marine fabrics, there is little reason not to employ that skill to maintain your own sails. This chapter offers a number of sail-maintenance projects that will add years to sail life and save you money in the bargain.

In these pages you will find detailed instructions for more than two dozen projects, but they represent only a sampling of the useful items you can make for your boat with modest canvasworking skills. Don't be shy about modifying these projects or about striking out on your own. The possibilities are endless.

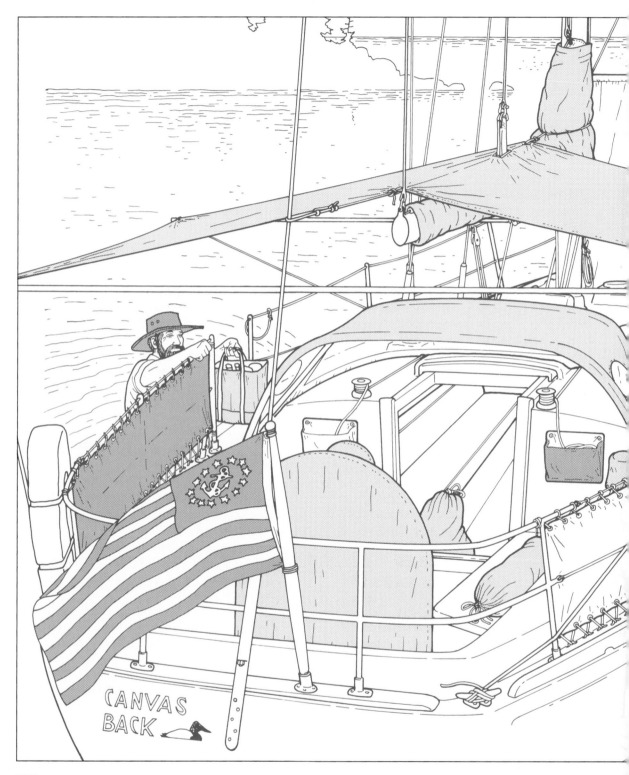

CANVAS
BACK

WHAT YOU NEED

Canvas has a long tradition on the water, equal in importance to wood and rope in the construction and operation of ships and boats for at least the last 2,500 years. Lashed to spars, canvas provided propulsion. Spread above deck, it provided respite from the elements. Tacked down and painted, canvas waterproofed decks. Spread between bulkheads, it cradled off-duty sailors. It continues to serve all those functions today, and more.

Despite this long history, many modern sailors tend to hold canvaswork at arm's length as a skill somehow beyond their grasp. This reluctance is especially surprising when you consider that an inexpertly fashioned canvas project doesn't put the boat at risk; the materials cost of even the most ambitious canvaswork project is likely to be less than an application of bottom paint; and for the time and money invested, canvas items offer the greatest benefit in appearance, convenience, or protection of virtually any boat improvement.

Learning to do your own canvaswork opens the door to scores of possibilities for inexpensively enhancing your boat and the pleasure of using it. Only a few simple skills are required to do journeyman canvaswork; anyone capable of sailing should have little difficulty mastering them.

Canvaswork projects are perfect for rainy days, the dead of winter, or the dog days of summer. The majority of a project (except for measuring and fitting) can be done indoors and away from the boat—at home, for example. You can complete an item in an uninterrupted effort or start and stop it over a period of weeks or months, whichever suits your temperament and the time available.

Like a trip around the buoys, you can probably get the job done quicker with the best equipment, but even an old boat is perfectly capable of completing the course. With not-for-profit canvaswork, completing the course is all that matters. Better tools may make a job easier or quicker, but they won't necessarily make it better. You need sharp scissors and a sewing machine that will make a decent stitch; beyond that, how good the finished item looks is up to you.

SEWING MACHINE BASICS

A lot of sailors own a swaging tool, a tension meter for the shrouds, or refrigeration gauges, but relatively few think of a sewing machine as a boat tool. In fact, a good sewing machine is one of the most valuable tools a sailor can own, often paying for itself on the first project.

FEATURES AND ADJUSTMENTS

The shape of the head and the location of some of the dials may differ from machine to machine, but most will have these basic features and adjustments:

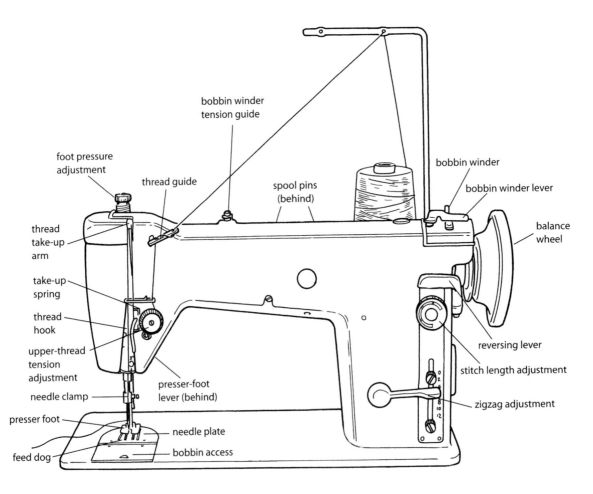

SELECTING A SEWING MACHINE FOR CANVASWORK

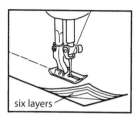

six layers

1 Take a piece of acrylic canvas with you. If you plan to do sail work, also take a piece of sailcloth. Make sure the machine will sew through at least six layers of your cloth. (When you hem two adjacent sides of a piece of canvas, you can have nine layers of cloth in the corner.)

2 Look at commercial machine outlets and major repair facilities rather than domestic sewing centers. A domestic machine will do the job, but you want a heavy-duty one capable of a basic, solid interlocking stitch, not a machine that does buttonholes and embroidery.

3 Look for a machine with vertical needle action. Bypass machines with slant needles.

4 Look for a long stitch. On most canvas projects, the longer the stitch, the better. You don't need a zigzag stitch for canvaswork, and heavy-duty straight-stitch machines can often be purchased very cheaply.

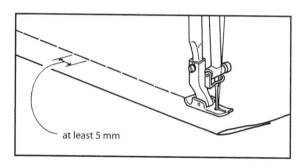

at least 5 mm

5 If you anticipate significant sail repair or sail construction, a zigzag stitch becomes essential. A 6-millimeter width is adequate, but wider is better.

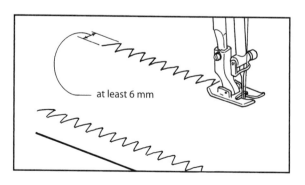

at least 6 mm

walking presser foot

6 Adjustable foot pressure is mandatory. A machine with a "walking" presser foot will handle heavy materials better.

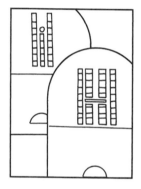

7 Interchangeable feed dogs are very useful, allowing the use of a wide feed dog on slippery fabric.

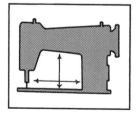

8 More underarm space is better.

OTHER TOOLS

Besides a capable sewing machine, the list of tools canvaswork requires is short. They are all inexpensive, so the difference in cost between a cheap tool and a quality one is only a few dollars. The quality tool will give better results and be less expensive in the long run.

FOR MARKING

A measuring tape, a *straight* yardstick, and a pencil are essential. A framing square can be useful. Use chalk to mark dark colors. Avoid pens and markers; ink will bleed through the material.

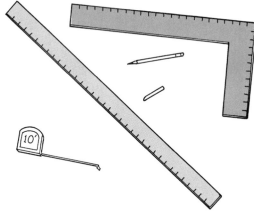

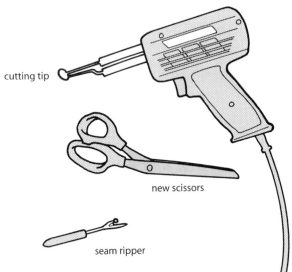

cutting tip

new scissors

seam ripper

FOR CUTTING

Start your canvaswork experience with a *new* pair of scissors. Lightweight vanadium-steel scissors (with brightly-colored plastic handles) cost under $10. Lefties—do yourselves a favor and get left-handed scissors. Nine-inch scissors are a convenient size. Also purchase a seam ripper. Cut sailcloth with a hotknife or a soldering iron.

FOR SEWING

Transfer tape looks like a narrow roll of brown-paper packing tape. When you apply it, then peel away the paper, only the adhesive remains. This lets you assemble two pieces or form a hem before you sew. Essential for sailcloth, it is also useful for canvaswork. You can accomplish much the same thing with a glue stick from an office supply store. You can also assemble pieces with heavy-duty straight pins.

If a project calls for a zipper or piping, you need a zipper foot for your sewing machine. Spare bobbins will minimize bobbin-winding interruptions.

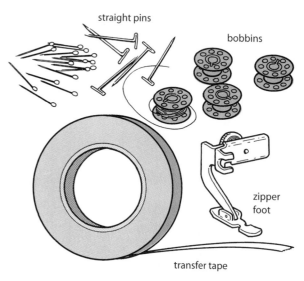

straight pins

bobbins

zipper foot

transfer tape

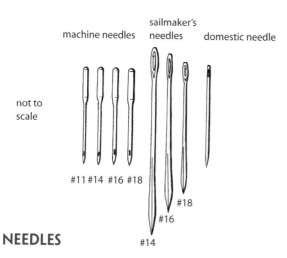

machine needles

sailmaker's needles

domestic needle

not to scale

#11 #14 #16 #18

#18

#16

#14

NEEDLES

Machine-needle sizes are logical—the larger the size, the larger the needle. Generally the heavier the fabric, the larger your needle should be. The smallest size you are likely to use is #12, the largest #22. A #18 needle is usually the best size for canvaswork, but if you have problems, try a larger needle. Needles should be designated "ball-point."

Just to confuse you, hand-sewing needle size decreases as the numbers increase. For handwork, a #16 sailmaker's needle is a good starting point.

FOR FINISHING

Durable grommet installation (spur grommets) requires a hole cutter and a good-quality die set. Except for the lightest-duty use, avoid the cheap die sets sold in washer grommet kits at hardware stores and marine outlets; you want a die set appropriate for spur grommets. You also need an installation tool for snap fasteners—about $5.

grommet die set

hole cutter

snap fastener installation tool

THREAD

You can stitch your canvaswork with variety-store thread, but it won't stand up to the sun and exposure. Unless you like restitching every year or two, it is sheer folly to use anything but polyester fiber thread, not spun polyester or wrapped polyester, or nylon. The kind of thread you need comes on a cone rather than a spool.

Virtually all lock-stitch machines require left lay (also called Z-twist) thread, so it has become standard; don't buy monofilament or thread that isn't twisted. "Bonded" polyester is preferable to "soft" finish. Thread designated V-92 is a good all-around weight, providing excellent strength and durability. For lighter fabrics and stitching that will not be exposed, V-69 can be a better choice. White is the only color you need.

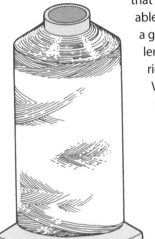

16-ounce cone

FABRIC

Choosing from among the endless array of patterns, colors, weaves, weights, and compositions of cloth available can seem daunting. For below-deck use, select any heavy-duty upholstery fabric in a pattern and color that complements the cabin. Just be sure the fabric is mildew- and stain-resistant, and that it isn't hot to sit or sleep on.

For exposed applications, choices are more limited. You will probably select acrylic canvas for most cover and awning applications, but you'll also find that natural canvas and a few other specialized fabrics are ideal for some marine uses.

ACRYLIC CANVAS

Most sailcovers are acrylic canvas. Once seemingly available only in blue, acrylic is today manufactured in a wide variety of colors and patterns. It is very UV-resistant, and most colors resist fading (red and some browns are the exceptions). Acrylic canvas "breathes" and is water-resistant, but it is susceptible to chafe damage. It is the best material for covers and a good choice for awnings. Common brands are Sunbrella, Acrylan, Diklon, and Sun Master.

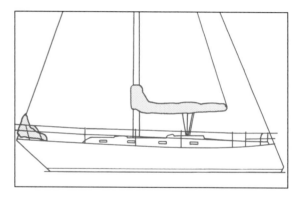

TREATED CANVAS

Natural canvas made of tightly woven cotton is a wonderful material, but its susceptibility to mildew and rot make it poorly suited to the marine environment. Treated canvas resists rot and mildew. Treated canvas is an excellent awning material, providing excellent UV-protection, and the natural fibers swell when wet to make the awning waterproof. Treated natural canvas is much less susceptible to chafe than acrylic canvas. Sunforger (Vivatex) and Terrasol are available in natural (off-white, called "colorless"), pearl (gray/green), and khaki; Permasol and Graniteville offer a variety of colors.

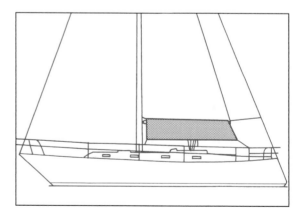

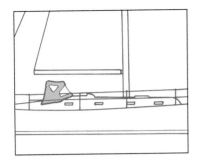

REINFORCED VINYL

Reinforced vinyl in the form of Naugahyde and similar fabrics was once the material of choice for almost all marine upholstery because it is waterproof. It is also hot in the summer, cold in the winter, sticks to bare skin, and promotes mildew because it doesn't breathe. Vinyl upholstery fabric remains the best choice for the exposed upholstery of powerboats, but has fewer advantages for sailboat use. Some vinyl-laminated polyester fabrics, such as Weblon, can be useful for Bimini awnings and dodgers.

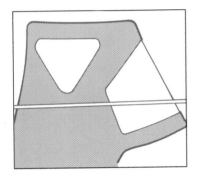

CLEAR VINYL

Clear vinyl is primarily used to put windows in dodgers and awnings. You can buy it by the yard, but if you want it to be water-clear, you will need to buy double-polished vinyl, sold in sheets (usually about 24 by 54 inches). For most uses, 0.020-inch thickness is the best choice—more flexible, easier to handle, and less expensive. Sheet clear vinyl is also available in 0.030-inch and 0.040-inch if added strength is necessary. Most clear vinyls cloud and darken with age; thick vinyls seem especially prone, perhaps because they are laminated from thinner material.

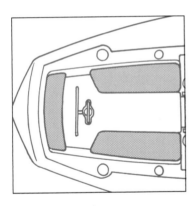

OPEN-WEAVE VINYL

Open-weave vinyl is woven polyester encased in polyvinyl chloride. Aside from marine uses, you have probably seen this fabric on lawn-furniture cushions and patio umbrellas. Open-weave vinyl is as waterproof as a screen door, but since it doesn't absorb or trap moisture, it is an ideal fabric for cockpit cushions, provided the enclosed foam is waterproof (closed cell). This fabric—Phifertex is perhaps the best-known brand—also makes good sheet bags and locker dividers. It is available in numerous colors and patterns. Machine-sewing open-weave fabric requires some special techniques.

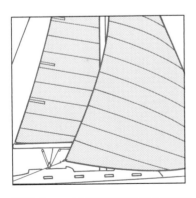

POLYESTER (DACRON)

Polyester fabric describes a lot of materials, including that awful double-knit in the leisure suit your brother-in-law still wears. For marine purposes, we are talking about sailcloth. Polyester, or Dacron, sailcloth is generally given a resin finish to help it hold its shape, but unfinished sailcloth is also available. Dacron makes great sails but poor covers and awnings. It quickly degrades in the sun, it is noisy in the wind, and UV radiation passes right through it, meaning it provides little protection from the sun. A subclass is vinyl-coated polyester fabric, such as Aqualon, popular for trailer-boat covers. This fabric has good abrasion resistance and color selection.

NYLON

Nylon cloth is used for light-air sails. It is commonly available in $3/4$-ounce (Stabilkote) and $1\frac{1}{2}$-ounce ("ripstop") weights. It is even less UV-resistant than Dacron, making it a poor choice for most canvaswork. Ripstop nylon can make a good light-air windscoop, but it creates an awful racket when the wind picks up. A soft, supple nylon cloth called oxford is available in 4- and 6-ounce weights. Nylon oxford cloth is often used for sailbags and similar items.

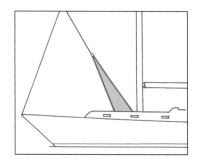

UPHOLSTERY FABRICS

There are hundreds of different upholstery fabrics, from silks and velvets to Herculons and Haitian cottons. Almost any upholstery fabric, in the right circumstances, can be used successfully in the cabin of a boat. Look for fabrics that are not excessively scratchy, hot, or subject to staining. Mildew resistance is a plus. For loose-cushion covers, washable fabrics will soon be appreciated. Buy a couple of yards of the cloth you are contemplating and sit on it, sleep on it, spill on it, and wash it (measure it first to check for shrinkage). If it passes all your tests AND you still like the pattern after a couple of weeks, it will likely be a good choice.

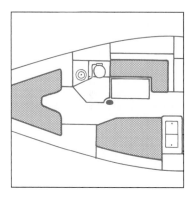

COLORS AND PATTERNS

COLORS AND PATTERNS ARE A MATTER OF TASTE, but there are some rules—guidelines really. Interior designers often rely on the color wheel to help in putting colors together. When the primary colors—red, yellow, and blue—are mixed, they form the secondary colors located between them on the wheel—orange, green, and violet. The warm colors (red, orange, yellow) are on the top half of the wheel; the cool colors (green, blue, violet) are at the bottom.

When you pick a color on the wheel, those on either side of it are *related* and will harmonize with it. The color opposite your selection is *complementary* and can be used success-fully as a contrasting color. The remaining colors are *discordant* and will have a jarring effect in combination. Select warm colors for a boat used in the often-dreary weather of the temperate zones; cool colors provide pleasant respite from the bright, hot tropics. The neutrals—white, black, gray, brown, and beige—aren't part of the color wheel (technically, they aren't colors) and can be used to good effect with any of the colors on the wheel. A color scheme should generally have an odd number of elements.

Patterns and textures add interest and make the cabin more "homey." But beware of excessively busy patterns; in a seaway, they can cause some people to feel queasy.

OTHER SUPPLIES

Most canvaswork projects require some method of attachment or closure, or both. Depending on the canvaswork project you take on, you will need some of the following hardware items. For bunk and settee cushions, you will also need an appropriate filler.

GROMMETS

Grommets provide a convenient means of tying awnings and covers in place. They can also provide additional ventilation. The grommets sold in most hardware stores and chandleries are washer grommets—adequate for only the lightest duty. For heavy-duty canvaswork you need spur grommets. If you fail to make the effort to obtain spur grommets, you are almost certain to regret that failing when the washer grommets pull out of the canvas. Spur grommets cost only pennies more than washer grommets; buy a one-gross box and you will cut the per-grommet cost and have enough grommets for a decade of personal projects. For general use, No. 2 grommets ($\frac{3}{8}$-inch hole) are usually a good size. Be sure your die set is for spur grommets.

spur grommet

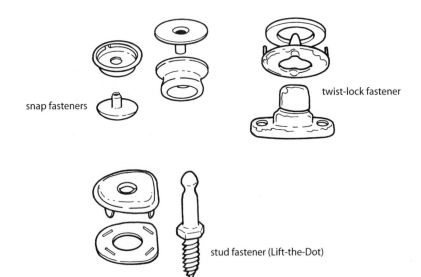

snap fasteners

twist-lock fastener

stud fastener (Lift-the-Dot)

SNAP FASTENERS

Snap fasteners are easy to install with an inexpensive installation tool. Be sure you buy good-quality snaps with bronze springs; cheap snap fasteners soon disintegrate in the marine environment. Stud fasteners (Lift-the-Dot) work similarly to snaps, but can be a better choice in some applications. Both snap and stud fasteners work better when the stress is mostly shear. Where the stress will be perpendicular to the fastener (lifting) a twist-lock fastener may be called for.

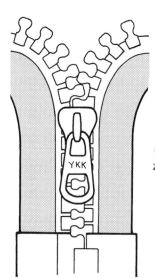

ZIPPERS

The easiest way to get the foam inside a cushion cover is through a zippered opening. Zippers are also useful for allowing a dodger window to be opened for ventilation, for extending a Bimini awning at anchor, and for allowing a cover to fit around a spar or other deck feature. Metal zippers have no place on a boat. Use only heavy-duty plastic zippers; the slide also *must* be plastic. The best are the YKK Delrin zippers. These come in two sizes—#5 and #10. The #10 zipper is larger and much stronger, and superior for almost any use imaginable aboard a boat. Select a #5 zipper only for light duty use or where a large zipper would be obtrusive.

VELCRO

Hook and loop tape (Velcro) has a number of uses aboard a boat, most notably as a secure way of attaching bug screens around hatches. It is also useful for holding cushions in place and for fastening covers and closing bags. Velcro is sometimes used to close cushion covers, but although it is cheaper than a zipper, it is also inferior for this purpose. Velcro is sold by the foot and is often available from discount suppliers. One inch is a good general-purpose width.

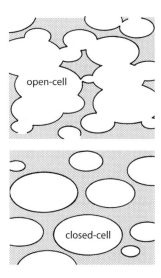

FOAM

Almost all cushions aboard boats are foam-filled. Open-cell foam (typically polyurethane) is the usual choice for settees and bunk cushions. If a cushion will be used for sleeping, adequate firmness is essential. Terms such as "Firm," "Extra Firm," etc., are meaningless. Select a foam that is compression-rated at at least 45 or 50 pounds (or with a density above 1.8 lb./cu. ft.). The best test is to try it; you may want 60- or 70-pound foam. Settee backs (not convertible to bunks) should be softer—try 30-pound. For cockpit cushions use only closed-cell foam (Airex or equivalent). Because closed-cell foam won't absorb water (open-cell foam is essentially a sponge), some sailors use it for all cushions, but closed-cell foam tends to compress rather than support. Sleeping on it may leave you with a backache, and when you roll over, your depression in the foam remains (for a while), making for a lumpy mattress. Buy 2-inch-thick closed-cell foam; 4 inches is a good thickness for open-cell foam.

GETTING YOUR MACHINE TO SEW

Learning to run a sewing machine is not difficult, but spending an hour or two with someone with good machine-sewing skill can accelerate the process. Mostly you need to know how to thread the machine and how to set thread tension. After that, getting a tight, uniform stitch in a particular material is mostly trial and error. Sit down with some scrap cloth and see what effect differing adjustments have. There is no substitute for practice.

OIL THE MACHINE

To operate properly, all sewing machines require *regular* and *thorough* oiling. Before starting every project, tilt the machine back and brush the mechanism free of lint and thread. Then, using sewing-machine oil, apply the specified number of drops to every spot shown in the manual. If you don't have a manual for your machine, put two or three drops of oil in every drilled hole in the mechanism parts and in every hole in the base and the head. Oil sliding mechanisms, such as the needle bar, and both sides of every bushing (or bearing the shafts rotate in). Run the machine (without thread) to distribute the oil. Wipe off any excess, then run several rows of stitching on scrap material.

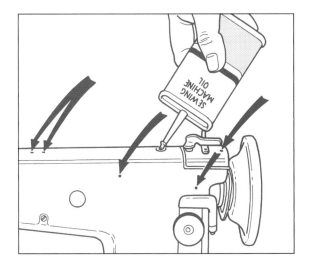

PULLING THREAD FROM A CONE

Spooled thread sits on a spool pin on the back side of the head, the spool rotating as the thread is pulled from it. But commercial-grade thread (long-strand polyester) comes on tubes or cones, and the thread must be pulled from the top. A length of coat hanger wire can easily be bent into a thread guide to feed commercial thread to your machine.

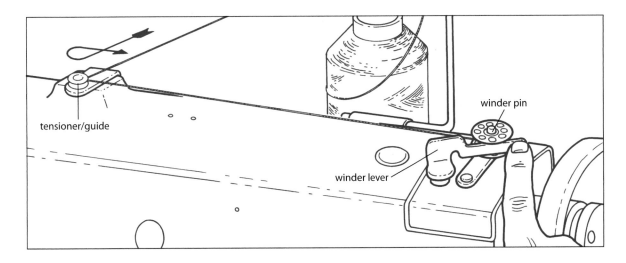

tensioner/guide

winder pin

winder lever

BOBBIN WINDING

Bobbin winders vary, but all operate in essentially the same way. Bring the thread from the cone through the tensioner/guide for the winder, and wrap several turns around an empty bobbin. (You will need fewer turns if you feed the end out through the hole in the bobbin's side.) Place the bobbin on the winder pin, paying attention to which way the pin rotates, then engage the drive wheel by pushing the winder lever. Running the machine winds the bobbin. Some machines have a knob on the balance wheel to release it so that the needle doesn't run when you are winding bobbins. The winder will automatically disengage when the bobbin is full.

THREADING THE MACHINE

Again, follow the instructions in your machine's manual. In general, pass the thread through the top thread guide, around the disks of the tensioner, over the take-up spring, under the thread hook, through the take-up arm, and down through the appropriate guides to the needle. The presser-foot lever must be up to release the tensioner disks. The top guide often has three holes for the thread to pass through (down-up-down), but passing the thread through the first hole, then looping it around the guide and down through the third hole sometimes helps prevent unwanted twist. Thread the needle from front to back or from left to right, depending on your machine. Pull out at least 6 inches of thread.

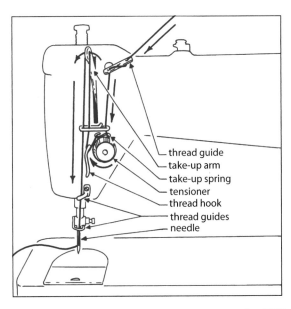

thread guide
take-up arm
take-up spring
tensioner
thread hook
thread guides
needle

BOBBIN TENSION

You adjust bobbin tension by tightening or loosening a tiny tension screw on the bobbin case. To remove the bobbin case from the machine, open the door in front of the needle plate—some slide, some lift. With the needle in the up position, grasp the bobbin-case latch lever and pull it, retrieving the case (and the bobbin). Release the lever and shake the bobbin out of the case. Drop in the fresh one, making sure it winds in the proper direction (usually clockwise from the open side of the case), and draw the end of the thread into the slit in the case and under the tension spring. The thread should pull smoothly but with resistance. If it pulls freely, tighten the tension screw slightly; if it pulls stiffly or unevenly, loosen the screw slightly. Leave several inches of thread hanging free and replace the bobbin case, snapping it in place. Pick up the bobbin thread by holding the top thread and rotating the balance wheel (top) away from you. When the needle returns to the top, pulling the top thread will bring up the bobbin thread.

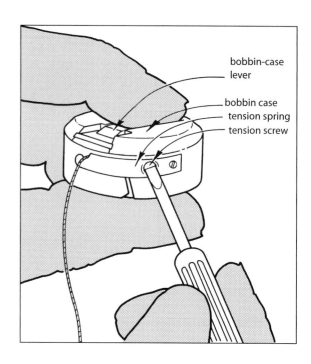

bobbin-case lever

bobbin case
tension spring
tension screw

STITCH LENGTH

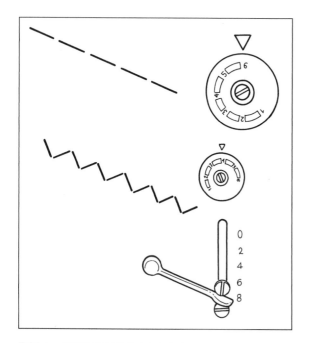

For almost all canvaswork, you want the longest stitch your machine is capable of sewing. Long stitches will minimize or eliminate needle puckers in acrylic canvas. Adjust the dial or lever to its maximum setting. The exception to this rule is sail seams, where you are using a zigzag stitch. In that instance you want square stitches—a 90-degree angle between stitches. The appropriate length will depend on how *wide* a stitch your machine can make.

FOOT PRESSURE

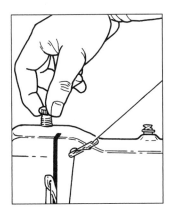

You don't need to adjust the foot pressure unless your machine feeds unevenly or skips stitches. In both cases, increasing the foot pressure may help. Some machines have only two settings—light and heavy. You want heavy—depress the button on top of the needle bar. Other machines have variable foot pressure that you adjust by turning a knurled knob at the top of the needle bar. Don't be afraid to crank it down if you're having problems.

UPPER-THREAD TENSION

After you get the machine set up for heavy material, you will normally need to make only upper-thread tension adjustments as you tackle canvas projects that vary in material and/or layers. The idea is to get the interlock between the two threads to be buried in the material. This is easy with soft fabric, more difficult with stiff acrylic canvas, and impossible with hard fabric like Dacron sailcloth. Sew a row of stitches through three layers of your fabric and examine them on both sides. If the bottom thread is straight, tighten the upper-thread tension. If the top thread is straight, loosen the upper-thread tension. If you have individual stitches on both sides, don't touch a thing. When you are unable to get the stitch you want, try adjusting the bobbin tension. Changing to a needle one size larger will also help.

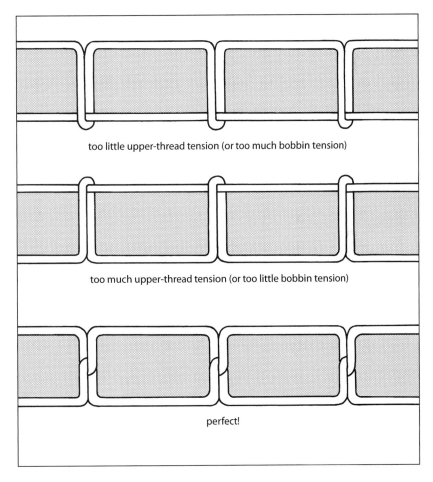

too little upper-thread tension (or too much bobbin tension)

too much upper-thread tension (or too little bobbin tension)

perfect!

DIAGNOSING PROBLEMS

You are likely to encounter some common problems. Here is a gallery of what they look like and how to cure them. Make all tension adjustments in small increments and run another test row of stitches.

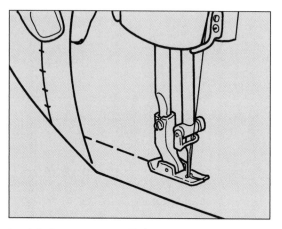

Straight bottom thread. Tighten upper-thread tension. Loosen bobbin tension. Change to larger needle.

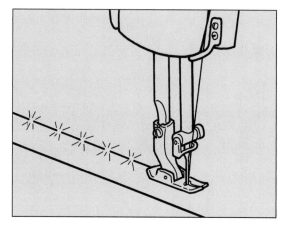

Puckered stitches. Increase stitch length. Change to smaller needle. Reduce *both* upper-thread tension and bobbin tension. Try lighter thread.

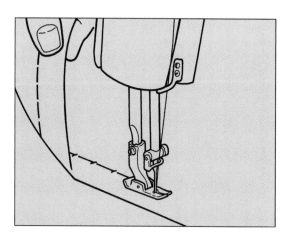

Straight top thread. Loosen upper-thread tension. Tighten bobbin tension. Make sure thread is feeding freely from tube or cone.

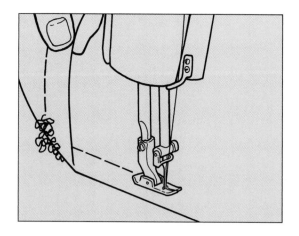

Bird's nest. Upper thread is not between tension disks. Presser foot is not down.

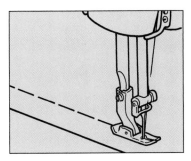

Broken thread. Loosen upper-thread tension. Make sure thread isn't jammed or snagged. Make sure needle is installed properly. Needle may be bent; install new needle. Try a larger needle.

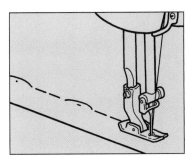

Skipped stitches. Increase presser-foot pressure. Change needle. Make sure fabric is feeding freely.

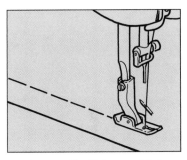

Broken needle. Make sure fabric feeds freely. Unjam top thread. Use a larger needle. Don't force too many layers under the foot. Apply less "helping" pull to cloth from backside of foot.

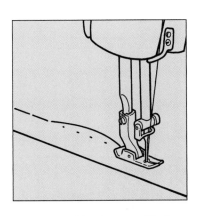

No stitch. Bobbin is empty. If bobbin isn't empty (i.e., broken lower thread), make sure bobbin spins freely in bobbin case. Clean bobbin shuttle and bobbin case, particularly under tension spring. Loosen bobbin tension.

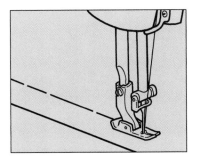

Uneven stitches. Make sure you are "feeding" the machine, not expecting it to pull the fabric. Raise feed dog (not all machines have feed-dog adjustment). Increase—or sometimes reduce—presser-foot pressure. Fit a roller presser foot. Replace worn feed dog. Help machine by pulling *lightly* on the fabric from behind the foot.

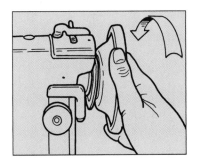

Machine doesn't run. No inertia; start the machine by turning the balance wheel by hand. Bobbin thread is jammed; work it free and clean out shuttle.

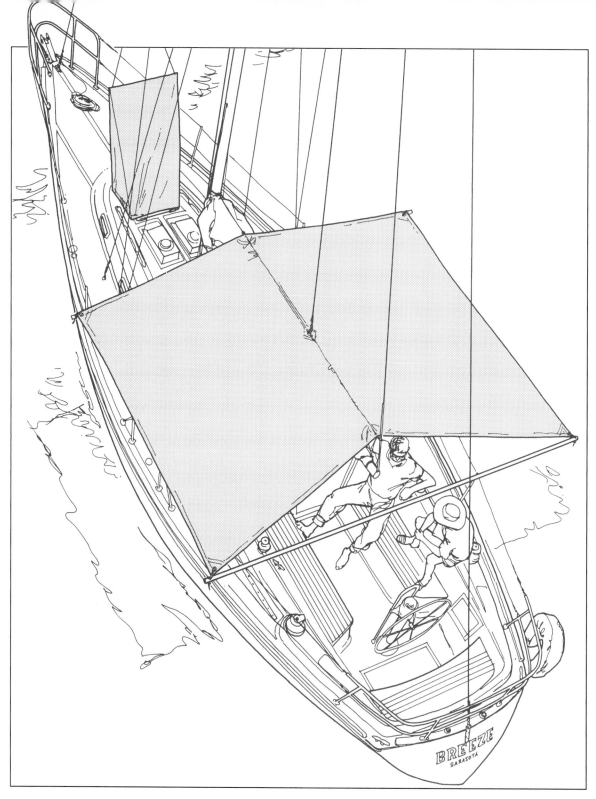

FLAT-SHEET PROJECTS

The first step toward becoming competent, even skillful, at doing your own canvaswork is to become comfortable with the sewing machine. Properly adjusted, the machine does all the work; you just feed it. There is little difference between stitching canvas on a sewing machine and making a scroll-cut in plywood on a bandsaw; you simply guide the material to keep the marked line at the front edge of the blade or, in this case, under the needle. To understand this better, draw a selection of spirals and geometric shapes on a piece of brown paper, then unthread your machine and "sew" the paper on the lines. This is also good practice for guiding the material.

Use some scrap fabric for your initial sewing efforts. Once you have mastered the coordination between guiding the material and applying the correct amount of pressure to the foot control for a comfortable sewing speed—and occasionally helping start the machine by hand-turning the balance wheel—it will be useful to do some experimental stitching. Start with a row of stitches through two layers of fabric. Tighten the upper-thread tension one hatch mark and make a second row of stitches. Tighten it another mark and sew. Number the rows and record the upper tension

setting for each, along with the bobbin tension, thread size (and type), needle size, stitch length, presser foot, material type, and number of layers. After you have tried four or five tension settings on either side of your initial setting, do the same thing again, but this time changing bobbin-tension settings. (Record bobbin-tension settings by sketching the orientation of the tension screw in the bobbin case.) Now try different needles. Different stitch lengths. Different presser-foot and feed-dog sets. Do the same thing all over with three layers of fabric. Then with four. This structured sequence will help you find the best *initial* settings for each sewing job. Some adjustment may be required because of differences in fabric, thread, or even humidity, but developing a notebook of initial settings for various fabrics and thicknesses can be a big timesaver.

When you can make your machine sew an even stitch through three layers of canvas, with the interlock buried, you are ready to tackle your first canvaswork project. An astonishing number of useful canvas items for your boat are simply a flat sheet of cloth with the edges hemmed. These are the easiest canvas items to make and are thus ideal for building your skills.

FENDER SKIRT

Dresses for your fenders don't work. They make the fender a giant roller, capable of painting your hull with creosote as tides or waves roll it up and down a piling. A skirt doesn't have this problem. Hang it from the rail between the fender and the hull.

Begin this project with a rectangular piece of canvas about 40 inches by 30 inches. Adjust these dimensions to suit; height should be slightly less than your boat's minimum freeboard. Treated natural canvas will be easier on your hull and resist abrasion better than acrylic canvas, and it costs less.

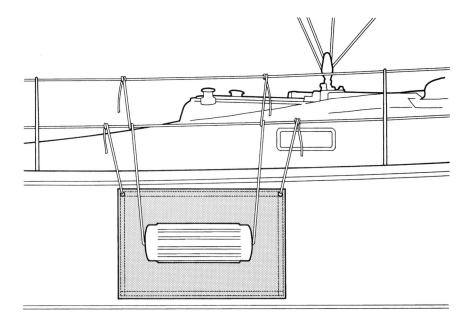

LOCKING STITCHES AT THE START AND FINISH

TO PREVENT STITCHES FROM PULLING OUT where the sewing starts or finishes, get in the habit of locking the first few stitches. If your machine has a reverse lever, sew about $3/4$ inch backwards, then release the lever and sew right over these stitches to lock them. At the finish, back-sew over the last $3/4$ inch of the stitching. If your machine won't sew backwards, lift the needle and foot after you sew about $3/4$ inch and reposition the fabric to the start of the stitching, then sew again right over the first stitches. Finish the same way.

SEWING A DOUBLE HEM

1 Fold in the sides (not the top and bottom) 2 inches and rub a crease into the canvas with the back of your scissors. Sew the fold down with a row of stitches ¼ inch in from the folded edge.

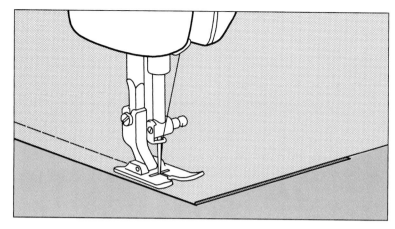

2 Turn ½ inch of the raw edge under and rub it with your scissors. Run a row of stitches ¼ inch from this new fold. The result is a 1½-inch *double-rubbed* hem, or just a double hem. You will use this kind of hem *every* time you want a finished edge.

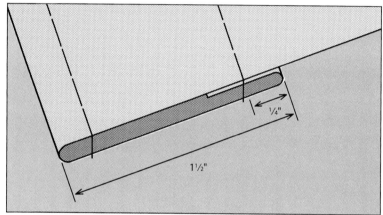

3 Hem the top and bottom edges the same way. Where the inner edges of the hems cross, you have *nine* layers of material! You may have to help your machine across these spots. Note that the finished dimension is 4 inches smaller than the cut size: *You must always allow extra material for hems and seams.*

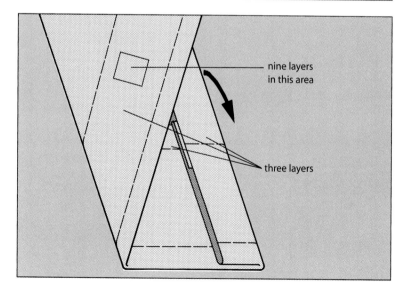

nine layers in this area

three layers

INSTALLING GROMMETS

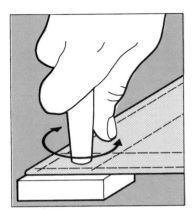

1 With the cutter that accompanies the grommet die set, cut holes in the center of the squares formed by the overlapping hems at the two top corners. Back the cloth with a piece of wood. You will extend the life of the cutter by twisting it rather than hammering it.

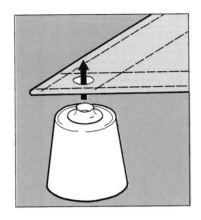

2 For most common applications, including this one, use #2 *spur* grommets. Seat the male half of the grommet on the die and put the hole in the cloth over it.

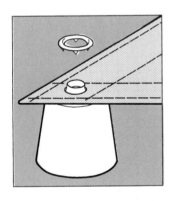

3 Fit the female half of the grommet—the ring—on top of the cloth over the protruding male half.

4 Insert the grommet setter, making sure the grommet is still seated on the die and that the setter is vertical. Tap the setter lightly to roll the edge and compress the two halves together. Finish with a harder blow to set the grommet. (If you are using a washer grommet, set it tightly enough that you can't twist it in the material.)

ANOTHER LAYER OF PROTECTION

FOR NORMAL USE a canvas skirt is more than adequate, but if your boat lies alongside most of the time, constantly riding against fenders, lining the inside of the canvas with terry cloth will be easier on your hull. Double hem the terry cloth at the bottom (not necessary if you are using a bath towel), then sew it to the canvas along the sides and top only, turning the edges of the terry cloth under.

LEE CLOTHS

ee cloths hold you securely in your bunk when the boat heels. The only construction difference between a fender skirt and a lee cloth is the addition of reinforcing webbing in the hem that gets fastened to the bunk—that and the choice of material. Lee cloths spend most of their lives stowed under the bunk cushion, so natural fibers are not a good choice. Dacron sailcloth is strong and has good moisture-shedding qualities, but acrylic canvas is also suitable and more comfortable against bare skin. If ventilation is a problem, use open-weave Phifertex.

MEASURING AND CUTTING

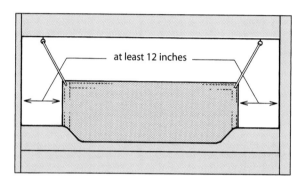

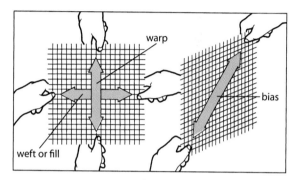

1 To allow for air circulation and to avoid claustrophobia, leave at least a foot open at both ends of a bunk: i.e., a 6½-foot bunk needs a 4½-foot (54-inch) lee cloth. For a finished height of about 18 inches, add 5 inches for the cushion thickness, 2 inches for screwing the cloth down, and 4 inches for hem allowance. Cut size is 58 (54 + 4) inches by 29 (18 + 5 + 2 + 4) inches.

2 Woven cloth is stable along the *grain* of the fabric, i.e., parallel to the threads, but stretches and distorts when pulled *on the bias*—diagonal to the thread lines. Unless there is a specific reason to cut a piece on the bias, always lay out your pieces with the grain. Canvas generally has a "square" weave—yarns running lengthwise (warp) and those running across (weft or fill) are the same—so it makes little difference whether you align a part with the cloth edge or perpendicular to it.

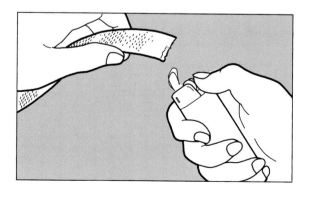

3 Cutting with scissors is quicker and easier than using a hotknife. When a sailcloth item will be double hemmed, hotknifing isn't necessary. You need a piece of 1-inch webbing—Dacron or nylon—the finished length of your lee cloth. Cut the webbing with your hotknife, or play a lighter flame over the ends to fuse the threads (see the sidebar "Using a Hotknife" on page 871).

FABRICATING

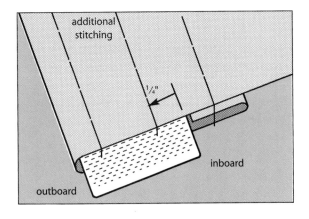

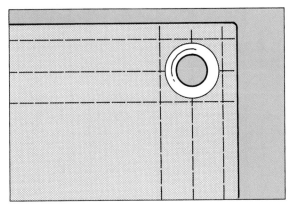

1 As illustrated on page 773, "Sewing a Double Hem," put a 1½-inch double-rubbed hem on all four sides of the lee cloth. Slip the webbing into the fold of the bottom hem before you sew it. Run an additional line of stitches ¼ inch outboard of the inboard edge of the webbing.

2 Install #2 spur grommets in the two top corners of the finished cloth.

INSTALLING

1 With the heated tip of an ice pick, melt mounting holes through the bottom edge of the lee cloth about 6 inches apart and centered in the webbing. Remove the bunk cushion and use stainless steel screws (# 8) and finishing washers to screw the webbing-reinforced edge of the cloth near the outboard edge of the bunk.

2 For light-duty use, the corners can be tied to overhead handrails, but for maximum security, through-bolt strapeyes or eyebolts to the overhead in appropriate locations. Tie lines to the grommets with bowlines or stopper knots, and make them long enough to allow the use of a trucker's hitch for plenty of purchase so the cloth can be pulled drum tight.

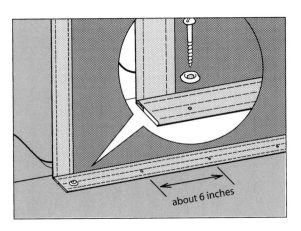

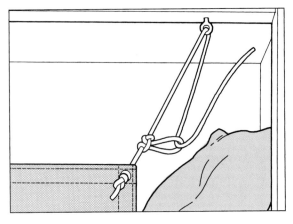

TRUCKER'S HITCH

THE TIGHTER you tie the lee cloth, the more comfortable it will be. The easiest way to get additional purchase on the lashings is with a trucker's hitch. Here is one way to tie this useful knot.

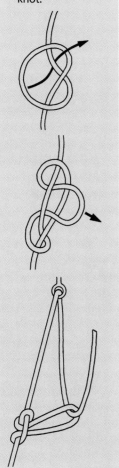

WEATHER CLOTHS

Also called spray dodgers, weather cloths provide protection from wind and spray, and they give a cockpit added privacy. Weather cloth construction is identical to a fender skirt except that the sides may not be parallel, and you may need a cutout for a line to pass through or for access to a cleat or block. Acrylic canvas is the fabric of choice.

1 Measure from the top lifeline to the deck, and from the stanchion on which the forward end laces to the one on which the aft end laces. The cloth can simply pass around intermediate stanchions. If you intend to lace the cloth to a curved rail, it will be easier to make the cloth straight and accommodate the curve with the lacing. A 2-inch hem allowance instead of 4 inches gives a finished dimension 1 inch smaller than the opening all around.

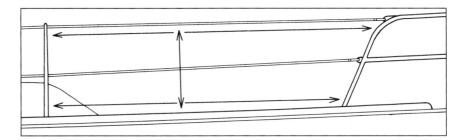

2 Sew a 1½-inch double-rubbed hem around the perimeter (see page 773, "Sewing a Double Hem.") For the best look, fold the hem onto the inside surface of the weather cloth; that means that opposing weather cloths are not identical, but rather mirror images.

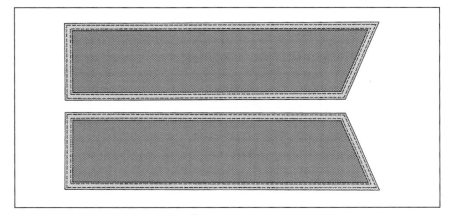

HEMMING CURVES AND CUTOUTS

1 Make the needed cutout after the cloth has been hemmed all around. In the following example, the cutout is a semicircle. The finished opening will be ¹/₂-inch larger than the cutout.

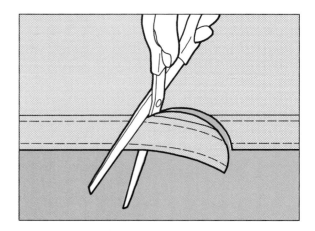

2 Cut a 2¹/₂-inch-wide arc of cloth matching the cutout on its inside edge. The legs of the arc should extend ¹/₂ inch beyond the hemmed edge of the weather cloth. (Use this same technique to put a curved hem on one end of the weather cloth to accommodate a curved stern railing.)

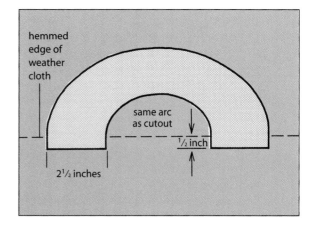

3 Place the arc on the outside (hems are on the inside) of the weather cloth, lined up with the cutout and extending ¹/₂ inch beyond the edge on either side. Sew the arc in this position with a row of stitches ¹/₂ inch from the inside edge.

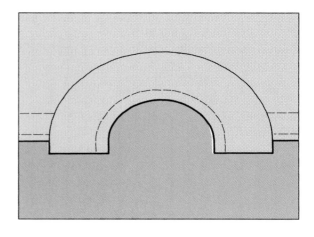

4 With your scissors, snip through the raw edges of both pieces, making a cut perpendicular to and about $^1/_8$ inch shy of the stitching. Repeat this every $^1/_2$ inch (every inch for larger radii) all along the curve, being very careful not to cut closer to the stitching than $^1/_8$ inch.

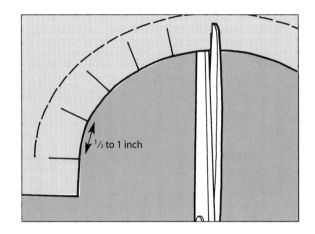

5 The slits allow the concave edge to expand, so you can fold the arc from the outside of the weather cloth to the inside. Turn under the raw edges of the legs of the arc and run a row of stitches following the contour and about $^1/_2$ inch from the edge.

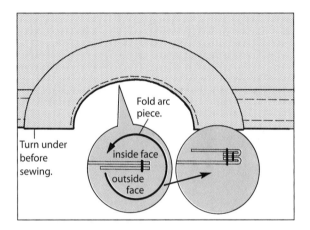

6 Fold under and sew down the outside edge of the arc piece. In soft fabric you can deal with the excess fabric that results by sewing in evenly spaced darts—triangular pleats—but on stiff canvas it is better to remove this extra fabric by V-cutting the hem of a convex edge before folding it under.

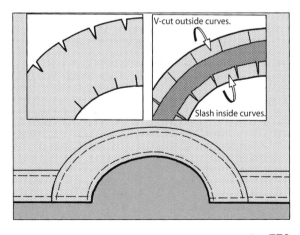

INSTALLING WEATHER CLOTHS

1 Install #2 spur grommets at each corner and evenly spaced 6 to 8 inches all around the perimeter.

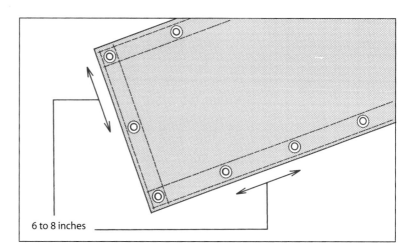

6 to 8 inches

2 Tie the cloth in place with short lengths of light line at the corners. Install small strap eyes on the deck, centered between each pair of grommets in the bottom edge.

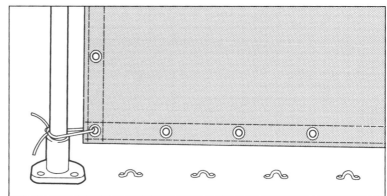

3 Use a continuous length of ³/₁₆-inch Dacron line to lace the cloth in place. The line will move and wear less if you throw in a half hitch every time the line passes over the lifeline, around a stanchion, or through an eye.

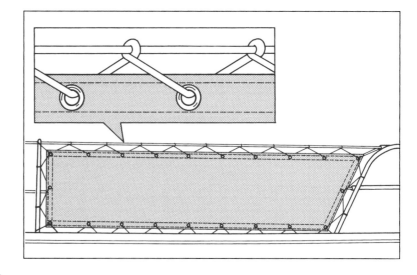

APPLIQUÉ—PUTTING LETTERS ON YOUR WEATHER CLOTHS

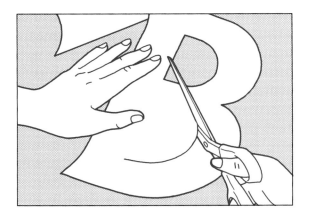

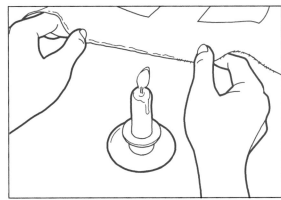

1 Cut letters from a contrasting fabric. If you want them to last as long as acrylic weather cloths, use acrylic canvas for the letters also.

2 Seal the raw edges of acrylic canvas by passing them quickly through a flame. Practice this skill first on scrap material.

3 Position the letters on the cloth the way you want them, then attach them with an office-supply glue stick. It is a good idea to rig the weather cloth and view the lettering actually on the boat before you sew it in place permanently.

4 Set the zigzag width to about 4 millimeters (6 mm is the typical maximum setting), dial the stitch length down to about 3 mm, and adjust the tension. *Overcast* the edges of the letters; that is, sew around their perimeters with one side of the stitch just off the edge of the letter. Don't forget the inside edges of closed letters.

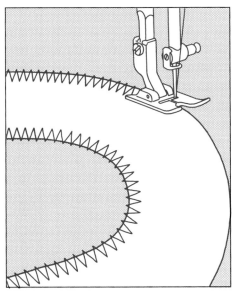

POCKETS

POCKETS SEWN to the inside of weather cloths can be very handy for holding charts, sunglasses, lotion, and innumerable other items. Instructions for fabricating patch pockets are included in the next chapter, "The Pocket."

FLAGS

Signal flags were once essential aboard boats for communication. Today their uses are more ceremonial, but a few flags can be required equipment. Most flags are easy to make. For flags that will be bright, durable, and fly well, select 4-ounce oxford nylon. The most common size is 12 by 18 inches, but 24-inch flags are a better fit for boats larger than about 35 feet.

USEFUL FLAGS

Foxtrot—disabled

Oscar—man overboard

Victor—require assitance

Q FLAG

A vessel entering a foreign country is required to fly the Q flag, indicating that it is under quarantine until officials issue clearance. The Q flag is solid yellow.

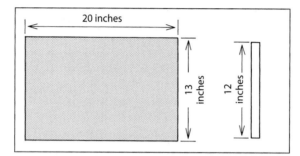

20 inches

13 inches

12 inches

Fold once.

½ inch

Fold again, then sew both edges of hem.

1 Cut the cloth an inch wider and 2 inches longer than the desired finished size: for a 12- by 18-inch flag, cut the cloth 13 by 20 inches. Cut a 12-inch length of 1-inch webbing.

2 Center the webbing on one short side, overlapping the cloth ½ inch. Stitch down the center of the overlap. Using the edges of the webbing as guides, fold the cloth over, then fold it over again. Stitch ¼ inch from the inboard and outboard edges of the hem.

3 Starting with the opposite short side, put a ¼-inch double-rubbed hem on the remaining three sides. Fold ¼ inch of cloth under, then fold it again another ¼ inch and sew it down with two rows of stitches. For your initial tries at this, gluing the hem down first with transfer tape or a glue stick may give you better results.

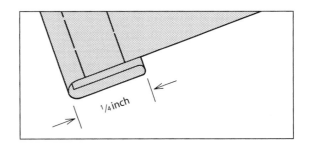

¼ inch

4 Put two #2 spur grommets near the ends of the reinforced edge.

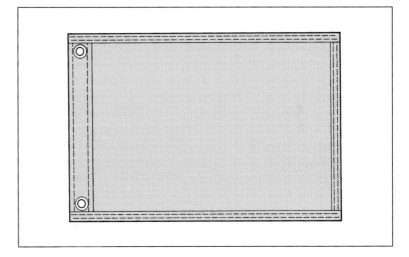

FLAT-FELLED SEAMS

WHEN BOTH SIDES OF THE FABRIC will be visible, join pieces with a *flat-felled seam*. The most secure method is to overlap the two pieces ½ inch and stitch down the center of the overlap. Fold the top piece of fabric under at the raw edge of the overlap, then flip the other piece over to enfold the other raw edge. This is a good place to use transfer tape to hold the fabric in position for sewing. Stitch near both edges of the seam to hold it flat.

This method has the advantage of having an internal row of stitches entirely protected from the sun, so when the exposed stitching begins to fail, the item will not fall apart.

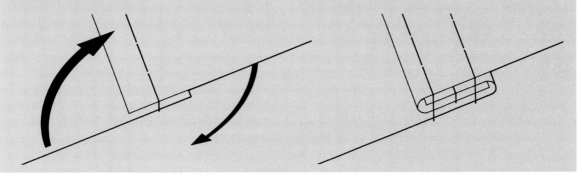

DIVER'S FLAG

Anytime a diver is in the water, the law requires the display of a diver's flag. Fly this flag from the spreader when you are near the boat, or attach it to a float-mounted pole tethered to you.

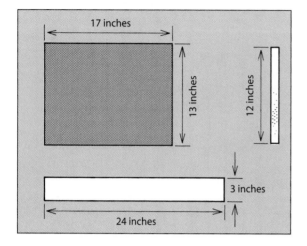

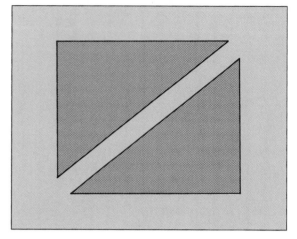

1 For a 12- by 18-inch flag, cut the red material 13 by 17 inches. You also need a strip of white material 3 inches wide and a couple of inches longer than the diagonal distance across the red—in this case, make the strip 24 inches long.

2 Draw a straight diagonal line between opposite corners of the red fabric and cut the piece in half on this line.

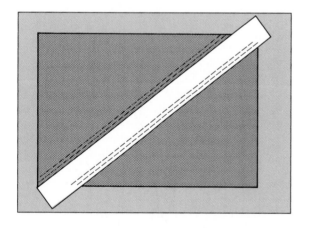

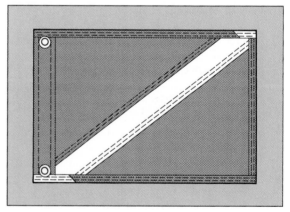

3 Sew the white strip to one of the diagonal edges with a ½-inch flat-felled seam (see page 783). Seam the other diagonal edge to the opposite side of the strip, aligning them as shown for the *flat-felled seam*.

4 Trim away the extra white material and finish the edges of the flag exactly like the Q flag on page 782.

WINDSCOOP

There are lots of windscoop designs, but this one has the advantage of being simple and big, the latter especially important on hot days when the wind is lethargic. The disadvantage is that the boat needs to more or less face the wind, a problem in current or at the dock.

Treated canvas is a good material choice because it is quiet and chafe-resistant, but you can't put it away wet. Acrylic canvas requires less care, but you will need chafe patches where it touches the open hatch. Stay away from spinnaker cloth: the ability to "fill" easily is not a benefit with this design, and the crackle of the nylon when the bow gets off the wind will drive you crazy.

1 Open the forward hatch to about 45 degrees and make a paper pattern of a three-sided box that lies flat against the hatch and sits on the deck. You are only interested in the bottom edge of this pattern.

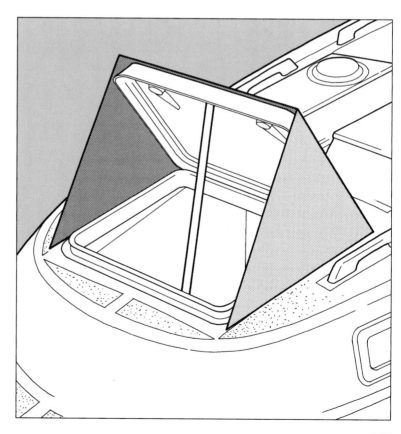

2 You can make this scoop as wide as you want, but a good rule of thumb is to make it about 2½ times the width of the hatch. The height is limited only by the diagonal distance to the headstay, but as a practical matter you will get ample height from two panels of 46-inch material, which will require only a single seam. For a 20-inch hatch, hem two 50-inch lengths of fabric side to side. Because you are joining finished edges (*selvages*), sew the pieces together with a simple ½-inch overlap seam. Overcast the edges with a zigzag stitch if you like.

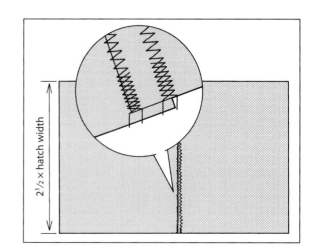

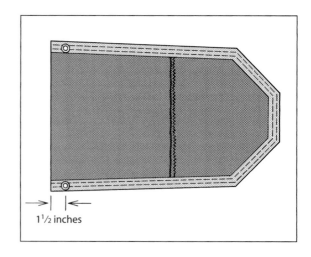

3 Center the bottom of the paper pattern along one of the short sides and trace its two angular edges onto the canvas. If you used the 2½-times rule, the pattern should fall an inch or two short of the edges of the cloth panel. If you made your scoop wider, extend the pattern line about 2 inches on either side, then connect it with a straight line to the top corners of the scoop. Cut on the lines.

4 Put a 1½-inch double-rubbed hem on all edges except the top. Install #2 spur grommets in the two side hems 1½ inches from the raw edge.

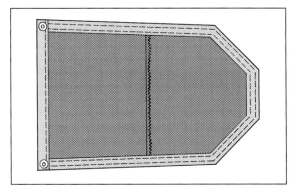

5 Finish the top edge with a 1½-inch double-rubbed hem, but omit the outboard row of stitches. This provides the pocket for the spreader.

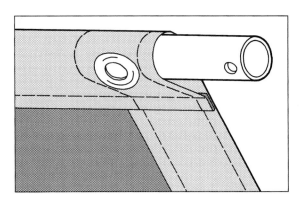

6 Cut a length of aluminum tubing or metal electrical conduit (EMT) to the finished width of the scoop and slide it into the pocket. Mark it with the location of the grommets. Remove it and drill ⅜-inch holes in the conduit slightly outboard of the marks; this way the hoist lines will also prevent the canvas from bunching on the spreader. Sand the edges of the holes.

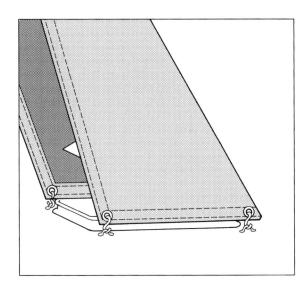

7 Install grommets at the four corners of the bottom edge, then install small strap eyes on deck at the locations of these grommets. S-hooks closed around the grommets expedite installation. Note that the hatch can be closed without removing the scoop.

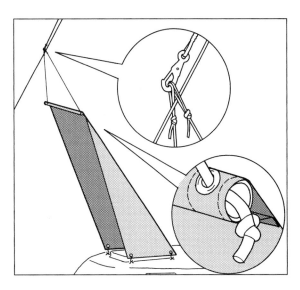

8 Put stopper knots on the ends of two lengths of ¼-inch Dacron line and thread them from inside the spreader out through the grommet. Tie bowlines in the other ends of the lines and hoist them forward of the headstay. Some experimentation will be required to find the right length, but the taut lines should be in the same plane as the top of the scoop.

HARBOR AWNING

Perhaps you're wondering if an awning isn't too far advanced for an entry foray into canvaswork. Shouldn't awnings come later in the book? No. A harbor awning, in a typical manifestation, is nothing more than a bigger panel of canvas, hemmed all around, with grommets on the corners, and perhaps with the addition of corner reinforcements and spreader pockets.

The best material for a harbor awning is treated canvas in the natural off-white color. The natural fibers of treated canvas stand up well to handling, and harbor awnings given intermittent use can easily last 15 or 20 years. Natural fibers also swell when wet, making the fabric genuinely waterproof. Acrylic canvas depends on a coating to make it waterproof, and the proofing soon wears off awnings that are often folded and handled. Avoid dark colors, especially for tropical use; the radiated heat from a dark awning can be nauseating.

AWNING DESIGN

1 A flat awning has internal battens to spread it. It can be the easiest type to put up, but the most awkward to stow. It handles sudden windstorms well, and it can be inclined toward the sunny side for later shade.

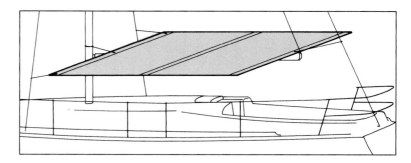

2 A tent awning is the easiest to construct and the easiest to stow. It is typically stretched between the mainmast and the backstay or the mizzenmast, with the four corners tied down to the shrouds, the lifelines, or both.

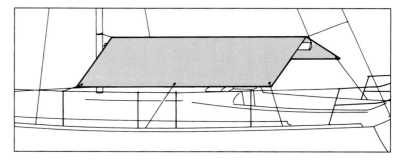

3 A pole awning is a tent awning with external spreaders. The spreaders allow the awning to be set higher for standing room and to extend beyond the rail for longer-lasting shade. The awning and spreaders are stowed separately.

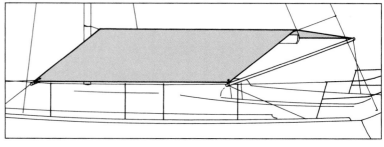

MEASURING FOR YOUR AWNING

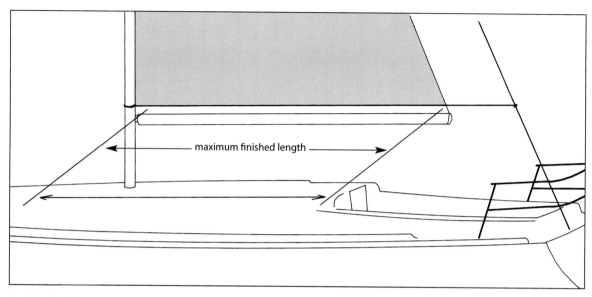

1 Tie a line between the mast and the backstay (or mizzen). The maximum finished length of your awning is the length of this line between the mast and the topping lift less an allowance for tensioning.

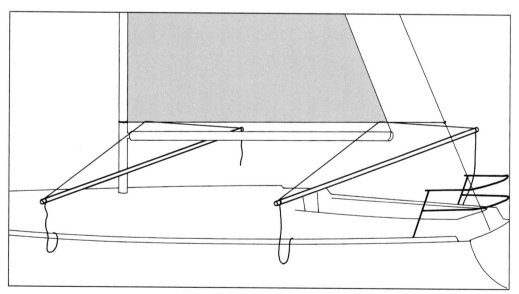

2 Tie lines from the ridgeline to your planned corner tie-off points. If you are making a flat awning, these lines must run straight across the ridgeline; if you are making a tent or pole awning, the lines will form an apex over the ridgeline. If you plan to use spreaders, simulate them now with reaching poles, boathooks, or what have you.

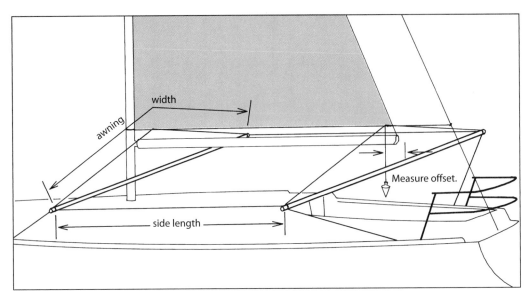

width

awning

Measure offset.

side length

3 Tie fore-and-aft lines between the tie-off points. These simulate the sides of the awning, which will essentially be straight. If there is any rigging inside of these lines, you will have to make the awning smaller or install a zipper (see page 822) to allow the awning to fit around it.

These lines also let you observe the limits of the shade as the day progresses. The distance between the corner tie-offs, measured over the ridgeline, gives the widths of your awning forward and aft.

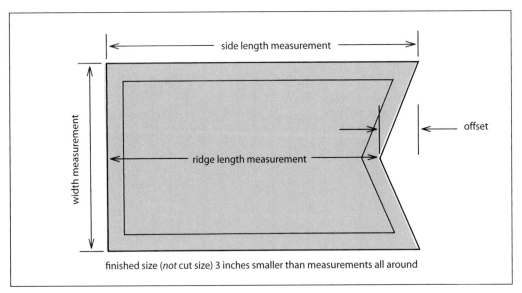

side length measurement

width measurement

ridge length measurement

offset

finished size (*not* cut size) 3 inches smaller than measurements all around

4 If your awning isn't a rectangle, measure the fore-and-aft distance to the mast or topping lift from a straight line between the tie-offs so you can duplicate the shape when you cut the material. Put all your measurements

on a sketch of the awning. Now reduce the length and width by 6 inches: you need at least 3 inches of space at each tie-off point to allow tensioning, and you want the pull at the corners to be diagonal.

MAKING THE PANEL

1 Seams should always run athwartship on an awning so rain runs along, not under, them. Cut the canvas with a 4-inch hem allowance, plus an additional 3 inches for tent or pole awnings. If the awning width isn't uniform, be sure each panel is long enough for its location. Sew the panels together with a 1-inch overlap seam, sewing down the middle of the overlap with your widest zigzag stitch (with the stitch length adjusted to give a square stitch). Overcast both edges with additional rows of zigzag stitching—this is identical to triple-stitched seams on a sail.

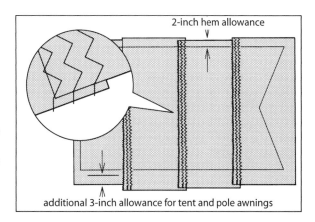

2-inch hem allowance

additional 3-inch allowance for tent and pole awnings

2 Straighten up the sides using scissors. If you allowed the extra 3 inches, cut a 3-inch-wide strip from one edge and set it aside. The length of the assembled panel, like the width, should be 4 inches longer than the finished size.

3 Cut a slight hollow into the side edges—about 1 inch for every 6 feet of length. This keeps the edge from flapping, just like leech hollow does in a sail.

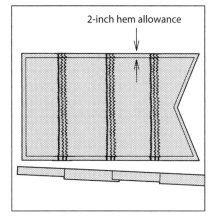

2-inch hem allowance

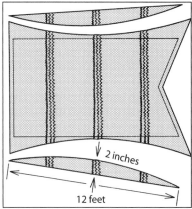

2 inches

12 feet

4 Sew reinforcement patches to the unhemmed panel. Add two layers of cloth at the corners, in the middle of the front and back edges (and the side edges if your awning will be fastened there), and at lift points in the center. Don't install lift patches now if the awning will have a ridge rope. For each reinforcement location, cut two patches to match the grain of the panel, one about 4 inches and the other about 6 inches on a side or in diameter. Align the large patch 2 inches from the edge and sew down the turned-under diagonal edge or curved edge. Slip the small patch under the large one and stitch $1/4$ inch inside its diagonal or curved edge. Make lift patches oval or diamond shaped, also with the top patch hemmed.

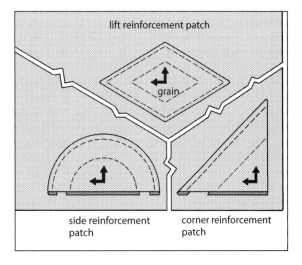

lift reinforcement patch

grain

side reinforcement patch

corner reinforcement patch

FROM PANEL TO AWNING

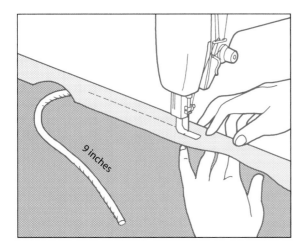

2 Rope the awning continuously all the way around, stopping about a foot short of where you started. Join the ends with a short splice, cutting half the yarns out of each strand to maintain the rope's diameter. Sew down the remaining section to enclose the splice. Now turn the raw edge under $\frac{1}{2}$ inch and sew it down all around.

1 Roping the edge doubles or triples an awning's life and quiets the edges. Use $\frac{3}{8}$-inch three-strand Dacron line. Trim and hem the corners for a mitered hem (see below). Put the zipper foot on your machine with the needle on the right side. Starting about one-third of the way across one end of the awning, fold the edge over 2 inches, slide the rope into the fold, and stitch up against it. Leave 9 inches of rope free and keep the rope straight and taut as you sew. If the zipper foot is long, corners may be troublesome: do the best you can.

3 If you elect not to rope the awning, put a normal $1\frac{1}{2}$-inch double-rubbed hem in it all around, mitering the corners. Whether you hem or rope, your stitching should catch the unsewn edges of the reinforcing patches.

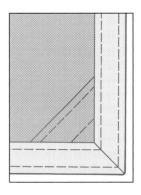

MITERING A HEMMED CORNER

YOU CAN REDUCE the bulk of hemmed corners by mitering them. Fold both edges over the normal hem amount and rub them to crease the material. Unfold them and cut the corner off diagonally $\frac{1}{2}$ inch from the intersection of the creases. Put a $\frac{1}{4}$-inch double-rubbed hem in this diagonal edge. Now put your regular double-rubbed hem in the sides. This way you need only to sew through six layers of cloth, instead of nine, and you get a flatter corner.

$\frac{1}{2}$ inch from the intersection of the creases

fold creases

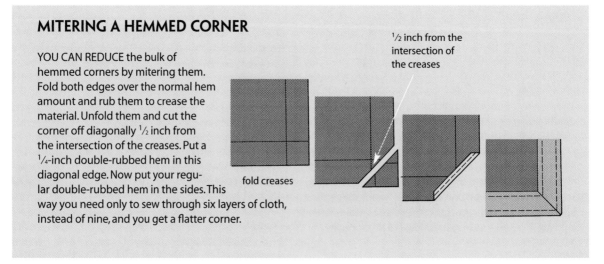

4 Flat awnings require batten pockets at the ends and sometimes in the middle. Cut strips of canvas about 1 inch wider than 3 times the diameter of your battens and just shorter than the width of the awning. Draw a straight line across the awning inboard of the anticipated grommet locations and a second line inboard of the first by the batten diameter. Hem the ends of the strip, then sew one edge on the outboard line. Fold the strip over, turn the raw edge under $1/2$ inch, and sew this edge on the inboard line to form a pocket. Sew one end closed, insert the batten, and sew the other end closed. Metal electrical conduit (EMT) makes good awning battens, but tape the ends to reduce chafe.

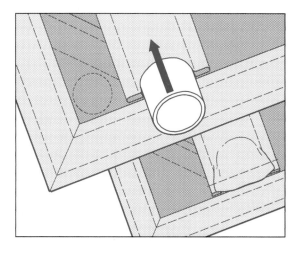

5 You can make battens removable by sewing an overlapping flap over one end of the pocket instead of stitching it closed. Batten pockets also need not fully enclose the batten: 6-inch pockets at either end will hold a batten securely. If the batten telescopes, it can be easily removed from end pockets.

6 Peaked awnings need a ridge rope. Do not install a ridge rope by folding the awning in half and sewing the rope into the fold: this concentrates all the stress on the stitching. The proper way is inside a pocket, and you have a 3-inch-wide strip of canvas set aside just for this purpose. Splice eyes around nylon thimbles in both ends of a length of $3/8$-inch Dacron rope, so that the distance between the eyes is the same as the distance between the planned location of the two center grommets on the awning. Strike a straight line on the underside of the awning between the grommet locations, and capture the ridge rope on this line with the canvas strip and your zipper foot, turning under all raw edges.

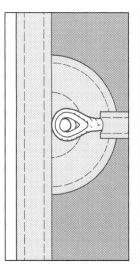
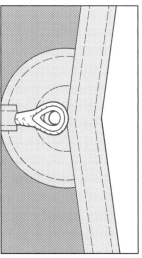

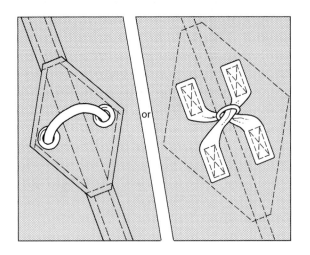

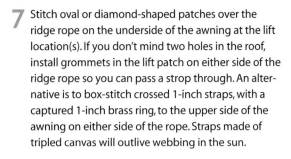

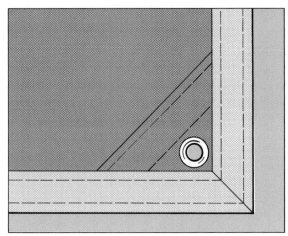

7 Stitch oval or diamond-shaped patches over the ridge rope on the underside of the awning at the lift location(s). If you don't mind two holes in the roof, install grommets in the lift patch on either side of the ridge rope so you can pass a strop through. An alternative is to box-stitch crossed 1-inch straps, with a captured 1-inch brass ring, to the upper side of the awning on either side of the rope. Straps made of tripled canvas will outlive webbing in the sun.

8 Install the perimeter grommets, setting them back far enough from the edge to take full advantage of the reinforcement patches.

EXTERNAL SPREADERS

Minimize wear to your awning by attaching the spreaders to the securing lines rather than to the awning. External spreaders are sometimes attached with eyes and snaphooks, but the easiest method is to put two stopper knots in a tie line and drop it into a slot in the end of the spreader, where tension holds it quite securely. To use this method, you must put solid plugs in the ends of hollow spreaders.

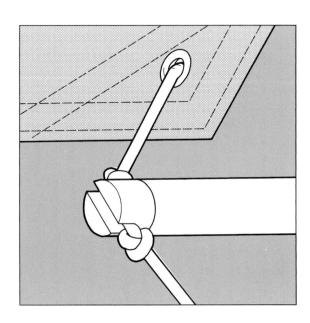

SIDE CURTAINS

Some sailors make side curtains a permanent feature of their harbor awning, rolled up and tied along the edge when not in use. Unfortunately, integral side curtains can double the bulk of an awning. Removable side curtains offer better flexibility. They can be attached with zippers, but lacing allows a single curtain to be located anywhere around the awning's edge.

1 Make lace-on side curtains exactly like a fender skirt, but with grommets spaced every 6 to 8 inches along one side to match the mid position of corresponding grommets in the edge hem of the awning. Corner grommets on the bottom edge allow you to secure the bottom. For additional flexibility install a couple of intermediate grommets on the bottom edge.

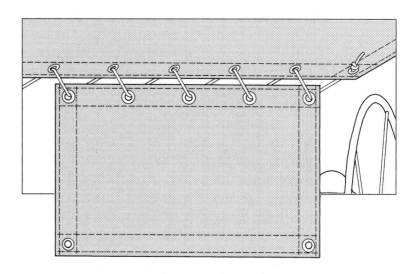

2 Lacing is hardly onerous, but you can easily make the side curtains button to the awning. Cut inch-long pieces of $^1/_4$-inch hardwood dowel and drill them with two $^1/_8$-inch holes about $^1/_2$ inch apart. Thread them as shown with $^1/_8$-inch braided Dacron flag halyard.

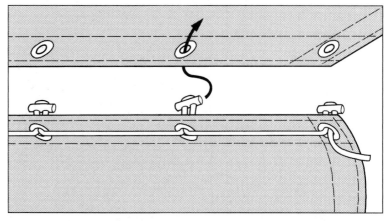

3 To leave side curtains attached when they aren't needed, roll them up and tie them with short lengths of line or webbing (shoe laces are ideal) passing through every third or fourth grommet.

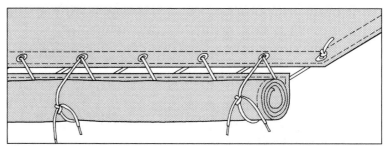

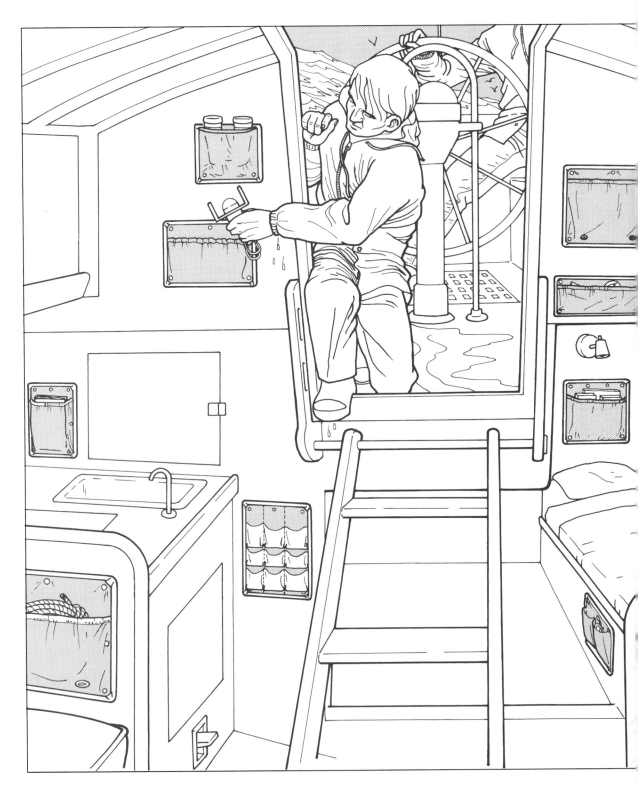

THE POCKET

Pockets are just as handy on a boat as they are in jeans, jackets, or kangaroos. Boats have an amazing affinity for gathering small items that then disappear when actually needed. Pockets are marvelous at helping you get a handle on that problem.

Pockets also provide storage possibilities for the odd-shaped spaces and inaccessible nooks on a boat that would otherwise be wasted. Buying a larger boat isn't the only solution to running out of space; with a little ingenuity and a few yards of fabric, you can substantially increase the useful space within the confines of your hull.

Pockets don't just confine: they also protect, holding their contents in a padded embrace. Pockets mounted high in lockers, out of harm's way, can be the safest place for fragile items. On the back of a cabinet door they can quell the rattle of pot lids. Or lying against the hull and stuffed with soft goods, a fabric pocket protects both the hull and the loose items in a locker.

Once you have mastered putting a hem in the perimeter of a flat sheet, the pocket is the next logical step for broadening the value of this new-found skill. In its simplest incarnation, the pocket is nothing more than a doubled flat sheet with the sides sewn together. Make the fold short of the middle and you end up with a flap that can be given grommets for hanging the pocket or snaps for closing it—or both.

In this book we have room to detail only a few of the most useful pocket items, but the variety of ways to take advantage of the pocket's utility aboard a boat is limited only by your imagination. Anytime you are looking for a way to stow an item out of the way or, ironically, to keep it immediately at hand, you will do well to ponder how a pocket might serve as more than a repository for your idle hands.

HANGING STORAGE POCKETS

You can never find the key to the water-fill cap? Sat on another pair of sunglasses? Dive fins come out of the cockpit locker distorted? Easily fabricated hanging canvas pockets can solve all of these problems and dozens more like them.

SELECTING THE FABRIC

You need the chafe resistance of treated natural canvas if the pocket will contain heavy items like tools or winch handles. For most other applications, choose acrylic canvas, taking advantage of the color variety to make it easier to remember what is in a specific pocket. For even easier identification, make the pocket from clear vinyl or acrylic canvas with a vinyl front. Ripstop nylon (spinnaker cloth) makes excellent pockets for clothes and other lightweight items. Linens and blankets will stay fresher in open-weave Phifertex bags; Phifertex also makes an excellent laundry bag.

BIND, DON'T HEM

If you hem your canvas before folding it into a pocket, the edges can become excessively bulky. Avoid this by finishing the edges with binding tape. Binding tape is a narrow strip of vinyl or cloth (white Orlon or acrylic in matching colors) with finished edges; ¾-inch is a good general-purpose width. Fold the tape over the raw edge(s) of the canvas and sew it down—with a zigzag stitch if your machine is capable. Dart the tape at corners. Seamed edges in canvas will be stronger if you sew the parts together first, then bind the edges.

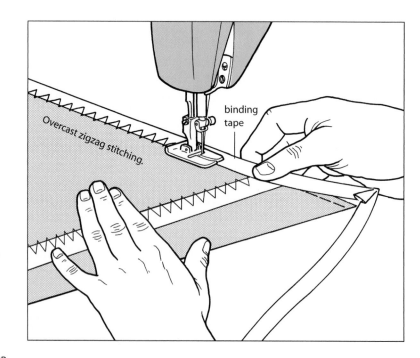

Overcast zigzag stitching.

binding tape

MAKING A POCKET

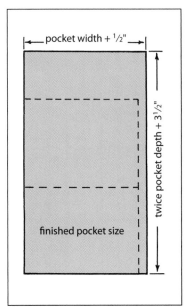

pocket width + ¹⁄₂"

twice pocket depth + 3¹⁄₂"

finished pocket size

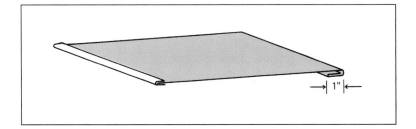

1"

1 Cut a rectangle of fabric ¹⁄₂ inch wider than the interior width of the planned pocket and about 3¹⁄₂ inches longer than twice the desired depth.

2 Put a 1-inch double-rubbed hem in one end. Hem or bind the opposite end.

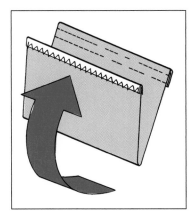

3 With the 1-inch hem to the back, fold the fabric to position the bound edge about 2 inches below the hemmed edge, then seam the sides.

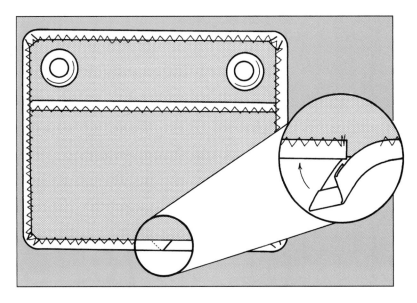

4 Bind the entire perimeter, cutting the end of the binding tape on a diagonal and folding it under to finish. Install #2 spur grommets in the corners of the triple-thickness flap.

CLEAR POCKETS

Make clear vinyl pockets, ideal for manuals and doc-
uments and for a conglomeration of small items, as
with any other fabric. Binding tape makes the vinyl
easier to sew—don't seam vinyl first. Be sure you are
using your longest stitch. Mounted clear pockets
are more attractive with a canvas back. In this case,
cut the front and back separately and assemble
them with binding tape. You can leave the top edge
of the vinyl raw.

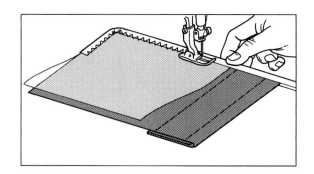

CLOSURES

1 If you want a closing flap rather than one for hanging,
omit the double-rubbed hem and reduce the cut size
appropriately.

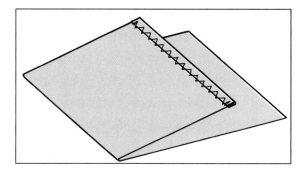

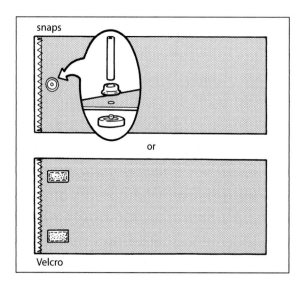

snaps

or

Velcro

2 Install half of your closure in the material before you
fold it into a pocket. For snaps, pierce the material
with a heated ice pick or awl, fit the stud, and set it
with a snap setter. For a Velcro closure, sew around
the perimeter of a horizontal strip of loop tape. If the
flap needs to be adjustable, substitute two vertical
strips.

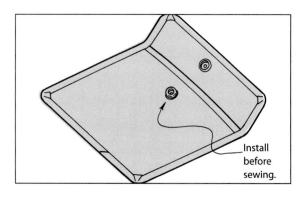

Install
before
sewing.

3 Finish the pocket, fill it to see where the flap half of
the closure belongs, then install the closure in the
flap.

Pockets made from canvas or clear vinyl that close with a zipper—like a bank bag—are especially useful aboard a boat. A YKK #5 plastic zipper is recommended, but you can also use a common dress zipper.

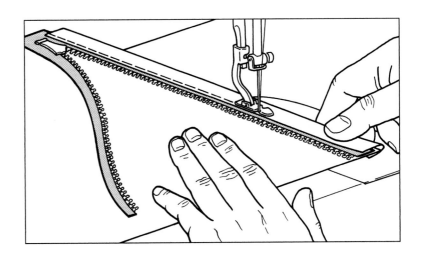

1 When you cut the material, omit the flap altogether. Use your zipper foot and a zipper slightly shorter than the pocket's width. Unzip the zipper and, with the zipper pull tab down, align the cloth edge of each half with an end edge of the fabric and sew them together with binding tape.

2 Bind the open sides, turning the binding tape under at both ends.

3 Turn the finished bag inside out.

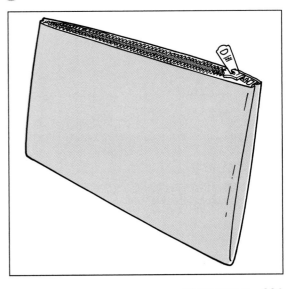

TOOL ROLLS

Square toolboxes are often a poor fit in round sailboats. By contrast, canvas tool rolls are easy to stow, keep tools quiet, provide instant accounting, and can be oiled to provide rust protection. The only fabric choice for tool rolls is treated canvas.

1 With a cloth tape, measure the surface-to-surface distance over the widest point of each tool you want to include in the roll. Add $\frac{1}{2}$ inch to each measurement and record them. Add all these dimensions together plus 2 inches to determine the cut width. The cut length should be 3 inches more than twice the length of the longest tool in the roll.

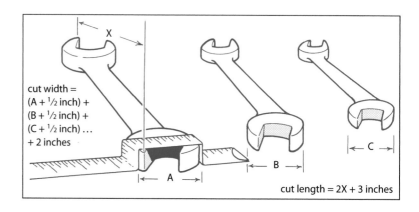

cut width =
$(A + \frac{1}{2}$ inch$)$ +
$(B + \frac{1}{2}$ inch$)$ +
$(C + \frac{1}{2}$ inch$)$ ...
+ 2 inches

cut length = 2X + 3 inches

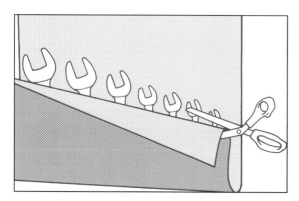

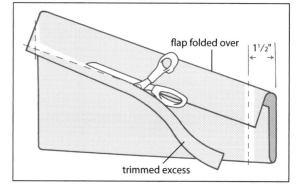

flap folded over

$1\frac{1}{2}$"

trimmed excess

2 Arrange the tools on the fabric from longest to shortest and fold the fabric to pocket them. Push each tool down to seat it against the fold, then fold the top of the front diagonally to expose enough of each tool to allow it to be easily identified and removed. Cut the fabric on this second fold line.

3 Fold the flap diagonally over the tops of the tools and cut away excess canvas to make the width of the flap even. Align the edge of the flap on one side by trimming it, and on the other side by trimming $1\frac{1}{2}$ inches from the side of the pocket.

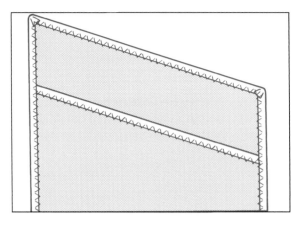

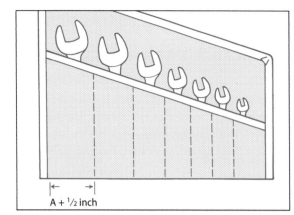

4 Trace the angled edge of the pocket onto the back panel to mark it, then remove the tools and bind this edge. Fold the pocket to the trace lines and seam the sides, then bind over the raw edges.

5 Along the front face, mark the width of each pocket per your recorded measurements, then extend a perpendicular line to the top of the pocket. Run a line of straight stitches on each pencil line, and be sure to backstitch the upper ends.

6 On the long side of the roll, just above half the *pocket* height, sew the middle of a shoelace or a length of cloth binding tape to the edge with three rows of stitching. This is the tie, and you can determine the appropriate length for it by putting the tools in the roll and rolling it up. If you use binding tape, hem the ends.

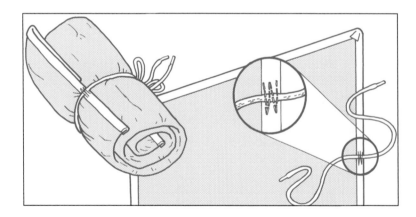

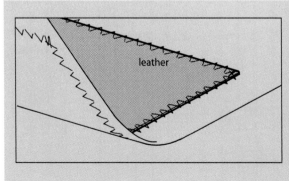

LEATHER LINING

YOU CAN GREATLY EXTEND the life of a pocket that holds heavy items, such as a tool roll, by lining the bottom of the pocket with leather. Before folding and stitching the pocket, center a 3-inch-wide strip of leather on the fold line and sew it down all around with an overcasting zigzag stitch; then finish the pocket normally. This can also be done along the flap's fold line for the same purpose.

SHEET BAGS

With the sails cranked in, there can easily be 100 feet or more of sheet tail jumbled in the cockpit. Aside from aesthetics, a pile of line can be a safety hazard. Get control of this situation with a sheet bag or two. You can use a standard hanging pocket as a sheet bag, but a slightly different construction technique yields a pocket better suited for the bulk.

1 In this bag, the front and back are separate pieces. Cut the back to your desired finished dimension, plus 1½ extra inches in the height dimension. The back piece of an 18 by 10 bag—a good size—would be 18 by 11½ inches. Cut the front piece the same height but 4 inches wider (22 by 11½ inches).

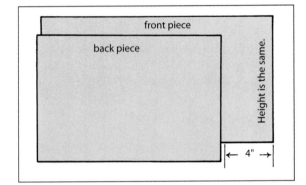

2 Put a ¾-inch (both folds) double-rubbed hem in the top of the back piece. Put a 2-inch *casing* in the top edge of the front, with ¼ inch of the raw edge turned under. A casing differs from a double-rubbed hem only in the absence of the second row of stitching near the fold.

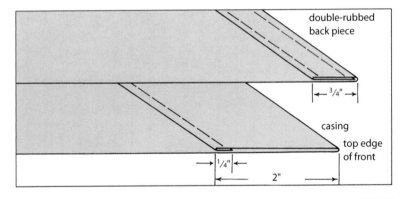

3 Mark a length of ¼-inch bungee cord the designed width of your bag. Feed it through the casing and sew the end about ½ inch from the edge. (If you can't get bungee under the foot of your machine, use 2-inch waistband elastic doubled lengthwise.) Pull the other end until the mark is outside, then sew this end down the same way. Trim the bungee at the stitching at both ends.

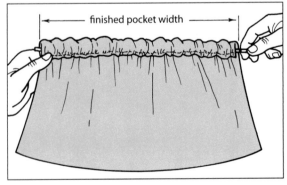

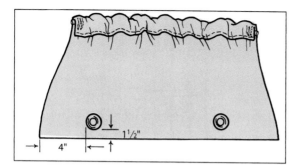

4 Install grommets in the front, placing their edges 1½ inches from the bottom and 4 inches from the sides. These are drains, but you don't want them to interfere with the bottom seam.

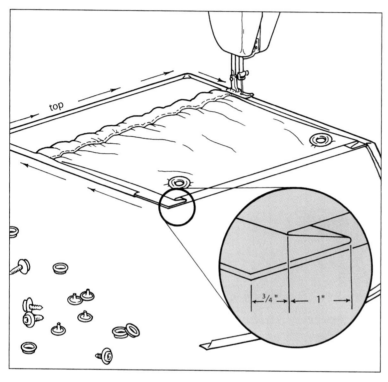

5 Bind the two halves together. Begin on one side and sew toward and across the top. When you get to the bottom corner, take out half of the excess front material with a 1-inch *pleat* positioned ¾ inch from the side. Bind across the bottom, putting a matching pleat on the opposite side.

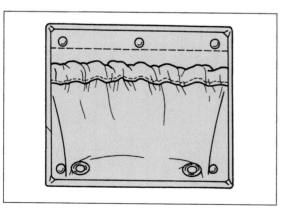

6 Install snap fasteners in all corners and one in the middle of the top flap. Screw matching studs to the boat where you want to mount the bag. If you put a couple of additional studs inside the cockpit locker, you will also have a perfect place to stow sheets when they aren't in use.

MULTI-POCKET BAGS

Drawer cabinets, those gizmos with a dozen or so little clear-plastic drawers for nuts and bolts and little parts, useful though they might be, aren't very practical aboard a sailboat. The multi-pocket bag is an effective alternative. Use acrylic or treated canvas for the back, clear vinyl (from a roll) for the front.

1 Determine where the bag will be mounted—on the inside of a cabinet door, for example—and cut the canvas back with a 1-inch allowance on the height dimension.

2 Determine the number of pockets you want, reserving $\frac{1}{2}$ inch of the canvas at the top and bottom for mounting. Be sure the pockets will be wide enough or shallow enough to allow you to reach the bottom. Cut strips of vinyl—one strip for each row of pockets. Determine the strip lengths by adding to the canvas width 4 inches for every pocket across. In other words, if you plan three pockets across a 15-inch piece of canvas, cut the vinyl strips 27 inches long [15 + (3 x 4) = 27].

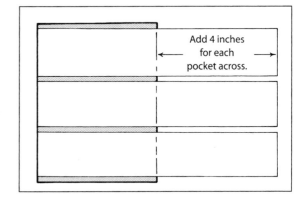

Add 4 inches for each pocket across.

3 To provide sturdy mounting strips, align lengths of Dacron or nylon webbing with the top and bottom edges of the canvas and sew them near the inner edge of the webbing. Half-inch webbing is ideal, but wider is fine if that's what you have.

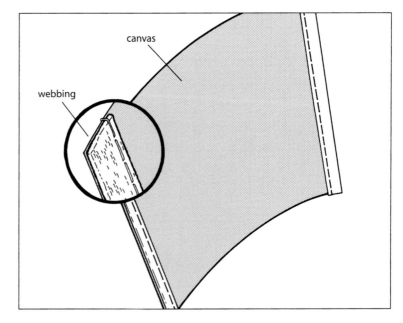

canvas

webbing

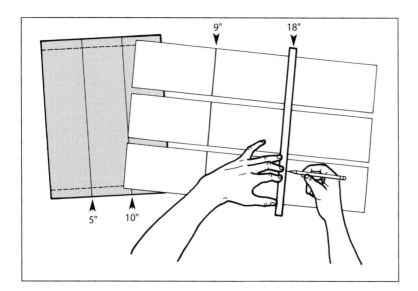

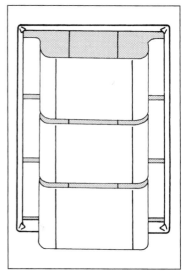

4 Assuming equal pockets, divide the canvas with vertical pencil lines (on the opposite side of the fabric from the webbing) into the number of pockets across—here with lines at 5 and 10 inches. Similarly mark the plastic strips into the same number of equal divisions; in this case the divisions are 9 inches apart (27 ÷ 3 = 9).

5 Abut the vinyl strips long edge to long edge, and align them with one edge of the canvas and ½ inch from the top and bottom. Bind them to the canvas, then continue with the binding all the way around, capturing the free edges of the webbing at the top and bottom, and the opposite ends of the vinyl strips on the other side.

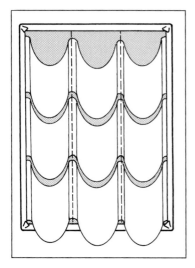

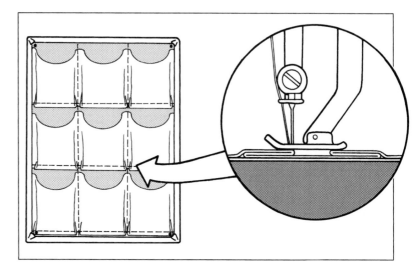

6 Align the divider marks on the vinyl with those on the canvas and sew them together on the lines.

7 Pleat the pockets at the bottom and sew across. Melt holes on the four corners and mount the bag with screws and finishing washers.

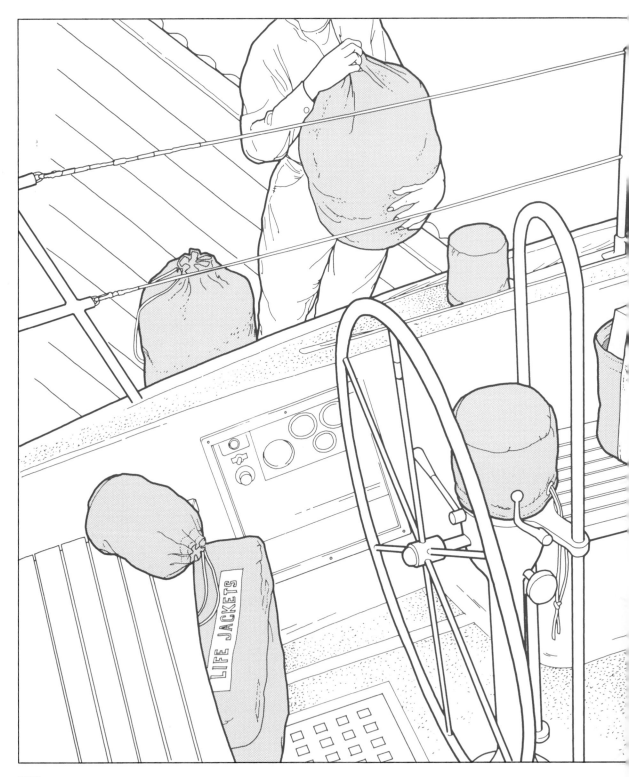

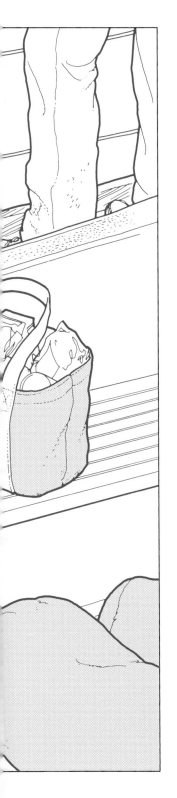

THE BAG

Not everything you want to stow, carry, or protect will fit into a pocket. Bulky items need a bag with a two-dimensional bottom. The distinction here is easier to understand if you think of the pocket as a canvas envelope and the bag as a canvas box.

The box-like shape of a canvas bag makes it extremely handy for transporting items to and from the boat. Grocery bags also serve, but who hasn't had the experience of the wet bottom of a paper bag suddenly turning loose? If it happens as you are passing the bag aboard, it can be a major event.

Canvas tote bags are readily available at reasonable prices, some intended specifically for marine use. The drawback to ready-made bags is that they are too often not the best size for the use you have in mind. A typical chandlery tote is 6 or 7 inches wide, making a spool of rope or a pressure cooker an odd fit. And while a pillowcase may be fine for transporting soiled linens and towels, getting the laundered and folded items back aboard neatly calls for a bag big enough to swallow the stack. Such a bag is hard to purchase but easy to construct.

Turn a bag bottom-up and you have a hood. Whether it is a hatch, a binnacle, or an outboard motor you want to protect, the cover is simply a bag of the appropriate dimension with a drawstring, snaps, or other fastening system around the opening.

Making a canvas bag is only slightly more involved than making a pocket, as you will see soon enough. By making one or two of the items detailed in this chapter, you will add to your comprehension and skill level. At the very least make a couple of tote bags for your boat; you will find them so handy that additional bags will soon be on your list of things to do.

ONE-PIECE TOTE BAG

Every sailor can find a good use for a canvas tote bag. A bag measuring 1 foot on every side is extraordinarily versatile, but a larger bag may be better for clothes or linens. Conversely, the weight of a cubic foot of hand tools may dictate a smaller bag for a tool tote. Treated canvas, because of its chafe-resistance and strength, is the best fabric for tote bags.

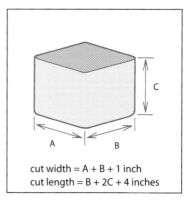

cut width = A + B + 1 inch
cut length = B + 2C + 4 inches

1 Determine the bottom and height dimensions of the finished bag. Cut the fabric 1 inch wider than half the bottom circumference, and 4 inches longer than the narrower bottom dimension plus twice the height of the bag. For a cubic-foot bag, that is 25 inches by 40 inches.

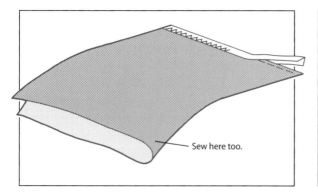

Sew here too.

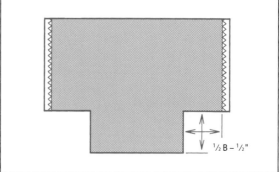

$\frac{1}{2}$ B – $\frac{1}{2}$"

2 Fold the fabric in half across the long dimension and run seams $\frac{1}{2}$ inch from the side edges to form a pocket. Bind the seamed edges.

3 Cut square notches at the corners at the folded edge, making their equal sides $\frac{1}{2}$ inch less than half the narrower bottom dimension. Measure the notch from the fold and from the seams, *not* the edge of the cloth.

PATCH POCKETS

A POCKET OR TWO ON THE INSIDE OR OUTSIDE of your tote bags will keep small items from getting lost at the bottom. Cut a piece of canvas an inch or so larger than the desired pocket. Rub a $\frac{1}{2}$-inch fold on all the edges, then double-rub the top edge (catching the two side folds) and sew in this hem. Now place the pocket wherever you want it on the bag—with the folded edges inside—and sew around three sides. A vertical row of stitches in the middle of a large, loose pocket will give you two smaller but tighter pockets.

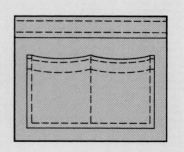

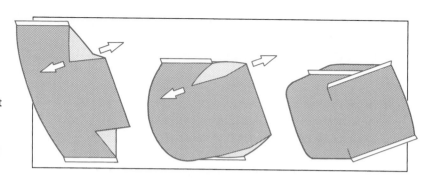

4 Separate the inside corners of the notches, pulling them apart until the notches become straight slits. Seam the slits 1½ inches from the raw edges, and bind them.

5 Turn the finished bag rightside out and put a 1½-inch double-rubbed hem around the top edge.

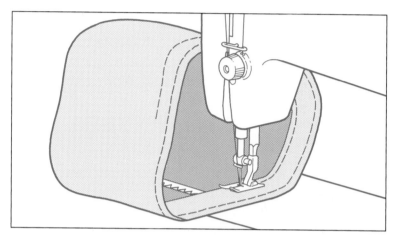

6 Sew 1½-inch webbing to the sides for handles. For strength and durability make the handles pass across (under) the bottom. Mark two parallel lines from hem to hem about a quarter of the bag's width from each side. In a single continuous length, align the webbing to the lines and sew it to the bag along both edges. For carrying ease the handles should loop at least a foot above the bag.

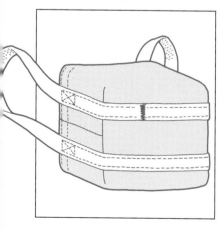

RIGID BOTTOM

SAILORS OFTEN PREFER the rigidity of a box for transporting paint and other liquids, but a bag with a rigid bottom can be just as secure and a lot easier to tote. Make a canvas pocket the size of the bottom of the bag, with a ½-inch flap along the long dimension. Cut a piece of hardboard (Masonite) to fit tightly inside the pocket. Place the empty pocket—flap side up—flat in the bottom of the bag and sew it in place along the flap. Turn the bag inside out and insert the hardboard, then reverse the bag again and fold the rigid bottom down into place. If you want rigid sides as well, find a box that will just fit inside the bag.

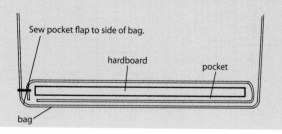

Sew pocket flap to side of bag.

hardboard

pocket

bag

HATCH COVER

If you want to cover a modern flush hatch, you need a hemmed flat sheet with snap fasteners in the four corners, but for a traditional hatch that stands proud, you need a hood—essentially a shallow bag. Acrylic canvas is the fabric of choice: It is UV-resistant and will match the boat's other canvas covers. Attach the hood with snaps, or with a drawstring if you prefer not to screw studs to your hatch.

SNAP-ON COVER

1 Measure from one bottom edge, over the hatch and back to the other bottom edge. Do this in both directions and add 3-inch hem allowances to get the cut size.

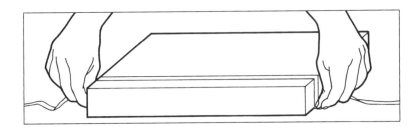

2 Drape the canvas over the hatch and crease it with your thumb to mark the corners.

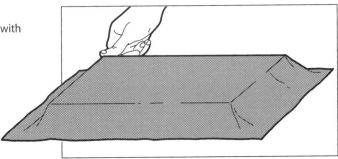

3 Fold the canvas diagonally at one corner to align adjoining edges; the corner mark should fall on the fold. About ¼ inch beyond the mark, run a row of stitches perpendicular to the raw edges. Repeat for the remaining three corners. These are called *darts*.

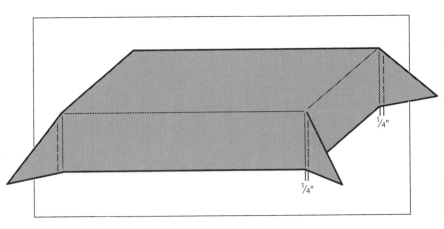

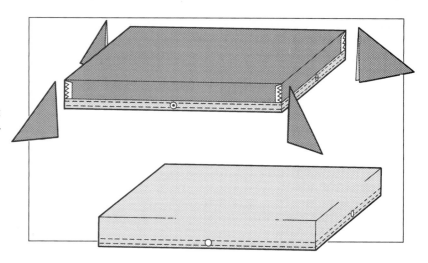

4 Check for fit and move the seams in or out if necessary. When the cover is snug (but not too tight), cut off the excess fabric beyond the seams and bind the edges. Put a ¾-inch (both folds) double-rubbed hem (inside) all around and install snap fasteners.

DRAWSTRING COVER

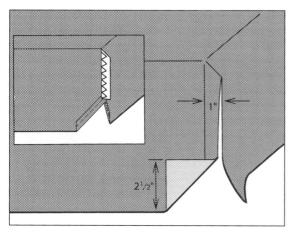

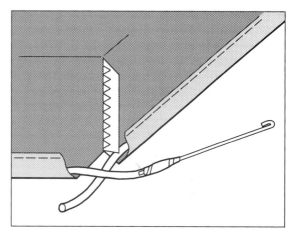

1 Increase the hem allowance to 4 inches. *Before* sewing the corner seams, cut excess material off 1 inch beyond the corner marks. Turn the bottom corners back 2½ inches and sew them down. Trim the cloth parallel to the stitching. Now seam and bind the corners.

2 Fold the edges ½ inch, then 1 inch, and stitch along the inside fold only to put a 1-inch casing in the sides for the drawstring. Tape a length of ⅛-inch flag halyard to a piece of stiff wire and thread the line through the casing until both ends exit at the same corner.

3 Turn the cover rightside out and fit it over the hatch. Pull the ends of the drawstring to fold the cover under the bottom edge, then tie the ends together. If you don't want to tie the cover each time, use bungee rather than flag halyard, but your cover won't be quite as secure.

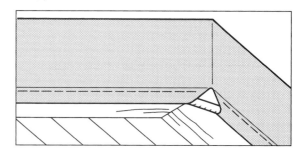

TWO-PIECE DUFFEL BAG

DRAWING A CIRCLE

THE DIAMETER OF MOST duffels will be beyond the capacity of a drawing compass. Tie two loops in a length of thread so that the distance between the loops is equal to the *radius* (half the diameter) of the circle you want to draw. Slip a straight pin through one loop and stick the pin into the cloth where you want the center of the circle. Holding the pin upright with one hand, insert the lead of a pencil into the other loop, then trace your circle by keeping the thread taut as you mark.

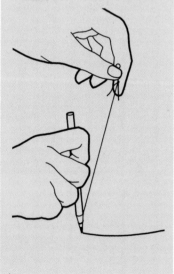

Duffel bags differ from tote bags in that their primary function is to contain rather than carry. They come in all sizes, from a small ditty bag for the ship's clothespins to a large sailbag for the drifter, but their construction is essentially the same. They are traditionally cylindrical because a circular bottom is the best at evenly distributing the load, but you can just as easily make the bottom another shape. They also traditionally close with a drawstring, but for use as luggage it is now more common to enclose the open end and put a zipper in the side. For a drawstring bag, select a fabric that will gather readily, such as oxford nylon.

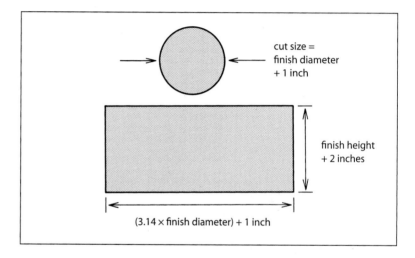

cut size = finish diameter + 1 inch

finish height + 2 inches

(3.14 × finish diameter) + 1 inch

1 Cut the circular bottom piece 1 inch larger than the finish diameter of the bag. The dimensions for the rectangular piece are 1 inch more than 3.14 (π) times the finish diameter and 2 inches more than the finish height. A ditty bag 8 inches in diameter and 10 inches deep requires a 9-inch circle of fabric and a rectangle 12 inches by 26⅛ inches.

2 Fold the rectangle in half and seam and bind the edges opposite the fold to form a tube.

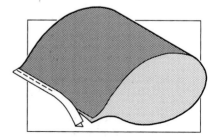

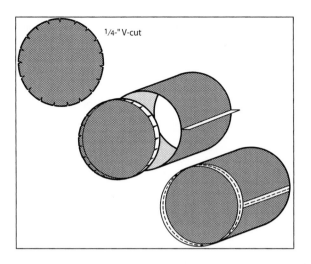

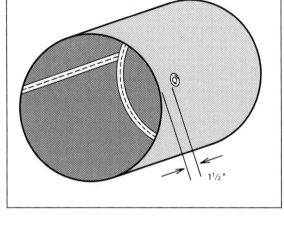

3 Put a series of ¼-inch V-cuts around the perimeter of the circular piece. Fit the circle into one end of the tube and pin or staple it in position; seam tape or glue probably won't hold. Sew the pieces together ½ inch from the edge. Remove the pins or staples and bind the seam.

4 Turn the bag rightside out and install a grommet for the drawstring to exit, placing the outside *edge* of the grommet 1½ inches from the raw edge of the bag's mouth. For a large bag, install a second grommet on the opposite side of the bag; large bags close easier with two drawstrings.

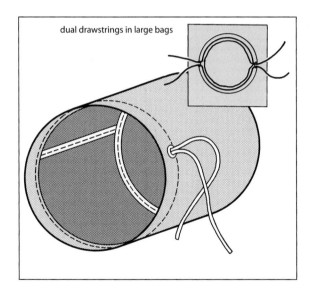

5 Thread the drawstring(s) through the grommet(s) so that the ends are outside and a bight of line is inside. Fold the edge to form a 1-inch casing with the drawstring inside and sew it closed, taking care not to let the needle catch the string.

6 A tight-fitting wooden bead slipped over the ends of the drawstring will hold the bag closed, or use a figure-8 knot. Tie the bitter ends of the drawstring(s) together.

WINCH COVER

No one claims that covered winches last longer, but they do require less maintenance. The time required to make the covers described here should be less than the time to tear down, clean, and lubricate a pair of winches one time. And these particular covers have the advantage of going on as easy as a baseball cap.

1 Using acrylic canvas, make a duffel bag (see previous project) just large enough to slip over and fully cover the winch. Omit the grommet and the drawstring, and add a second row of stitches near the fold of the casing to make it a double-rubbed hem. Omit the binding on the bottom seam.

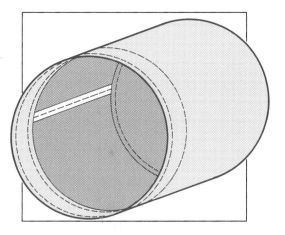

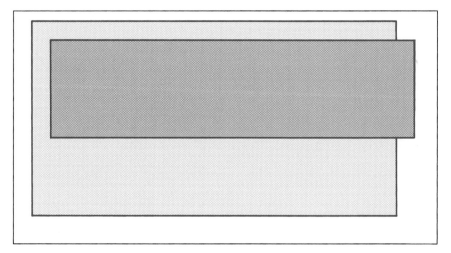

2 Cut a second rectangle of cloth the same length as the first but half the width. This piece should be softer cloth than acrylic canvas—oxford nylon is ideal.

3 Put a 1-inch casing in one long edge of the narrow rectangle. Feed ¼-inch bungee (or doubled waistband elastic) through the casing.

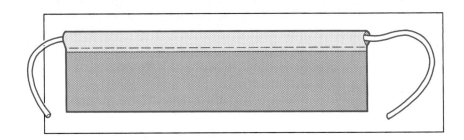

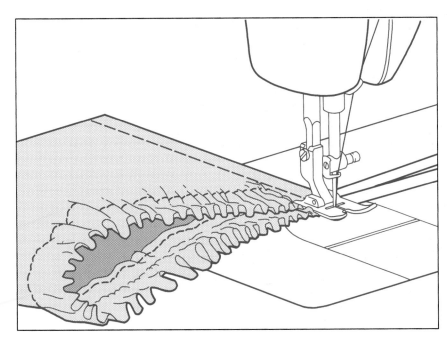

4 Fold the cloth in half and seam the ends together, stopping the machine—*with the needle down*— just before the foot reaches the elastic. Pull the ends of the elastic like a drawstring until the diameter of the tube is about halved, then continue the seam, sewing back and forth over the elastic several times to secure the ends. Snip off the excess elastic and bind the seam.

5 Slip the inside-out bag through the tube and align the raw edges. Seam and bind the tube to the bag. When you turn the bag rightside out, it now has an internal elastic skirt. Reach inside the cover and spread the elastic over the winch to hold the cover in place.

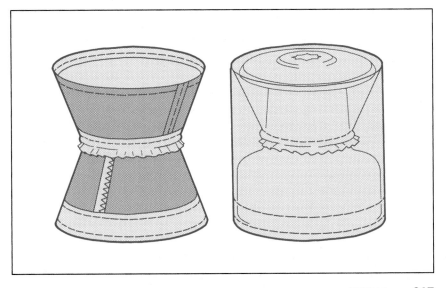

LIFE-JACKET BOX

In 1995 the law changed to require wearable flotation devices aboard virtually all boats. Flotation cushions are no longer adequate even for the dinghy. That may mean you are carrying additional life jackets aboard your boat. In any case, it is a sign of good seamanship to have life jackets not just aboard but readily accessible.

A soft box secured in the cockpit or on deck can keep jackets from becoming buried in a locker and assure they will be instantly at hand in an emergency. You can make a jacket-storage bag from acrylic canvas, but the material of choice is Weblon—a nylon-reinforced vinyl.

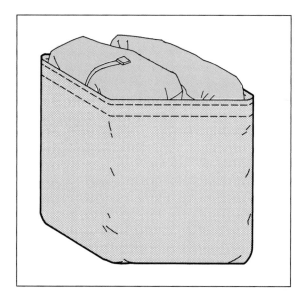

1 Stack all your life jackets as compactly as possible and determine the size bag required to contain them. They should fill the bag to the top. Fabricate a one-piece tote bag (see page 810) to these dimensions. Omit the handles, but add straps or fasteners as needed to secure the bag in the selected location.

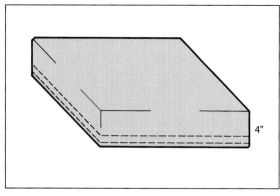

4"

2 Using the bottom dimensions of the tote bag, fabricate a hatch cover (see page 812) with 4-inch sides. This is the lid of your box.

3 Sew several strips of 1-inch Velcro hook tape along the inside edge of the lid at both ends and on one side. Slip the lid over the bag to mark the locations for the corresponding strips of loop tape, then sew them to the bag.

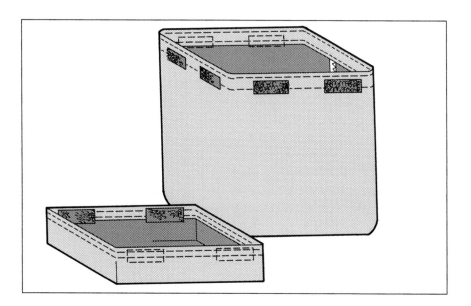

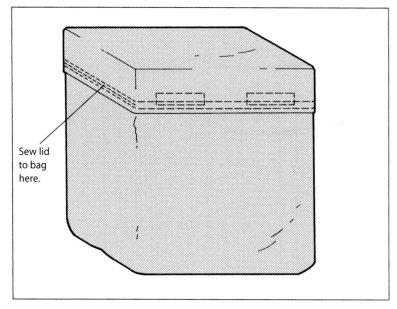

Sew lid to bag here.

4 Carefully fit the side of the bag without Velcro onto the corresponding side of the lid and sew them together with a row of stitches near the bottom edge of the lid. Fill the box with life jackets and close the lid.

THE CLOSED BOX

The life-jacket "box" ending "The Bag" is actually two bags, not a closed box. The distinction is easy to make: a rectangular bag has five sides, a closed box has six.

It would seem that all we have to do to make a bag into a closed box is add a side, but do *just* that and you better make sure that whatever you want the box to contain is already in there. Also the seams, or at least the last one, are going to be on the outside because there is no way to turn a closed box inside out.

The solution to this is to put an opening in one of the sides. The opening allows you to reverse the box so all seams are on the inside, and it allows you to fill the box *after* you sew it. Some kind of closure will be needed. This is most often a zipper, but you can also close the opening with snaps, Velcro, or even lacing.

Loose cushions are nothing more than a closed box stuffed with padding. This is true whether they are settee cushions, bunk cushions, or cockpit cushions, whether they are an inch or 6 inches thick, and whether they are perfectly square or have the arrowhead shape of the V-bunk. The construction of a cover for an odd-shaped cushion is exactly the same as for one with all right angles.

If you made a duffel bag from "The Bag," you already have *almost* all the skills needed to re-cover old cushions or make new ones. You may still need some help getting the top to align squarely with the bottom; installing a zipper will be easier if you know a couple of tricks; and you should know how to make and install piping to give the seams a finished look. But none of these added requirements are any more difficult than those we have already mastered. All are fully explained in this chapter.

The closed box is the neatest of the canvas containers and surely the most satisfying to construct. Master it and you can take on any onboard canvas project with confidence.

BOLSTER

Blankets, sweaters, and other bulky items can quickly fill limited stowage space. At the same time, most settees—designed to fit the space, not your back—are too upright for comfort. Help both problems by storing blankets and sweaters in a canvas bolster that doubles as lumbar support. Choose a fabric that feels comfortable, preferably one you can throw in the wash.

1 Make a size determination based on planned use or by measuring the bundle you want to enclose. A fat bolster at the end of a settee provides a comfortable arm rest. For lumbar support, limit the diameter to about 6 inches. Cut two identical circles with a 1-inch seam allowance. Also allow 1 inch on the "length" dimension of the rectangular piece and add the total *width* of the zipper to the "around" dimension. A bolster 8 inches in diameter and 16 inches long would require two 9-inch circles of fabric and a rectangle measuring 17 by 26⅝, assuming a 1½-inch-wide zipper (see step 1 of "Two-Piece Duffel Bag," page 814).

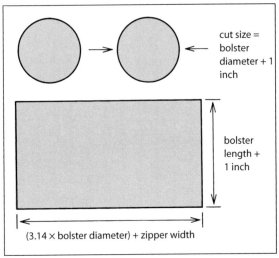

cut size = bolster diameter + 1 inch

bolster length + 1 inch

(3.14 × bolster diameter) + zipper width

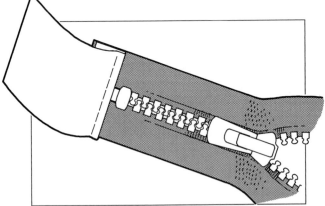

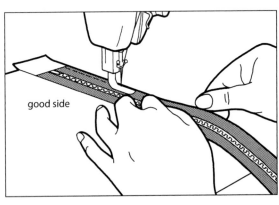

good side

2 Select a zipper slightly shorter than the finished length of the bolster. The tape that extends beyond the teeth at either end of the zipper should provide an overall length longer than the bolster's finished length. If it doesn't, extend the closed end with webbing or a strip of fabric.

3 For perfect zipper alignment, place the zipper—tab down—on top of the good side of the fabric and align the two edge-to-edge and centered side-to-side. Sew them together near the edge.

4 Fold the material so the fold lies down the center of the zipper. Use the zipper foot to topstitch the fabric parallel to the fold, catching both layers of fabric and the zipper tape, but taking care not to sew close enough to the zipper's teeth to interfere with the operation of the slider.

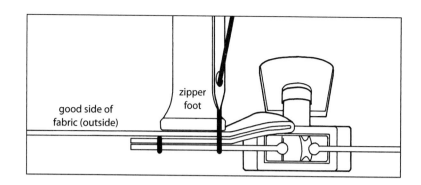

good side of fabric (outside)

zipper foot

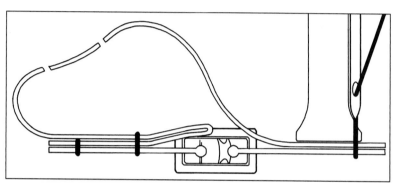

5 Fold the fabric in half inside out, aligning the exposed edge of the zipper with the raw edge of the cloth, and sew them together. Unzip the zipper, then fold and topstitch this side just like the other one.

6 Zip the two halves back together with the tube inside out. Notch the two circles and sew them in the ends exactly like sewing the bottom in a duffel (see "The Bag"). Open the zipper and turn the finished bolster rightside out.

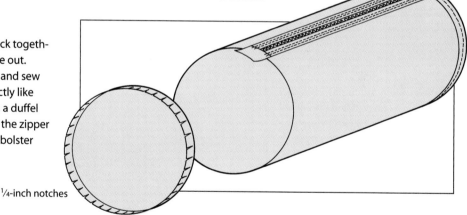

¼-inch notches

ZIPPERS

FOR OUTSIDE USE SELECT only YKK #10 Delrin zippers. Below deck the smaller YKK #5 zipper may be preferable. Complete zippers—called jacket zippers—allow the separation of both halves and come in a range of lengths. Zipper is also available in continuous length—called zipper tape—for applications that don't require separation, such as a bolster, bag, or cushion closure. You can use a jacket zipper for these applications, but zipper tape may be cheaper. Use only plastic sliders aboard a boat.

ZIPPERED DUFFEL BAG

The only difference between a bolster and a zippered duffel is the handle and the choice of fabric. Make duffel bags from acrylic canvas.

1 Strike a pair of lines around the finished bag 3 or 4 inches either side of the center. Sew a continuous length of webbing to the bag on these two lines so the handle loops overlap at the zipper by 5 or 6 inches. Stitch the handles only to the lower half of the bag.

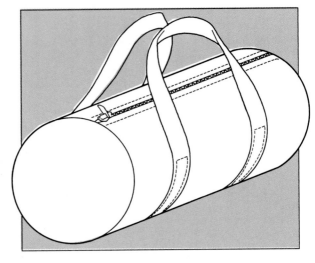

2 If you want padded handles, use 2-inch webbing. Mark the center of the handle loops. Cut two 6-inch lengths of $^3/_8$-inch rubber hose and use your zipper foot to sew them into a fold in the webbing and centered on the mark. Sew across the webbing at the ends of the hose.

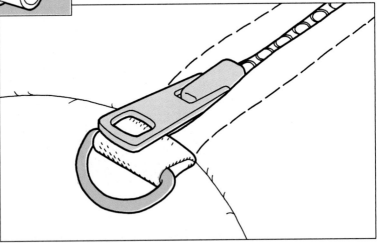

3 To make your duffel lockable, fold a short length of webbing around a small D-ring and sew it into the end seam at the "open" end of the zipper *at the time you are installing that end*. A small lock between the slider tab and the D-ring will prevent casual opening of the bag.

PIPING

You may find a bolster more attractive finished with piping, also called *welt cord*. *Piping* is a fabric bead that gives exposed seams a finished look and effectively hides the stitching even when the seam is under stress. Extruded piping is available in a variety of colors and sizes for use with vinyl fabrics. For woven cloth, you are more likely to make your own piping by wrapping a strip of matching or contrasting cloth around cord.

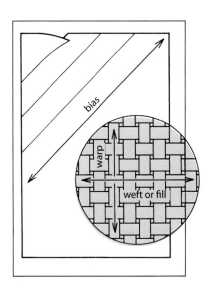

1 Piping generally handles better if the fabric is cut on the bias, i.e., diagonally (see page 775, "Measuring and Cutting"), but to save fabric the strips are often cut from scrap, which usually means with the grain. It isn't likely to matter much, and if you have a patterned fabric, you may want to cut it with the grain anyway to match the pattern.

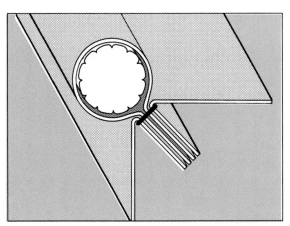

2 Piping size can vary from subtle to bold, and you can buy appropriate cord from a fabric supplier. Keep in mind that the piping will be larger than the cord alone. The width of the fabric strips depends upon the size of the cord and your preferred seam allowance. Experiment with a scrap before you cut all the strips. Ideally you want the edges of the piping to align with the edges of the fabric when you sew the seams. For an attractive and easy-to-make contrasting piping, simply fold binding tape around flag halyard.

3 Cut all the strips for the needed piping and sew them end to end. A diagonal seam is preferred. For the joined pieces to align properly, position them perpendicular with their pointed corners extending beyond the strip edges by approximately the seam width. Butterfly the seam.

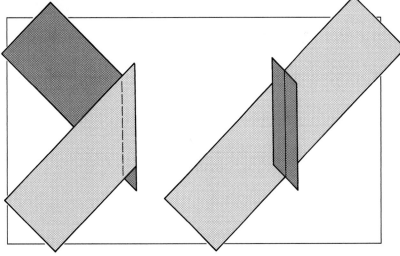

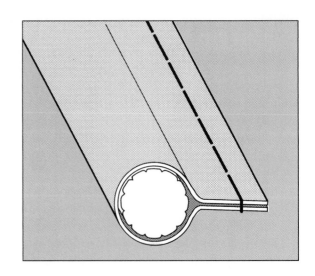

4 You can pin, staple, or glue the fabric around the cord to baste it, but the surest and often quickest method is to sew it. Place the row of stitches well away from the cord so they won't show in the finished seam.

5 Install piping or welt by simply sewing it between the two pieces of fabric being seamed. If you cut the strips to the right width, all the raw edges will align. Use a zipper foot to place the stitches as close to the cord as possible. This makes the piping neatly tight and hides any basting stitches. Slash the raw edges to let the cord turn corners easily.

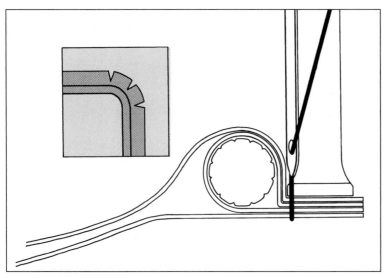

COCKPIT CUSHIONS

Cockpit cushions provide a good opportunity for a first foray into upholstery. Good cockpit cushions—meaning made of closed-cell foam and covered with weather-resistant fabric—are a marvelous addition to any boat.

The best fabric for cockpit cushions is acrylic canvas. Besides being weather-resistant, it resists staining, is comfortable against the skin, and dries quickly. Avoid dark colors if the cushions will have strong sun exposure.

Another popular fabric for cockpit cushions is Phifertex. This open-weave fabric comes in a wide variety of light colors designed for outdoor use. It doesn't shield the foam from moisture, but since closed-cell foam doesn't absorb water—an essential characteristic for outdoor cushions—this foam and

fabric combination dries very quickly. The vinyl coating does tend to yellow with age.

Reinforced vinyl is another choice; it wears well, cleans easily, and is waterproof. But vinyl tends to be sticky and uncomfortable against bare skin. Even open-weave Phifertex can exhibit this trait. Solid reinforced vinyls also tend to trap moisture against the foam, culturing mold and mildew inside the cover. Some vinyls quickly harden and crack in the sun.

Use only closed-cell foam for cockpit cushions. Typically made of ethylene vinyl acetate (EVA), closed-cell foam is readily available in 1- and 2-inch thicknesses (approximately). The thicker size will be more comfortable.

1 Cut paper patterns for the best cushion configuration for your cockpit. Multiple cushions can be better than trying to pad the entire area with two cushions. Smaller cushions are easier to stow and can do double duty as back cushions. Cushions slightly larger than the hatch underneath allow locker access without disturbing the other seating. Do try to avoid separations in the most likely seating locations. Note the back edge on each pattern to help later in zipper placement.

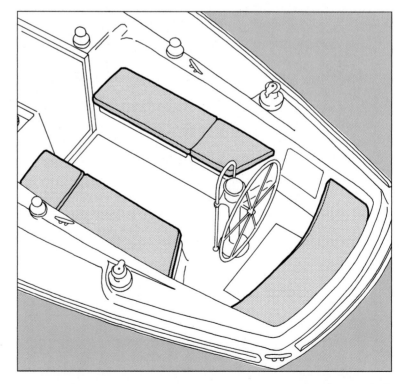

2 Closed-cell foam shrinks with age, so cut each cushion $\frac{1}{2}$ inch larger all around than your paper patterns. Mark the foam and cut on the lines with a just-sharpened fillet knife, drawing the knife in the same direction several times for each cut.

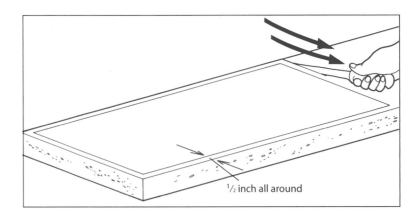

½ inch all around

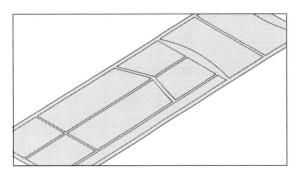

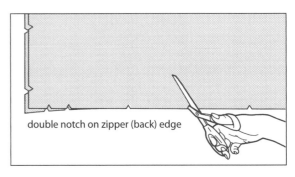

double notch on zipper (back) edge

3 Each cushion requires a matching top and bottom, but if your material has a "good" side, be sure the top and bottom are mirror images, not duplicates. Use the paper patterns to lay out the material, again adding ½ inch all around, but this time as a seam allowance. It is a good idea to lay out all the pieces—including the strips for the sides and the piping—before you make any cuts.

5 The strip of cloth that joins the top and bottom is called the *boxing*. It is easier to fabricate the boxing in two sections, one containing the zipper. Cut two strips of fabric a couple of inches longer than the length of the zipper and 1⅛ inches wider than half the thickness of the foam (assuming your zipper is 1½ inches wide). The zipper should be slightly shorter than the back side of the cushion. Sew the zipper, edge aligned and tab down, to the good side of one of the strips, then fold the strip along the center of the zipper and sew it again. Attach the second strip to the opposite edge of the zipper in the same manner.

4 With the two cut pieces aligned good side to good side, make matching shallow notches in their hem allowances a couple of inches from either side of the corners. Put similar notches every foot or so along the sides. These notches will help you align the top and bottom when you sew the cover together. Double-notch one corner on the zipper edge for easy orientation.

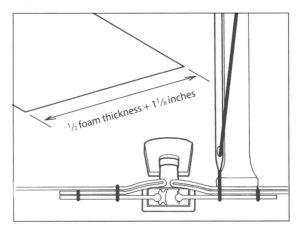

½ foam thickness + 1⅛ inches

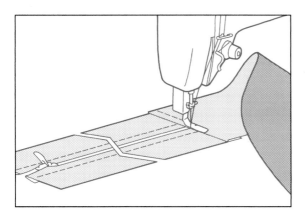

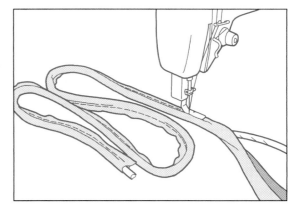

6 Subtract the length of the zipper assembly from the circumference of the cushion, then add about 3 inches to get the length of the remaining boxing. Cut this strip ¾ inch wider than the foam thickness. With a ½-inch seam allowance on each side, this provides a finished width ¼ less than the foam, which improves the cover's fit. Hem one end of the boxing and sew it to the zipper assembly, taking care to keep the edges straight.

7 Cut the needed strips of fabric for the piping, sew them together, and baste them shut with the cord inside. Make up enough piping for all the cushions in a continuous length, cutting it as you use it. Extruded vinyl piping eliminates this step for vinyl or Phifertex covers. Small piping—perhaps ⅛-inch cord—is generally preferable for cockpit cushions. A contrasting piping can give cushions a bit of extra pizzazz.

8 Starting at the zipper end, sew the boxing to one of the cover pieces with the piping sandwiched between. Leave about 2 inches of boxing and piping unstitched at your starting point. When you arrive there again, cut the boxing so it will overlap the end of the zipper by about an inch, allowing an extra ½ inch to turn the raw end under. Cut molded piping to abut. Cut covered piping to overlap about an inch, then snip the basting to open the piping, and cut the overlap amount off the cord. Turn about ½ inch of the piping fabric under and slip the starting end of the piping inside so that the cord now butts end to end. Be sure the finish end of the boxing is on the outside of the zipper assembly, then finish seaming the edge.

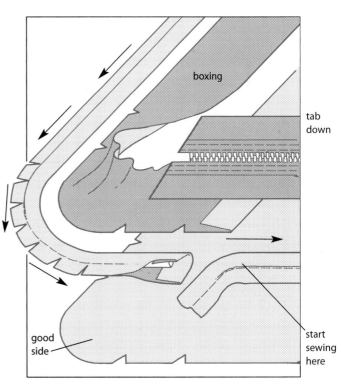

boxing

tab down

good side

start sewing here

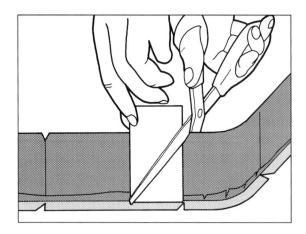

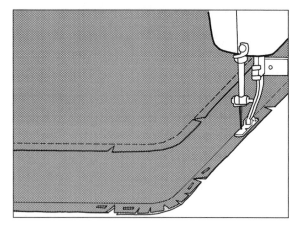

9 Locate each of the alignment notches in the assembled cover piece and transfer it straight across the boxing, making corresponding notches in the seam allowance of the boxing. A business card makes a handy square. As long as the notches line up with the ones already in the remaining cover piece when you sew it, the top and bottom will also be aligned.

10 Staple the second cover piece to the boxing with the notches aligned before you start sewing. This helps, but it doesn't prevent alignment problems, which can still arise as you sew around corners. Starting short of the separation in the boxing, sew the second cover to the boxing, watching the notches. If they get off more than $1/8$ inch, stop, take the last run of stitches out, and do it again. You can adjust the alignment somewhat by putting some tension on either the cover or the boxing as the machine drags it under the foot.

SEWING AROUND CORNERS

WHEN YOU GET TO THE CORNER OF A CUSHION COVER, you will get a better finished result if you round the corner slightly. Stop the machine—with the needle buried—an inch or so before the corner. Use your scissors to put two or three slashes in the seam allowance of the boxing and the piping where they will make the turn. Continue sewing until the needle is almost at the corner; then, with the needle again buried, rotate the material around the needle about 30 degrees. Turn the balance wheel by hand to make a single stitch, then rotate the bottom fabric an additional 30 degrees. Make one more hand-driven stitch, then rotate the fabric 30 degrees one more time. You want to end up with the needle $1/2$ inch from the new edge and the foot pointed in the right direction to continue sewing. With a little practice, that is just what will happen. Trim the extra material to the edge of the boxing before you turn the cover inside out.

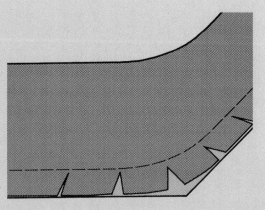

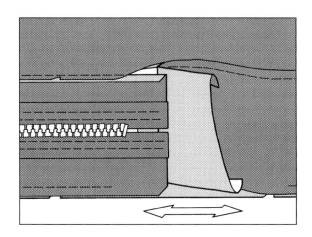

11 Leaving the two ends of the boxing open allows your stitching path around the second cover to be slightly shorter or longer than the first one. The length of the boxing will self-adjust; just make sure the end fold is perpendicular. It isn't necessary to stitch across this end unless it offends your sense of symmetry because of the stitching at the other end of the zipper.

12 Unzip the cover and turn it rightside out, working the corners out with your fingers. Fold the foam and insert it into the cover, unfolding it inside. Try to limit the stress on the ends of the zipper. Work the foam until the corners are properly positioned, then close the zipper. Ta da!

KEEPING COCKPIT CUSHIONS IN PLACE

WHEN A SAILBOAT HEELS, cockpit cushions tend to slide off the seats. A short fiddle on the front edge of the seats will stop this, but unless the fiddle is removable, it will be an annoyance when the cushions aren't in place. The traditional way of securing cushions without a fiddle is with snap fasteners in a flap along the back of the cushion. Seam the ends of a lengthwise-folded strip of canvas and reverse it to put the seams inside. When you assemble the cover, sew this strip between the piping and the boxing on the bottom of the backside. For reversible cushions, put a matching flap in the top seam; the unused flap will lie flat behind the cushion when not in use. Install two or three snaps (or a strip of Velcro loop tape) in the flaps and attach their mates to the cockpit seat.

For an alternative that may be better because it doesn't take up space behind the cushion, you'll need two lengths of webbing, two boat snaps (small snaphooks), and two strap eyes. Thread the webbing through the boat snaps and box-stitch them to the boxing on either side so that the snaphooks just reach the back edge of the cushion. Install the strap eyes on the seat. Abutting cushions can attach to the same eyestrap. Center the webbing top to bottom for reversible cushions.

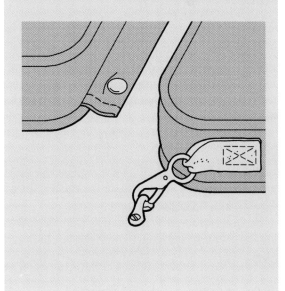

SETTEE UPHOLSTERY

Reupholstering loose below-deck cushions is exactly like covering cockpit cushions, with an occasional twist. For example, the top of a bunk cushion may be wider than the bottom to accommodate the flare of the hull, or a corner may be notched to fit around a removable "filler" cushion. And the style of the cushion may require a technique different from all-around boxing.

Some below-deck soft furniture may not be loose-cushion. For example, settee backrests often have a solid framework, typically a plywood back. Don't be put off by this; built-in backrests are often easier to cover than loose cushions.

FABRIC

Fabric choices for below-deck use are unlimited. Boat upholstery is likely to get wet occasionally—from an open hatch, a deck leak, or a wet bathing suit—so don't select a delicate fabric; but otherwise you can use any fabric suitable for your sofa at home. Keep in mind that bold patterns may require matching from cushion to cushion. Synthetics are more stain-resistant, but some tend to be hot, especially for sleeping. Fabrics intended for automotive upholstery can be especially durable in a boat. Vinyl bottom panels, commonly seen on factory cushions, have little to recommend them.

FOAM

Think about replacing the foam when you reupholster. Factory cushions are often too thin, and old foam goes soft. Choose polyurethane foam, not closed-cell EVA. Closed-cell foam tends to "deflate" over time as you sit or lie on it, becoming harder the deeper your shoulders and hips sink. Reinflation also takes time, so earlier depressions remain as you reposition, making for uncomfortable sleeping.

Polyurethane foam is rated by the weight required to compress it, but rating systems vary among manufacturers. You probably want 50- to 60-pound foam, but the best test is to put the piece on the floor and lie on it. Always err to the firm side. Don't buy "loaded" foam. Backrests, if they don't double as bunks, should be 25- to 35-pound foam.

As with closed-cell foam, cut polyurethane foam about $1/2$ inch oversize all around. Polyurethane foam doesn't shrink, but the extra foam will tighten the covers.

BEVELED CUSHIONS

Cushions lying against the hull may not have square sides. That causes the top and bottom pieces to have different dimensions, and the boxing on the beveled side will be wider than that on the square sides.

1 Outline the top and bottom pieces separately. Use the old cover or the foam as a pattern, adding a ½-inch seam allowance all around. If you have new foam cut ½-inch oversize, cut the fabric the same size as the foam.

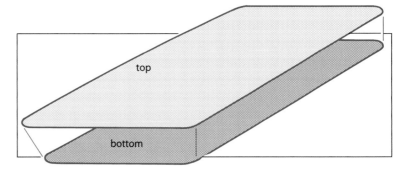

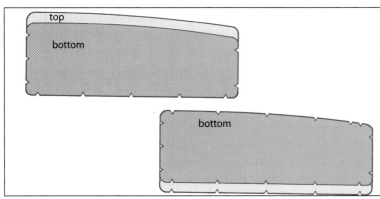

2 Alignment notches remain essential. With the two pieces good side to good side, align the three square edges and notch them in the seam allowance. Now slide the pieces to align the beveled edge and notch it.

3 Measure the width and length of the beveled edge on the foam and make your zipper assembly ¾ inch wider and 1 inch longer (see page 822). Cut the remaining boxing ¾ inch wider than the thickness of the foam and allow a couple of inches of extra length, being certain to get the length measurement from the larger of the cover pieces.

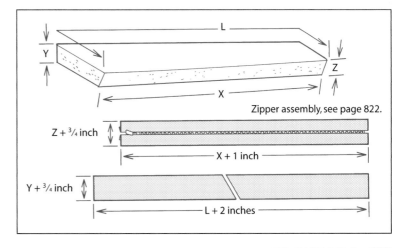

Zipper assembly, see page 822.

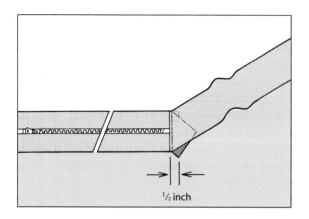

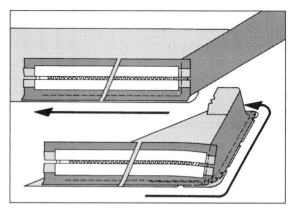

4 Fold one end of the boxing to match the bevel angle and sew it on top of one end of the zipper assembly, overlapping ½ inch. The length of the fold and the width of the zipper assembly should be the same. Trim the excess fabric.

5 This seam should align exactly with the intersection of straight side and the beveled side. To make that happen, place it about ⅛ inch shy of the corresponding corner on the larger of the cover pieces and sew back from it almost to the beginning of the zipper assembly (including piping if applicable). Now go back to where you started and sew in the opposite direction around the rest of the cover, stopping just short of completing the circuit.

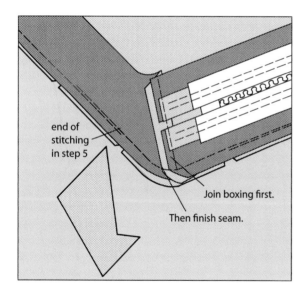

end of stitching in step 5

Join boxing first.

Then finish seam.

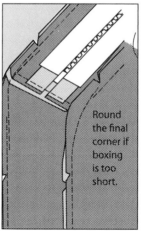

Round the final corner if boxing is too short.

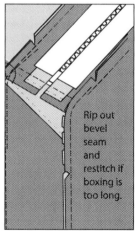

Rip out bevel seam and restitch if boxing is too long.

6 Fold the end of the boxing to match the bevel, locating the fold by estimating where it needs to be to end up precisely at the corner when you finish the seam. Sew the fold on top of the zipper assembly, overlapping a uniform ½ inch. Trim the excess boxing and finish the seam.

7 Transfer the alignment notches from the cover piece to the raw side of the boxing; then sew on the other cover piece starting from the zipper assembly. If you are diligent in keeping the pieces aligned, you shouldn't encounter any problems, but if the boxing runs slightly short, rounding the final corner to solve it won't matter. If it runs long, rip out the bevel seam and adjust it to fit.

BULL-NOSED CUSHIONS

Piping can be an irritant to bare legs, and twin hard ridges between cushions can be especially annoying when the settee is used as a bunk. Simply omitting the welt from a box cushion isn't very satisfactory. A better solution is the bull-nosed cushion.

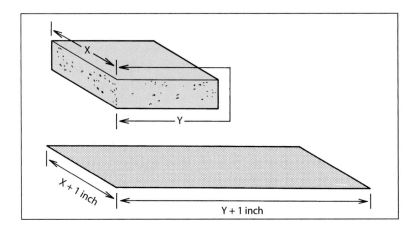

1 From the back edge of the foam, measure across the top, the front, and the bottom, and back again to the back edge and add 1 inch to get one dimension of the main piece of fabric. Add 1 inch to the width of the foam for the other dimension. The double width of the cover piece may be confusing, so pay close attention to the orientation of patterned fabric.

2 Measure the side dimensions of the foam and add 1 inch to both to get the side boxing. Two pieces are required. Use a compass to mark a perfect semicircle at one end and cut the boxing pieces to shape. Put alignment notches at the noon, 3 o'clock, and 6 o'clock positions.

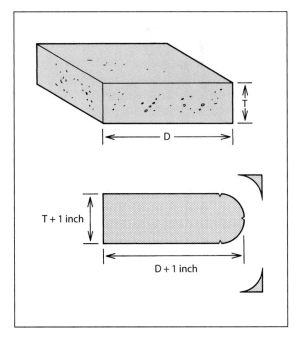

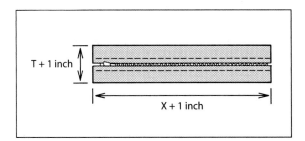

3 Make a zipper assembly 1 inch longer and wider than the foam's back dimensions (see page 822).

4 Fold the main piece in half and notch it at the fold on both sides. Unfold it and align one of these notches with the center (3 o'clock) notch of one of the boxing pieces. Sew from the notch to the back edge, running the machine by hand initially while you sew the curve of the boxing to the straight edge of the cover piece. Turn the assembly around and start again at the notch—overlapping a few stitches—to sew the other edge of the boxing to the cover.

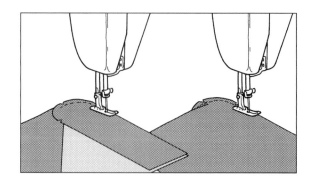

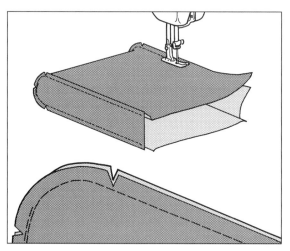

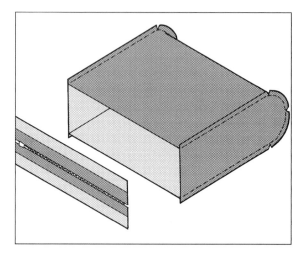

5 Transfer the noon and 6 o'clock notches across to the opposite edge of the cover with a square. Install the second piece of boxing the same way as the first, taking care to get the alignment right.

6 Trim the back edges of the cover to match the length of the side boxing, then staple the zipper assembly into the opening of the cover and seam it in place. Remove the staples. Open the zipper and turn the finished cover rightside out.

TRIMMING FOAM FOR BULL-NOSED CUSHIONS

TO GET A BULL-NOSED cushion to take the right shape, the front of the filling needs to be round. Rounding the foam requires special machinery, but you can approximate the rounded edge by putting five facets on the front edge. To hold the knife blade at 30 degrees, make the jig shown. Reversing the jig also allows it to hold the blade at 60 degrees. Make four cuts, then wrap the cushion with *polyester batting*.

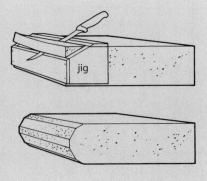

CENTER-WELT CUSHIONS

Center-welt cushions give an overstuffed look. They are most appropriate when at least two sides of the cushion will show. Center-welt cushions require a soft fabric, and the foam should be wrapped in batting.

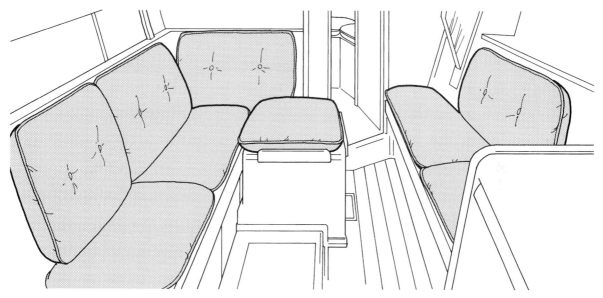

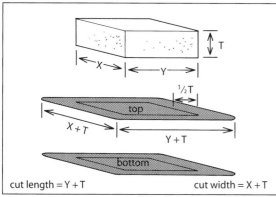

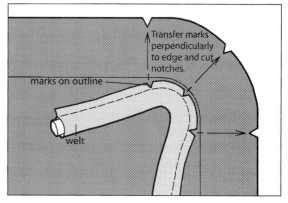

1 Add the thickness of the foam to the length and width dimensions to get the cut size of the two pieces of fabric required. Round the corners. Draw an outline on the back side of the fabric half the thickness of the foam from the edge.

2 Thick welt is the usual choice for center-welt cushions. Put three evenly spaced notches in the welt so that when you shape the welt to the outline and put the center notch at the center of one of the rounded corners, the other two notches fall on the straight sides of the outline just beyond where the curvature of the corner starts. Use the notched cord to mark the outline with these three points at every corner.

3 Transfer these three points at each corner perpendicularly to the edge and notch their locations in the seam allowance. Replace the welt on the outline, aligning the initial three notches with the initial three marks; then align the welt all the way around the outline and notch it at the other nine marks on the outline.

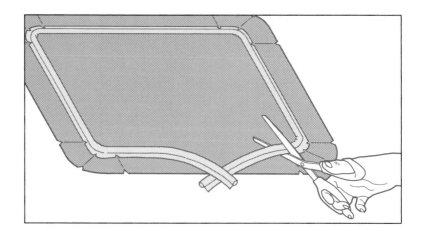

4 Fold the fabric back along the back edge of one of the cover pieces and sew it to a zipper so that the unsewn edge of the zipper replaces the raw edge of the fabric. Assemble the cover by sewing the welt around one cover piece, gathering the fabric at each corner to make the wide-spaced notches along the edge of the fabric align with the closer-spaced ones in the piping. Turn the assembly over and sew the second piece on the same way.

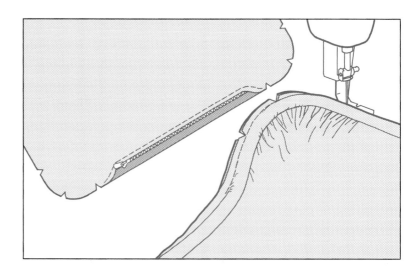

POLYESTER BATTING

IN ADDITION TO ROUNDING THE FRONT EDGE of a bull-nosed cushion, a layer of polyester batting, also called *wadding*, can give any style foam cushion some initial softness. Batting also tends to improve the cover fit. Polyester batting comes in a variety of weights; select a wadding about $1/2$ inch thick for wrapping cushions. Lay it on loose, or tack it in place with spray adhesive. If your foam will be batting wrapped, don't take the $1/4$ inch out of the boxing width measurements.

BACKRESTS

Built-in backrests are usually assembled on a thin backing of plywood. If they are self-contained, they are typically held in place with interlocking brackets. Try sliding the backrest straight up to free it. Otherwise, look for hidden fasteners.

A backrest can be unboxed or boxed on two, three, or four sides, depending on the cushion design. To get a perfect fit, always mark the fabric first where it should fold over the plywood.

Attach the fabric with closely spaced Monel staples installed diagonally, starting at the center of the top edge and working out in both directions at the same time. Do the bottom edge, then the sides the same way. Work the corners carefully, folding them under smoothly and gathering the fabric evenly if the backrest isn't boxed.

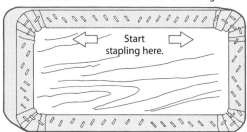

Mark where fabric should fold over backing.

Start stapling here.

BUTTON TUFTING

Tufting was once essential to hold cotton or hair padding in place. With solid foam padding, buttons are more decorative than functional, but they *can* keep backrest fabric from sagging.

The easiest and best way to get covered buttons is to take a piece of your fabric to an upholstery shop and let them press the buttons for you on a special machine. You can also cover your own using covered button forms from a dress shop, but these won't be quite as durable.

Mark the location of the buttons on the fabric and on the backing material of a backrest. Drill the backing. Fold a length of heavy waxed thread and run the folded end through the ring of a button, then open the fold and draw it over the top of the button to lock it. Thread both loose ends of the tie into a long needle and punch it through the mark in the fabric and out the drilled hole. Remove the needle and thread the ends through the two holes of a backer button. Pull the ends until the button is at the depth you want, then tie the ends together.

You can also button loose cushions in a similar manner, using a covered button on both sides. But keep in mind that buttoning prevents you from removing covers to clean them without cutting off the buttons.

PLEATED FABRIC

The pleated look, especially on a backrest, can be a nice design feature. The simplest route to the pleated look is to pleat the fabric beforehand, then construct the cushion in the normal way. Joining panels with diagonal pleats can create an interesting pattern.

You need extra fabric width—about $1/2$ inch per pleat. Pleats can be any width, but 1 to 4 inches is normal. Mark your fabric *on the good side* with parallel lines spaced $1/2$ inch farther apart than your desired pleat width.

Cut a piece of $1/4$-inch foam to the same size as your fabric and stitch it around the perimeter to the back side. You can also use polyester batting. Fold the fabric along your first pleat line and run a row of stitches $1/4$ inch inside the fold in the cloth. Because of the added bulk, the stitch line will be more than $1/4$ inch from the folded edge of the foam; to put the stitch line in the correct place, you'll have to experiment with how wide you want the seam to appear.

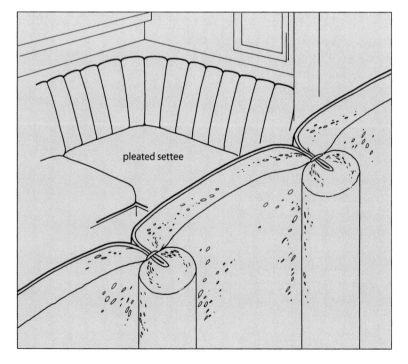

pleated settee

Continue folding and sewing until the entire piece is pleated, then cut the cover pieces you need from the pleated fabric. The finished cover may lie better if you have trimmed off the loop of foam or batting over the fabric folds.

CUSTOM UPHOLSTERY

Re-covering some items aboard, such as a navigator's seat, may require alternative techniques. The proper approach is to carefully remove the old cover, noting on a pad exactly how it is attached. The only new attachments you are likely to encounter are *tack strips* and *shaping flaps*. A tack strip is typically a flat strip of metal with tack-like barbs. The fabric wraps over the strip with the tacks protruding through the folded-under edge, then the covered strip is hammered into a wooden frame to yield a finished edge. Shaping flaps are usually just extra wide seams that are sewn or stapled down before fitting the cover completely to give the finished cover a concave shape.

With the cover removed, notch and label adjoining edges, then rip out the stitching and separate the cover into its component pieces. Use them as patterns for the new pieces—including the alignment notches—then simply reassemble and reinstall the cover the same way you took it apart.

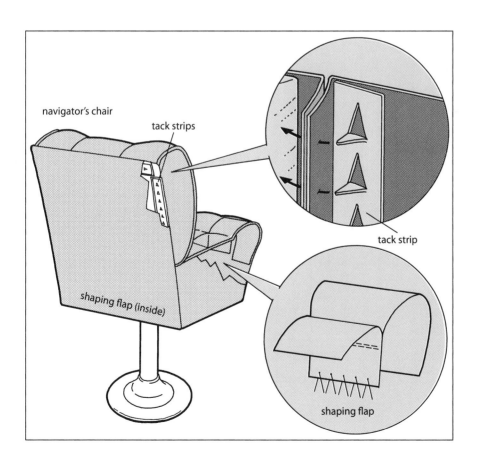

navigator's chair

tack strips

tack strip

shaping flap (inside)

shaping flap

CUSTOM CANVAS

What if you want a sun cover for a sailboard? Is that much different from the zipper pockets we learned to make in "The Pocket"? Sew the folded edge to the contour of the board and trim away the excess canvas ½ inch beyond the stitch line. Contour the raw edges as well. The remaining steps are the same as for any zipper bag: Sew the raw edges to opposite sides of a full-length zipper, then seam and bind the ends.

How about a cover for the dink's outboard when it is rail-mounted? Nothing more than an appropriately sized bag with a drawstring or straps to secure it. (Give it handles and you will always have a tote bag in the dinghy.)

What about a secure way to get your cutlery to the beach for a picnic or cookout? Is what you need significantly different from a tool roll?

Most canvas items aboard a boat are some form of one of the four categories already covered, perhaps with a little shaping here, an extra seam there. Most, yes, but not all. A sailcover, for example, is more closely related to a sports jacket than a bag or a pocket. And a spray dodger may put you in mind of a convertible top for an old MG. Can the boatowner fabricate these odd-shaped canvas items? Of course.

If the project you have in mind is a replacement, the old item will serve as a pattern for each piece of fabric and as a guide to their assembly. Simply notch the seam allowances and label the pieces, then disassemble the item by ripping the seams. Lay the components on your new fabric—paying attention to the grain—and trace around them. Include the notches. Cut out the new pieces, then assemble them according to your notations.

If you don't have an old item to use as a pattern, then make one—using paper (or pattern fabric) and tape. Once you get the paper item to fit, cut it into pieces that will lie flat on your fabric—which generally means along the tape lines. Use a straightedge and a flexible batten when you trace the pattern to help you with the edges, and always remember to add seam and hem allowances as required. If your pattern fits, the item you make from it will also fit.

SAILCOVERS

Leave sails out continually in strong sunlight and they will be damaged in a single season, destroyed in three or four; but keep them covered and they will give a weekend sailor decades of use. Given that the cost of a sail is about 20 times that of a sailcover, it makes sense to have a cover and use it, and most sailors do. When the old one is faded or threadbare, making a new one is straightforward. Use acrylic canvas for all the usual reasons. Never make a sailcover from vinyl or any other fabric that doesn't "breathe."

1 If you don't have an old cover to use as a pattern, think of a sailcover as two wedge-shaped pieces of fabric seamed together on their longest edges, then lopped off on the pointed ends to let them wrap straight around both mast and boom. The distance from the front of the mast to the end of the boom gives the length of this truncated wedge. The height is measured from the bottom of the boom to a point about 6 inches above the dropped headboard. The seamed edge is usually concave to better match the contour of the furled sail; determine its exact shape by measuring from the bottom of the boom (and the front of the mast) to the center of the furled sail—around its bulk—taking measurements every 6 inches near the mast and every 2 feet once the curve flattens out.

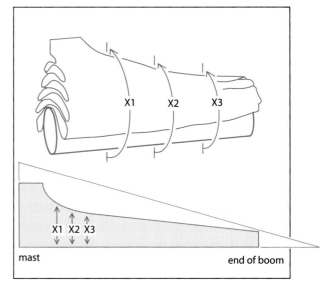

2 Add a ¹/₂-inch seam allowance to the curved side and a 6-inch fitting allowance to the boom end. Add 2 inches to all the other sides if you will close the cover with hooks and lacing, 4 inches if you plan to use twist fasteners. Lay out the two halves of the cover on the fabric. You can overlap the narrow ends to conserve fabric if both sides of the fabric are the same; if not, you must make the second piece the mirror image of the first. The fabric will probably be too narrow to accommodate the full height dimension of the cover; lay the excess out onto a paper extension, then transfer it back onto the fabric, allowing an extra inch of fabric along the edge that joins the main piece.

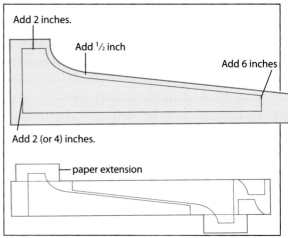

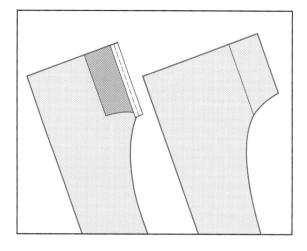

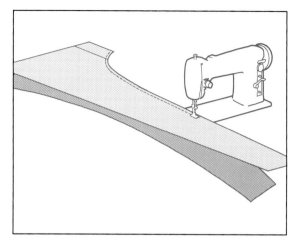

3 Sew the extension pieces to the main pieces with ½-inch seams. Bind these seams.

4 Sew the two cover halves together along the curve, good side to good side, placing the stitches ½ inch from the raw edges. Remove any pins or staples you used to baste the pieces together.

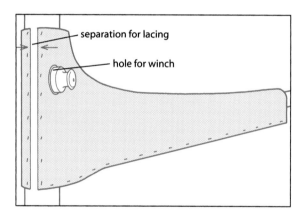

separation for lacing

hole for winch

5 Rub a 1½-inch (both folds) double-rubbed hem on the bottom and front edges and staple them to hold them temporarily. Place this cover "blank" over the sail and check it for fit. The edges should be a couple of inches apart for hook-and-lace fastening; for twist buttons they should overlap a couple of inches. Note any adjustments required. Mast-mounted winches may interfere with the fit; carefully position the cover and cut a hole in it to let the winch protrude. Also mark where you want the cover to end on the mast and boom and leave a 3-inch hem allowance.

6 After making all fit adjustments, bind the center seam. Open the two panels flat and fold the seam onto one of them, then sew it down with two parallel rows of topstitching. Trim the blank per your fitting marks and put a 1½-inch double-rubbed hem all around.

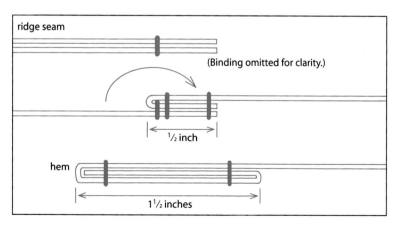

ridge seam

(Binding omitted for clarity.)

½ inch

hem

1½ inches

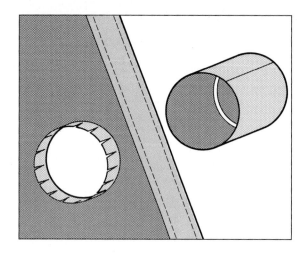

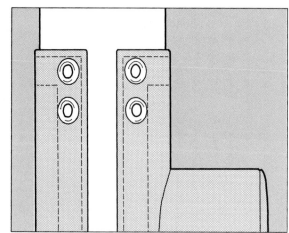

7 Cut a circle 2 inches larger than the winch hole and sew it inside an appropriately sized canvas tube to make a cover for the winch (see "Two-Piece Duffel Bag," page 814). Turn this boot rightside out. Cut a series of ³⁄₈-inch slits around the perimeter of the hole in the cover to allow the edge to fold in, then mate the raw edge of the boot with the edge of the hole and sew them together. Bind the seam.

8 Regardless of your closure system, install four grommets near the top of the front edges to allow the collar of the cover to be laced tightly against the mast. Having the collar tight prevents water penetration that leads to mildew. If the cover overlaps (for twist-lock fastening), set one pair of grommets back from the edge to allow tensioning.

9 For a hook-and-lace closure, install sailhooks on one side with a pair of grommets opposite. Place the hooks every 6 inches on the front of the mast, every 18 inches along the bottom of the boom. Hooks can be hand-sewn to the canvas or attached with pop rivets and washers. If you use pop rivets, be sure the proud side of the rivet is on the hook side of the cloth. Tie the lacing to the first pair of grommets (top and forward) and run it inside the cover, exiting the tandem grommets to capture the hook. Leaving the other end loose allows you to adjust the fit of the cover.

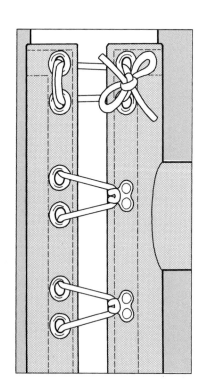

A SHORTCUT

SAILCOVERS DIE MOSTLY FROM HORIZONTAL EXPOSURE TO THE sun. If the hems that contain the hooks and grommets for closing the cover—around the boom and around the mast—are in good shape, save time and take advantage of the machine installation of the hardware by cutting off the old hems and seaming them to the edges of your new cover.

10 For a twist-button closure, install matching Common Sense studs and eyelets in the hems, using the same spacing as for the sailhooks above. Install them so that the fabric is overlapping, not pinched together. Use a heated knife to melt the slits for the prongs. Press the prongs through the slits and bend them with pliers over the appropriate backing plate. Cut the cloth from the center of the eyelet with a hotknife or a soldering iron *after* the eyelet is installed.

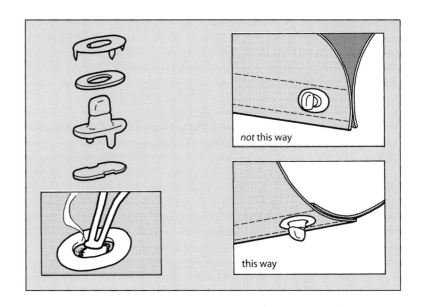

not this way

this way

11 Functionally it doesn't matter that a lace-on cover is slightly "open" on the front of the mast, but if you want a closed look, cut and hem a strip of canvas 4 inches wide and the same length as the height of the cover. Sew this flap to the inside of one side of the cover, or sew it to the outside and close it over the lacing with Velcro.

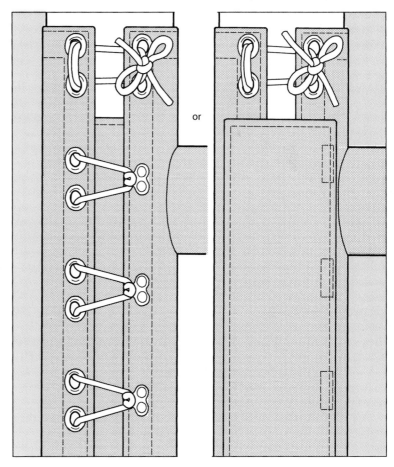

or

BOAT COVERS

In northern climes, a winter cover that keeps water off the deck prevents the damage caused when the water that has found its way into deck cracks freezes and expands. Storage covers are common, but boats *in use* are rarely covered despite the fact that the inconvenience of a cover may be more than offset by a significant reduction in maintenance. Covers are especially beneficial for varnished brightwork, but they also extend the life of caulking, plastic portlights, teak oil, covered hardware, and even surface gelcoat or paint; and they keep the decks clean and dry.

The waterproof and chafe-resistant nature of treated canvas makes it a good choice for a winter cover, but it must be kept clean to avoid mildew. It must also be stored clean and dry when not in use.

For regular in-season use, a light polyester fabric is sometimes selected because it makes a light, soft cover. Except for limited water-resistance, soft polyester (not sailcloth) isn't a bad choice if you don't mind replacing the cover every three or four years. Treated canvas is another possibility, but if you don't keep it clean, especially of bird droppings, mildew will quickly destroy it. For a carefree water-resistant cover that will last a decade or longer for in-season use, use acrylic canvas.

A day-use cover is basically a tarp—a flat sheet of canvas—shaped to the contour of the rail and pierced to let spars, wires, and other vertical features protrude. It can lie flat on the deck where it adds the least windage, or it can peak, tent-like, over the boom or some other support.

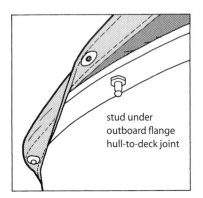

stud under outboard flange hull-to-deck joint

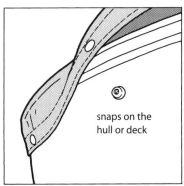

snaps on the hull or deck

1 Start this project by deciding how the cover will be attached. This affects the amount of overhang all around and how the edges should be finished.

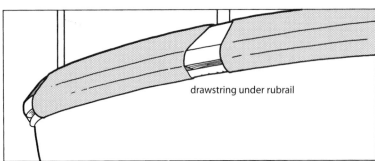

drawstring under rubrail

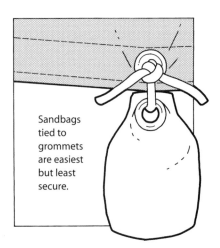

Sandbags tied to grommets are easiest but least secure.

2 Decide how the cover will fit around the mast. A zipper to one side is typical; making the cover in two parts is another choice. An overlap will be virtually watertight for a boat on a mooring, but if the boat can't clock to the wind, the overlap is likely to open.

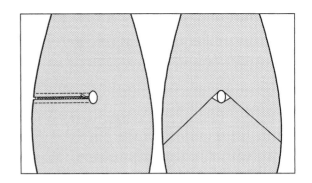

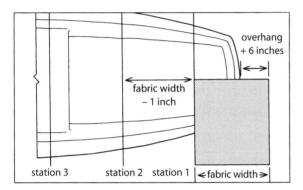

3 Starting at the stern, divide the boat into stations. The first station should be forward of the stern by the width of your cloth less 6 inches and the planned overhang. The remaining stations, all the way to the bow, should be 1 inch less than the width of your fabric apart. Measure them on the centerline of the boat if the cover will lie on deck, or along the ridgeline if the cover will be elevated over a support.

4 Begin construction by making up a blank—a piece of fabric roughly the size of your planned cover plus allowances for fitting. At the first station measure the distance from the centerline or ridgeline to the side rail and add to it the overhang plus 6 extra inches. Double this sum to get the length of the first panel. Make a similar measurement at the next station to get the length of the next panel. When you reach the longest station, cut two panels to that length—the length of a panel is determined by the longer of the two stations that border it. Continue measuring panel lengths all the way to the bow.

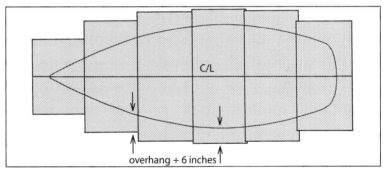

MILDEW LOVES THE DARK

THE BIGGEST PROBLEM WITH DAY-USE BOAT COVERS, aside from taking them off and putting them back on, is that they make the cabin dark. Add hot, humid weather into the mix and mildew quickly sets up housekeeping in your absence. The solution is open cutouts over transparent hatches. If that strategy lets more rain onto your deck than you think desirable, seal these openings with a clear vinyl window. The "Dodger" section at the end of this chapter contains instructions for installing vinyl windows.

5 Cut the panels and sew them together in the order you measured them, aligning their centerlines. Because the full-width panels have selvage edges (see page 786), a 1-inch overlap seam, triple zigzag stitched, is appropriate. Otherwise, use a flat-felled seam (see page 783).

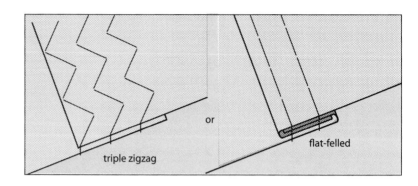

triple zigzag   or   flat-felled

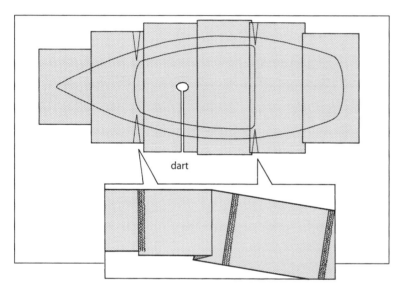

dart

6 Spread the blank on the boat so that it would overhang evenly all around if shrouds, stays, and stanchions weren't in the way. This requires making the mast cutout. Sew darts into the edge of the blank in line with slope changes on the centerline or ridge line to remove excess fabric at the rail. More extensive contouring to fit the cover to the shape of the cabin is generally unnecessary, but if you want to contour it, this is the time.

7 The cover will drape over low deck features, but cut holes for the windlass, cowl ventilators, and other features that interfere with the fit. Make boots (see "Sailcovers") and sew them into the holes for the windlass and other protuberances you want covered. For a day-use cover, you may want ventilators to remain uncovered; in that case, bind the edge of the holes.

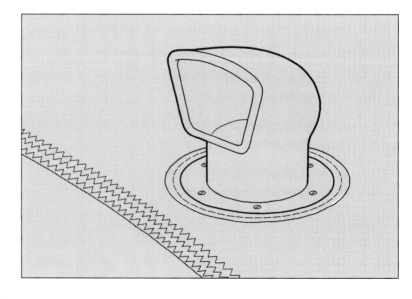

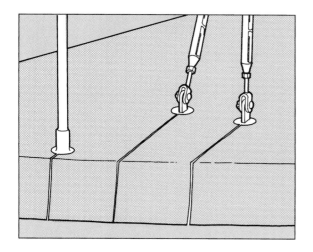

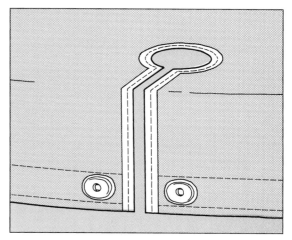

8   Working from the dock or a dinghy and taking care that the centerline of the blank remains aligned with the centerline of the boat, make a cutout for every penetrating feature at or near the rail. Slit the blank from each cutout to the edge. Mark the perimeter of the finished cover, accounting for your fastening system.

9   Add an appropriate hem allowance and trim the edge. Bind the raw edges of all the cutouts and slits. Hem the perimeter of the cover and install the planned fasteners.

TAILORING

A COVER THAT LIES ON DECK WILL HAVE A NEATER appearance if it is tailored to the contour of the forward end of the trunk cabin. Cut the blank straight across, using the deck corners of the cabin to position the cut. Cut three paper patterns, one for the outline of the cabin on the deck, one for the outline of the forward edge of the cabintop and sides, and one duplicating the front surface of the cabin. Taped together these three patterns should neatly enclose the forward end of the cabin. Mark them on the centerline.

Cut the forward section of the blank to the deck-contour pattern, and the aft section to the cabin contour pattern, adding ¾-inch seam allowances. Cut an additional piece of canvas the shape of your front-surface pattern, also with ¾-inch allowances. Seam the three pieces together with ½-inch flat-felled seams.

Use the same technique to tailor your cover to accommodate a doghouse or any other deck contours.

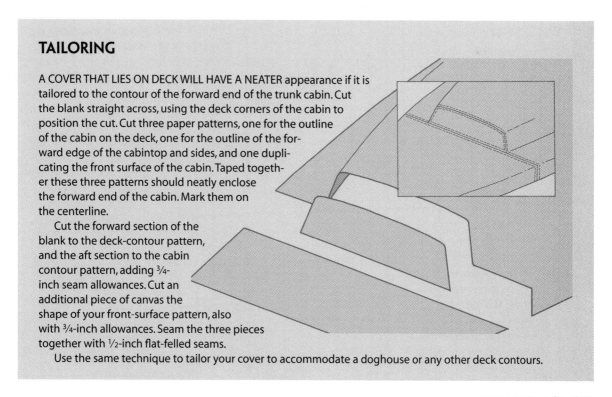

BIMINI AWNING

A Bimini awning is another flat-sheet project, hemmed on the sides and given casings on the ends shaped to the contour of the supporting frame. Because the frame adjusts to the cloth, a perfect fit requires only reasonably accurate end contours. Reinforced vinyl and acrylic canvas make good Bimini tops. Acrylic canvas will need to be sprayed with a proof coating every couple of years to keep water from penetrating.

THE FRAME

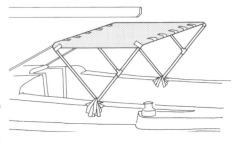

1   If you're starting from scratch, you need a frame for the top. Make a mock-up from plastic water pipe and elbow fittings. Cover it with Kraft paper or pieces of old bed sheet, then sail with it. Does it interfere with the mainsheet? Does the boom clear? Can you get to the jib winches? Can you go forward easily? Can you see to trim the sails? Will the top fold out of the way? Work out the problems you discover.

2   Aluminum tubing is a common frame material, but it distorts easily. Stainless steel tubing is a better choice although heavier and more expensive. Steel tubing should be $^7/_8$ or 1 inch (OD) with a wall thickness of 0.049 or 0.065 inch. Bend the bows on a bender fashioned from $^3/_4$-inch plywood. Make the radius at least 12 inches to avoid flattening or kinking. Making the bends short of 90 degrees so that the width between the ends prior to mounting is 8 or 10 inches wider than the distance between the mounting sockets will introduce curvature to the top when you install the bows, strengthening the frame and improving water shedding.

BENDER

nailed to base   1 x 2
                           2 x 4
                    nailed to lever
radius at
least 12
inches
$^3/_4$-inch plywood   pivot bolt
washers between

3   Install the frame and space the bows with webbing with loops sewn in the ends, and in the middle if you have intermediate bows. Position and install (temporarily) the tie-down straps.

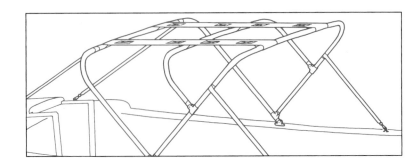

THE PATTERN

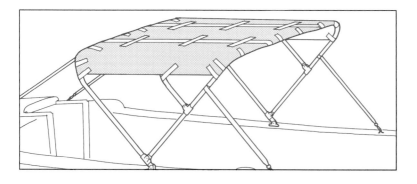

1 If you are making a replacement top, take apart the old top as a pattern. For a new top, cover the spread frame with paper or pattern material taped tightly around the bows.

2 Mark the pattern material along the forwardmost edge of the forward bow and the aftmost edge aft. Decide how far down the sides you want the top to reach and mark both sides fore and aft. Mark the locations of the tie-down straps. If the frame has intermediate bows, trace them along both sides on the underside of the pattern.

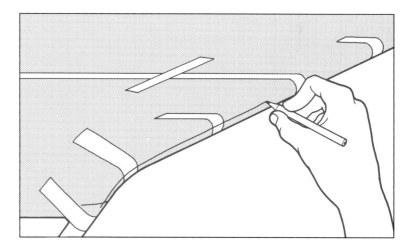

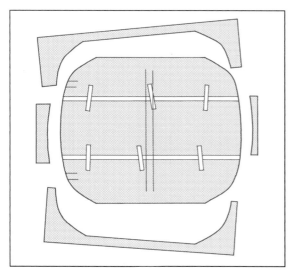

3 Remove the pattern material. Connect the side marks with straight lines, then cut out the pattern.

THE TOP

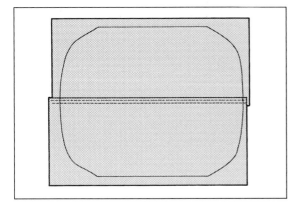

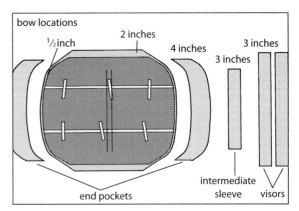

1. Sew two or more panels together—as required—to make a blank large enough to accommodate your pattern. The seam(s) should run fore and aft. With an odd number of seams, put the center seam in the center of the top. With an even number, place the center panel at the top's center. Sew the panels together with flat-felled seams.

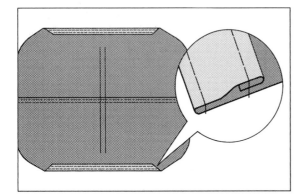

3. Put a 1½-inch double-rubbed hem (½ inch turned under) on both sides of the top.

4. Mark the location of the tie-down straps on the end-pocket pieces and make arched cutouts. Hem or bind the cutouts. Hem the ends and the concave side of the end pockets, and the ends and one side of the center pocket(s).

2. Trace the pattern onto your fabric, adding a ½-inch allowance to the ends and a 2-inch allowance to the sides. Mark the intermediate bow location(s). Cut out two end-pocket pieces about 4 inches wide (including allowances) that exactly match the contour of the ends of the top piece but 3 inches shorter. Sleeves for intermediate bows are straight strips about 3 inches wide and two-thirds the top's width. Cut two 3-inch-wide visor strips 3 inches shorter than the curved ends of the top piece.

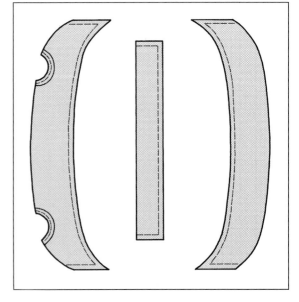

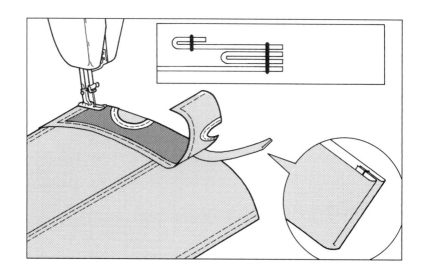

5 Fold the visor strips in half lengthwise—good side inside—and seam the ends ½ inch from the edge. Reverse the fold to put the seams inside. Align the raw edges and sew the top and the end pockets together—good side to good side—with the visor strip between them.

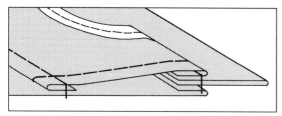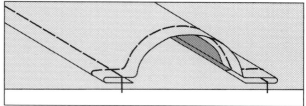

6 Fold the end pockets over and press the seam flat, then sew the hemmed side (not the ends) to the top piece. Sew the raw edge of the intermediate pocket(s) to the underside of the top along one of the marks then fold it over and sew the hemmed

edge along the other mark. If you want your top removable without dismantling the frame, attach the hemmed edges of the pockets with jacket zippers rather than sewing them.

7 Install the Bimini by sliding the loose bows through the appropriate sleeves. Remember to install the stitched loops of the tie-down straps at the sleeve cutouts as you insert the bows. Mount the bows and adjust the straps.

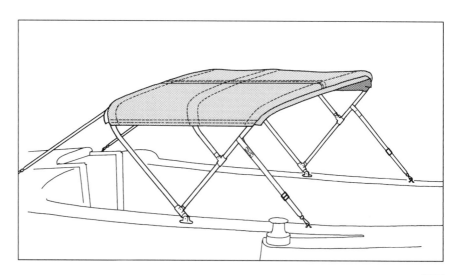

DODGER

It may be helpful to think of a dodger as a short Bimini awning (preceding project) with a windshield and side curtains. The frame is basically the same as a two-bow Bimini frame. Aluminum tubing is *not* appropriate for a dodger frame; the rigidity of stainless steel is essential. For the best visibility, use 0.020 polished sheet vinyl for the windshield.

DESIGN

1. As with the Bimini, making a water-pipe mock-up is a smart first step. Can you easily enter and exit the companionway? Does the boom clear? The winch handles? How will the lower edge of the windshield cross the companionway slide? Can you stand at the helm and see *over* the dodger when the windshield is salt-fogged? Get off the boat: Does the dodger look too short? Too high? Too boxy? Windshield too vertical?

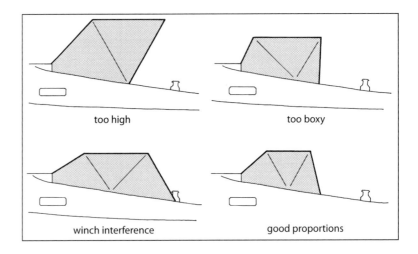

too high

too boxy

winch interference

good proportions

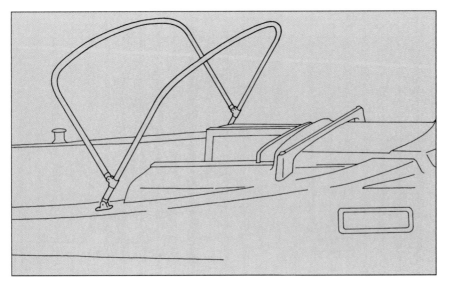

2. Bend the bows and install the frame (see "Bimini Awning— The Frame," step 2). A large radius gives the dodger a rounded look that on many boats is more pleasing. Underbend the bows slightly to make the ends wider apart than their sockets, which introduces curvature to the center of the bow when you mount it.

3 Cover the mounted and guyed frame with paper or pattern fabric. Work all wrinkles out of the pattern material. Tape a separate piece of pattern fabric to the forward bow and to the deck to represent the windshield portion of the dodger. Add "wings" to close the sides of the dodger. Draw in the outlines of clear panels for the windshield and side ports. Mark seam locations.

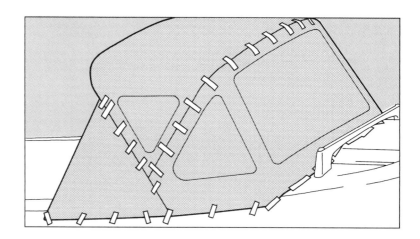

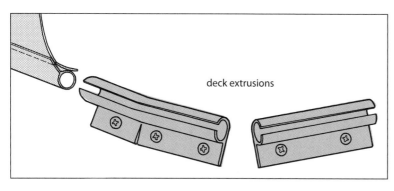

deck extrusions

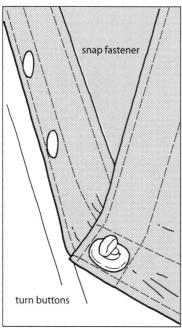

snap fastener

turn buttons

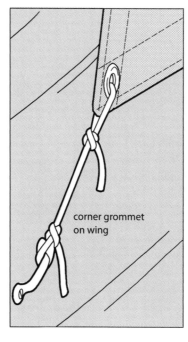

corner grommet on wing

4 Work out all attachment issues. The most waterproof method of attachment is a boltrope in the edge of the dodger that slides through a deck-fastened extrusion. Cutting the mounting flange allows the extrusion to be bent moderately; for more radical turns, install the extrusion in sections. Alternatively, attach the front edge with turn buttons and the sides with snap fasteners. Snaps won't work on the front edge because the upward pull will unsnap them. The wings typically have a corner grommet for a lacing.

ASSEMBLY

1 Cut the pattern apart on the seam lines. Cut the top piece from your fabric, remembering to add a ½-inch seam allowance. Also cut the wing pieces, giving them an extra 1½-inch allowance for a wide hem on the two free sides. Cut grommet-reinforcement corner patches (two) for each wing and install them under the hems.

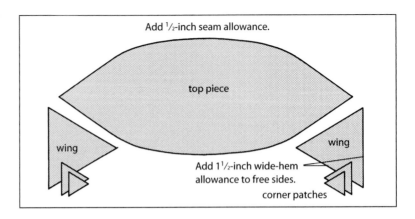

2 The windshield is typically divided into three pieces joined with zippers, which allows you to open the center panel for ventilation. The easiest way to fabricate the windshield section is to frame the vinyl pieces with hemmed canvas strips. Folded strips give a finished appearance inside and out, and they make the vinyl easier to sew. Always use your longest stitch on vinyl. Place zippers on the inside of the windshield and oriented to unzip up.

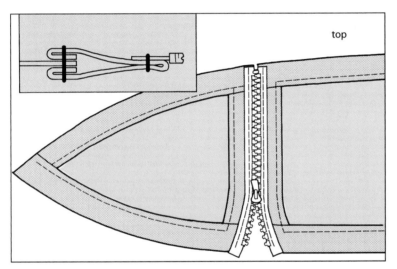

3 Cut two 4-inch-wide sleeve pieces to match the forward and aft contours of the top piece. The forward sleeve need only be 3 or 4 feet long: it simply holds the forward bow in position. Make the back sleeve long enough to extend about halfway through the side curves of the bow. Hem the ends and concave sides. If you want the dodger to be easily removable, sew #10 jacket zippers to the hemmed sides.

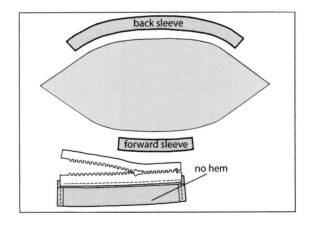

4 A dodger quickly becomes your preferred handhold. Cut a 3-inch-wide strip of leather or reinforced vinyl to protect the aft edge of the dodger.

5 Install the clear side ports. Cut the vinyl 1 inch larger than the finish size on all sides, and sew it to the inside surface of the top piece in the appropriate location. Cover the vinyl with Saran wrap to keep the foot of your sewing machine from sticking. Cut the canvas 1 inch inside the stitch line. Do not make this cutout *before* you sew the vinyl in place. Make a regular series of $3/8$-inch slits in the curved portions of the cut edge, then fold $1/2$ inch under and topstitch it down.

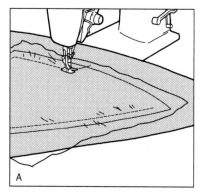

A

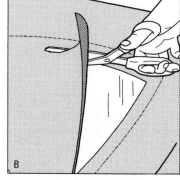

B

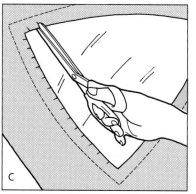

C

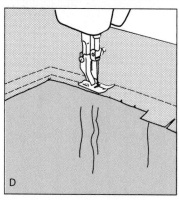

D

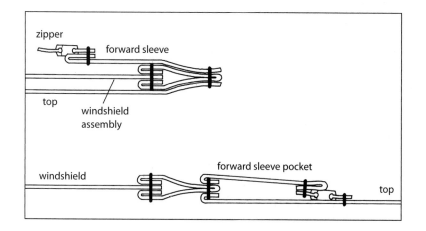

6 Sew the top, the windshield assembly, and the forward sleeve together, sewing in both directions from the centerline to assure proper alignment. Fold the pocket piece under, pressing the seam flat, and sew the pocket's aft edge or its zipper to the top.

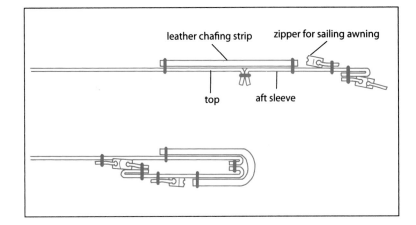

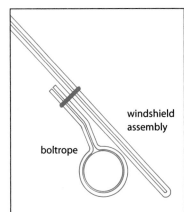

7 Sew the top, the aft sleeve, and the wings together. Where the wings and sleeve overlap, be sure the wing piece is in the middle. Open the seam flat and sew the leather chafing strip to both the sleeve and the top. If you plan to have a sailing awning that attaches to the dodger, now is also the time to sew on the dodger half of the jacket zipper. Fold the sleeve under, pressing the seam flat, and sew its aft edge or its zipper to the top.

8 Install the dodger on the frame and mark the locations for the fasteners. Remove the dodger and install appropriate fasteners in it. Install grommets in the reinforced corners of the wings. If you are using bolt rope, sew the rope inside a canvas strip or binding tape (similar to piping—see page 825), then sew the tape to the inside of the bottom edge of the windshield assembly.

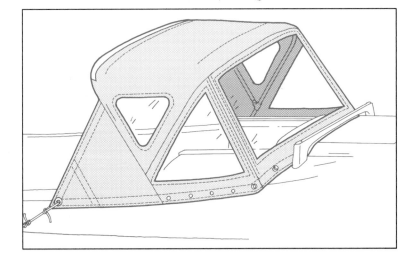

9 Reinstall the dodger and guy the aft bow in position. Mark the deck for the boltrope extrusion and/or the deck half of the various fasteners. Working from the center out in both directions, smooth the top and install and fasten each fastener in turn to get even tension on the canvas. Install strap eyes below and behind the wing grommets and use a lacing to tension the installed dodger.

SAILING AWNING

YOU CAN QUICKLY CONSTRUCT A SIMPLE SAILING AWNING for your dodger from an appropriately sized flat sheet of canvas. Put a casing in one end and hem the remaining three edges. Insert a stiff batten into the casing and sew half of a jacket zipper to the other end. Zip the zipper to its mate (see step 7 above), tie the batten to the backstay, and sail in the shade.

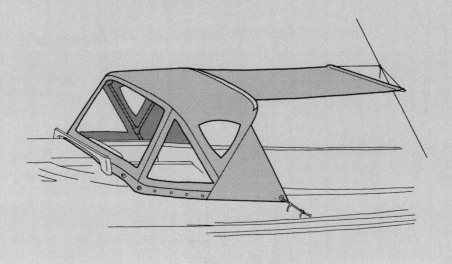

SAIL REPAIR

The most significant canvas item on a sailboat is the sail. Is it advisable, or even possible, to apply your new or improved canvasworking skills to sail repair?

Consider this. The most basic canvas item, as we have already seen, is a flat sheet with edges hemmed and grommets installed in the corners. The difference between a lee cloth and a harbor awning is mostly a matter of scale, plus the addition of perimeter features like corner reinforcement and perhaps a rope in the hem. Start with a triangular sheet of fabric and you end up with something that looks an awful lot like a sail.

Wait a minute! Sails aren't flat. Neither are awnings or lee cloths when they're doing their job. Okay, it is true that most sails have built-in shape, a certain amount of fullness behind the luff, but by now you know how to introduce such fullness— even if you don't know that you know. Remember the hatch cover in "The Bag"—a flat piece of canvas with darts in the four corners? Dart just two corners and you end up with fullness behind one edge— just like a sail.

Anyway, the fullness doesn't matter for repairs to the sail's perimeter, and since "shape" is almost always confined to the forward third of the sail, the aft two thirds *is* flat. Besides that, every panel of cloth is flat, so repairs confined to a single panel have no effect on sail shape.

Restitching a sail, however, can be significantly more challenging than other flat-sheet projects for two reasons: fabric and size.

Dacron sailcloth, especially new cloth, is stiff and slick. While softer fabrics adjust to hide minor sewing indiscretions, sailcloth is as unforgiving as plywood. Even the slightest misalignment shows up as a pucker or a wrinkle, and the fabric is so slippery that pinching two pieces together is like squeezing a wet bar of soap. Fortunately there is a simple solution: When sewing sailcloth, glue every seam together before you sew it. Transfer tape or a glue stick make this easy.

The complications of size are not quite as easily overcome. Size is of little consequence for repairs near the edge, but finding a way to get the presser foot into the middle of a 500-square-foot sail can be a real challenge. It is possible that your sail may be too big or your machine's underarm space too small to meet this challenge, but you won't know unless you try. Aside from size, sail repair is just another flat-sheet project.

Sails aren't really flat, and it is a good idea to understand what gives them shape so you don't unwittingly change it. Some high-tech racing sails have the shape "molded" into the sail, but all others are shaped by some combination of two basic techniques.

LUFF ROUND

If you round the leading edge—the *luff*—of a sail, straightening it when you hoist the sail moves excess fabric back into the sail. This gives the sail fullness behind the luff. Luff round alone was adequate to shape cotton sails, but the stiffness of resin-impregnated Dacron tends to restrict the effectiveness of this technique. Dacron sails are still given rounded luffs, but a second technique is required to move the draft back from the luff.

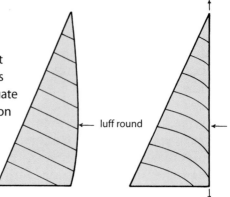

luff round

BROADSEAMING

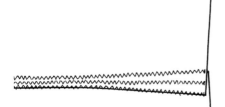

Broadseaming is nothing more than increasing the overlap of two panels as you seam them together toward the edge. It works much like a dart, removing cloth from the edge of the sail. This results in more cloth in the center of the sail than at the edge. This bagginess gives the finished sail its draft and is controlled by where the broadseams begin and how much the overlap increases.

LEECH HOLLOW

The aft edge—the *leech*—of unbattened sails is typically given a concave contour. This is not to shape the sail but rather to tighten the edge to keep it from fluttering. The amount of hollow is typically about 2 percent of the length of the leech, but varies according to the intended use of the sail. The leech may also be tightened with a broadseam or two at the aft edge of the sail.

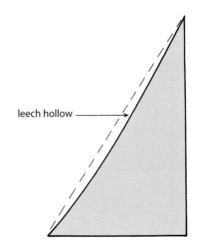

leech hollow

FIRST AID

Ben Franklin was onto something with that "stitch in time" thing. Almost every sail problem begins with a single broken thread. Spot a problem early and you significantly limit the extent of the repair required.

TAPE

The easiest way to close a seam or tear is with fabric tape. Special sail-repair tapes in 2- or 3-inch widths are available, and the better ones will last a season when properly applied. Duct tape, although unsightly, also does an admirable job. Place the damaged section on a flat surface and clean both sides with an alcohol-dampened cloth to remove oils and displace moisture. Apply the tape to both sides of the sail, extending it well beyond the damage. Press the patch with a roller or pound it with a mallet or a shoe. Tape also makes excellent chafe patches.

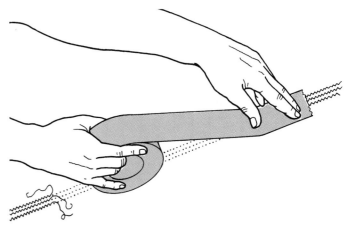

GLUE

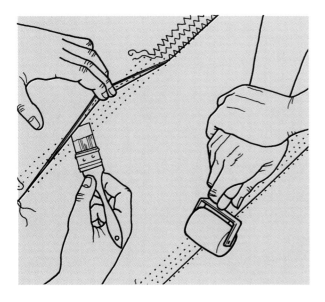

Contact cement is another way to quickly patch a large tear or a split seam. Some glues permanently stain sailcloth, but in an emergency a stained seam may be a minor concern. Coat the sail and the patch, or both surfaces of an open seam. Keep the two parts apart while the adhesive dries tack-free, then carefully align the two sides and press them together. Such a repair will be quite strong. If you don't have sailcloth aboard, you can cut a patch from some canvas item or an old foul-weather jacket. The glue in your inflatable repair kit is contact cement.

HAND-SEWING

The best way to repair a tear or split is to sew a patch in place or restitch the seam, but hand-sewing, if there is much of it, is slow and tedious. For general-purpose sail repair, select a #16 needle with a triangular shank. Use waxed polyester sail twine. A sewing palm will make the work much easier.

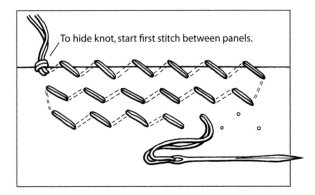

To hide knot, start first stitch between panels.

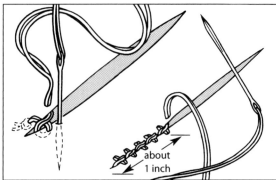

about 1 inch

1 Hand-sew split seams and loose tabling (edge binding) by passing the needle through the original holes. This assures correct alignment. If the split is in the middle of the sail, the repair goes much quicker with a person on both sides of the sail feeding the needle back and forth. The finished job looks like a row of slanted stitches. The twine is much stronger than machine thread, so there is little reason to fill the other side of the zigzag.

2 Repair tears in the fabric with a herringbone stitch, also called a *sailmaker's darn*. Knot the end of the doubled twine to start the repair. Make four or five stitches per inch and place them well back from the edges. Pull the stitches tight enough to bring the torn edges together, but not so tight that you introduce a pucker. Tie off and tuck the loose end.

USING A SAILMAKER'S PALM

HOLD THE THREADED NEEDLE between your thumb and forefinger and seat the eye end into the dimpled metal guard. Stick the point of the needle into the cloth, then release your grip on the needle and push it straight through with the palm. It is important, especially when sewing through several layers, not to let the needle get out of column or you may break it. You will quickly learn to feel when your palm pressure is directly down the center of the needle. When most of the needle has been pushed through the cloth, grip it again and pull it the rest of the way. Reseat it in the metal guard and you are ready for the next stitch.

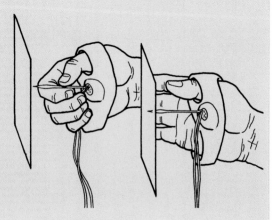

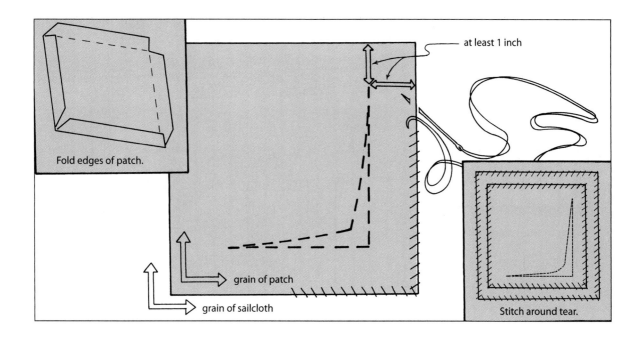

Fold edges of patch.

at least 1 inch

grain of patch

grain of sailcloth

Stitch around tear.

3 Sew repair or chafe patches to the sail with a flat seaming stitch. Always align the grain of a patch with the grain of the sail. Sewing around a patch is easier if you pin or glue it in place. Adhesive-backed sail tape or sailcloth is ideal for sewn patches. Seal or fold the edges of plain sailcloth. Sew with the patch on top, pushing the needle down through the sail, then back up through the sail and patch in one motion. Pull each stitch snug before making the next one. Place a second row of stitches around the tear.

REPAIR KIT

NO MATTER HOW WELL YOU MAINTAIN your sails, splits and tears are an ever-present possibility. Brand-new racing sails have been holed by the wadding from the starting cannon. Just a few sail-repair items aboard can save the day. Start your kit with a roll of sail-repair tape. Inexpensive nylon "ripstop" is adequate for weekend repairs, but for offshore sailing put stronger and stickier adhesive-backed Dacron tape in your kit.

Your kit should include a dozen or so triangular sailmaker's needles in sizes #16 and #14 and a cone of prewaxed sail twine. If you have a spinnaker aboard, throw in a package of heavy domestic needles and a tube of heavy polyester thread. A leather palm is essential for pushing a thick needle through multiple layers of sailcloth. Also include a small pair of scissors, a seam ripper, and a block of beeswax.

In addition to the tape, it is a good idea to have a couple of yards of Dacron sailcloth aboard. A piece of leather will also be handy for chafe patches. Throw in a couple of jib hanks and a couple of sail slides with their attendant hardware, and you are ready for most contingencies.

EXAMINING YOUR SAILS

The best way to catch that first broken stitch is to carefully examine your sails at least once a year—more often if they see daily use. Don't be afraid to tug at a seam if it looks suspect; now is the time to find out if it is about to let go.

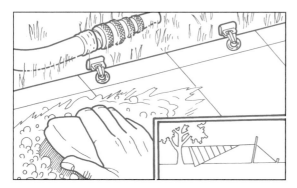

1 Washing the sail first is a good idea. Spread it on the lawn and scrub it with a soft brush and a mild detergent, then rinse thoroughly. Wash the opposite side. Hang the sail by the head and tack to let it dry. Never machine-wash a sail! Forget about trying to remove stains; any chemicals strong enough to succeed are also likely to damage either the fabric or the resin.

2 Spread the sail on the lawn, remove your shoes, then crawl all over the sail dragging your finger over *every* seam. This forces you to look at every stitch. Mark every problem with a single tied stitch of brightly colored thread; pencil marks are too easily overlooked, and a strip of tape can peel off. You can use a pencil *in addition to* the thread flag to outline the extent of the needed repair.

3 Check each of the batten pockets. Battens often chafe against the inside of the pocket. Holding the sail up to the light may reveal thinning fabric.

4 Check the headboard for loose rivets or worn stitching. Check the tack and clew for chafe and problems with eye or ring installations. Check the leech for wear. Examine boltropes or their casings. Check the attachment of every hank or slide.

RESTITCHING SEAMS

By far the most common sail repair is restitching. Stitches stand proud on the hard sailcloth and are the first thing damaged when the sail chafes. Thread also weakens with exposure and age.

1 For Dacron sailcloth, use a #18 or larger needle in your machine. Most stitch problems you are likely to encounter can be solved by increasing the needle size. Set the stitch length to the maximum, then adjust the zigzag width to sew a "square" pattern—each stitch about 90 degrees to the previous one. Sailcloth is too hard for the interlock between upper and lower threads to pull into the fabric, so when the upper tension is right, the threads will form a tight knot on the underside at each stitch.

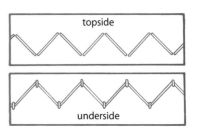

topside

underside

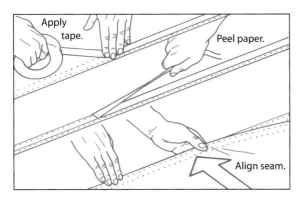

Apply tape.

Peel paper.

Align seam.

2 Baste the seam together. If some of the old stitching is still in place, leave it to maintain the alignment of the panels. If the panels are separated, use seam tape to rejoin them, carefully aligning the old stitch holes as you stick the panel edges together. You can also align and baste the panels with long hand stitches through corresponding stitch holes.

3 Sewing a sail is often easier if you get the machine down on the floor so you don't have to lift the sail. Sit in the lotus position and operate the foot pedal with your knee. You can handle short repairs alone, but a helper will make restitching long splits much easier.

4 Roll the sail like a scroll and feed it under the foot of your machine. Clamp the ends of the rolls or put tight lashings on the sail after it is under the foot to keep the roll diameters small. Stitch along the edge of the top panel, placing one side of the zigzag stitch just off the edge. Slide the sail out and turn it over to put the bottom panel on top. Sew along its edge. Finish the repair with a third row of stitches between the first two.

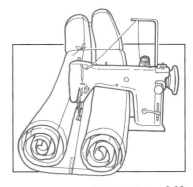

PATCHING A TEAR

You are hoisting away when the belly of the sail finds the end of an unprotected cotter pin. It happens. As long as you can get the sail under the arm of your machine, repairing a tear is not very difficult, and except for a small visual reminder of your indiscretion, the sail will be none the worse for the incident. If the tear crosses a seam, patch each panel independently, then sew them back together.

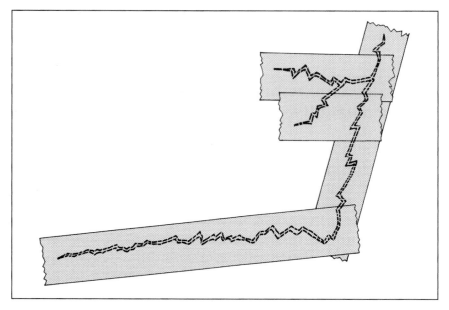

1 Spread the torn portion of the sail over a flat surface and realign all the torn edges. Take great care to get the cloth back into its original alignment. Tape the tear closed. Almost any tape will do. Don't let the tape extend far beyond the tear.

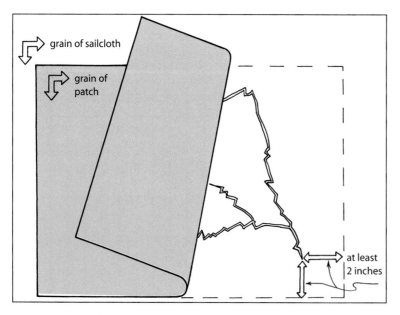

grain of sailcloth

grain of patch

at least 2 inches

2 Use a soldering iron or a hotknife to cut a rectangular patch of sailcloth similar in weight to the sail. Make the patch large enough to overlap the tear by at least 2 inches, keeping in mind that the grain of the patch must match the grain of the panel. Use seam tape or a glue stick to attach the patch to the sail on the side opposite the tape.

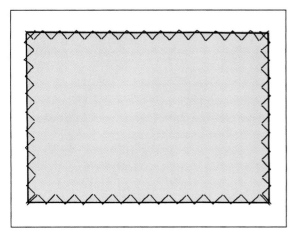

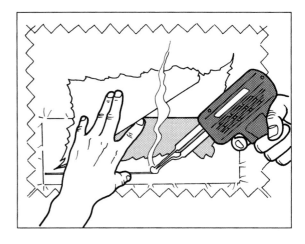

3 Stitch around the perimeter of the patch with a square zigzag stitch.

4 Turn the sail over and peel the tape. Slide a shield between the sail and the patch (through the tear) and carefully use a hotknife to cut the sail 1 inch inside the patch stitching.

USING A HOTKNIFE

WHENEVER POSSIBLE, CUT synthetic sailcloth with a hotknife. This seals the edges so that a hem is generally unnecessary, making the sail smoother and reducing weight. The usual hot knife is nothing more than a common soldering gun with a special "burning" tip that looks like a flat vertical disk. Placing a smooth, heat-resistant surface—such as a ceramic tile—under the cloth will help make your cuts easy and uniform.

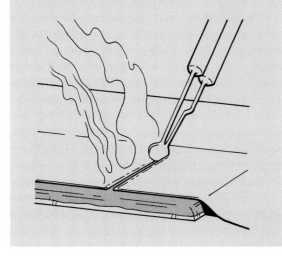

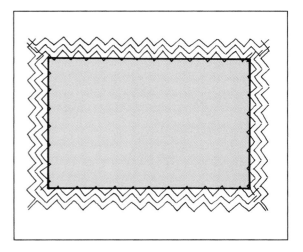

5 Sew around the edges of the rectangular hole. Add a third row of stitches between the first two.

Sometimes the damage is so severe or the cloth so weak that replacing a section of a panel is a better alternative. This can be simple or complicated, depending on where the panel is and how much needs to be replaced. You need sailcloth of approximately the same weight as the original.

1 Decide how much of the panel you want to replace. The job will be significantly easier if the replacement doesn't involve the edge of the sail. With a pencil, trace onto both adjoining panels the edge of the section you are replacing. Use a framing square to mark cut lines across the panel perpendicular to the edges.

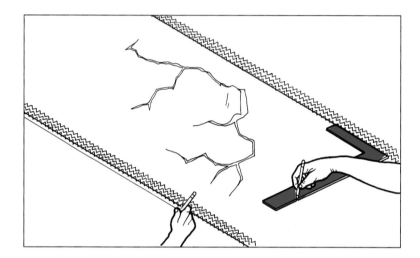

2 Hotknife the replacement panel 2 inches longer than the distance between your two cross-panel lines. Place the new panel on the old one and see how closely their widths match. The standard sailcloth width is more or less 36 inches. If they match perfectly, the side lines you traced will be an accurate guide. If the new panel is wider, measure the difference and move one of the edge lines out that distance. If the new panel is narrower, note the difference so you can move a guideline in after you remove the old panel.

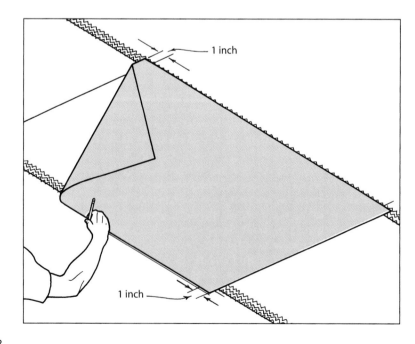

1 inch

1 inch

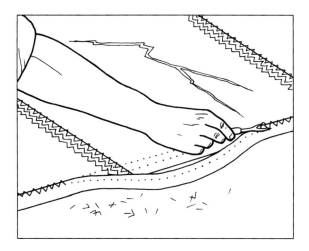

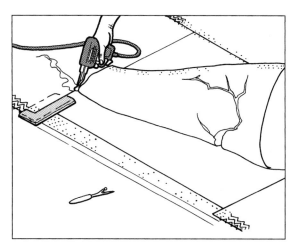

3 If the replacement extends to the edge of the sail, use a seam ripper to unstitch any casing, tabling, or hems that cross the panel.

4 Rip the panel seams, opening them a couple of inches beyond the cross-panel pencil lines. Use a hotknife to cut the panel on the lines, taking care not to touch the adjacent panels with the knife.

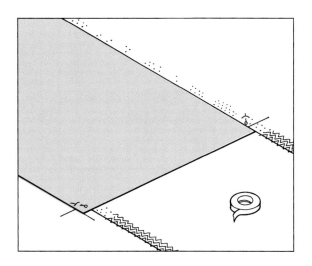

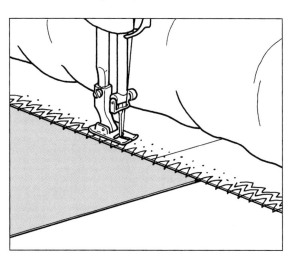

5 Redraw the guidelines if necessary, then glue the new panel into position with seam tape or a glue stick, taking great care to align the edges perfectly with the guidelines. The replacement panel should evenly overlap the sail 1 inch at each end (unless it extends to the sail's edge). Use pins or staples to reinforce the adhesive at the corners of the replacement.

6 Roll the sail (if necessary) and sew one edge of the replacement panel. Start and finish the stitching far enough beyond the panel to reseam the sections not removed. Put in all three rows of stitches.

7 Unroll the sail and seam one end of the replacement.

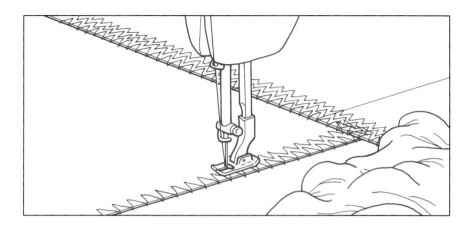

8 Lay the sail flat and make sure the unsewn edge is properly aligned with your guideline. Roll the sail again and seam this edge.

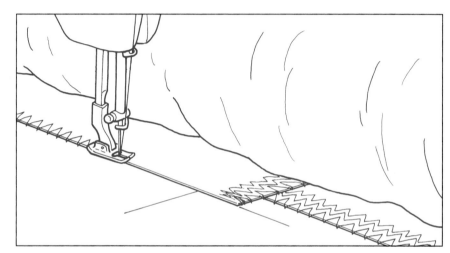

9 Seam the end of the panel or, if it extends to the edge of the sail, use the old panel as a pattern to trim it to the appropriate contour. Hem the edge or reattach the loose tabling or casing.

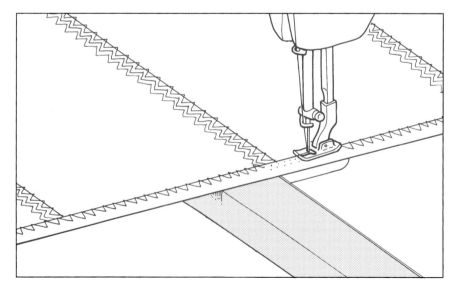

BATTEN POCKET REPAIRS

Battens chafe inside their pockets. Worn stitching is easy enough to repair. Damage to the cloth is somewhat more difficult, but easier than panel replacement because all the sewing is near an edge of the sail.

SPLIT POCKET OPENING

Repair the leech end of batten pockets by hand-sewing the seams with waxed sail twine. The twine resists the chafe of the batten better than machine thread. Use a round stitch—five stitches per inch—to close and/or reinforce the end seam. Put a couple of stitches at the top of the pocket opening.

TORN CLOTH

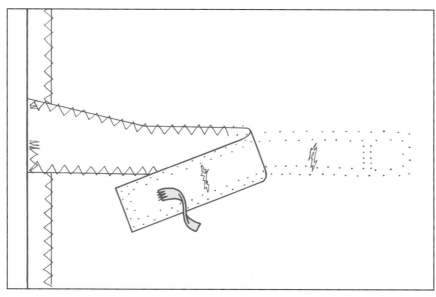

1 Rip the seams to release the pocket at the damaged end. To make an effective repair, partially separate the pocket from the sail; if you don't, the aft edge of a patch will close the pocket. If the pocket has an elastic tensioner, unstitch it from the sail.

2 Repair sail damage with a patch on the opposite side of the sail from the pocket. This avoids creating an edge inside the pocket that can catch the batten. For the same reason, rather than cutting out the damage (see "Patching a Tear," page 870), reduce the length of your square zigzag by about half and sew over the torn or worn spot to capture it.

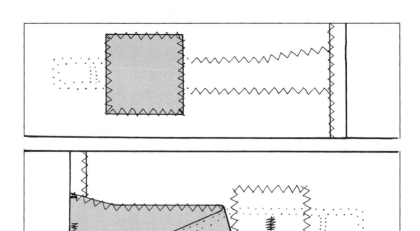

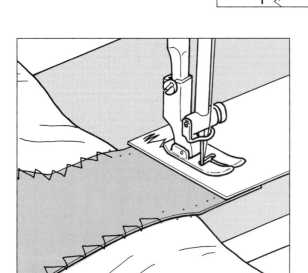

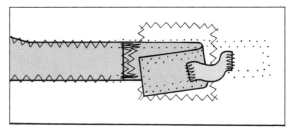

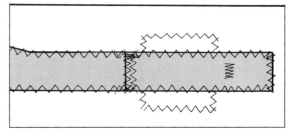

3 Repair pocket damage by cutting off the damaged end and replacing it. To avoid an edge inside the pocket, sew the new piece on top of the old one.

4 Restitch the elastic tensioner, then glue the edges of the pocket to the sail and sew them back down.

CHAFE PROTECTION

Avoid damage to your sail with strategically located chafe patches. Likely locations are where the mainsail bears against the spreaders off the wind and where the foot of a genoa rubs the pulpit or lifelines.

1 Mark the outside limits of the chafing area. Powdered chalk can help.

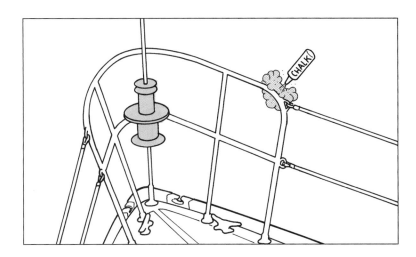

2 With a hotknife, cut matching sailcloth patches for both sides of the sail. Be sure the grain of the patch will match the grain of the sail where it will be applied. Make the patches a couple of inches larger than the protected area to avoid subjecting the stitching to chafe. Use seam tape to apply one patch, then glue the second in place on the opposite side, aligning it to the first. Sew down the edges of both patches at the same time.

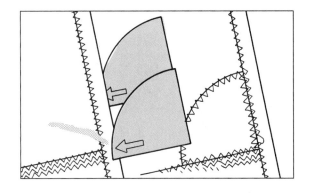

3 Use leather for edge protection. Make edge patches large enough to fold around the edge and protect both sides.

CLEW DAMAGE

Heavy loads at the clew can distort and even tear a sail. Rebuilding the clew with additional corner patches may exceed the capacity of a domestic sewing machine, but you can still effect a strong and long-lasting repair. Cut three 18-inch lengths of 1-inch webbing and pass them through the eye or D-ring. Pull them tight against the forward edge of the ring and hand-sew them to the sail—one along the foot, one along the leech, and one midway between the other two. Make long zigzag stitches to minimize perforation. Protect the webbing with a leather butterfly if needed. Use the same technique to reinforce leech cringles and the tack.

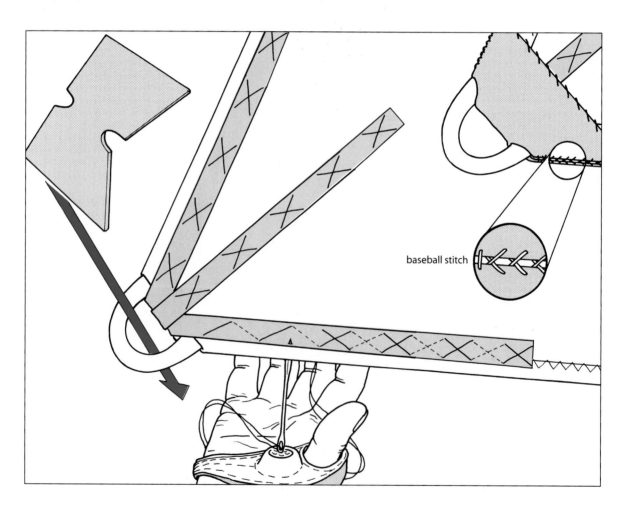

baseball stitch

Like shoestrings, leech lines break, and tying them back together just doesn't work. Replacing a leech line is easy. The best leech line is braided Dacron, often sold as flag halyard. The most common size is ⅛ inch, but light sails are often built with 1/16-inch line.

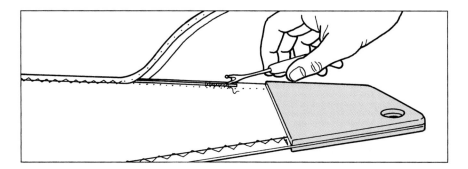

1 Rip the leech tabling seam at the head of the sail to expose the end of the line. It is usually sewn down, so cut the stitches to release it.

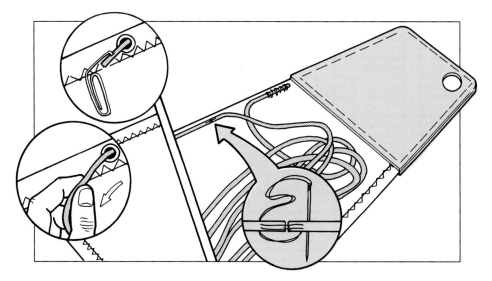

2 If the line broke at the eyelet near the clew—the usual spot—you can save some effort by fishing out the end with a straightened paper clip with a small hook bent on the end. Sew a new length of the same diameter line to the top of the sail, then attach its loose end to the old line with a couple of loops of thread sewn through the lines. Pull the new line through the tabling with the old one.

3 If the old line broke inside the sail, pull the remaining piece out from the top. Sew on a new line. Cut a 10-inch length of coat-hanger wire and round one end with a file. Nick the wire near the other end. Make a couple of stitches through the line, then tie the thread to the wire at the nick. Use a push-pull action to thread the wire through the tabling and out the bottom eyelet.

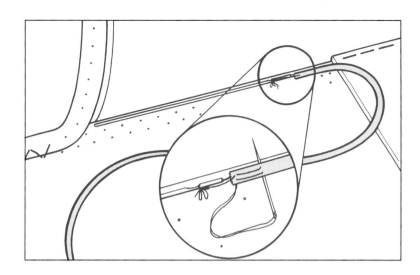

4 Restitch the tabling at the top of the sail. A pair of buttons cut from stiff leather make leech-line adjustment easy. Add them if your sail doesn't have them. On a headsail protect the buttons from snagging on shrouds with a stiff covering flap sewn only along its top and forward edges.

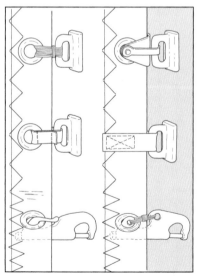

HANKS AND SLIDES

Plastic slides break and the lashings that hold hanks to the sail chafe through. Hanks and slides can be attached in a number of ways. You are most likely to reattach a hank or slide the way it was originally, but if a hank or slide attachment is a recurring problem, consider one of the alternative attachment methods shown.

INDEX

DC circuits *(continued)*
    components of, 103, 718–19;
    continuity testing, 484; engine
    installation diagram, 729; failures
    of, 103; faults, 730–31; fires
    aboard boats and, 103, 413;
    grounded circuits, 480; inspec-
    tion of, 91, 134; interference from
    circuitry, 111, 113; maintenance
    schedule, 589; mapping, 410,
    482–86; neatness of, 470–72;
    overload protection, 466–68;
    panel location, 472; polarity, 422;
    routing, 460–61; safety precau-
    tions, 411; starting circuits, 719;
    start switch, 730; symbols for dia-
    grams, 478–82; troubleshooting,
    490–91; 24-volt systems, 458;
    types of, 423–25, 477, 481–82;
    visual inspection of, 593; warning
    circuits, 740–41; winterizing, 600.
    See also battery entries; voltage
    drop
DC wiring: bundled wires, 472; con-
    struction of, 454–55; failure, rea-
    sons for, 453; fire dangers, 413;
    insulation, 107, 459–60; labeling
    runs, 470–71; neatness of,
    470–72, 491; routing, 460–61;
    size and length recommenda-
    tions, 107–8, 413, 455–58; types
    of, 107–8, 459
deadlights, 158–60, 163
deck hardware: backing plates, 43;
    bedding/rebedding, 43, 150–53;
    inspection of, 43–46; materials
    for, 44; mounting, 43, 154;
    removal of, 299–300
deck hatches. *See* hatches
decks: alligatoring, 35; breakout, 36;
    care, 31; construction, 31; craz-
    ing, 35; design of, 31, 181; hat-
    shaped stiffeners, 230–31; hull-
    to-deck joints, 32–34; inspection,
    128; leaks, 144–45; painting,
    189–90, 299–300, 386–90; repairs
    to, 31, 145, 181–203; stress
    cracks, 35–36, 182–84; teak
    decks, 195–203; voids, 36. *See
    also* nonskid surfaces

deck-stepped masts, 53
deep-cycle batteries: characteristics,
    436, 437, 721; discharge of, 445;
    equalization phase, 516; plate
    thickness, 433
delamination of cored construction:
    alligatoring, 35; impact damage
    repairs, 252–53; inspection for,
    37, 127, 128; outer skin separa-
    tion repair, 220–21; percussion
    testing, 15, 37; signs of, 219
depth sounders, 359, 420, 442
designer reputation, 115, 116
diesel tanks. *See* fuel tanks
diodes: bridge rectifier, 512, 726;
    galvanic isolators, 559, 561; iso-
    lating diodes, 528, 530, 727;
    testing/troubleshooting, 503,
    527–28, 561
direct-cooled engines, 657, 671
direct current. *See* DC entries
disk sanders, 294, 305
diver's flag, 784–85
docklines, 122
dodgers and awnings, 750, 843;
    awning design, 788; batten pock-
    ets, 793; Bimini awning, 852–55;
    dodger, 856–60; harbor awning,
    788–95; inspection of, 47; ridge
    rope, 793–94; roping the edge,
    792; sailing awning, 861; side
    curtains, 795; spray dodgers,
    777–81; spreaders, 794
dropboards, 40
duffel bags, 814–15, 824–26
duplex wire, 455
dust control, 308–9, 344, 382
dust masks, 298

E
ear plugs, 175, 306
electrical connections: AC circuits,
    555; bare wire connections, 465;
    corrosion, 110, 491; crimp connec-
    tions, 462–63; heat-shrink connec-
    tions, 465; inspection of, 107;
    materials for, 413, 462; neatness
    of, 470–72; soldered connections,
    464–65; terminal strips, 471–72;
    types of, 462; wire nuts, 465

electrical equipment: adding to
    boat, 409–10; circuit breakers for,
    468; inspection of, 110; inverter
    for powering, 445; load calcula-
    tions, 105, 410, 420, 443–44,
    505–6; needs aboard, 409; over-
    load protection, 468; polarity
    and, 422; troubleshooting, 490.
    See also specific equipment
electrical systems. *See* AC circuits;
    DC circuits
electrical system troubleshooting,
    487; fuses, 489; interconnected
    problems, 488; lights, 488, 489;
    multimeter features, 494–95;
    multimeter functions, 496–97;
    multimeter tests, 498–506; odors,
    490; starting problems, 488; test
    light testing, 492–93; wiring,
    490–91
electricity: baseball analogy, 415;
    generation of, 426, 511; load cal-
    culation, 105, 420; load calcula-
    tions, 410, 443–44, 505–6; mea-
    surement of, 416, 496, 497, 505;
    Ohm's Law, 418; power equation,
    419; ripple, 527; safety precau-
    tions, 411–14; terminology,
    415–20
electrolyte: gel-cell batteries, 436;
    maintenance, 450; safety precau-
    tions, 412; testing, 105, 452
electronic equipment: circuit break-
    ers for, 468; electric load of, 442;
    inspection of, 112–13, 121; light-
    ning protection for, 581; location
    of, 112–13, 413; navigation
    equipment, 105, 420; overload
    protection, 468; polarity and, 422
emergency tiller, 101
engine controls and instruments:
    ammeters, 732–33, 739; control
    cables, 737; engine-stop controls,
    732–33, 736, 742; gauges,
    732–33; gear-selector controls,
    735, 742; location of, 732–33; oil
    pressure gauge, 732–33, 739,
    743; tachometers, 732–33,
    737–38, 743; throttle controls,
    732–34, 742; visual inspection of,

polarity: AC (alternating current), 427, 549; of alternators, 519; DC circuits, 422; tester for AC circuits, 549, 554; testing, 495, 560

polycarbonate sheets (Lexan): characteristics, 162; cutting, 161, 162

polyester (Dacron) fabrics, 760

polyester resin: chemical linking of, 209; hardener for, 177, 207; temperature and cure time, 207; types of, 206–7

polyethylene tanks, 75

polysulfide sealants, 148, 149, 150, 285

polyurethane foam, 763, 832

polyurethane paints: coat requirements, 385; dust control with, 382; glass for flow testing, 382; pace of work with, 383; roller application, 382–83; sanding, 384; single-part (urethane modified alkyd), 277, 318; spray application of, 381; surface preparation for, 189–90; thinning, 381, 382; tipping techniques, 383; two-part (linear polyurethane), 277, 309, 378–85

polyurethane sealants, 148, 149, 150, 285

polyurethane varnish, 280, 311, 335

polyvinyl alcohol (PVA), 178, 206, 374

portholes/portlights: adhesive sealants and, 150; bedding/rebedding, 157–60; frames, 163, 300; inspection of, 42; replacing, 42, 161–62, 300, 395; ventilation and, 83

potential (electricity), 416

power: AC (alternating current), 428; definition, 419; equation for, 419, 420; increases in, 417; load calculations, 105, 420, 505–6; measurement of, 417. See also electricity

power factor, 546

power loss formula, 490

pox, 18, 241–43, 364

Practical Sailor, 123

price of a boat, 123

primary wire, 455

print-through of fabric, 11

propane, 78, 79

propellers: corrosion control, 577; Cutless bearings, 27, 28, 127; inspection of, 27–28, 127; painting, 359; ratings for, 597

propeller shafts: alignment of, 92; zinc collars, 28, 577

P-type alternators, 519

pulleys: alternators, 520–21; inspection of, 91; pulley ratio, 509, 727

pulpits, 45

pumps, 420, 441, 442, 443. See also specific pumps

Q

Q flag, 782–83

quality indicators, 115, 136

R

racing application of bottom paint, 357

racing enamel, 283

radar, 420, 442

radio-frequency grounding, 476, 569, 579–80

radios: electric load of, 420, 442; grounding, 578. See also ham radios; single-sideband radios

rags, 298

random-bit sanders, 295, 305

raw-water circuit: antisiphon valve, 669; components of, 656–57; exhaust injection elbow, 656–57, 708–9, 711–12, 717; faults, 672–73; filters, 657; filters/strainers, 658–59, 672; heat exchangers, 656, 657, 665–68, 673; hoses and clamps, 656–57, 670–71; maintenance schedule, 589; oil coolers, 665–68, 673; pump access, 88, 95; pumps, 600, 656, 657, 659–64, 672; startup survey, 595; temperature recommendations, 95; temperature troubleshooting, 614–15; thermostats, 671; through-hull fitting and valve, 656–57, 658;

types of cooling, 657; visual inspection of, 593; winterizing, 600; zinc anodes, 667–68

reactance, 428, 546

rectifiers, 512, 726

refinishing products, 275–87

refrigeration units: electric load of, 105, 420, 442, 443; location of, 79

regulators: alternator/regulator wiring, 517–20; attached, 518; charging times and, 507, 727; dual, 513; external, 518; fooling, 513–14, 727; function of, 510, 511–12, 515, 722; inspection of, 109; internal, 517; maintenance, 726; manual controller, 514; overcharge protection, 512–14; smart, 516; three-step regulator, 514–15, 727; troubleshooting, 522–28

reinforcement patches, 791

reserve minutes, 441

resistance (electricity): measurement of, 417, 496, 497, 505; Ohm's Law, 418; parallel circuits, 424; series circuits, 423

respirator, 298

ridge rope, 793–94

ridge seam, 845

rigging, 49; failure, 49; inspection of, 49, 130–31; tension of, 64; types of, 60–61

ripple, 527

rod rigging, 61

roller covers: cutting, 292; frames for, 292; storage, 318; types of, 291

roller furling, 66

roller techniques: gelcoat application, 375; paints, 317; polyurethane paints, 382–83

routers, 320

rpm readings: idle rpm, 609, 694; maximum rpm, 597, 609; no-load rpm, 596–97, 608

rubber roller, 320

rubbing compound, 173

rubrails, 395

rudderpost, 98–99

rudders: construction of, 26–27, 263; grounding damage, 255; inspection of, 24–27, 127; repairs to, 261–63; types of, 24–26; weeping, 261–62

starting batteries, 434, 435, 444, 720
starting circuits, 467, 468, 719
start switch, 730
stays. *See* shrouds and stays
steel tanks, 75
steering systems, 98–101, 129
storage pockets, 798–800
stowage, availability of, 83
stray current: bonding system protection from, 576–77; corrosion from, 558; isolation transformers and, 559; testing for, 506, 563
stress cracks: decks, 35–36, 182–84; gelcoat, 17, 128; prevention, 183
stringers, 71
strippers. *See* chemical strippers
stuffing box, 88, 93
suitability of boat, 115, 116
surface preparation for finishes: chemical stripper, 304, 305; cleaning, 301, 312; degreasing, 301; dust removal, 308–9; importance of, 273, 299; paint adhesion testing, 302; paint compatibility testing, 302, 312, 380; polyurethane paints, two-part, 189–90; sanding techniques, 305–7; silicone, removing, 302; trim and hardware removal, 299–300, 312; wetting down work area, 309
surge protection, 520, 581
surveys of boats: advantages of professional survey, 7; costs of professional survey, 7, 138–39; reasons for professional survey, 137; report following survey, 139; surveyor, finding a, 137–38; survey process, 139; surveys by owner, 7; 30-minute survey, 125–36
swaged fittings, 62, 131
swimmers, risks to, 556–57
switches, 469–70, 503. *See also* specific switches

T

tachometers, 732–33, 737–38, 743
tack rags, 344
tack strips, 841
tangs, 56

tanks, 75–76, 576–77. *See also* specific tanks
tape, 356
teak: cleaning, 195, 196, 330–31; finishes for, 329; lightening, 195, 330; oil finishes, 330–33; sealers, 279, 334
teak decks: bung replacement, 199–200; caulk failure signs, 198; caulking, 197–98; caulk recommendation, 198; cleaning, 195, 196; lightening, 195; plank replacement, 201–3; surfacing, 197
television, 420, 442
terminal strips, 471–72
test lights, 492–93
thermostarts, 696
thermostats, 684–85; coolant systems, 680–81; inspection of, 680; location of, 674; purpose of, 675; raw-water circuit, 671, 673; testing, 680–81
thin-film Teflon bottom paint, 283
thinner, 291
30-minute survey, 125–36
thread, 758
throttle controls, 732–34, 742
through-hull fittings: bedding for, 29; corrosion of, 506; inspection of, 29, 134; isolating, 576; materials for, 29; raw-water circuit, 658; replacing, 167–68; seacock inspection, 80–81
throw-away brushes, 288
tiller steering: emergency tiller, 101; inspection of, 99, 129
timing gears, 631
tin-based paints, 271, 283
tin-plated wire, 413, 454, 459
tin snips, 320
tipping techniques, 317, 383
toggles, 63
toluene, 287
toolkit, 744–45
tool rolls, 802–3, 843
topside enamel, 276
tote bag, 810–11
tracks and travelers, 46
transducers, painting, 359
transfer tape, 757, 863

transmissions: access to, 88; maintenance schedule, 589; ratings for, 597; startup survey, 596
trim: finishes for, 311; installation of, 300, 327; removal of, 299–300
trucker's hitch (knot), 777
tufting, 839
tung oil, 279, 332
turbochargers, 622–23, 709, 714–15, 717
turnbuckles: as belt tensioner, 520; inspection of, 63
12-volt circuits, 411. *See also* DC circuits
24-volt systems, 458

U

Underwriters Laboratories (UL) wire standards, 459
upholstery: fabrics for, 761; inspection of, 85; replacing, 832, 841; shaping flaps, 841; tack strips, 841
urethane modified alkyd paints, 277, 318. *See also* polyurethane paints
urethane varnish. *See* polyurethane varnish
Used Boat Guide (BUC Research), 123
Used Boat Price Guide (NADA), 123

V

value of a boat, 123
valves, 628–29, 631–33, 639
vangs, 60
vaporproof selector switches, 103
varnish: advances in, 270; appearance of, 335; bleaching wood, 338–39; brand selection, 274–75; bubbles in, 342; can opening and resealing, 312–13, 342; characteristics, 335, 341; coat requirements, 343; dust control with, 344; filters for, 313, 342; for interior wood, 311; maintenance, 347; safety protection, 298; stripping old, 335, 336–38; surface preparation for, 299–309, 340; thinning, 341; tools for, 273; touching up, 347; types of, 280, 335; UV-inhibitor additives, 335, 347; when to use, 341

varnishing techniques: brush techniques, 315–16, 343; finish coats, 345–46; masking tape, 356; preparatory coats, 343, 344; sanding between coats, 343; wire for unloading brush, 315, 342

V-belts, 674, 682–83, 684–85

Velcro, 763

VHF radios, 420, 442

Victor flag, 782

vinyl bottom paints, 282, 357

vinylester resin, 207

vinyl fabrics, 760

vinyl sewing tips, 859

voltage drop: definition, 456; formula for wire size, 456, 457, 458; heat from, 490; Kirchoff's Law, 501; measurement of, 499, 501; power loss formula, 490; wiring recommendations, 108

voltage regulator. See regulators

voltmeters: AC (alternating current), 428; battery testing, 451, 498, 500, 722; engine-panel gauges, 732–33, 739; function of, 496; modification to, 500; testing with, 498–501, 560, 725

volts/voltage: AC (alternating current), 427–28, 546; definition, 416; increases in, 417; Ohm's Law, 418; power equation, 419

W

wadding, 838

warning circuits, 732–33, 740–41

water intrusion: keel ballast, 21; rudders, 26; tests for moisture, 19, 38; wet core, 38

waterline, finding, 360

water-powered generators, 507, 542

water tanks, 76

water temperature gauge, 732–33, 739, 743

watts: definition, 417; power equation, 419

weather cloths, 750, 777–81

weeping keels, 14, 256

weeping rudders, 261–62

welt cord, 825–26

wet-cell batteries: characteristics, 435, 719–20; charging of, 447; construction of, 432–33; discharge of, 445; self-discharge, 434; testing, 105

wet-exhaust systems, 709, 713

wet sanding, 306

wetting down work areas, 309

wheel steering: inspection of, 129. See also cable steering; geared steering

winches: covers, 816–17, 846; inspection of, 44, 129

wind generators, 507, 537–42 windlass: electric load of, 420, 442; inspection of, 121

windscoop instructions, 785–87

windshields, 856, 858–60

winterizing engines, 600–601

wire markers, 470

wire rigging, 60–61

wire rope: breaking strength of, 65; inspection of, 131

wood: bleaching, 338–39; cleaning after sanding, 308; masts, 572; mast step rot, 53; rot, 38; rot, testing for, 74, 133; sandpaper recommendation, 306; spreaders, 53. See also wood finishes

wooden hulls, 9

wood finishes: oil finishes, 330–33; sealers, 334; types of, 278–80, 311; wood types and, 329

wood trim. See trim

Y

yacht brokers, 123, 138

Z

zinc anodes, 576; painting, 359; propeller shaft collars, 28, 577; raw-water circuit, 667–68

zinc-oxide based paints, 283

zippered duffel bags, 824–26

zipper pockets, 801

zippers, 763, 822–23

7/07